Benson and Hedges

Cricket Year

Benson and Hedges

Cricket Year

Eighteenth Edition

September 1998 to September 1999

Written by **Jonathan Agnew**

with additional contributions by
Qamar Ahmed
Mark Baldwin
Tony Cozier
Ralph Dellor
Neal Manthorpe
Jim Maxwell
Sarah Potter
Bryan Waddle

BLOOMSBURY

First published in 1999 by
Bloomsbury Publishing Plc
38 Soho Square
London W1V 5DF

A copy of the CIP entry for this book is available from the
British Library .

ISBN 0 7475 4546 4

10 9 8 7 6 5 4 3 2 1

Written by Jonathan Agnew

with additional contributions by
Qamar Ahmed
Mark Baldwin
Tony Cozier
Ralph Dellor
Neal Manthorpe
Jim Maxwell
Sarah Potter
Sa'adi Thawfeeq
Telford Vice
Bryan Waddle

Designed by Bradbury and Williams
Statistics by Wendy Wimbush
Picture research by David Munden
Typeset by Book Creation Services, London

Printed by Bath Press, Great Britain

Contents

Sponsor's Message

With the new millennium just around the corner, the past 12 months have turned out to be a year of change for Benson and Hedges, and for cricket. Most obviously there has been the alteration to the format of our own competition, which became briefly the Benson and Hedges Super Cup. As I am sure you are all aware we return to the original Benson and Hedges Cup competition next year.

Sadly, in December 1998 David Lemmon, who had been responsible for editing this book since its inception 18 years ago, died after a brief illness. All those who were associated with the *Benson and Hedges Cricket Year* during that time had come to know David well and appreciated the hard work involved in compiling a complete record of all first-class cricket played throughout the world in the last 12 months, and producing it within a month of the end of the English cricket season. We will miss him. However, we are delighted that Jonathan Agnew has assumed the mantle of Editor. Jonathan is familiar to all those who listen to *Test Match Special* and to cricket followers in general in his role as the BBC's cricket correspondent. We also remember his cricketing exploits for Leicestershire and with England, for whom he played three Test matches against Australia, West Indies and Sri Lanka in 1984 and 1985.

Jonathan has brought his own brand of humour and opinion to this, the 18th edition of the *Benson and Hedges Cricket Year*. In a section devoted to the World Cup he has included his personal view of England's early departure from the competition and Australia's nail-biting semi-final tie against South Africa, which took them to the Final and their ultimate victory over Pakistan on 20 June. Jonathan has also co-opted the help of such eminent overseas commentators from *Test Match Special* as Tony Cozier, to bring you their personal observations of cricket in their country.

In August, the Benson and Hedges Super Cup was won by Gloucestershire, the first silverware to be taken home to Bristol since 1977, when they won the Benson and Hedges Cup, beating Kent by 64 runs. The Super Cup Final was blessed with beautiful weather and an enthusiastic crowd who were thrilled to see the Gloucestershire captain, Mark Alleyne, score an inventive 112 before being bowled by Craig White, to win him not only the Gold Award, but also the Trophy for his county. It was quite a moment for all of us at Lord's and those watching on Sky TV to finally see Jack Russell collecting his medal after being such a loyal servant to Gloucestershire over the past 18 years.

Next year, the tournament returns to its old format with all 18 counties playing in zonal rounds before the quarter- and semi-final stages. The Benson and Hedges Cup Final will be played at Lord's Cricket Ground on Saturday 10 June.

We hope you approve of the changes made to the 18th edition of the Benson and Hedges Cricket Year, and enjoy the new look that Jonathan Agnew and Bloomsbury have created, which will, I hope, make it more fun to read as well as being a highly useful reference book.

At the end of the English cricket season, which has seen the carnival of the World Cup as well as Channel 4's acclaimed new-look cricket coverage led by Mark Nicholas, we wish Nasser Hussain the best of luck in leading England to South Africa during the winter. Jonathan's views on England's successes and failures will feature prominently in the 19th edition of the *Benson and Hedges Cricket Year*.

Barry Jenner
Director, Benson and Hedges

Foreword

Before I sit and write a single word in this, the 18th edition of the Benson and Hedges Cricket Year, I must pay tribute to David Lemmon.

David was the original editor of the Cricket Year, and his death last winter saddened everyone who has enjoyed the pleasure of his company in press boxes up and down the country. He is greatly missed, nowhere more so than at Lords – and also at his beloved Highbury.

It was only when I was asked to succeed David that I realised what an enormous task he had undertaken for the past 17 years. This was complicated further this year by the fact that this edition had to be written and compiled in half the time. That was one of the reasons behind my decision to approach renowned journalists and commentators such as Tony Cozier, Jim Maxwell, Qamar Ahmed and Mark Baldwin, and there is no doubt that the book benefits significantly from their knowledge and experience. My special thanks must go to Wendy Wimbush who overcame all the odds, undertook a crash course in surfing the World Wide Web, and has managed to produce all of the statistics that appear in the book.

There are many other alterations that I hope regular readers of the Benson and Hedges Cricket Year will enjoy. The lay-out has been transformed with an entire colour section devoted to the World Cup. The main focus of the book is England and the England cricket team which has meant a deliberate trimming of the coverage of relatively insignificant matches elsewhere. This has also made space available for specific features. Amongst others, there is a tribute to the former Australian captain, Mark Taylor, by Jim Maxwell and Tony Cozier reports on another remarkable year in the life of Brian Lara.

Given the shortage of time (and my inexperience at this sort of thing!) it is inevitable that there will be an omission, or two. It is worth noting that the situation in Sri Lanka has made it extremely difficult to record their domestic season, not least because, at the time of writing, the two leading clubs, Colombo Cricket Club and Bloomfield Cricket Club are involved in a dispute over who actually won the title! It may very well be that an account of the 1999 Sri Lankan domestic season will have to wait until next year.

However, I hope that you, the reader, will enjoy the new Benson and Hedges Cricket Year. I hope it is easy on the eye, and that it gives an accurate and refreshing account of the international and domestic cricket played throughout the world in 1998–99.

Jonathan Agnew

Acknowledgments:
Qamar Ahmed, DJM Armstrong, Mark Baldwin, Sarah Barlow, Fiona Butchart, Tony Cozier, Ralph Dellor, Les Hatton, David Llewellyn, Neal Manthorpe, Jim Maxwell, Mohan Menon, David Munden at Sportsline Photographic, Melanie Porte, Sarah Potter, Andrew Sansom, Sa'adi Thawfeeq, William Turrell, Telford Vice, Bryan Waddle, Beatriz Waller, John Ward, Frank Wheeldon, Wendy Wimbush.

The symbol * indicates not out or wicketkeeper according to context

OCTOBER 1998

Australia beat Pakistan in Rawalpindi to win Test series one-nil (above) – *page 343*.
Zimbabwe defeat India in Harare to record their second Test victory – *page 300*.

JANUARY 1999

Australia beat England in Sydney to win the series three-one – *page 260*.
West Indies are humiliated in South Africa, losing the series five-nil (right) – *page 224*.
Pakistan beat India in Madras by 12 runs – *page 331*.

NOVEMBER 1998

Australia trounce England in Perth to take a one-nil lead in the Ashes series – *page 251*.
South Africa beat West Indies in the final of the Wills Trophy in Dhaka.
India defeat Zimbabwe in the final of the Champions Trophy in Sharjah (left) – *page 275*.

FEBRUARY

India beat Pakistan in Delhi by 212 runs – *page 332*.
Pakistan beat Sri Lanka in the final of the Asia Test Championship (below) – *page 243*.
South Africa thrash West Indies six-one in their one-day series – *page 230*.

DECEMBER 1998

Australia retain the Ashes by defeating England in Adelaide (right) – *page 254*.
England win the Boxing Day Test in Melbourne by 12 runs – *page 256*.
Zimbabwe beat Pakistan in first Test in Peshawar – *page 253*.
South Africa record victories over West Indies in Port Elizabeth and Durban – *page 218*.
New Zealand beat India in Wellington – *page 281*.

MARCH

South Africa win in Wellington to take the series one-nil (right) – *page 290*.
Australia beat West Indies in Port of Spain. Brian Lara leads West Indies to victories in Jamaica and Barbados – *page 310*.

APRIL
Australia fight back to defeat West Indies in Antigua and draw the series two-two (left) – *page 317*.
Pakistan win the Coca Cola Cup in Sharjah, beating India in the final – *page 276*.

MAY
World Cup begins (below left and bottom). England, West Indies, Sri Lanka, Kenya, Bangladesh, Scotland and Holland are knocked out of the qualifying stage – *page 181*.

JULY
England beat New Zealand in first Test at Edgbaston – *page 11*. New Zealand record their first Test victory at Lord's to level the series one-one (right) – *page 14*.

AUGUST
Gloucestershire defeat Yorkshire to win Benson and Hedges Super Cup Final – *page 161*.
New Zealand beat England at the Oval to win the series two-one – *page 20*.
Gloucestershire record a remarkable double by defeating Somerset to win the NatWest Trophy (below) – *page 171*.

JUNE
World Cup semi-finals: Australia beat South Africa and Pakistan defeat New Zealand – *page 207*. Australia beat Pakistan in final – *page 210*.

SEPTEMBER
Adam Hollioake's Surrey clinch the PPP Healthcare County Championship (right) – *page 102*.
Lancashire win the first division of the CGU National Cricket League – *page 150*.

opposite: Philip Tufnell surrounded by pigeons as England lose the series against New Zealand two-one. *David Munden/Sportsline Photographic*

Other chapter openers:
pages 6–7: A general view of Lord's.
David Munden/Sportsline Photographic

page 181: Australia get their hands on the World Cup. *David Munden/Sportsline Photographic*

page 213: Newlands in Cape Town with Table Mountains in background.
Gordon Brooks/Sportsline Photographic

page 237: Shahid Afridi is being congratulated by his team-mates on taking splended catch on the fifth day of the Calcutta Test.
Mueen ud din Hameed/Sportsline Photographic

page 245: Jason Gillespie celebrates in style after trapping Darren Gough lbw, Australia v. England at Perth. *David Munden/Sportsline Photographic*

page 273: Shoaib Akhtar and teammates ready for a joyride in the Opel car given to Shoaib after he was declared Man of the Series, Sharjah April 1999.
Mueen ud din Hameed/Sportsline Photographic

page 279: Kiwi captain Stephen Fleming.
David Munden/Sportsline Photographic

page 299: Zimbabwe cricketing brothers Andy and Grant Flower. *David Munden/Sportsline Photographic*

page 307: Celebations at West Indies dramatic victory over Australia at Kensington Oval.
Gordon Brooks/Sportsline Photographic

page 329: Chidambaram Stadium, Madras, India.
David Munden/Sportsline Photographic

page 341: Pakistan cricket team in colours.
David Munden/Sportsline Photographic

page 361: Romesh Kaluwitharna, Sri Lanka batsman.
David Munden/Sportsline Photographic

INTRODUCTION

By Jonathan Agnew

England players Alan Mullally and Neil Fairbrother during the
1999 World Cup. England failed to qualify for the Super Six
stage of the tournament.

David Munden/Sportsline Photographic

On December 31st, England's cricketers will gather on Cape Town's Waterfront for a party to usher in the next century. Or, at least, that is the impression they will give to passers-by. For when the champagne glasses are raised towards Table Mountain, and Allan Mullally, bashing away on his guitar, leads the chorus of 'Auld Lang Syne', the likelihood is that the toast will be one of relief: to the closing of the final decade of the twentieth century – the most grisly chapter in English cricketing history – and an end to the last year in particular.

There will be no better opportunity in our lifetime to make a fresh start. In the last 12 months, England lost five and won only two of the nine Tests they played. Both of the draws they achieved (at Brisbane and Manchester) would almost certainly have been defeats had the weather not intervened, so England stagger into the new century at the bottom of the unofficial but, nonetheless authoritative, world rankings. English cricket is teetering on a precipice, and the only people who can argue against that are either those whose job it is to do precisely that, or those who have their heads firmly stuck in the sand – or possibly both.

The authorities will argue that changes are being made and, to an extent, that is true. There is no doubt that huge efforts are being made to encourage youngsters to take up cricket and, finally, we have in Kate Hoey a Sports Minister who will promote the playing of competitive team sports in our schools.

That is good news. But until the England cricket team wins more matches than it loses and creates a positive image for itself, all of that hard work will be wasted. Youngsters need heroes and role models and, with all the will in the world, you would be hard pushed to suggest that anyone in the current England team is a sporting icon.

We have just experienced the first battle for promotion and relegation in the county championship. We have heard and read of the extra competitiveness in the final round of matches that has been introduced as a result of splitting the competition in two, but this misses the point entirely. The quality of the cricket was exactly the same – mediocre – and the game between Derbyshire and Hampshire at the very end of the summer proved beyond doubt that the good old art of collusion – so popular during the days of three-day cricket – is still alive and well.

Next April, the players from nine counties will start the season knowing that they cannot win the major trophy of English cricket. In fact they cannot even compete for it. Their sponsors know it, too. So do their supporters. The following April, six of those same nine counties will experience that feeling again. And, in all probability, the next April, too. Believe

Lord's, the headquarters of cricket, played host to the final of the 1999 World Cup.
David Munden/Sportsline Photographic

me, a second division county cricket ground will be the gloomiest of places; hardly a cricketing nerve centre that will attract the next generation of first-class players. Chopping up the championship was a short-sighted, ill-fated decision generated, largely, by a combination of panic and self-interest. I believe that it will do precisely nothing to improve the standard of England's cricketers. In fact, the reverse is true; particularly when one bears in mind that, from next summer, England's leading players will all be on central contracts. They will hardly appear in county cricket with the obvious, inevitable result being a further and rapid decline that will make the gap between county cricket and Test cricket wider still.

It is that gap that must be the focus of our attention. How can we raise the standard of our game in order to make the English team competitive once again? The obvious solution is to have the very best cricketers playing against each other on a level above that of the current county championship: a regional tournament consisting of no more than six teams.

The concept of regional cricket is hardly new and, I agree, it does not sound terribly sexy. However, unlike many of the critics who oppose its

Above: The 1998–99 season saw a return to form of Australian cricketer Shane Warne.
David Munden/Sportsline Photographic

Below: The Australian team celebrate after winning the 1999 World Cup.
David Munden/Sportsline Photographic

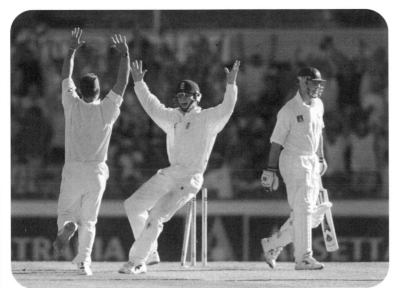

A rare moment of celebration for the England team during the Ashes tour, as Darren Gough takes the wicket of Colin Miller to complete a hat-trick.
David Munden/Sportsline Photographic

Muttiah Muralitharan, Saqlain Mushtaq and Anil Kumble all brightening up the county circuit, there is a great temptation to sit back and claim that we can still attract the best in the world. But any shred of complacency can be dismissed by merely a glance at the startling performances, this year, of Saqlain and Murali. They took 124 wickets between them at a rate of one wicket every five overs. True, they are quite outstanding, brilliant bowlers who will produce exceptional results. Stuart Law, on the other hand, cannot get into the Australian team, but he scored over 400 more runs in six fewer innings than anyone else. Law hit eight centuries – two more than Jamie Cox, another Australian, who has little prospect of ever representing his country. The gulf between our first-class cricketers and those from overseas is growing wider by the season and, as yet, I can see nothing in place that will halt England's decline. How I long to be proved wrong.

introduction, I appreciate, through experience, the effect it would have upon county cricketers. I know what an added incentive would have been provided on a slow day at Grace Road 15 years ago if we had played knowing that the regional team was being chosen – by the England selectors – immediately afterwards. I might have had the chance of competing directly with, say, Neal Radford, Graham Dilley, Gladstone Small, Neil Foster and Greg Thomas with places in the next Test team at stake. I would have to earn that right, of course, and bowling my boots off for Leicestershire would only be the start. Now fast-forward a few years and decide which one spinner you would choose to have in your hypothetical South East team: Ian Salisbury, Peter Such, Phil Tufnell or Min Patel? Not only would you have the added competition under such a scheme, but also the improved quality and that is what will be lacking next summer.

There is no shortage of either in the Sheffield Shield and we must congratulate Australia on an outstanding year. Their comfortable victory in the Ashes series was to be expected, but their revival in the World Cup following an exhausting tour of the West Indies was a triumph. It coincided with the return to form of two wonderful cricketers, Glenn McGrath and Shane Warne, who will both be playing county cricket in 2000. With Shoaib Akhtar,

Another England wicket falls in the Test series against New Zealand. England lost the series and sank to the bottom of the unofficial world rankings.
David Munden/Sportsline Photographic

ENGLAND

New Zealand in England
Sri Lanka 'A' in England
England 'A' in Zimbabwe
and South Africa
Australia Under-19 in England
PPP Healthcare County Championship

First-Class Averages
CGU National League
Benson and Hedges Super Cup
NatWest Trophy
Oxford and Cambridge Universities
Minor Counties

NASSER HUSSAIN

To be appointed captain of the England cricket team is to assume one of the toughest roles in international sport. Following England's early exit from the World Cup, a new direction was sought and Nasser Hussain shrugged off a token challenge from Mark Ramprakash to become the third man to lead England in only 16 months. Can he focus a volatile temperament and lead England out of the wilderness?

BY JONATHAN AGNEW

If supporters of English cricket had sought retribution during a deeply depressing summer, they were presented with a succession of scapegoats. A season that began amidst so much optimism – people were even suggesting that England might win the World Cup, for goodness sake! – ended with casualties strewn every which way. David Lloyd, the coach, jumped overboard before the ECB could fire him. Alec Stewart, the captain, was sacked after England failed to qualify for the second stage of the World Cup. Mike Gatting and Graham Gooch, two of England's most prominent cricketers of the 1980s and 90s, were removed from the selection panel before the final Test. In fact, the only area of the English game that was devoid of casualties was in the administrative department, and it can only be a matter of time before the pressure starts to mount within the offices of the ECB.

There was little option than to remove Stewart. His position, as I recorded when he was originally appointed, was never going to be long term because he is such a valuable player. The captaincy was another burden to add to his already long list of responsibilities. It is true that his part in the unseemly wrangling over the players' World Cup payments did little to strengthen his position with the authorities, and while Stewart viewed his sacking as unfair, the fact is that World Cups do mark the end of a cycle. After their poor performance, England had to change direction and move forward with a new man at the helm.

And so it was that Nasser Hussain stepped up from the ranks. There was a time when it seemed highly unlikely that he would ever be trusted with the ultimate

Andy Caddick responded magnificently to Hussain's call.
David Munden/ Sportsline Photographic

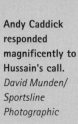

responsibility: Hussain was volatile, angry and anything but a team man. In fact, as recently as 1998 when the successor for Mike Atherton was being sought, Hussain was viewed highly suspiciously by those at the top, including those who would have to make the decision. That only 12 months later, Hussain was made captain of England is testimony to his sudden development, reformation and new-found maturity.

He is a proud man in every way. Born in Madras, he is not only aware of his roots, but also recognises the opportunity that now exists to promote cricket amongst the Asian population in the United Kingdom. His father, Joe, has been stereotyped as the archetypal 'pushy father' (something he admits to, by the way) and Nasser has inherited that same drive and determination. In fact, in many ways, Nasser Hussain is more of an Australian than an Indian or Englishman.

This is no bad thing. At a time when English cricket is on its knees, it requires someone with an 'edge' to lead the recovery. True, the game must always be played in the right spirit – if not, cricket simply is not worth playing – and there have been times when Hussain has stood his ground despite the most blatant of edges, and got away with it. His two centuries of the 1996 series against India both contained the most astonishing and bare-faced reprieves. That Hussain can stand there, take the inevitable abuse that follows and still carry on batting says much for his single-minded attitude, if not a great deal for his observation of the niceties of the game.

Tactically, he has enjoyed a good start. He appears to be very much a 'hands on' captain who, despite being a brilliant slip fielder, will prefer to spend time at mid-off. Here he can both encourage the bowler and control him. His field placings were intelligent and had been carefully thought out. The fact that England's batsmen played like lemmings was no reflection on Hussain's leadership at all.

But what impressed me the most about Hussain during the summer was something that I really should not have found the least bit surprising: his willingness to recall the 'difficult' characters, Phil Tufnell and Andy Caddick. It was a clear message from the captain, a man who had also been labelled selfish, awkward and aggressive in the past, that skilled players will be

tolerated, even accepted by the team under his leadership. Caddick immediately repaid every ounce of faith his captain had shown in him by bowling and, importantly, batting out of his skin. It was nothing less than Hussain would have expected from him.

So we wish Nasser well as he begins his first tour overseas as captain of England. His temperament will be tested and stretched to the limit by the South Africans, who are bent on revenge following their defeat in England in 1998. It will require a cool head, pride and commitment, and a great deal of luck for England to succeed. Hussain can do nothing about the luck and has already shown his grit and determination when playing for England. But a cool head? This might very well prove to be his greatest test.

Nasser Hussain has been charged with lifting England from the bottom of the unofficial world rankings.
David Munden/Sportsline Photographic

NEW ZEALAND IN ENGLAND
By Jonathan Agnew

Less than a fortnight after the hugely disappointing World Cup Final, the second half of England's international summer was underway. Much had changed, however, since the opening game of the World Cup in mid-May. Alec Stewart had been fired as captain and although he muttered darkly about having been made a scapegoat for England's failings, he was allowed, nonetheless, to line up at Edgbaston alongside the new captain, Nasser Hussain of Essex. David Lloyd, the coach, was also missing at Birmingham; the only difference between his and Stewart's dismissals being that Lloyd jumped before he was pushed.

Not only did England have a new captain, they had a new coach, too. However, as if to illustrate perfectly the extent to which the tail wags the dog at the England and Wales Cricket Board, Glamorgan would not allow Duncan Fletcher to answer England's call immediately because he was contracted at Sophia Gardens until the end of the season. Therefore, a rather curious press conference was staged to herald England's new dawn: attended by both Hussain and Fletcher – who had never met each other before – it announced that Fletcher could not take up his post until 1 October. Thus, England were coach-less for a series that they simply had to win in order to restore much-needed public respect and confidence. It was an absurdly – and quite unnecessarily – chaotic start.

Pundits had been anticipating this series against New Zealand for at least two years; not, I must confess, because of the prospect of bright, entertaining cricket between two enlightened cricket teams. No! This was the window of opportunity that English cricket would have to embrace and use as a rare chance to blood the next generation of Test cricketers. A tough tour in South Africa lay ahead, followed by series against Zimbabwe and West Indies. This was the moment to act.

Following his late withdrawal from the Sydney Test in January, Mike Atherton's international career appeared to be over. He was still having treatment for his back condition, which was preventing him from playing regularly for Lancashire, and with Darren Gough nursing a shin injury England would be without their most experienced batsman and their cutting edge.

New Zealand, on the other hand, had enjoyed a good World Cup. Beaten semi-finalists, they had

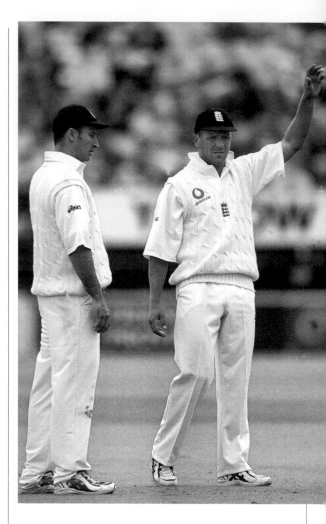

New England captain Nasser Hussain takes advice from previous captain Alec Stewart.
David Munden/Sportsline Photographic

shown themselves to be businesslike and well drilled under the guidance of their Australian coach, Steve Rixon, who was to leave his post after this series. Geoff Allott had been one of the successes of the World Cup and if the conditions favoured seam bowling, New Zealand's attack might very well outclass that of England. That having been said, the reality was that England had beaten New Zealand on their last two tours 'down-under' and in the unofficial *Wisden* world rankings, New Zealand sat two uncomfortable positions below England, right at the bottom of the table. This was the battle of the also-rans, and the marketing men were all too aware of it.

FIRST TEST
1, 2 and 3 July 1999 at Edgbaston

England's line-up for the first match of Hussain's reign was vastly different from the one that lost the final Test against Australia in Sydney, and the changes were widely applauded. Hussain – rather more sympathetic towards the difficult but talented characters at England's disposal than his predecessors – immediately restored Phil Tufnell and Andy Caddick to the ranks. Most of Tufnell's off-the-field antics have been well documented, but the fact remains that he, more than any other spinner in England, is likely to win a Test match. Caddick's omission from the tour of Australia had been nothing short of scandalous. Lacking in confidence, Caddick does not always endear himself to his colleagues (or those, at least, who do not know him) but he is a first-rate bowler who would have shaken up the Australians at the WACA in the winter.

Alex Tudor was the sole survivor from England's attack in Sydney. Gough was unavailable, but Dean Headley and Peter Such were dropped, along with Graeme Hick (for the seventh time), John Crawley and wicketkeeper Warren Hegg.

Possibly because of my experience at Leicestershire – where we got through six county captains at a rate of almost one per year – I have always argued against retaining recently sacked captains. It seems to me that they add nothing positive to what is supposed to be a new environment and can only cause rifts and cliques amongst the team. Stewart was, in my view, extremely fortunate to remain involved, not least because of his role in the unseemly row over pay before the World Cup, but principally because he honestly considered himself to have been unfairly treated by the selectors. Had Hussain not been made of tougher stuff, this could have undermined his position.

The balance of England's team was affected once again by the decision to bring in a specialist wicketkeeper – 20-year-old Chris Read – rather than give the gloves to Stewart. Thus England went into the game with six batsmen, four bowlers and two wicketkeepers: an expensive luxury a team as destitute as England's really cannot afford for long.

Having witnessed the excitable and passionate support by the Asian community during the World Cup, the selection of Aftab Habib – born in Reading of Pakistani parents – was laudable. Habib had scored heavily for Leicestershire and was rated by his captain, James Whitaker, higher than two other worthy contenders, Ben Smith and Darren Maddy. The survival of cricket in England surely depends upon the involvement of the ethnic minorities, and this England team contained two players with Caribbean connections, two (including the captain) with Asian backgrounds, a bowler who was born in England but raised in Australia and an 'anglicised' New Zealander.

The Edgbaston pitch was a concern. 'I hope it lasts five days,' admitted the groundsman, Steve Rouse. In fact, the game was over halfway through the third afternoon.

Geoff Allott celebrates dismissing Alec Stewart for 0 in the first Test.
David Munden/Sportsline Photographic

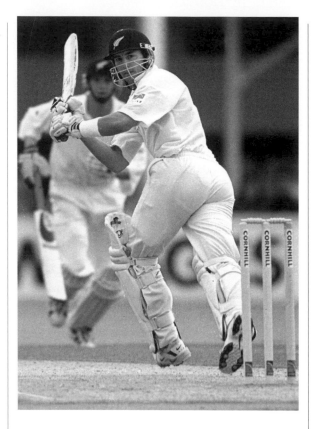

Adam Parore leg glances Alan Mullally for four during his innings of 73 in the first Test at Edgbaston.
David Munden/Sportsline Photographic

On a cloudy morning, New Zealand won the toss and decided to bat. It was a wise decision based on the realisation that the pitch would not improve as time went by. Roger Twose fell in the first over, and New Zealand were soon 73 for 4 as the ball swung and zipped about all over the place. Adam Parore was badly missed by Stewart, who simply did not see the ball fly past him in the slips and while Dion Nash kept an end up, Parore cashed in on some wayward, over-excitable bowling. In desperation, Hussain finally turned to Tufnell. The captain, himself, clung on to a superb diving catch at slip to remove the obdurate Nash, and Tufnell ran through the tail to finish with 3 for 22. Word from the England dressing room that evening was that a total of 275 to 300 was par: even having applied the necessary dose of 'spin' to that assessment, 150 seemed far more realistic.

The second morning was equally humid and overcast and, as we suspected, New Zealand's bowlers revelled in the conditions. They were helped by the quite appalling run-out of Butcher by Hussain, and that moment of madness sparked a collapse of six wickets for 19 runs. Coming together at 45 for 7, Caddick and Tudor batted with common sense, putting on exactly 70 before Caddick edged Nash to Parore for 33. Mullally fell first ball as usual, and when Tufnell was taken at slip, Tudor remained undefeated on 32. It had been a promising, uncomplicated innings but England remained 100 behind. In these conditions, that lead was worth double.

Caddick's innings must have done wonders for his confidence, because he now charged in like a man possessed. Before New Zealand could wake up to the disaster that was about to overwhelm them, they were 46 for 6 and then an unbelievable 52 for 8. Caddick claimed five wickets, but Tudor's support bowling was far from convincing. Doull, batting at number ten, seized his opportunity and threw the bat with great effect while his captain, Fleming, stood firm at the other end. It was Tufnell who, once again, wrapped up the innings by first having Fleming caught at the second attempt by Read and then having Doull comfortably stumped for 46 from only 50 balls. Tufnell clinched those two vital wickets within only 13 balls of coming on to bowl to give him match figures of 5 for 29. Caddick's overdue recall was worth 8 for 89.

In succumbing for 107, New Zealand set England 208 to win – surely 100 runs fewer than they would have liked – but Stewart fell third ball in the gloom before the close of the second day to leave England on 3 for 1, still 205 runs away from an unlikely victory.

The third morning was fresh and bright – a stark contrast to the weather on the previous two days in which 31 wickets had fallen. Despite the obvious change in the conditions, New Zealand were still favourites to wrap up the match.

However, despite their success at bowling under pressure in the World Cup, New Zealand's bowlers completely blew it. Doull, who bowled magnificently in the first innings, seemed consumed by nerves. Allott, too, lost all control. Butcher immediately grabbed the initiative and, gradually, so did Tudor, the nightwatchman, to the extent that he took control. The first seven overs of the morning cost 43 runs.

Nash found Butcher's inside edge but Hussain continued the positive approach that Tudor was now very obviously enjoying. Anything wide of the off-stump was flayed through the covers by the tall fast

FIRST TEST – ENGLAND v. NEW ZEALAND
1, 2 and 3 July 1999 at Edgbaston, Birmingham

NEW ZEALAND

	First Innings		Second Innings	
RG Twose	c Thorpe, b Mullally	0	lbw, b Caddick	0
MJ Horne	lbw, b Caddick	12	c Read, b Mullally	1
SP Fleming (capt)	c Thorpe, b Tudor	27	c Read, b Tufnell	25
NJ Astle	c Read, b Butcher	26	c Read, b Mullally	9
CD McMillan	c Thorpe, b Caddick	18	c Butcher, b Mullally	15
CL Cairns	c and b Caddick	17	c Read, b Caddick	3
*AC Parore	c Read, b Mullally	73	c Stewart, b Caddick	0
DJ Nash	c Hussain, b Tufnell	21	c Read, b Caddick	0
DL Vettori	c Hussain, b Tufnell	1	b Caddick	0
SB Doull	c Butcher, b Tufnell	11	st Read, b Caddick	46
GI Allott	not out	7	not out	0
	b 1, lb 5, w 1, nb 6	13	b 1, lb 4, w 1, nb 2	8
		226		**107**

	First Innings				Second Innings			
	O	M	R	W	O	M	R	W
Mullally	26.4	5	72	2	16	3	48	3
Caddick	27	12	57	3	14	3	32	5
Tudor	11	2	44	1	5	2	15	–
Butcher	7	2	25	1				
Tufnell	17	9	22	3	2.1	0	7	2

Fall of Wickets
1–0, 2–19, 3–55, 4–73, 5–103, 6–104, 7–189, 8–191, 9–211
1–0, 2–5, 3–17, 4–39, 5–46, 6–46, 7–52, 8–52, 9–106

ENGLAND

	First Innings		Second Innings	
MA Butcher	run out (Horne/Doull)	11	c Parore, b Nash	33
AJ Stewart	lbw, b Allott	1	b Allott	0
N Hussain (capt)	b Doull	10	(4) b Allott	44
GP Thorpe	c Astle, b Allott	6	(5) not out	21
MR Ramprakash	c Parore, b Cairns	0		
Aftab Habib	b Cairns	1		
*CMW Read	c sub (CZ Harris), b Nash	1		
AR Caddick	c Parore, b Nash	33		
AJ Tudor	not out	32	(3) not out	99
AD Mullally	c Parore, b Nash	0		
PCR Tufnell	c Fleming, b Cairns	6		
	b 8, lb 11, nb 6	25	b 7, lb 2, nb 5	14
		126	(for 3 wickets)	**211**

	First Innings				Second Innings			
	O	M	R	W	O	M	R	W
Allott	14	3	38	2	15	0	71	2
Doull	12	6	17	1	7	0	48	–
Vettori					6	1	22	–
Cairns	9.4	3	35	3	4	0	18	–
Nash	11	6	17	3	7	0	29	1
Astle					1	1	0	–
McMillan					3.4	0	14	–

Fall of Wickets
1–5, 2–26, 3–28, 4–33, 5–38, 6–40, 7–45, 8–115, 9–115
1–3, 2–76, 3–174

Umpires: SA Bucknor & P Willey
TV Umpire: R Julian
Toss: New Zealand
Debuts: Aftab Habib & CMW Read
Man of the Match: AJ Tudor

England won by seven wickets

Alex Tudor celebrates as he reaches 50 not out, taking England to victory in the first Test. He went on to make 99 not out, the highest score ever by an English nightwatchman.
David Munden/Sportsline Photographic

bowler and he displayed his West Indian roots with some delightful calypso flicks though mid-wicket.

By the time Hussain lost his stumps to an in-swinger, the game was already England's. The only question was whether Tudor would reach one of the most remarkable Test centuries of all time. His Surrey team-mate, Graham Thorpe, appeared to do his best to thwart him by scoring at every opportunity, and the top-edged pull that flew to the boundary to win the match took Tudor to 99 not out from 119 balls: the highest score ever made by an English nightwatchman.

New Zealand's shattered bowlers left the field shamefaced, and Hussain escaped with an unlikely victory that broke the losing sequence for new captains that dated back to Bob Willis' first Test in 1982.

SECOND TEST
22, 23, 24 and 25 July 1999 at Lord's

England's record at Lord's in recent years has been atrocious. Many reasons have been offered to explain this, but the most likely of all is that visiting teams are inspired by the realisation of the childhood dream of playing a Test match at the home of cricket. 'Inspired' is a word not often directed at the England team, but following on the heels of their victory at Edgbaston – and the

Matt Horne cuts during his century in the second Test at Lord's.

Philip Brown/Sportsline Photographic

elevation of Alex Tudor to hero status – the odds were on England overcoming the Lord's hoodoo once and for all.

However, right from the start, England's plans were shambolic. Darren Gough – missing at Edgbaston – finally turned out for Yorkshire against Warwickshire and, on a pitch of dubious quality, took enough wickets to cause a stir. But no sooner was his name being pencilled into the selectors' notebooks, than Gough went lame again and ended the season with his leg encased in plaster. Next, Tudor withdrew at infuriatingly short notice for the second time in his short international career. The England camp was furious that Surrey had booked Tudor in for a scan on his troublesome knee on the eve of the Test, without telling them. A 'hotspot' was identified, Tudor pulled out and, on the Wednesday evening, poor old Angus Fraser was contacted in Taunton and told to head for Lord's. Even this caused problems. The County Ground, Taunton was locked up for the night and Fraser could not get his kit out of the pavilion! Early next day – the morning of the Test – Fraser packed his bags and headed east. As he reached the Hogarth roundabout in West London, Fraser heard the announcement on *Test Match Special* that Headley was playing so, remarkably calmly, Fraser merely went all the way round the roundabout and drove the three hours back to Taunton!

New Zealand had their injury problems, too. Simon Doull, who had bowled so well in the first innings at Edgbaston, withdrew and was replaced by an opening batsman, Matthew Bell.

Winning the toss in cloudy conditions, Nasser Hussain opted to bat first, and in no time Butcher was back in the dressing room for 8. Stewart knew, following his performance at Edgbaston, that the full glare of the spotlight was focused on him and he responded by scoring a half-century that even he would recognise as having been scratchy. However, in the company of Hussain, he had raised England to 79 for 1.

Mark Ramprakash is trapped by Dion Nash, second Test.
Philip Brown/Sportsline Photographic

After lunch, England's innings fell apart in the face of some accurate, innovative, but hardly devastating seam bowling from Nash and Cairns. Four wickets fell for 23 from 45 balls including Aftab Habib who was bowled in exactly the same 'walking' manner that had brought about his downfall at Birmingham. The middle order was swept away – Cairns' slower ball deceived the ducking Read quite delightfully – and only Caddick, who made a typically determined 18, joined Stewart and Hussain (61) with double figures. Hussain was the last man out, giving Cairns his sixth wicket, to complete an all too familiar tale. Having been dismissed for only 186, England had their work cut out.

At 45 for 2, and with Bell and Fleming back in the pavilion, England were still in the hunt. But Horne and the dogged Twose combined in a stand of 121 in 42 patient overs. Stewart and Tufnell missed difficult half-chances and the game was slipping through England's fingers. But, in the final half-hour of the second day, Caddick found a fuller length to remove McMillan after Headley had nipped out Horne for exactly 100 and Twose for 52. A little nervously, New Zealand sent out their nightwatchman, the bespectacled Vettori.

Next day, Vettori led a charge with the bat that was to be the undoing of England. Hussain broke a finger in the gully that prevented him from taking any further part in the match (and the following Test, too) as Vettori cut and carved his way to 54 in a swashbuckling partnership of 70 with Cairns. When the fun was over, New Zealand's lead was 172.

SECOND TEST – ENGLAND v. NEW ZEALAND
22, 23, 24 and 25 July 1999 at Lord's, London

ENGLAND

	First Innings		Second Innings	
MA Butcher	c Parore, b Cairns	8	c Astle, b Vettori	20
AJ Stewart	c Fleming, b Nash	50	b Vettori	35
N Hussain (capt)	c Parore, b Cairns	61	absent injured	
GP Thorpe	c Astle, b Cairns	7	b Cairns	7
MR Ramprakash	lbw, b Nash	4	(3) c Parore, b Astle	24
Aftab Habib	b Nash	6	(5) c Astle, b Allott	19
*CMW Read	b Cairns	0	lbw, b Nash	37
AR Caddick	$ run out (Horne/Astle)	18	c Fleming, b Allott	45
DW Headley	lbw, b Cairns	4	(6) c Fleming, b Allott	12
AD Mullally	c Astle, b Cairns	0	(9) c Twose, c Cairns	10
PCR Tufnell	not out	1	(10) not out	5
	b 5, lb 8, nb 14	27	b 5, lb 3, nb 7	15
		186		**229**

	First Innings				Second Innings			
	O	M	R	W	O	M	R	W
Allott	10	1	37	–	16.4	6	36	3
Cairns	21.1	1	77	6	25	6	67	2
Nash	23	11	50	3	25	9	50	1
Astle	7	3	9	–	4	2	6	1
Vettori					31	12	62	2

Fall of Wickets
1–35, 2–79, 3–102, 4–112, 5–123, 6–125, 7–150, 8–165, 9–170
1–55, 2–71, 3–78, 4–97, 5–123, 6–127, 7–205, 8–216, 9–229

NEW ZEALAND

	First Innings		Second Innings	
MJ Horne	c Hussain, b Headley	100	lbw, b Caddick	26
MD Bell	lbw, b Headley	15	not out	26
SP Fleming (capt)	c Read, b Mullally	1	not out	5
NJ Astle	c Read, b Mullally	43		
RG Twose	c Caddick, b Headley	52		
CD McMillan	c Read, b Caddick	3		
DL Vettori	c Thorpe, b Tufnell	54		
*AC Parore	b Caddick	12		
CL Cairns	b Caddick	31		
DJ Nash	c Mullally, b Tufnell	6		
GI Allott	not out	1		
	b 1, lb 24, w 2, nb 13	40	b 2, nb 1	3
		358	(for 1 wicket)	**60**

	First Innings				Second Innings			
	O	M	R	W	O	M	R	W
Mullally	27	7	98	2	5	0	21	–
Caddick	34	11	92	3	10	4	18	1
Headley	27	7	74	3				
Tufnell	27.1	7	61	2	8	2	19	–
Butcher	3	0	7	–				
Ramprakash	1	–	1	–				

Fall of Wickets
1–43, 2–45, 3–112, 4–232, 5–239 , 6–242, 7–275, 8–345, 9–351
1–37

$ TV Decision
Umpires: MJ Kitchen & RE Koertzen
TV Umpire: NT Plews
Toss: England
Man of the Match: MJ Horne

New Zealand won by nine wickets

Chris Read is completely fooled by a Chris Cairns slower ball.
Philip Brown/Sportsline Photographic

This was the hour of reckoning for England's batsmen who, facing the prospect of defeat, had to play with absolute concentration and tenacity. In fact, possibly due to the woeful examples set by the openers Butcher and Stewart, England set New Zealand only 58 to win. Butcher threw his wicket away in the last over before tea, attempting to heave Vettori for six over mid-wicket. Shortly after the break, Stewart aimed to slog Vettori against the spin and out of the rough – a testing combination at the best of times – and was horribly bowled for 35. The only resistance was offered by Read and Caddick – again – who put together a stand of 78. Without it, England would have been sunk by an innings. It is worth recording that Mullally reached double figures – just.

Horne was bowled by Caddick for 26, but New Zealand were never likely to falter and their victory, inside four days, was their first at Lord's in 13 attempts. England's effort was roundly condemned, and not without some justification. The Daily Telegraph announced that England was the 'lowest of the low'. It was slightly premature in doing so because that status would actually be achieved the following month.

THIRD TEST
5, 6, 7, 8 and 9 August 1999 at Old Trafford

Much of the pre-Test speculation focused on the England captaincy. Until the day before the match, Hussain was still uttering optimistic noises about being able to play despite his broken finger. However, on the Wednesday afternoon he had to concede that it was not an option, and announced that he was handing the reins to Mark Butcher. Given that Butcher had played what was indisputably the most irresponsible stroke of the series in the previous Test, it seemed a curious reward. Indeed, such was the recklessness of England's batting in the two Tests to date, that Butcher – among others – was extremely fortunate still to be in the team. That these players did remain said a great deal about the cosy environment in and around the England dressing room. It would change shortly, but not quite yet.

Aftab Habib was dropped after only two Tests; Peter Such and Mike Atherton returned and so, for the seventh time, did Graeme Hick. More condemnation. This was to have been a series in which the selectors introduced a sensible youth policy that would stand England in good stead for the forthcoming tour of South Africa, and beyond. Rumours of disagreements in the selection meeting prior to the match swept around the cricketing circuit. Unconfirmed reports suggested that Mike Gatting and Graham Gooch had enlisted the support of Hussain to outnumber the forward-thinking chairman, David Graveney. Whatever the truth of it all, Hick's return was a surprising move particularly when it was announced that he was not selected with his bowling in mind. Given that Old Trafford had been a spinner's paradise for the whole summer, this made little sense.

Neither did England's final selection. The pitch, which had already been used twice this season, looked rough and promised to take spin, but in insisting that Read keep wicket rather than Stewart, England went into the match with only two seam bowlers, Caddick and Headley, with Tufnell and Such providing the spin. The attack looked alarmingly threadbare.

Neither side wanted to bat last and when Fleming called wrongly, Butcher was clearly delighted.

Craig McMillan sweeps during his century in the third Test at Old Trafford.
David Munden/Sportsline Photographic

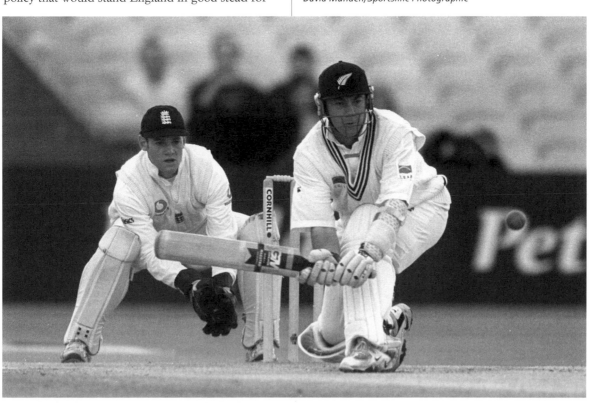

Dean Headley plays the ball past Stephen Fleming, third Test.
David Munden/Sportsline Photographic

However, that was before England batted. Twenty-nine overs were lost on the first day at the end of which England had crawled to 108 for 5. It was torpid, unattractive cricket, not helped by the pitch which Barry Richards described as a 'shocker' and Peter Marron, the groundsman, awarded two points out of ten. Devoid of any pace and with uneven bounce, the pitch strangled the life out of batting and New Zealand's excellent attack made run-scoring all but impossible. This, explained Fleming later, proved to be their form of attack. Hick received a terrible leg before decision from umpire Tiffin, with whom he used to play club cricket in Zimbabwe, to bring to an end an innings of 12, made up entirely of boundaries.

Chris Harris has produced few devastating spells in Test cricket but, on the second morning, he dismissed Headley and Read in one over, leaving Ramprakash with his familiar duty of shepherding the tail-enders through another crisis. In Such he found just about the least likely ally in English cricket and together they put on 31 precious runs in 72 minutes. Such's contribution was a 51-ball 0, and he departed, with bat proudly raised, to a standing ovation in recognition of the second-longest duck in Test history. This seemed to inspire Tufnell who also hung around for half an hour. He, at least, got off the mark before leaving Ramprakash stranded on 69 not out.

Before New Zealand had scored a run in reply, Thorpe dropped Horne at slip off Caddick. It was the worst possible start and Horne responded by going for his strokes in what were, amazingly, improving conditions.

THIRD TEST – ENGLAND v. NEW ZEALAND
5, 6, 7, 8 and 9 August 1999 at Old Trafford, Manchester

ENGLAND

	First Innings		Second Innings	
MA Butcher (capt)	c Fleming, b Cairns	5	lbw, b Nash	9
MA Atherton	c Parore, b Cairns	11	c Astle, b Vettori	48
AJ Stewart	c Parore, b Nash	23	not out	83
GP Thorpe	c Bell, b Vettori	27	not out	25
GA Hick	lbw, b Nash	12		
MR Ramprakash	not out	69		
DW Headley	c Fleming, b Harris	18		
*CMW Read	b Harris	0		
AR Caddick	$ run out (Harris/Parore)	12		
PM Such	c Bell, b Vettori	0		
PCR Tufnell	c Astle, b Nash	1		
	b 6, lb 10, w 5	21	b 9, lb 7	16
		199	**(for 2 wickets)**	**181**

	First Innings				Second Innings			
	O	M	R	W	O	M	R	W
Cairns	34	12	72	2	11	1	54	–
Nash	31.1	15	46	3	10	3	26	1
Astle	11	5	14	–	3	1	7	0
Vettori	25	7	35	2	26	12	48	1
Harris	8	4	16	2	18	6	30	0

Fall of Wickets
1-13, 2-54, 3-60, 4-83, 5-104, 6-133, 7-133, 8-152, 9-183
1-19, 2-118

NEW ZEALAND

	First Innings	
MJ Horne	b Caddick	39
MD Bell	c Atherton, b Headley	83
SP Fleming (capt)	lbw, b Such	38
NJ Astle	c Such, b Caddick	101
RG Twose	lbw, b Such	20
CD McMillan	not out	107
*AC Parore	c Butcher, b Such	10
CL Cairns	c Caddick, b Tufnell	41
DJ Nash	c Caddick, b Such	26
CZ Harris	b Tufnell	3
DL Vettori	not out	2
	b 6, lb 17, nb 3	26
	(for 9 wickets, dec.)	**496**

	First Innings			
	O	M	R	W
Caddick	39	11	112	2
Headley	31	4	115	1
Tufnell	46	12	111	2
Such	41	11	114	4
Hick	1	0	8	–
Butcher	2	0	13	–

Fall of Wickets
1-46, 2-110, 3-263, 4-280, 5-321, 6-331, 7-425, 8-476, 9-487

$ TV Decision
Umpires: DR Shepherd & R Tiffin
TV Umpire: KE Palmer
Toss: England
Man of the Match: CD McMillan

Match drawn

New Zealand bowler Dion Nash appeals for lbw against Graham Thorpe.
David Munden/Sportsline Photographic

All of New Zealand's top order chipped in as England's paltry 199 was quickly overtaken. In front of a sparse crowd, McMillan and Cairns rammed the point home, McMillan's undefeated 107 containing three sixes and nine fours. Fleming declared with a lead of 297 and a minimum of 151 overs in which to bowl England out. New Zealand were perfectly placed to take a lead in the series. Butcher's poor trot continued; he fell leg before to Nash for 9, but Stewart then came out with all guns blazing to put on 99 with Mike Atherton. It was some of the brightest English batting of the series and was ended by a cruel umpiring decision, this time by David Shepherd. He dispatched Atherton to an alleged catch at slip off Vettori – bowling into the rough – on a startling absence of evidence. The shot itself might have been ill-judged, but the decision was poor.

An exciting final day beckoned with England still 179 runs behind with eight wickets left. However, play could not begin until 2pm because of heavy overnight rain and it returned after only 24 overs to wash out the match. England had their draw which kept the series level, but such was the lack of enthusiasm and appetite for the task that, once again, angry voices were raised in the media. This resulted in the sacking of both Gooch and Gatting as selectors and the announcement that Duncan Fletcher, the coach-elect, would choose the team for the final match with Hussain and Graveney.

FOURTH TEST
19, 20, 21 and 22 August 1999 at The Oval

It is not inconceivable that there will be a time when we will recall the events of this match and declare this to be the game that, finally, exposed English cricket for the second-rate, smug and listless business it has now become. This was the weekend that England sunk to the bottom of the unofficial league of Test-playing countries and, after the mocking headlines had forcibly emphasised the point, many were left genuinely concerned about the future of the game.

Not, apparently, the officials at the ECB who immediately went into overdrive. 'The game is safe and in good hands,' was their message, and they pointed to the undeniable success of the England Under-19 and England 'A' teams. That was missing the point. It is from that moment, as promising and ambitious international cricketers, that England's players lose their way. Until that is addressed with a new, fresh and invigorating environment surrounding 'Team England' and a competitive, completely restructured first-class competition is introduced, England's Test team will continue to struggle.

What made the defeat at the Oval particularly galling to England's supporters was the fact that they should have won the game. Even those of us who, through years of watching England, have become hardened to inexplicable collapses, reckoned that they could not possibly blow this one. We should have known better, of course.

Stung by the criticism at Old Trafford, England were keen to put on a show of unity, with much emphasis being placed on 'body language'. This is merely another word for enthusiasm, and it saddens me to think that this is something you have to 'put on' when playing for England. However, Hussain's surprising decision to put New Zealand in to bat, in apparently blameless conditions, seemed to have

Rain, seen through a window, stops play for the final time on the last day of the third Test. The match was abandoned as a draw.
David Munden/Sportsline Photographic

Mark Ramprakash dives and holds onto a blinding catch to dismiss Adam Parore off Philip Tufnell for 0.
David Munden/Sportsline Photographic

paid dividends when the visitors slipped to 104 for 7. As we discovered throughout the match, this was almost entirely due to the tentative, nervous frame of mind the batsmen from both teams had developed. Terrified of losing the match – and with it the series – the batsmen were consumed by self-doubt and it was this, rather than terrors either in the pitch or in the bowling attacks, that accounted for the low scores.

Fleming, the captain of New Zealand, seemed particularly badly affected. His innings of 66 not out took five and a half hours of absolute concentration and a remarkable lack of shots. He was shown up when Vettori at number ten emerged to play his second important innings of the series. He plundered England's bowling to the tune of 51 as 66 runs were added in only 12 overs on the second morning. New Zealand's last three wickets had added 132 priceless runs. How many runs, we mused, will England's last three men (Mullally, Tufnell and the new cap Giddins) muster in the match? The answer was seven.

Atherton opened the innings with Darren Maddy of Leicestershire, and the experienced man was dismissed first, caught by Fleming at slip. Maddy soon followed, beautifully deceived by Vettori who, finding a surprising amount of spin, rattled Maddy's off-stump with a perfect arm-ball.

England were soon 87 for 4 when Vettori exposed Stewart's unease against spin bowling and four runs later, Hussain, unbelievably, pulled Cairns straight to the deep square leg fielder who had been deliberately set for the shot. Hussain, in distress, hung his head and apart from another fighting 30 from Ramprakash, the lower order was blown away to leave England 83 runs behind. Cairns took 5 for 31 to further illustrate the advances he has made on the tour.

Having made such a hash of their dominant position at Edgbaston, the onus was now on New Zealand's batsmen to drive home their advantage. But, once again, nerves struck. 39 for 6 became 79 for 7 and England were cock-a-hoop. Giddins, Caddick and Mullally had steadily worked their way through some feeble batting, but as they rested, Cairns came out to play the most influential innings of the series. This was the knock that made the difference between victory and defeat. He clubbed four towering sixes

FOURTH TEST – ENGLAND v. NEW ZEALAND
19, 20, 21 and 22 August 1999 at The Oval, London

NEW ZEALAND

	First Innings		Second Innings	
MJ Horne	c Caddick, b Irani	15	lbw, b Giddins	10
MD Bell	c Stewart, b Mullally	23	c Irani, b Caddick	4
SP Fleming (capt)	not out	66	c Thorpe, b Caddick	4
NJ Astle	c Stewart, b Caddick	9	c Irani, b Giddins	5
RG Twose	c Maddy, b Giddins	1	c Stewart, b Giddins	0
CD McMillan	b Tufnell	19	lbw, b Mullally	26
*AC Parore	c Ramprakash, b Tufnell	0	b Caddick	1
CL Cairns	b Mullally	11	c and b Mullally	80
DJ Nash	c Ramprakash, b Caddick	18	not out	10
DL Vettori	lbw, b Tufnell	51	c Ramprakash, b Tufnell	6
SB O'Connor	lbw, b Caddick	1	b Tufnell	6
	b 9, lb 9, w 2, nb 2	22	lb 4, w 1, nb 5	10
		236		**162**

	First Innings				Second Innings			
	O	M	R	W	O	M	R	W
Caddick	33.1	17	66	3	17	4	35	3
Mullally	26	12	34	2	11	2	27	2
Giddins	16	4	41	1	10	3	38	3
Tufnell	16	3	39	3	16	3	58	2
Irani	11	3	38	1				

Fall of Wickets
1–39, 2–45, 3–54, 4–62, 5–87, 6–87, 7–104, 8–157, 9–235
1–15, 2–15, 3–22, 4–22, 5–37, 6–39, 7–79, 8–149, 9–156

ENGLAND

	First Innings		Second Innings	
MA Atherton	c Fleming, b Nash	10	c Parore, b Nash	64
DL Maddy	b Vettori	14	c Fleming, b Nash	5
N Hussain (capt)	c Bell, b Cairns	40	c Parore, b O'Connor	9
GP Thorpe	c Fleming, b Cairns	10	c Fleming, b O'Connor	44
*AJ Stewart	b Vettori	11	c Bell, b Nash	12
MR Ramprakash	c Parore, b Cairns	30	c Parore, b Nash	0
RC Irani	lbw, b Cairns	1	c Parore, b Vettori	9
AR Caddick	b O'Connor	15	c Bell, b Vettori	3
AD Mullally	c Bell, b Vettori	5	c Twose, b Cairns	3
PCR Tufnell	not out	0	run out (Nash)	1
ESH Giddins	lbw, b Cairns	0	not out	0
	b 1, lb 5, w 5, nb 6	17	b 2, lb 3, nb 7	12
		153		**162**

	First Innings				Second Innings			
	O	M	R	W	O	M	R	W
Cairns	19	8	31	5	15.1	3	50	1
Nash	14	5	40	1	14	3	39	4
O'Connor	13	3	30	1	11	3	32	2
Vettori	33	12	46	3	16	6	36	2
Astle	1	1	0	–				

Fall of Wickets
1–25, 2–29, 3–46, 4–87, 5–91, 6–94, 7–141, 8–153, 9–153
1–23, 2–45, 3–123, 4–143, 5–143, 6–148, 7–157, 8–160, 9–161

Umpires: G Sharp & S Venkataraghavan
TV Umpire: JH Hampshire
Toss: England
Debuts: ESH Giddins & DL Maddy
Man of the Match: CL Cairns
Players of the Series: AR Caddick (E) and CL Cairns (NZ)

New Zealand won by 83 runs

TEST MATCH AVERAGES
England v. New Zealand

ENGLAND

Batting	M	Inns	NO	HS	Runs	Av	100	50
MA Atherton	2	4	0	64	133	33.25	–	1
N Hussain	3	5	0	61	164	32.80	–	1
AJ Stewart	4	8	1	83*	215	30.71	–	1
MR Ramprakash	4	6	1	69*	127	25.40	–	1
GP Thorpe	4	8	2	44	147	24.50	–	–
AR Caddick	4	6	0	45	126	21.00	–	–
MA Butcher	3	6	0	33	86	14.33	–	–
DW Headley	2	3	0	18	34	11.33	–	–
CMW Read	3	4	0	37	38	9.50	–	–
Aftab Habib	2	3	0	19	25	8.33	–	–
PCR Tufnell	4	6	3	6	14	4.66	–	–
MD Mullally	3	5	0	10	18	3.60	–	–

Played in one Test: ESH Giddins 0 & 0*; GA Hick 12; RC Irani 1 & 9; DL Mullally 14 & 5;
PM Such 0; AJ Tudor 32* & 99*

Bowling	Overs	Mds	Runs	Wkts	Av	Best	10/m	5/inns
AR Caddick	174.1	62	412	20	20.60	5–32	–	1
PCR Tufnell	132.1	36	317	14	22.64	3–22	–	–
AD Mullally	111.4	29	300	11	27.27	3–48	–	–

Also bowled: MA Butcher 12–2–45–1; ESH Giddins 26–7–79–4; DW Headley 58–11–189–4;
GA Hick 1–0–8–0; RC Irani 11–3–38–1; MR Ramprakash 1–0–1–0; PM Such 41–11–114–4;
AJ Tudor 16–4–59–1

Fielding Figures
11 – CMW Read (ct 10/st 1); 5 – GP Thorpe, AR Caddick; 4 – AJ Stewart; 3 – N Hussain,
MR Ramprakash, MA Butcher, 2 – AD Mullally, RC Irani; 1 – MA Atherton, DL Maddy, PM Such

NEW ZEALAND

Batting	M	Inns	NO	HS	Runs	Av	100	50
MD Bell	3	5	1	83	151	37.75	–	1
CD McMillan	4	6	1	107*	188	37.60	1	–
SP Fleming	4	7	2	66*	166	33.20	–	1
NJ Astle	4	6	0	101	193	32.16	1	–
CL Cairns	4	6	0	80	183	30.50	–	1
MJ Horne	4	7	0	100	203	29.00	1	–
DL Vettori	4	6	1	54	114	22.80	–	1
DJ Nash	4	6	1	26	81	16.20	–	–
AC Parore	4	6	0	73	96	16.00	–	1
RG Twose	4	6	0	52	73	12.16	–	1

Played in two Tests: GI Allott 7* & 0*, 1*
Played in one Test: SB Doull 11 & 46; CZ Harris 3; SB O'Connor 1 & 6

Bowling	Overs	Mds	Runs	Wkts	Av	Best	10/m	5/inns
DJ Nash	135.1	52	297	17	17.47	4–39	–	–
CL Cairns	139	34	404	19	21.26	6–77	–	2
DL Vettori	137	50	249	10	24.90	3–46	–	–
GI Allott	55.4	10	182	7	26.00	3–36	–	–

Also bowled: NJ Astle 27–13–36–1; SB Doull 19–6–65–1; CZ Harris 26–10–46–2;
CD McMillan 3.4–0–14–0; SB O'Connor 24–6–62–3

Fielding Figures
14 – AC Parore; 10 – SP Fleming; 7 – NJ Astle; 6 – MD Bell; 2 – RG Twose

Above: Alec Stewart pulls a ball from Dion Nash but will be caught at square leg in England's second innings.
David Munden/Sportsline Photographic

off Tufnell and raced to 80 from only 94 balls. His partnership with Nash, who made 10 not out, was worth 70 in only 71 minutes and, from chasing only 160 to win the series, England were set 246.

Again, there were early losses: Maddy and Hussain this time, but by the close of the third day, Atherton and Thorpe had steered England to within 155 runs of victory with eight wickets in hand.

And that was how the fourth and final day was so perfectly set up. Much depended on Atherton's wicket – everyone was aware of that – and on how New Zealand's attack stood up to the pressure but the favourites had to be England.

New Zealand broke through after 32 runs had been painstakingly added when Thorpe was taken, low at first slip, by Fleming off the left-arm swing bowler, O'Connor. Twenty runs later, the big one: Atherton inside-edged a catch to Parore as he aimed a pull off Nash to depart for 64 and when Ramprakash was caught off the very next ball, New Zealand knew they were well on their way to victory. Stewart casually pulled Nash to square leg and Irani fell to Vettori on the stroke of lunch: New Zealand had captured five wickets for 66 in the session.

We did not expect any heroics from the tail and were not provided with any. Tufnell's run-out, in which he ended up on all fours, was as comical as it was pathetic and Mullally's hopeless slog to mid-on, where Twose held a simple catch, handed victory to New Zealand.

As he appeared on the balcony, Hussain was booed and jeered by a large group of England spectators who were genuinely angered by England's effort. 'I am proud of the way the team fought in this match,' he insisted afterwards, in which case Hussain stood very much alone.

Left: New Zealand all-rounder Chris Cairns celebrates the two-one series win with Champagne.
David Munden/Sportsline Photographic

VODAFONE CHALLENGE

Somerset v. New Zealand
25, 26, 27 and 28 June 1999 at Taunton
Somerset 554 (GJ Kennis 175, PS Jones 105,
ARK Pierson 66, RJ Turner 59) and 146
New Zealand 420 (CD McMillan 121, MJ Horne 91,
AC Parore 80) and 282 for 4 (NJ Astle 88*, CL Cairns
74*, KA Parsons 4 for 61)
New Zealand won by six wickets

Gregor Kennis, released by Surrey after three years
in 1997 and offered a new contract by Somerset only
after injury ruled out Mark Lathwell for the season,

Chris Cairns, the New Zealand all-rounder, came of age on
the tour of England.
David Munden/Sportsline Photographic

responded to a rare chance in the first eleven by
hitting the New Zealand attack for 175. His five and
a quarter hour innings contained 35 fours and, on
the second morning, the likely Kiwi attack for the
First Test was again thrashed – by tailenders Steffan
Jones and Adrian Pierson – as Somerset ran up 554.
Jones reached a maiden first-class ton from 146 balls
and was eventually out for 105. Pierson made 66
and the pair equalled the county record eighth-
wicket stand of 172 – set in 1983 at Leicester by
none other than Viv Richards and Ian Botham. New
Zealand, however, bounced back with 420 – Craig
McMillan hitting form with 121 – and then the
whole nature of the game changed with Somerset
being bundled out for just 146 in their second
innings. Keith Parsons raised hopes of a Somerset
win by removing the first four Kiwi batsmen, but
then Nathan Astle (88 not out) and Chris Cairns
(74 not out) provided a match-winning stand.

Hampshire v. New Zealand
9, 10, 11 and 12 July 1999 at Southampton
New Zealand 370 for 9 dec. (DJ Nash 135*, DL Vettori
50) and 247 for 9 dec. (DJ Nash 62, SD Udal 5 for 102)
Hampshire 297 (GW White 121, JP Stephenson 54,
DJ Nash 7 for 39) and 227 for 9 (M Garaway 55,
M Keech 50, DL Vettori 5 for 92)
Match drawn

This was Dion Nash's match, with the New
Zealander dominating the first three days like a
latter-day Richard Hadlee. Nash scored 135 not out
and 62, and added career-best bowling of 7 for 39 to
his career-best first-innings hundred as Hampshire
were bowled out for 297 early on day three. On the
fourth and final day, however, Nash was given only
seven overs as he was understandably rested – and
Hampshire hung on for a draw at 227 for 9 and a
£2,750 reward from sponsors Vodafone. New
Zealand were 56 for 5 in their first innings, but
Daniel Vettori (50) and Simon Doull (49 from
number ten) supported Nash well. Giles White made
a first innings 121 for Hampshire, and Vettori
narrowly failed to spin the Kiwis to victory with 5 for
92 on the final afternoon.

Kent v. New Zealand
15, 16, 17 and 18 July 1999 at Canterbury
Kent 201 (ET Smith 72, CL Cairns 7 for 46) and 417 for
9 (ET Smith 111, A Symonds 102, MJ Banes 53)
New Zealand 591 (MJ Horne 172, NJ Astle 121,
RG Twose 73, DJ Nash 66*, DA Scott 4 for 151)
Match drawn

A run-feast at Canterbury ended in a draw with the New Zealanders just unable to finish off a below full-strength county side on the final afternoon. Kent's first innings of 201 was a dreadful underachievement, well though Chris Cairns bowled for his 7 for 46. New Zealand then batted on and on to score 591, Matthew Horne hitting 172, Nathan Astle 121 and both Roger Twose and Dion Nash going well past 50. Ed Smith, however, followed up his first innings 72 with an assured 111 and Andrew Symonds also underlined his vast potential with 102.

Derbyshire v. New Zealand
28 July 1999 at Derby
New Zealand 369 for 6 (50 overs) CD McMillan 86, MJ Horne 73, MD Bell 70
Derbyshire 239 for 8 (50 overs) AS Rollins 111*
New Zealand won by 130 runs

A curious one-day fixture it might have been, in the middle of the Cornhill Test series, but the New Zealanders had a fine time of it in the sunshine. Matt Horne, Matthew Bell and Craig McMillan (89 from 69 balls) all went well past 50 – and a below-strength Derbyshire conceded an astonishing 91 from the last five overs. An excellent 111 not out from acting captain Adrian Rollins ensured the county's reply was not without some merit – but New Zealand's 50-over score of 369 for 6 was always far out of reach.

Leicestershire v. New Zealand
30, 31 July and 1 August 1999 at Leicester
Leicestershire 125 (AJ Penn 6 for 51) and 333 (VJ Wells 101, PA Nixon 99, SB O'Connor 6 for 65)
New Zealand 260 (DL Vettori 112, AJ Penn 69*, J Ormond 5 for 63) and 202 for 2 (CD McMillan 85*, SP Fleming 82*)
New Zealand won by nine wickets

Andrew Penn, summoned from Surrey League club Esher because of injury to other fast bowlers, enjoyed an unexpected call-up into the New Zealand ranks by taking 6 for 51 as Leicestershire were tumbled out for 125. Penn, who plays for Central Districts and had three one-day international appearances to his name, then hit 69 not out, adding 91 for the eighth wicket with Daniel Vettori, whose 112 was a maiden first-class hundred. Jimmy Ormond's five wickets failed to stop New Zealand building a sizeable first innings lead. Leicestershire, at 107 for 5, seemed to be heading for a heavy defeat but Vince Wells (101) was joined by Paul Nixon (99) in a determined stand. An

eventual second-innings total of 333, in which Shayne O'Connor took 6 for 65, left the Kiwis to make 199. Craig McMillan, finding true form, hit 85 not out and Stephen Fleming kept pace with 82 not out as New Zealand romped home by nine wickets.

Middlesex v. New Zealand
11 August 1999 at Southgate
Middlesex 239 for 8 (50 overs) MR Ramprakash 85, AJ Penn 4 for 54
New Zealand 200 (46.5 overs) PN Weekes 4 for 27
Middlesex won by 39 runs

Mark Ramprakash eased his way to 85 off 119 balls as Middlesex scored 239 for 8 from their 50 overs at Southgate, Andrew Penn's four wickets coming at some cost. But a lacklustre New Zealand batting performance ended with them being bowled out for 200, Craig McMillan top-scoring with 42. Richard Johnson, back after a six-week lay-off following a groin operation and then a strained rib muscle, took the last two Kiwi wickets.

Essex v. New Zealand
13, 14, 15 and 16 August 1999 at Chelmsford
New Zealand 236 (NJ Astle 54) and 217 (RG Twose 91, RSG Anderson 4 for 39)
Essex 493 (DDJ Robinson 200, SD Peters 99, DR Law 63*, SB O'Connor 5 for 130)
Essex won by an innings and 40 runs

Essex won themselves £11,000 from sponsors Vodafone by inflicting a heavy innings defeat on the New Zealanders just days before the final Test against England. Ronnie Irani, captaining Essex in the absence of resting England captain Nasser Hussain, led the way with 3 for 24 as New Zealand were dismissed for 236 on the opening day. Then came almost two days of grinding as the Essex batsmen followed their instructions to the letter and kept the tourists toiling in the field. Darren Robinson, who came into the game averaging less than 20 in the championship, made a career-best 200 and his sixth-wicket stand of 206 with Stephen Peters was just two runs short of the county record. Peters, disappointingly for the 20-year-old, was out hooking for 99, but Danny Law followed up his first innings 3 for 48 with 63 not out as Essex reached 493. At the end of the third day New Zealand, clearly disheartened, were 94 for 4, and little resistance remained. Roger Twose was last out for a fighting 91 but Ricky Anderson, one of seven uncapped players in the Essex side, took 4 for 39.

SRI LANKA 'A' IN ENGLAND
By Mark Baldwin

New Zealand v. Sri Lanka 'A'
7 July 1999 at Milton Keynes
New Zealand 243 for 6 (50 overs) RG Twose 84,
MD Bell 55
Sri Lanka 'A' 244 for 7 (48.1 overs) A Gunawardene
79, TM Dilshan 77
Sri Lanka 'A' won by three wickets

Fine batting by Avishka Gunawardene (79) and
Tuwan Dilshan (77) took Sri Lanka 'A' breezing
past New Zealand's 50-over total of 243 for 6 at
Milton Keynes. Roger Twose top-scored for the
Kiwis with 84 but the Sri Lankans triumphed by
three wickets. More than a month later, at the end
of their seven-week tour, the Sri Lanka 'A' manager,
Stanley Jayasinghe, said he would be writing to
the New Zealand Cricket Board to register an
official complaint about racist sledging during
the match.

Lancashire v. Sri Lanka 'A'
9, 10 and 11 July 1999 at Old Trafford
Sri Lanka 'A' 277 (SI de Saram 89, ID Austin 6 for 43)
and 274 (A Gunawardene 62, PP Wickremasinghe 62,
IS Gallage 54*, G Yates 5 for 54)
Lancashire 271 (JJ Haynes 80, NH Fairbrother 55,
PP Wickremasinghe 4 for 56) and 101 (R Herath
6 for 45)
Sri Lanka 'A' won by 179 runs

Mike Atherton's second comeback of the summer
brought only the embarrassment of a heavy defeat
for Lancashire against a Sri Lankan side who
outbowled and outfought a county team also
bolstered by the presence of four other
internationals in Fairbrother, Flintoff, Lloyd and
Austin. Atherton initially spent 30 balls making just
a single, and in the second-innings collapse to 101
he was the first of Rangana Herath's six victims –
making only five runs. A fine 80 by wicketkeeper
Jamie Haynes helped Lancashire get to within six
runs of Sri Lanka's first-innings 277, which was built
on 89 from de Saram and included the first first-
class wickets of the season for Austin, who ended
with 6 for 43. But Lancashire had no answer to a
brilliant last-wicket stand of 134 between
Wickremasinghe (62) and Gallage (54 not out) and,
led by slow left-armer Herath, the Sri Lankan
spinners looked more threatening than the
Lancastrian trio of Yates, Schofield and Keedy.

Northamptonshire v. Sri Lanka 'A'
15, 16 and 17 July 1999 at Northampton
Northamptonshire 314 (DJG Sales 87,
GP Swann 75*, ASA Perera 7 for 73)
and 313 for 7 dec. (GP Swann 130*,
RJ Warren 51)
Sri Lanka 'A' 86 (DJG Sales 4 for 25) and
385 (TM Dilshan 115, S Kalavitigoda 63,
SI de Saram 61, KJ Innes 4 for 85)
Northamptonshire won by 156 runs

A terrible first-innings batting performance
cost the Sri Lankans dearly as Northants beat
them by 156 runs and with a day to spare. Suresh
Perera took 7 for 73 on the opening day, but David
Sales (87) and Graeme Swann (75 not out)

**Gunawardene top-scored for Sri Lanka 'A' in their victory
over Lancashire.**
Mueen ud Din Hameed/Sportsline Photographic

took advantage of a rare chance to take on international opposition in a Northants first-innings total of 314. Sales then picked up 4 for 25 as the Sri Lankans crumbled pitifully to just 86 all out and Northants, with 313 for 7 declared second time around, chose to rub in their superiority rather than enforce the follow-on. It also enabled the younger Swann brother to rattle up 130 not out – his hundred taking just 88 balls – and take his unbeaten match run aggregate to 205. Sri Lanka fought well in their second innings, Dilshan hitting 115, but they were eventually winkled out for 385.

Essex v. Sri Lanka 'A'
21, 22, 23 and 24 July 1999 at Chelmsford
Sri Lanka 'A' 364 (TM Dilshan 86, RP Arnold 70, NC Phillips 4 for 42) and 525 for 7 dec. (HPW Jayawardene 89, LPC Silva 80, S Kalavitigoda 73, A Gunawardene 72, ASA Perera 71*)
Essex 442 (RC Irani 153, AP Grayson 125)
Match drawn

A match totally dominated by the bat ended, predictably, in a draw with the third innings yet to be completed. Tim Phillips, a left-arm spinner just out of Felsted School, made a worthy first-class debut by taking 4 for 42 in the Sri Lankans' first-innings 364. Ronnie Irani made 153 and Paul Grayson 125 as Essex won a 78-run first-innings lead, but then no less than five Sri Lanka batsmen topped 70 without going on to three figures as the tourists batted out time to reach a mountainous 525 for 7.

Durham v. Sri Lanka 'A'
26 July 1999 at Chester-le-Street
Durham 290 for 6 (50 overs) JA Daley 81, JJB Lewis 57, MP Speight 54
Sri Lanka 'A' 208 (37.4 overs) LPC Silva 71
Durham won by 82 runs

Jimmy Daley launched Durham's 50-over innings with an innings of 81 from 125 balls, but it was the explosive batting of wicketkeeper Martin Speight that set this game alight. Speight's 54 took him just 26 balls and, with 121 runs flowing from the final ten overs, Durham reached an imposing 290 for 6. The Sri Lankans tried to match their six-per-over asking rate, and Silva in particular played well for his 71, but they lost wickets too rapidly and were eventually all out for 208 with 12.2 overs still remaining.

First-Class County Select XI v. Sri Lanka 'A'
28 July 1999 at Chester-le-Street
First-Class County Select XI 276 for 6 (50 overs) DL Maddy 110, VS Solanki 53
Sri Lanka 'A' 251 for 9 (50 overs) ASA Perera 75, A Gunawardene 62
First-Class County Select XI won by 25 runs

Darren Maddy underlined his credentials as a possible Test batsman with a commanding 110 from 144 balls as a First-Class County Select XI defeated the Sri Lankan tourists by 25 runs. Vikram Solanki hit a run-a-ball half-century and economical bowling from Ed Giddins, who took 2 for 25 from his ten overs, was chiefly responsible for Sri Lanka falling short of the Select XI's 50-over total of 276 for 6. Avishka Gunawardene hit a 78-ball 62 and, down the order, Suresh Perera smote 75 off 74 balls.

Surrey v. Sri Lanka 'A'
30, 31 July and 1 and 2 August 1999 at The Oval
Surrey 322 (BC Hollioake 69, GP Butcher 54, IJ Ward 50, RP Arnold 4 for 74) and 182 (JN Batty 64, NRG Perera 4 for 35, R Herath 4 for 43)
Sri Lanka 'A' 232 (A Gunawardene 77, JD Ratcliffe 6 for 48) and 251 (TM Dilshan 127)
Surrey won by 21 runs

A closely contested game ended with Surrey the winners by just 21 runs. Ben Hollioake, Ian Ward and Gary Butcher all hit half-centuries as Surrey totalled 322, and Avishka Gunawardene replied with an attractive 77. But Jason Ratcliffe took 6 for 44 with his little-used seamers as Sri Lanka fell away to 232 and it took some fine spin bowling from Herath and Perera to limit Surrey to 182 second time around. Tuwan Dilshan then led the Sri Lankan victory charge with a plucky 127, but he failed to find substantial support and eventually fast bowler Carl Greenidge, the son of Gordon, wrapped up Surrey's victory by taking the last two wickets.

Worcestershire v. Sri Lanka 'A'
10, 11, 12 and 13 August 1999 at Worcester
Worcestershire 237 for 7 dec. (NE Batson 72, DA Leatherdale 52, VS Solanki 50) and 222 for 9 dec. (GR Haynes 60*)
Sri Lanka 'A' 243 for 9 dec. (RP Arnold 68, VS Solanki 4 for 41) and 84 for 0 (TM Dilshan 51*)
Match drawn

There was an extraordinary start to this scheduled four-day match...or, rather, no start at all. The

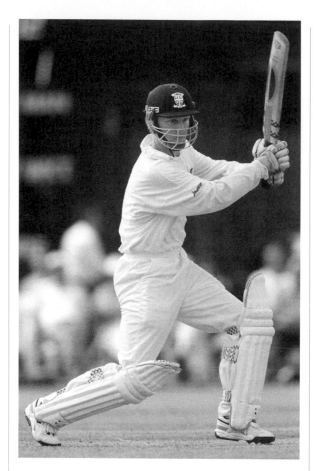

Jonathan Lewis made 57 to steer Durham to an 82-run win over Sri Lanka 'A'.

David Munden/Sportsline Photographic

Sri Lankans, having travelled back to England from the short Denmark leg of their tour, found that their entire playing kit had gone missing en route. The start was therefore delayed and when, at 4pm, the kit had still not turned up, the day's play was called off. A decent-sized crowd, which had waited patiently, was reimbursed. Thankfully, the kit arrived overnight – but the start to the second day was also delayed...because of the eclipse! Then rain interrupted proceedings for 28 overs in mid-afternoon, allowing Worcestershire to reach only 237 for 7 by the close – at which point they declared. Nathan Batson made a career-best 72 and both Vikram Solanki and David Leatherdale half-centuries, and Solanki then took 4 for 41 with his improving off-breaks as Sri Lanka replied with 243 for 9 declared on the third day. By the close Worcestershire were 48 for 2 and, on the final day,

looked at one point to be in some trouble despite Solanki's 49 – in which he passed 1,000 first-class runs for the season. But Gavin Haynes scored a responsible 60 not out, guiding the tail to safer waters and eventually the home side declared again at 222 for 8. The Sri Lankans, technically needing 217 in 24 overs, galloped to 84 for 0 from 15 overs before settling for the draw.

Sussex v. Sri Lanka 'A'
15 August 1999 at Hove (floodlit)
Sri Lanka 'A' 186 for 6 (36 overs) RP Hewage 92*
Sussex 182 for 8 (36 overs)
Sri Lanka 'A' won by 10 runs (D/L Method: Sussex target 192 off 36 overs)

The Sri Lankans won a close contest, under the Duckworth-Lewis formula, following a short interruption for rain. Pradeep Hewage made an entertaining 92 not out from 120 balls in Sri Lanka 'A's 36-over total of 186 for 6 – although a paying audience of only 103, in a crowd little more than 200 strong, were alone in seeing it. Sussex, set 192 after the weather intervened, required 14 from the final over after Tony Cottey (47) and James Carpenter (39) had hit out, but Justin Bates and Billy Taylor, the ninth-wicket pair, could muster only four.

MCC v. Sri Lanka 'A'
17, 18, 19 and 20 August 1999 at Shenley Park
Sri Lanka 'A' 188 for 9 dec. and 169 for 9 dec.
(TM Dilshan 64, JH Dawes 5 for 45, RD King 4 for 41)
MCC 102 for 4 dec. and 201 for 8
Match drawn

The intended showpiece finale to Sri Lanka A's tour, at the lovely Hertfordshire ground of Shenley Park, proved a damp squib as rain washed away all but 5.4 overs of the opening two days. MCC captain Andy Flower, one of three Zimbabwe Test players in the select side, did his best to open up the game by declaring at 102 for 4 in reply to Sri Lanka's first-innings 188 for 9 declared. Dilshan, by far the classiest visiting batsman in a team severely depleted by senior international call-ups back in Colombo, scored 64 to steady his side and set up yet another declaration at 169 for 9. This left MCC a target of 256 from 46 overs, but Chinmay Gupte, the opener, fretted 31 overs for 44 and – despite some frantic hitting by Flower, Paul Strang and Neil Johnson, the match was drawn with MCC on 201 for 8.

ENGLAND 'A' IN ZIMBABWE AND SOUTH AFRICA
By Ralph Dellor

In January 1994, the England 'A' team lost a first-class match against Natal in Durban. Between then and January 1999, teams travelling under the England 'A' flag had journeyed to India, Bangladesh, Pakistan, Australia, Kenya and Sri Lanka without losing another first-class encounter and, apart from one slightly worrying passage of play against the ZCU President's XI, never appeared likely to lose that proud record on this expedition to Southern Africa.

Throughout the trip, this party demonstrated an unquenchable will to win; a team spirit whereby the whole is truly more than the sum of the parts and a refusal to accept defeat. In fact, the players showed all the qualities for which the full Test team has striven for so long while finding them so elusive. Manager Phil Neale and coach John Emburey deserve their share of the credit for ensuring that these players were fine ambassadors for English cricket both sides of the boundary.

Not all the players on this tour advanced their claims for recognition at Test level, but few if any returned to England without improving their game. Andrew Flintoff did enough to earn immediate inclusion in the World Cup squad, having made significant strides with his batting and getting fit enough to bowl again. He lost two stone between the end of the English season and the start of the tour and, with a strict exercise regime devised by fitness consultant Nigel Stockill and the first woman physiotherapist on an England tour, Ann Brentnall, he appeared capable of becoming the genuine all-rounder that England have been seeking for so long.

Graeme Swann could also fill the role, as an off-spinning all-rounder. He took every opportunity on responsive pitches, but needs to tighten his batting technique in order to eliminate too adventurous strokes early in his innings. Chris Read's batting did show significant improvement to go with his outstanding wicketkeeping, earmarking him for his place in the summer's Tests. Steve Harmison managed to get enough overs under his belt by the end of the tour to build up to a pace quick enough to inconvenience established batsmen. Then there was the captain: Michael Vaughan batted well enough to suggest that he could step up a class in the near future, while his leadership qualities were always evident. On and off the field, there was no doubt that he was a natural leader who commanded the respect and enthusiastic support of his team. Vaughan also enjoyed a happy knack of winning the toss, only once calling incorrectly.

After a lengthy period of acclimatisation, reduced in value by the continual rain in Harare, the tour began with two one-day matches. The Country Districts XI were not, as the name might suggest, a collection of rustics arriving at the ground on a hay wain. Eight of their number had represented Zimbabwe in international cricket. They were defeated by seven wickets and the Academy XI would surely have gone the same way had not a torrential downpour ended proceedings before even Duckworth-Lewis could come into play.

So much rain fell that the first two days of a scheduled four-day fixture against Mashonaland were washed out, and the first of the hastily rearranged one-day matches went the same way. However, the second was played on what proved to be an inadequate pitch leaving England 'A' comfortable winners.

Moving out of the capital to the provincial town of Kwekwe, the tourists at last found some warm, sunny weather and even warmer hospitality. The opposition was pretty hot as well with the Flower brothers, representing the ZCU President's XI, putting on a batting masterclass. They established a first-innings lead of 226, but more disciplined batting from England 'A' in the second innings meant that they had moved in front by 101 runs when the captains shook hands on the draw.

Back in Harare, the first 'A' Test might have been a triumph for England and Darren Thomas had the rain not dashed any chance of a result. The Glamorgan bowler took a career-best 8 for 50 in Zimbabwe's much interrupted first innings. England went for quick runs in an attempt to manufacture a contest in the time remaining, but a total wash-out on the final day rendered even this admirable strategy futile.

England's superiority was allowed to blossom in the second Test in Bulawayo. Mal Loye was in imposing form with innings of 90 and 86 already behind him. His 133 was the cornerstone of the first innings, lasting a shade over six hours and containing 19 elegant fours. Zimbabwe were showing resistance until a spell of 4 for 6 from 5.1 overs after lunch on the third day by Swann gave England a first-innings lead of 160. That was extended by Vaughan (131) and Flintoff (88) so that Zimbabwe required 471 to win in a minimum of 145 overs. Swann and Dean Cosker formed a telling spin duo to take four wickets each to leave England winners by 193 runs on the stroke of tea on the final day.

The first one-day 'A' international in Bulawayo was a thriller, with England winning from a most unlikely position. Needing to score at 5.26 an over at the outset, Vikram Solanki set up the possibility of a win with an innings of charm and excitement marking him out as a batsman with a rare talent to be cherished. When Paul Franks was controversially run out off a no-ball, 41 were needed off 29 balls with three wickets in hand. At the fall of the ninth wicket – Solanki for 70 – the last pair of Read and Cosker needed 25 from 19 balls. They got home with three balls unused among scenes of great and justified celebration in the England party.

Vaughan, Read and Duckworth-Lewis took England to victory in the second match by four wickets, but Vaughan was missing from the third match with a leg injury. Maddy took over the captaincy and busied himself with 12 bowling changes in the Zimbabwe innings, including bringing himself on four times. Again Duckworth-Lewis featured in another narrow victory for England, this time by two wickets.

The ECB financed the extension of the tour for two matches in South Africa to ensure a testing finale. By this stage, however, England 'A' had become a formidable unit themselves too strong for less committed opposition. Vaughan and Maddy's opening partnership of 151 against Gauteng at The Wanderers in Johannesburg proved to be merely the prelude to a blistering innings of 145 from Flintoff, against whom the South Africans found it near impossible to bowl. On a poor pitch, Swann bowled splendidly to take five wickets and enforce the follow-on and, with Cosker taking five second-innings wickets, England needed a mere 27 to win – a task achieved in 15 balls.

Maddy's first century of the tour against the President's XI at Newlands in Cape Town provided the platform for an adequate first-innings total. The South Africans trailed by 151 before being set 440 to win after another good Flintoff innings and, less expected, some improvised hitting from Harmison at the end. Harmison bowled with pace and aggression at the start of the final innings of the tour, but substantial partnerships on a still sound batting surface presented difficult obstacles. However, like every other obstacle placed in its path, the team overcame them to win by 46 runs with 8.2 overs of the final hour remaining and so ensure a triumphant conclusion to a successful tour.

Zimbabwe Country Districts v. England 'A'
16 January 1999 at Harare Sports Club
Zimbabwe Country Districts 195 (49.4 overs)
England 'A' 196 for 3 (45.2 overs) MB Loye 86, DL Maddy 52
England 'A' won by seven wickets

Zimbabwe Cricket Academy XI v. England 'A'
18 January 1999 at Harare South Country Club
Zimbabwe Cricket Academy XI 196 for 9 (50 overs)
England 'A' 72 for 1 (16.5 overs)
Match abandoned

Mashonaland v. England 'A'
20, 21, 22 and 23 January 1999 at Old Hararians Ground, Harare
The match was scheduled for four days but no play was possible on the first two days. Two one-day games were scheduled at the same venue for the third and fourth days but rain prevented any play on 22 January.

Mashonaland v. England 'A'
23 January 1999 at Old Hararians Ground, Harare
England 'A' 159 (44 overs)
Mashonaland 86 (36.1 overs)
England 'A' won by 73 runs

Zimbabwe Cricket Union President's XI v. England 'A'
26, 27, 28 and 29 January 1999 at Kweke Sports Club
England 'A' 267 (MGN Windows 69, A Flintoff 61) and 327 for 7 (MB Loye 90, MP Vaughan 78, MGN Windows 66)
Zimbabwe Cricket Union President's XI 493 (A Flower 194*, GW Flower 130, DP Viljoen 70)
Match drawn

Zimbabwe 'A' v. England 'A'
2, 3, 4, 5 and 6 February 1999 at Alexandra Sports Club, Harare
Zimbabwe 'A' 160 (SD Thomas 8 for 50) and 20 for 1
England 'A' 192 (A Flintoff)
Match drawn

Zimbabwe 'A' v. England 'A'
9, 10, 11, 12 and 13 February 1999 at Queen's Sports Oval, Bulawayo
England 'A' 383 (MB Loye 133, VS Solanki 65, DL Maddy 64, AR Whittall 4 for 88, BC Strang 4 for 107) and 310 for 6 dec. (MP Vaughan 131, A Flintoff 88)
Zimbabwe 'A' 223 (AM Blignaut 58, DP Viljoen 57, GP Swann 4 for 52) and 277 (TN Madondo 57, DA Cosker 4 for 54, GP Swann 4 for 104)
England 'A' won by 193 runs

Chris Read's outstanding wicketkeeping during the England 'A' tour earned him a place in the summer's Tests.
David Munden/Sportsline Photographic

Zimbabwe 'A' v. England 'A'
16 February 1999 at Queen's Sports Club, Bulawayo
Zimbabwe 'A' 262 (49.4 overs) SV Carlisle 80, DP Viljoen 73
England 'A' 263 for 9 (49.3 overs) VS Solanki 70, A Flintoff 57
England won by one wicket

Zimbabwe 'A' v. England 'A'
18 February 1999 at Alexandra Sports Club, Harare
Zimbabwe 'A' 154 (46.1 overs) PJ Franks 4 for 34
England 'A' 154 for 6 (39.1 overs)
England won by four wickets (D/L method: England target 151 off 47 overs)

Zimbabwe 'A' v. England 'A'
20 February 1999 at Alexandra Sports Club, Harare
Zimbabwe 'A' 179 (44.1 overs) CB Wishart 65, A Flintoff 4 for 22

England 'A' 183 for 8 (44.1 overs)
England won by two wickets (D/L method: England target 183 off 45 overs)

Gauteng v. England 'A'
25, 26, 27 and 28 February 1999 at Wanderers, Johannesburg
England 'A' 447 for 9 dec. (A Flintoff 80, MP Vaughan 76, DL Maddy 73) and 27 for 0
Gauteng 262 (Z De Bruyn 62, GP Swann 5 for 77) and 211 (AJ Seymore 74, AM Bacher 64, DA Cosker 5 for 57)
England 'A' won by ten wickets

United Cricket Board President's XI v. England 'A'
4, 5, 6, 7 and 8 March 1999 at Newlands, Cape Town
England 'A' 350 (DL Maddy 135, A Flintoff 70) and 288 (A Flintoff 80, MB Loye 60)
United Cricket Board President's XI 199 (CC Bradfield 61, DN Crookes 52) and 393 (M van Jaarsveld 147, JM Kemp 61*, FC Brooker 56, SJ Harmison 4 for 79)
England 'A' won by 46 runs

ENGLAND 'A' AVERAGES
in Zimbabwe and South Africa

BATTING

	M	Inns	NO	HS	Runs	Av	100	50
A Flintoff	5	8	1	145	542	77.42	1	5
DL Maddy	4	7	1	135	329	54.83	1	2
MB Loye	4	7	0	133	336	48.00	1	2
MP Vaughan	5	8	0	131	336	42.00	1	2
MGN Windows	4	6	0	69	217	36.16	–	2
VS Solanki	4	6	1	65	169	33.80	–	1
CMW Read	5	8	2	47	154	25.66	–	–
GP Swann	5	9	1	48	176	22.00	–	–
DA Cosker	5	6	2	28*	68	17.00	–	–
SJ Harmison	3	4	2	21*	27	13.50	–	–
SD Thomas	4	6	2	14*	50	12.50	–	–
RWT Key	3	5	0	25	52	10.40	–	–

Played in two matches: JD Lewry 16 & 1
Played in one match: MM Betts 1; PJ Franks 8

BOWLING

	Overs	Mds	Runs	Wkts	Av	Best	10/m	5/inns
SD Thomas	129.2	34	331	18	18.38	8–50	–	1
DA Cosker	203.1	51	504	22	22.90	5–57	–	1
GP Swann	201.5	43	538	21	25.61	5–77	–	1
JD Lewry	47	18	129	5	25.80	3–45	–	–
SJ Harmison	113	35	272	7	38.55	4–79	–	–

Also bowled: MM Betts 18.4–4–62–2; A Flintoff 99.2–33–203–2; PJ Franks 19–4–46–0; DL Maddy 9–2–19–0; VS Solanki 4–0–11–0; MP Vaughan 12–2–32–0; MGN Windows 2–0–7–0

FIELDING FIGURES

12 – CMW Read (11 ct/1 st); 8 – GP Swann; 7 – VS Solanki; 6 – DL Maddy; 4 – A Flintoff, RWT Key, MB Loye; 3 – MGN Windows; 1 – DA Cosker, SJ Harmison

BROADCASTING RIGHTS

The final year of the century saw more upheaval in the broadcasting boxes than any other time in cricket's history. Three major networks – BBC, BSkyB and Channel 4 – all enjoyed live coverage of parts of the international season and county cricket which, while providing welcome funds for the England and Wales Cricket Board, made the business of watching the game utterly exhausting. Even armed with the latest copy of the *Radio Times*, it was impossible to work out which competition – and, in the case of the NatWest Trophy, which round of the competition – was being broadcast where and, indeed, when. The scheduling of the television coverage was almost as infuriating and as hard to follow as the lay-out of the domestic fixture list: and that is saying something.

The triumphant manner in which the England and Wales Cricket Board ended 60 years of BBC television coverage still irritates many people in Television Centre. That will ease in time, particularly when we consider the high-handed manner in which the negotiations were conducted in the past – before there was any realistic competition – and also the refusal of BBC schedulers to show the highlights at a sensible time in early evening. Indeed, until that stumbling block is overcome, the chances of BBC TV winning the rights back again are remote – and rightly so.

BY JONATHAN AGNEW

Competition is always healthy and, given its current state, the English game was extremely fortunate to have three networks bidding for the broadcasting rights. Had the negotiations taken place during this past summer, it is difficult to believe that the television companies would have valued the game nearly as high as when England and South Africa were enjoying a tight series in 1998. And yet competition amongst broadcasters can have a detrimental effect on the viewer and, for that matter, the listener. Channel 4's negotiators homed in on the ECB's marketing aim to attract what it described as 'the new faces of cricket'. This particular concept featured photographs of the most unlikely cricket followers you could imagine, who appeared to be either high on drugs or recently escaped from a nearby institution – or, most likely, both. It was an absolute fallacy and anyone with an ounce of cricketing intelligence knew as much. However, having struck that same chord, Channel 4 now finds itself under pressure to be 'different': to attract these 'new faces of cricket' to Test matches. We have 'snickometers' and 'skylines'. Cybil Ruscoe interviews soap stars from *Brookside* who just happened to be sitting in the front row of the Old Trafford pavilion an hour before play. The 'analyst' – housed in what appears to be a dungeon – gives us graphic replays of Phil Tufnell's batting technique.

Now, these are all fascinating innovations that might very well brighten up a day's play – and that is the point. Channel 9 do not need 'snickometers' or 'skylines'. Tony Greig does not disappear down a manhole and reappear as 'the analyst'. Quite simply, there is no need to dress up Australian cricket. Or South African cricket. Or any other cricket, for that matter, except England's.

Cricket coverage must not be 'dumbed down' in order to attract the next generation of spectators to the game, and cricket viewers should not need to be bombarded with gadgets and gizmos in order to be entertained. We wait with bated breath to see what Talk Radio will serve up in South Africa. You can be sure that it will be 'different' for no other reason than to show the ECB that they are trying their hardest to attract a 'different' type of listener: a new face, or two, to the game. The fact is that broadcasters – and writers, too – can only go so far in selling the game. The onus is very much on the board and England's cricketers to deliver a quality product; and then leave the rest to us.

AUSTRALIA UNDER-19 IN ENGLAND

27 July 1999 at Eton College
South England Under-19 XI 229 for 5
(50 overs) C Taylor 65
Australia Under-19 XI 232 for 1
(44.3 overs) M Klinger 89*, L Williams 83*,
D Harris 50
Australia Under-19 XI won by nine wickets

28 July 1999 at Eton College
South England Under-19 XI 164 (43.2 overs)
MA Carberry 56
Australia Under-19 XI (165 for 0) AM Rowe 79*,
S Clingeleffer 72*
Australia Under-19 XI won by ten wickets

30 July 1999 at Canterbury
England Under-19 XI 239 for 8
(50 overs) MA Gough 86, A Voges
4 for 48
Australia Under-19 XI 229 for 7
(50 overs) D Harris 58
England Under-19 XI won by 10 runs

1 August 1999 at Chelmsford
England Under-19 XI 234 for 9 (50 overs)
GR Haywood 56
Australia Under-19 XI 236 for 6 (49.1 overs)
L Williams 93
Australia Under-19 XI won by four wickets

2 August 1999 at Hove (floodlit)
Australia Under-19 XI 250 (50 overs)
L Williams 85, MPL Bulbeck 4 for 57
England Under-19 XI 226 (47.1 overs)
RJ Logan 558, M Clarke 4 for 41
Australia Under-19 XI won by 24 runs

4, 5 and 6 August 1999 at Arundel Castle CC
Australia Under-19 XI 360 for 4 dec.
(B Oliver 159*, D Harris 104) and 247 for 5 dec.
(D Harris 67)
Development of Excellence XI 242 (L Sears 52)
and 178
Australia Under-19 XI won by 187 runs

8 August 1999 at Lakenham, Norwich
Australia Under-19 XI 79 for 3
(23.1 overs)
England Cricket Board XI did not bat
Match abandoned

9, 10 and 11 August 1999 at Sleaford CC
North England Under-19 XI 321 for 7 dec.
(RKJ Dawson 61, D Clapp 59, J Sadler 58) and
232 for 6 dec. (H Jones 82, J Sadler 70)
Australia Under-19 XI 302 for 3 dec.
(M Klinger 124*, L Williams 61, AM Rowe 58)
and 254 for 7 (N Hauritz 26*)
Australia Under-19 XI won by three wickets

First Youth 'Test Match'
17, 18, 19 and 20 August 1999 at Edgbaston
Australia Under-19 XI 173 (MPL Bulbeck 4 for 45)
and 196 (A Voges 52*)
England Under-19 XI 171 (DR MacKenzie
4 for 23) and 202 for 2 (MA Gough 95,
IN Flanagan 60)
England Under-19 XI won by eight wickets

Second Youth 'Test Match'
23, 24, 25 and 26 August 1999 at Bristol
Australia Under-19 XI 153 (L Williams 55) and
159 for 3 (M Klinger 55*)
England Under-19 XI 322 for 9 dec. (IR Bell 90,
IN Flanagan 65)
Match drawn
*No play was possible on the second
and third days*

Third Youth 'Test Match'
1, 2 and 3 September 1999 at Chester-le-Street
Australia Under-19 XI 424 (S Clingeleffer 135,
M Clarke 111, RJ Logan 4 for 86)
England Under-19 XI 84 (M Johnson 4 for 16) and
(following on) 233 (MA Gough 59, MA Carberry 50,
B Oliver 6 for 38)
*Australia Under-19 XI won by an innings and
107 runs*

PPP HEALTHCARE COUNTY CHAMPIONSHIP
By Mark Baldwin

Mark Baldwin writes on county cricket for
The Times, *and since 1988 has covered 11 England
or England 'A' tours.*

English county cricket came to a crossroads in
1999 and, hardly pausing to plot and plan its
onward journey, plunged on down the difficult
road ahead without scarcely a sideways glance.

A summer of huge change in the domestic game
flashed past indeed, with the tribulations of the
England team merely encouraging the urgings-on of
many a loud-voiced expert: 'On, on you go! On to
the promised land!'

If ever there was a time for cool minds, and a calm
and measured approach, this past summer was it.
But what we got, I fear, was more reckless driving
from all those desperate to get their hands on the
wheel and rush on. It will, of course, inevitably lead
to casualties and, possibly, a nasty pile-up.

England threw out a long-term Test match
strategy, built up promisingly under Alec Stewart
and David Lloyd against South Africa and Australia,
because the selectors picked the wrong team for
the World Cup. The result was a foul-up in a Test
series against New Zealand. And, on the domestic
front, a move to a two-division championship has
been flung into the bubbling pot because it is,
allegedly, the secret ingredient that will soon have
us tasting the sweetness of lasting international
success. What a mess.

Two-division cricket at one-day level is an
acceptable way to jazz up that product, although
one sizeable downside is that it can affect crowds by
denying counties the chance to play a local rival. For
instance, Gloucestershire and Somerset met only (by
sheer chance) in the final of the NatWest Trophy.
Next season Warwickshire and Worcestershire will
meet again in the championship (thanks to
Warwickshire's controversial relegation to the
second division), but not in more financially-
lucrative one-day matches. Floodlit, high-summer
one-day derbies should be a highlight of limited-
overs county fare.

Two-division championship cricket, however, will
merely lead to more counties spending increased
amounts on overseas imports, or 'tried-and-trusted'
county pros just below England level, in the craving
for top nine status. Funding of youth schemes will
become secondary to the desire for a quick fix in the
club's senior side.

In next year's split championship Kent will not
play Sussex, Somerset will not play Gloucestershire,
Notts will not play Derbyshire, and Surrey will not
play Middlesex. But, much more damagingly, Ben
Hollioake and Andrew Flintoff and Darren Maddy
and many other young players of promise will not
get the chance to face Glenn McGrath, Shoaib
Akhtar or Jacques Kallis in first-class competition.
David Sales, Graeme Swann, Paul Franks and
both Michael Powells (for instance) will not get
an opportunity to mix it with Shane Warne,
Saqlain Mushtaq, Muttiah Muralitharan and Anil
Kumble. Is this really going to improve the ability of
young cricketers charged with raising the standard
of our national team?

Or will we just get an even more cynical version,
given the financial and marketability losses that
will accompany banishment to the 'second-class'
lower division, of what we had in 1999? That,
just to remind you, was a depressing stream of
pitches quite unfit for four-day cricket (without
one single tangible penalty!) and, at the last,
collusion-based controversy in the championship
shake-up and weather-based controversy in the
one-day shake-up.

What seems to have been forgotten in all the tub-
thumping in the written and electronic media
(mostly from those who see very little county
cricket) is that England's immediate and long-term
future depends on what we do with the cream of
our youth between the ages of 18 and 23.

And the answer is not to impose ill-thought-out
theory on the championship game, and leave the
majority of our youngsters less well-off than they
were originally, but to invest heavily and
unreservedly in the coming generation.

Flintoff, Hollioake, Swann, Sales, Harmison,
Davies, Trescothick, Key, Solanki, Franks, Read,
Nash and their like should not be playing much
county cricket anyway. The senior England players
won't be from 2000 onwards, what with seven Tests
and ten one-day internationals, which further
devalues the 'improved' championship.

English cricket has, for ten years now, spent much
money on 'A' team winter tours – but has failed to
follow through to its logical and proper conclusion a
system which would sort out those with
international ability and temperament, and give
them the year-round, structured international
experience that should be the only reckoner.

England 'A', which would include the sort of
players named above, ought to be playing at least
five shadow 'Tests' every summer – against incoming

Surrey take on Middlesex at Lord's on a September evening.
Philip Brown/Sportsline Photographic

touring teams on good pitches such as Taunton or Chelmsford – plus at least nine one-day internationals. Next summer there will be a July one-day triangular between England, West Indies and Zimbabwe. Why not include England 'A' as well, and give these lads some incentive? Perhaps England 'A', and not England, would get into a quadrangular final! It would certainly concentrate a few minds!

Virtually all the consistent, true world-class players England have cherished in their history had made their international debuts by the time they were 21 or 22: players like Larwood, Trueman, Statham, Underwood, Willis, Botham; Hutton, Compton, May, Cowdrey, Knott, Gower, Gooch and Atherton.

Central control of England players should extend to those in the crucial years after they perform so well at Under-19 level. If they haven't broken into the full Test team within four years then they can return full-time to the county circuit – well-coached, experienced in the realities of top-level cricket and with a burning desire to prove they still have a future.

As for 'toughening up' the championship, why not siphon off some of the £1 million annual hand-out each county gets from the ECB, and put it towards prize-money? Eighteen 'entrance fees' of £200,000, for instance, would bump up the championship to a £4 million-plus event, together with sponsorship monies. If you win, you get £1 million, with each subsequent place graded so that a top nine finish would bring sizeable reward and a bottom-of-the-table finish a loss of most of the £200,000 'stake'. And centrally employ groundsmen, too, while you're at it, to ensure fair play.

One of the many nonsenses and non sequiturs of a confusing, jumbled and unsettling county summer was that Gloucestershire could finish bottom of the so-called premier competition – the championship that is supposed to breed our England stars – and yet still rake in, by some distance, the third-highest amount of prize money (£110,400).

ROUND 1: 13–17 APRIL 1999

13, 14, 15 and 16 April
at Chester-le-Street
Worcestershire 152 (52.1 overs) (DA Leatherdale 85,
SJE Brown 6 for 25) and 137 for 7 (EJ Wilson 58*)
Durham 303 for 6 dec. (78 overs) (PD Collingwood 56,
JE Morris 55, DC Boon 54, JJB Lewis 52)
Match drawn
Durham 11 pts, Worcestershire 6 pts

at Chelmsford
Essex 252 (86.1 overs) (PJ Prichard 91) and 150
Leicestershire 424 (136.1 overs) (CC Lewis 139,
PA Nixon 121, RC Irani 4 for 59)
Leicestershire won by an innings and 22 runs
Leicestershire 20 pts, Essex 4 pts

at Old Trafford
Sussex 351 for 8 dec. (118.4 overs) (MTE Peirce 77,
RR Montgomerie 62)
Lancashire 301 for 8 dec. (69.3 overs) (MJ Chilton 87,
MA Robinson 4 for 62)
Match drawn
Lancashire 10 pts, Sussex 11 pts

at Lord's
Middlesex 254 (95.5 overs) (DC Nash 62*,
JL Langer 55, JBD Thompson 4 for 61) and 381 for 4
(JL Langer 241*)
Kent 286 (109.1 overs) (RWT Key 86, A Symonds 69,
JP Hewitt 5 for 50)
Match drawn
Middlesex 10 pts, Kent 10 pts

at The Oval
Surrey 342 (129.2 overs) (IJ Ward 78, MA Butcher 68,
AM Smith 4 for 93) and 229 for 7 dec. (MA Butcher
101, AM Smith 5 for 42)
Gloucestershire 213 (72.2 overs) (THC Hancock 53,
IDK Salisbury 5 for 44) and 209 for 5
(MGN Windows 98*)
Match drawn
Surrey 11 pts, Gloucestershire 9 pts

14, 15, 16 and 17 April
at Edgbaston
Warwickshire 323 (112.1 overs) (DR Brown 142,
DL Hemp 64, DE Malcolm 6 for 116)
Northamptonshire 167 for 6 (47.4 overs)
(G Welch 5 for 47)
Match drawn
Warwickshire 9 pts, Northamptonshire 8 pts

**Chris Lewis of Leicestershire scored his first championship
century for five years.**
David Munden/Sportsline Photographic

Leicestershire had more to fear from the 'sudden-
death' element of this championship season than
anyone else. Having won the title two years out of
the last three it would, surely, be grossly unfair if
they were dispatched to the second division on the
strength of one below-par season? Their captain,
James Whitaker, was fit to return after spending the
entire 1998 season on the physiotherapist's couch,
and his players responded by securing the only
victory of the opening round.

Michael Kasprowicz, their Queensland opening
bowler, took six wickets on his Leicestershire debut,
including that of Essex's Paul Prichard for 91, but
the most telling contributions came from Chris
Lewis and Paul Nixon. In Leicestershire's second
innings, they piled up 228 runs for the sixth wicket
to rescue the champions from potential difficulty at
153 for 5. Lewis scored 139 – his first championship
century for five years – and Nixon 121 enabling
Leicestershire's bowlers to wrap up victory on the
fourth day.

Many fixtures were hit by the weather, most
notably at Edgbaston where rain washed out the

final day. A century by Dougie Brown and 64 from David Hemp thwarted Devon Malcolm's attempt to create mayhem. Malcolm seized 6 for 116, but Northants soon found themselves in trouble at 167 for 6. Graeme Welch took the first five wickets to fall, only for the rain to have the final say.

Durham almost pulled off an unlikely win at Riverside against Worcestershire, who were rescued by Elliott Wilson. Playing only his sixth championship match, Wilson – batting at number five – survived 41 traumatic overs as Worcestershire, 151 runs behind on first innings, suddenly slumped to 68 for 6. With the help of Lampitt and Illingworth, disaster was averted but Durham, with their lively and youthful seam attack, had sounded an early warning.

Two days' play were washed out at Old Trafford but there was still time for Mark Chilton – who had scored the first first-class century against Cambridge University the previous week – to make a composed 87. Playing against Sussex in the absence of the injured Mike Atherton, Chilton added 100 in 21 overs with Graham Lloyd as Lancashire replied to Sussex's 351 for 8 declared.

A combination of rain and a defiant Matthew Windows frustrated Surrey at the Oval. Set an unlikely 359 to win – thanks to a fine century from Mark Butcher – Gloucestershire were soon 7 for 2 and then, to the last ball of the final morning, 57 for 3. Windows settled in and with help, first from Mark Alleyne and then Jack Russell, saw Gloucestershire to within 20 overs of safety, at which point the rain duly arrived.

The loss of virtually all of the opening day wrecked the opening match of the season at Lord's. Justin Langer made an unbeaten 241, his highest score for Middlesex who had decided merely to bat out the final day. This after Kent had their chance to push for a win with both Langer and the nightwatchman Hewitt being dropped early in the morning.

Round 2: 19–24 April 1999

19, 20, 21 and 22 April
at Edgbaston
Warwickshire 356 for 7 (104 overs) (TL Penney 73, KJ Piper 66, DR Brown 55*)
Somerset did not bat
Match drawn
Warwickshire 8 pts, Somerset 7 pts

20, 21, 22 and 23 April
at Derby
Derbyshire 168 for 4 (69.5 overs) (AS Rollins 79*)
Glamorgan did not bat
Match drawn
Derbyshire 4 pts, Glamorgan 5 pts

at Leicester
Nottinghamshire 117 for 5 (40 overs)
Leicestershire did not bat
Match drawn
Leicestershire 6 pts, Nottinghamshire 4 pts

Paul Nixon had a 228-run partnership with Chris Lewis to take Leicestershire to victory at Chelmsford.
David Munden/Sportsline Photographic

at Lord's
Middlesex v. Lancashire
No play was possible – 4 pts each

at Worcester
Surrey 223 (43.4 overs) (BC Hollioake 55, CG Liptrot
5 for 51, SR Lampitt 4 for 47)
Worcestershire 15 for 1 (5 overs)
Match drawn
Worcestershire 8 pts, Surrey 5 pts

21, 22, 23 and 24 April
at Southampton
Hampshire 252 (86.1 overs) (WS Kendall 93,
MJ McCague 4 for 65)
Kent 135 for 7 dec (51.4 overs)
Match drawn
Hampshire 9 pts, Kent 8 pts

at Hove
Northamptonshire 391 for 8 dec (116 overs)
(ML Hayden 119, RJ Warren 88, D Ripley 50*)
Sussex 104 (50.2 overs) (RK Rao 52*, DE Malcolm
6 for 39) and (following) on 209 for 1
(RR Montgomerie 113*)
Match drawn
Sussex 7 pts, Northamptonshire 12 pts

at Headingley
Yorkshire 282 (113.4 overs) (GM Hamilton 81*,
AM Smith 4 for 73) and 148 for 6 dec. (J Lewis 4 for 60)
Gloucestershire 169 (42.2 overs) (GM Hamilton 4 for
26) and 180 (D Gough 4 for 27)
Yorkshire won by 81 runs
Yorkshire 18 pts, Gloucestershire 4 pts

Yorkshire, like Leicestershire in the first round of
championship games, were the one side to avoid the
worst efforts of the April showers. World Cup-
bound pair Darren Gough and Gavin Hamilton
provided the cutting edge for Yorkshire to
overpower Gloucestershire and secure an important
early-season win. Hamilton took seven wickets and
Gough six, but the Scotland all-rounder would have
pipped the England fast bowler for any Man of the
Match award because he also scored 95 unbeaten
runs. Hamilton showed why many pundits had
already announced him as an England Test player of
the future with a first-innings 81 not out, a career
best, on a pitch offering unpredictable bounce and
sometimes excessive movement for the seamers.
Mike Smith and Jon Lewis did their best to keep
Gloucestershire in the match, but even without the

Queensland's Matthew Hayden took on the captaincy of
Northamptonshire.
David Munden/Sportsline Photographic

injured Silverwood and Hutchison the five-pronged
Yorkshire pace attack had far more bite. Matthew
Windows added to the good impression he had
made as an England 'A' winter tourist with innings
of 39 and 28 but Yorkshire were even good enough
to beat the weather as well as Gloucestershire.

Poor bowling from Somerset, after their new
captain Jamie Cox had won the toss, allowed
Warwickshire to reach the heights of 356 at
the end of the first day at Edgbaston. But then it
rained. This was unlucky for the home side who
had put themselves into a position of some strength
on a green, seaming pitch. Robust batting came
from numbers two to seven in the order, following
the early loss of Knight to Bulbeck. Wagh made
44, Hemp 47 and skipper Neil Smith 37 – but
in between came half-centuries for Trevor Penney,
Keith Piper and Dougie Brown. Penney, with
73 from 170 balls, held the innings together
while first Piper, with an impudent 66, and
Brown, with ten thumping fours in his unbeaten
55, took the attack to Somerset. In the end, though,
the weather mocked groundsman Steve Rouse's

Chris Liptrot of Worcestershire claimed five wickets against Surrey.
David Munden/Sportsline Photographic

Herculean efforts to get the game started at all on day one.

At Derby, a game that started two days and 90 minutes late, due to rain, was then abandoned as a draw when the elements made play impossible at all on the scheduled final day. A determined, unbroken stand of 114 between Adrian Rollins and Dominic Cork dominated what play there was, following an early slide to 54 for 4, and in many ways that was fitting. Rollins, after missing two months of the 1998 season with a back injury, wanted to show he is capable of shoring up the top order following the departure of Kim Barnett, while skipper Cork was desperate to indicate his commitment to the cause in the wake of the internal winter squabbles which led initially to his resignation and then to his dramatic reinstatement. Rollins finished on 79 not out, with Cork unbeaten on 45.

The 1998 county champions, meanwhile, were also enduring a frustrating few days. Just 40 overs were possible, on the third day. The South African-born Noel Gie, whose family moved to England when he was seven, was 33 not out when more rain

ended the contest, and he added a promising 59 for the fifth wicket with Chris Read, the England 'A' wicketkeeper.

For Nottinghamshire fans there was also the comforting sight of their former talismanic skipper Clive Rice back in a tracksuit as the county's new cricket supremo. Rice, when appointed during the winter, had simply made it clear to his new charges – only Tim Robinson and Paul Johnson remain from his own playing days at Trent Bridge – that they either do things his way, or leave!

At Lord's the match between Middlesex and Lancashire saw no play at all. At least both counties had the consolation of four points when the contest was eventually abandoned as a draw.

At Worcester Alec Stewart, Graham Thorpe and Adam Hollioake were all looking for batting practice ahead of the World Cup – but the trio managed just 17 runs between them in Surrey's only innings. Indeed, the weather allowed Worcestershire to bat for only five overs in reply on the third day, following two wash-outs, before it descended again to prevent any further action. Chris Liptrot, a 19-year-old apprentice electrician from Wigan giving county cricket a try, enjoyed himself with a five-wicket haul – including the scalp of Ben Hollioake whose 60-ball 55 was the best Surrey could offer. But it was Stuart Lampitt who spoiled the England trio's day, Stewart and Hollioake senior being taken at second slip and Thorpe hitting a return catch. Alex Tudor, not included in the World Cup squad but very much a part of England's immediate future, snapped up the wicket of Philip Weston just before the rains came again.

A staunch 93 from Will Kendall, his second-highest score in county cricket, was the focal point of Hampshire's first innings at Southampton, after the match had got under way a day late. Kendall battled away for 243 minutes until he was sixth out, at 224, attempting to clip Martin McCague to leg and giving instead a return catch off a leading edge. McCague took four wickets to go some way to putting behind him a forgettable 1998 in which he played only ten matches because of injury and took just 27 wickets. Kent were 18 for 3 at the close of the second day but rain prevented any play on the scheduled third day and also led to a token mid-afternoon start on the fourth. David Fulton's 41, and 33 for Alan Wells, could not stop them from sliding to 135 for 7 before, mercifully for all concerned, time ran out.

Queensland's Matthew Hayden came to the Northants captaincy with a career batting average in excess of 54, despite having played just seven Tests for Australia in five years. At Hove he underlined his quality against all but the very highest class of bowling with an effortless century of natural power. Surviving a difficult high chance at gully off Mark Robinson when 39, the big Aussie left-hander inspired Russell Warren to join him in a third-wicket stand worth 165. The Sussex attack was going through the motions by the time David Ripley set up the declaration but, either side of tea on day two, Devon Malcolm was the complete opposite. Even at 36 Malcolm is still regarded as the fastest English-qualified bowler...when the mood is right. Dev's radar was spot on as, with the new ball, he took 4 for 27 in 13 overs and, after a blank third day, he took his tally to 6 for 39 to condemn Sussex to a follow-on. Only Rajesh Rao kept out Malcolm and co in that first innings, with a brave unbeaten 52, but when they batted again Malcolm could not repeat his magic. Century-maker Richard Montgomerie, supported ably by first Toby Pierce and then skipper Chris Adams, won an honourable draw for his side.

ROUND 3: 28 APRIL–2 MAY 1999

28, 29 and 30 April
at Chester-le-Street
Hampshire 366 (116.4 overs) (WS Kendall 105, DA Kenway 70*, AN Aymes 51) and 66 for 2
Durham 167 (59.4 overs) (SJ Renshaw 4 for 43) and (following on) 264 (DC Boon 61*, MA Gough 59, JA Daley 56, JP Stephenson 4 for 48)
Hampshire won by eight wickets
Hampshire 20 pts, Durham 4 pts

at Chelmsford
Warwickshire 271 (93.5 overs) (NMK Smith 69) and 86 (MC Ilott 6 for 38)
Essex 191 (105.1 overs) (ESH Giddins 4 for 42) and 168 for 3 (PJ Prichard 59, N Hussain 59)
Essex won by seven wickets
Essex 16 pts, Warwickshire 6 pts

at Canterbury
Kent 141 (49 overs) (MJ Walker 53, KJ Dean 4 for 34) and 220 (MA Ealham 88*, TM Smith 4 for 38)
Derbyshire 300 (90.1 overs) (DG Cork 82, AS Rollins 71, MJ Slater 65, MA Ealham 4 for 75, DW Headley 4 for 103) and 62 for 0 wicket
Derbyshire won by ten wickets
Derbyshire 19 pts, Kent 4 pts

at Trent Bridge
Nottinghamshire 417 (122.5 overs) (P Johnson 126, JER Gallian 82, A Sheriyar 4 for 96) and 35 for 0
Worcestershire 172 (57.4 overs) (VC Drakes 5 for 49) and 279 (VS Solanki 91, GA Hick 89, VC Drakes 4 for 60)
Nottinghamshire won by ten wickets
Nottinghamshire 20 pts, Worcestershire 3 pts

28, 29, 30 April and 1 May
at Cardiff
Sussex 222 (88.3 overs) (S Humphries 57, SP Jones 5 for 31) and 265 (MTE Peirce 123, RSC Martin-Jenkins 52, RDB Croft 5 for 82)
Glamorgan 149 (66.1 overs) (RJ Kirtley 5 for 49) and 341 for 4 (SP James 153, RDB Croft 58*)
Glamorgan won by six wickets
Glamorgan 16 pts, Sussex 5 pts

at Bristol
Gloucestershire 297 (129.5 overs) (MW Alleyne 76, KJ Barnett 51, ARC Fraser 4 for 53) and 215 (PCR Tufnell 5 for 61)
Middlesex 268 (110.1 overs) (MR Ramprakash 101, J Lewis 5 for 79) and 245 for 8 (OA Shah 60)
Middlesex won by two wickets
Middlesex 18 pts, Gloucestershire 6 pts

at Leicester
Leicestershire 388 (115 overs) (CC Lewis 108, DL Maddy 86, G Chapple 5 for 92, RJ Green 4 for 86) and 215 (Aftab Habib 79, MP Smethurst 4 for 47)
Lancashire 241 (83.1 overs) (A Flintoff 86) and 255 (NT Wood 82)
Leicestershire won by 107 runs
Leicestershire 20 pts, Lancashire 5 pts

at Northampton
Northamptonshire 248 (83.1 overs) (RJ Bailey 75, JP Taylor 71, MP Bicknell 4 for 48) and 338 (AL Penberthy 88, DJG Sales 69, AJ Tudor 5 for 64)
Surrey 286 (79.3 overs) (AJ Hollioake 96, MA Butcher 52) and 301 for 2 (GP Thorpe 138*, AD Brown 66*, IJ Ward 63)
Surrey won by eight wickets
Surrey 18 pts, Northamptonshire 5 pts

29, 30 April, 1 and 2 May
at Taunton
Somerset 468 for 9 dec. (137 overs) (J Cox 173, M Burns 63, RJ Turner 53) and 26 for 4 (CEW Silverwood 4 for 11)
Yorkshire 148 (63.2 overs) (AR Caddick 4 for 24) and

345 (D Byas 90, A McGrath 75, MPL Bulbeck 4 for 79)
Somerset won by six wickets
Somerset 20 pts, Yorkshire 3 pts

The championship season finally got away under full sail, with results in all nine matches and some sort of pattern at last emerging following a weather-bedevilled start to a schedule already suffering from a confusing, convoluted fixture list and the onrush of the World Cup.

Leicestershire became the only county with two wins, thanks to an efficient seeing-off of struggling Lancashire at Leicester, while Yorkshire stumbled badly against Somerset at Taunton. Other winners in this round of games were: Hampshire, Essex, Derbyshire, Nottinghamshire, Glamorgan, Middlesex and Surrey.

Four of the nine matches in this round of games, however, finished inside three days. The weather clearing was a relief in many ways, but it also served to reveal the first instance this season of a recurring trend in championship cricket – that four-day cricket, the supposed saving of the English game not so long ago, was becoming a product in danger of contravening the Trades Description Act.

Chris Lewis won the battle of the all-rounders at Grace Road, outperforming Andrew Flintoff despite another beefy innings of 86 by the youthful Lancashire giant. Ironically, the original 'Beefy' – Ian Botham – turned up on the third morning of this fine match to do some banging of the drum himself in a temporary role of World Cup ambassador. Had Botham been around on the first two days he would have enjoyed Flintoff's straight hitting – including one six crunched back over Alan Mullally's head – after no doubt wondering along with the rest of English cricket why the infuriating Lewis has not made even more of his great talent. On day one Lewis reached 77 not out, pushing Leicestershire beyond 300 after Darren Maddy's dedicated 86, and on the second morning he pushed on to 108, his second successive championship hundred, in a vital last-wicket stand with Matthew Brimson finally worth 123. Then Lewis took 3 for 18 as Lancashire fell short in their own first innings and, after Aftab Habib's high-quality 79, helped to make sure of Leicestershire's superiority by hitting a rapid 37 and snapping up the important wicket of visiting skipper John Crawley just before the close of day three. Nathan Wood fought hard against the tide, but there was only one winner after that.

Yorkshire fought back hard against Somerset at Taunton, in a match which just managed to scrape

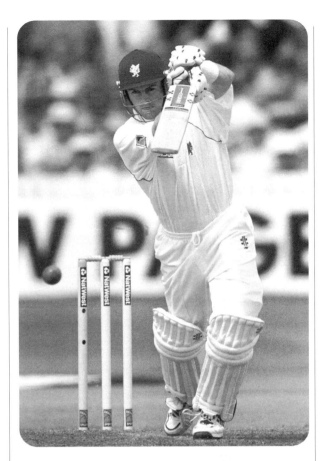

Jamie Cox scored a magnificent 173 runs in his first championship innings for Somerset.
David Munden/Sportsline Photographic

into the fourth day, but victory for the Cider County represented a personal triumph for Jamie Cox, their new overseas signing and captain. The 29-year-old Tasmanian vice-captain, a six-footer with a guardsman's bearing, marked his first championship innings with a brilliant 173, batting for 325 minutes and 247 balls, and with most of his 25 fours coming from textbook strokes straight back past the bowler or through the covers. Michael Burns and Rob Turner lent valued support as Somerset demoralised Yorkshire by running up a total of 468 for 9 declared. Then came Caddick. The fast bowler, then still in the England wilderness despite his 105 championship wickets in 1998, ripped the heart out of Yorkshire's first innings with a remarkable spell of 4 for 24 from 20 overs on a largely unresponsive pitch. Steffan Jones and Keith Parsons benefited from operating in Caddick's slipstream and, by the close of the second day, Yorkshire were 16 for 1

(Caddick striking again with the wicket of Michael Vaughan) as they followed on after being dismissed for just 148. The 19-year-old Matt Bulbeck took four of Yorkshire's first seven second-innings wickets, but David Byas (90) and Anthony McGrath (75) at least prevented a rout. Chris Silverwood then took a touch of shine off Somerset's fine win by picking up 4 for 11 as they made heavy weather of a victory target of just 26.

Dramatic left-arm swing bowling by Mark Ilott, who followed up two successes of the previous evening in an overall spell of 6 for 38, laid waste to Warwickshire's second innings at Chelmsford and earned Essex their first championship win at their headquarters since May 1997. Ilott also turned the match on its head as Warwickshire, with an 80-run lead on first innings, were tumbled out for just 86. Paul Prichard and Nasser Hussain both made 59 to ensure Essex reached their 167-run target with few alarms – and the 1998 wooden spoonists were back in business. In fact, Essex had reduced a frail-looking Warwickshire top order to 84 for 6 by lunch on the first day, before Neil Smith, the captain, counter-attacked with 69 and Graeme Welch added an unbeaten 48 to a solid lower-order effort. Essex's first innings was uninspired, dull fare, with Ed Giddins and Tim Munton sharing seven wickets. Ilott, though, certainly livened things up.

Hampshire, who were to prove the early season's surprise packet, overwhelmed Durham by eight wickets at the Riverside after posting a first-innings 366 based on Will Kendall's championship-best 105. Derek Kenway contributed a career-best 70 not out and Adrian Aymes, pushed up the order by Robin Smith, made 51. Simon Renshaw's intelligently varied medium pace brought him 4 for 43 as Durham were dismissed for 167 and then, after Dimitri Mascarenhas had struck twice on the second evening, Nixon McLean and John Stephenson (4 for 48) worked their way through the rest of the Durham batting. Local lads Michael Gough and Jimmy Daley salvaged some pride with 59 and 56 respectively, and skipper David Boon remained defiant on 61 not out, but as Smith rushed Hampshire to victory with an unbeaten 30 it was difficult to foresee Durham having anything other than a season of hard toil.

Unfancied Derbyshire also made sure of a good start to the new campaign by turning over Kent in their own Garden of England backyard. Canterbury regulars were disgruntled to see Kent bowled out for just 141 on the first day, with Matthew Walker's 53 the only score of note, and then to collapse again to

Dominic Cork, the Derbyshire captain, proved himself a true all-rounder in the match against Kent, taking four wickets in the match and making 82 in the first innings.
David Munden/Sportsline Photographic

58 for 6 second time around when they faced a deficit of 159. Mark Ealham, with an unbeaten 88, took the game – just – into the third day, and there was some late belligerence too from Matthew Fleming and Martin McCague. But Kent could have no complaints about their ten-wicket mauling. Kevin Dean followed up his first innings 4 for 34 with 3 for 60, Trevor Smith took a second-innings 4 for 38 and Phil DeFreitas chipped in as always. Michael Slater and Adrian Rollins made sure of continued Derbyshire dominance in the second half of the opening day with an opening stand of 131. But this match belonged to Dominic Cork, emerging triumphantly from a winter of discord at Derby with his position as captain strengthened and with his team right behind him. Cork took two Kent wickets in each innings but, in between, played the innings of the match. Cork's 82 took three hours, contained

two sixes and nine fours, mixed fine stroke-play with determined defence as a winning lead was steadily built, and was the performance of a true all-rounder.

Another side to win by ten wickets were Nottinghamshire, with the rejuvenated Paul Johnson hitting 126, captain Jason Gallian (82) passing 50 for the first time in 13 innings since taking over the captaincy the previous July, and new overseas signing Vasbert Drakes picking up 5 for 49 and 4 for 60. Worcestershire, weakened by the absences of Moody, Lampitt and Newport, could offer only a second-innings stand of 204 for the third wicket between Graeme Hick and Vikram Solanki after being forced to follow on. Nottinghamshire's 417 put them in control, but this victory – and the manner of it – was just what Clive Rice wanted on his return to Trent Bridge as the county's new cricket manager.

Surrey moved into second place in the PPP table, behind Leicestershire, as Graham Thorpe led a dazzling chase towards a 300-run win target on the final day at Northampton. Thorpe finished 138 not out, Ian Ward made 63 and Alastair Brown an unbeaten 66 as Surrey waltzed home by eight wickets. Until Thorpe broke loose it had been a finely contested game, with Northants responding to a slight first-innings deficit by reaching 338 second time around. Tony Penberthy and David Sales put on a rapid 111 as they moved to 88 and 69 respectively but, throughout, this match benefited from a pitch of pace and bounce which reflected great credit on groundsman David Bates. Alex Tudor and Martin Bicknell won the pace battle against Devon Malcolm and Paul Taylor – with Malcolm looking faster even than the tyro Tudor despite giving him 15 years. Bicknell, one of the circuit's most consistent performers, took four wickets in each innings and Tudor's second-innings haul of 5 for 64 was central to Surrey's success. Northants, in fact, were 91 for 7 on the first day before Taylor (71) joined Rob Bailey (75) in an unlikely eighth-wicket stand of 117 in 34 overs. Adam Hollioake made a very good 96 in Surrey's first-innings 286 – hitting Malcolm back over his head for six and then advancing down the pitch to Taylor to strike some of his 15 fours.

The tightest finish in this round of games was at Bristol, where Middlesex ended an unwanted sequence of 16 first-class matches without success by beating Gloucestershire by two wickets. At one stage 127 for 4, as they chased 245, Middlesex were boosted by a fifth-wicket stand of 88 between Owais Shah (60) and Paul Weekes (40). But Jon Lewis, in a lively spell, dismissed them both – and when Hewitt and Cook followed Middlesex were suddenly 231 for 8. David Nash and Angus Fraser made sure of victory, but it was tense at the end. Lewis had taken 5 for 79 in Middlesex's first-innings 268, a total built around Mark Ramprakash's five-hour 101, but Phil Tufnell was the real architect of Gloucestershire's downfall after the West Country county had earned a hard-fought 29-run halfway lead. Shah played an important part with the ball, too, taking 3 for 33 with his underrated off-breaks, but Tufnell's 5 for 61 was the main reason Gloucestershire failed to rub in their advantage after reaching 152 for 4. Hancock, Hewson and Dawson all fell short of a half-century after batting promisingly. The Gloucestershire first innings was founded on 51 from Kim Barnett, 76 by Mark Alleyne, and 36 from Jack Russell, who shepherded the tail effectively but was surely coming in far too low at number eight.

Glamorgan made 341 for 4 to beat Sussex at Cardiff, the highest fourth-innings total made for victory on the ground. Steve James spearheaded the effort with 153, sharing in century stands for the second and third wickets with Adrian Dale and Keith Newell, who made 41 against his former

Alex Tudor: the Surrey fast bowler who spent much of the summer on the sidelines.
David Munden/Sportsline Photographic

county. Then, when James fell at 269, Robert Croft and Adrian Shaw continued the drive to the finishing post with an unbroken stand of 72. Croft ended on 58 not out, in addition to his 5 for 82 in the Sussex second innings of 265. It was a real triumph for Glamorgan, who lost skipper Matthew Maynard to an accident that occurred during fielding practice following the first day. Maynard caught his right little finger in the turf, and broke it, and was consequently unable to bat as Glamorgan slumped to 149 in reply to Sussex's first-innings 222, in which 20-year-old Simon Jones – son of former Glamorgan and England fast bowler Jeff Jones – bagged 5 for 31 in his fourth championship match. Glamorgan's first innings would have been an even grimmer affair but for a three-hour, career-best 49 by Dean Cosker, who had gone in as a nightwatchman. For Sussex, Shaun Humphries made a first-innings 57 and, second time around, a laborious but valuable 123 by opener Toby Pierce was followed by a brisk 52 from Robin Martin-Jenkins.

ROUND 4: 14–17 MAY 1999

14, 15 and 16 May
at Trent Bridge
Nottinghamshire 251 (69.2 overs) (MPL Bulbeck 5 for 58) and 246 (JER Gallian 76, VC Drakes 55*, PW Jarvis 4 for 76)
Somerset 234 (66.3 overs) (JID Kerr 51, MN Bowen 5 for 66) and 232 (J Cox 83, VC Drakes 4 for 70)
Nottinghamshire won by 31 runs
Nottinghamshire 18 pts, Somerset 5 pts

14, 15, 16 and 17 May
at Stockton-on-Tees
Kent 301 for 8 dec. (95.1 overs) (AP Wells 111, A Symonds 78) and 121 for 5 (J Wood 4 for 47)
Durham 93 (47.1 overs) (MM Patel 5 for 18) and 325 (JJB Lewis 132, MA Gough 67, JBD Thompson 7 for 89)
Kent won by five wickets
Kent 19 pts, Durham 3 pts

at Cardiff
Glamorgan 260 (89.3 overs) (A Dale 108, BW Gannon 6 for 80) and 312 for 6 dec. (A Dale 113, I Dawood 102)
Gloucestershire 109 (38.5 overs) (SL Watkin 5 for 31) and 291 (JN Snape 63*, MGN Windows 57, THC Hancock 55, SD Thomas 4 for 81)
Glamorgan won by 172 runs
Glamorgan 18 pts, Gloucestershire 4 pts

at Southampton
Hampshire 352 (96.2 overs) (RA Smith 69, AD Mascarenhas 62, A Sheriyar 7 for 130) and 91 for 3
Worcestershire 184 (54.3 overs) (RK Illingworth 91*, AC Morris 5 for 59) and 258 (VS Solanki 84, AC Morris 5 for 52)
Hampshire won by seven wickets
Hampshire 20 pts, Worcestershire 4 pts

at Old Trafford
Northamptonshire 404 for 8 dec. (130.1 overs) (MB Loye 100, DJG Sales 96) and 256 for 0 dec. (ML Hayden 130*, RJ Bailey 113*)
Lancashire 350 for 6 dec. (100 overs) (M Watkinson 116, MJ Chilton 102) and 121 (DE Malcolm 4 for 37)
Northamptonshire won by 189 runs
Northamptonshire 18 pts, Lancashire 6 pts

at The Oval
Essex 262 (108.5 overs) (PJ Prichard 103) and 204 (SG Law 64, RJ Hyam 51, AJ Tudor 4 for 42)
Surrey 195 (71.4 overs) (MC Ilott 4 for 44) and 272 for 6 (AD Brown 110*)
Surrey won by four wickets
Surrey 16 pts, Essex 6 pts

at Edgbaston
Warwickshire 315 (91.2 overs) (A Singh 58, DR Brown 51, NMK Smith 51, PAJ DeFreitas 6 for 92) and 319 (DR Brown 74, TL Penney 59, DG Cork 5 for 88)
Derbyshire 286 (81.5 overs) (BJ Spendlove 63, AS Rolling 51, AF Giles 4 for 63) and 264 (SP Titchard 73, AF Giles 4 for 62, NMK Smith 4 for 90)
Warwickshire won by 84 runs
Warwickshire 19 pts, Derbyshire 6 pts

at Headingley
Yorkshire 160 (62.4 overs) (D Byas 62, RL Johnson 4 for 56) and 313 (A McGrath 142*, GS Blewett 73, SJ Cook 4 for 83)
Middlesex 249 (102.2 overs) (MR Ramprakash 84, MJ Hoggard 4 for 56) and 226 for 5 (JL Langer 127*, PN Weekes 65*)
Middlesex won by five wickets
Middlesex 17 pts, Yorkshire 4 pts

Obstetrician Dr Julian Thompson delivered Kent their first championship victory of the season with career-best bowling figures of 7 for 89 as Durham, following on 208 runs behind, folded in their second innings, despite a first-wicket stand of 179 between Jon Lewis and Michael Gough. The former scored his eighth first-class hundred, the latter passed his

Alex Morris of Hampshire claimed his maiden five-wicket haul in the first innings against Worcestershire and then improved on his figures in the second innings.
David Munden/Sportsline Photographic

previous championship best of 62. But Kent had a few wobbles on the way to the 118 they required for victory when John Wood picked up three wickets in the 18th over of the innings; fortunately captain Matthew Fleming mastered the bowling and the fading light to smash 26 off 16 balls. Having been turned into a three-day match by the weather, which postponed proceedings for 24 hours, there was a point when it looked as if it would not run the three. First Alan Wells, surviving two chances on nought and four, reached his highest championship score for Kent, an innings crafted over five hours; then Andrew Symonds weighed in with his best to date for the county, allowing Fleming to declare. Then slow left-arm bowler Min Patel found some appreciable turn and helped to bowl out Durham for 93.

The absence of captain Matthew Maynard, who broke a finger while playing football, and the prolific opener Steve James, made not a jot of difference to Glamorgan's power to score runs. They managed a substantial first-innings score against Gloucestershire, despite Ben Gannon, who became the first bowler to take five wickets on his debut for Gloucestershire since Brian Wells in 1951. Adrian Dale resisted everything that was sent down to him and having been dropped on three in the first innings reached a deserved hundred; he then did the double with another century second time around, the first time he has achieved the feat. Stand-in opener, wicketkeeper Ismail Dawood shared in a second-wicket stand of 211 as he posted his maiden first-class hundred. Acting captain Steve Watkin, who knocked over five batsmen as Gloucestershire were skittled for 109, had chosen not to enforce the follow-on, possibly mindful of the fact that the visitors' side contained two spinners. Gloucestershire's remaining seven second-innings wickets fell in just over three hours of the final day. The win was all the more remarkable since the appalling injury list meant that there were just three capped players in the Glamorgan eleven.

For a brief spell Hampshire found themselves at the top of the county championship for the first time since June 1992; then Surrey too won their match and they had to content themselves with second spot. For their victory Hampshire can thank their burly, pony-tailed Yorkshireman Alex Morris, who recorded his maiden five-wicket haul in the first innings and then bettered it as Worcestershire, ravaged by injuries and World Cup calls, subsided next time around. Hampshire did lose wickets on their way to the win, but their opponents had left too small a difference to give their bowlers a chance to whip out Hampshire before they had knocked off the 91 needed. There were positives to emerge for Worcestershire, who were without Phil Newport, Stuart Lampitt, Tom Moody, Graeme Hick and Paul Pollard: among these was Alamgir Sheriyar, a pacy left-arm bowler who got the ball to swing and shouldered the burden of being his side's strike and stock bowler. His first-innings figures read more like a spinner's, but his return of 7 for 130 was a personal best. His ten wickets in the match, the third time he has achieved the feat in his career, promised better things for later on.

Northamptonshire captain Matthew Hayden, a Queenslander, could take much of the credit for Mike Watkinson reaching the 11th hundred of his first-class career in Lancashire's first innings. Watkinson, the non-striker on seven at the time, claimed he was obstructed by off-spinner Graeme Swann when taking a quick single, Paul Taylor's throw arriving in wicketkeeper David Ripley's gloves with the batsman yards out. Hayden withdrew the appeal and the Lancashire batsman went on to score a further 109 runs. There were four other centurions

Alastair Brown made an unbeaten 110 for Surrey against Essex.

David Munden/Sportsline Photographic

during this rain-affected match. Lancashire's Mark Chilton reached his maiden championship hundred in the first innings, Mal Loye having got to three figures for the opposition; when Northamptonshire batted again, and because Lancashire had opted to bat on, the home side had to resort to 'cafeteria' bowling. Hayden and Rob Bailey both profited, striking a century apiece, but the only satisfaction to be gleaned from all that was the fact that with Devon Malcolm firing them in like a teenager, and Swann nipping in for three wickets, Lancashire were bowled out for next to nothing.

The Trent Bridge pitch was reported because 15 wickets fell on the first day's play between Notts and Somerset, but it was viewed as merely 'sporting' after an inspection. The match did not make it into a fourth day. There was also some kind of fear that spectators would not do so either because the gates to Trent Bridge were locked to keep out the football fans of Nottingham Forest and Leicester. And not long after Forest had been relegated from the FA Premiership, Nottinghamshire completed their second win of the season. For long moments while Somerset captain Jamie Cox was at the crease in the second innings, victory did not look such a certainty. Nottinghamshire wicketkeeper Chris Read

confirmed what everyone already knew, that he has a lot to offer with bat and gloves. In this match it was his work behind the stumps which caught the eye, and the ball. Nine catches in the match, six in Somerset's second innings, underlined his potential. Vasbert Drakes with a second-innings half-century and six wickets in the match deserved praise, as did Mark Bowen for his first-innings return of 5 for 66 and seven wickets in the game. Cox apart, no one managed to get even a half-decent score in the second innings.

It was a match of hits and misses at The Oval and Surrey's Alastair Brown featured strongly in both categories. His miss was at slip in the second innings when Essex wicketkeeper Barry Hyam was on one. The hits were match-winning ones as Brown blasted his way to an unbeaten 110, the 19th hundred of his first-class career. On the way he shared in a stand of 72 with wicketkeeper Jon Batty, who had also been guilty of a glaring miss when Hyam was on ten – the generosity of Messrs Brown and Batty had allowed Hyam to reach his maiden first-class fifty. Brown smacked his way to his first fifty of 58 balls and before being joined by Batty had put on 87 for the sixth wicket with Ben Hollioake. For Essex, who had dominated proceedings until Brown was unleashed on them, there was the welcome sight of three figures alongside opener Paul Prichard's name, his decision to give up the captaincy at the end of last season clearly beginning to pay dividends. His last championship hundred was in August 1997 – a double ton against Kent at Canterbury. This one at The Oval was his first against Surrey and left him needing to repeat the feat against Glamorgan and Hampshire to complete a full set against all the first-class counties.

Derbyshire's five seamers were no match for the balanced offensive unit put out by Warwickshire. Spinners accounted for 13 of the 20 Derbyshire wickets to fall and while Dominic Cork, who had opted to field on winning the toss, and veteran Phillip deFreitas also picked up 13 wickets between them the cost was greater. There were some bright moments for Derbyshire, notably Ben Spendlove's first-innings half-century – his maiden first-class fifty on the ground where he took two Test catches when he fielded as a substitute for England last year – and Adrian Rollins' fifty; while Stephen Titchard, down from Lancashire to seek a change of fortune, scored a fine 73 in the second innings. But Warwickshire always had the edge. Dougie Brown scored fifties in each innings and Anurag Singh captivated the first-day crowd with his fluent and stunningly executed

58, which reminded watchers of the potential he had shown as a schoolboy when he scored 16 centuries in schools and youth cricket in his final year at King Edward's in Birmingham. Trevor Penney was forced to take over as wicketkeeper because Tony Frost was suffering from back spasms; the Zimbabwean then weighed in with a second-innings 59.

It may have been anger; it may have been hunger, but whatever the motivation Middlesex's Justin Langer was certainly moved to compile a match-winning century against Yorkshire. On the third day, when Anthony McGrath looked to have swung things Yorkshire's way with the highest score of his career, Middlesex believed that they had caught the batsman when he had reached 57: Langer was the slip fielder, Paul Weekes the unlucky bowler. McGrath survived and indeed remained undefeated. So Middlesex went into the last day with three wickets already down and a further 183 runs needed for victory. Langer made his intentions and his feelings clear when he hammered Ian Fisher's first two deliveries of the day for four. Nightwatchman Simon Cook hung around for another 49 minutes, and once Langer had been joined by Weekes the writing was on the scoreboard. The pair shared an undefeated stand of 143 in 33.3 overs, Weekes reaching 65, and Langer 127, an innings which included 16 fours and occupied 203 balls. The Yorkshire attack was shorn of the services of Darren Gough, Gavin Hamilton and the injured Paul Hutchison, but Matthew Hoggard and Chris Silverwood did put in some encouraging spells.

ROUND 5: 19–22 MAY 1999

19, 20 and 21 May
at Derby
Northamptonshire 270 (81.1 overs) (AL Penberthy 98, PAJ DeFreitas 5 for 48) and 261 (ML Hayden 111)
Derbyshire 466 (101 overs) (MJ Slater 171, SP Titchard 136) and 66 for 2
Derbyshire won by eight wickets
Derbyshire 20 pts, Northamptonshire 6 pts

at Taunton
Somerset 453 (137.2 overs) (PD Bowler 138, M Burns 109, RJ Turner 52*, J Ormond 5 for 85) and 37 for 1
Leicestershire 173 (49.5 overs) (JID Kerr 7 for 23) and 313 (Aftab Habib 147, JM Dakin 62, AR Caddick 5 for 79)
Somerset won by nine wickets
Somerset 20 pts, Leicestershire 3 pts

19, 20, 21 and 22 May
at Chelmsford
Yorkshire 311 (114.2 overs) (MP Vaughan 100, MJ Wood 53) and 435 for 5 dec. (MP Vaughan 151, D Byas 90, A McGrath 54)
Essex 335 (90 overs) (SG Law 159) and 237 (SG Law 113*, ID Fisher 5 for 73)
Yorkshire won by 174 runs
Yorkshire 19 pts, Essex 7 pts

at Old Trafford
Nottinghamshire 181 (58.3 overs) (AG Wharf 54*, PJ Martin 5 for 43) and 291 (JER Gallian 120*, G Keedy 5 for 67)
Lancashire 141 (56.2 overs) (PJ Franks 4 for 24, VC Drakes 4 for 55) and 332 for 7 (GD Lloyd 120*, G Chapple 55, RD Stemp 4 for 114)
Lancashire won by three wickets
Lancashire 16 pts, Nottinghamshire 4 pts

at Lord's
Middlesex 256 (84.5 overs) (PN Weekes 61, SJ Cook 51) and 339 (MA Rose 116, MR Ramprakash 62, AC Morris 5 for 79)
Hampshire 379 (104.4 overs) (WS Kendall 85, DA Kenway 75*, PJ Hartley 58, SJ Cook 4 for 108, TF Bloomfield 4 for 109) and 219 for 4 (WS Kendall 78*, GW White 64)
Hampshire won by six wickets
Hampshire 20 pts, Middlesex 6 pts

at Hove
Gloucestershire 294 (115.2 overs) (THC Hancock 66, RC Russell 64) and 302 for 8 dec. (RC Russell 85, MGN Windows 50, RJ Kirtley 4 for 75)
Sussex 145 (55.5 overs) (AM Smith 4 for 36) and 455 for 8 (MJ Di Venuto 162, PA Cottey 126)
Sussex won by two wickets
Sussex 16 pts, Gloucestershire 6 pts

at Edgbaston
Warwickshire 321 (111 overs) (DL Hemp 144, MA Wagh 60, A Sheriyar 6 for 104) and 253 for 6 dec. (TL Penney 71*, A Singh 69)
Worcestershire 203 (95 overs) (G Welch 4 for 57) and 320 (CG Liptrot 61, PR Pollard 58, AF Giles 4 for 64)
Warwickshire won by 51 runs
Warwickshire 19 pts, Worcestershire 5 pts

Australians dominated the match between Derbyshire and Northants: Michael Slater for Derbyshire and Matthew Hayden for Northamptonshire. Sandwiched somewhere in

Derbyshire's Michael Slater made a maiden championship century against Northamptonshire in May.
David Munden/Sportsline Photographic

between was a meaty filling from Englishman Stephen Titchard. Phil DeFreitas maintained his run of form with another five-wicket haul in the first innings. Tony Penberthy got close to three figures, but Slater and Titchard both beat him to the mark, followed by Hayden in Northants' second innings. Slater's century was a welcome one, it being his maiden championship hundred in his second season with Derbyshire. Making full use of an easy paced pitch he launched into the Northants attack and powered to three figures in 143 balls. The onslaught continued as he took just 46 more to reach 150. He and Titchard put on a record 294 for Derbyshire against Northants. Titchard brought up his first

hundred for Derbyshire with a five; luck not being on Northamptonshire's side, there were four overthrows when the former Lancashire batsman stole a single. Although Hayden had a dart and thumped 111, the task of setting a big enough target for victory proved beyond even his huge capabilities and a win was achieved with a day to spare.

Yorkshire suffered yet again at the hands of an Australian batsman, although at least on this occasion they did finish up as the winners, unlike the previous two times when Jamie Cox and Justin Langer steered Somerset and Middlesex to victory respectively. This time though, Essex's Stuart Law really hammered them, scoring not one, but two centuries, in, as it turned out, a hopeless cause. Yorkshire had the man to combat that. Law did not have a monopoly on hundreds in each innings. Yorkshire opener Michael Vaughan, who had captained England 'A' with a deal of success in the winter, was up to the challenge. If his first day's effort was a pleasure to witness, his second-innings hundred was masterful, and in complete contrast to the approach of the more powerfully built Law. Vaughan's 151, his third championship hundred against Essex, put the match way out of their reach. And left-arm spinner Ian Fisher, playing only his fourth championship match, claimed his second five-wicket haul to ensure that Vaughan's work was not wasted. Law was a determined opponent and his defiant, unbeaten hundred showed the rest of his team-mates what was possible; unfortunately they did not follow his lead.

After 29 wickets had fallen in two days at Old Trafford, Nottinghamshire captain Jason Gallian could not be blamed for thinking that he had batted his side into an impregnable position with his unbeaten 120 second time around. A target of 332 looked way beyond Lancashire's abilities, given their abysmal first-innings performance, when they had conceded a first-innings advantage. Gallian's noble effort, which lasted a shade under five hours, was the 14th hundred of his first-class career and was all the more satisfying having been scored against his former colleagues. However, Lloyd, who is nothing if not a gambler, decided to end an appalling trot by going on the offensive and suddenly the impossible passed through the realms of the improbable and into reality. He too scored 120 not out and received invaluable support from John Crawley, the Lancashire captain, who sadly fell just short of fifty but did enough to set the Lancashire cause on the right track. Lloyd really dug in for victory. It was a century made under pressure and particularly gratifying for that. In all he faced 165 balls and hit 16 fours and one six and had some vital support from Glen Chapple, who made a competent 55.

There was youth on show in abundance at Lord's and some rising stars, including Hampshire's Derek Kenway and Will Kendall and Middlesex's Simon Cook, but the tidal wave of emotion when Mike Roseberry reached his hundred engulfed everything else on a tense fourth day. It was Roseberry's first championship century for five years, his last having been made for Middlesex against Durham, the county he joined and spent four harrowing years with until his return to Lord's last winter. It would have been a fairy-tale ending if the effort Roseberry had put into his second innings – the 20th hundred of his first-class career – had been rewarded with a Middlesex win, but the only element of fairy tale about this was that the result was grim for Middlesex. That was despite a maiden first-class fifty by Cook and an impressive spell of first-innings bowling that earned him four wickets for the second innings on the trot to confirm his all-round potential. But in Kenway and Kendall and, in the second innings, Giles White, Hampshire possessed

Michael Vaughan, Yorkshire's opening batsman, scored a century in both innings at Chelmsford.
Sportsline Photographic

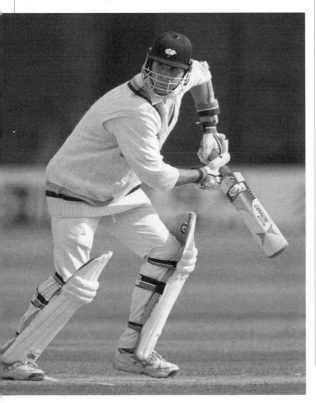

the match-winning batsmen after Alex Morris, with a third five-wicket haul in four innings, had helped to undermine the Middlesex second innings.

It was a far from champion-like performance from Leicestershire, who suffered their first defeat in the competition since August 1997. They were out-batted and out-bowled by Somerset throughout the three days. Peter Bowler, having shed the captaincy and its concomitant responsibility, scored his second hundred of the summer and the 33rd of his career, while Mike Burns dispelled the impression that he is purely a one-day slogger with a cultured maiden first-class century as they added 214 for the fourth wicket. In-form wicketkeeper Robbie Turner maintained his remarkably good run with an unbeaten fifty. Leicestershire were never in the hunt when they replied to Somerset's imposing first-innings total. All-rounder Jason Kerr claimed a career-best 7 for 23 – the best figures by a Somerset player against Leicestershire – as the champions followed on. At one stage he had a spell of 5 for 6 in 19 balls. When they followed on, Aftab Habib underlined his abilities with a 241-ball hundred, which included 22 boundaries as he and Jon Dakin put on 115 for the sixth wicket, but Andy Caddick took over as the spearhead of the Somerset attack and returned admirable figures of 5 for 79.

Sussex, having avoided the follow-on by just one run and been outplayed for three of the four days by Gloucestershire, turned the match on its head as they recorded their highest fourth-innings score to beat Gloucestershire by two wickets, victory arriving in the last over of the match. Heroes of the day were Sussex's overseas star Michael Di Venuto and their close season signing from Glamorgan, Tony Cottey. The pair of them dug in from the start of the final day, which they resumed on 127 for 3, still an imposing 325 runs away from the target of 452. By the time they were parted they had added 256 for the fourth wicket. Di Venuto had looked commanding, and Gloucestershire must have regretted a missed chance, Jon Lewis spilling a catch at long leg on the evening of the third day when he had made 53. Cottey too reached his hundred, the 22nd of his first-class career. It then fell to Umer Rashid, with a career-best 44 not out to steer them home. Gloucestershire, who recorded their first three-figure opening partnership since 1997 in the first innings between Jack Russell and Tim Hancock, also passed 300 for the first time in the season.

Worcestershire got to within a tantalising nine minutes of forcing a draw with Warwickshire. Weakened by injury and international calls, there

The Australian, Michael Di Venuto, hit three centuries for Sussex.
Stephen Laffer/
Sportsline Photographic

was no Graeme Hick, no Tom Moody (both on World Cup duty), and Philip Weston, Stuart Lampitt and Reuben Spiring were all injured or ill. Phil Newport was making his first appearance since undergoing knee surgery last year and the side was littered with raw recruits. Two of them, Chris Liptrot, a 19-year-old seam bowler and Nathan Batson gave Warwickshire a scare on the final day, Liptrot reaching his maiden first-class half-century and Batson scoring a career-best 42. But Warwickshire were just too strong. For the fifth innings on the trot at Edgbaston they passed 300 in the first innings and probably would have done so second time around had they not declared when 371 runs ahead leaving Worcestershire to score more runs than any other side has ever managed in a fourth innings to beat Warwickshire. There was a sound hundred from David Hemp in the first innings, the tenth of his career and his fifth for Warwickshire. Mark Wagh and Anurag Singh, rival Varsity captains two years ago – the former with Oxford, the latter, Cambridge – also hit form with the bat.

ROUND 6: 26–29 MAY 1999

26, 27 and 28 May 1999
at Worcester
Worcestershire 164 (58.1 overs) (PR Pollard 52) and 160 (SD Thomas 4 for 48)
Glamorgan 127 (46 overs) (A Sheriyar 4 for 49) and 149
Worcestershire won by 48 runs
Worcestershire 16 pts, Glamorgan 4 pts

26, 27, 28 and 29 May 1999
at Gloucester
Essex 273 (94.3 overs) (AP Grayson 62, PJ Prichard 61, AM Smith 4 for 45) and 344 for 8 (SG Law 125, TC Walton 71, RC Irani 64)
Gloucestershire 408 (128 overs) (MGN Windows 118, JN Snape 98*, RC Irani 4 for 43)
Match drawn
Gloucestershire 12 pts, Essex 10 pts

at Canterbury
Leicestershire 369 (128.4 overs) (BF Smith 73, Aftab Habib 60, IJ Sutcliffe 55) and 346 for 9 dec. (DL Maddy 93, MS Kasprowicz 52, JBD Thompson 4 for 79)
Kent 420 (124.5 overs) (A Symonds 177, DP Fulton 64, DJ Millns 5 for 62) and 92 for 3
Match drawn
Kent 11 pts, Leicestershire 11 pts

at Lord's
Sussex 430 (149 overs) (CJ Adams 130, MTE Peirce 98,
RR Montgomerie 69) and 81 for 7
Middlesex 233 (83 overs) (MR Ramprakash 81,
MA Robinson 4 for 85) and (following on) 358
(OA Shah 75, PN Weekes 62, MR Ramprakash 59,
RSC Martin-Jenkins 4 for 58)
Match drawn
Middlesex 7 pts, Sussex 12 pts

at The Oval
Somerset 199 (67.3 overs) (RJ Turner 67, MP Bicknell
4 for 72) and 405 (KA Parsons 77, ME Trescothick 76,
RJ Turner 68, J Cox 54, R Amin 4 for 87)
Surrey 558 for 9 dec. (172 overs) (DJ Bicknell 114,
IDK Salisbury 100*, JD Ratcliffe 86, IJ Ward 76,
MP Bicknell 69) and 49 for 3
Surrey won by seven wickets
Surrey 19 pts, Somerset 1 pt

27, 28 and 29 May
at Trent Bridge
Nottinghamshire 324 (86.3 overs) (PJ Franks 61)
and 333 (P Johnson 92, MP Dowman 67*)
Hampshire 203 (72.5 overs) (RA Smith 68, VC Drakes
4 for 63) and 193 (RA Smith 55, PJ Franks 4 for 25)
Nottinghamshire won by 261 runs
Nottinghamshire 19 pts, Hampshire 5 pts

at Headingley
Durham 114 (37 overs) and 211 (JJB Lewis 74, C White
4 for 63)
Yorkshire 310 (90.2 overs) (D Byas 68, A McGrath 62,
J Wood 7 for 58) and 16 for 1
Yorkshire won by nine wickets
Yorkshire 19 pts, Durham 4 pts

By the time rain arrived on the final day of their
match with Essex, there was already too much for
Gloucestershire to do. They had to winkle two more
Essex batsmen and at that point would have needed
to have scored 210 runs for victory. They were
undone by Stuart Law, who reached his third
hundred in four innings as he and Irani shared a
fourth-wicket stand of 139 in the second innings,
Irani making, for him, a subdued 64. It was a match
littered with odd incidents. Irani's decision to bat on
a slow and true wicket on Archdeacon Meadow
looked to have backfired with four Essex men,
including the acting captain, back in the pavilion
with just 25 runs on the board, swing bowler Mike
Smith doing much of the damage, at one point
boasting figures of 8–4–14–3. Having bottomed out

at the ridiculous, it swung back with a century
partnership between the Pauls, Prichard and
Grayson. Play was interrupted by a swarm of bees,
day two, the players taking refuge in the shadow of
Gloucester Cathedral until the coast was clear.
Former Northamptonshire players did well. Jeremy
Snape (Gloucestershire) was left stranded on 98
and Tim Walton (Essex) knocked off a rapid 71
second time around.

Andrew Symonds had planned some hunting and
fishing this summer, the Australian close season, on
the Queensland coast; instead he was hunted and
brought over to Kent as replacement for Carl
Hooper. After a modestly promising start he blazed
into big-hitting mode against Leicestershire by
scoring an outstanding first century for Kent and the
16th of his career. His 177 was far and away the
highest score of a high-scoring game – 1,227 runs
were amassed over the four days – and contained
three sixes and 22 fours. During his onslaught on

Andrew Symonds was brought in to replace Carl Hooper at
Kent this summer. After a modest start, he scored an
outstanding 177 against Leicestershire.
David Munden/Sportsline Photographic

the third morning Symonds took 18 off one Darren Maddy over and appeared to be on the point of scoring a century before lunch. Another Aussie, Mike Kasprowicz, signed for his bowling, starred with the bat on the final day. Having hit a useful 32 in the first innings, he then weighed in with his maiden championship fifty which helped Leicestershire captain James Whitaker to declare, leaving Kent a target of 296 off a minimum of 42 overs – a total they never made any pretence of chasing. Whitaker, who missed the whole of last season with a knee injury, suffered a torn calf muscle, an injury caused, he thought, by him compensating for a weak joint.

A total of 17 leg before decisions and seven more bowled told as much of a story about the Lord's pitch as the batting, which swung between the supreme and the mundane. Chris Adams' first 98 runs were a sight to behold. Enthralling and exhilarating. He moved to his century on the second morning and having been dropped on 115, scored a further 15 runs, but in far more muted style. Mark Ramprakash burrowed in on the low, slow strip for 81 first time round, which kept Middlesex in the hunt, and later in the same day, when Middlesex followed on 197 runs adrift, smacked a second half-century. When the second innings was completed, with some more telling contributions this time from Owais Shah and Paul Weekes, as well as a swishing swipe of 49 from Jamie Hewitt (dropped on 10) it all looked over for Middlesex. There was simply the formality for Sussex of knocking off the 162 needed for victory in 43 overs. Instead they found themselves teetering on the brink of defeat at 81 for 7 as they fumbled against the spin of Phil Tufnell in the darkness as a violent storm gathered and ultimately drove them off for good with ten overs remaining, leaving Middlesex thwarted and frustrated.

At The Oval, all five warning lights were on, indicating that conditions were bordering on the subterranean, when Surrey came out to thrash and smash their way to the 47 runs they needed off the five overs remaining in the match. Having dominated that game for much of the time it was not exactly the finish that the home team would have envisaged. They lost Mark Butcher in the first over, Ben Hollioake in the next, both run out. As the storm closed in so did the field. Alastair Brown was given a gentlemanly second warning by Andy Caddick that he could have been run out backing up; the drama was heightened by the rolls of thunder overhead. Eight were needed off the last

Paul Johnson of Nottinghamshire, narrowly missed a century against Hampshire.
David Munden/Sportsline Photographic

over and Brown and Jason Ratcliffe got there with a ball to spare. There were some fine individual performances, notably Darren Bicknell's first-innings hundred in his third outing of the season. It was the 31st of his career. Ian Salisbury scored a maiden hundred, and his leg spin earned him six wickets in the match. Surrey's left-arm spinner Rupesh Amin was well worth his four wickets after a marathon 54 overs in the innings. For Somerset, Robbie Turner scored a half-century in each innings.

Worcestershire escaped a possible fine and censure after 18 wickets fell on the first day of their match against Glamorgan. A further 19 fell on the second day and they recorded their first win of the season on the third day. They were hampered by the

DERBYSHIRE CCC

Home Ground:
Derby
Address:
County Ground, Nottingham Road,
Derby DE21 6DA
Tel: 01332 383211
Email: derby@ecb.co.uk
Directions:
By road: From the south, exit M1 at junction 25, follow A52 into Derby. The ground is off Pentagon Island. From the north, exit M1 at junction 28, join A38 into Derby and then follow directional signs.
Capacity: 4,000
Other grounds used: Chesterfield
Year formed: 1870

Chairman: Trevor Bowring
Secretary/General Manager: John Smedley
Cricket Manager: Colin Wells
Other posts:
Commercial Manager: Keith Stevenson; County Development Officers: John Brown, Colin Davies; Head Groundsman: Barry Marsh
Captain: Dominic Cork
Coaching contact: John Brown 01332 383211
County colours: Blue, brown and gold

HONOURS

COUNTY CHAMPIONSHIP
1936
SUNDAY LEAGUE
1990
BENSON & HEDGES CUP
1993
GILLETTE CUP/NATWEST TROPHY
1981

CGU National Cricket League nickname:
DERBYSHIRE SCORPIONS

Website:
www.dccc.co.uk

enforced absence of their captain Tom Moody and Graeme Hick, but this win ended a run of three defeats for them and it was done with ruthless efficiency. It took them 17 overs of the final morning to complete the job. Paul Pollard's first-day fifty remained the highest individual score of the match, when he held up one end for an admirable 170 minutes. But the rest of his Worcestershire team-mates contrived to let the score slip from 70 for 1 to 164 all out. Yet Glamorgan fared little better as they slumped to 16 for 4 before Michael Powell weighed in with a bold 42 off 60 balls. The second day followed the pattern of the first, by now doubts about the pitch and its bounce had permeated everyone's helmet. Only Vikram Solanki for Worcestershire and Alun Evans seemed to get to grips with it. Alamgir Sheriyar underlined his fine qualities with some excellent swing bowling, in and out. Phil Newport also picked up wickets in his second match of the season.

Hampshire arrived at Trent Bridge as championship leaders, but left with their tails between their legs, and their lead whittled away. Paul Franks emerged in this match with his stature as an all-rounder greatly enhanced. The former England Under-19 player top-scored in the first innings, then picked up seven wickets in a match which Nottinghamshire – a more potent side under the influence of Clive Rice, their former captain and now director of cricket – had wrapped up inside three days. It was Hampshire's first defeat of the season. In that final innings only captain Robin Smith stood between his side and total ignominy, but even he could not do it all alone. Profligate first-innings bowling by Hampshire, who conceded 73 extras, and an inadequate first dig, when again only Smith, with the first of his two half-centuries in the match, laid the dodgy foundations which eventually saw the whole structure of the Hampshire challenge undermined. They were also undone by a superb innings from veteran and former Nottinghamshire captain Paul Johnson. His 92 off 69 balls deserved to have been a hundred. He and Tim Robinson are the only squad members who were around in Rice's time as a player.

Durham have found Yorkshire one of the sides most difficult to resist in their first-class existence. This was Yorkshire's sixth championship success over them and their third win in five matches this season. That the match went into a third day by 90 minutes was as much due to the weather as it was to the resistance of eighth-wicket pair Martin Speight and John Wood, who battled on gamely until they

had amassed 54, before Wood was out just one run away from levelling the scores. Yorkshire still lost Michael Vaughan when they needed two more runs for victory, but it was always a formality after Durham's first-innings capitulation on a pitch which saw 16 wickets fall on the first day. Speight top-scored with 23, half his unbeaten second-innings knock. With 60-odd apiece from David Byas and Tony McGrath Yorkshire were always in the driving seat. Even when opener Jon Lewis made the highest individual score of the match there was little that Durham could do to stave off the inevitable. Craig White's four wickets second time around and some economical spells from Chris Silverwood and Ryan Sidebottom left Yorkshire with a paltry total to chase for victory.

ROUND 7: 2–5 JUNE 1999

2, 3, 4 and 5 June
at Derby
Yorkshire 117 (46.3 overs) (PAJ DeFreitas 4 for 37) and 308 for 8 dec. (A McGrath 76, RJ Blakey 70*, DG Cork 5 for 66)
Derbyshire 206 (72.2 overs) (RMS Weston 72, MJ Hoggard 5 for 47, CEW Silverwood 4 for 59)
Match drawn
Derbyshire 9 pts, Yorkshire 8 pts

at Chester-le-Street
Somerset 300 for 9 dec. (75.1 overs) (RJ Turner 95, MPL Bulbeck 76*) and 199 (M Burns 50*)
Durham 312 (81.5 overs) (JE Morris 100, JJB Lewis 68, KA Parsons 5 for 57)
Match drawn
Durham 11pts, Somerset 11pts

at Ilford
Essex 354 for 9 dec. (101.5 overs) (AP Grayson 159*, SG Law 56) and 218 for 3 dec. (SG Law 107*, N Hussain 59)
Hampshire 324 (102.5 overs) (RA Smith 96) and 36 for 2
Match drawn
Essex 12 pts, Hampshire 11 pts

at Bristol
Lancashire 351 for 9 dec. (78.1 overs) (A Flintoff 158, GD Lloyd 55, J Lewis 4 for 101)
Gloucestershire did not bat
Match drawn
Gloucestershire 8 pts, Lancashire 8 pts

at Tunbridge Wells
Surrey 271 (99.1 overs) (DJ Bicknell 57)
Kent 71 (35.3 overs) (AJ Tudor 5 for 30, MP Bicknell 4 for 32) and (following on) 172
Surrey won by an innings and 28 runs
Surrey 18 pts, Kent 4 pts

at Leicester
Glamorgan 291 (102.1 overs) (MJ Powell 71*, DJ Millns 4 for 30)
Leicestershire 259 (62.3 overs) (BF Smith 82, Aftab Habib 73, SD Thomas 4 for 66, SP Jones 4 for 70)
Match drawn
Leicestershire 10 pts, Glamorgan 10 pts

at Northampton
Nottinghamshire 220 (74.3 overs) (P Johnson 61, RT Robinson 61, DE Malcolm 4 for 52) and 209 for 3 (P Johnson 83*)
Northamptonshire 484 for 3 dec. (94 overs) (ML Hayden 170, AJ Swann 154, DJG Sales 81, RJ Warren 57*)
Match drawn
Northamptonshire 12 pts, Nottinghamshire 6 pts

at Horsham
Sussex 301 for 9 dec. (83.2 overs) (MTE Peirce 75, RR Montgomerie 66, MJ Di Venuto 64, A Sheriyar 4 for 102)
Worcestershire 124 (48.4 overs) (JD Lewry 6 for 63) and (following on) 255 for 9 (GA Hick 334)
Match drawn
Sussex 11 pts, Worcestershire 8 pts

at Edgbaston
Middlesex 216 for 8 dec. (84.3 overs) (PN Weekes 57) and 15 for 0
Warwickshire 70 for 2 dec.
Match drawn
Warwickshire 7 pts, Middlesex 5 pts

Robert Turner of Somerset showed remarkable consistency with bat and gloves this summer.
David Munden/Sportsline Photographic

Rain robbed the match between Derbyshire and Yorkshire of a start – the first day was a wash-out – and a finish. If there was a moral victory it was Derbyshire's after grinding out a first-innings lead. Robin Weston's first substantial score of the season saw his side to a solitary batting bonus point. Silverwood underlined his abilities with four Derbyshire wickets, while the youngster Matthew Hoggard claimed five for the first time this season. But despite the promise shown by the young pace bowlers and some spirited second-innings resistance from the likes of Tony McGrath, Richard Blakey, Chris Silverwood and Ian Fisher, and given the time that was lost to rain, there was every chance that Yorkshire would lose. There just seemed to be less fragility to the Derbyshire batting. Yorkshire's first-innings effort would have been even more shameful and pathetic had it not been for Craig White. Phil DeFreitas and Dominic Cork proved irresistible then, and Cork blasted batsmen aside in the second innings as he picked up his first five-wicket haul of the summer. The draw was certainly a setback for Yorkshire, but they still squeezed into third place; Derbyshire remained in a form of stasis, 11th for the third week running.

The confrontation between Durham and Somerset was littered with little coincidences, and lashed with a lot of rain, which guaranteed a draw. Somerset gave a first-class debut to Ian Jones, the first recruit to the Durham Academy in 1995 and released after a handful of second-team appearances. He made Durham suffer in the second innings with a stubborn 35 as nightwatchman. Jones' boyhood friend Melvyn Betts was dropped for the match, which pitted Tasmania's past and present captains, David Boon of Durham and Jamie Cox of Somerset, against each other. For a while Durham's attack, when the match really got under way on the second day, threatened to run through Somerset cheaply, then wicketkeeper Robbie Turner got his head down and got to within five runs of a deserved hundred – his fourth half-century on the trot and fifth of a productive period in which he has also been claiming his fair share of victims with the gloves. When it was their turn to bat, John Morris scored a stunning century: the man really can turn it on when the mood takes him – his hundred arrived off 112 balls. Unfortunately he was promptly out, caught at long leg after hitting two successive boundaries to reach three figures.

If the weather, which cost this game between Essex and Hampshire the first day and bite-sized chunks of a couple more, ensured that proceedings would end in a draw, the players on both sides certainly went out to make it entertaining. And Essex reached a

notable landmark in their first innings as they amassed maximum batting bonus points for the first time in a championship game since the beginning of September 1997. For that they had Paul Grayson's career-best score to thank and a pugnacious contribution from Australian Stuart Law. Grayson's unbeaten 159, the fifth century of his career and his fourth for Essex, was made in a shade under seven hours. He and Law added a brisk 85 for the third wicket – Grayson's share a modest 24 – then it was Hampshire's turn and captain Robin Smith emerged for a belligerent and competent 96. He fell to a sizzling slip catch by Darren Robinson. It helped draw Hampshire to within sight of the Essex first-innings total, but there just was not enough time either to leave a sensible target or for Hampshire to go for it. Not that this prevented Essex from having a stab at it. Law smacked his fourth hundred in six innings, scoring at a run a ball to leave Hampshire to get 249. It was too much.

What little of the match between Gloucestershire and Lancashire was permitted to be played certainly contained some of the most exhilarating cricket of the season thus far. Play did not get under way until the third day and just seven and a half overs were bowled on the final day, at which point Lancashire declared their first innings having acquired the fourth batting bonus point that they were looking for and their opponents having garnered a fourth bowling point to boot. Unfortunately Gloucestershire were unable to emerge from the dressing room. But at least Andrew Flintoff had done his stuff. In a display of power-hitting and timing not seen since Ian Botham in his pomp, Flintoff became only the second Lancashire player since the war to score a hundred before lunch, the other being David Green who achieved the feat against Glamorgan in 1964. Flintoff, still only 21, needed 61 balls to reach three figures. His first fifty came in 43 balls, the next took

Andrew Flintoff of Lancashire became only the second Lancashire player since the war to score a hundred before lunch. It was the fastest authentic century since 1986.
David Munden/Sportsline Photographic

DURHAM CCC

Home Ground:
Chester-Le-Street
Address:
County Ground, Riverside,
Chester-Le-Street, Co.
Durham DH3 3QR
Tel: 0191 387 1717
Email: marketing@durham-ccc.org.uk
Directions:
By rail: Chester-Le-Street Station (approximately five
minutes away by taxi).
By road: Easily accessible from A1(M). Nearby car parking
on match days at a cost of £3.00 per day.
Capacity: 10,000
Other grounds used:
Darlington CC (Feethams); Hartlepool CC;
Stockton CC 01642 672835.
Year formed: 1882

Chairman: Don Robson
Chief Executive: Mike Candlish
Cricket Executive: Geoff Cook
Other posts: First Team Coach: Norman Gifford
Captain: David Boon
Vice-captain: Nick Speak
County colours:
Yellow, blue, burgundy

HONOURS

NONE AS YET

**CGU National Cricket League
nickname:**
DURHAM DYNAMOS

Website:
www.durham-ccc.org.uk

him 18 – with only 11 scoring shots. He reached a career-best 158, off 105 balls, with 134 of those runs coming in boundaries, five of them sixes. It was the fastest authentic hundred since Viv Richards smashed a 48-ball century against hapless Glamorgan in 1986.

The weather, which also played a hand in the outcome between Kent and Surrey, made sure that everyone had to hang around at the Nevill Ground for 23 balls on the fourth day, at which point Martin Bicknell delivered the coup de grace when he had Dr Julian Thompson leg before for three. Victory, their fourth on the trot, took Surrey to the top of the championship table and was just reward for the way they tackled the tricky conditions. While some described it as a sporty pitch, only Darren Bicknell adopted a sensible approach. He stuck around, the superglue of the Surrey first innings, for the best part of four and a half hours, compiling the highest individual score of the match, 57, and ultimately guaranteeing that Surrey would not have to bat again. Kent were reduced to a shambles by the extra pace of Alex Tudor (5 for 30) and Martin Bicknell (4 for 32) in the first innings. That they scrabbled to 71 was little short of miraculous. When they followed on, exactly 200 in arrears, they appeared to have learned little from their first-innings torment. Only Robert Key applied himself, spending almost two hours for a gritty 31. Jason Ratcliffe, at best an occasional bowler, picked up a career-best 3 for 28.

The first day between Leicestershire and Glamorgan, like so many other matches around the country, was a wash-out. The second was also heavily diluted by rain, and in the 35 overs allowed, Glamorgan, having been put in to bat, managed to get to the brink of three figures without losing a wicket, although they should have. Steve James was put down at fourth slip before he had scored and wicketkeeper Paul Nixon chased 40 yards to take a top edge only to drop the ball. Glamorgan were eventually able to double their batting points for the season, their only bag coming against Gloucestershire in May. David Millns wrapped up the Glamorgan innings on the fourth day and Leicestershire rattled up two batting bonus points. There was something of a dramatic collapse, Leicestershire having cruised to 235 for 5 before losing their remaining wickets for the addition of a further 24 runs. At least Ben Smith and Aftab Habib made solid-looking half-centuries, but the defending champions still showed some worrying signs of frailty. Their attack had not been helped by the withdrawal of England left-arm paceman Alan

Mullally, who had cited mental and physical exhaustion after England's World Cup exit.

Nottinghamshire's Paul Johnson and Tim Robinson held together the first innings against Northants with identical scores as they revealed patience on a pitch which showed evidence of turn on the first day. Overnight though something must have happened because the new order at Northamptonshire, captain Matthew Hayden and Alec Swann reduced the pitch to a feather bed as they flayed the bowling to all parts. Hayden, the left-hander from Queensland, scored 126 of his mammoth innings before lunch, reaching his fourth century of the season off only 93 balls. When he was out 50 deliveries later he had smashed three sixes and 24 fours. Swann, who had scored a hundred in his only previous first-class game against Cambridge University earlier in the season, hit four sixes and 20 fours in his accomplished 154. The bowling figures read like a horror story, spinners Richard Stemp and Richard Bates being hammered for 158 and 83 respectively, and not a wicket between them. Thankfully the weather, which had robbed the game of the first day, intervened on the final one, although Johnson looked like saving it on his own, hitting his second half-century of the match.

A couple of returning heroes dominated proceedings at Horsham in a match that Sussex could and should have won. It could be argued that in this instance they suffered a bout of Hick-cups. Graeme of that ilk, newly returned from World Cup duty with England, marked his first innings back with a duck, but more than made up for it in the second with a match-saving hundred, the 105th of his enigmatic first-class career. It was yet another flawless gem which frustrated Sussex attempts to take advantage of their near total domination of this match. They owed much of that to Jason Lewry, their left-arm pace bowler, who had been out of action following a shoulder injury the previous August and a relapse on the England 'A' tour with England last winter. He chipped in with six of the best, including Hick, to hustle out Worcestershire first time around and help enforce the follow-on. Unfortunately he was then unable to repeat the feat. Captain Chris Adams, who is turning into more than just a useful standby, had the honour of dismissing the Hick, but even after he fell there was little chance of victory, although they got to within one wicket, because the storm clouds had got within sight of the ground to end play early.

There was an acrimonious final day at Edgbaston after the first three largely became hostages to the weather. Warwickshire's frustration was fuelled by the knowledge that they had the means to have kept the elements at bay and perhaps have provided enough time for something to be contrived. But the ban on flat coverings this season has made redundant the famous 'Brumbrella' which has done so much to keep play going in the past. Neither captain could agree a suitable target for Warwickshire to chase: Middlesex muttered something in the region of 280, Warwickshire whispered 250 and ne'er the twain would meet. So Middlesex crawled to a solitary batting point, something which had taken them until the fourth day to achieve. Paul Weekes did his batting average no harm as he struck his fourth half-century in six innings. Then Warwickshire, denied a fourth bowling point by their opponents, declared when they were safely past the follow-on figure for the loss of just two wickets with Nick Knight looking comfortable as he reached a modest 27. That declaration prevented Middlesex from picking up any bowling points and the game dribbled to a soggy, unsatisfactory draw.

ROUND 8: 9–12 JUNE 1999

9, 10 and 11 June
at Chelmsford
Derbyshire 285 (102 overs) (RMS Weston 129*) and 131 (RSG Anderson 5 for 37)
Essex 281 (96 overs) (N Hussain 141, ME Cassar 5 for 51) and 136 for 1 (AP Grayson 74*, N Hussain 56*)
Essex won by nine wickets
Essex 18 pts, Derbyshire 6 pts

at Cardiff
Middlesex 462 for 9 dec. (140.5 overs) (PN Weekes 140*, MA Roseberry 84, ARC Fraser 56 retired hurt, SD Thomas 4 for 84)
Glamorgan 108 (32.4 overs) (TF Bloomfield 5 for 36) and (following on) 241 (MJ Powell 83*)
Middlesex won by an innings and 113 runs
Middlesex 20 pts, Glamorgan 3 pts

at Basingstoke
Hampshire 206 (77 overs) (CEW Silverwood 5 for 43) and 124 (MJ Hoggard 4 for 45)
Yorkshire 192 (75.5 overs) (RJ Blakey 59, PJ Hartley 8 for 65) and 141 for 4 (D Byas 95)
Yorkshire won by six wickets
Yorkshire 16 pts, Hampshire 5 pts

at Southport
Warwickshire 217 (85.5 overs) (NV Knight 82, M Muralitharan 7 for 44) and 211 (NV Knight 64, M Muralitharan 7 for 73)
Lancashire 144 (49 overs) (JP Crawley 55, ESH Giddins 5 for 50) and 265 (JP Crawley 76, WK Hegg 58)
Warwickshire won by 19 runs
Warwickshire 17 pts, Lancashire 4 pts

9, 10, 11 and 12 June
at Leicester
Leicestershire 272 (85.2 overs) (Aftab Habib 60, CC Lewis 56, AJ Tudor 7 for 77) and 239 for 4 (Aftab Habib 70*, DL Maddy 52)
Surrey 501 (131.2 overs) (MA Butcher 259, IJ Ward 57, AD Mullally 5 for 106)
Match drawn
Leicestershire 9 pts, Surrey 12 pts

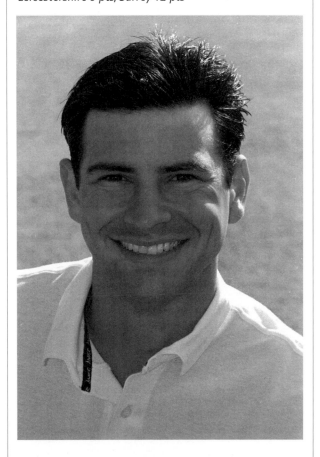

Matt Cassar of Derbyshire picked up a maiden five-wicket haul against Essex at Chelmsford.
David Munden/Sportsline Photographic

ESSEX CCC

Home Ground:
The County Ground, Chelmsford
Address:
County Cricket Ground, New Writtle Street,
Chelmsford, Essex CM2 0PG
Tel: 01245 252420
Prospects of play: 01245 287921
Email: administration.essex@ecb.co.uk
Directions:
By rail: Chelmsford Station eight minutes' walk
away
By road: M25 then A12 to Chelmsford.
Exit Chelmsford and follow AA signs
to 'Essex Cricket Club'.
Capacity: 6,000
Other grounds used: Castle Park, Colchester; Valentine's
Park, Ilford; Southchurch Park, Southend-on-Sea.
Year formed: 1876

Chairman: DL Acfield
Secretary/General Manager: PJ Edwards
Cricket Consultant: KWR Fletcher OBE
Other posts: Bowling Coach: Geoff Arnold;
2nd XI Coach/Captain: John Childs
Captain: Nasser Hussain
Vice-captain: Ronnie Irani
Coaching contact:
Norman Bambridge 01245 266794
County colours: Blue, gold and red

HONOURS

COUNTY CHAMPIONSHIP
1979, 1983, 1984, 1986,
1991, 1992
SUNDAY LEAGUE
1981, 1984, 1985
REFUGE ASSURANCE CUP
1989
BENSON & HEDGES CUP
1979, 1998
GILLETTE CUP/NATWEST TROPHY
1985,1997

CGU National Cricket League nickname:
ESSEX EAGLES

Website:
www.essexcricket.org.uk

at Northampton
Durham 317 (99 overs) (DC Boon 57) and 216
(PD Collingwood 72)
Northamptonshire 190 (63 overs) (ML Hayden 68,
N Killeen 6 for 20, SJ Harmison 4 for 58) and
298 (DJG Sales 84, GP Swann 62, RJ Warren 55,
SJE Brown 5 for 99)
Durham won by 45 runs
Durham 19 pts, Northamptonshire 4 pts

at Bath
Gloucestershire 346 (118.1 overs) (KJ Barnett 88,
RC Russell 86) and 144 for 7 (AR Caddick 4 for 55)
Somerset 138 (62.3 overs) (BW Gannon 4 for 38,
IJ Harvey 4 for 41) and (following on) 351 (RJ Turner
107, J Cox 58, M Burns 53)
Gloucestershire won by three wickets
Gloucestershire 19 pts, Somerset 4 pts

at Hove
Sussex 336 (112.3 overs) (MJ Di Venuto 136,
RR Montgomerie 70, DW Headley 4 for 74) and
317 for 8 dec. (UBA Rashid 73, MJ Di Venuto 71,
JBD Thompson 4 for 77)
Kent 336 (115.5 overs) (MA Ealham 74, A Symonds 54,
MJ Walker 51, MA Robinson 4 for 75) and 42 for 0
Match drawn
Sussex 11 pts, Kent 11 pts

The only thing that went Derbyshire's way at
Chelmsford was the toss. They were crippled by no
fewer than nine injuries which stripped the seam
cupboard bare. It meant a surprise recall for the 39-
year-old Simon Base, and Paul Thomas, formerly of
Worcestershire, was registered on the Tuesday, two
days before the match. Consolation was not exactly
what Dominic Cork would have been looking for,
but he got it anyway in the form of a maiden first-
class century from Robin Weston, an unbeaten one
at that. Thereafter Essex dominated in every
department, from Nasser Hussain's first century for
his county since September 1997 – and the 38th of
his career – to Ricky Anderson's first five-wicket
haul in his third championship match. There was an
altercation between Cork and Hussain over a
replacement ball during the latter's innings, but at
least Cork's decision to turn to Matthew Cassar
proved an effective surprise weapon. Cassar picked
up his maiden five-wicket haul. But Hussain had the
last word with a half-century in the second innings
after Anderson had induced a dramatic collapse as
Derbyshire lost their last eight wickets for 32 runs
and the match inside three days.

**Mark Butcher of Surrey scored his first-ever double century
against Leicestershire in June.**
David Munden/Sportsline Photographic

Middlesex picked up their seventh championship victory in a row against Glamorgan and the Welsh county played like the underdogs that statistic implies. There was the merest scrap of resistance from Michael Powell in the second innings, but absolutely no support from any of his more experienced team-mates. The continued absence of captain Matthew Maynard was keenly felt, but that is no excuse for the abject surrender in their two innings. If they had watched Middlesex more closely they might have learned a thing or two from their opponents, for whom Paul Weekes scored a commanding and admirable century, his tenth, as he and Mike Roseberry showed application. Opener Roseberry spent four and a quarter hours over his worthy 84, as he continues to rediscover all the powers he lost at Durham. Angus Fraser also scored a half-century as Middlesex built an imposing first-innings score. Darren Thomas was the pick of the home side's bowlers. Tim Bloomfield returned a career-best 5 for 36 in Glamorgan's first innings, but the wickets were more evenly distributed second time around when Middlesex ran out winners with a day and the best part of two sessions to spare.

Hampshire suffered a defeat against Yorkshire – a defeat that was particularly hard on Hampshire's Peter Hartley. Firstly, it was his superlative effort which had got Yorkshire into a jam initially with a magnificent 8 for 65; secondly it was Yorkshire who decided two years ago that the paceman was surplus to requirements. He gave them eight good reasons to regret their decision as he helped Hampshire into a first-innings lead, but, unhappily, Hampshire's batsmen then let him down with a capitulation that left Yorkshire with very little to do to record their fourth victory of the season with a day and a half to spare. Chris Silverwood's five wickets in the first innings, his first of the summer, went a long way to keeping Hampshire in check. In the second it was Matthew Hoggard's turn with four wickets. Gavin Hamilton, the Scotland World Cup player with aspirations to play for England, also did well with bat and ball, while wicketkeeper Richard Blakey top-scored in Yorkshire's disappointing first innings. Captain David Byas led the way to victory with a fine 95. His only false shot came when he attempted to bring up his hundred with a six. He paid for his impetuosity but by then he had made it a formality.

There cannot be many bowlers who have claimed 14 wickets in a match only to finish on the losing side, but that is precisely what happened to Muttiah Muralitharan at Southport. The Sri Lankan Test off-spinner mesmerised the Warwickshire batsmen taking 7 for 44, then 7 for 73 in the second innings. That match analysis was Lancashire's best for 35 years. It was also the best at Trafalgar Road, surpassing Wasim Akram's 13 for 137 against Somerset in 1994. Not that Warwickshire had had a hint of the trouble ahead after winning the toss and electing to bat. The openers were coping admirably with the four seamers Lancashire employed ahead of Muralitharan. Then it all changed. Murali came on to bowl the 17th over and within another four he had made the breakthrough removing Mark Wagh. But the real problems started when he switched to the Sea End. Then the ball really began to turn. Only Nick Knight looked to have any idea of how to handle it, if a half-century in each innings is anything to go by. But Warwickshire had Ed Giddins, whose five wickets in the first innings were augmented by three more in the second. And Dougie Brown weighed in with vital wickets as well.

Surrey deserved victory at Grace Road if only for Mark Butcher's superb double century, the first of his career. They had the champions on the ropes, just ten runs to the good, four second-innings wickets down, a man injured and a whole day to see out. But the rain has never been sentimental and gives everyone and everything an equal dousing. So it was that Surrey were confined to barracks as the drizzle dribbled down the dressing-room windows, leaving them to ponder on what had gone before. Butcher was textbook in everything he did. He smacked 30 boundaries and a couple of sixes – both taken off Matthew Brimson, Leicestershire's left-arm spinner. His faultless innings had followed Alex Tudor's career-best 7 for 77 as he restricted the defending champions to an inadequate first-innings score. It needed, and got, a competent performance second time around when Aftab Habib underlined his class with an unbeaten 70 as he guided Leicestershire's noses in front, with valuable assistance from Darren Maddy and later Paul Nixon. Then the weather did its bit for the Leicestershire cause.

Durham's previous victory had been on D-Day 1998. It was the bowlers who won this match for them. Neil Killeen claimed a career-best 6 for 20 in the first innings and former Northamptonshire left-arm paceman Simon Brown picked up his second five-wicket haul of the summer in the second innings, while the promising Stephen Harmison weighed in with seven in the match. Sadly the Durham batsmen do not produce the goods as regularly as their colleagues in the other department. Captain David Boon's first-innings 57 was the top score by the eventual victors, the next highest being paceman John Wood's unbeaten 49. In the second innings Killeen came within four runs of completing a career-best double as he reached 45. Northampton in contrast have plenty of batsmen capable of making runs. Captain Matthew Hayden had four centuries coming into this match. He passed fifty again in the first innings, but he flew solo. When they saw what had to be done second time around there was a flurry of fifties, but Durham tails were up and the efforts of David Sales, Graeme Swann and Russell Warren were in vain.

By the time Somerset got their batting act together it was far too late to save things. Gloucestershire had too tight a grip on affairs, a grip that they had applied from the first day when Jack Russell, revelling in his new role of opening bat, and veteran Kim Barnett, compiled a century stand for the second wicket. When Ben Gannon and Australian Ian Harvey took advantage of some indifferent Somerset batting in the first innings to pick up four wickets apiece and ensure Somerset had to follow on, it was just a matter of time. Somerset wicketkeeper Robbie Turner, who may well win a place on tour after showing remarkable consistency with bat and gloves this summer, had top-scored with a paltry 36 in the first innings. He improved significantly on that when he batted in the second innings. His 107, the seventh hundred of his career, took the match into a fourth day with additional help from Jamie Cox and Mike Burns, who had already smacked useful half-centuries. The perspiration was pouring off Gloucestershire brows when they were reeling at 87 for 5 as Andrew Caddick found pace and movement on a slowish wicket, but Martyn Ball steered them home.

Sussex were not interested in setting a remotely gettable target for Kent; for their part Kent were clearly disinterested in chasing anything at all and anyway the rains came, ending the argument and bringing a potentially exciting game to a damp finish. There was still much to cheer. Michael Di Venuto, Sussex's Tasmanian left-hander scored his second hundred of the season, then added a half-century in the second innings. His was an unflappable, assured performance as he reached three figures for the 11th time in his career. Richard Montgomerie proved yet again that he is no stodgy opener. He passed fifty for the fifth time and it was a pity that he was unable to turn it into his second hundred for Sussex. Then there was Umer Rashid.

The slow left-arm bowler left Middlesex last season to try his luck on the south coast and he produced a personal-best 3 for 41, modest, but a sign that he has the potential. He followed that up with a useful second-innings 70. Kent supplied a clutch of half-centuries and David Graveney, the chairman of selectors, watched Dr Julian Thompson pick up four second-innings wickets.

ROUND 9: 15–18 JUNE 1999

15, 16 and 17 June
at Trent Bridge
Warwickshire 316 (98.3 overs) (DL Hemp 100, VC Drakes 6 for 71) and 142 (VC Drakes 6 for 39, PJ Franks 4 for 52)
Nottinghamshire 327 (93 overs) (CMW Read 160, CM Tolley 51, ESH Giddins 4 for 46) and 76 (TA Munton 4 for 20, ESH Giddins 4 for 31)
Warwickshire won by 55 runs
Warwickshire 19 pts, Nottinghamshire 7 pts

at Headingley
Yorkshire 271 (97.3 overs) (MP Vaughan 71, UBA Rashid 4 for 41) and 157 (JD Lewry 4 for 59)
Sussex 192 (58.1 overs) and 239 for 5 (RR Montgomerie 110, CJ Adams 58)
Sussex won by five wickets
Sussex 16 pts, Yorkshire 6 pts

15, 16, 17 and 18 June
at Southampton
Leicestershire 405 (126 overs) (BF Smith 154, MS Kasprowicz 73, SJ Renshaw 4 for 124) and 317 for 8 dec. (DL Maddy 108, DI Stevens 61, JP Stephenson 4 for 67)
Hampshire 382 (126 overs) (RA Smith 78, AN Aymes 60, WS Kendall 52, JS Laney 50, DJ Millns 4 for 47) and 222 for 8 (JS Laney 99, J Ormond 4 for 93)
Match drawn
Hampshire 11 pts, Leicestershire 11 pts

at Canterbury
Kent 332 (122.1 overs) (MV Fleming 94, RWT Key 92, SL Watkin 5 for 47) and 317 for 4 dec. (DP Fulton 126*, MJ Walker 93, ET Smith 61)
Glamorgan 544 (159.3 overs) (MP Maynard 170, SP James 103, AW Evans 50, MM Patel 4 for 93)
Match drawn
Kent 9 pts, Glamorgan 11 pts

Pacy left–arm bowler Alamgir Sheriyar of Worcestershire had match figures of 9 for 145 against Somerset at Worcester.
David Munden/Sportsline Photographic

at The Oval
Lancashire 194 (73.2 overs) (AJ Tudor 4 for 60) and 260 (WK Hegg 94, MA Atherton 52, MA Butcher 4 for 30, AJ Tudor 4 for 81)
Surrey 298 (97.5 overs) (AJ Stewart 95, M Muralitharan 6 for 87) and 161 for 6 (M Muralitharan 4 for 67)
Surrey won by four wickets
Surrey 18 pts, Lancashire 4 pts

at Worcester
Worcestershire 308 (128.4 overs) (PJ Newport 65*, GA Hick 50, AR Caddick 4 for 55) and 200 (SR Lampitt 51*, AR Caddick 5 for 48)
Somerset 193 (61.2 overs) (RJ Turner 63, A Sheriyar 4 for 49) and 289 (M Burns 105, RJ Turner 58, A Sheriyar 5 for 96)
Worcestershire won by 26 runs
Worcestershire 18 pts, Somerset 3 pts

A couple of Smiths forged steely innings at Southampton, but neither was able to fashion a

victory. Ben Smith recorded his first hundred of the season – the 12th of his career – a perfect example of a captain leading from the front. It was a mature innings lasting a shade over seven hours and containing 16 boundaries. Mike Kasprowicz scored a career-best 73 which helped Leicestershire top 400. Enter Robin Smith, also leading his side. Having watched Jason Laney and Will Kendall perish on reaching their half-centuries, Smith hammered his way into the 70s, hitting the ball as hard as he has ever done. Wicketkeeper Adrian Aymes, who had not reached double figures in his previous seven innings, then knocked off a useful 60. Darren Maddy's second-innings hundred and a career-best 61 from Darren Stevens in his first championship match of the season meant Leicestershire were able to set a challenging 341 off what turned out to be 88 overs. But Laney's 99 apart, the rest of the Hampshire line-up struggled to make any serious runs let alone reach the target. James Ormond, ordinarily a medium fast out-swing bowler, resorted to what he had been practising in the nets and his off-spin claimed 4 for 93.

There was an acrimonious finish at Canterbury when David Fulton, starved of a big innings since the previous August, stood his ground on 31 and went on to reach an unbeaten 126, only the sixth hundred of his first-class career. Fulton claimed that he was unsure whether Dean Cosker, at second slip, had hung on to a catch at the second attempt. When the players turned to the umpires to settle the dispute, Ken Palmer said he was unsighted by Darren Thomas's follow-through, so benefit of the doubt, and a lot of dark glances, went to the batsman. Glamorgan's activities were overshadowed by the fate of their Zimbabwean coach Duncan Fletcher, who attended the interview which led to his appointment as England coach on the opening day of the game. Matthew Maynard returned to action in style with the 44th hundred of his career, Steve James scored his second of the summer to wrest the initiative from Kent and earn Glamorgan a substantial first-innings lead as they topped 500 for the first time since May 1998, this after Robert Key and captain Matthew Fleming had pulled Kent back into the match while Steve Watkin was making inroads. But dropped catches and Fulton's good fortune conspired to help Kent battle to a draw.

Chris Read may have finished on the losing side but the way he hauled his team back into the match having come in at a parlous 59 for 5 revealed a strength of character that caught the eye of the England selectors. Soon he was to graduate to the

GLAMORGAN CCC

Home Ground:
Cardiff
Address:
Sophia Gardens, Cardiff CF1 9XR
Tel: 01222 409380
Fax: 01222 409390
Email: glam@ecb.co.uk
Directions:
By rail: Cardiff Central Train Station.
By road: From north, A470 and follow signs to Cardiff until
junction with Cardiff by-pass then A48 Port Talbot and City
Centre, Cathedral Road is situated off A48 for Sophia
Gardens. From east, M4 Junction 29 then A48,
Capacity: 4,000
Other grounds used: Pontypridd, Mid Glamorgan; St Helens,
Swansea; Rhos-on-Sea, Colwyn Bay; Pen-Y-Pound Ground,
Abergavenny.
Year formed: 1888

Chairman: Gerard Elias QC
Cricket Secretary: Mike Fatkin
Director of Cricket: Alan Jones
Other posts: First XI Coach: Duncan Fletcher;
Deputy Chairman: Hugh Davies
Captain: Matthew Maynard
Coaching contact: Indoor centre 01222 419307
County colours: Navy blue and yellow/gold

HONOURS

COUNTY CHAMPIONSHIP
1948, 1969, 1997
SUNDAY LEAGUE
1993

CGU National Cricket League
nickname:
GLAMORGAN DRAGONS

Website:
www.glamorganccc.cricket.org.uk

David Fulton of Kent made an unbeaten 126 in the match against Glamorgan.
David Munden

full Test team after this 208-ball effort which contained 24 fours. It was his maiden first-class hundred and took the best part of five hours. It was also the highest score by a Nottinghamshire wicketkeeper since Deryck Murray's 166 almost 30 years ago. The shame of it was that the 20-year-old Devonian could not repeat even a fraction of it second time around when Nottinghamshire, requiring just 132 runs to win, subsided lamentably to 76 all out. Vasbert Drakes, stunned by the death of his brother in Barbados during the game, returned match figures of 12 for 110, but the Nottinghamshire upper order then failed to come to terms with a pitch which saw 18 wickets fall on the third and final day. All this was after David Hemp had scored his second century of the season.

On an Oval wicket that offered seamers a little bit of what they fancied on the first day, it was Sri Lankan off-spinner Muttiah Muralitharan who still grabbed all the attention – and the wickets. He had another bag of ten in a match, yet incredibly he finished on the losing side for a second successive match. Perhaps the presence of four left-handed batsmen in the Surrey line-up went some way to defusing his match-winning potential; there certainly seemed to be a policy of farming out the Sri Lankan's overs to the left-handers where possible. But it was a right-hander, Alec Stewart, who top-scored – just – in the match. The England opener, and captain as he still was at the start of the game, battled his way to a characterful 95. After Warren Hegg's gutsy 94 second time around and a burst of wickets late on the third day from the two spinners Muralitharan and Gary Keedy, it looked as if Lancashire might just nick it. But the fourth morning saw Darren Bicknell (a left-hander who faced 49 Muralitharan deliveries) and wicketkeeper Jonathan Batty, who only had to tackle 22 balls from the Sri Lankan, steer Surrey safely to their fifth win in eight outings.

Michael Burns is a punishing batsman, as the second hundred of his career and the season proved. Unfortunately, apart from wicketkeeper Rob Turner who scored fifties in each innings for the second time this season, the former Warwickshire gloveman received precious little support at New Road. Instead it was fast bowler Alamgir Sheriyar who stole the limelight. His figures of 9 for 145 took him to within three of his half-century, but the left-arm seamer is as much a workhorse for Worcestershire as well. He sent down almost 45 overs, nearly as many as his support men Stuart Lampitt and Chris Liptrot managed between them, during the match. With Phil Newport playing out his final championship season, the full burden will soon shift to Sheriyar's willing shoulders; Worcestershire must make sure he is not bowled into the ground, which is actually what he did to Somerset. Andy Caddick also picked up nine wickets in the match. But Somerset were always up against it after conceding a first-innings lead to Worcestershire. Half-centuries from Graeme Hick and Newport, the latter's an unbeaten 65, went a long way to putting victory beyond their opponents' reach.

The alarming lack of form shown by Yorkshire's Australian Test opener Greg Blewett continued with a paltry 17 runs against Sussex to take him to a worrying 289 runs in 16 innings. In contrast, the Sussex opener Richard Montgomerie's move to the south coast from Northamptonshire has revived a flagging career. His meaty 110, his second hundred of the summer, was a major factor in Sussex's second championship victory of the season. Last summer Montgomerie struggled to amass 222 at fewer than 20; this year he is poised to hit 1,000. This was only the second championship victory by Sussex at

Headingley since 1966, when they accomplished the win in two days, and they never looked anything but in control from Umer Rashid's four first-innings wickets to Chris Adams' second-innings 58. For Yorkshire there were very few bright spots. Darren Gough returned after a long absence and performed tolerably well, picking up a total of four wickets, but generally the bowling lacked penetration. As for the batting – extras aside – only Michael Vaughan got past 50. Second time around only Gavin Hamilton and captain David Byas made it into the thirties, but neither could get beyond that.

ROUND 10: 29 JUNE–3 JULY 1999

29, 30 June, 1 and 2 July
at Old Trafford
Lancashire 298 (105.4 overs) (MJ Chilton 71, A Flintoff 52, JP Crawley 51, PM Such 7 for 36) and 209 for 7 dec. (JP Crawley 64, PM Such 6 for 77)
Essex 207 (69 overs) (AP Grayson 63, SG Law 51, M Muralitharan 7 for 73) and 182 (AP Grayson 76, M Muralitharan 6 for 61)
Lancashire won by 118 runs
Lancashire 18 pts, Essex 5 pts

30 June, 1 and 2 July
at Maidstone
Kent 164 (55.2 overs) (TM Munton 6 for 44 including a hat-trick) and 199 (ET Smith 52, DR Brown 4 for 37)
Warwickshire 116 (32.4 overs) (JDB Thompson 4 for 48) and 156 (MM Patel 6 for 43)
Kent won by 91 runs
Kent 16 pts, Warwickshire 4 pts

at Northampton
Worcestershire 102 (38 overs) (TM Moody 63*) and 384 (VS Solanki 126, TM Moody 63, JP Taylor 5 for 105)
Northamptonshire 197 (51.5 overs) (GP Swann 62, SR Lampitt 4 for 28) and 177
Worcestershire won by 112 runs
Worcestershire 16 pts, Northamptonshire 4 pts

30 June, 1, 2 and 3 July
at Swansea
Hampshire 345 (118.3 overs) (AN Aymes 89, RA Smith 63, SL Watkin 4 for 45)
Glamorgan 162 (53.2 overs) (PJ Hartley 4 for 54) and 177 (SP James 53, SD Udal 6 for 47)
Hampshire won by an innings and 6 runs
Hampshire 19 pts, Glamorgan 4 pts

at Bristol
Nottinghamshire 269 (108.4 overs) (P Johnson 85, RT Robinson 64, IJ Harvey 5 for 76) and 201 (U Afzaal 59, P Johnson 59, J Lewis 7 for 56)
Gloucestershire 317 (101 overs) (RJ Cunliffe 84, KJ Barnett 56) and 154 for 3
Gloucestershire won by seven wickets
Gloucestershire 19 pts, Nottinghamshire 6 pts

at Lord's
Middlesex 210 (76.5 overs) (AJ Strauss 61, AJ Harris 5 for 63, P Aldred 4 for 54) and 221 (DC Nash 71*, KJ Dean 4 for 60)
Derbyshire 366 (117.2 overs) (RMS Weston 124, ID Blackwell 60, MJ Slater 53) and 66 for 1
Derbyshire won by nine wickets
Derbyshire 20 pts, Middlesex 5 pts

at Taunton
Somerset 503 for 8 dec. (156 overs) (J Cox 111, PCL Holloway 110) and 94 for 2
Sussex 165 (41.5 overs) (CJ Adams 56, MJ Di Venuto 52) and (following on) 431 (MJ Di Venuto 105, RSC Martin-Jenkins 70, UBA Rashid 69, WG Khan 51, MPL Bulbeck 4 for 101)
Somerset won by eight wickets
Somerset 20 pts, Sussex 1 pt

at The Oval
Surrey 335 (106 overs) (IDK Salisbury 53, IJ Ward 51, BC Hollioake 50, SJ Harmison 5 for 76) and 247 for 6 dec. (JD Ratcliffe 91, BC Hollioake 71)
Durham 217 (92.5 overs) (JE Morris 78, Saqlain Mushtaq 5 for 72, IDK Salisbury 4 for 57) and 139 (Saqlain Mushtaq 7 for 38)
Surrey won by 226 runs
Surrey 19 pts, Durham 5 pts

1, 2 and 3 July
at Leicester
Yorkshire 52 (28.3 overs) (J Ormond 4 for 16) and 251 (RJ Harden 69, C White 52)
Leicestershire 297 (97.4 overs) (DL Maddy 158*) and 7 for 1
Leicestershire won by nine wickets
Leicestershire 18 pts, Yorkshire 4 pts

Surrey stretched their lead at the top by overwhelming bottom team Durham at The Oval while Warwickshire, beaten by Kent, saw their second-place spot claimed by unsung Hampshire.
    Robin Smith's spirited side took advantage of a poor performance by Glamorgan at Swansea to

GLOUCESTERSHIRE CCC

Home Ground:
Bristol
Address:
The Sun Alliance Ground, Nevil Road,
Bristol BS7 9EJ
Tel: 0117 910 8000
Directions:
By road: M5, M4, M32 into Bristol: exit at second
exit (Fishponds/Horfield), then third exit – Muller
Road. Almost at end of Muller Road (bus station on right),
turn left at Ralph Road. Go to the top, turn left and then
right almost immediately into Kennington Avenue. Follow
the signs for County cricket.
Capacity: 8,000
Other grounds used: College Ground, Cheltenham;
Kings School, Gloucester
Year formed: 1870

Chairman: John Higson
Director of Cricket: Andy Stovold
Other posts: Chief Executive: CL Sexstone; Youth
Development Officer: Richard Holdsworth
Captain: Mark Alleyne
Coaching contact: Andy Stovold, Director of Coaching
0117 910 8004
County colours: Blue, brown, gold, green and red, sky
blue

HONOURS

BENSON & HEDGES CUP
1977, 1999
GILLETTE CUP/NATWEST TROPHY
1973, 1999

**CGU National Cricket League
nickname:**
GLOUCESTERSHIRE GLADIATORS

Website:
www.glosccc.co.uk

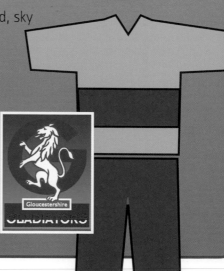

HAMPSHIRE CCC

Home Ground:
Southampton
Address:
County Ground, Northlands Road,
Southampton SO15 2UE
Tel: 01703 333788
Fax: 01703 330121
E-mail: enquiries.hants@ecb.co.uk
Directions:
By rail: Southampton Central - one mile.
By road: M3 to J14 then follow A33 to city centre.
Situated in Northlands Road off the Avenue (A33).
From M27, exit junction 5 and follow signs to City
Centre.
Capacity: 4,500
Other grounds used: United Services Ground,
Portsmouth; Mays Bounty, Bounty Road, Basingstoke.
Year formed: 1863

Chairman: Brian Ford
Chief Executive: Tony Baker
Director of Cricket: Tim Tremlett
Other posts: Marketing manager: Mike Taylor
Captain: Robin Smith
Vice-captain: Sean Udal
Coaching contact: Tony Middleton, Cricket
Development Officer 01703 333788
County colours: Navy blue, old gold

HONOURS

COUNTY CHAMPIONSHIP
1961, 1973
SUNDAY LEAGUE
1975, 1978, 1986
BENSON & HEDGES CUP 1988,
1992
GILLETTE CUP/NATWEST TROPHY
1991

CGU National Cricket League nickname:
HAMPSHIRE HAWKS

Website:
www.hampshire.cricket.org

triumph by an innings and six runs – despite the loss of the entire second day to rain. Off-spinner Shaun Udal took nine wickets in the match, including a second-innings 6 for 47, as Glamorgan were hustled out for 162 and 177. Hampshire's 345, which set up the follow-on, was based initially on an aggressive 63 by Smith and then a combative 89 from wicketkeeper Adrian Aymes. Glamorgan missed Aymes on 23, when Dawood fluffed a stumping chance off Robert Croft, and only Steve Watkin (4 for 45) and Steve James, with a second-innings 53, offered much resistance in a dismal Welsh effort.

Saqlain Mushtaq and Ian Salisbury were too much for Durham, who by contrast had only the left arm of 18-year-old debutant Graeme Bridge and the occasional off-breaks of opener Michael Gough to offer in the way of spin on a dry, dusting pitch. Surrey, delightedly winning the toss and batting in the knowledge that their own top-class spinners would now bowl the bulk of their overs later in the match, were perhaps guilty of letting an air of superiority spill over into arrogance and carelessness as they slid to 225 for 7 despite 51 from Ian Ward and 50 off 54 balls from Ben Hollioake. But Salisbury, with 53 from number nine, added 71 for the eighth wicket with Jon Batty (44) to haul them up to 335. Steve Harmison's 5 for 76 was a worthy effort, but soon Saqlain and Salisbury were getting to work with the ball. John Morris made a classy 78 but Durham were dismissed for 217 as Saqlain finished with 5 for 72 and Salisbury 4 for 57. Surrey now plundered quick second-innings runs, with Jason Ratcliffe hitting 91 from 108 balls, with two sixes and 13 fours, and Ben Hollioake also striking two sixes in his 71. A declaration came at 247 for 6 but, as it transpired, Surrey had almost had enough with their first-innings lead alone: Durham were cut down for 139 as Saqlain wove a web that brought him 7 for 38 from 21 overs. Leg-spinner Salisbury wrapped up the crushing win, opener Jon Lewis last out for a fighting 46, and Surrey coach Keith Medlycott said: 'I would have paid very good money to have seen spin bowling of that quality'.

Saqlain's match tally of 12 wickets was topped, however, at Old Trafford, by two other spinners. Peter Such, of Essex, had career-best match figures of 13 for 213 yet was completely overshadowed by Muttiah Muralitharan. The magical Sri Lankan, Saqlain's only rival as the world's best off-spinner, took 13 for 134 as Lancashire won by 118 runs and, at last, began to pull themselves up from the lower reaches of the PPP table. Such had to work hard for his first innings 7 for 136 as Lancashire reached 298 on the back of a solid top-order performance. Mark Chilton (71) and John Crawley (51) put on 117 for the first wicket, while Andy Flintoff (52) and Warren Hegg (43) added typically robust runs later on. To stay in the match, however, Essex had to get a first-innings lead and – thanks to Muralitharan – they failed by some distance. Paul Grayson scored a dedicated 63 and Stuart Law a flamboyant 51 – the pair demonstrating in different ways that Murali could be played – but 207 was inadequate as Muralitharan picked up 7 for 73. Crawley then hit 64 as Lancashire, despite Such chipping away with 6 for 77, moved to a declaration. Grayson again impressed with 76, showing great technique against the spinning ball and batting for six hours and 44 minutes in the match, but Muralitharan's 6 for 61 condemned Essex to 182 all out and defeat. Muralitharan, starting with his 13-wicket haul in The Oval Test of August 1998, had now taken 53 wickets in eight consecutive innings in England – putting him level with the achievement of Hedley Verity in 1933 and just behind Charles Townsend (1898) and Tich Freeman (1932) who both took 55 wickets in their golden stretches.

Derbyshire beat Middlesex at Lord's for the first time since 1961, their nine-wicket victory being thoroughly deserved for some disciplined but lively seam and swing bowling. Andrew Harris, his 5 for 63 a first five-wicket analysis since 1996, and Paul Aldred (4 for 54) made the first incisions into the disappointing Middlesex batting, with Andrew Strauss (61) the only performance of substance. Robin Weston, emerging as a young middle-order batsman of promise, compiled a second successive championship hundred and Ian Blackwell underlined his all-round ability with a hard-hit 60. Middlesex, facing a substantial first-innings deficit, were only saved from the ignominy of defeat within three days by David Nash, who hit a jaunty unbeaten 71. Kevin Dean, excellent throughout, returned second-innings figures of 4 for 60.

In a remarkable game at Northampton it was difficult to know whether to heap praise on Worcestershire for a classic comeback victory against the odds, or to condemn Northants for a performance which bore all the hallmarks of the 'soft' cricket that the authorities deplore. Northants had their opponents 2 for 4 on the first morning, then took a first-innings lead of 95, and finally had Worcestershire reeling again at 47 for 4 second time around. But, by the end of the third day, Northants had lost by 112 runs and – shamed – had tumbled into 17th position in the PPP table. Paul Taylor and Devon Malcolm were the chief destroyers as Worcestershire were bowled out for 102 on day one, Tom Moody playing a lone hand with 63 not out. But, by the eventual close at 7.45pm, no less than 23 wickets had fallen with Worcestershire in trouble again after themselves dismissing Northants for 197. Seven of the first 12 batsmen out walked off with ducks to their name – and the hapless Paul Pollard completed a pair inside seven and a half hours. Hayden was stupidly run out and several Northants batsmen got themselves out when seemingly well set. The pitch, though encouraging seam, did not misbehave and only Graeme Swann's enterprising 62 kept Northants on top. But on the second day, which began with an obligatory pitch inspection by Chris Wood and Harry Brind of the ECB, the course of the match changed with Vikram Solanki seizing back the initiative for Worcestershire. Even the early exit of Graeme Hick failed to disturb Solanki, who found in Moody and then David Leatherdale partners willing to match his determination to mix attack with watchful, sensible defence. Suddenly, with technique at last being married with application in the time-honoured fashion, batting did not look such a hazardous occupation. Solanki went on to 126, with a six and 22 fours, and the day ended with Steve Rhodes and Phil Newport stretching the Worcestershire lead still further. A victory target of 290 asked questions of resolve that the Northants batsmen answered only too quickly: they didn't have any. Swann again escaped condemnation, finishing unbeaten on 27, but the rest was a mess as Northants were bowled out for 177.

Wickets tumbled too on the first day at Maidstone, 20 of them to be precise as Kent followed up their inadequate 164 by bowling out Warwickshire for a pathetic 116. Again, as at Northampton, the umpires did not consider the pitch at The Mote to be responsible. Once more, it was simply a case of bad batting. Tim Munton put the skids under Kent initially, taking his first hat-trick in 15 seasons, Robert Key being quickly followed back into the pavilion by David Fulton, leg before playing down the wrong line, and Trevor Ward, bowled off-stump. Perhaps that unsettled Kent, especially as Munton was only playing due to injuries to Allan Donald, Neil Smith and Ashley Giles, but Martin McCague shook them out of it with a beefy 46 from down the order. Julian Thompson, continuing his fine season with four

more wickets, was supported by Mark Ealham as Warwickshire failed to take control. Kent's second-innings 199 was built upon a fine 52 from Ed Smith, one of the few to display a straight bat, and – on a surface promoting scant turn – Warwickshire then contrived to allow Min Patel to return figures of 6 for 43 as they slumped to 156 and defeat by 91 runs. When slow left-armer Patel first came on, towards the end of the second day, it was like a shock to spectators following 181 overs of seam.

The underrated Jon Lewis turned a Bristol battle Gloucestershire's way with a second-innings haul of 7 for 56 against Nottinghamshire. Lewis had a spell of 3 for 8 in 6.5 overs on the first hour of the final day, tipping the balance of a hard-fought contest and leaving the home side to make just 154 in 81 overs for victory. Jack Russell's 46, and another classy innings by Rob Cunliffe, who added 45 to his 84 earlier in the match, ensured there was no alarm. Cunliffe, surprisingly playing his first game of the season, was joined by Kim Barnett (56) as Gloucestershire claimed a useful first-innings lead. Paul Johnson was Cunliffe's only rival as the game's best batsman – following up a first-innings 85 with a run-a-ball 59. Notts were 178 for 2 at one stage on the opening day, thanks to Johnson and Tim Robinson (64), but only Usman Afzaal (59) kept Johnson company in the second innings. Russell will long remember this match, too, because it contained his 1,000th first-class catch – a tally that puts him in an elite seven-man wicketkeeping list behind Bob Taylor, John Murray, Herbert Strudwick, Alan Knott, Jim Parks and Brian 'Tonker' Taylor.

Somerset had to overcome the lack of a front-line spinner, the absence on Test duty of Andy Caddick, and injuries during the game to their seam attack as they outfought Sussex over four hard days at Taunton. Hundreds from Piran Holloway and Jamie Cox, whose 23 fours were all on the off side or straight, enabled Somerset to build a huge first-innings 503 for 8 declared, and initially its vastness seemed to inhibit Sussex who were tumbled out for just 165. But, following on, they produced a far sterner effort, with Michael Di Venuto adding 105 to his first-innings 52. Di Venuto, though, was disgusted to lob up a return catch to his fellow Tasmanian, Cox, who joyously celebrated his first first-class victim. Cox's ropy off-breaks could tease out no other, however, and Robin Martin-Jenkins and Umer Rashid put on 102 for the sixth wicket as Somerset grew worried. Martin-Jenkins fell to the second new ball for 70 and, on the final morning,

Peter Bowler scored 149 for Somerset against his former club, at Derby.
David Munden/Sportsline Photographic

Matt Bulbeck (4 for 101) and Keith Parsons (3 for 69) closed Sussex out. Rashid made 69 but perhaps Sussex could have escaped had Di Venuto not fallen for Cox's baubles and had skipper Chris Adams not got out recklessly after blasting 42 from just 33 balls. Di Venuto did have the consolation, however, of trapping Cox leg before for 28 – his first championship wicket! – as Somerset knocked off the runs required for victory.

A brilliant 158 not out by Darren Maddy was the major difference at Leicester as the home side trounced Yorkshire by nine wickets to maintain their championship challenge. Another poor pitch was the first impression as Yorkshire crumbled to just 52 all out – their lowest score since 1973. James Ormond took 4 for 16, and later followed it up with several second-innings wickets, but in between Maddy made the pitch look docile as he guided Leicestershire to 297 and a match-winning lead. By the close of the opening day Maddy was 85 not out, and on the second morning he continued to look a different class to the rest of the batsmen on show. A first Test cap looked just around the corner as Maddy carried his bat and as Chris Lewis, with 23, made the next highest score. Maddy was not finished, though, because on the third day he grabbed the ball to take 2 for 7 with his medium-pacers – splitting a stubborn sixth-wicket stand between Richard Harden (69 in 88 overs) and Craig White (52) after injury problems began to afflict Ormond, Mike Kasprowicz and Lewis. Maddy then hit the winning runs after Leicestershire were forced, just, to bat again.

ROUND 11: 9–12 JULY 1999

9, 10 and 11 July
at Cardiff
Glamorgan 185 (68 overs) (AP Cowan 6 for 47) and 122 (RC Irani 4 for 29)
Essex 444 (133 overs) (SG Law 140, SD Peters 81, PJ Prichard 73)
Essex won by an innings and 137 runs
Essex 20 pts, Glamorgan 3 pts

at Lord's
Northamptonshire 223 (72.3 overs) (GP Swann 78, TF Bloomfield 4 for 53) and 88 (JP Hewitt 4 for 6)
Middlesex 96 (32.4 overs) (JP Taylor 4 for 23, DE Malcolm 4 for 49) and 218 for 3 (JL Langer 117*)
Middlesex won by seven wickets
Middlesex 16 pts, Northamptonshire 5 pts

KENT CCC

Home Ground:
Canterbury
Address:
St Lawrence Ground,
Old Dover Road,
Canterbury,
Kent CT1 3NZ
Tel: 01227 456886
Fax: 01227 762168
Directions:
By rail: Canterbury East/West.
By road: AA roadsigns
Capacity: 10,000
Other grounds used: The Mote, Maidstone;
The Neville, Tunbridge Wells
Year formed: 1870

Chairman: CF Openshaw
Chief Executive: Paul Millman
Director of Cricket: John Wright
President: Anthony Levick
Captain: Matthew Fleming
Vice-captain: Trevor Ward
Coaching contact: Alan Ealham 01227 456886
County colours: Blue and white

HONOURS

COUNTY CHAMPIONSHIP
1906, 1909, 1910, 1913, 1970,
1977, 1978
SUNDAY LEAGUE
1972, 1973, 1976, 1995
BENSON & HEDGES CUP
1973, 1976, 1978
GILLETTE CUP/NATWEST TROPHY
1967, 1974

CGU National Cricket League nickname:
KENT SPITFIRES

Website:
www.kentcountycricket.co.uk

Somerset's Piran Holloway scored an unbeaten century against Middlesex at Taunton.
David Munden/Sportsline Photographic

9, 10, 11 and 12 July
at Derby
Derbyshire 359 (124 overs) (RMS Weston 156, KM Krikken 56, BJ Spendlove 51, AR Caddick 4 for 72) and 194 (AR Caddick 4 for 56)
Somerset 361 (138.4 overs) (PD Bowler 149, M Burns 72, P Aldred 5 for 74, AJ Harris 5 for 101) and 196 for 2 (J Cox 89*)
Somerset won by eight wickets
Somerset 18 pts, Derbyshire 6 pts

at Chester-le-Street
Durham 392 (121 overs) (PD Collingwood 106, MA Gough 62, MP Speight 60, PJ Franks 4 for 80, VC Drakes 4 for 88) and 304 for 8 dec. (JJB Lewis 118, JE Morris 78, VC Drakes 4 for 70)
Nottinghamshire 353 (107 overs) (P Johnson 83, GF Archer 81, U Afzaal 60, MM Betts 4 for 79) and 248 (RT Robinson 80, P Johnson 70*, JER Gallian 69, MA Gough 4 for 49)
Durham won by 95 runs
Durham 20 pts, Nottinghamshire 8 pts

at Worcester
Kent 119 (55.5 overs) (TM Moody 4 for 27, A Sheriyar 4 for 43 including a hat-trick) and 350 (MV Fleming 138, VS Solanki 4 for 62)
Worcestershire 106 (44 overs) (DN Patel 4 for 31) and 343 (GA Hick 99, JBD Thompson 4 for 58)
Kent won by 20 runs
Kent 16 pts, Worcestershire 4 pts

Somerset and Middlesex made the most significant moves up the PPP table during this round of championship games, progressing to third and fourth places respectively. Kent won a remarkable, thrilling encounter at Worcester – while Durham's coming of age as a championship force was confirmed as several of their bright, younger players contributed to victory over Nottinghamshire.

Peter Bowler enjoyed Somerset's eight-wicket win at Derby with 192 runs, for once out, against his former club. How ironic, as he was completing a first-innings century of stern application that, off the field, Derbyshire were hosting their annual former players' reunion. Yet the match had begun promisingly for Derbyshire, with the in-form Robin Weston going to his third hundred in successive championship fixtures. Weston's 156, a career-best, lifted him into second place in the national batting averages. Only William Storer, Peter Kirsten and Kim Barnett had hit three championship hundreds in successive matches for Derbyshire before Weston, who added 144 for the sixth wicket with Karl Krikken. But Bowler's seven-hour 149, and a stand of 136 with Michael Burns (72), brought Somerset back into the match and Derbyshire's attack was clearly weakened by the absence through injury of Cork, DeFreitas and Dean. Derbyshire struggled to 130 for 5 by the close of the third day and, on the final day, Andy Caddick (4 for 56) and Paul Jarvis (3 for 30) further undermined their resolve. That left Somerset to score 193 in 69 overs and, under the calm influence of their skipper Jamie Cox (89 not out), the result was not in doubt.

A disintegration by Northants, in their second innings, allowed Middlesex the chance to earn themselves a fine comeback victory at Lord's. Graeme Swann's punchy 78 had brought a recovery from 30 for 5 on the first morning in which Tim Bloomfield took 4 for 10 inside 27 balls. And, after reaching 223, Northants ran through the Middlesex batting to dismiss them for 96, Devon Malcolm and Paul Taylor sharing eight wickets. But then came a startling lack of backbone as Middlesex fought back in the field through Angus Fraser (3 for 16 in 15 overs) and Jamie Hewitt, who had the fine return of 4 for 6 from ten overs. Russell Warren top-scored with 25, only three batsmen reached double figures and Northants were shot out for just 88. Middlesex, needing 216, then reached the close of the second day on 157 for 3 and, next morning, completed victory by seven wickets. Australian Justin Langer, finishing 117 not out, exposed by his own efforts the complete inadequacy of the English batting on view in the game. Seventeen wickets fell on the first day, and 16 on the second, but once again the pitch – though having to be reported – was deemed acceptable.

The match of the round was, undoubtedly, at Worcester where no less than 20 wickets tumbled on the opening day but which lasted easily into the fourth day. Kent eventually won by just 20 runs – a triumph for their captain, Matthew Fleming, and for their collective nerve and determination. An Alamgir Sheriyar hat-trick provided the first drama: Fulton and Ward (who had fallen in Munton's hat-trick a week before at Maidstone) were this time followed by Andrew Symonds as Kent plunged to 14 for 5. Robert Key, concentrating exclusively on keeping out the seaming ball, took 65 minutes over his nought, but Kent's lower order did manage to score some runs as they took the total to 119. Astonishingly their modest efforts were rewarded as, by the end of the day, Kent had taken a 13-run first-innings lead. Min Patel continued his good season, picking up 4 for 31 as Worcestershire plunged to 106 all out. Key and David Fulton hinted at more permanence at the crease at the start of the Kent second innings, but it was not until the emergence of Fleming at number seven that the attack began to be directed back at the bowlers. Fleming, well-supported by his lower order, went on to equal his career-best with 138, from 173 balls and with two sixes and 18 fours, but the match was really won by a courageous last-wicket stand of 101 between Fleming and Julian Thompson.

Thompson, who has opened the batting for Kent League side Tunbridge Wells, made 23 and – eventually – Worcestershire set out needing to make 364 for victory. While Graeme Hick was in full flow it seemed a doddle. Hick went from 50 to 92 in only 25 deliveries but then, backing up too far in search of a single when David Leatherdale swept at Patel, he was run out for 99 by Dean Headley's swoop at backward square leg and swift return to the bowler. Nevertheless, Worcestershire were 280 for 6 at the end of the third day and, next morning, had got to within 32 runs of victory with three wickets left when Fleming opted to take the second new ball – four overs late. Headley and Thompson, kept back to ensure they were as fresh as possible in sultry conditions, responded to their challenge and Kent had won a memorable contest.

Durham tasted championship victory on home soil for the first time since May 1998 by seeing off Notts by 95 runs at Chester-le-Street. It also took them off the bottom of the table. Paul Collingwood hit his

Graeme Hick was dismissed for 99 against Kent.
David Munden/Sportsline Photographic

second championship century, from 168 balls and with two sixes and 14 fours, to ensure that opener Michael Gough's hard work at the top of the order was not wasted. Gough scored 62 and was confirmed, during this game, as England's Under-19 captain for the upcoming 'Test' series against Australia Under-19s. Martin Speight's 60 also helped to lift Durham to an imposing first-innings total but Notts replied solidly with Paul Johnson (83), Graeme Archer (81) and Usman Afzaal (60) all in the runs. Mel Betts returned to form with 4 for 79 but Durham needed the dedication of opener Jon Lewis (118) and the stroke-play of John Morris (78), the pair putting on 137 for the second wicket, to pull away from Notts again. A declaration left Notts to make 344 in 83 overs, but they did not get close despite reaching 185 for 2 after a fine stand between Tim Robinson (80) and Jason Gallian (69). Johnson was left stranded on 70 not out as the middle and lower order was routed by Gough and Harmison. Gough took a career-best 4 for 49 with his fledgling off-spin, his six-foot-five-inch frame enabling him to

extract bounce as well as some turn from the pitch. Left-arm paceman Harmison did what all budding fast bowlers should be able to do: he blew away the tail to finish with 3 for 33. Notts, third at the end of May, continue their free fall down the table and Clive Rice, the cricket manager, was unsparing in his criticism. Only Johnson, Drakes, Read and Franks, he said, had justified their places in the team during the season so far.

At Cardiff, and still waiting for the availability of their new overseas player Jacques Kallis, Glamorgan were crushed by Essex by an innings and 137 runs. Ashley Cowan's career-best 6 for 47 was instrumental in their decline to 185 all out on the first day, and then Stuart Law had a lot of fun by hitting 140 and spearheading Essex's drive to 444. Paul Prichard (73) and Stephen Peters (81) were other major contributors, while Mark Ilott's lower-order 44 rubbed salt into the Welsh wounds. By the close of the second day Glamorgan were 6 for 2 in their second innings, Ilott striking twice with the new ball. It went no better on the third day, and soon Glamorgan were bowled out for 122, Irani taking 4 for 29 and only Michael Powell and Alun Evans showing any lasting signs of resistance.

Nick Knight, Warwickshire's vice-captain, failed to reach three figures in the championship.
David Munden/Sportsline Photographic

ROUND 12: 13–17 JULY 1999

13, 14, 15 and 16 July
at Edgbaston
Warwickshire 253 (87.2 overs)
(NV Knight 59, DL Hemp 53,
D Gough 4 for 62) and 182
(NV Knight 51)
Yorkshire (53.3 overs) (A McGrath
75, ESH Giddins 4 for 59) and
224 for 7 (GM Hamilton 75*,
MP Vaughan 52)
Yorkshire won by three wickets
Yorkshire 17 pts, Warwickshire 6 pts

14, 15 and 16 July
at Southend
Middlesex 113 (39.1 overs)
(RSG Anderson 5 for 36) and 140
(AP Grayson 4 for 16)
Essex 429 (152 overs) (N Hussain 99,
RC Irani 70, SG Law 58, AP Cowan
52*)
Essex won by an innings and 176 runs
Essex 19 pts, Middlesex 2 pts

LANCASHIRE CCC

Home Ground:
Old Trafford
Address:
Old Trafford, Manchester M16 0PX
Tel: 0161 282 4000 (switchboard)
0161 282 4040 (ticket office)
Directions:
By rail: Manchester Piccadilly or Victoria then Metro link to Old Trafford (station alongside ground).
By road: M63, Stretford slip road (junction 7) on to A56; follow signs.
Capacity: 21,500
Other grounds used: Blackpool (Stanley Park); Liverpool (Aigburth); Southport (Trafalgar Road); Lytham (Church Road).
Year formed: 1864

Chairman: Jack Simmons
Chief Executive: Jim Cumbes
Director of Cricket: Dav Whatmore
Other posts: Secretary: Dave Edmundson; Second XI Coach: PR Sleep
Captain: John Crawley
Coaching contact: Terry Holt, Cricket Centre Manager 0161 282 4033
County colours: Red, blue, green

HONOURS

COUNTY CHAMPIONSHIP
1881, 1897, 1927, 1927, 1928, 1930, 1934
JOINT CHAMPIONS
1878, 1882, 1889, 1950
NATIONAL LEAGUE
1999
BENSON & HEDGES CUP
1984, 1990, 1995, 1996
GILLETTE CUP/NATWEST TROPHY
1970, 1971, 1972, 1975, 1990, 1996, 1998

CGU National Cricket League nickname:
LANCASHIRE LIGHTNING

Website:
www.lccc.co.uk

14, 15, 16 and 17 July
at Cheltenham
Worcestershire 591 for 7 dec. (164.3 overs) (VS Solanki 171, WPC Weston 139, GA Hick 122) and 68 for 5 (AM Smith 4 for 47)
Gloucestershire 231 (84.1 overs) (THC Hancock 58, KJ Barnett 53, A Sheriyar 6 for 101) and (following on) 425 (KJ Barnett 106, MCJ Ball 70*, THC Hancock 64, J Lewis 62, PJ Newport 4 for 57)
Worcestershire won by five wickets
Worcestershire 20 pts, Gloucestershire 2 pts

at Blackpool
Lancashire 556 for 6 dec. (157 overs) (MA Atherton 268*, MJ Chilton 71, NH Fairbrother 59, WK Hegg 53) and 19 for 0
Glamorgan 282 (106.2 overs) (A Dale 112, SD Thomas 54, M Muralitharan 6 for 104, CP Schofield 4 for 55) and (following on) 289 (MJ Powell 96, WL Law 53, M Muralitharan 4 for 72, CP Schofield 4 for 71)
Lancashire won by ten wickets
Lancashire 20 pts, Glamorgan 3 pts

at Guildford
Surrey 171 (41.3 overs) (AJ Hollioake 63*, NAM McLean 4 for 63, PJ Hartley 4 for 66) and 482 (GP Thorpe 164, MA Butcher 94, IJ Ward 55)
Hampshire 322 (91.5 overs) (NAM McLean 70, DA Kenway 63, MP Bicknell 4 for 75) and 175 (Saqlain Mushtaq 6 for 44)
Surrey won by 156 runs
Surrey 16 pts, Hampshire 7 pts

at Arundel
Leicestershire 566 for 8 dec. (172 overs) (Aftab Habib 160*, DJ Stevens 130, MS Kasprowicz 52, CC Lewis 51, VJ Wells 51, JJ Bates 5 for 154)
Sussex 319 (120.5 overs) (WG Khan 88, MT Brimson 4 for 69) and (following on) 214 (NJ Wilton 55, MT Brimson 5 for 51)
Leicestershire won by an innings and 33 runs
Leicestershire 20 pts, Sussex 4 pts

15 and 16 July
at Chester-le-Street
Derbyshire 241 (76.4 overs) (KM Krikken 88, DG Cork 53, SJE Brown 6 for 84) and 130 (MM Betts 4 for 34)
Durham 346 (89 overs) (JE Morris 119, NJ Speak 57, MA Gough 53, DG Cork 5 for 106) and 29 for 3
Durham won by seven wickets
Durham 18 pts, Derbyshire 5 pts

Surrey staged a memorable comeback victory against neighbours and title rivals Hampshire, but their lead at the top of the PPP table was cut to 24 points as Leicestershire earned the maximum 20 points for beating Sussex.

Guildford was the venue for Surrey's 16-point triumph but, after being bowled out for just 171 on day one, the leaders looked in trouble. Hampshire, unfazed by the presence of ten internationals in the Surrey line-up, were level at 171 for 6 by the close of an eventful opening day with Derek Kenway on 61 not out. Kenway added just two runs on the second morning but Nixon McLean – who had taken 4 for 63 in the Surrey first innings – then thrashed a career-best 70 from just 52 balls and, with Shaun Udal unbeaten on 30, Hampshire reached 322 and a lead of 151. First time around only Adam Hollioake, with 63 not out, had held up the Hampshire bowlers but now Surrey's top batsmen got going. Mark Butcher made 94 and Ian Ward 55 before Graham Thorpe played one of the most decisive innings of the summer. Ignoring the steady fall of wickets at the other end, Thorpe strode on. In the end it took a direct hit from Jason Laney to run him out for 164, but the left-hander's highly disciplined innings, plus useful efforts of 40 from Ally Brown and 35 from Martin Bicknell, took Surrey to a total of 482 and an overall lead of 331. It was too much for Hampshire. Saqlain, who had picked up only 1 for 77 in the first innings, now took 6 for 44 after Bicknell (3 for 50) had made the initial breakthrough. Robin Smith, 33 not out when Hampshire began the final day on 99 for 4, could manage only 46 as his side were dismissed for 175.

Leicestershire not only closed the gap slightly on Surrey with their hard-fought innings win at Arundel, but also pushed Hampshire back into third place. The key to Leicestershire's victory was a huge first-innings total of 566 for 8 declared, based on Darren Stevens' maiden first-class hundred (a knock of 130), an attractive 160 not out by Aftab Habib and half-centuries for Vince Wells, Chris Lewis and Mike Kasprowicz. Slow left-armer Matthew Brimson then bore the brunt of the responsibility for bowling out Sussex twice – especially with both Lewis and Kasprowicz suffering injury niggles – and he bore it well. Brimson had match figures of 9 for 120 but Alan Mullally and Darren Maddy took useful wickets too in the first and second innings respectively. Wasim Khan hit a cultured 88 in the Sussex first innings of 319.

Yorkshire's three-wicket win over Warwickshire at Edgbaston was notable not just for hauling the

Graham Thorpe scored 164 at Guildford in July. It was one of the most decisive innings of the summer and took Surrey to victory over Hampshire.

David Munden/Sportsline Photographic

White Rose county back into the top half of the table again but also for the decision to give Darren Gough a comeback from injury. Gough, who had missed the first Test against New Zealand, was not expected to play but reported no reaction to a net the previous day and was thrown in. He ended up with 4 for 62, after an unsurprisingly tentative start, but not before Nick Knight (59) and David Hemp (53) had laid the foundations for a score of 253. Yorkshire suffered a first-innings deficit of 40 despite Anthony McGrath's 75 but were still in the game when Warwickshire were bowled out for 182, Knight again standing firm initially with 51. By the close of the third day, chasing 223, Yorkshire were 170 for 6 but that already

represented something of a recovery from 103 for 6. The men responsible were Gavin Hamilton, coming in at number eight, and Richard Harden. Their stand was eventually worth 84, of which Harden made just 25, but Hamilton was a heroic 75 not out when victory was clinched.

A miserable batting performance by Middlesex, in both innings, helped Essex towards a third win in four games – and a fourth championship victory out of four with Nasser Hussain leading them. Hussain made 99 in an Essex first-innings total of 429, Ronnie Irani weighing in with 70 and both Stuart Law and Ashley Cowan hitting fifties. That total gave them a massive lead over Middlesex, shot out for 113 on the first day with Ricky Anderson snatching a career-best 5 for 36. On the third day it was the Essex spinners, though, who completed the rout as the Southend pitch grew dry and dusting. Peter Such took 3 for 42 but Paul Grayson finished with 4 for 16 as Middlesex folded for just 140.

Lancashire's ten-wicket mauling of Glamorgan at Blackpool was most notable for the promising performance of 20-year-old leg-spinning all-rounder Chris Schofield, who had analyses of 4 for 55 and 4 for 71 and, in the second innings especially, even outbowled Sri Lankan wonderman Muttiah Muralitharan. The match also heralded the true re-emergence after injury of Michael Atherton, the former England captain taking advantage of friendly batting conditions on the first day to amass a career-best 268 not out. Chilton, Fairbrother and Hegg all chipped in too, with half-centuries, and Glamorgan looked demoralised by the time they ended the second day on 193 for 6. Adrian Dale went on to score 112, and Darren Thomas hit 54, but the Welshmen were soon following on and finding life just as difficult against the spinners. Muralitharan, perhaps tiring, added only 4 for 72 to his first-innings 6 for 104 and at least two young Glamorgan batsmen, Michael Powell and Wayne Law, impressed observers with defiant knocks of 96 and 53 respectively. Lancashire's win took them up to near halfway in the table.

A remarkable last-wicket stand of 130 between Martyn Ball (70 not out) and Jon Lewis (62) failed to save Gloucestershire from defeat at Cheltenham. But at least they made Worcestershire work hard for the win that looked to be keeping them on course for a top nine finish – Tom Moody's side then losing five wickets as they attempted to knock off a modest 66-run victory target on the final afternoon. Worcestershire had dominated the first three days, running up a mammoth 591 for 7 declared on the

LEICESTERSHIRE CCC

Home Ground:
Grace Road, Leicester
Address:
County Ground,
Grace Road,
Leicester LE2 8AD
Tel: 0116 2832128
Directions:
By road: Follow signs from city centre, or from southern ring road from M1 or A6.
Capacity: 5,500
Other grounds used: None
Year formed: 1879

Chairman: R Goadby
Chief Executive: D G Collier
Director of Cricket: Jack Birkenshaw
Captain: Vince Wells.
Coaching contact: Russell Cobb 0116 2440965
County colours: Dark green and scarlet

HONOURS

COUNTY CHAMPIONSHIP
1975, 1996, 1998
SUNDAY LEAGUE
1974, 1977
BENSON & HEDGES CUP
1972, 1975, 1985

CGU National Cricket League nickname:
LEICESTERSHIRE FOXES

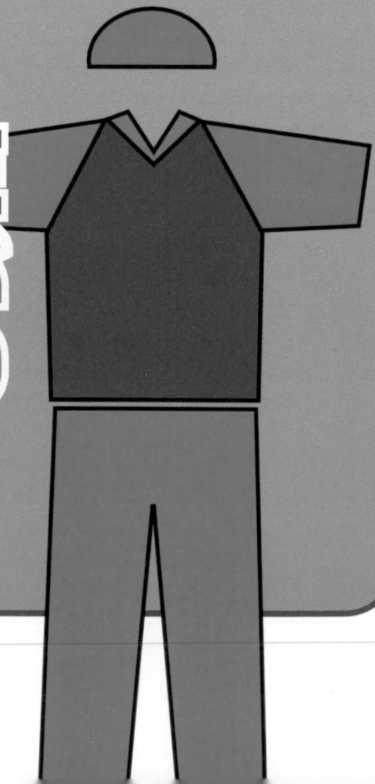

Website:
www.leicestershireccc.com

Leicestershire's Ben Smith on his way to 138 against Worcestershire.

David Munden/Sportsline Photographic

back of 139 from Phil Weston, 122 from Graeme Hick (his 106th first-class hundred) and 171 from Vikram Solanki, and then dismissing their opponents for 231. Alamgir Sheriyar kept up his prolific season with 6 for 101 and, following on, Gloucestershire were 185 for 4 by the end of the third day. Kim Barnett, on 61 overnight, went on to 106 and then came that magnificent last-wicket partnership, finally broken when Solanki bowled Lewis. But it was still too little, too late, and Mike Smith's 4 for 47 new-ball burst was mere additional consolation.

No one enjoyed Durham's two-day victory over Derbyshire more than John Morris, who had 12 seasons at Derby from 1982. Morris struck a brilliant 119, his second fifty taking only 31 balls, to help Durham establish a sizeable first-innings lead after bowling Derbyshire out for 241 on the opening day. Karl Krikken made 88 and Dominic Cork 53 in an 89-run eighth-wicket stand, but by the close Durham were 89 for 1 and approaching a position of strength. Morris, supported by Michael Gough and Nick Speak, made sure they did not waste it and soon Derbyshire were down and out. Simon Brown and Steven Harmison were irrepressible with the new ball – Harmison looking particularly potent with his extra pace and bounce – and then Melvyn Betts charged in to finish things off with 4 for 34. Durham lost three wickets in reaching a tiny victory target, but their third win in four matches was also their first inside two days.

ROUND 13: 20–25 JULY 1999

20, 21, 22 and 23 July
at Scarborough
Northamptonshire 517 for 7 dec. (159.4 overs)
(AL Penberthy 123*, D Ripley 107, DJG Sales 101,
RJ Warren 87) and 61 for 2
Yorkshire 289 (94.5 overs) (GS Blewett 98, D Byas 50,
DE Malcolm 4 for 106) and (following on) 407
(GS Blewett 190, GM Hamilton 84*, RJ Harden 50)
Match drawn
Yorkshire 8 pts, Northamptonshire 12 pts

21, 22 and 23 July
at Derby
Sussex 271 (62.5 overs) (CJ Adams 92, DG Cork 6 for
113) and 176 (MTE Peirce 55, PAJ DeFreitas 6 for 41)
Derbyshire 226 (54.5 overs) (MA Robinson 6 for 88)
and 136 (JD Lewry 7 for 38)
Sussex won by 85 runs
Sussex 18 pts, Derbyshire 5 pts

at Cheltenham
Durham 552 (157 overs) (DC Boon 139, NJ Speak 110, JE Morris 74, JJB Lewis 59, MP Speight 56)
Gloucestershire 202 (66.1 overs) (SJE Brown 5 for 78) and (following on) 223 (MW Alleyne 64, MGN Windows 53, N Killeen 5 for 44)
Durham won by an innings and 127 runs
Durham 20 pts, Gloucestershire 2 pts

at Trent Bridge
Kent 191 (61.2 overs) (RWT Key 50, WM Noon 7 catches) and 222 (AG Wharf 4 for 75)
Nottinghamshire 88 (39.1 overs) (MA Ealham 5 for 30) and 237 (VC Drakes 80, U Afzaal 62, JBD Thompson 6 for 63)
Kent won by 88 runs
Kent 16 pts, Nottinghamshire 4 pts

at Edgbaston
Surrey 483 (136 overs) (AD Brown 108, IJ Ward 82, GP Butcher 70, ESH Giddins 6 for 90)
Warwickshire 227 (75.1 overs) (NV Knight 94, IDK Salisbury 5 for 49) and (following on) 133 (Saqlain Mushtaq 5 for 32, IDK Salisbury 4 for 46)
Surrey won by an innings and 123 runs
Surrey 20 pts, Warwickshire 3 pts

21, 22, 23 and 24 July
at Southampton
Lancashire 492 (139.5 overs) (JP Crawley 101, GD Lloyd 85, NH Fairbrother 83, MJ Chilton 51) and 93 for 2
Hampshire 181 (67.1 overs) (A Flintoff 5 for 24) and (following on) 402 (JS Laney 95, DA Kenway 92, RA Smith 77, MD Muralitharan 7 for 114)
Lancashire won by eight wickets
Lancashire 20 pts, Hampshire 2 pts

at Taunton
Somerset 297 (86.4 overs) (M Burns 74, RJ Turner 73) and 523 for 3 dec. (ME Trescothick 190, PCL Holloway 114*, J Cox 114)
Middlesex 355 (109 overs) (JL Langer 96, PN Weekes 65) and 271 for 1 (JL Langer 127*, OA Shah 110*)
Match drawn
Somerset 10 pts, Middlesex 12 pts

22, 23, 24 and 25 July
at Worcester
Leicestershire 291 (115.5 overs) (IJ Sutcliffe 110, VS Solanki 4 for 64) and 316 for 9 dec. (BF Smith 138)
Worcestershire 133 (69.2 overs) (JM Dakin 4 for 27)

and 353 for 4 (WPC Weston 157, GA Hick 59)
Match drawn
Worcestershire 8 pts, Leicestershire 10 pts

Surrey pulled further ahead at the top of the PPP championship in this round of matches. Two days after they trounced Warwickshire, with Saqlain and Salisbury again to the fore, Leicestershire were frustrated by a fine Worcestershire rearguard action at Grace Road. High-riding Hampshire also lost, but Kent and Durham scored significant wins.

Ian Salisbury took nine wickets and Saqlain Mushtaq seven as Warwickshire, bowled out for 227 and 133 at Edgbaston, lost by an innings and 123 runs. A century by Alastair Brown, whose 108 took little more than two hours, with a six and 14 fours, dominated the opening day – although the consistent Ian Ward also made 82. Gary Butcher's 70, containing 13 boundaries, then helped to boost Surrey's first-innings total to 483 and only Ed Giddins, with 6 for 90, troubled the Surrey stroke-makers. Nick Knight opened up with 94 in reply, but soon the Surrey spin twins were getting to work and by the end of the second day Warwickshire had slid to 223 for 9. Salisbury finished them off early the next morning, to give himself figures of 5 for 49, and in the Warwickshire second innings picked up a further 4 for 46. Saqlain also revelled in the conditions, taking 5 for 32 as Surrey swept to a 20-point haul. Warwickshire looked lacklustre in defeat, their players reported to be aggrieved at the club's decision to pass over the long-serving and loyal Dominic Ostler for a benefit in the year 2000, in addition to general concern about the way director of cricket Phil Neale had been moved aside for the impending return of Bob Woolmer.

Kent moved up to fourth place with a third successive win, Mark Ealham (5 for 30) and Martin McCague (3 for 33) destroying the Nottinghamshire first innings and Julian Thompson (6 for 63) also proving too much for them as they tried in vain to reach 326 for victory on a seaming pitch at Trent Bridge. Notts' second-innings 237, with Usman Afzaal making 62 and Vasbert Drakes a flamboyant 80, was in fact the highest total of the match – not that it was much consolation for a Notts side who slid further down the table to 15th after what was a fourth successive defeat. Wicketkeeper Wayne Noon will remember the match though, because he claimed a club-record seven catches – beating the six taken four times by Bruce French – in what was only his second championship appearance of the season. Robert Key dug in for a good fifty as Kent totalled 191 on day one, but by the close Notts were 18 for 2 in reply and on the following day collapsed to 88. Kent were 79 for 5 in their second innings, with Ed Smith (38) standing alone in a shaky top order, but the Kent lower order pulled their total up to 222 – and the overall lead was more than enough.

Hampshire took just two points from an eight-wicket defeat by Lancashire, although they made a brave attempt to extricate themselves from a sticky position. Lancashire opened up with a massive 492, John Crawley (101) hitting his first century of the season and Graham Lloyd (85) and Neil Fairbrother (83) making other significant contributions. Hampshire then folded to 181, but what was most remarkable about their first innings was that Muttiah Muralitharan took only a single wicket. Andrew Flintoff, instead, was the destroyer with a career-best 5 for 24. Following on, however, Hampshire's spirit was apparent in an opening stand of 212 between Jason Laney and Derek Kenway – both born within the county. Laney, on 95, was bowled on the charge against Muralitharan, and Kenway (92) also failed to reach three figures. On the third evening Hampshire were 303 for 3 with Robin Smith still there but, although he went on to 77 and Giles White made 47, a rapid collapse followed a high point of 348 for 3. Glen Chapple had White caught at the wicket and, suddenly, Muralitharan had figures of 7 for 114 as the lower order disintegrated.

Durham, bottom of the table little more than a fortnight earlier, moved into the top half when they slaughtered Gloucestershire by an innings and 127 runs. A first-innings total of 552 proved far too intimidating to a Gloucestershire side by now concentrating hard on their one-day form and the fast-approaching Benson and Hedges Super Cup final and NatWest Trophy quarter-final. David Boon and Nick Speak made hundreds, John Morris made 74 from 80 balls, and both Jon Lewis and Martin Speight topped fifty. Simon Brown swept aside Gloucestershire's first innings for just 202 with 5 for 78, and when they followed on only Mark Alleyne (64) and Matt Windows (53) lingered awhile. Neil Killeen, the medium-pacer, grabbed 5 for 44 as Gloucestershire were bundled out for 223 to complete a miserable Cheltenham festival. All 20 wickets taken by Durham went to locally raised bowlers – a measure of the north-east talent now beginning to emerge as a real force on the county circuit.

Somerset's meeting with Middlesex at Taunton finished as a draw – with the pitch just getting

Ian Salisbury was at the forefront of Surrey's attack in the match against Warwickshire in July. He took a total of nine wickets, taking his team to victory.
David Munden/Sportsline Photographic

better. Justin Langer (96) and Paul Weekes (65) gave their side a seemingly useful first-innings advantage, after Somerset had been dismissed for 297 on the first day. Michael Burns made 74, Rob Turner 73 and Matt Bulbeck a robust unbeaten 43 but, by the close, with Bulbeck striking twice with the new ball,

MIDDLESEX CCC

Home Ground:
Lord's Cricket Ground
Address:
Lord's Cricket Ground,
St John's Wood, London NW8 8QN
Tel: 0171 289 1300
Email: enquiries.middx@ecb.co.uk
Directions:
By underground: St John's Wood on Jubilee Line
(five minutes walk).
By bus: 13, 82, 113 stop along east side of
ground; 139 at south west corner; 274 at top
of Regent's Park
Capacity: 28,000
Other grounds used: Uxbridge; Southgate
Year formed: 1864

Chairman: Phil Edmonds
Secretary: Vinny Codrington
Senior Coach: Mike Gatting
Other posts: Second Team Captain and
Coach: Ian Gould
Captain: Justin Langer
Coaching contact: Middlesex Cricket & Squash Centre
0181 346 8020
County colours: Navy

HONOURS

COUNTY CHAMPIONSHIP
1903, 1920, 1921, 1947,
1949 (JOINT), 1976, 1977 (JOINT),
1980, 1982, 1985, 1990, 1993
SUNDAY LEAGUE
1992
BENSON & HEDGES CUP
1983, 1986
GILLETTE CUP/NATWEST TROPHY
1977, 1980, 1984, 1988

**CGU National Cricket League
nickname:**
MIDDLESEX CRUSADERS

crusaders

Website:
www.middlesexccc.co.uk

20-year-old Chris Read, Nottinghamshire and England wicketkeeper, proved himself outstanding with both bat and gloves this season.

David Munden/Sportsline Photographic

Middlesex were 61 for 3. Thirteen wickets fell on that first day, but then only 11 more in the remainder of the match. Somerset made a huge 523 for 3 declared second time around – Marcus Trescothick including 31 fours and a six in his 190, and both Jamie Cox and Piran Holloway adding hundreds – and even Angus Fraser was going for more than four an over as the bat held total sway. On the final afternoon, batting out time, Langer scored 127 not out and Owais Shah an unbeaten 110 with Middlesex closing on 271 for 1.

Yorkshire's fighting comeback to achieve a draw against Northamptonshire at Scarborough was based on a remarkable return to form for Greg Blewett. In 22 previous championship innings the Australian had struggled to reach a total of 330 runs. Now he was making 288 in one match. A first-innings 98 by Blewett was not enough to stave off the follow-on – Yorkshire being bowled out for 298 in reply to a Northants total of 517 for 7 declared, in which David Sales made 101 and Russell Warren 87 to lead a recovery from 17 for 3. But the real story was the 214-run stand between David Ripley (107) and Tony Penberthy (123 not out) which was just 15 short of the county's seventh-wicket record, set in 1926.

Yorkshire, second time around, were 141 for 4 by the close of the third day, but Blewett raced on to 190 and Richard Harden kept him company with 50 and Gavin Hamilton with 84 not out. Northants could not get Yorkshire out quickly enough: they were left with a 12-an-over target and although Graeme Swann swatted 38 off 19 balls it was never on.

Dominic Cork took 6 for 113 in Sussex's first innings, and Phil DeFreitas 6 for 41 in the second – but still Derbyshire lost. Sussex had Chris Adams (92, including two sixes and 18 fours) to thank for reaching 271 on the opening day, and Derbyshire could only reach 226 in reply. Mark Robinson, bowling straight on a helpful Derby track, took 6 for 88 but the real bowling match-winner was Jason Lewry. The Sussex left-arm paceman took centre stage after Sussex had scored a second-innings 176 – Toby Pierce hitting an important 55 and DeFreitas's haul moving him up to 999 first-class career wickets. Lewry finished with a career-best 7 for 38 as Derbyshire crumbled to 136, few batsmen applying themselves.

Leicestershire's hopes of retaining their title, meanwhile, took a knock as Worcestershire held on in some style for a draw at Leicester. Despite missing six players through either Test calls or injury, Leicestershire took control by reaching 291 in their first innings, Iain Sutcliffe hitting 110, and then bowling out Worcestershire for just 133. Jon Dakin (4 for 27) and Tim Mason (3 for 32) were the destroyers but, after Leicestershire drove on to 316 for 9 declared in their second innings, Ben Smith scoring 138, Worcestershire's batsmen proved no soft touch. By the close of the third day they were 138 for 1 in their second innings, with opener Philip Weston unbeaten on 81. On the final day he went on to reach 157, while Graeme Hick had to be content with 59. At 353 for 4, Worcestershire had really earned their extra four points for the draw.

ROUND 14: 30 JULY–2 AUGUST 1999

30, 31 July and 1 August
at Trent Bridge
Nottinghamshire 232 (63.1 overs) (P Johnson 85, CMW Read 67, P Aldred 4 for 47, AJ Harris 4 for 54) and 153 (53.3 overs) (DG Cork 4 for 46)
Derbyshire 263 (76.5 overs) (SP Titchard 59, PJ Franks 4 for 77) and 123 for 4
Derbyshire won by six wickets
Derbyshire 18 pts, Nottinghamshire 5 pts

at Northampton
Northamptonshire 579 (131 overs) (DJG Sales 303*,
D Ripley 94, AP Cowan 4 for 69)
Essex 355 (115.5 overs) (SG Law 117, PJ Prichard 74,
MK Davies 5 for 61) and (following on) 143 (MK Davies
4 for 23)
Northamptonshire won by an innings and 81 runs
Northamptonshire 20 pts, Essex 8 pts

30, 31 July, 1 and 2 August
at Cardiff
Durham 448 (167 overs) (NJ Speak 103, MP Speight
97*, JJB Lewis 50, SD Thomas 5 for 64) and 185
(PD Collingwood 51, RDB Croft 7 for 70)
Glamorgan 387 (119 overs) (A Dale 79, SP James 65,
AD Shaw 53, NC Phillips 6 for 71) and 247 for 7
(AW Evans 88*, JH Kallis 60, NC Phillips 6 for 97)
Glamorgan won by three wickets
Glamorgan 18 pts, Durham 6 pts

at Northampton
Northamptonshire 111 (40.2 overs) (MPL Bulbeck 5 for
45) and 226 (AL Penberthy 53, MPL Bulbeck 5 for 63)
Somerset 422 for 9 dec. (164.3 overs) (KA Parsons 80,
J Cox 69, JID Kerr 64)
Somerset won by an innings and 85 runs
Somerset 19 pts, Northamptonshire 3 pts

at Headingley
Worcestershire 90 (26 overs) (PM Hutchison 6 for 35)
and 287 (VS Solanki 70, SR Lampitt 66*, TM Moody 56)
Yorkshire 374 (108.5 overs) (GM Hamilton 94*, D Byas
67, A McGrath 51, A Sheriyar 4 for 94) and 4 for 1
Yorkshire won by nine wickets
Yorkshire 20 pts, Worcestershire 4 pts

An outstanding innings of 303 not out by David
Sales dominated this small round of games, inspiring
Northamptonshire to a much-needed win against
Essex. Derbyshire and Glamorgan were the other
victors – Glamorgan's win taking them off the
bottom of the PPP table.

Sales, the 21-year-old who made a double hundred
on his first-class debut in 1996, became the first
Englishman to reach 1,000 runs for the season
during his epic innings, and was also awarded his
county cap. Northants, at one stage 58 for 6,
recovered to score 579 – an incredible
transformation based on a county-record seventh-
wicket stand of 293 in 63 overs between Sales and
David Ripley. For Ripley, the wicketkeeper, it was
his third involvement in a county-record stand.
Initially, Essex made a good fist of things in reply,

with Stuart Law hitting 117 and Paul Prichard 74.
But slow left-arm Michael Davies then began to
weave a web around the visiting batsmen that
resulted in Essex folding from an overnight 258 for
3 to 355 all out and, following on, being dismissed
for a desultory 143. Davies added 4 for 23 to his
first-innings 5 for 61.

Glamorgan's three-wicket win against Durham at
Cardiff was that modern-day rarity – a four-day
match fully worthy of the description, and
progressing to a natural finish deep into the final
day quite free either of interruption or contrivance.
Nick Speak made 103 on the opening day and
Martin Speight motored on to 97 not out on the
second as Durham reached 448. Glamorgan made a
positive reply, with Adrian Dale (79) and Steve
James (65) giving them a fine start on the way to
387. Nicky Phillips, with 6 for 171, earned himself a
bizarre-looking career-best. With the pitch
beginning to take turn – another requirement of
four-day cricket – Robert Croft stepped in to swing
the match back towards Glamorgan. Croft's 7 for 70
was his best return since 1992 and, having bowled
out Durham for 185, the Welsh county were left to
chase 247 in 66 remaining overs. At 81 for 4 the
outcome was in the balance, but Jacques Kallis
made 60 and Alun Evans an inspired 88 not out
from 113 balls. Phillips, the former Sussex off-
spinner, improved his career-best figures again to
6 for 97 but could not prevent Glamorgan's first
championship victory since the middle of May.

Tension is never far from the surface when local
rivals Nottinghamshire and Derbyshire meet, and
such was the case again when Dominic Cork and
Vasbert Drakes eyeballed each other in a mid-pitch
confrontation following the refusal of Derbyshire
wicketkeeper Karl Krikken to walk when Notts
claimed a slip catch off Drakes' bowling. That
incident spiced up a Derbyshire first-innings total
of 263, which gave them a slim but handy lead of
31 on a Trent Bridge pitch that always kept the
seamers interested. Paul Johnson's 85 and Chris
Read's 67 was the outstanding batting in Notts' 232,
in which Paul Aldred and Andrew Harris shared
eight wickets and Phil DeFreitas, in removing
Usman Afzaal, claimed the 1,000th first-class
scalp of his career. DeFreitas and Aldred then
took three more wickets each in the Notts second
innings, but it was Cork who had the last laugh
with 4 for 46. Notts, shot out for 153, had set
Derbyshire just 123 to win and, by the close of the
second day, they were 44 for 0. The next morning
brought a six-wicket victory.

ROUND 15: 4–9 AUGUST 1999

4, 5, 6 and 7 August
at Chester-le-Street
Sussex 231 (76.3 overs) (PA Cottey 53, N Killeen
4 for 46) and 192 (UBA Rashid 55, SJE Brown
6 for 64)
Durham 141 (44.2 overs) (JD Lewry 4 for 36)
and 274 (JA Daley 80, PD Collingwood 50,
JD Lewry 5 for 86)
Sussex won by 8 runs
Sussex 17 pts, Durham 4 pts

4 and 5 August
at The Oval
Glamorgan 101 (40.5 overs) (BC Hollioake 5 for 51)
and 84 (Saqlain Mushtaq 5 for 18)
Surrey 309 (95 overs) (AD Brown 124,
MP Bicknell 57)
Surrey won by an innings and 124 runs
Surrey 19 pts, Glamorgan 4 pts

4, 5 and 6 August
at Derby
Lancashire 224 (90.5 overs) (G Chapple 83,
P Aldred 6 for 83) and 235 (G Lloyd 104, P Aldred
7 for l01)
Derbyshire 132 (52.25 overs) (PJ Martin
5 for 51, M Muralitharan 4 for 22) and 135
(M Muralitharan 7 for 39)
Lancashire won by 192 runs
Lancashire 17 pts, Derbyshire 4 pts

at Southgate
Middlesex 291 (118.3 overs) (DC Nash 92,
BL Hutton 59, VC Drakes 6 for 64, PJ Franks
4 for 96) and 120 (VC Drakes 5 for 49)
Nottinghamshire 306 (110 overs) (JER Gallian
74, GF Archer 56, P Johnson 55, PN Weekes
4 for 50) and 108 for 2 (U Afzaal 52)
Nottinghamshire won by eight wickets
Nottinghamshire 19 pts, Middlesex 6 pts

at Canterbury
Kent 541 (152.1 overs) (A Symonds 132,
MA Ealham 80, RWT Key 77) and 53 for 3
Essex 350 (134.5 overs) (RC Irani 127*,
MA Ealham 4 for 51) and (following on) 243
(SG Law 104*, RC Irani 52)
Kent won by seven wickets
Kent 20 pts, Essex 5 pts

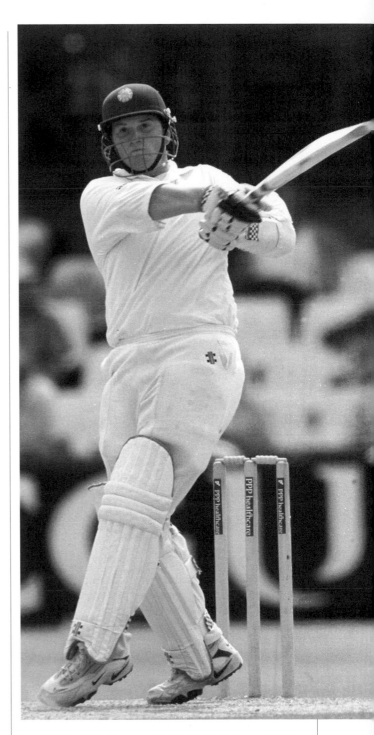

**David Sales of Northamptonshire during his innings of 303
not out against Essex.**
David Munden/Sportsline Photographic

Chris Adams, the captain of Sussex, was chosen for England's winter tour of South Africa.

David Munden/Sportsline Photographic

5, 6, 7 and 8 August
at Bristol
Gloucestershire 380 (138.5 overs) (RC Russell 94*, MW Alleyne 75, RJ Cunliffe 52, JP Stephenson 5 for 60, SD Udal 5 for 96) and 96 for 8
Hampshire 253 (94.1 overs) (JS Laney 97, WS Kendall 55, MJ Cawdron 5 for 35)
Match drawn
Gloucestershire 11 pts, Hampshire 8 pts

6, 7, 8 and 9 August
at Leicester
Warwickshire 306 (102.5 overs) (DP Ostler 87, MJ Powell 52, J Ormond 5 for 108)
Leicestershire 353 for 8 dec. (89 overs) (VJ Wells 109*, DL Maddy 59, J Ormond 50*)
Match drawn
Leicestershire 12 pts, Warwickshire 10 pts

Muttiah Muralitharan's magnificent contribution to Lancashire's season came to an end with another major wicket haul in the victory against Derbyshire which pushed John Crawley's team further up the PPP table. The Derbyshire batsmen, in truth, had little idea of how to counter Muralitharan's vicious turn – and, one by one, they perished, offering nothing more in retaliation than the slog-sweep. Muralitharan took 11 for 61 in the match, including second-innings figures of 7 for 39, and it brought his wicket tally to 66 from just 12 innings. The Sri Lankan had five match hauls of more than ten wickets in six matches – and his bowling average was a stunning 11.77. Lancashire, however, did not

NORTHAMPTONSHIRE CCC

Home Ground:
Northampton
Address:
The County Ground, Wantage Road,
Northampton NN1 4TJ
Tel: 01604 514455
Fax: 01604 514488
Directions:
By rail: Castle Station, three miles.
By road: M1 to J15, A508 and follow RAC signs.
RAC signs from all other areas. Parking on ground when
space permits otherwise ample local street parking.
By coach: regular service from Greyfriars coach station.
Capacity: 4,250
Other grounds used: Campbell Park, Milton Keynes.
Year formed: 1878

Chairman: Lynn Wilson
Chief Executive: Stephen Coverdale
Director of Excellence: David Capel
Director of Cricket: Bob Carter
Captain: Matthew Hayden
Vice-captain: David Ripley
Coaching contact: Ian Lucas 01604 632917
County colours: Claret and gold

HONOURS

BENSON & HEDGES CUP
1980
GILLETTE CUP/NATWEST TROPHY
1976, 1992

CGU National Cricket League nickname:
NORTHAMPTONSHIRE STEELBACKS

Website:
www.nccc.co.uk

have everything their own way, despite dismissing Derbyshire for 132 and 135, with Peter Martin picking up 5 for 51 on the second day. Lancashire's opening-day total of 224 owed much to Glen Chapple who first put on 71 with Warren Hegg for the seventh wicket and then another 82 for the ninth wicket with Richard Green. And, in the Lancashire second innings, after Paul Aldred had single-handedly reduced them to 91 for 5 on his way to figures of 7 for 101, Graham Lloyd pulled it round to 235 with an important knock of 104.

Leaders Surrey, meanwhile, kept marching on with the two-day innings thrashing of feeble Glamorgan. Duncan Fletcher, seeing out his time with the Welshmen before taking up the England coaching job, kept his players in the dressing room for a 45-minute talking-to after they had folded to 84 all out 15 minutes after tea. In the first innings Glamorgan only made 101 and, in between, Surrey ran up 309 with Alastair Brown smashing 124 and Martin Bicknell 57 from down the order. Brown, though, was missed on 10 and 34. Ben Hollioake had the first five-wicket analysis in Glamorgan's first innings, picking up 5 for 51 in a sustained spell of swing bowling, but Saqlain was the more predictable destroyer second time around with 5 for 18. It was Surrey's ninth victory in 12 matches and, as they began to stretch away for the title, only a broken cheekbone to wicketkeeper Jon Batty, suffered batting against Simon Jones and bad enough for him to be detained in hospital overnight, removed some of the gloss attached to having two extra days off.

The closest game in this round of matches came at the Riverside where Durham, needing 282 and beginning the final day on 153 for 4, fell short by just eight runs. Sussex had Jason Lewry to thank for their 17-point haul, the left-arm paceman picking up 5 for 86, his third five-wicket return of a summer interrupted by injury. Sussex made 231 on the opening day, Tony Cottey top-scoring with 53 and Neil Killeen taking 4 for 46 for the home side, who then slipped disappointingly to 141 all out with Lewry (4 for 36) and James Kirtley (3 for 19) doing most of the damage. Sussex, 42 for 4 at the end of the second day with all the wickets falling to Simon Brown with the new ball, recovered to 192 as Umer Rashid hit 55 and skipper Chris Adams stroked 49. David Boon helped steady Durham's victory chase with 42 but Jimmy Daley carried most of the home team's hopes into the fourth day – going on to make 80. Paul Collingwood scored 50, but it was not quite enough.

Kent fought their way to a hard-earned seven-wicket victory against Essex, with seven overs to spare, in a contest that was a good advertisement for the way four-day cricket should be played. The game also took place before the usual fine crowds and unique festival atmosphere of Canterbury Week, a mixture of ingredients to prove that championship cricket can still be pretty tasty. Kent's first-innings 541 was built initially on a solid and sensible 77 from opener Rob Key but mainly on a superb fifth-wicket stand of 207 between Andrew Symonds (132) and Mark Ealham (80). Martin McCague also had some late fun with a big-hitting 48 but by the close of the second day Essex were 174 for 3 with Ronnie Irani 61 not out. The all-rounder remained unbeaten on 127, being helped in a last-wicket stand of 69 by Ricky Anderson (44), but Ealham took 4 for 51 and Essex were still dismissed for 350. Following on, they began the final day on 38 for 3 and struggled on to make 243. Stuart Law at one stage looked like denying Kent, finishing 104 not out, but the turning point came when Irani, on 52, drove Min Patel to mid-off. Matthew Fleming could not stop the ball cleanly, and Irani called for the single. But the ball rebounded across the pitch to Julian Thompson at mid-on and the fast bowler took careful aim before coolly throwing down the bowler's stumps. After the Irani run-out McCague steamed in to take 3 for 10 in 22 deliveries and – in the end – a target of 53 proved relatively straightforward.

Nottinghamshire's first championship win since late May intensified the gloom beginning to surround Middlesex, and the eight-wicket victory was a personal triumph for Barbadian Vasbert Drakes. The fast bowler opened up on day one with a remarkable spell of 18–10–14–3 and went on to bowl 33 overs in the day. Middlesex, 257 for 7 overnight, reached 291 due to David Nash (92) and Ben Hutton (59), but Drakes ended with six wickets and Paul Franks four. Notts, with skipper Jason Gallian scoring 74 and Paul Johnson and Graeme Archer half-centuries, earned themselves a small lead before Drakes took over again. This time his figures were 5 for 49, including Justin Langer bowled for nought, and, with Franks getting 3 for 32, Middlesex were humbled at 120 all out. Usman Afzaal hit 52 to make sure there were no jitters in reaching a win target of just 105.

Matthew Bulbeck, soon to represent England Under-19s against their Australian counterparts, took match figures of 10 for 108 as Somerset swept aside a spineless Northamptonshire at Wantage Road. Bulbeck's bag included a career-best 5 for 45 as Northants tumbled to 111 in their first innings, Graham Rose also cashing in on the home batsmen's inadequacies with 3 for 20. Somerset, given a good start by Jamie Cox (69), kept Northants in the field for nine and a half hours before declaring at 422 for 9. There were contributions all the way down the order, but Keith Parsons (80) and Jason Kerr (64) prolonged the Northants suffering by adding 76 for the eighth wicket. Tony Penberthy (53) put up the only resistance of note, in a 49-run stand with Graeme Swann, before Northants were bowled out for 226 and condemned to defeat by an innings.

At Headingley, Worcestershire never recovered from being shot out for just 90 on the first morning. They were actually 14 for 5 at one stage, Paul Hutchison making an inspired comeback from injury by taking 6 for 35 in his first championship appearance of the season. The young left-arm quickie, who was forced to remodel his delivery stride after having to come home early from the previous winter's England 'A' tour of Zimbabwe with a back injury, produced an irresistible spell of swing bowling and was well supported by Gavin Hamilton (3 for 35). Yorkshire, showing up the batting conditions for what they really were, had surged to 276 for 6 by the close of the first day, with David Byas (67) and Anthony McGrath (51) chiefly responsible. Hamilton, with 94 not out, then ensured Yorkshire's lead was a match-winning one and Worcestershire, despite totalling 287 in their second innings with half-centuries from Solanki, Lampitt and Moody, only just managed to make Yorkshire bat again. A nine-wicket win was just the tonic Yorkshire were looking for ahead of their NatWest Trophy semi-final.

Rain, which washed away the final day, spoilt an intriguing finish at Bristol where Gloucestershire, at 96 for 8 in the second innings, were 223 runs ahead of a Hampshire side struggling to regain their fine early-season form. A memorably idiosyncratic unbeaten 94 by Jack Russell, following 75 by Mark Alleyne and 52 from Rob Cunliffe, guided Gloucestershire to a first-innings 380. Jason Laney then replied with a sparkling 97, supported by Will Kendall (55), but Michael Cawdron – at last making a first-class debut after five years and 27 one-day games – followed up a hard-hit 42 by taking 5 for 35 to reduce Hampshire to 253.

The weather also ruined Leicestershire's game against Warwickshire at Leicester, which began two days after the main body of matches. There was no play at all on the second day, Warwickshire eventually totalling 306 with Dominic Ostler top-scoring with 87 and James Ormond taking 5 for 108 and being awarded his county cap. On the final day

Leicestershire concentrated on knocking up some batting bonus points and, with Vince Wells unbeaten on 109 and Ormond not out 50, following Darren Maddy's 59, they eventually reached 353 for 8 just before time ran out.

ROUND 16: 17–21 AUGUST 1999

17, 18, 19 and 20 August
at Southampton
Hampshire 353 for 7 dec. (120 overs) (DA Kenway 102, GW White 92, WS Kendall 51, G Welch 4 for 120) and 46 for 0
Warwickshire 351 (108.1 overs) (DL Hemp 69, PJ Hartley 5 for 88)
Match drawn – no play was possible on the first day
Hampshire 12 pts, Warwickshire 11 pts

at Northampton
Northamptonshire 341 (118.4 overs) (AL Penberthy 92, AJ Swann 57, MJ Cawdron 5 for 54) and 84 for 3
Gloucestershire 260 (110.5 overs) (RJ Cunliffe 108, RC Russell 50, MK Davies 6 for 65)
Match drawn
Northamptonshire 11 pts, Gloucestershire 10 pts

18, 19, 20 and 21 August
at Colchester
Durham 350 for 8 dec. (104.4 overs) (JA Daley 105, DC Boon 75, MP Speight 70, RSG Anderson 4 for 70)
Essex 215 (69.5 overs) (SG Law 94, N Killeen 4 for 61)
Match drawn – no play was possible on the first two days
Essex 8 pts, Durham 12 pts

at Colwyn Bay
Nottinghamshire 228 (59.2 overs) (AG Wharf 78, U Afzaal 52, SL Watkin 6 for 75) and 302 (U Afzaal 97, P Johnson 53, RDB Croft 5 for 60)
Glamorgan 648 for 4 dec. (187 overs) (SP James 259*, MJ Powell 164, JH Kallis 101, MP Maynard 81)
Glamorgan won by an innings and 118 runs
Glamorgan 20 pts, Nottinghamshire 1 pt

at Lord's
Leicestershire 228 (68 overs) (IJ Sutcliffe 58, JM Dakin 56*, RL Johnson 4 for 50) and 225 for 7 dec. (JM Dakin 57*, MS Kasprowicz 54*, ARC Fraser 5 for 63)
Middlesex 137 (40.3 overs) (MS Kasprowicz 5 for 42) and 273 for 6 (OA Shah 108, RA Kettleborough 93)
Match drawn – no play was possible on the first day
Middlesex 8 pts, Leicestershire 9 pts

NOTTINGHAMSHIRE CCC

Home Ground:
Trent Bridge
Address:
Trent Bridge,
Nottingham NG2 6AG
Tel: 0115 982 3000
Fax: 0115 945 5730
Email: administration.notts@ecb.co.uk
Directions:
By road: Follow signs from Ring Road, towards
city centre.
Capacity: 14,500 (16,000 during Test
Matches/ODIs)
Other grounds used: Worksop
Year formed: 1841

Chairman: A Bocking
Chief Executive: Mark Arthur
First XI Manager: Clive Rice
Secretary: Brian Robson
Captain: Jason Gallian
Coaching contact: John Cope, Cricket
Development Manager
County colours: Green and gold

HONOURS

COUNTY CHAMPIONSHIP
1907, 1929, 1981, 1987
SUNDAY LEAGUE
1991
BENSON & HEDGES CUP
1989
GILLETTE CUP/NAT WEST TROPHY
1987

**CGU National Cricket League
nickname:**
NOTTINGHAMSHIRE OUTLAWS

Website:
www.trentbridge.co.uk

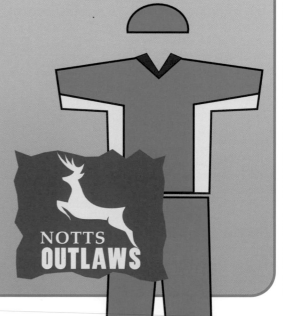

NOTTS
OUTLAWS

SOMERSET CCC

Home Ground:
Taunton
Address:
The Clerical Medical County Ground,
Taunton,
Somerset TA1 1JT
Tel: 01823 272946
Directions:
By road: M5 junction 25. Follow A358 to town
centre. Signposted from there.
Other grounds used: None
Year formed: 1875

Chairman: Richard Parsons
Chief Executive: Peter Anderson
Director of Coaching: Dermot Reeve
Captain: Jamie Cox.
Vice-captain: Marcus Trescothick
Coaching contact: A Moulding, Cricket
Development Officer 01823 272946
County colours: Black, white and maroon

HONOURS

SUNDAY LEAGUE
1979
BENSON & HEDGES CUP
1981 1982
GILLETTE CUP/NATWEST TROPHY
1979, 1983

**CGU National Cricket League
nickname:**
SOMERSET SABRES

unofficial **Website:**
www.busco.demon.co.uk

at Taunton
Kent 504 (134.1 overs) (DP Fulton 86, ET Smith 83, MA
Ealham 75, SA Marsh 73*, MV Fleming 50, ARK Pierson
4 for 131) and 279 for 6 dec. (RWT Key 125)
Somerset 361 for 6 dec. (111 overs) (RJ Turner 138*,
PCL Holloway 65)
Match drawn
Somerset 10 pts, Kent 10 pts

at Hove
Surrey 224 (69.3 overs) (MP Bicknell 67, AJ Hollioake
61, RSC Martin-Jenkins 4 for 50, RJ Kirtley 4 for 61)
and 315 for 7 dec. (DJ Bicknell 115, AD Brown 59)
Sussex 115 (45 overs) (MTE Peirce 51, Saqlain Mushtaq
7 for 19) and 217 (CJ Adams 72, IDK Salisbury 4 for 45)
Surrey won by 207 runs
No play was possible on the first day
Surrey 17 pts, Sussex 4 pts

at Kidderminster
Worcestershire 316 (104.1 overs) (VS Solanki 75,
EJ Wilson 54, GA Hick 51, PAJ DeFreitas 5 for 86)
and 245 (GA Hick 60, P Aldred 6 for 81)
Derbyshire 382 (104.5 overs) (AS Rollins 101,
A Sheriyar 4 for 142) and 183 for 4 (ID Blackwell 62*)
Derbyshire won by six wickets
Derbyshire 20 pts, Worcestershire 7 pts

19, 20 and 21 August
at Old Trafford
Yorkshire 67 (38.2 overs) (RJ Green 4 for 21) and 277
(D Byas 66, PJ Martin 5 for 67)
Lancashire 314 (71.3 overs) (A Flintoff 160) and 34 for 0
Lancashire won by ten wickets
Lancashire 19 pts, Yorkshire 4 pts

Saqlain Mushtaq provided one of the most dramatic
analyses of the summer as Surrey pushed on
remorselessly towards the PPP title with a 207-run
victory. Single-handedly, to all intents and purposes,
Saqlain dismantled the Sussex first innings at Hove
with figures of 14–8–19–7. Sussex, by the close of
the opening day, did not think they were doing
badly. First they had Surrey reeling at 55 for 6, only
to see a seventh-wicket stand of 121 between Adam
Hollioake (61) and Martin Bicknell (67) raise the
championship leaders to 224. Yet, when stumps
were drawn that evening, Sussex were moving along
quite nicely at 99 for 2 in reply. How it changed
when morning came! Soon, impotent under
Saqlain's sorcery, they had been bowled out for just
115 and Surrey, second time around, made no errors
with the bat. Darren Bicknell scored 115 and

Alastair Brown 59 as, from just 69.5 overs, Surrey
rattled up 315 for 7 declared. Chris Adams fought
hard with 72, and Michael Di Venuto made 41, but
Saqlain picked up a further 3 for 78 and his spin
partner Ian Salisbury 4 for 45 as Sussex were
dismissed for 217.

At Old Trafford there was an astonishing start to
the Roses fixture with Yorkshire being bundled out
for 67 – their lowest total against Lancashire for 31
years. Only three batsmen reached double figures as
Richard Green, Peter Martin and Glen Chapple ran

**Martin Bicknell had an outstanding season for Surrey, taking
71 wickets at only 18 runs apiece.**
David Munden/Sportsline Photographic

amok. Michael Vaughan, amid the carnage, even managed to set a record – for someone not getting out for nought – by taking 46 balls and 59 minutes to get off the mark. By the close of a truncated first day Lancashire were 91 for 3 – and on the second day they stretched their lead to match-winning proportions by reaching 314. Andrew Flintoff certainly found no terrors in the pitch, thumping a career-best 160 from 162 balls with two sixes and 25 fours. Flintoff scored 111 of his runs in 98 balls before lunch on the second day. Yorkshire at least showed a bit of fight in their second innings, with David Byas scoring 66 in a total of 277. But Martin ended up with 5 for 67 and Lancashire, after knocking off the few runs needed for a ten-wicket win, celebrated a further move up the table.

Derbyshire were another county making a significant move upwards, in their case from 13th to eighth courtesy of a six-wicket victory against Worcestershire at Kidderminster. Vikram Solanki (75) added 93 in 18 overs with Graeme Hick (51), and Elliott Wilson made 54 in a Worcestershire first innings of 316. But Phil DeFreitas took 5 for 86 and put the unfortunate Paul Pollard out of the game. Pollard, back after having his left index finger broken against Kent at Tunbridge Wells in early June, was struck in exactly the same spot by a DeFreitas delivery...with the same result. Adrian Rollins, one of the most underrated batsmen on the circuit, then lifted three sixes in an innings of 101 from 167 balls that also contained ten fours. Ian Blackwell scored 48 and DeFreitas 41, and the net result of a solid batting effort was a lead of 66. Paul Aldred then stepped in, taking 6 for 81 as Worcestershire were bowled out for 245, despite 60 from Hick. And Derbyshire rounded off a highly competent performance by knocking off the 180 they required in just 37.4 overs – Blackwell caning an unbeaten 62 from only 35 balls.

Glamorgan, enduring a wretched season, began to have some fun at last with a comprehensive innings and 118-run win against equally struggling Nottinghamshire at Colwyn Bay. The match started sensationally with Steve Watkin causing havoc with high-class new-ball bowling to leave Notts shell-shocked at 9 for 6. A brave seventh-wicket stand of 132 between Usman Afzaal (52) and Alex Wharf (78) was followed by a gutsy unbeaten 49 from Paul Franks. But a total of 228 was always going to be a long way short – and so it proved as Glamorgan gleefully piled up 648 for 4. Steve James led the destruction of the Notts attack with 259 not out – a career-best, his fifth hundred in successive matches

Stephen James of Glamorgan scored a career-best 259 not out against Nottinghamshire.
David Munden/Sportsline Photographic

against Notts and the highest post-war individual score for Glamorgan. Jacques Kallis chipped in with 101, the promising Michael Powell 164, and skipper Matthew Maynard rubbed much salt into the visitors' wounds with 81 from 58 balls. It was Glamorgan's biggest total for 60 years and although Afzaal hit 97, Notts were bowled out for 302 with Robert Croft looking back to his best form with 5 for 60.

Elsewhere, in a round of matches bedevilled by the weather, there were only draws. At Northampton there was, however, a maiden first-class century for Rob Cunliffe and some more eye-catching left-arm spin from the emerging Michael Davies as Gloucestershire were bowled out for 260 in reply to Northants' 341. Tony Penberthy's 92 and Michael Cawdron's 5 for 54 were other performances of note.

Derek Kenway hit 102 and Giles White 92 for Hampshire against Warwickshire at Southampton, while at Taunton it was the pitch as much as bad weather which had the final say. Kent ran up 504, with sizeable contributions from Ed Smith, David Fulton, Mark Ealham and Steve Marsh, but Rob Turner replied with 138 not out, completing his 1,000 runs for the season as Somerset reached 361 for 6 declared. On a dull final day Rob Key hit 125 as the match meandered to a close.

Two days were washed out at Colchester, and when the match finally began on day three Jimmy Daley moved to a third first-class hundred in a Durham total of 318 for 6 declared. Stuart Law hit 94 in an Essex reply of 215, Neil Killeen taking 4 for 61. But then the time ran out.

Leicestershire had the best of the drawn encounter with Middlesex at Southgate, although the home side made a brave stab at victory on the final day. Owais Shah hit 108 and Richard Kettleborough 70 not out. Earlier in the game both Mike Kasprowicz and Angus Fraser returned five-wicket hauls for the first time in the season. Kasprowicz, and Jon Dakin, also impressed with the bat.

ROUND 17: 24–27 AUGUST 1999

24, 25 and 26 August
at Canterbury
Northamptonshire 69 (23.1 overs) (JBD Thompson 6 for 27) and 86 (MA Ealham 6 for 35)
Kent 167 (53.2 overs) (SC Willis 67, DE Malcolm 5 for 65, JP Taylor 4 for 55)
Kent won by an innings and 12 runs
Kent 16 pts, Northamptonshire 4 pts
No play was possible on the first day

at Trent Bridge
Nottinghamshire 184 (44.4 overs) (JER Gallian 50, GM Hamilton 5 for 30, CE White 4 for 44) and 144 (C White 4 for 32)
Yorkshire 185 (66.1 overs) (RJ Blakey 60, PJ Franks 5 for 52) and 144 for 7
Yorkshire won by three wickets
Yorkshire 16 pts, Nottinghamshire 4 pts

A hamstring injury curtailed Gavin Hamilton's season with Yorkshire, but he was selected to tour South Africa with England.
David Munden/Sportsline Photographic

SURREY CCC

Home Ground:
The Foster's Oval
Address:
The Foster's Oval, Kennington,
London SE11 5SS
Tel: 0171 582 6660
Directions:
By rail: Vauxhall, SouthWest Lines, five
minutes walk away.
By underground: Northern Line, Oval Tube 100 yds
away; Victoria Line, Vauxhall is five minutes away.
By road: Situated on A202 near junction of A24
and A3 south of Vauxhall Bridge.
By bus: 36 and 185 from Victoria
Capacity: 16,500
Other grounds used: Guildford Cricket Club, Woodbridge
Road, Guildford.
Year formed: 1845

Chairman: Michael Soper
Chief Executive: Paul Sheldon
Director/Coach of Cricket:
Other posts: Cricket Manager: Keith Medleycott; 2nd XI
Coach: Alan Butcher.
Captain: Adam Hollioake
Vice-captain: Mark Butcher
Coaching contact: Ken Barrington Centre 0171 582
6660; Cricket Development, Nescafe Courses 0171
582 6660; Surrey County Cricket Centre, Peter Brett
01483 598880.
County colours: Brown & silver

Website:
www.surreyccc.co.uk

HONOURS

COUNTY CHAMPIONSHIP
1890, 1891, 1892, 1894, 1895,
1899, 1914, 1952–1958, 1971, 1999
SUNDAY LEAGUE
1996
BENSON & HEDGES CUP
1974, 1997
GILLETTE CUP/NATWEST TROPHY
1982

CGU National Cricket League
nickname:
SURREY LIONS

24, 25, 26 and 27 August
at Derby
Surrey 350 for 9 dec. (101.3 overs) (IJ Ward 103,
GP Thorpe 89) and 1 for 1
Derbyshire 154 (57.2 overs) and (following on) 196
(DG Cork 53, AS Rollins 53, Saqlain Mushtaq 5 for 59,
MP Bicknell 4 for 46)
Surrey won by nine wickets
Surrey 20 pts, Derbyshire 4 pts

at Chester-le-Street
Middlesex 222 (81.5 overs) (MR Ramprakash 53, OA
Shah 52, SJ Harmison 4 for 51) and 180 (PN Weekes
56, N Killeen 5 for 50, SJ Harmison 4 for 49)
Durham 290 (112.3 overs) (JJB Lewis 98, RL Johnson 4
for 102) and 113 for 4
Durham won by six wickets
Durham 18 pts, Middlesex 5 pts

at Chelmsford
Somerset 246 (72.3 overs) (PCL Holloway 60,
DJ Thompson 4 for 46) and 256 for 9 (J Cox 54,
PCL Holloway 52, RSG Anderson 4 for 66)
Essex 544 (139.4 overs) (SG Law 263, DDJ Robinson
112, AP Grayson 50, PS Jones 4 for 126)
Match drawn
Essex 12 pts, Somerset 6 pts

at Cardiff
Glamorgan 300 for 8 dec. (118 overs) (JH Kallis 94,
MP Maynard 72, RDB Croft 57*, A Richardson 4 for 75)
Warwickshire 341 (102.4 overs) (MJ Powell 136,
DL Hemp 73, NV Knight 64, RDB Croft 5 for 89)
Match drawn
Glamorgan 11 pts, Warwickshire 10 pts
No play was possible on the first day

at Southampton
Sussex 375 (105.3 overs) (MJ Di Venuto 93, JJ Bates
57, PA Cottey 54, CJ Adams 53, SD Udal 4 for 102)
Hampshire 76 (30.1 overs) (RJ Kirtley 7 for 21) and
(following on) 570 for 6 dec. (WS Kendall 201,
AN Aymes 111*, GW White 77, RA Smith 66)
Match drawn
Hampshire 8 pts, Sussex 12 pts

at Leicester
Leicestershire 214 (62.4 overs) (MS Kasprowicz 61,
MJ Cawdron 5 for 54) and 347 for 7 dec. (Aftab Habib
141, JM Dakin 124)
Gloucestershire 166 (57.4 overs) and 170
(THC Hancock 68, J Ormond 4 for 34, MS Kasprowicz
4 for 61)

Leicestershire won by 225 runs
Leicestershire 17 pts, Gloucestershire 4 pts

at Worcester
Worcestershire 227 (72.3 overs) (SJ Rhodes 74,
PJ Martin 5 for 52) and 88 for 2 dec.
Lancashire 217 (55 overs) (A Sheriyar 4 for 86)
Match drawn
Worcestershire 9 pts, Lancashire 9 pts
No play was possible on the first and second days

Surrey were left a mere eight points away from
the PPP championship title, with three rounds of
fixtures in hand, when they overwhelmed
Derbyshire by nine wickets at Derby – despite
some weather interruption.

A first-innings 350 was built on opener Ian Ward's
maiden first-class hundred, in his 51st innings, but
Graham Thorpe (89) and Alastair Brown provided
the scintillating stroke-play. Derbyshire, bowled out
for 154, were 28 for 1 by the close of the third day
after being asked to follow on. Saqlain Mushtaq (5
for 59) and Martin Bicknell (4 for 46) then wrapped
the home side's second innings for 196, although
Adrian Rollins and Dominic Cork both fought
hard with 53s. James Pyemont, the 25th player
used by Derbyshire in a summer beset by injuries,
became the first to record a king pair on his debut
for the county.

Durham's players were also celebrating at the
Riverside, a six-wicket win against Middlesex very
much keeping alive their ambition to play in the first
division of the championship in the year 2000. A
fifth win of the season, their most since joining the
championship in 1992, was based on some incisive
seam and swing bowling from Steve Harmison (8 for
90 in the match), Simon Brown and Neil Killeen.
Middlesex, dismissed for 222 first time around, with
only Mark Ramprakash and Owais Shah topping
fifty, then slumped to 180 in their second innings
with Killeen finishing with 5 for 50. In between,
Durham totalled 290, with Jon Lewis grinding out
a determined 98, and a modest victory target was
reached with few alarms.

One of the most exciting finishes of the week
came at Chelmsford...and left no winner. Essex,
inspired by the continued excellence of Stuart Law,
came within one wicket of beating Somerset – but
the West Country county hung on grimly in the final
session to provide a fine advertisement for the
benefit of four draw points. Fine captaincy by
Nasser Hussain was a feature of the first day, in
which Somerset were bowled out for 246 with David

Thompson taking 4 for 46. By the close of day two Law was 135 not out and, on the third day, Law motored on in the company of Darren Robinson to give Essex a huge lead of 298. Law's 263 was the sixth-highest individual score made for the county, and his eighth three-figure innings of the championship season – leaving him just one ton short of equalling the Essex record. Somerset were 31 for 1 overnight, but on the final day battled for survival to provide a fascinating spectacle. Ricky Anderson looked to have swung the match Essex's way with a determined afternoon spell, and he finished with 4 for 66, but Andrew Caddick led the rearguard action by batting 95 minutes for 10 not out. In the end Caddick and Adrian Pierson, the number eleven, held out for the last 10.2 overs.

Tough cricket was conspicuous by its absence, however, at Canterbury as a feeble Northamptonshire batting effort gifted victory to Kent. Rain ruled out play on the first day but, on the second morning, there was drama aplenty as Northants plunged to 69 all out. Batsman after batsman seemed to have little idea against the seam and swing of Julian Thompson, who finished with 6 for 27 after a truly remarkable spell of 6 for 2 in 23 balls. Kent, in turn, found themselves on 41 for 7 as Devon Malcolm (4 for 22) and Paul Taylor (3 for 29) led a fightback but wicketkeeper Simon Willis then put supposedly front-line batsmen to shame with a forthright 67. Thompson also made 22 not out from number eleven, a significant innings in the context of the match, and Kent rallied to 167. Mark Ealham, who had taken 3 for 18 in the Northants first innings, then took 6 for 35 as the visitors crumbled once more to 86 all out. It was batting to be ashamed of, and pitch inspector Peter Eaton, representing the England and Wales Cricket Board, quite rightly found nothing wrong with the surface.

Leicestershire, by now resigned to seeing their championship title pass to Surrey, nevertheless roused themselves to the tune of seeing off Gloucestershire by 225 runs at Grace Road. The visitors, desperate to escape from the lower regions of the table, had the better of the opening day with Michael Cawdron taking 5 for 54, his third five-wicket haul in his third first-class match. But Leicestershire, whose 214 owed much to tail-ender Mike Kasprowicz's 61, hit back by dismissing Gloucestershire for 166. Hundreds by Aftab Habib (141) and Jon Dakin (124) then guided Leicestershire to a second-innings 347 for 7 declared and, with James Ormond and Kasprowicz sharing eight wickets, Gloucestershire were sent packing to

170 all out. Habib's century, by the way, was the first time he had passed fifty since being dropped by England a month earlier.

Yorkshire showed true grit on the way to a three-wicket victory against Nottinghamshire at Trent Bridge. On a green surface the match was always going to be a low-scoring affair and Notts' 184, based on Jason Gallian's 50, looked a dominant total when Yorkshire slid to 39 for 5 in reply. But Craig White and Gavin Hamilton, who earlier had taken 4 for 44 and 5 for 30 respectively, aided a recovery led by Richard Blakey (60) and despite Paul Franks's 5 for 52 Yorkshire eventually reached 185. White's 4 for 32 then undermined the Notts second innings, which raised only 144, but Yorkshire were reeling again at 43 for 6 before staging another fightback. Hamilton made a pugnacious 43 not out, once more revealing his fine temperament, and Chris Silverwood finished 25 not out with some fearless big-hitting as the finishing line approached. Notts, meanwhile, escaped a points penalty for a pitch on which 17 wickets fell on the first day – but an ECB panel described the surface as 'poor' and the club were warned that points would indeed be docked if a pitch was reported again during the next 12 months.

Hampshire showed great resolve at Southampton to achieve a draw with neighbours and rivals Sussex, having been bundled out for just 76 in their first innings by James Kirtley (7 for 21). That meant a follow-on, Sussex having earlier totalled 375 with Michael Di Venuto top-scoring with 93, but Hampshire's batsmen were more than equal to the task. Will Kendall made 201, being awarded his county cap by Robin Smith as he walked off the field, and Adrian Aymes ended 111 not out. Smith had himself scored 66, and Giles White made 77 as Hampshire ran up 570 for 6 declared.

Rain washed away the first two days at Worcester, condemning Worcestershire and Lancashire to a draw, while the same result occurred at Cardiff, where play began only at 4.40pm on the second day and both Glamorgan and Warwickshire settled for the collection of bonus points and the four apiece available for the draw. Peter Martin had figures of 5 for 52 in Worcestershire's 227 while, in a Lancashire reply of 217, the country's leading wicket-taker Alamgir Sheriyar had the extraordinary figures of 18–6–86–4. Jacques Kallis (94), Matthew Maynard (72) and Robert Croft (57 not out) took Glamorgan to 300 for 8 declared, and Croft's return to form with the ball earned him 5 for 89 as Warwickshire replied with 341, in which Michael Powell hit 136.

SUSSEX CCC

Home Ground:
Hove
Address:
County Ground, Eaton Road, Hove,
East Sussex BN3 3AN
Tel: 01273 827100
Fax: 01273 771549
Email: Fran@sccc.demon.co.uk
Directions:
By rail: Hove station is a ten-minute walk.
By road: Follow AA signs. Street parking at no cost.
Capacity: 5,500
Other grounds used: Eastbourne, Horsham, Arundel
Year formed: 1839

Chairman: Don Trangmar
Chief Executive: Tony Pigott
General Manager: David Gilbert
Other posts: Vice-chairman: John Snow;
Cricket Manager/Coach: Peter Moores;
Media Relations Officer: Francesca Watson
Captain: Chris Adams
Vice-captain: Tony Cottey
Coaching contact: For private and group coaching contact
Cricket Department: 01273 735143.
County colours: Dark blue, light blue gold

HONOURS

SUNDAY LEAGUE
1982
GILLETTE CUP/NATWEST TROPHY
1963, 1964, 1978, 1986

CGU National Cricket League nickname:
SUSSEX SHARKS

Website:
www.sccc.demon.co.uk

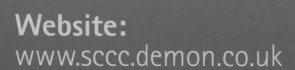

WARWICKSHIRE CCC

Home Ground:
Edgbaston
Address:
County Ground,
Edgbaston,
Birmingham, B5 7QU
Tel: 0121 446 4422
Directions:
By rail: New Street station, Birmingham
By road: M6 to A38M, to city centre, then follow
signs to County Ground.
Capacity: 20,000
Other grounds used: None
Year formed: 1882

Chairman: MJK Smith
Chief Executive: Dennis Amiss
Director of Cricket: Phil Neale
Other posts: Warwickshire Cricket Board's
Director of Cricket: Richard Cox; Head
Groundsman: Steve Rouse
Captain: Neil Smith
Vice-captain: Nick Knight

HONOURS

COUNTY CHAMPIONSHIP
1911, 1951, 1972, 1994, 1995
SUNDAY LEAGUE
1980, 1994, 1997
BENSON & HEDGES CUP
1994
GILLETTE CUP/NATWEST TROPHY
1989, 1993, 1995

**CGU National Cricket League
nickname:**
WARWICKSHIRE BEARS

The Bears

Website:
www.warwickccc.org.uk

Round 18: 31 August–4 September 1999

31 August, 1 and 2 September
at Eastbourne
Essex 179 (N Hussain 61, RSC Martin-Jenkins 4 for 58)
and 155 (RJ Kirtley 6 for 37)
Sussex 271 (90.4 overs) (RR Montgomerie 83,
PA Cottey 72) and 64 for 2
Sussex won by eight wickets
Sussex 18 pts, Essex 4 pts

1 and 2 September
at The Oval
Nottinghamshire 115 (44.3 overs) and 233
(U Afzaal 104, IDK Salisbury 4 for 66, Saqlain Mushtaq
4 for 100)
Surrey 199 (58.5 overs) (VC Drakes 4 for 53) and 153
for 0 (MA Butcher 81*, IJ Ward 55*)
Surrey won by ten wickets
Surrey 16 pts, Nottinghamshire 4 pts

1, 2 and 3 September
at Old Trafford
Durham 226 (87.3 overs) (JA Daley 66,
JJB Lewis 61, CP Schofield 5 for 66) and 197
(NJ Speak 66)
Lancashire 437 (142 overs) (JP Crawley 158, GD Lloyd
86, NC Phillips 4 for 171)
Lancashire won by an innings and 14 runs
Lancashire 20 pts, Durham 4 pts

at Leicester
Leicestershire 343 (104.4 overs) (PA Nixon 72,
VJ Wells 68, TM Smith 5 for 87) and 197
(DI Stevens 60, PA Nixon 51, TM Smith
5 for 63)
Derbyshire 308 (82 overs) (PAJ DeFreitas 105,
KM Krikken 60, MS Kasprowicz 4 for 70) and
235 for 6 (AS Rollins 113)
Derbyshire won by four wickets
Derbyshire 19 pts, Leicestershire 7 pts

1, 2, 3 and 4 September
at Northampton
Hampshire 357 (124 overs) (WS Kendall 98,
RA Smith 94, GW White 55) and 167
(DA Kenway 52, MK Davies 6 for 49, GP Swann
4 for 46)
Northamptonshire 342 (116.3 overs) (RJ Warren 110,
RJ Bailey 92, D Ripley 67, PJ Hartley 4 for 59) and 183
for 6 (AJ Swann 57, SD Udal 4 for 80)
Northamptonshire won by four wickets
Northamptonshire 18 pts, Hampshire 7 pts

at Scarborough
Kent 302 (96.2 overs) (MS Ealham 59, MJ McCague
53, CEW Silverwood 5 for 67) and 226 (ET Smith 55,
CEW Silverwood 4 for 57)
Yorkshire 389 (130.1 overs) (MP Vaughan 153,
RJ Harden 64, CEW Silverwood 53*, DW Headley
4 for 105) and 141 for 5 (MP Vaughan 50)
Yorkshire won by five wickets
Yorkshire 20 pts, Kent 6 pts

2, 3 and 4 September
at Taunton
Somerset 203 (56.3 overs) (GD Rose 50,
OT Parkin 4 for 38, SD Thomas 4 for 40) and 280
(ME Trescothick 167)
Glamorgan 113 (42.1 overs) (GD Rose 4 for 14) and
151 (AR Caddick 6 for 47, GD Rose 4 for 56)
Somerset won by 219 runs
Somerset 17 pts, Glamorgan 4 pts

at Edgbaston
Gloucestershire 132 (41.5 overs) (JN Snape 57,
A Richardson 8 for 51) and 206
Warwickshire 167 (68.4 overs) (AM Smith 5 for 41)
and 174 for 9 (DP Ostler 76)
Warwickshire won by one wicket
Warwickshire 16 pts, Gloucestershire 4 pts

Adam Hollioake, born just one week before Surrey
last won the county title, in 1971, lifted the PPP
trophy with pride at The Oval following a two-day
trouncing of Nottinghamshire.

Surrey, in fact, had gone into the game needing
just eight points to clinch the championship –
with two rounds of games still to go – but their
12th victory in 15 matches made bonus point
calculations irrelevant.

Hollioake, the Surrey captain, praised the true
squad effort that had earned his county the most
coveted domestic honour. Six players, including
himself, had missed large chunks of the season due
to international commitments – but Surrey had
never faltered after moving to the top of the table at
the beginning of June. 'It's fantastic, the best
moment of my career,' said Hollioake, 'when you
play with guys day in and day out and then win the
championship it is the best feeling'.

Surrey certainly made short work of lowly Notts,
bowling them out for just 115 on the opening day,
spinners Saqlain Mushtaq and Ian Salisbury sharing
six wickets and Mark Patterson, a 25-year-old
Belfast-born fast bowler who has represented
Ireland in the ICC Trophy, picking up 3 for 25.

Eighteen wickets fell on the first day, with Surrey reaching the close at 199 for 8 thanks largely to a stand of 78 between Alec Stewart (49) and Alastair Brown (34). But the pitch was blameless, according to umpires Mervyn Kitchen and John Steele, and Notts certainly made a better fist of their second innings after quickly finishing off the Surrey first innings on the second morning.

Usman Afzaal made 104, and Paul Johnson 41, as Saqlain, ironically, struggled to find any sort of rhythm. Afzaal hit 15 boundaries, from 172 balls, but suddenly the Surrey spin twins began to get going. Saqlain ended up with 4 for 100 and Salisbury 4 for 66 and Surrey needed 150 inside 23 overs to wrap up the title on 2 September. Mark Butcher and Ian Ward, the openers, batted as if already high in celebration – Butcher smashing 81 not out from 72 balls and Ward an unbeaten 55 from 67 balls.

It was exhilarating stuff and, up in the committee room, Surrey president Micky Stewart – captain in the 1971 season – looked down with pride as his son Alec and the rest of the 1999 squad took their bows amid the champagne spray.

Elsewhere, Lancashire's late season surge up the PPP table continued as they swamped Durham by an innings and 14 runs – a sixth win in seven matches taking them into third place and ensuring first division championship cricket in the year 2000.

Durham actually started the match, at Old Trafford, in fine style with openers Jimmy Daley (66) and Jon Lewis (61) putting on 144 for the first wicket. But then it all went wrong, with 20-year-old leg-spinner Chris Schofield taking five wicket in the space of 43 balls to transform his figures from 0 for 58 to 5 for 66. Durham, in all, lost their last eight wickets in 19 overs for 33 runs and their 226 was totally inadequate. Lancashire then proved just how inadequate by building a total of 437 over the next four sessions, John Crawley capitalising on a Durham attack weakened by injury to score 158. Graham Lloyd thrashed 86 off 111 balls, in his uncomplicated way, and on the second day Durham even had their 46-year-old batting coach Graham Gooch acting as a substitute fielder after Lewis had been hit on the head at silly point. Nick Speak made 66 against his old county in Durham's second innings but Schofield and Peter Martin each took three wickets as the visitors slid to 197.

Leicestershire, the fallen champions, had their hopes of taking runners-up spot severely dented by Derbyshire, who continued to confound the experts with a magnificent four-wicket win at Leicester that took them into the top half of the PPP table. At first Leicestershire seemed to be setting solid foundations themselves, reaching 343 in their first innings after wobbling at 111 for 4. Vince Wells (68) and Paul Nixon (72) provided the middle-order mixture of cussedness and know-how, although Trevor Smith, a 22-year-old seamer from Derby, fully deserved his return of 5 for 87. Derbyshire then slumped to 102 for 6 but the innings was eventually transformed by the power-hitting of Phil DeFreitas. The former England fast bowler, who has largely underachieved as a batsman both at county and international level, came in at 141 for 7 and produced an exhilarating knock of 105, his seventh first-class hundred. With Karl Krikken supporting gamely

Surrey win the trophy for the first time in 28 years. Alec Stewart celebrates in style.
David Munden/Sportsline Photographic

WORCESTERSHIRE CCC

Home Ground:
Worcester
Address:
New Road, Worcester WR2 4QQ
Tel: 01905 748474
Fax: 01905 748005
Directions:
By rail: Worcester Foregate Street Station, half a mile from ground. Worcester Shrub Hill Station, one mile from ground.
By road: From the north, M5 junction 6 then follow signposted route to Worcester and city centre, then take A44 for New Road
By bus: Midland Red West Nos 23-6.
Capacity: 4,500
Other grounds used: Kidderminster CC, Chester Road North, Kidderminster
Year formed: 1865

Chairman: John Elliott
Secretary: The Reverend Michael Vockins OBE
Senior Coach: Bill Athey
Other posts:
Coach: Damian D'Oliveira; Assistant Secretary: Mark Tagg
Captain: Tom Moody
Vice-captain: Graeme Hick
Coaching contact: Allan Scrafton, Cricket Development Admin Officer 01905 429147
County colours: Green, black and white

HONOURS

COUNTY CHAMPIONSHIP
1964, 1965, 1974, 1988, 1989
SUNDAY LEAGUE
1971, 1987, 1988, 1991
BENSON & HEDGES CUP
1991
GILLETTE CUP/NATWEST TROPHY
1994

CGU National Cricket League nickname:
WORCESTERSHIRE ROYALS

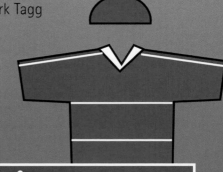

Website:
www.wccc.co.uk

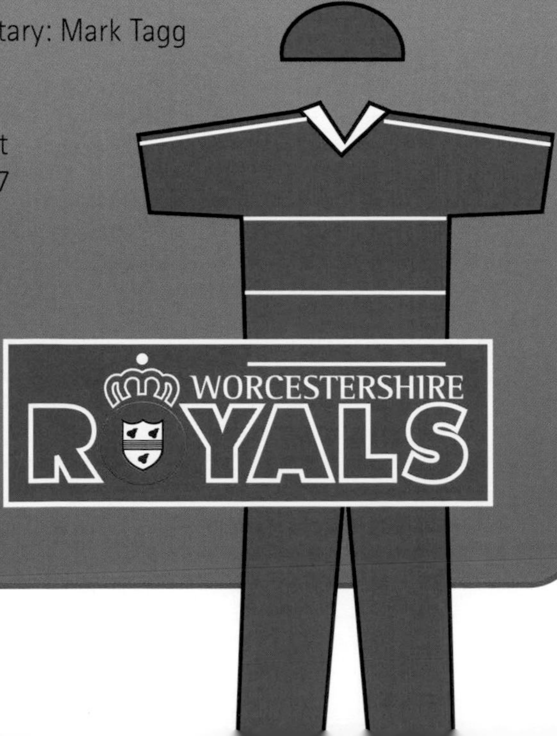

Adam Hollioake parades the trophy for Surrey. 'A monkey could have captained this team!' he said.
David Munden/Sportsline Photographic

with 60, Derbyshire reached 308 – and the fightback continued with Smith again to the fore. Darren Stevens made 60 and Nixon 51, but Smith earned himself the first ten-wicket match haul of his two-year career with a fine 5 for 63. A 123-run opening stand between Adrian Rollins and Steve Stubbings then gave Derbyshire the perfect launchpad towards a victory target of 233 and Rollins went on to score a match-winning 113.

Tony Cottey, Nick Wilton and the rest of the Sussex team had the last laugh at Eastbourne as England and Essex captain Nasser Hussain arguably tried to play the wrong sort of tough cricket in a match that did not last beyond lunch on the third day. Hussain made 61, the only score of note, as Essex were dismissed for 179 on the first day – losing their last five wickets for three runs in 21 balls as Robin Martin-Jenkins picked up 4 for 58. By the close Sussex were 122 for 3 and in charge, but before play on the second morning wicketkeeper Wilton suffered a dislocated shoulder in a warm-up accident. Sussex asked if, when they came to field again, a specialist substitute 'keeper could be drafted in – but Hussain, as technically is his right, refused. Sussex totalled 271, in which Richard Montgomerie made 83 and Cottey 72, and then Cottey took the wicketkeeper's gloves for the Essex second innings. Paul Prichard and Hussain both got ducks, Cottey snapped up two catches late in the day, and by stumps Essex were in some trouble at 121 for 5. Opener Paul Grayson, 42 not out, fell immediately the next morning and, with James Kirtley bowling straight and fast for 6 for 37, Essex were shot out for 155. Sussex, left with a modest target, won a satisfying victory by eight wickets.

Young English cricketers were playing decisive roles in all the games in this championship round, which was heartening news as a dismal summer for the England national team drew near its end. Nowhere was this more evident than at Northampton where two youthful spinners – Graeme Swann and Michael Davies – combined to earn Northants a four-wicket win over Hampshire. Swann and Davies, the classical English double act of off-breaks and slow left-arm, initially checked the Hampshire first innings to 357 after Will Kendall (98) and Robin Smith (94) had put on 145 and threatened to post a huge total. Then, after Northants had replied with 342, based on Rob Bailey's 92 and a superb seventh-wicket stand between Russell Warren (110) and David Ripley (67), Hampshire were blown away by the young spin twins. From 95 for 0 (Derek Kenway 52 and Jason Laney 43) Hampshire collapsed to 167 all out against the turning ball. The last five wickets fell for seven runs in 24 balls, Davies finishing with 6 for 49 and Swann 4 for 46. Alec Swann then added 57 to his first innings 44 before his younger brother Graeme completed what he had helped to start by hitting a robust 26 not out to join Warren (39 not out) in the decisive stand. Curiously, there were no less than 14 ducks in the match – out of 36 dismissals. Some sort of record?

A heart-warming, old-fashioned sort of championship match was fought out between Yorkshire and Kent in the splendid surroundings of Scarborough. Michael Vaughan and Chris Silverwood, one chosen for England's winter tour earlier in the week and the other miffed at his exclusion, were the dominant personalities as Yorkshire ran out five-wicket victors late on the final day. Four successive days of glorious weather merely served to enhance the product – which was a slap in the face for those critics decrying the decline of county cricket. Crowds totalling more than 12,000 for the match also told a story at odds with much of the opinion being expressed in the popular media. On the first day Kent recovered well from 92 for 5, the sturdy figure of Mark Ealham (59) leading the way and Martin McCague (53), Min Patel (49) and Steve Marsh (46) all playing their part. Silverwood, swinging the ball consistently away at pace, took 5 for 67. Yorkshire, resuming on 10 for 1, ground their way to 290 for 7 on the second day – opener Vaughan a picture of concentration in a chanceless 133 not out. Dean Headley took four wickets but, on the third morning, Vaughan went on to 153 and Silverwood won his side a healthy advantage with a hard-hit 53 not out. As Yorkshire officials predicted a £50,000 profit for the festival, Kent declined to 148 for 6 by the close – Ed Smith offering a dedicated 55 but slow left-arm Ian Fisher taking 2 for 11 from 13 overs to help to exert a stranglehold. On the final day Kent struggled to 226, Julian Thompson hitting 44 and Marsh 31 but Silverwood finishing with 4-57. Vaughan then struck 50 from just 58 balls but the surge to victory slowed at 93 for 5 and Kent sniffed a late chance. Young Gary Fellows, however, seized the moment with a confident unbeaten 34 and Yorkshire pushed Kent down to fifth while moving themselves up into third place.

At Taunton Marcus Trescothick, the 23-year-old biffer from Bath, made 167 out of Somerset's second-innings 280 to take the match out of Glamorgan's reach on a pitch which no other batsman could master. The quality of seam bowling was high, though, especially from Andy Caddick who took 6 for 47 to wrap up a 219-run victory. Glamorgan, dismissed for 113 on an opening day in which Somerset were themselves bowled out for 203, could make only 151 second time around with Michael Powell's 40 their top score in the match. Graham Rose was Somerset's other hero. Back at last from injury problems that threatened to wreck his whole season, the faithful 35-year-old all-rounder hit 50 in Somerset's first innings and then returned analyses of 4 for 14 and 4 for 56.

Alan Richardson, in only his fourth championship appearance, took 8 for 51 to shock Gloucestershire at Edgbaston and also claim the best figures of the season. The match ultimately produced a gripping finish, Warwickshire scraping home by one wicket, with number 11 Richardson at the crease, but the first day belonged totally to the 24-year-old from Staffordshire. Hitting the seam regularly, and getting bounce from his height, Richardson claimed four scalps in his 11-over new-ball spell and then returned after lunch to take four more in the space of 17 balls. Gloucestershire, initially rallying from 33 for 5 through an 89-run partnership between Ian Harvey (33) and Jeremy Snape (57), were bowled out for 132 and Richardson said he was 'in dreamland'. He also had the modesty, too, to admit he thought he had bowled better two weeks earlier when picking up only one hard-earned wicket against Hampshire! Gloucestershire, however, were still very much in the game as they dismissed Warwickshire for 167 in reply, Nick Knight top-scoring with 39 and Mike Smith claiming 5 for 41. Matt Windows, Mark Alleyne, Harvey and Martyn Ball then all got past 30 but failed to reach 40 as Tim Munton and Ashley Giles chipped away. Gloucestershire's eventual 206 left Warwickshire to score 172 and it was a desperately close-run thing. Dominic Ostler's 76 finally proved crucial but Alleyne's decision to keep off-spinner Ball in the attack backfired after Warwickshire's ninth wicket had fallen with six more runs needed. Richardson played and missed at the one ball he was to face, and Giles, after hitting a two, then slog-swept Ball for six to clinch victory in some style. Gloucestershire's defeat meant they were the first county to be condemned to second division championship cricket next season.

ROUND 19: 8–12 SEPTEMBER 1999

8, 9 and 10 September
at Bristol
Gloucestershire 150 (48.1 overs) (P Aldred 6 for 34) and 212 (THC Hancock 71, MGN Windows 55, TM Smith 5 for 69, PAJ DeFreitas 4 for 35)
Derbyshire 203 (76.3 overs) (RMS Weston 52, BW Gannon 5 for 42) and 161 for 4 (AS Rollins 95)
Derbyshire won by six wickets
Derbyshire 17 pts, Gloucestershire 4 pts

at Northampton
Northamptonshire 509 (133.4 overs) (DJG Sales 205, D Ripley 105)
Leicestershire 311 (112.4 overs) (Aftab Habib 51, GP Swann 5 for 85, MK Davies 4 for 87) and (following on) 143 (GP Swann 6 for 41)
Northamptonshire won by an innings and 55 runs
Northamptonshire 20 pts, Leicestershire 6 pts

at Headingley
Glamorgan 498 (140.2 overs) (MP Maynard 186, MJ Powell 70, MA Wallace 64*)
Yorkshire 140 (39.2 overs) (SL Watkin 4 for 35) and (following on) 306 (RJ Blakey 123, OT Parkin 4 for 54)
Glamorgan won by an innings and 52 runs
Glamorgan 20 pts, Yorkshire 3 pts

8, 9, 10 and 11 September
at Chester-le-Street
Durham 255 (100.4 overs) (JJB Lewis 76, DC Boon 54, TA Munton 7 for 91) and 235 (DC Boon 72, DR Brown 7 for 66)
Warwickshire 285 (100.3 overs) (MJ Powell 117, DL Hemp 51, J Wood 5 for 75, N Killeen 4 for 62) and 115 (N Killeen 4 for 57)
Durham won by 90 runs
Durham 18 pts, Warwickshire 6 pts

at Chelmsford
Worcestershire 308 (97.2 overs) (GA Hick 101, RC Irani 4 for 51, RSG Anderson 4 for 74) and 365 for 9 dec. (GA Hick 150, DN Catterall 60)
Essex 303 (102.1 overs) (RC Irani 103, N Hussain 71, A Sheriyar 4 for 70) and 265 for 4 (AP Grayson 105, N Hussain 65)
Match drawn
Essex 11 pts, Worcestershire 11 pts

David Hemp, Warwickshire's stylish left–hander, hit two first class centuries in 1999.

David Munden/Sportsline Photographic

at Southampton
Somerset 493 for 6 dec. (165 overs) (J Cox 216, PD Bowler 103*, PCL Holloway 58) and 255 for 2 dec. (J Cox 129*, ME Trescothick 86)
Hampshire 413 (150.2 overs) (AN Aymes 115*, JS Laney 63, DA Kenway 61, MPL Bulbeck 4 for 58)
Match drawn
Hampshire 7 pts, Somerset 11 pts

at Old Trafford
Kent 410 (117.5 overs) (A Symonds 99, AP Wells 86, DW Headley 72, MV Fleming 55, CP Schofield 4 for 103) and 159 (G Yates 6 for 64)
Lancashire 312 (88.2 overs) (GD Lloyd 81, NH Fairbrother 63, MM Patel 8 for 115) and 258 for 6 (GD Lloyd 84, JP Crawley 57, MM Patel 4 for 120)
Lancashire won by four wickets
Lancashire 19 pts, Kent 8 pts

YORKSHIRE CCC

Home Ground:
Headingley
Address:
Headingley Cricket Ground,
Leeds LS6 3BU
Tel: 0113 278 7394
Fax: 0113 278 4099
Email: cricket@yorkshireccc.org.uk
Other grounds used: Scarborough
Year formed: 1863

Chairman: Keith Moss
Chief Executive: Chris Hassell
Cricket Development Manager: Steve Oldham
Other posts:
President: Sir Lawrence Byford;
Director of Coaching: Martyn Moxon;
Club Coach: Doug Padgett;
Groundsman: Andy Fogarty
Captain: David Byas
Coaching contact: Academy Coach: Arnie
Sidebottom; Cricket Development Officer: MK Bore
County colours: Oxford blue, Cambridge blue and gold

HONOURS

COUNTY CHAMPIONSHIP
1893, 1896, 1898, 1900, 1901,
1902, 1905, 1908, 1912, 1919,
1922, 1923, 1924, 1925, 1931,
1963, 1966, 1967, 1968
BENSON & HEDGES CUP
1987
SUNDAY LEAGUE
1983
GILLETTE CUP/NATWEST TROPHY
1965, 1969

**CGU National Cricket League
nickname:**
YORKSHIRE PHOENIX

Website:
www.yorkshireccc.org.uk

Glamorgan's Matthew Maynard laid the foundations of an innings rout of Yorkshire by scoring 186.
David Munden/Sportsline Photographic

9, 10 and 11 September
at Hove
Sussex 275 (103.4 overs) (RR Montgomerie 59, VC Drakes 4 for 68) and 315 (MTE Peirce 95, MJ Di Venuto 90)
Nottinghamshire 199 (71.5 overs) and 132 (JD Lewry 4 for 23)
Sussex won by 259 runs
Sussex 18 pts, Nottinghamshire 4 pts

9, 10, 11 and 12 September
at Lord's
Surrey 585 (150.2 overs) (AD Brown 265, AJ Hollioake 116)
Middlesex 284 (107.2 overs) (AJ Strauss 98) and (following on) 499 for 5 dec. (MR Ramprakash 209*, RA Kettleborough 69, DC Nash 56*, BL Hutton 50)
Match drawn
Middlesex 7 pts, Surrey 11 pts

Lancashire powered into second place in the PPP table by beating Kent, at Old Trafford, in a match in which sunshine stopped play late on the third afternoon.

Blinding reflections from the corrugated metal roof of the new £500,000 media centre, at the Stretford End, drove the players off at 4.45pm – and they did not return! With the sun still blazing from the sky Jim Cumbes, the Lancashire chief executive, said: 'People always complain about the Manchester weather, but this is a new one!'

Fortunately, this bizarre episode did not affect the outcome of an intriguing contest – and a stirring fightback by Lancashire. A dry, bare surface and the inclusion of three spinners by Lancashire told its own story before the start but Kent, after winning the toss, took the game to the home side in no uncertain terms. Andrew Symonds, with 99, and Alan Wells (86) both reacted to the loss of two early wickets by attacking, and this theme of controlled aggression was carried on by the rest of the Kent order. Matthew Fleming hit 55 and Dean Headley was so successful against the spinners that, by the end of the day, he was 60 not out and Kent's total stood at 388 for 9. That became 410 all out next morning, with Headley last out for 72, and Kent seemed to be moving into a position of great strength when Min Patel wheeled away for 40 consecutive overs to finish with 8 for 115. There was not much support for Patel from the other end but, despite Graham Lloyd's 81 and 63 from Neil Fairbrother, Lancashire were still dismissed for 312. Now, though, Kent's fragile batting let them down. Gary Yates took 6 for 64 with his steady off-spin as Kent were bowled out for 159, and by the time the sun intervened Lancashire were 117 for 3 as they chased 258. A tense final day could have belonged to Patel (4 for 120), but instead Lloyd (84) seized the initiative and eventually Lancashire got home by four wickets.

Leicestershire's demise continued apace at Northampton where the 1998 champions, suffering from a depleted attack, lost by an innings to the rejuvenated home side. Northants' victory was based on telling contributions from three of the country's brightest young players: David Sales, Graeme Swann and Michael Davies. First, Sales. Northants were actually 138 for 5 before the 21-year-old Sales was joined by wicketkeeper David Ripley. Together they added 285 in 57 highly entertaining overs, with Ripley reaching 105 and Sales ending the opening day unbeaten on 183. His power off both the front and back foot was electrifying and on the second morning Sales went on to 205; three of his first five first-class hundreds have been converted into 200 or more. Kevin Innes finished 47 not out, and the Northants total of 509 proved far too intimidating. By the close of the second day Leicestershire were on the ropes at 225 for 7, Aftab Habib making 51 but Swann and Davies beginning to get in amongst the visiting batsmen. An unbeaten 44 from Carl Crowe hoisted Leicestershire up to 311, but Swann ended with 5 for 85 and Davies 4 for 87. Following on, Leicestershire fell apart – bowled out for 143 with Swann grabbing a career-best 6 for 41 (and his first match haul of more than ten wickets) and Davies 2 for 32.

Majestic batting by Matthew Maynard, whose 186 lit up Headingley, was the prelude to an innings rout of Yorkshire by Glamorgan which made a mockery of the two counties' respective standings in the PPP table. Before the game Yorkshire were harbouring hopes of a runners-up spot, while Glamorgan were battling to avoid the wooden spoon. That looked laughable as, over three days, Yorkshire were completely outplayed by a team that – in the brave new world of the year 2000 – will be in a supposedly inferior division. Maynard went past 20,000 first-class runs during an innings that contained 21 fours and, once more, questioned why he has won so few Test caps in an era of England underachievement. Michael Powell supported well with 70 and, towards the latter end of Glamorgan's 498, 17-year-old debutant Mark Wallace, a talented wicketkeeper, scored 64 not out. Steve Watkin then undermined the Yorkshire first innings, taking 4 for 35 as they crumbled to 140 all out and, by the close of the second day the White Rose county had wilted again to 93 for 5 as they followed on. Owen Parkin, whose new ball burst of 3 for 19 in six overs put the skids under Yorkshire's second innings, finished with 4 for 54. Yorkshire reached 306 only because of a devil-may-care last wicket stand of 78 between Richard Blakey (123) and last man Ryan Sidebottom (48 not out).

Derbyshire all but assured themselves of first division status by beating bottom club Gloucestershire by six wickets at Bristol. Paul Aldred was their star on day one, his 6 for 34 taking his season's wicket tally to 47 – as many as his total scalps for the previous four years of his professional career. Gloucestershire, bowled out for just 150, did hit back by dismissing Derbyshire for 203, Ben Gannon picking up 5 for 42, but a second-innings total of 212 was not enough. Trevor Smith (5 for 69) and Phil DeFreitas (4 for 35) were the chief wicket-takers this time around, and then Adrian Rollins played another of his no-nonsense top-order innings to settle the issue. Rollins thumped three sixes in a 116-ball 95 and, with Robin Weston adding an unbeaten 43 to his first innings 52, Derbyshire cantered to victory.

Hampshire, nursing injuries to several leading bowlers and desperate to hang on to a top-nine berth, prepared a batting paradise at Southampton and, thanks mainly to Adrian Aymes, got the high-scoring draw they were looking for. Jamie Cox stroked 216, a career-best, as Somerset reached 493 for 6 declared, while Peter Bowler's 103 not out was his third century against Hampshire – the first two being for Leicestershire and Derbyshire! By the close of the second day Hampshire were 126 for 0 in reply but, although openers Jason Laney (63) and Derek Kenway (61) both got out early on the third morning, Aymes steered Hampshire to 413 with a determined century. On the final day, an academic exercise, Cox became the first Somerset player to hit a double hundred and a hundred in the same match – reaching 129 not out before a declaration at 255 for 2. Marcus Trescothick continued his fine late season form with 86.

Durham's dream of upsetting the odds and making the first division took another sizeable step towards reality at the Riverside. David Boon, their redoubtable captain, was in the vanguard against Warwickshire, scoring 54 and 72 in a relatively low-scoring game, but there were other heroes too – on both sides. Tim Munton, for instance, ploughed through over after over on the first day – into a fierce headwind – to take six wickets, and the big Warwickshire seamer finished with 7 for 91 as Durham totalled 255. Jon Lewis' 76 was an important innings on the opening day, but young Michael Powell then seemed to be playing an even more vital one as he reached 111 not out by the halfway stage. Warwickshire, however, collapsed to 285 all out – Powell making 117 – with John Wood (5 for 75) and Neil Killeen (4 for 62) leading the

Yorkshire's Ian Fisher made a half-century against Surrey.
David Munden

counter-attack. Durham, in their second innings, were wobbling at 56 for 4 before Boon was joined by Paul Collingwood (42) in a partnership worth 122. Dougie Brown took 7 for 66 but Durham's 235 meant a target of 206 for Warwickshire on a pitch beginning to offer the seamers variable bounce. David Hemp added 49 to his first-innings 51 on the fourth morning but 85 for 2 became a sad 115 all out as the unsung Killeen (4 for 57) was joined by Wood (3 for 22) and Steve Harmison (2 for 20) in a demolition job. To make matters worse for Warwickshire – not to mention South Africa – fast bowler Allan Donald managed just 20 wicketless overs in the match before breaking down again with more ankle trouble.

Graeme Hick made the 107th and 108th first-class hundreds of his career as Worcestershire frustrated Essex's hopes of victory at Chelmsford. Unhappily for Worcestershire, however, they ended up being frustrated by Essex on the final day, and a draw condemned them to second division championship cricket next season. Hick's tons took him past Colin Cowdrey and Andrew Sandham into 15th place on the all-time list of century-makers, level with Pakistan's great run machine Zaheer Abbas. His first here shared the honours, on day one, with Ronnie Irani and Ricky Anderson, who took 4 for 51 and 4 for 74 respectively as Worcestershire were dismissed for 308. Irani then shone with the bat, hitting a defiant 103 as Essex replied with 303. Nasser Hussain contributed a delightful 71, and Barry Hyam batted sensibly for 49 not out to secure a third batting point. On the third day Essex thought they had taken the upper hand, trimming Worcestershire to 99 for 5. But they should have known that Hick was the key. His 150, from 172 balls with three sixes and 19 fours, was a magnificent display of effortless power and, fortunately for Worcestershire, both Steve Rhodes and Duncan Catterall hung around long enough to figure in sizeable stands with their captain. Ultimately, though, Paul Grayson's 105 and Hussain's 65 gave Essex the final word.

An epic 265 by Alastair Brown, an innings which beseeched the England selectors to think of him as substantially more than just a supposed one-day specialist, was the highlight of a high-scoring draw at Lord's. Not far behind came Mark Ramprakash's unbeaten 209 on the last day and a half: and his message to selectors who had recently left him out of the winter tour to South Africa would have been undoubtedly more earthy. Adam Hollioake made 116 in Surrey's mammoth 585, but Brown's eight-hour effort dominated the innings and he even had the energy to figure in a ninth-wicket stand of 95 with Ian Salisbury after reaching his maiden double hundred. Salisbury (3 for 74) and Martin Bicknell (3 for 47) then seemed to be setting up a Surrey push for victory, as Middlesex were dismissed for 284, but the new champions were denied by Ramprakash's technical brilliance and utter determination. Ben Hutton (50), Richard Kettleborough (69) and David Nash (56 not out) all played support acts.

Sussex maintained hopes of first division status by overwhelming Nottinghamshire by 259 runs at Hove. Richard Montgomerie (59) and Robin Martin-Jenkins, with a robust 46, underpinned a Sussex first innings of 275 and the seam and swing of Jason Lewry (3 for 72) and Mark Robinson (3 for 36) sent Notts spiralling to 199 in reply. The match was taken right away from the visitors by Toby Pierce (95) and Michael Di Venuto (90) and, sure enough, after Sussex had totalled 315, Notts crumbled to 132 all out as Lewry (4 for 23) and Robinson (3 for 33) again went about their business with relish.

ROUND 20: 15–18 SEPTEMBER 1999

15 and 16 September

at Edgbaston
Sussex 99 (40 overs) (TA Munton 7 for 36) and 176
(PA Cottey 73, AF Giles 5 for 63)
Warwickshire 207 (48.1 overs) (NMK Smith 71, T Frost
66, JD Lewry 5 for 59) and 71 for 3
Warwickshire won by seven wickets
Warwickshire 17 pts, Sussex 4 pts

15, 16, 17 and 18 September

at Derby
Hampshire 362 for 8 dec. (104 overs) (AN Aymes 86,
JS Laney 67, RA Smith 64, AD Mascarenhas 51) and
199 for 5 dec.
Derbyshire 277 for 9 dec. (PAJ DeFreitas 54) and 282
(PAJ DeFreitas 61, DG Cork 51, NAM McLean 4 for 87)
Hampshire won by 2 runs
Hampshire 20 pts, Derbyshire 5 pts

at Cardiff
Glamorgan 227 (76.1 overs) (MJ Powell 67) and 204
for 3 (SP James 111, WL Law 64)
Northamptonshire 294 (75.4 overs) (RJ Warren 72)
Match drawn
Glamorgan 9 pts, Northamptonshire 9 pts

at Canterbury
Gloucestershire 350 for 6 dec. (77.5 overs) (KJ Barnett
125, IJ Harvey 123) and 173 for 5 (MGN Windows 113*)
Kent 482 (127.1 overs) (AP Wells 100, MV Fleming 99,
MM Patel 67, SA Marsh 60)
Match drawn
Kent 10 pts, Gloucestershire 12 pts

at Leicester
Leicestershire 322 (90.5 overs) (DI Stevens 98, VJ Wells
57, N Killeen, 7 for 85) and 74 for 4
Durham 278 (102.1 overs) (DC Boon 53,
MS Kasprowicz 5 for 75)
Match drawn
Leicestershire 11 pts, Durham 10 pts

at Trent Bridge
Nottinghamshire 349 (92.3 overs) (JER Gallian 118
GE Welton 76, RT Robinson 66, DJ Thompson 4 for 54)
and 151
Essex 188 (61.2 overs) (SG Law 64) and (following on)
432 for 7 dec. (N Hussain 143, PJ Prichard 110,
DS Lucas 5 for 104)
Essex won by 120 runs
Essex 16 pts, Nottinghamshire 7 pts

at Taunton
Lancashire 322 (84 overs) (GD Lloyd 144, JP Crawley
64, AR Caddick 8 for 113)
Somerset 376 for 6 (118 overs) (GD Rose 123*,
ME Trescothick 78, KA Parsons 76*)
No play was possible on the fourth day
Match drawn
Somerset 12 pts, Lancashire 9 pts

at The Oval
Yorkshire 115 (44.2 overs) (CG Greenidge 5 for 60,
MP Bicknell 4 for 38) and 213 for 9 dec. (RJ Blakey 71,
ID Fisher 51)
Surrey 128 (33 overs) (GP Thorpe 58*, CEW Silverwood
5 for 28) and 57 for 4
Match drawn
Surrey 8 pts, Yorkshire 8 pts

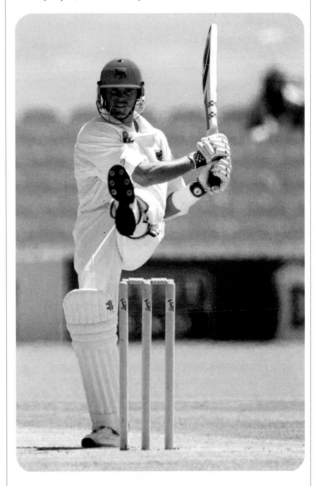

**Greg Blewett, the Australian batsman, struggled to come to
terms with conditions in England.**
David Munden/Sportsline Photographic

at Worcester
Worcestershire 465 for 9 dec. (141.2 overs) (VS Solanki 155, EJ Wilson 116, DN Catterall 60, PCR Tufnell 5 for 107)
Middlesex 235 (66.5 overs) (AJ Strauss 62) and (following on) 235 for 1 (MR Ramprakash 87*, AJ Strauss 71*)
Match drawn
Worcestershire 12 pts, Middlesex 7 pts

Controversy at Derby brought an explosive end to the championship season, with Warwickshire finishing in the dreaded tenth place thanks to Hampshire's thrilling, two-run win against Derbyshire. The cricket on the last day at Derby was superb, cut and thrust stuff which ended with Derbyshire bowled out for 282 as Peter Hartley juggled a drive from Simon Lacey before completing a caught and bowled. It was what happened on the previous day that caused uproar and – on Warwickshire's instigation – an official England and Wales Cricket Board enquiry.

Warwickshire had, by then, completed a two-day rout of Sussex at Edgbaston to push themselves into the coveted top nine. First division status beckoned, but only if Derbyshire failed to get two batting bonus points and lost the match – or if Hampshire were beaten. A draw would have been enough for Derbyshire...and Warwickshire.

Hampshire captain Robin Smith was prepared to do whatever it took to give his side the chance of the victory they needed. Derbyshire captain Dominic Cork had two priorities – first to ensure division one membership, and secondly (but only then) to push on in search of fourth place and a share of the prize money offered by sponsors PPP Healthcare.

Hampshire, in the first four sessions, had batted well to reach 362 for 8 declared with Jason Laney and Smith making sixties at the top of the order and Adrian Aymes (86) and Dimitri Mascarenhas (51) putting on 127 in 51 overs. A final fling came when Aymes and Nixon McLean thrashed 49 in just four overs to make it the highest total Derbyshire had conceded all season.

Now Hampshire needed wickets, but by the close Derbyshire had gone watchfully to 143 for 3 and, when the third day began, the home side's single ambition was to get to 250 and clinch their own first division status. For a while it seemed as if they would fall short. Wickets tumbled, until Phil DeFreitas and number nine Lacey came together in a stand of 67. Then, though, DeFreitas sliced to cover and Derbyshire were 231 for 8. Smith was, at this time, off the field nursing a groin strain, and he had left his deputy Shaun Udal in charge out on the

field. But everyone connected with the match knew that, should Derbyshire fail to secure a second batting point, they would have no option but to seek a draw and the subsequent four extra points.

In addition, poor weather was forecast for the final day and, with time ticking away, Hampshire felt they had to keep the game open. Warwickshire officials felt unacceptable collusion between the two captains went on – but both Cork and Smith argued that they were only doing what was in the best interests of their own counties. Smith offered Cork a projection: would he be prepared to accept a chase of what turned out to be 285 in a generous 127 overs (with the extra time included in the calculations in case of rain interruptions)? Cork indicated he would be interested and Hampshire, sensing their best chance to win the game, then clearly allowed Derbyshire an immediate opportunity to reach their initial goal. Out on the field, Udal declined to bring back his strike bowler McLean to polish off the Derbyshire tail. Instead, he threw the ball to occasional leg-spinner Giles White. Soon Derbyshire, with Lacey going to 31 not out, not only breezed past 250 but also motored on to 277 for 9 before declaring 85 runs in arrears.

Almost immediately, Trevor Smith struck twice in three balls to remove Laney and Will Kendall and Hampshire were 13 for 2. But, instead of trying to press home this advantage, Cork honoured his earlier deal with his opposite number and brought on a motley collection of part-time bowlers – including his wicketkeeper Karl Krikken. Hampshire, unsurprisingly, went quickly to the third declaration of the game, at 199 for 5, and Derbyshire had the target that had been agreed.

By now, however, Derbyshire's members had forgotten their earlier joy at knowing first division status had been achieved. They did not approve of what they had seen in the Hampshire second innings, and loud boos accompanied the Derbyshire players when they left the field to prepare to bat again.

By the close of a remarkable day Derbyshire were 109 for 4 and the cricket on show was again hard and uncompromising. But the damage was done. Warwickshire cried foul, but Hampshire skipper Smith said: 'It should not make any difference if these things happen in the first or last matches of the season. No-one complains when matches finish in two and a half days because of sub-standard pitches.' Sussex captain Chris Adams also got involved, saying he had no sympathy for Warwickshire because, he felt, they had employed sharp practice themselves by preparing a 'result-pitch' at Edgbaston for a last game of the season

Somerset's Andrew Caddick had figures of 8 for 113 in the first innings against Lancashire – a great end to an outstanding season.
David Munden/Sportsline Photographic

they knew they had to win. 'There's a saying in sport – what goes around, comes around,' said Adams.

Meanwhile, on the final day, Cork (51) and DeFreitas (61) battled magnificently in their team's cause and Lacey, despite having his hand broken by a McLean lifter near the end, made a heroic 42 before offering Hartley the catch that provoked wild Hampshire celebrations. Hampshire, in fact, went into seventh place and Derbyshire finished ninth. And Warwickshire, ironically one of the prime movers for change to a two-division championship, were left to fume as the ECB cleared both Hampshire and Derbyshire, and their captains, of any wrong-doing.

Durham also clinched a place in the so-called 'elite', taking the ten points they required from a draw with Leicestershire at Grace Road in a match that only began on day two because of heavy rain. Neil Killeen was the bowling hero, bowling his seamers with an accuracy the rest of the Durham attack could not match to take 7 for 85 as Leicestershire were dismissed for 322. With four bowling points in the bag, Durham now required a minimum of two for batting. At 165 for 4 the target of 250 seemed some way off but David Boon (53) and Paul Collingwood (38) added 74 to make it

almost a formality. Fittingly, Boon had made a crucial contribution to Durham's 278, and as the match meandered to a draw amid last day rain Boon was able to reflect with huge satisfaction that he had taken his Durham side into the first division in what was the last first-class match of his great career.

Somerset, Kent and Yorkshire were the other sides to book their places in the first division with rain-affected draws – finishing in fourth, fifth and sixth place respectively behind the top three of champions Surrey, runners-up Lancashire and third-placed Leicestershire.

At Taunton no play was possible on the final day, with Somerset 376 for 6 in reply to Lancashire's 322 in what had already been a rain-affected contest. The opening day, however, had offered exhilarating cricket with Graham Lloyd making a brilliant if unorthodox 144 off 151 balls and Andrew Caddick capping a triumphant personal season with figures of 8 for 113. Once more, given the encouragement of some pace and bounce in a splendid Taunton pitch, Caddick produced four top-class spells. With 196 wickets in two seasons, Caddick has finally earned the respect of even his previous detractors. Marcus Trescothick hit 16 fours in his 78 when Somerset replied, and Graham Rose (123 not out) put on an unbroken 167 with Keith Parsons (76 not out) for the seventh wicket.

Kent had a chance of snatching third place in the PPP table when Gloucestershire slipped to 108 for 5 in their second innings at Canterbury. The visitors were then still 25 runs adrift, but Matt Windows made 113 not out and Jeremy Snape stayed with him on 21 not out as Gloucestershire recovered to 173 for 5. Only 23 minutes of play had been possible on the first day, but Gloucestershire were boosted to 350 for 6 declared by a stand of 223 for the fifth wicket between Kim Barnett (125) and Ian Harvey (123). Kent, needing a draw, had any nerves put to rest by Alan Wells's 100, which included two sixes and 15 fours, but Matthew Fleming (99), Steve Marsh (60) and Min Patel (67) then pushed the total up to 483.

Yorkshire, playing Surrey at The Oval, sat through a washed-out first day and then, on a rain-affected second, struggled to 50 for 5 with Carl Greenidge (son of Gordon) picking up three wickets after becoming the 21st player used by the champions in this PPP campaign. On the third morning Yorkshire were dismissed for 115, and it was only that good because of a last wicket stand of 43 between Richard Harden (36 not out) and Ian Fisher (31). Chris Silverwood then bowled superbly to take 5 for 28, and Surrey limped to 128 all out simply because Graham Thorpe

(58 not out) was a class above any other batsman on view. Yorkshire were 91 for 6 in their second innings, with Martin Bicknell doing most of the damage, but recovered to 213 thanks to David Byas (71) and another gutsy effort in the lower order by Fisher (51). More weather problems meant there was time only for Surrey to reach 57 for 4, and the game was drawn.

Curiously, four matches took place between counties who will be together in division two in the year 2000 – besides the four (described above) between those destined for division one.

Warwickshire's win against Sussex was achieved in five sessions, although the Edgbaston surface survived an official inspection by the ECB's Harry Brind and Chris Wood following the fall of 20 wickets on day one. Tim Munton started the carnage, taking 7 for 36 from 20 overs as Sussex were skittled for 99 – but Warwickshire were fielding again by the end of the day after being dismissed themselves for 207. Their first-innings lead owed almost everything to a seventh-wicket stand of 124 between skipper Neil Smith (71) and wicketkeeper Tony Frost (66) that rescued them from the depths of 50 for 6. Jason Lewry swung the ball appreciably to take 5 for 59 but – after play before lunch on the second day had been washed out – Sussex were soon in trouble again. Only a fighting 73 from Tony Cottey lifted them to 176 and, as the light faded, Nick Knight hit a quick unbeaten 40 to take Warwickshire past their target of 69 with just three wickets down.

Essex at least ended a forgettable season with a victory, beating Nottinghamshire by 120 runs to push themselves up to 12th place. Notts totalled 349 in their first innings, Tim Robinson making a cultured 66 in his last championship appearance before retirement after Jason Gallian (118) and Guy Welton (76) had initially mocked Nasser Hussain's decision to bowl first. When Essex were then bowled out for 188 by Alex Wharf and Chris Tolley, with only Stuart Law (64) looking anything like his normal self, there seemed to be just one winner. But, following on, Essex reached the close of the third day at 266 for 1 and, on the final morning, Hussain pressed on to 143. He had put on 221 for the second wicket with Paul Prichard (110) to provide the base for an eventual declaration at 432 for 7. Notts, by now on the back foot, were tumbled out for 151 – after Mark Ilott and Ronnie Irani had left them reeling at 10 for 5 with potent new ball spells.

Glamorgan batsmen old and new, Steve James and Michael Powell, both passed 1,000 first-class runs for the season at Cardiff – James for the fifth successive summer and Powell for the first time. In a rain-affected draw, Powell scored 67 in Glamorgan's first innings 227 and – after Northamptonshire had replied with 204 – James hit 111 as the Welsh county reached 204 for 3 in their second innings. There was no play at all on the final day.

The match between Worcestershire and Middlesex, at New Road, was also a draw. Vikram Solanki hit a stylish 155 and Elliott Wilson 116 as Worcestershire piled up 465 for 9 declared despite Phil Tufnell's 5 for 107. Middlesex, despite an opening stand of 117 between Andrew Strauss (62) and Ben Hutton, slid to 235 all out and a follow-on. Strauss and Hutton responded with another century opening partnership, this time of 103, and on a much-shortened final day Mark Ramprakash (87 not out) helped Strauss (71 not out) take their unbroken second wicket stand to 132.

PPP HEALTHCARE COUNTY CHAMPIONSHIP FINAL TABLE

	M	W	L	Drawn	Bat Pts	Bowl Pts	Total Pts
Surrey (5)	17	12	–	5	36	34	264
Lancashire (2)	17	8	4	5	37	55	208
Leicestershire (1)	17	5	3	9	43	61	200
Somerset (9)	17	6	4	7	38	56	194
Kent (11)	17	6	4	7	34	60	194
Yorkshire (3)	17	8	6	3	21	64	193
Hampshire (6)	17	5	5	7	45	58	191
Durham (14)	17	6	7	4	34	66	188
Derbyshire (10)	17	7	8	2	34	61	187
Warwickshire (8)	17	6	5	6	35	56	187
Sussex (7)	17	6	5	6	29	60	185
Essex (18)	17	5	7	5	38	63	181
Northamptonshire (15)	17	4	7	6	35	64	171
Glamorgan (12)	17	5	7	5	26	57	163
Worcestershire (13)	17	4	6	7	18	65	159
Middlesex (17)	17	4	5	8	24	52	156
Nottinghamshire (16)	17	4	11	2	27	57	140
Gloucestershire (4)	17	2	9	6	26	62	136

1998 season in brackets

Top nine teams will compete in Division One in 2000; bottom nine will form Division Two.

Somerset are ahead of Kent by virtue of having scored more runs, the result between them having been a draw. Derbyshire are ahead of Warwickshire by virtue of having more wins.

FIRST-CLASS AVERAGES

BATTING

	M	Inns	NO	HS	Runs	Av	100	50
SG Law	17	29	4	263	1833	73.32	8	6
TM Dilshan	5	10	1	127	562	62.44	2	3
JL Langer	12	22	4	241*	1048	58.22	4	2
J Cox	18	30	2	216	1617	57.75	6	6
ML Hayden	9	15	2	170	745	57.30	4	1
RJ Turner	19	27	4	138*	1217	52.91	2	10
N Hussain	12	20	1	143	988	52.00	2	8
DJG Sales	18	29	4	303*	1291	51.64	3	5
AD Brown	17	26	4	265	1127	51.22	4	2
DJ Nash	8	11	3	135*	395	49.37	1	2
PD Bowler	17	27	8	149	931	49.00	4	-
GA Hick	13	22	0	150	1063	48.31	4	6
MJ Powell (Gm)	16	26	4	164	1060	48.18	2	5
CC Lewis	10	13	2	139	520	47.27	2	2
GM Hamilton	11	20	8	94*	567	47.25	-	4
MJ Horne	9	15	0	172	670	44.66	3	1
MA Atherton	9	15	2	268*	578	44.46	1	2
NJ Astle	10	15	1	121	617	44.07	3	2
GB Loveridge	7	10	0	126	427	42.70	1	2
RA Smith	18	29	3	96	1110	42.69	-	10
D Ripley	15	22	6	107	683	42.68	2	3
GD Lloyd	17	26	1	144	1066	42.64	3	6
P Johnson	16	29	3	126	1104	42.46	1	10
SP James	16	25	1	259*	1017	42.37	4	3
MR Ramprakash	16	28	3	209*	1056	42.24	2	7
DA Kenway	19	31	6	102	1055	42.20	1	7
GP Thorpe	13	21	4	164	708	41.64	2	2
BW Byrne	6	11	2	94	374	41.55	-	2
MJ Di Venuto	16	28	2	162	1067	41.03	3	5
JJB Lewis	16	28	0	132	1146	40.92	2	8
A Symonds	14	25	2	177	940	40.86	3	4
VS Solanki	19	35	2	171	1339	40.57	3	6
Aftab Habib	18	29	3	160*	1055	40.57	3	6
ET Smith	14	25	2	111	931	40.47	1	6
MP Maynard	13	18	1	186	685	40.29	2	2
JH Kallis	6	9	0	101	362	40.22	1	2
MA Butcher	16	28	1	259	1077	39.88	2	4
SP Fleming	9	15	3	127	476	39.66	1	2
QJ Hughes	8	13	2	101	435	39.54	1	3
WS Kendall	19	32	2	201	1186	39.53	2	7
MV Fleming	17	25	4	138	830	39.52	1	4
RC Irani	21	34	5	153	1121	38.65	4	3
AS Rollins	15	28	3	113	965	38.60	2	5
JS Laney	11	19	1	99	691	38.38	-	6
A Flintoff	13	21	2	160	727	38.26	2	2
GD Rose	9	11	2	123*	342	38.00	1	1
DL Maddy	18	30	2	158*	1060	37.85	2	4
MPL Bulbeck	15	15	8	76*	265	37.85	-	1
JP Crawley	15	25	2	158	870	37.82	2	6
DL Vettori	10	14	2	112	453	37.75	1	4
IJ Ward	18	30	3	103	1018	37.70	1	9
CD McMillan	10	16	2	121	525	37.50	2	1
ME Trescothick	15	24	0	190	898	37.41	2	3
RJ Warren	18	29	4	110	935	37.40	1	6
NJ Speak	10	17	2	110	561	37.40	2	2
Imraan Mohammed	9	16	2	110	520	37.14	1	2
RR Montgomerie	15	27	1	113*	962	37.00	2	6
DC Nash	17	27	8	92	696	36.63	-	4
AP Grayson	20	32	2	159*	1083	36.10	3	6
AN Aymes	18	27	5	115*	791	35.95	2	5
KDM Walker	7	8	0	132	286	35.75	1	1
TM Moody	5	10	2	63*	286	35.75	-	3
EJ Wilson	9	17	2	116	536	35.73	1	3
MGN Windows	17	30	3	118	960	35.55	2	5
RJ Bailey	14	23	2	113*	743	35.38	1	3
JA Claughton	7	13	4	85	318	35.33	-	3
MJ Powell (Wa)	9	14	0	136	494	35.28	2	1
M Burns	19	27	1	109	915	35.19	2	5
DL Hemp	18	29	0	144	1014	34.96	2	6
RMS Weston	15	26	2	156	838	34.91	3	2
BF Smith	14	21	0	154	732	34.85	2	2
PN Weekes	16	28	4	140*	828	34.50	1	6
MP Dowman	9	15	3	67*	412	34.33	-	3
NV Knight	14	23	2	94	719	34.23	-	6

FIRST-CLASS AVERAGES

BATTING

	M	Inns	NO	HS	Runs	Av	100	50
RP Arnold	5	10	1	70	307	34.11	-	2
DC Boon	16	27	2	139	839	33.56	1	7
CL Cairns	7	10	1	80	302	33.55	-	2
AJ Hollioake	13	18	2	116	534	33.37	1	3
MP Bicknell	15	17	4	69	432	33.23	-	3
CJ Adams	17	31	2	130	956	32.96	1	5
RC Russell	17	30	6	94*	790	32.91	-	5
PJ Prichard	16	26	0	110	852	32.76	2	6
VJ Wells	13	20	2	109*	588	32.66	2	3
AP Wells	10	15	0	111	490	32.66	2	1
RI Cunliffe	7	13	0	108	421	32.38	1	2
PCL Holloway	19	32	5	114*	869	32.38	2	5
MA Wagh	13	21	1	216*	643	32.15	1	1
A Gunawardene	4	8	0	77	257	32.12	-	3
WK Hegg	16	24	3	94	670	31.90	-	3
AJ Swann	12	18	0	154	573	31.83	2	2
JER Gallian	19	34	3	120*	985	31.77	2	5
MJ Slater	10	18	1	171	540	31.76	1	2
JE Morris	15	25	0	119	792	31.68	2	4
GP Swann	18	27	4	130*	727	31.60	1	4
DJ Bicknell	11	17	1	115	504	31.50	2	1
AL Penberthy	18	25	2	123*	718	31.21	1	4
GS Blewett	12	23	2	190	655	31.19	1	2
A Dale	16	26	0	113	809	31.11	3	1
PC McKeown	5	8	1	75	216	30.85	-	2
MA Ealham	13	22	3	88*	585	30.78	-	5
PA Nixon	18	29	2	121	828	30.66	1	3
MJ Chilton	18	30	3	106*	827	30.62	2	4
AJ Strauss	9	17	1	98	488	30.50	-	4
GW White	16	28	1	121	818	30.29	1	4
UBA Rashid	10	18	3	73	454	30.26	-	3
A McGrath	16	30	2	142*	831	29.67	1	6
MTE Peirce	17	31	0	123	919	29.64	1	6
U Afzaal	16	30	2	104	828	29.57	1	6
SR Lampitt	14	19	5	66*	413	29.50	-	2
M Keech	8	13	1	50	353	29.41	-	1
NW Ashley	5	9	0	96	264	29.33	-	2
KJ Barnett	15	26	1	125	727	29.08	2	4
SD Peters	11	15	2	99	374	28.76	-	1
M Watkinson	8	13	1	116	345	28.75	1	-
THC Hancock	17	30	0	71	858	28.60	-	7
AJ Stewart	12	20	2	95	511	28.38	-	3
JM Dakin	11	18	2	124	454	28.37	1	3
DI Stevens	11	20	0	130	562	28.10	1	3
DDJ Robinson	17	29	1	200	786	28.07	3	1
PA Cottey	17	29	1	126	780	27.85	1	4
SP Titchard	17	31	4	136	752	27.85	1	2
DR Brown	16	25	1	142	666	27.75	1	3
KA Parsons	15	21	3	80	499	27.72	-	3
OA Shah	17	32	2	110*	829	27.63	3	3
RJ Harden	10	19	3	69	438	27.37	-	3
D Byas	17	34	2	95	875	27.34	-	8
MP Vaughan	17	34	1	153	895	27.12	3	3
KJ Innes	8	11	3	47*	217	27.12	-	-
RWT Key	19	33	2	125	836	26.96	1	5
BC Hollioake	13	20	0	71	538	26.90	-	4
DG Cork	14	22	2	82	535	26.75	-	4
DP Fulton	17	29	2	126*	722	26.74	1	3
MS Kasprowicz	16	23	4	73	507	26.68	-	5
WL Law	5	9	0	64	240	26.66	-	2
JA Daley	14	24	1	105	609	26.47	1	3
NH Fairbrother	12	19	0	83	503	26.47	-	4
WPC Weston	11	21	-	157	554	26.38	2	1
MJ Walker	14	23	2	103*	553	26.33	1	3
RG Twose	8	13	0	91	341	26.23	-	3
PAJ DeFreitas	13	18	1	105	441	25.94	1	2
AD Mascarenhas	14	20	2	62	465	25.83	-	2
MP Speight	17	27	5	97*	566	25.72	-	4
SJ Lacey	6	8	2	42	154	25.66	-	-
PS Jones	9	14	3	105	281	25.54	1	-
AR Danson	6	10	4	30*	153	25.50	-	-
RJ Blakey	17	31	4	123	684	25.33	1	4
JN Batty	15	20	5	64	379	25.26	-	1
G Chapple	13	18	2	83	402	25.12	-	2

FIRST-CLASS AVERAGES

BATTING

	M	Inns	NO	HS	Runs	Av	100	50
S Kalavitigoda	6	11	0	73	276	25.09	-	2
RT Robinson	12	22	1	80	525	25.00	-	4
NT Wood	6	9	0	82	225	25.00	-	1
GP Butcher	5	8	0	70	199	24.87	-	1
ID Blackwell	10	16	2	62*	347	24.78	-	2
MJ McCague	10	13	2	53	272	24.72	-	1
PD Collingwood	17	28	0	106	692	24.71	1	4
AJ Tudor	10	13	4	99*	222	24.66	-	1
TL Penney	15	24	3	73	517	24.61	-	3
AW Evans	15	24	3	88*	512	24.38	-	2
KM Krikken	12	19	3	88	389	24.31	-	3
MA Roseberry	12	21	1	116	483	24.15	1	1
AC Parore	6	8	0	80	193	24.12	-	2
MW Alleyne	17	29	1	76	672	24.00	-	3
NMK Smith	15	21	0	71	504	24.00	-	3
ID Fisher	11	16	5	51	261	23.72	-	1
SJ Rhodes	18	30	5	74	591	23.64	-	1
GF Archer	15	28	1	132	635	23.51	1	2
JP Pyemont	11	19	2	90*	398	23.41	-	3
BJ Hyam	18	26	4	51	514	23.36	-	1
SA Marsh	15	22	2	73*	466	23.30	-	2
DP Ostler	7	11	0	87	250	22.72	-	2
MD Bell	8	13	1	83	272	22.66	-	1
DJ Millns	6	9	3	47	136	22.66	-	-
IJ Harvey	12	19	0	123	429	22.57	1	-
JN Snape	17	29	6	98*	518	22.52	-	3
DA Leatherdale	19	34	3	85	693	22.35	-	3
MCJ Ball	12	19	4	70*	333	22.20	-	1
JP Pyemont	11	19	1	90*	398	22.11	-	3
BL Hutton	8	15	0	59	331	22.06	-	2
IJ Sutcliffe	16	27	0	110	590	21.85	1	2
I Dawood	7	12	0	102	262	21.83	1	1
CMW Read	19	31	1	160	653	21.76	1	1
RK Illingworth	16	26	5	91*	457	21.76	-	1
G Welch	14	21	6	48*	326	21.73	-	-
K Newell	8	11	0	46	239	21.72	-	-
MB Loye	13	20	0	102	433	21.65	2	-
HPW Jayawardene	4	8	0	89	173	21.62	-	1
BJ Spendlove	7	13	0	63	279	21.46	-	2
SD Stubbings	5	10	0	45	213	21.30	-	-
MA Gough	12	20	0	67	424	21.20	-	4
JID Kerr	14	19	1	64	381	21.16	-	2
JD Ratcliffe	13	20	1	91	402	21.15	-	2
AF Giles	16	23	5	123*	375	20.83	1	-
ID Austin	5	8	2	45*	125	20.83	-	-
AD Shaw	12	16	1	140	312	20.80	1	-
IDK Salisbury	17	19	2	100*	353	20.76	1	1
CP Schofield	10	14	4	39*	205	20.50	-	-
T Frost	12	18	1	66	348	20.47	-	1
PJ Hartley	12	15	6	58	183	20.33	-	1
NE Batson	5	10	1	72	181	20.11	-	1
RA Kettleborough	8	15	0	93	300	20.00	-	2
PR Pollard	11	21	2	60	377	19.84	-	3
TC Hicks	7	10	1	54	178	19.77	-	1
GE Welton	9	17	1	76	316	19.75	-	1
RG Halsall	7	9	1	76	157	19.62	-	i
TC Walton	6	8	0	71	155	19.37	-	i
JPB Barnes	6	9	0	45	174	19.33	-	-
JP Stephenson	15	24	2	136	425	19.31	1	i
RJ Green	10	10	5	27	96	19.20	-	-
JJ Bates	6	10	0	57	190	19.00	-	1
RDB Croft	15	21	4	58*	322	18.94	-	2
RSC Martin-Jenkins	14	24	2	70	413	18.77	-	2
ME Cassar	14	24	3	42	393	18.71	-	-
DW Headley	14	19	3	72	297	18.56	-	1
WG Khan	5	9	0	88	167	18.55	-	2
TR Ward	8	13	0	101	240	18.46	1	-
PJ Newport	11	19	3	65*	295	18.43	-	1
AR Caddick	17	23	5	45	331	18.38	-	-
SJ Cook	10	16	3	51	237	18.23	-	1
MC Ilott	12	17	1	44	290	18.12	-	-
MJ Cawdron	6	9	2	42	126	18.00	-	-
DJ Eadie	4	8	2	52*	108	18.00	-	1
C White	17	31	4	52	521	17.96	-	1

FIRST-CLASS AVERAGES

BATTING

	M	Inns	NO	HS	Runs	Av	100	50
GR Haynes	8	12	2	60*	177	17.70	-	1
JB DeC Thompson	14	19	9	44	176	17.60	-	-
JJ Bull	6	11	0	49	193	17.54	-	1
JP Hewitt	13	21	1	49*	350	17.50	-	1
SD Udal	15	21	6	40	261	17.40	-	-
TM Smith	8	9	6	20*	52	17.33	-	-
JP Taylor	17	21	2	71	316	16.63	-	1
IN Flanagan	6	10	0	52	165	16.50	-	1
AF Gofton	5	8	1	37*	115	16.42	-	-
AG Wharf	16	26	3	78	370	16.08	-	1
VC Drakes	17	30	3	80	427	15.81	-	2
AP Cowan	17	24	3	52*	332	15.80	-	1
PJ Martin	14	19	5	30*	220	15.71	-	-
N Killeen	12	19	3	46	251	15.68	-	-
BJ Collins	7	11	2	46	141	15.66	-	-
NJ Wilton	6	10	0	55	156	15.60	-	1
A Singh	5	10	0	69	154	15.40	-	2
Saqlain Mushtaq	7	8	5	25*	46	15.33	-	-
JH Louw	7	13	1	82	183	15.25	-	2
DA Cosker	13	18	4	49	212	15.14	-	-
SD Thomas	18	26	2	54	352	14.66	-	1
PJ Franks	16	27	3	61	348	14.50	-	1
SJ Renshaw	12	13	6	28	101	14.42	-	-
DR Hewson	5	10	0	40	144	14.40	-	-
CEW Silverwood	13	20	2	53*	259	14.38	-	1
CG Liptrot	11	16	6	61	142	14.20	-	1
MM Patel	18	24	3	67	290	13.80	-	1
MJ Wood	17	33	0	53	451	13.66	-	1
JD Lewry	12	19	7	30*	163	13.58	-	-
J Lewis	14	23	3	62	266	13.30	-	1
CM Tolley	4	8	0	51	106	13.25	-	1
J Ormond	13	17	3	50*	183	13.07	-	1
ARK Pierson	13	13	3	66	129	12.90	-	1
ARC Fraser	12	16	5	56rh	142	12.90	-	1
NAM McLean	14	19	3	70	206	12.87	-	1
MT Brimson	14	16	6	36*	127	12.70	-	-
AJ Harris	7	11	7	8*	48	12.00	-	4
KP Dutch	6	10	0	23	119	11.90	-	-
NC Phillips	6	9	0	42	105	11.66	-	-
PCR Tufnell	16	21	4	48	198	11.64	-	-
GI Allott	6	8	6	13*	23	11.50	-	-
S Humphries	11	18	2	57	176	11.00	-	1
RJ Kirtley	15	23	5	32	194	10.77	-	-
RL Johnson	6	8	0	39	86	10.75	-	-
SJE Brown	15	23	8	29*	160	10.66	-	-
DJ Roberts	5	8	1	34*	73	10.42	-	-
PM Such	20	24	11	20	134	10.30	-	-
MN Bowen	11	21	8	19	130	10.00	-	-
TF Bloomfield	11	17	9	17*	80	10.00	-	-

Qualification: 8 innings, average 10.00

BOWLING

	Overs	Mds	Runs	Wkts	Av	Best	10/m	5/inns
Saqlain Mushtaq	290.5	90	660	58	11.37	7-19	2	7
M Muralitharan	386.2	122	777	66	11.77	7-39	5	8
DJ Nash	232	84	548	34	16.11	7-39	-	2
DJ Millns	142.3	35	372	23	16.17	5-62	-	1
MJ Cawdron	101.5	30	266	16	16.62	5-35	-	3
AC Morris	172	51	497	28	17.75	5-52	1	3
JD Ratcliffe	99	27	269	15	17.93	6-48	-	1
N Killeen	411.3	114	1070	58	18.44	7-85	-	4
MP Bicknell	545.4	157	1346	71	18.95	4-32	-	-
GM Hamilton	277.1	64	825	43	19.18	5-30	-	1
JB DeC Thompson	434.1	64	1265	64	19.76	7-89	-	3
TA Munton	409.1	107	1028	52	19.76	7-36	-	3
R Herath	154	45	377	19	19.84	6-45	-	1
CEW Silverwood	405.2	87	1204	59	20.40	5-28	-	3
AM Smith	450.1	127	1168	57	20.49	5-41	-	2
PJ Martin	446.4	134	1028	50	20.56	5-43	-	4
TM Smith	183.4	34	646	31	20.83	5-63	1	3
AR Caddick	763.5	249	1900	91	20.87	8-113	-	5

FIRST-CLASS AVERAGES

BOWLING

	Overs	Mds	Runs	Wkts	Av	Best	10/m	5/inns
RC Irani	395.2	101	1084	51	21.25	4-29	-	-
P Aldred	362.4	85	1063	50	21.26	7-101	1	5
MK Davies	423.3	137	857	40	21.42	6-49	-	3
DL Maddy	85.4	22	260	12	21.66	3-5	-	-
PAJ DeFreitas	477.2	125	1284	59	21.76	6-41	-	4
PJ Hartley	393	93	1176	54	21.77	8-65	1	2
CL Cairns	234.2	56	701	32	21.90	7-46	1	3
IDK Salisbury	558.2	145	1315	60	21.91	5-44	-	2
ESH Giddins	381.3	102	1142	52	21.96	6-90	-	2
MJ Hoggard	215.1	58	619	28	22.10	5-47	-	1
DG Cork	427.3	96	1229	55	22.34	6-113	-	4
J Wood	247.4	61	805	36	22.36	7-58	-	2
AJ Tudor	297.3	70	895	40	22.37	7-48	-	3
VC Drakes	586.2	131	1794	80	22.42	6-39	2	5
G Yates	131.1	42	315	14	22.50	6-64	-	2
SR Lampitt	287.1	70	888	39	22.76	4-28	-	-
SJE Brown	475	112	1448	63	22.98	6-25	-	5
RJ Kirtley	514.3	133	1504	65	23.13	7-21	-	3
OT Parkin	155.4	39	491	21	23.38	4-38	-	-
A Richardson	190.3	43	539	23	23.43	8-51	1	1
SB O'Connor	134.2	32	447	19	23.52	6-65	-	2
MN Bowen	264	53	872	37	23.56	5-66	-	1
PJ Franks	513	124	1489	63	23.63	5-52	-	1
MC Ilott	310.4	85	900	38	23.68	6-38	-	1
JD Lewry	381.4	84	1330	56	23.75	7-38	1	4
MA Ealham	339.2	73	981	41	23.92	6-35	-	2
AF Giles	447.4	145	938	39	24.05	5-28	-	2
PJ Newport	274.4	77	747	31	24.09	4-57	-	-
SD Thomas	447.2	78	1480	61	24.26	5-64	-	1
J Ormond	406.1	89	1283	52	24.67	5-63	-	3
A Sheriyar	609.2	119	2273	92	24.70	7-130	1	4
MM Patel	674.3	209	1568	63	24.88	8-115	1	3
SL Watkin	421.3	121	1087	43	25.27	6-75	-	3
RSG Anderson	378.3	85	1273	50	25.46	5-36	-	2
PCR Tufnell	577.3	155	1223	48	25.47	5-61	-	2
RSC Martin-Jenkins	370.2	100	1074	42	25.57	4-50	-	-
C White	354	70	1058	41	25.80	4-32	-	-
M A Butcher	180	49	445	17	26.17	4-30	-	-
S D Udal	497.3	124	1336	50	26.72	6-47	-	3
A Dale	136.5	46	407	15	27.13	3-29	-	-
G Keedy	265.4	73	711	26	27.34	5-67	-	1
MS Kasprowicz	485.5	106	1458	53	27.50	5-42	-	2
AD Mullally	310.4	93	771	28	27.53	5-106	-	1
AP Cowan	393.1	66	1267	46	27.54	6-47	-	1
DR Brown	232.5	57	717	26	27.67	7-66	-	1
SJ Harmison	565.5	120	1775	64	27.73	5-76	-	1
A Flintoff	145.4	30	419	15	27.93	5-24	-	1
IJ Harvey	296.1	77	876	31	28.25	5-76	-	1
RL Johnson	133.3	30	453	16	28.31	4-50	-	-
MPL Bulbeck	425.4	101	1456	51	28.54	5-45	1	3
DJ Thompson	184	30	685	24	28.54	4-46	-	-
KJ Innes	137	37	429	15	28.60	4-85	-	-
DE Malcolm	484.5	90	1726	60	28.76	6-39	-	3
ARC Fraser	435.1	113	1093	38	28.76	5-63	-	1
GP Swann	560.1	131	1641	57	28.78	6-41	1	2
AJ Harris	229.3	44	752	26	28.92	5-63	-	2
MP Smethurst	126.1	29	377	13	29.00	4-44	-	-
MM Betts	175.1	41	583	20	29.15	4-34	-	-
JP Hewitt	311.1	69	1022	35	29.20	5-50	-	1
JP Stephenson	310	57	1086	37	29.35	5-60	-	1
KA Parsons	285.1	80	823	28	29.39	5-57	-	1
J Lewis	492.2	134	1444	49	29.46	7-56	1	2
ME Cassar	164	34	562	19	29.57	5-51	-	1
OA Shah	99.1	14	326	11	29.63	3-33	-	-
JP Taylor	507.2	119	1427	48	29.72	5-105	-	1
G Welch	269.3	47	927	31	29.90	5-47	-	1
MA Robinson	520.4	140	1438	48	29.95	6-88	-	1
BW Gannon	259.3	47	992	33	30.06	6-80	-	2
VS Solanki	158.3	47	514	17	30.23	4-41	-	-
JM Dakin	219.1	59	575	19	30.26	4-27	-	-
TF Bloomfield	266.3	45	1007	33	30.51	5-56	-	1
PM Such	702	192	1710	55	31.09	7-136	1	2
JH Kallis	95	12	345	11	31.36	3-52	-	-
RDB Croft	521.4	135	1412	45	31.37	7-70	1	4
MV Fleming	266.3	64	726	23	31.56	3-59	-	-

FIRST-CLASS AVERAGES

BOWLING

	Overs	Mds	Runs	Wkts	Av	Best	10/m	5/inns
NAM McLean	471	105	1489	46	32.36	4-63	-	-
PW Jarvis	201.2	43	619	19	32.57	4-76	-	-
MT Brimson	316.5	98	784	24	32.66	5-51	-	1
CP Schofield	324	82	951	29	32.79	5-66	-	1
DL Vettori	469	155	1051	32	32.84	5-80	-	2
RJ Sidebottom	275.3	70	789	24	32.87	3-16	-	-
CG Liptrot	194.1	49	665	20	33.25	5-51	-	1
CJ Adams	120	28	333	10	33.30	3-37	-	-
NMK Smith	190.3	47	540	16	33.75	4-90	-	-
IDK Fisher	162	42	476	14	34.00	5-73	-	1
M Watkinson	137	30	413	12	34.41	3-43	-	-
RJ Green	212.2	46	692	20	34.60	4-21	-	-
JID Kerr	305.2	68	1075	31	34.67	7-23	-	1
BC Hollioake	249.5	49	801	23	34.82	5-51	-	1
SJ Cook	276.4	60	954	27	35.33	4-83	-	-
MJ McCague	235	44	754	21	35.90	4-36	-	-
CC Lewis	191.1	51	585	16	36.56	3-18	-	-
SJ Renshaw	381.3	93	1125	30	37.50	4-43	-	-
NC Phillips	212	41	677	18	37.61	6-92	1	2
AP Grayson	319.2	98	849	22	38.59	4-16	-	-
GD Rose	219.2	61	657	17	38.64	4-14	-	-
AL Penberthy	266.5	84	735	19	38.68	3-13	-	-
PN Weekes	316.1	68	890	23	38.69	4-50	-	-
DW Headley	457.5	93	1442	37	38.97	4-74	-	-
DP Mather	142.2	26	469	12	39.08	3-44	-	-
AG Wharf	335.3	65	1216	31	39.22	4-30	-	-
GI Allott	163.1	32	593	15	39.53	3-22	-	-
KDM Walker	142	31	479	12	39.91	3-65	-	-
G Chapple	337.5	93	964	24	40.16	5-92	-	1
PS Jones	255.2	50	845	21	40.23	4-126	-	-
SP Jones	208	31	776	19	40.84	5-31	-	1
MP Vaughan	137.1	26	424	10	42.40	2-19	-	-
MW Alleyne	367	109	1000	23	43.47	3-36	-	-
UBA Rashid	218.3	67	664	15	44.26	4-41	-	-
DA Cosker	322	81	844	19	44.42	3-100	-	-
RG Halsall	168	35	491	11	44.63	3-64	-	-
VJ Wells	176	47	473	10	47.30	2-2	-	-
ID Blackwell	250.1	69	595	12	49.58	3-30	-	-
AD Mascarenhas	308	98	868	17	51.05	2-2	-	-
RK Illingworth	336.4	92	767	15	51.13	3-58	-	-
MCJ Ball	266	69	723	13	55.61	3-38	-	-
ARK Pierson	271.2	52	789	13	60.69	4-131	-	-
RD Stemp	325.5	89	974	16	60.87	4-114	-	-
A Symonds	207.1	37	761	12	63.41	2-48	-	-
JN Snape	277.1	71	804	12	67.00	3-67	-	-
TC Hicks	181.1	28	672	10	67.20	2-61	-	-
GB Loveridge	209.4	25	830	11	75.45	2-59	-	-

Qualification: 10 wickets in 8 innings

The following bowlers took 10 wickets in fewer than 8 innings:-

MJ Saggers	59.5	13	192	12	16.00	4-26	-	-
KJ Dean	66.4	14	198	12	16.50	4-34	-	-
JM de la Pena	63.5	19	240	13	18.46	6-18	1	1
D Gough	96.3	20	319	17	18.76	4-27	-	-
PM Hutchison	65.5	16	263	13	20.23	6-35	-	1
CG Greenidge, Jr	76.4	20	231	11	21.00	5-60	-	1
ASA Perera	66.5	9	253	11	23.00	7-73	-	1
IS Gallage	80.5	24	235	10	23.50	3-18	-	-
DS Lucas	103.5	23	394	15	26.26	5-104	-	1
SM Sheikh	96.5	18	338	12	28.16	4-25	-	-
CD Crowe	92	14	348	11	31.63	3-63	-	-
JJ Bates	141	46	356	11	32.36	5-154	-	1

LEADING FIELDERS

69 – RJ Turner (67 ct/2 st); 61 – CMW Read (59 ct/2 st); 60 – RC Russell (55 ct/5 st);
56 – JN Batty (49 ct/7 st); 53 – AN Aymes (51 ct/2 st, SJ Rhodes (51 ct/2 st);
50 – MP Speight (48 ct/2 st), DC Nash (46 ct/4 st), PA Nixon (46 ct/2 st); 49 – WK Hegg (45 ct/4 st);
47 – BJ Hyam(46 ct/1 st); 43 – D Ripley (40 ct/3 st); 41 – RJ Blakey; 35 – SA Marsh (28 ct/7 st);
31 – AD Brown (30 ct/1 st), KM Krikken (30 ct/1 st); 30 – NV Knight; 29 – SG Law;
27 – GF Archer, ME Trescothick; 26 – AD Shaw (25 ct/1 st); 25 – PD Collingwood, A Flintoff,
WS Kendall; 24 – D Byas, T Frost (23 ct/1 st); 23 – CJ Adams, AC Parore; 21 – MJ Chilton,
VS Solanki; 20 – MW Alleyne, I Dawood, MJ Di Venuto, SP Fleming, S Humphries (18 ct/2 st)

WOMEN'S CRICKET

"Women? Inside the MCC pavilion at Lord's? It will never happen!" Well, this year it did; and not before time.

BY SARAH POTTER

Even Old Father Time seemed to swivel his stooped back away from the biting north wind that blew a snowstorm over Lord's on the opening day of the season. No amount of hiding, though, could disguise the zing of excitement rippling through the Victorian splendour of the pavilion. Women were in there and ten had been honoured with life memberships.

Perfect timing, since the sense of expectation was running through the women's game like Muralitharan runs through county batsmen. Merger with the England and Wales Cricket Board enabled the appointment of the former Middlesex and Kent wicketkeeper, Paul Farbrace, as England coach and ensured an international summer series against India.

These wristy, spinning entertainers had not toured here since 1986 and neither side was sure of the other. They did not meet in the last World Cup, staged in India during December 1997, and both lost in the semi-finals; England to New Zealand, India to the eventual winners, Australia.

This three-match one-day series and one-off Test would, then, decide who could claim to be the third best team in the world. Since both teams already have one eye trained on the next World Cup in New Zealand in December 2000, and since so many modern-day cricketers cannot act without first thinking about psychology, it was a claim that seemed important.

England were already on the back foot, since Jan Brittin, their prolific opening batsman, had packed up her spikes – and picked up an OBE in the Queen's honours list – and Barbara Daniels, the National Manager of Women's Cricket at

Karen Smithies, England Ladies cricket captain.
David Munden/Sportsline Photographic

the ECB, had opted for a year out. Farbrace, and specialists like Graham Dilley, had put in plenty of winter work with the England squad but these gaps would be hard to fill from a domestic game still building its foundations.

Step forward, then, Karen Smithies. Not a new name, since the flame-haired all-rounder has captained England since that glorious, unexpected World Cup triumph at Lord's in 1993 – for which she too collected an OBE. It was the left-hander's grit and skill that salvaged reward for England when home ambitions were being ambushed by India.

Old Trafford played host to the opening one-day international in early July. The track was shaved and baked, mean on pace and bounce. A pity, since the Sky television cameras followed every low-scoring ball. England could muster only 128 runs in their 50 overs, while India's four spinners must have thought they were bowling in Calcutta, so far did the ball turn.

Nonetheless, with team spirit worn like a proud badge, England almost defended their total. Until, that is, a tall and elegant stroke-player from Delhi decided it was about time her country won an international on English soil. Anjum Chopra scored a half-century as faultless as it was decisive and, despite a tense, last-over finish, England were beaten by one wicket.

Worse was to follow as, three days later in Northampton, India secured the series. The tourists demonstrated their versatility, for this time the pitch had zip and bounce. Bat overcame ball, or, more specifically, Chopra overcame Clare Connor.

The left-handed opener drove, cut and pulled her way to her maiden international century. Again, it was the innings that made the difference. Connor, England's new vice-captain, would have been proud to play it, for the Sussex all-rounder considers herself more of a batsman than bowler. She may have to adjust her thoughts since it was her left-arm spin that inked her name into the record books.

Hat-tricks are rare in women's international cricket – only three had ever been achieved – but Connor, bowling in wraparound shades, managed the feat in the last over of the Indian innings to take her match haul to five wickets.

England needed something to spark them for Farbrace and his charges were being outplayed. An action replay looked likely at Trent Bridge, where India scorched the already parched turf with attacking stroke-play. Their 220 total loomed large, especially when England's familiar tumble of wickets began. For the second time in a week Charlotte Edwards could not last the first over and, despite their obvious talent, Kathryn Leng and Jane Cassar are not reliable in the middle order.

Smithies, however, is a born fighter and did not allow the dispiriting loss of partners to deflect her. Her undefeated 110 was as good an innings as I have seen, certainly the bravest. Having run her heart out in partnerships with Sue Redfern and Melissa Reynard, she heaved the last ball of the match to the mid-on boundary, evading two diving fielders. It was the four runs England needed for victory.

So to the Test match at Shenley. Sudha Shah, India's coach, admitted during the first day's play that her team had not recovered from the disappointment. Perhaps that was the reason India only just managed to avoid the follow-on. Edwards at last found form, scoring her maiden Test century in the first innings, while Smithies managed a half-century in both innings.

England's captain has become the cement binding too many ordinary bricks. With Edwards, she was the only one to score at more than a run an over – inexcusable given the reliable wicket. Under unstinting sunshine the Test did, though, sparkle on the last day. India spun themselves back into it and their batsmen really ought to have ensured victory.

Still, England do fight – even if their incessant clapping and shouting too often spills over into unacceptable gamesmanship – and a flurry of late wickets almost claimed the match. The realists in the camp will acknowledge, though, that it was the tourists who had played the more positive cricket and, as such, deserved their silverware.

So there is much grafting, searching and grooming to be done if England are to lift the World Cup next year. Just maybe, though, the real reason for optimism is that Farbrace and his players have the will – if not yet the poise – to rise to the challenge. Old Father Time will surely swivel back to salute that.

CGU NATIONAL LEAGUE
By Mark Baldwin

17 April 1999: Division One
at Leicester
Leicestershire 152 for 7 (40 overs)
Hampshire 17 for 2 (5.4 overs)
Match abandoned
Leicestershire 2 pts, Hampshire 2 pts

The new, jazzy, two-division National League began in less than captivating style. It rained.

Poor weather kept away spectators, with less than 1,000 turning up at Grace Road for the meeting of the freshly-named Leicestershire Foxes and the Hampshire Hawks. But why was this game scheduled on a day that saw Leicester's rugby team, the Tigers, playing at home? At least the hardy souls who came to see a small piece of cricket history being made had some action to watch – although Leicestershire struggling to reach 152 for 7 from (ironically) a reduction to 40 overs was hardly thrill-a-minute entertainment. Soon, however, there was no entertainment at all – with Hampshire 17 for 2 from 5.3 overs in reply, the rain came. The only noteworthy event of the whole afternoon, in fact, was the first instance of a 'fee hit' in county cricket. A John Stephenson no-ball in the 32nd over gave Dominic Williamson the chance of a free swing at the next delivery. Williamson, to his eternal credit, marked the moment by stepping back towards square leg and carving the ball past short third man to the boundary.

18 April 1999: Division Two
at Chester-le-Street
Surrey 175 for 7 (26 overs)
Durham 186 (25.4 overs) DC Boon 55
Surrey (4 pts) won by 2 runs
(D/L method: Durham target 189 in 26 overs)

at Lord's
Middlesex 239 for 6 (45 overs) JL Langer 71,
MA Roseberry 64
Nottinghamshire 177 (44.1 overs) P Johnson 57,
PN Weekes 4 for 43
Middlesex (4 pts) won by 62 runs

Durham's Dynamos scored 11 more runs than Surrey at Chester-le-Street, and in two balls less, but under the Duckworth-Lewis system it was not enough to tame the Lions. Adam Hollioake, the

Dominic Cork could not lead Derbyshire out of the CGU second division.
David Munden/Sportsline Photographic

Surrey captain, held his nerve in a dramatic final over to take his side to a two-run win. Durham needed just four runs from the final over, with three wickets in hand, but contrived to lose as both Jon Lewis and Simon Brown were run out and Neil Killeen was caught at mid-on. Surrey were 52 for 1 when a hailstorm forced a rescheduling of a 26-over-per-side match, and that was the signal for some frantic hitting from Ben Hollioake, whose 45 occupied only 33 balls. Three of his four sixes were from successive deliveries from Paul Collingwood. For a long while, however, Durham seemed in control with David Boon making 55 off 39 balls from the top of the order.

The first National League match to be played at Lord's was a low-key affair, with a meagre crowd shivering in pale sunlight and a chill wind and the game being the first of many in this competition to go on far too late into a Sunday evening. Vasbert Drakes and Chris Read did well to add 59 in nine overs as Nottinghamshire tried in vain to match Middlesex's 239 for 6, but the light was so gloomy that many of the few spectators who braved the elements had opted to go home by then – both to warm themselves up and to get themselves ready for the working week ahead. Justin Langer (71) and the returning Michael Roseberry (64) put on 131 to set up the victory, while for Notts only Paul Johnson (57 off 67 balls) looked like threatening the Crusader march.

The match between Kent and Lancashire at Canterbury was rained off.

24 April 1999: Division Two
at Taunton
Somerset 223 (43.4 overs) PCL Holloway 54, MM Betts 4 for 39
Durham 171 (39.2 overs)
Somerset (4 pts) won by 52 runs

Somerset earned themselves a winning start to their second division campaign by outgunning Durham by 52 runs at Taunton. Piran Holloway's 54, plus some solid middle-order contributions, took the home side to 223 and although they wastefully left eight balls unused it proved too much for a Durham side which fell away from 151 for 5.

25 April 1999: Division One
at Chelmsford
Lancashire 301 for 6 (45 overs) A Flintoff 143, JP Crawley 84
Essex 298 (44.5 overs) RJ Rollins 87, SG Law 55
Lancashire (4 pts) won by 3 runs

at Southampton
Kent 208 for 8 (45 overs)
Hampshire 130 for 1 (28 overs) JP Stephenson 71*
Hampshire (4 pts) won by 21 runs
(D/L method: Hampshire target 156 in 34 runs)

at Edgbaston
Worcestershire 287 for 4 (45 overs) WPC Weston 125, PR Pollard 70
Warwickshire 113 (21.4 overs) DA Leatherdale 4 for 23
Worcestershire (4 pts) won by 117 runs
(D/L method: Warwickshire target 231 in 29 overs)

at Headingley
Gloucestershire 145 (36 overs) C White 4 for 25
Yorkshire 147 for 8 (43.2 overs)
Yorkshire (4 pts) won by two wickets

Andrew Flintoff flayed the Essex attack with an exhibition of brutal hitting at Chelmsford. Flintoff, entering at number five when Lancashire were 68 for 3, scored 143 off a scarcely creditable 66 balls with nine sixes and 15 fours. The power he generated with his huge frame, natural timing and straightforward technique was quite awesome. John Crawley, overshadowed but outstanding too, hit 84 from 108 balls, and the pair's fourth-wicket stand of 179 in 20 overs lifted Lancashire to an intimidating 301 for 6. Amazingly, Essex almost won the game. When their last man was run out off the final ball they were just four runs short of victory, a thrilling chase being sustained mainly by Robert Rollins whose 87 off 51 balls would have captured the headlines on any other day.

Two breaks for rain aided Hampshire's attempt to overhaul Kent's 208 for 8 at Southampton. John Stephenson finished 71 not out when the weather brought a premature end to Hampshire's efforts of making 156 from 34 overs, under the Duckworth-Lewis method. But, at 130 for 1, they were ahead of the asking rate anyway.

After taking eight overs to get off the mark, Philip Weston, the Worcestershire opener, smashed six sixes and 11 fours in a 124-ball 125 to spearhead his side's 117-run mauling of local rivals Warwickshire at Edgbaston. Weston and Paul Pollard (70) put on 149 for the first wicket, and a total of 287 for 4 was a formidable one. Warwickshire then slumped to 27 for 2 off seven overs before emerging, following an hour's rain break, to find their target readjusted to 231 from 29 overs. David Leatherdale (4 for 23) benefited most from the frenzied, unsuccessful slogging that then ensued.

The batting of Darren Gough rescued Yorkshire at Headingley. Chasing Gloucestershire's modest 145, Yorkshire slid to a nervy 114 for 7 before Gough joined the young batsman Gary Fellows to score 15 and add a crucial 26 in the evening gloom. Earlier Craig White had followed up his 4 for 25 to hit 49.

25 April 1999: Division Two
at Lord's
Glamorgan 208 (44.5 overs) A Dale 57, RDB Croft 53
Middlesex 173 for 9 (45 overs)
Glamorgan (4 pts) won by 35 runs

at The Oval
Surrey 207 for 9 (45 overs) AL Penberthy 4 for 48
Northamptonshire 211 for 6 (43.2 overs)
MB Loye 55
Northamptonshire (4 pts) won by four wickets

at Hove
Derbyshire 181 for 7 (45 overs) DG Cork 61*
Sussex 137 for 3 (36 overs) RR Montgomerie 61*,
CJ Adams 57
Sussex (4 pts) won by 11 runs
(D/L method: Sussex 126 in 36 overs)

Glamorgan's long-overdue first batting effort of the season was bolstered by half-centuries from both Adrian Dale and Robert Croft, and a total of 208 was too much for Middlesex at Lord's. Steady new-ball bowling from Owen Parkin and Steve Watkin then undermined the Middlesex reply, with Keith Dutch's 29 being the highest score in an innings which finally petered out to 173 for 9 in near darkness at 7.45pm.

A breezy 55 from opener Mal Loye, and an unbroken stand of 60 for the seventh wicket between Tony Penberthy and Graeme Swann, took Northants to a four-wicket win against fancied Surrey at The Oval. Penberthy had earlier picked up 4 for 48 as Surrey coughed and spluttered their way to 207 for 9.

Skilful slow left-arm bowling from their new signing, Umer Rashid, set up victory for Sussex against Derbyshire on a painfully slow Hove pitch. Rashid took 3 for 13 from his nine overs and only a combative 61 not out from Dominic Cork hauled Derbyshire up to 181 for 7. A second-wicket stand of 122 between Richard Montgomerie and Chris Adams then looked to be sweeping Sussex to victory but rain and bad light interrupted. Most people in the small crowd had left the ground by the time the match was officially called off at 7.30pm – but Sussex didn't mind. They won by 11 runs under the Duckworth-Lewis regulations.

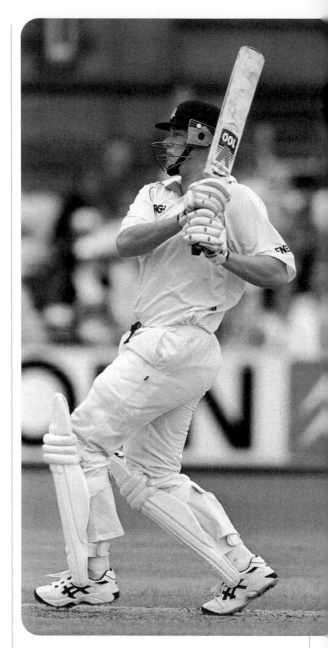

Andrew Flintoff scored 143 to smash the Essex attack and bring victory to Lancashire.
David Munden/Sportsline Photographic

3 May 1999: Division One
at Bristol
Gloucestershire 199 for 9 (45 overs)
THC Hancock 57, JN Snape 56
Lancashire 177 (42.1 overs) KJ Barnett 4 for 29
Gloucestershire (4 pts) won by 22 runs

at Southampton
Hampshire 168 (44.2 overs) AF Giles
4 for 29
Warwickshire 172 for 3 (29.4 overs) DL Hemp 72*,
TL Penney 55
Warwickshire (4 pts) won by seven wickets

at Canterbury
Leicestershire 239 for 4 (45 overs) CC Lewis 116*,
PA Nixon 96*
Kent 243 for 7 (37.2 overs) A Symonds 95
Kent (4 pts) won by three wickets

at Worcester
Worcestershire 212 for 5 (45 overs)
DA Leatherdale 70*, GR Haynes 66
Yorkshire 213 for 7 (44.2 overs)
D Byas 87
Yorkshire (4 pts) won by three wickets

Two cricketers irked not to be involved in the imminent World Cup lit up the stage at Canterbury, where Kent won a fine match against Leicestershire by three wickets. First, Chris Lewis scored 116 not out from just 111 balls, with a six and 12 fours, and put on 220 in 32 overs with Paul Nixon, whose unbeaten 96 took only 93 balls. Matthew Fleming, the Kent captain, conceded 77 runs from his nine overs and a total of 239 for 4 was a challenging one. Enter Andrew Symonds: the Australian, Kent's new overseas signing, blitzed 95 from 63 balls to shock the visitors.

Hampshire were thrashed by seven wickets at home to Warwickshire, scoring only 168 after surprisingly deciding to bat first and then seeing their own bowling attack flayed to all parts of Southampton by David Hemp (72 not out) and Trevor Penney (55).

Aggressive half-centuries from Jeremy Snape and Tim Hancock, plus some inspired slow-medium floaters from Kim Barnett, who took 4 for 29, was too much for Lancashire in front of an animated 3,000 crowd at Bristol. Gloucestershire recovered from 43 for 4 to reach 199 for 9 and then Lancashire, following an opening stand of 73, fell apart to be dismissed for 173.

Yorkshire, spearheaded by skipper David Byas's 87, held their nerve in a tight finale at New Road to beat Worcestershire by three wickets. Gavin Haynes made 66 and David Leatherdale 70 not out, but a feature of Worcestershire's 212 for 5 was the potent new-ball bowling of Chris Silverwood, with 3 for 30.

Despite a half-century by Paul Johnson, Middlesex defeated Nottinghamshire at Lord's.
David Munden/Sportsline Photographic

3 May 1999: Division Two
at Chester-le-Street
Durham 189 for 9 (45 overs) JA Daley 90
Middlesex 192 for 2 (39.4 overs)
MA Roseberry 77*
Middlesex (4 pts) won by eight wickets

at Cardiff
Glamorgan 220 for 7 (45 overs) AW Evans 108
Derbyshire 195 for 8 (45 overs)
Glamorgan (2 pts) won by 25 runs

at Northampton
Sussex 198 (45 overs) PA Cottey 62
Northamptonshire 130 (38.3 overs) UBA Rashid
4 for 32, MA Robinson 4 for 34
Sussex (4 pts) won by 68 runs

at Trent Bridge
Nottinghamshire 237 for 8 (45 overs)
Surrey 226 (44.3 overs) IJ Ward 80, MN Bowen
4 for 46
Nottinghamshire (4 pts) won by 11 runs

Yorkshire's captain, David Byas, leads his team to victory over Worcestershire.
David Munden/Sportsline Photographic

Mike Roseberry was a happy man after his unbeaten 77 guided Middlesex to an eight-wicket win against his former club Durham at the Riverside. It was, in fact, a solid batting effort by the visitors after Durham, thanks to Jimmy Daley's 90 from 114 balls, made a barely adequate 189 for 9.

Tight bowling by Mark Robinson (4 for 34) and Umer Rashid (4 for 32) eased Sussex to a 68-run win against Northamptonshire at Wantage Road. A gutsy 62 by Tony Cottey was the other reason for Sussex's success as they totalled 198.

Alun Evans was the undoubted star of the show at Cardiff, and he showed unrestrained glee when reaching his maiden one-day hundred. Evans' 108 was the basis of a good score of 220 for 7, and no Derbyshire batsman could get going in reply. A committed all-round display in the field by Glamorgan restricted their visitors to 195 for 8 and clinched victory by 25 runs.

An outstanding 80 from 81 balls by Ian Ward was not enough to prevent Surrey going down by 11 runs to Nottinghamshire at Trent Bridge. A dashing 38 from 23 balls by Paul Johnson provided early momentum in Notts's 237 for 8, and an unbroken ninth-wicket stand of 58 between Alex Wharf and Mark Bowen also made a big difference. Notts struck an early blow by dismissing Alastair Brown cheaply but Ward made a game of it.

23 May 1999: Division One
at Chelmsford
Essex 220 for 9 (45 overs) RC Irani 55
Yorkshire 223 for 7 (44.3 overs)
Yorkshire (4 pts) won by three wickets

at Old Trafford
Lancashire 186 for 8 (45 overs) MJ Rawnsley 4 for 27
Worcestershire 187 for 4 (40.2 overs) PR Pollard 66,
KR Spiring 56
Worcestershire (4 pts) won by six wickets

at Edgbaston
Kent 170 for 7 (45 overs)
Warwickshire 176 for 6 (44.1 overs)
Warwickshire (4 pts) won by four wickets

Yorkshire's Matthew Wood is rapidly becoming the scourge of Essex in the former Sunday League competition. He registered his best score of 65 not out against the same opponents at Scarborough last year. This time on Essex turf he was again unbeaten just shy of his half-century. He had come in with 99

Matthew Wood is making a habit of frustrating Essex.
David Munden/Sportsline Photographic

needed off 15 overs and, showing a maturity beyond his 22 years, steered Yorkshire to the target with three balls to spare. Earlier Ronnie Irani had made a disciplined half-century in Essex's inadequate total.

The appearance of WCJ Athey (playing for his fourth county) at Old Trafford merely served to underline the crisis at Worcestershire thanks to World Cup calls and injuries. Athey, who had been hastily registered with Lord's just before the match,

finished on the winning side with an unbeaten 22 although much of the groundwork had been done by Reuben Spiring and Paul Pollard. Matthew Rawnsley weighed in with four wickets as Lancashire were restricted to a very gettable total.

The Warwickshire Bears and the Kent Spitfires suffered a relatively low-scoring match with no one on either side getting into the 40s. Kent's decision to bat first did them little good. Trevor Ward was quickly dismissed while opening partner Ed Smith took 13 overs to score 14. Then Matthews, Fleming and Walker made the highest individual scores in the match, reaching 39. Warwickshire were up to it though, with Trevor Penney and Tony Frost seeing them home, the latter hitting a six off the first ball of the last over to win the match.

23 May 1999: Division Two
at Derby
Durham 219 for 6 (45 overs) JJB Lewis 85, DC Boon 66
Derbyshire 224 for 6 (43.5 overs) PAJ DeFreitas 61, MJ Slater 51
Derbyshire (4 pts) won by four wickets

at Taunton
Surrey 184 for 9 (45 overs)
Somerset 185 for 4 (38.3 overs) PD Bowler 70, RJ Turner 63
Somerset (4 pts) won by six wickets

at Hove
Sussex 181 (44.2 overs) CJ Adams 71, RR Montgomerie 54
Glamorgan 127 (38.1 overs)
Sussex (4 pts) won by 54 runs

The Durham Dynamos' cause was not helped by the late withdrawal of John Morris after he was hit on the foot by Melvyn Betts in the pre-match nets. They were still given the best start with an opening stand of 128 between David Boon, who contributed 66, and Jon Lewis, who top-scored with a good-looking 85. But they fell away towards the end. Phil DeFreitas, who reached his half-century with a runner after straining a leg on 42, and Michael Slater who hit 51 made sure of a comfortable victory.

Peter Bowler and Rob Turner led Somerset's annihilation of the Surrey Lions with a 115-run stand for the third wicket. Wicketkeeper Turner scored at better than a run a ball; Bowler's 70 occupied 109 balls. The match got off to a dramatic start when Surrey, put in by the Sabres, lost three wickets in the first two overs. The third of those was bizarre. Ben Hollioake played Steffan Jones defensively towards mid-on, but his back foot slid against the stumps just hard enough to dislodge a bail.

A century stand between Sussex Shark's captain Chris Adams and Richard Montgomerie, followed by some controlled bowling and excellent out-cricket snuffed out the Dragons' fire completely. Glamorgan, still without captain Matthew Maynard, had no one who was able to go on the counter-attack and try to dominate the Sussex attack. Montgomerie scored his 54 from 67 balls. He and Adams hit 15 boundaries between them, which constituted the Sussex total of fours; Glamorgan managed just nine boundaries in all.

30 May 1999: Division One
at Gloucester
Gloucestershire 188 for 9 (45 overs)
Worcestershire 138 (42.2 overs)
Worcestershire (4 pts) won by 50 runs

at Leicester
Lancashire 208 (44.3 overs) GD Lloyd 55*
Leicestershire 156 (41.1 overs)
Lancashire (4 pts) won by 52 runs

at Edgbaston
Essex 238 for 5 (45 overs) N Hussain 81,
DDJ Robinson 53
Warwickshire 109 (28.5 overs) RC Irani 4 for 13
Essex (4 pts) won by 129 runs

at Headingley
Hampshire 132 for 7 (45 overs
Yorkshire 136 for 2 (18.3 overs) C White 67
Yorkshire (4 pts) won by eight wickets

Spin dominated the encounter between the Gloucestershire Gladiators and the Worcestershire Royals, with 34 overs being sent down for a total of eight wickets for 92 runs, which just about summed events up. The King's School pitch was a slow one, with only Kim Barnett able to show how it should be played. Jeremy Snape, like Barnett another of Gloucestershire's imports over the winter, produced a useful all-round performance with a tidy innings and some neat off-spin bowling. Paul Pollard top-scored for the Royals with 29.

Andrew Flintoff did what a streaker failed to do, namely enliven a chilly day at Grace Road with an excellent all-round performance which went a long way to helping Lancashire Lightning secure victory. While the likes of Graham Lloyd, with an unbeaten 55 off 80 balls, and Neil Fairbrother (31 runs off 42 balls) were providing a steady flow of runs for the cause, Flintoff emerged to smash 29 off 16 deliveries, including two sixes and three fours. He then held a catch and took two wickets.

Nasser Hussain was a man with a mission at Edgbaston. Or so he appeared. In the wake of England's ignominious exit from the World Cup he vented his disappointment on the very ground where they had lost to India. His 114-ball 81 was the mainstay of the Essex innings. He shared a first-wicket stand of 124 with Darren Robinson, who also scored a half-century. Then Ronnie Irani steamed in to take four wickets for just 13 runs and the lacklustre Bears were left with sore heads.

The Hampshire Hawks were first strangled by Darren Gough, Chris Silverwood and Ryan Sidebottom. They were then subjected to a flogging around Headingley as Craig White smashed his way to 67 off only 48 balls: two sixes and nine fours were hit by the Australian-born Yorkshireman, and his assault included 20 runs off one Simon Renshaw over. Hampshire had neither the batting nor the bowling to cope. Their top scorer was John Stephenson with 37.

30 May 1999: Division Two
at Cardiff
Glamorgan 214 for 5 (45 overs) A Dale 74*
Northamptonshire 208 (45 overs) AL Penberthy 60
Glamorgan (4 pts) won by 6 runs

at Lord's
Middlesex 155 for 8 (45 overs)
Sussex 156 for 1 (41.3 overs) MJ Di Venuto 79*
Sussex (4 pts) won by nine wickets

at Trent Bridge
Nottinghamshire 228 for 9 (45 overs) CMW Read 62,
MPL Bulbeck 4 for 40
Somerset 229 for 5 (42.5 overs) J Cox 101,
PCL Holloway 74
Somerset (4 pts) won by five wickets

at The Oval
Surrey 153 (44.1 overs)
Derbyshire 154 for 4 (39.5 overs)
Derbyshire (4 pts) won by six wickets

The premature loss of Steve Watkin with a back spasm, after he had bowled just three and a half overs, was not enough to stop the Glamorgan Dragons secure their third victory of the season. But it was close. Thanks to Tony Penberthy's half-century, the Northamptonshire Steelbacks needed 13 runs to win from the last three deliveries and that came down to six off the last ball, from which Paul Taylor was run out. Adrian Dale had done much of the hard work with the bat, scoring his second National League fifty of the season.

Stifling cricket and a slow pitch conspired to present everyone with a dull, low-scoring match at Lord's. Middlesex Crusaders could not get the runs flowing fast enough. Wicketkeeper David Nash top-scored with 37 not out, an innings which contained a solitary four; Chris Adams picked up three wickets for a miserly 22 runs. Sussex maintained their unbeaten record thanks to Michael Di Venuto's highest National League score of the season as he and Adams put on an unbroken 91 for the second wicket and victory.

Somerset kept their 100 per cent record, but at a price. Andy Caddick suffered a ricked back and Marcus Trescothick was carried off after twisting a knee. But captain Jamie Cox went on and thumped a century as he and Piran Holloway put on 171 for the second wicket. Chris Read had salvaged some pride for Nottinghamshire with his highest score in this form of the game, while Matthew Bulbeck picked up four fortuitous wickets.

The appearance, at The Oval, of coach Colin Wells for his first senior competitive match since 1996 underscored Derbyshire Scorpions' problems with injuries. Two players made their debuts for Derbyshire: Michael Deane, a pace bowler, who took three Surrey wickets for 42, and Anthony Woolley, who bowled tidily and economically, in a largely featureless Surrey innings. Stephen Titchard revealed application by hitting an unbeaten 44 to steer Derbyshire home with more than five overs to spare.

6 June 1999: Division One
at Ilford
Gloucestershire 224 for 9 (45 overs)
MW Alleyne 59, RC Russell 58*,
RC Irani 4 for 49
Essex 204 (42.5 overs)
Gloucestershire (4 pts) won by 20 runs

England's captain Nasser Hussain made 81 for Essex as they thrashed Warwickshire by 129 runs.
David Munden/Sportsline Photographic

at Tunbridge Wells
Worcestershire 182 for 5 (38.4 overs) VS Solanki 55
Kent 102 (21.1 overs) MJ Rawnsley 5 for 26
Worcestershire (4 pts) won by 67 runs
(D/L method: Kent target 170 in 26 overs)

at Leicester
Warwickshire 212 for 7 (45 overs) NV Knight 102*
Leicestershire 205 for 9 (42 overs) BF Smith 66
Leicestershire (4 pts) won by one wicket
(D/L method: Leicestershire target 205 in 42 overs)

While Danny Law was laying all about him with a lot of abandon and a certain amount of luck, it looked as if Essex Eagles, who had got off to a fine start thanks to Stuart Law and Darren Robinson, might overhaul the Gloucestershire Gladiators. Essex bowler Ronnie Irani picked up his second four-wicket haul in the competition in six days, including those of Mark Alleyne and Jack Russell, who each scored half-centuries – Russell's unbeaten. However, Gloucestershire's bowlers were that much tighter and they got home with two overs to spare.

It took a while for the Kent target to be calculated under the Duckworth-Lewis method but the 170 from 26 overs was beyond their capabilities. Matthew Rawnsley claimed a Sunday-best return of 5 for 26, easy pickings for the slow left-arm spinner, while Alamgir Sheriyar's pace accounted for three other Kent batsmen. Vikram Solanki, who shared in an inventive stand of 76 in 15 overs with Gavin Haynes (33), made an entertaining 55 after Paul Pollard retired hurt after being struck on the finger.

Nick Knight's first one-day hundred for 12 months was a salient reminder of his undoubted talents in the short game. His unbeaten 102 was his third in one-day cricket, but it was first since the last game of the 1997 AXA League. The pity of it was that it was in vain. Leicestershire's Alan Mullally stole his thunder, hitting the winning runs off the last ball of the match after Ben Smith had scored a useful 66 off 65 balls, including two sixes and five fours. Paul Nixon and Mullally saw them home.

6 June 1999: Division Two
at Derby
Glamorgan 207 for 8 (45 overs) AW Evans 52, GM Roberts 4 for 23
Derbyshire 205 (42.2 overs) ID Blackwell 97
Match tied (D/L method: Derbyshire target 206 in 44 overs)
Derbyshire (2 pts), Glamorgan (2 pts)

at Chester-le-Street
Somerset 231 for 9 (45 overs) PD Bowler 56
Durham 195 for 6 (39 overs)
Somerset (4 pts) won by 5 runs (D/L method: Durham target 201 in 39 overs)

at Northampton
Northamptonshire 201 for 9 (38 overs) RJ Warren 61
Middlesex 121 (22.1 overs) AL Penberthy 4 for 17
Northamptonshire (4 pts) won by 338 runs (D/L method: Middlesex target 160 in 26 overs)

Ronnie Irani enjoyed an excellent all-round season that led to his recall for England in the final Test.
David Munden/Sportsline Photographic

Somehow there is not quite the same thrill to a tied match when Duckworth-Lewis has been applied to the proceedings. Glamorgan scored two more runs than Derbyshire, yet it was a tie. Ian Blackwell did his damnedest to win the game for the Scorpions, but when he was last man out with scores level it was the Dragons who had the sting in the tail. Derbyshire had had to re-register Simon Base and Frankie Griffith for the game. Alun Evans had earlier scored a 42-ball half-century for Glamorgan.

The Duckworth-Lewis system was at its best at the Riverside Ground. The mathematical calculations left Durham needing 45 from five overs and they fell narrowly short. Before Martin Speight's dismissal Durham had been three runs in front; when he edged a catch behind they slipped to minus four and ultimately the target proved beyond them. Peter

Bowler, back after a back injury, passed a landmark 5,000 runs in the competition on the way to his 56 off 83 balls.

A burst of three wickets from Northamptonshire's Devon Malcolm and an economical mopping-up spell of 4 for 17 in three overs by Tony Penberthy ensured that Middlesex were left well short of the revised target of 160 from 26 overs under the Duckworth-Lewis method. Only Owais Shah, with 37 off 30 balls, showed any fight. Russell Warren's 61, with other valuable contributions from captain Matthew Hayden, Rob Bailey and Kevin Innes enabled Northamptonshire to reach an imposing total in their 38 overs.

13 June 1999: Division One
at Chelmsford
Kent 245 (45 overs) A Symonds 85
Essex 225 (43.1 overs) N Hussain 65
Kent (4 pts) won by 20 runs

at Bristol
Leicestershire 214 (45 overs) IJ Harvey 5 for 41
Gloucestershire 176 (41.1 overs)
Leicestershire (4 pts) won by 38 runs

at Basingstoke
Yorkshire 191 for 9 (45 overs) A McGrath 75
Hampshire 164 (42.1 overs) MP Vaughan 4 for 31
Yorkshire (4 pts) won by 27 runs

at Edgbaston
Warwickshire 127 (44.4 overs) PJ Martin 5 for 28
Lancashire 130 for 4 (21.5 overs)
Lancashire (4 pts) won by six wickets

Ashley Cowan and Barry Hyam provided Kent with some ticklish moments as they added 27 in just 13 balls for the eighth wicket, raising hopes of an Essex win, especially after the century opening stand between Nasser Hussain and Darren Robinson. However the last three wickets fell in seven balls and Andrew Symonds' very fine innings was not wasted. At one point Symonds seemed certain of a century, blasting his way effortlessly to 85 off 79 balls with the help of two sixes and half a dozen fours.

Leicestershire's innings petered out after being given such a good start by Darren Stevens and Iain Sutcliffe, but it mattered not because Gloucestershire seemed to lack the stomach for a fight. This despite Ian Harvey's 5 for 41, his first such league haul. Stevens was fairly thundering

along at a shade under a run a ball when he was taken by Mark Alleyne; during his innings Stevens had struck a six, the ball striking the press box window some 90 yards away at mid-wicket without breaking any glass.

A spell of four wickets for seven runs in five overs by Michael Vaughan proved critical to Yorkshire maintaining their 100 per cent record. Until then Hampshire were looking good for the victory with Robin Smith well set. Then came a brilliant catch by Greg Blewett and Hampshire went to pieces. But Yorkshire had also suffered a collapse, crashing to 88 for 6 before Anthony McGrath pulled them round with a stirring half-century of 102 balls with two sixes and eight fours.

Lancashire lived up to their sobriquet of Lightning as they dashed off the requisite runs for victory over the Bears in 23.1 overs, Andrew Flintoff thumping 45 off 35 balls, an onslaught which included 20 off one Ed Giddins over with two sixes and two fours. Warwickshire's innings had been hampered by controlled bowling from Mike Watkinson and Muttiah Muralitharan whose 18 overs cost 35 runs between them. Graeme Welch top-scored for the Bears, who were undone by Peter Martin's 5 for 28.

13 June 1999: Division Two
at Northampton
Northamptonshire 235 for 8 (45 overs) DJG Sales 54
Surrey 230 (45 overs) GP Thorpe 70
Northamptonshire (4 pts) won by 5 runs

at Bath
Nottinghamshire 227 for 8 (45 overs)
Somerset 231 for 3 (39.5 overs) PD Bowler 86,
PCL Holloway 70*
Somerset (4 pts) won by seven wickets

at Hove
Durham 161 (42.3 overs)
Sussex 162 for 3 (25.5 overs) MJ Di Venuto 72*,
CJ Adams 64
Sussex (4 pts) won by seven wickets

The Surrey Lions needed a six off the last over bowled by Northamptonshire's Kevin Innes to win, but it proved beyond Darren Bicknell. It had been a thrilling match. Victory was set up as much as anyone as by David Sales, who had scored his 54 at exactly a run a ball and was supported by able contributions from Russell Warren and Tony

Martin Bicknell took a remarkable 7 for 30 as Surrey bowled Glamorgan out for only 44.

David Munden/Sportsline Photographic

Penberthy. Graham Thorpe took Surrey close to victory with his 70. Alastair Brown and Ben Hollioake both fell before the target was reached and Surrey were left out of it.

Peter Bowler's highest one-day score for Somerset and his third successive half-century in the National League went a long way to helping his team maintain their unbeaten record. Nottinghamshire's Paul Johnson had briefly threatened to make life awkward but having moved within sight of a half-century he fell to Piran Holloway at point. The fielder went on to score an unbeaten half-century sharing a stand of 127 with Bowler. It was the second time Holloway had reached 70 against the Outlaws in the league this season.

The haste with which Sussex raced to victory over Durham – they had 19 overs to spare – was as decent a reflection of the gulf between the two one-day sides as anything. Durham had begun at six an over but when John Morris fell they went to pieces. Michael Di Venuto and Chris Adams then ripped into the Durham attack amassing 126 runs for the second wicket in 1,901 balls, the former reaching his half-century in 45 balls, the latter needing just 36.

19 June 1999: Division One
at Southampton
Leicestershire 248 (42.4 overs) DL Maddy 89*
Hampshire 245 for 6 (45 overs) DA Kenway 53,
AD Mascarenhas 51*
Leicestershire (4 pts) won by 3 runs

at Worcester
Worcestershire 184 (45 overs) PR Pollard 53,
JN Snape 4 for 27
Gloucestershire 183 (44.5 overs)
Worcestershire (4 pts) won by 1 run

at Headingley
Essex 241 for 7 (45 overs) N Hussain 114
Yorkshire 194 (42.5 overs)
Essex (4 pts) won by 47 runs

The see-saw nature of the match between the Hampshire Hawks and the Leicestershire Foxes had both sides sensing victory at different times. It boiled down to Hampshire needing four off the last ball, but although Nixon McLean and Dimitri Mascarenhas had done valiantly, it was too much. All Hampshire managed was a single. A shame because Jason Laney and Derek Kenway had set off like express trains putting on 96 for the first wicket.

Matt Cassar of Derbyshire: a
handy performer with both bat and ball.
David Munden/Sportsline Photographic

Earlier Darren Maddy's unbeaten half-century was the backbone of his side's total.

There was a fantastic finish at New Road that could have been written for *Boy's Own.* Three balls remaining, two wickets wanted for a Worcestershire win, two runs for Gloucestershire to triumph. The wily Richard Illingworth, halfway through his over, undid Jon Lewis with a yorker, then he clung on to a throat-high catch to account for Mike Smith. Matt Windows top-scored for the visitors, while Reuben Spiring and Paul Pollard laid the foundation of the Worcestershire innings with a 94-run partnership for the first wicket.

A single-handed effort brought about Yorkshire's first defeat in the National League at the hands of Essex. Nasser Hussain was in commanding form as he compiled his maiden century in the former Sunday League competition. It occupied 131 balls and totally eclipsed anything that Yorkshire had to offer. Greg Blewett did reach his highest score in the competition to date, but it occupied 97 balls and generally the Essex bowling proved impossible to get away.

19 June 1999: Division Two
at Chester-le-Street
Northamptonshire 201 for 5 (33 overs) MI Hayden 86
Durham 137 (29.1 overs) GP Swann 5 for 35
Northamptonshire (4 pts) won by 77 runs

at Trent Bridge
Middlesex 197 for 8 (45 overs) MA Roseberry 50,
CM Tolley 4 for 34
Nottinghamshire 198 for 5 (41.3 overs) GF Archer 53*
Nottinghamshire (4 pts) won by five wickets

at Taunton
Derbyshire 243 for 7 (45 overs) ME Cassar 103,
ID Blackwell 78
Somerset 247 for 4 (42.2 overs) PCL Holloway 94*,
J Cox 78
Somerset (4 pts) won by six wickets

at The Oval
Surrey 187 (45 overs)
Glamorgan 44 (17 overs) MP Bicknell 7 for 30
Surrey (4 pts) won by 143 runs

There was the clash of the Australian captains at Chester-le-Street. In the blue corner David Boon of Durham; in the red corner Matthew Hayden of Northamptonshire. Boon was blue on two counts.

On a personal level his six runs were 80 short of Hayden's innings, which in turn went a long way to ensuring a comprehensive victory, albeit under the Duckworth-Lewis method. Graeme Swann's off-spin earned him his first five-wicket haul in the competition. Durham's attack, in contrast, was largely anonymous.

Mike Roseberry's second half-century in the competition this season confirmed a reawakening of his all-round batting skills, but he was unable to save Middlesex from a resounding defeat by the Outlaws. With Chris Tolley's left-arm seam bringing him four wickets, it required some controlled and disciplined bowling by Middlesex to salvage victory. The 15 wides they sent down told their own story. Although the promising Simon Cook picked up three wickets, there was a general lack of menace and accuracy.

At Taunton, the Derbyshire cause was rescued by Matthew Cassar and Ian Blackwell, the former recording his second hundred in the competition (his first in the 40-over format) as they dragged their team out of serious trouble at 40 for 4 with a stand of 138. The Cornish left-hander Piran Holloway then smashed a brilliant, unbeaten 94, hitting a six and ten fours from 112 balls as he helped Somerset to their target – and the top of the table – with 16 balls to spare.

Surrey's Martin Bicknell's career-best figures of 7 for 30 confirmed him as the single-handed destroyer of Glamorgan as the Dragons slumped to ignominious defeat in 17 overs. Amazingly it was not their lowest total: that came 20 years ago against Derbyshire in Swansea when they were skittled for 42. This time, for only the second time in domestic one-day history two bowlers had dismissed a side on their own, Ian Bishop, released by Somerset three years previously, mopping up the leftovers.

28 June 1999: Division Two
at Hove
Sussex v. Northamptonshire
No play was possible in this floodlit match
Sussex 2 pts, Northamptonshire 2 pts

29 June 1999: Division One
at Leicester (floodlit)
Yorkshire 231 for 6 (45 overs)
Leicestershire 131 (33.2 overs)
GM Hamilton 4 for 33
Yorkshire (4 pts) won by 100 runs

Gavin Hamilton made another telling contribution as Yorkshire overwhelmed Leicestershire by 100 runs at Leicester. In a day-night fixture, Yorkshire first totalled 231 for 6 before reducing the home side to 131 all out in just 33.3 overs, Hamilton finishing with 4 for 33.

3 July 1999: Division One
at Old Trafford (floodlit)
Essex 168 (44.2 overs) RC Irani 64, ID Austin 4 for 15
Lancashire 171 for 3 (35.5 overs) A Flintoff 52*, NH Fairbrother 50*
Lancashire (4 pts) won by seven wickets

Lancashire easily won their first day-night fixture of the season, bowling out Essex for 168 and then knocking off the runs for the loss of just three wickets. Ronnie Irani made 64, putting on 68 for the third wicket with Stuart Law (44) but the seam attack of Ian Austin (4 for 15), Peter Martin and Andy Flintoff was too much for the visitors. Flintoff, with a six and six fours in 52 not out, and Neil Fairbrother (50 not out from 73 balls) wrapped things up.

4 July 1999: Division One
at Maidstone
Warwickshire 219 for 8 (45 overs) A Singh 76, G Welch 71, DW Headley 5 for 43
Kent 221 for 9 (44.4 overs)
Kent (4 pts) won by one wicket

at Worcester
Hampshire 161 for 9 (45 overs) AD Mascarenhas 55, SR Lampitt 4 for 18
Worcestershire 162 for 3 (26.2 overs) TM Moody 55, GA Hick 54
Worcestershire (4 pts) won by seven wickets

Dean Headley was the Kent hero at Maidstone, in a thrilling victory over Warwickshire. Headley, who had already taken 5 for 43, including a spell of 4 for 7 in 17 balls, marched in to drive Graeme Welch back over his head for four – with three runs needed from three balls, but with just one wicket left. Warwickshire's 219 for 8 was based on a fluent 76 from Anurag Singh and a beefy 71 by Welch. Tim Munton bowled tidily but all but two of Kent's notoriously fragile top order made significant contributions. The late clatter of wickets, in the rush for victory, merely set up Headley.

Yorkshire's Gavin Hamilton enjoyed himself in the first ever floodlit match at Grace Road.
David Munden/Sportsline Photographic

An exhilarating onslaught by Tom Moody and Graeme Hick, who put on 95 in 12 overs for the second wicket, rushed Worcestershire to a seven-wicket victory over Hampshire that moved them back into second place in the division one table. Stuart Lampitt (4 for 18) was the bowling star in Hampshire's 161 for 9, Dimitri Mascarenhas providing the only real resistance with 55. Moody (55) reached his fifty from 49 balls and Hick (54) his from 47.

4 July 1999: Division Two
at Derby
Surrey 238 for 9 (45 overs) AD Brown 105,
KJ Dean 4 for 35
Derbyshire 174 (41.4 overs)
Surrey (4 pts) won by 64 runs

at Swansea
Sussex 201 for 8 (41 overs) CJ Adams 80*,
MJ Di Venuto 65
Glamorgan 121 (38.1 overs) UBA Rashid 5 for 24
Sussex (4 pts) won by 88 runs
(D/L method: Glamorgan target 210 in 41 overs)

at Lord's
Middlesex 207 for 6 (45 overs) MA Roseberry 83,
MR Ramprakash 57
Durham 182 (42 overs)
Middlesex (4 pts) won by 25 runs

at Northampton
Northamptonshire 182 for 5 (31 overs)
Nottinghamshire 118 for 9 (17 overs)
Northamptonshire (4 pts) won by 17 runs
*(D/L method: Nottinghamshire target 136
in 17 overs)*

Alastair Brown took control of Surrey's fixture at Derby by cracking 105 off 91 balls, an innings that contained three sixes and ten fours. Brown, coming in at 34 for 3, was seventh out at 229 as Surrey reached their highest score in the competition this summer. Derbyshire had no answer after Martin Bicknell had ripped out their first three wickets cheaply.

Michael Di Venuto raced to 50 from 44 balls, finally making 65 and putting on 109 for the second wicket with Chris Adams who remained 80 not out through the late slog. With a target upgraded by the Duckworth-Lewis method, Glamorgan collapsed insipidly. Umer Rashid, whose slow left-armers have been central to Sussex's one-day success this season, benefited to the tune of 5 for 24.

Mike Roseberry relished the 83 made against his former county Durham at Lord's and, together with Mark Ramprakash's 57, it took Middlesex to a winning total of 207 for 6. Angus Fraser lopped off the Durham top order with 3 for 29 and Paul Weekes picked up 3 for 38 as they were dismissed for 182.

Northamptonshire claimed a hollow victory in a match ruined as a fair contest by rain. A downpour initially drove the players off for 90 minutes halfway through the Northants innings, which then resumed as a 31-over contest. The rain then came again when Notts, chasing a revised target of 210 under the Duckworth-Lewis method, were 52 for 2 from eight overs. When play resumed again, at 7.10pm, the new target was 136 from 17 overs – an equation of 84 from nine remaining overs. Against Devon Malcolm in the half-light, Notts put up a gallant fight, to no avail.

13 July 1999: Division Two
at Chester-le-Street (floodlit)
Derbyshire 143 for 9 (33 overs) MJ Slater 50,
NC Phillips 4 for 13
Durham 146 for 3 (25.3 overs) DC Boon 61
Durham (4 pts) won by seven wickets

Durham's first day-night fixture, in front of a 4,000 crowd at the Riverside, brought their first win of the season in the competition. Cork and Slater put on 90 for Derbyshire's first wicket, but then came a collapse with off-spinner Nicky Phillips picking up 4 for 13 – a return which put him on top of the wicket-taking table for the competition. David Boon, with 61, made it a stroll for Durham: John Morris also made 31 as victory arrived with 7.3 overs to spare.

17 July 1999: Division One
at Edgbaston
Yorkshire 213 (44.5 overs) MP Vaughan 72,
A McGrath 71
Warwickshire 214 for 5 (44.1 overs) A Singh 61
Warwickshire (4 pts) won by five wickets

A competitive match ended with Graeme Welch smiting a decisive 27 not out from 17 balls to take Warwickshire past Yorkshire's 213 with five deliveries to spare. Earlier Welch had taken 2 for 18 in his nine overs, with Michael Vaughan (72) and Anthony McGrath (71) leading the way for Yorkshire. Anurag Singh (61) launched the Warwickshire reply in fine style, and Dominic Ostler hit a crowd-pleasing 42 not out.

18 July 1999: Division One
at Southend
Hampshire 259 for 9 (45 overs) JS Laney 106*
Essex 120 (23.4 overs) SJ Renshaw 45 for 40
Hampshire (4 pts) won by 139 runs

at Cheltenham
Gloucestershire 261 (44.5 overs) RC Russell 91*,
RJ Cunliffe 66, CEW Silverwood 4 for 44
Yorkshire 133 (35.5 overs) MCJ Ball 5 for 42
Gloucestershire (4 pts) won by 128 runs

Hampshire and Gloucestershire enjoyed crushing wins over Essex and Yorkshire, respectively, by running up an intimidating total and then bowling out their opponents convincingly.

Hampshire's 259 for 5, at Southend, was based on Jason Laney's 106 not out, and then Simon Renshaw and Peter Hartley tumbled out Essex for 120 in just 23.4 overs. Jack Russell, unbeaten on 91, and Rob Cunliffe, with 66, spearheaded Gloucestershire's progress towards 261 – and Martyn Ball rubbed in their superiority by taking 5 for 42 as Yorkshire slid to 133 all out.

18 July: Division Two
at Trent Bridge
Nottinghamshire 240 for 7 (45 overs)
GF Archer 75*
Glamorgan 214 (43.5 overs) MP Maynard 65,
PJ Franks 5 for 27
Nottinghamshire (4 pts) won by 26 runs

at Guildford
Surrey 225 for 9 (45 overs) PW Jarvis 4 for 28
Somerset 227 for 8 (43.2 overs) PCL Holloway 101*
Somerset (4 pts) won by two wickets

at Arundel
Sussex 297 for 5 (45 overs) CJ Adams 163,
JR Carpenter 60*
Middlesex 288 for 6 (45 overs) OA Shah 134,
JL Langer 51
Sussex (4 pts) won by 9 runs

A magnificent 163 by Chris Adams, during a run-feast at Arundel, was the highlight of three matches that saw victories for Sussex, Somerset and Nottinghamshire.

Adams' great knock was almost matched by Owais Shah, who hit 134, but in the end Middlesex were nine runs short of Sussex's 297 for 5.

Piran Holloway made an unbeaten 101 as Somerset overhauled Surrey's 225 for 9 at Guildford, and Paul Franks continued his development with 5 for 27 as Notts successfully defended 240 for 7 at Trent Bridge against Glamorgan.

Piran Holloway scored 101 not out for Somerset against Surrey.
David Munden/Sportsline Photographic

19 July 1999: Division One
at Old Trafford (floodlit)
Warwickshire 46 for 4 (10.2 overs)
Lancashire did not bat
Match abandoned: 2 pts each

20 July 1999: Division One
at Worcester (floodlit)
Worcestershire 250 for 6 (45 overs) GA Hick 110*
Leicestershire 248 (44.5 overs) BF Smith 74,
RK Illingworth 4 for 49
Worcestershire (4 pts) won by 2 runs

In their first floodlit game at Worcester, victory by just two runs took Worcestershire level with Leicestershire. Graeme Hick's 110 not out inspired Worcestershire to 250 for 6 but they were also boosted by 35 wides. Leicestershire's reply was brave, Ben Smith anchoring the run chase with 74 and Jon Dakin upping it with 36 from only 17 balls. Richard Illingworth, though, called on all his vast experience to take 4 for 49.

25 July 1999: Division One
at Cheltenham
Warwickshire 198 for 8 (45 overs) NMK Smith 61,
DP Ostler 53, MJ Cawdron 4 for 17
Gloucestershire 202 for 7 (44.5 overs) RC Russell 52
Gloucestershire (4 pts) won by three wickets

at Southampton
Hampshire 210 for 7 (45 overs) JP Stephenson 96
Lancashire 214 for 6 (44.3 overs) MA Atherton 95*
Lancashire (4 pts) won by four wickets

at Scarborough
Yorkshire 178 for 8 (45 overs) A McGrath 68
Kent 179 for 7 (42.4 overs)
Kent (4 pts) won by three wickets

The sides batting second won all three division one fixtures taking place, with Mike Atherton's unbeaten 95 perhaps the most significant innings played against a backdrop of England's Test defeat at Lord's.

Atherton guided Lancashire past a Hampshire total of 210 for 7, in which John Stephenson made 96 off 86 balls and hit Muttiah Muralitharan for four sixes. A start of 36 for 4, from the first 15 overs, cost Hampshire dear, however.

Michael Cawdron, still to play first-class cricket, had one-day best figures of 4 for 17 as Gloucestershire kept Warwickshire to 198 for 8, in which Neil Smith hammered 61 from 62 balls. Gloucestershire's reply, well launched by Hancock and Barnett, was carried on by Jack Russell (52), but it needed a well-paced 49 not out by Mark Alleyne to bring the curtain down on the Cheltenham festival with a home win. Alleyne, in fact, had to drive the penultimate ball from Ashley Giles for six to settle a wildly fluctuating contest.

Mark Ealham was the all-rounder at the heart of Kent's three-wicket win against Yorkshire at Scarborough. He took 3 for 29, after Julian Thompson's fine new-ball spell of 9–2–16–3, to restrict Yorkshire to 178 for 8. Anthony McGrath's 68 remained the only half-century of the match, but Will House launched the Kent reply with 39 off 36 balls and Ealham was on hand to steady the ship with 34 not out at the end.

25 July 1999: Division Two
at Derby
Northamptonshire 187 for 6 (45 overs)
Derbyshire 180 (44.5 overs) MJ Slater 59, KJ Innes 4 for 37
Northamptonshire (4 pts) won by 7 runs

at Pontypridd
Glamorgan 294 for 4 (45 overs) JH Kallis 155*, MP Maynard 79
Surrey 223 (39 overs) DJ Bicknell
Glamorgan (4 pts) won by 71 runs

at Cleethorpes
Nottinghamshire 246 for 4 (45 overs) JER Gallian 108*, GF Archer 52
Sussex 200 for 8 (45 overs) JR Carpenter 64*, CM Tolley 4 for 38
Nottinghamshire (4 pts) won by 46 runs

at Taunton
Somerset 218 (43.5 overs) ME Trescothick 110, KP Dutch 5 for 35
Middlesex 219 for 2 (39.1 overs) MA Roseberry 91*, KP Dutch 57, OA Shah 56
Middlesex (4 pts) won by eight wickets

Somerset and Sussex both suffered their first defeats in the competition, losing to Middlesex and Nottinghamshire respectively. Keith Dutch followed up his 5 for 35 with 57 as Middlesex triumphed by eight wickets at Taunton, and the home side's one-paced attack was exposed as Mike Roseberry (91 not out) and Owais Shah (56) put on 101 for the first wicket. Roseberry and Dutch then added 102 for the second wicket and Somerset's 218, in which Marcus Trescothick, the acting captain, made 110 – his highest score in the competition. Angus Fraser (9–3–17–2) and Jamie Hewitt had earlier reduced Somerset to 18 for 4 with the new ball before Trescothick and Keith Parsons added 131. Sussex were put to the sword by Jason Gallian, who anchored the Notts innings of 246 for 4 with an unbeaten 108. Chris Tolley then took 4 for 38 with his left-arm medium pace and James Carpenter's unbeaten 64 was defiance only.

Elsewhere, Northamptonshire edged out Derbyshire by seven runs at Derby, despite Michael Slater's 59, and Jacques Kallis made an imperious debut for Glamorgan in their defeat of Surrey at Pontypridd.

Kallis, the South African all-rounder sidelined by injury for a month after the World Cup, did not let down Welsh supporters who had been kept waiting for a first glimpse of their new overseas star. Reaching his hundred from 112 balls, he then accelerated majestically to 155 not out from 141 balls, with two sixes and 17 fours, and with Matthew Maynard (79) added a county competition record 204 for the third wicket. Darren Bicknell offered a late 62 but Surrey, overall, never looked like challenging Glamorgan's 294 for 4 and in the end were beaten by 71 runs. They now looked certain to stay in the second division.

1 August 1999: Division One
at Worcester
Kent 88 for 4 (16 overs)
Worcestershire did not bat
Match abandoned – 2 pts each

3 August 1999: Division One
at Bristol (floodlit)
Hampshire 211 for 9 (45 overs) JS Laney 61, DA Kenway 58, IJ Harvey 4 for 37
Gloucestershire 191 (43.1 overs) MW Alleyne 91, PJ Hartley 4 for 29
Hampshire (4 pts) won by 20 runs

Gloucestershire's players paraded the Benson and Hedges Super Cup at Bristol before the start of a day-night fixture attended by a crowd of almost 6,000. Mark Alleyne, the hero of Lord's, continued his good form with 91 – but Gloucestershire still fell 20 runs short of Hampshire's 211 for 9, in which Jason Laney and Derek Kenway both made half-centuries.

4 August 1999: Division One
at Edgbaston (floodlit)
Leicestershire 250 for 8 (45 overs) DI Stevens 82
Warwickshire 138 for 8 (34 overs) MS Kasprowicz 4 for 30
Leicestershire (4 pts) won by 71 runs
(D/L method: Warwickshire target 209 from 34 overs)

Anthony McGrath made 68 in Yorkshire's defeat by Kent.
David Munden/Sportsline Photographic

At Edgbaston a Leicestershire total of 250 for 8, built on an aggressive 82 from the promising Darren Stevens, was far too much for Warwickshire. Despite having their target reduced by rain the home side could only struggle to 138 for 8, Mike Kasprowicz taking 4 for 30, and were defeated by 71 runs.

8 August 1999: Division One
at Canterbury
Essex 139 (32 overs)
Kent 141 for 5 (31.5 overs)
Kent (4 pts) won by five wickets

at Headingley
Worcestershire 228 for 7 (45 overs) TM Moody 56, DA Leatherdale 54
Yorkshire 143 (37.2 overs) GR Haynes 4 for 31
Worcestershire (4 pts) won by 85 runs

Greg Blewett made an appropriately low key farewell to the Headingley crowd after a miserable summer in which he had the dubious distinction of having the worst individual record of all Yorkshire's overseas players. Worcestershire scored 228 for 7, with Tom Moody hitting 56 and David Leatherdale 54, before Yorkshire were shot out for 143 with Gavin Haynes claiming 4 for 31. Blewett made only 24, taking his run aggregate in 11 league matches to a measly 178. To make a bad day worse for Yorkshire, there were more than 10,000 spectators present to witness it.

In the other division one fixture Kent beat Essex by five wickets in a game reduced to 32 overs per side. Min Patel took 3 for 22 and Matthew Fleming 3 for 15 as Essex were bowled out for 139. At one stage Kent were wobbling on 20 for 4, but then Nigel Llong hit 40 and Mark Ealham finished 43 not out as Canterbury Week was wrapped up satisfactorily for the hosts with seven balls to spare.

8 August 1999: Division Two
at Chester-le-Street
Durham 134 (38.2 overs)
Sussex 135 for 2 (29.1 overs) MJ Di Venuto 72*
Sussex (4 pts) won by eight wickets

at Southgate
Somerset 205 for 4 (21 overs) J Cox 83, JID Kerr 56
Middlesex 187 for 7 (17 overs) JL Langer 84
Somerset (4 pts) won by 2 runs
(D/L method: Middlesex target 190 from 17 overs)

Following Mark Ramprakash's resignation, the Australian Justin Langer will lead Middlesex next season.
David Munden/Sportsline Photographic

at Northampton
Northamptonshire v. Derbyshire
No play possible – 2 pts each

at The Oval
Surrey v. Nottinghamshire
No play possible – 2 pts each

Leaders Sussex and Somerset both maintained their momentum at the head of the second division table with defeats of Durham and Middlesex respectively.

Sussex trampled all over Durham at the Riverside, Robin Martin-Jenkins taking 3 for 27 as the home side were dismissed for 134. Michael Di Venuto then struck 72 not out from 91 balls, and Chris Adams 41 from 36 balls, as victory came with eight wickets and 15.5 overs in hand.

Somerset, meanwhile, won a big-hitting contest at Southgate in a rain-affected match. First, in 21 overs, Somerset thrashed 205 for 4 with Jamie Cox needing only 51 balls for his 83 and Marcus Trescothick thumping four sixes in an unbeaten 15-ball 36. Another shower reduced Middlesex's target to 189 from 17 overs and, despite Justin Langer's remarkable 84 off 41 balls, they fell two runs short when Ben Hutton failed to make contact with the last ball, bowled by Paul Jarvis.

The Northants v. Derbyshire and Surrey v. Notts fixtures were abandoned due to rain.

10 August 1999: Division One
at Southampton
Essex 187 for 4 (33 overs)
Hampshire 188 for 7 (32.3 overs) RA Smith 97*,
RC Irani 5 for 33
Hampshire (4 pts) won by three wickets

at Old Trafford
Gloucestershire 178 for 8 (45 overs)
Lancashire 181 for 4 (44.2 overs) JP Crawley 80,
NH Fairbrother 66*
Lancashire (4 pts) won by six wickets

at Leicester
Kent 120 (36 overs) RWT Key 59, JM Dakin 5 for 30
Leicestershire 121 for 4 (27.4 overs) BF Smith 55*
Leicestershire (4 pts) won by six wickets

Lancashire stayed second after beating opponents
Gloucestershire by six wickets at Old Trafford.
Kim Barnett's 46 was the mainstay of the visitors'
178 for 8 and John Crawley, hitting 80 after being
re-appointed skipper for the year 2000, put on
113 in 24 overs with Neil Fairbrother (66 not out)
to ensure victory.

Robin Smith's 97 not out off 105 balls, his best
score of the season at that point, helped Hampshire
to a three-wicket win against Essex, with three balls
to spare in what became a 33-over match. Danny
Law (48) top-scored in Essex's 187 for 4 and Ronnie
Irani then took 5 for 33 to no avail.

Kent, unbeaten in one-day cricket since 6 June,
were thumped by six wickets by Leicestershire at
Grace Road. Rob Key, ninth out for 59, was the only
batsman to make any impression in Kent's 120 – and
then Ben Smith made 55 not out to guide the home
side home.

10 August 1999: Division Two
at Cardiff
Durham 198 for 7 (45 overs) NJ Speak 53
Glamorgan 189 for 7 (45 overs) A Dale 58
Durham (4 pts) won by 9 runs

at Southgate
Derbyshire 139 (33 overs)
Middlesex 114 (31.5 overs)
Derbyshire (4 pts) won by 25 runs

at Trent Bridge
Nottinghamshire 225 for 9 (45 overs) MP Dowman 52,
JP Taylor 4 for 41

Northamptonshire 228 (43.4 overs)
AL Penberthy 64*
Northamptonshire (4 pts) won by five wickets

at Hove
Sussex 167 for 8 (45 overs)
Somerset 168 for 2 (36.2 overs)
PCL Holloway 70*
Somerset (4 pts) won by eight wickets

Somerset won the first meeting between the
division's runaway top two, holding Sussex to just
167 for 8 from their 45 overs at Hove and then
romping to victory in front of a 3,500 crowd. Keith
Parsons and Steffan Jones took Somerset's bowling
honours, with three wickets each, and then Piran
Holloway hit 70 not out to anchor the reply. Jamie
Cox (41) and Michael Burns (39 not out) also played
their part in a comprehensive win.

Derbyshire won a low-scoring match against
Middlesex, despite being bowled out for 139,
and Durham squeezed past Glamorgan by just
nine runs after totalling 198 for 7 with Nick Speak
and Jimmy Daley to the fore. In the division's
other game Northamptonshire were led home
by Tony Penberthy's unbeaten 64 in reply to
Nottinghamshire's challenging 225 for 9. The Swann
brothers also starred under the Trent Bridge lights,
Alec launching the innings with 47 and Graeme
contributing an aggressive 34 just when acceleration
was needed.

12 August 1999: Division One
at Chelmsford
Essex 166 (43.4 overs) DDJ Robinson 74*,
JM Dakin 4 for 32
Leicestershire 169 for 5 (31.2 overs)
DI Stevens 68
Leicestershire (4 pts) won by five wickets

at Bristol
Kent 192 for 7 (45 overs) TR Ward 58
Gloucestershire 176 for 9 (45 overs)
RC Russell 52
Kent (4 pts) won by 16 runs

at Headingley (floodlit)
Lancashire 149 (44.1 overs)
Yorkshire 114 for 7 (40.2 overs)
Lancashire (4 pts) won by 14 runs
*(D/L method: Yorkshire target 128 from
40.2 overs)*

Ian Austin returned the remarkable figures of 9–6–8–2 as Lancashire maintained their title hopes by beating Yorkshire in a low-scoring day-night Roses encounter at Headingley. Lancashire were bowled out for 149, with Chris Silverwood taking 3 for 22, and then Yorkshire seemed to be cruising at 82 for 3 in the 27th over. But a middle-order stutter resulted in the home side sliding to 114 for 7 from 40.2 overs when rain began to fall at 10pm. No further play was possible, but few in the largely disappointed 10,000 crowd could quibble with the Duckworth-Lewis ruling that Lancashire were victors by 14 runs.

Leicestershire, meanwhile, kept up their own challenge for honours with a solid five-wicket win against bottom-of-the-table Essex at Chelmsford. Essex were dismissed for 166, Darren Robinson carrying his bat for 74, but then Darren Stevens (68) led the reply.

Trevor Ward's first half-century of the summer, against county opposition, helped Kent beat a Gloucestershire side out-of-sorts at Bristol. Facing Kent's 192 for 7, the home side slipped to 176 for 9 despite 52 from Jack Russell and 47 from Ian Harvey. Both Martin McCague and Julian Thompson picked up three wickets.

12 August 1999: Division Two
at Derby
Derbyshire 158 for 8 (45 overs)
Somerset 160 for 5 (30.2 overs) M Burns 50, TM Smith 4 for 38
Somerset (4 pts) won by five wickets

at Chester-le-Street
Nottinghamshire 163 for 7 (45 overs)
Durham 164 for 6 (42.5 overs) VC Drakes 5 for 31
Durham (4 pts) won by four wickets

at Northampton
Glamorgan 221 for 4 (45 overs) JH Kallis 72
Northamptonshire 168 (37.4 overs) GP Swann 63
Glamorgan (4 pts) won by 53 runs

at Hove (floodlit)
Surrey 144 (41.3 overs)
Sussex 145 for 3 (34 overs) CJ Adams 51
Sussex (4 pts) won by seven wickets

A crowd of 4,200 turned up at Hove to see Sussex continue their National League promotion drive at the expense of star-studded Surrey. If the home fans had any gripes, however, it was that the match finished too early after Surrey had staggered to just 144 all out through a series of ill-judged strokes from their clutch of England men. Billy Taylor took 3 for 22 and then Chris Adams, his current average 70 for the competition this season, belted an entertaining 51 to take Sussex racing past the winning post with seven wickets to spare.

Vasbert Drakes continued his prolific season by taking 5 for 31 at the Riverside, but Durham still got home by four wickets with 13 balls remaining as they successfully chased Nottinghamshire's 163 for 7. Jason Gallian scored 49 but Nick Speak's unbeaten 45 trumped it.

Somerset's 13th win in 14 one-day games, and their tenth out of 11 in the National League, all but secured their promotion to division one. Michael Burns hit 50 as Somerset took just 30.2 overs to overhaul Derbyshire's 158 for 8 at Taunton. Trevor Smith picked up 4 for 38, but Somerset cruised home by five wickets.

Glamorgan's 221 for 4 at Northampton was too much for the home team. Only Graeme Swann, with 63, offered any hope as Steve Watkin strangled the Northants innings with 3 for 15 in a superb spell of seam and swing bowling. Earlier Jacques Kallis had stroked 72, Steve James 48 and Matthew Maynard an unbeaten 41.

17 August 1999: Division One
at Old Trafford (floodlit)
Yorkshire 153 for 9 (45 overs)
Lancashire 143 for 5 (37.3 overs) NH Fairbrother 54*
Lancashire (4 pts) won by five wickets (D/L method because of floodlight failure: Lancashire target 1 for 42 from 42 overs)

Lancashire's drive towards the National League title continued in front of 12,626 fans at Old Trafford, but their day-night five-wicket win against Roses rivals Yorkshire was not without embarrassment. With Lancashire needing just 19 runs from 8.3 remaining overs, Yorkshire having earlier been dismissed for a paltry 153, the ground was plunged into darkness when the floodlights failed. After a 15-minute delay, in which the problem was solved, Lancashire's target was slightly reduced under the Duckworth-Lewis system – and the victory was duly achieved without any further fuss. Neil Fairbrother finished 54 not out, once more displaying all his experience of run chases as Lancashire rallied from being 19 for 3.

22 August 1999: Division One
at Colchester
Essex 117 (41.1 overs)
Warwickshire 118 for 4 (31 overs) NV Knight 50
Warwickshire (4 pts) won by six wickets

at Southampton
Gloucestershire 247 for 5 (45 overs)
RJ Cunliffe 63
Hampshire 169 (41.2 overs)
Gloucestershire (4 pts) won by 78 runs

at Leicester
Worcestershire 197 for 7 (45 overs)
VS Solanki 63
Leicestershire 186 for 9 (45 overs)
Worcestershire (4 pts) won by 11 runs

All three away teams won the day in this round of matches, with Worcestershire's 11-run victory over Leicestershire at Grace Road the most significant in terms of the title race.

Vikram Solanki's 63 was the basis of Worcestershire's 197 for 7, and the visitors always looked comfortable – despite a late assault from Dominic Williamson.

Gloucestershire's hopes of avoiding the drop to division two were boosted by their emphatic 78-run win over Hampshire, whose wicketkeeper Adrian Aymes was left out on disciplinary grounds after a run of 104 consecutive appearances. Aymes had received a one-match suspension following a scuffle with Essex's Paul Grayson in the previous National League fixture. Rob Cunliffe hit 63 in Gloucestershire's 247 for 5 at Southampton, and Kim Barnett 48. Mark Alleyne (41 not out) and Jack Russell (32 not out) plundered 57 from the last five overs. Martyn Ball then took 3 for 37 as Hampshire were bowled out for 169.

Paul Prichard's 20 was the top score in Essex's pathetic 117 at Colchester. Nick Knight then led Warwickshire's victory drive with 50 against some testing spin on a pitch patently unsuitable for one-day cricket.

22 August 1999: Division Two
at Colwyn Bay
Glamorgan 247 for 5 (45 overs) SP James 91,
JH Kallis 79
Nottinghamshire 147 (36.1 overs) RDB Croft
4 for 31
Glamorgan (4 pts) won by 100 runs

Chris Adams, captain of Sussex, gives the groundsman a helping hand in the Parks.
Philip Brown/Sportsline Photographic

at Lord's
Middlesex 156 for 9 (45 overs)
Northamptonshire 157 for 5 (42.2 overs)
Northamptonshire (4 pts) won by five wickets

at Taunton
Sussex 260 for 3 (45 overs) CJ Adams 115*,
PA Cottey 62*
Somerset 258 for 7 (45 overs) PD Bowler 53
Sussex (4 pts) won by 2 runs

The meeting of the division's top two, at Taunton, saw Sussex emerge the victors by just two runs after a high-quality encounter tarnished by a too-late finish. Chris Adams' unbeaten 115 occupied only 103 balls and Tony Cottey also hit a rapid 62 not out as Sussex amassed 260 for 3. Somerset's top order, led by Peter Bowler (53), all made contributions but, sadly, it was almost dark by the time eight runs were needed from the final over. Late finishes in the competition have been legion, following the failure of the authorities to sanction a starting time before 1.30pm. And, here, it was almost 8pm when the final over began. Somerset's batsmen could hardly see the ball.

A miserly spell of 9–4–12–3 by Kevin Curran set up Northants for a five-wicket victory against Middlesex at Southgate. David Nash (40 not out) and Angus Fraser (31) rallied Middlesex from 83 for 8 to 156 for 9 with a 73-run stand, but Northants were hardly stretched as they knocked off the runs. Middlesex, with this eighth defeat, were all but resigned to second division status again next season.

At Colwyn Bay, opener Steve James continued his remarkable hold over the Nottinghamshire bowlers as Glamorgan thrashed their visitors by 100 runs. James made 91 in Glamorgan's 247 for 5, although the real fireworks were provided by Jacques Kallis with 79 from 68 balls. Robert Croft (4 for 31) and Adrian Dale (3 for 19) wrapped up a miserable week for Notts.

29 August: Division One
at Canterbury
Yorkshire 161 for 8 (45 overs)
Kent 164 for 1 (31.3 overs) RWT Key 76*, TR Ward 70
Kent (4 pts) won by nine wickets

at Old Trafford
Leicestershire 166 for 8 (45 overs)
Lancashire 168 for 3 (42.2 overs) MA Atherton 64*
Lancashire (4 pts) won by seven wickets

at Worcester
Essex 131 for 9 (45 overs)
Worcestershire 133 for 2 (29.3 overs)
Worcestershire (4 pts) won by eight wickets

Worcestershire stepped up the pressure on leaders Lancashire by overwhelming Essex by eight wickets at New Road. The win kept them second, just two points adrift. Wickets were shared as Essex struggled to a 45-over total of just 131 for 9, but any murmurings about the quality of the pitch were lost in the acclaim for Graeme Hick, Worcestershire's captain. Hick got under way by striking Peter Such for six, four, six and when victory was clinched with more than 15 overs left, Hick was 45 not out from just 26 balls.

Lancashire, meanwhile, enjoyed a clinical victory over Leicestershire by seven wickets. On a mottled Old Trafford pitch, hardly ideal for one-day cricket, Leicestershire huffed and puffed their way to 166 for 8 with Aftab Habib top-scoring with 42. Mike Watkinson eased the pressure on the Lancashire batsmen by going in first and knocking up 49 in an opening stand worth 75 with Michael Atherton. Neither opener, though, could do much about Mike Kasprowicz who had figures of 9–2–11–0 at the end of his new-ball spell. John Crawley also contributed 39 but it was Atherton who saw Lancashire home with an unhurried, unbeaten 64.

Relegation began to loom for unhappy Yorkshire, whose once-bright season had by now dimmed to such an extent that this was their seventh successive National League defeat. All self-belief seemed lost as Yorkshire totalled 161 for 8 at Canterbury and then saw Kent romp home by nine wickets. Julian Thompson, with 1 for 16 from his nine overs, and Mark Ealham, with 3 for 26 from his, kept a stranglehold that only David Byas (46) and Gary Fellows (36) could break. Then Trevor Ward blazed away to reach 70 from 87 balls, and Robert Key was unbeaten on 76 when the end came 13.3 overs early.

29 August: Division Two
at Trent Bridge
Nottinghamshire 269 for 7 (45 overs) U Afzaal 57, JER Gallian 53
Derbyshire 261 for 9 (45 overs) ME Cassar 109, RMS Weston 56, VC Drakes 4 for 41
Nottinghamshire (4 pts) won by 8 runs

at The Oval
Surrey 221 for 7 (45 overs) GP Thorpe 84
Durham 219 for 8 (44 overs) MP Speight 60, IE Bishop 4 for 34
Surrey (4 pts) won by 2 runs

A fine game at Trent Bridge ended in memorable and remarkable fashion, fast bowler Vasbert Drakes taking four wickets with the first four balls of the final over to clinch a Nottinghamshire victory by eight runs. Derbyshire had made a spirited chase of Notts' 269 for 7, which featured an opening stand of 98 between Usman Afzaal (57) and Jason Gallian (53). Matthew Cassar led the charge, with 109 from 118 balls, and Robin Weston (56) helped him add 118 in 19 overs. The 45th over began with

Peter Bowler's half-century could not prevent Sussex's hard-fought victory at the top of the second division.

David Munden/Sportsline Photographic

Derbyshire requiring 10 more runs, but the deadly Drakes was inspired by the tension. He yorked DeFreitas and Rollins, then had Pyemont leg before, before yorking Lacey leg stump to all but wrap up the match in truly dramatic style. Derbyshire had lost seven wickets for 35 runs in six overs. Ironically, it was a Derbyshire fast bowler, Alan Ward, who had been the only man previously to take four in four in the competition. Ward did it in 1970, against Sussex at Derby, and the only other instance of the feat in English domestic one-day cricket came in 1996 when South African Shaun Pollock made an astonishing debut for Warwickshire, against Leicestershire at Edgbaston.

Surrey's chances of avoiding the wooden spoon improved at The Oval when Durham were squeezed out by two runs in an exciting finish. Graham Thorpe's classy 84 from 95 balls underpinned Surrey's 221 for 7 but Durham came out fighting and Martin Speight's 58-ball 60 seemed to have set them up. He and Jon Lewis added 101 in 16 overs but, in the end, the failure to bowl their overs quickly enough earlier in the game cost Durham dear. From the 44 overs they were allowed, as a penalty, they could only manage 219 for 8.

30 August 1999: Division One
at Canterbury
Kent 188 for 7 (45 overs)
Hampshire 106 (40 overs) DW Headley 4 for 21
Kent (4 pts) won by 82 runs

at Worcester
Worcestershire 206 for 6 (45 overs) GA Hick 89,
EJ Wilson 62
Warwickshire 210 for 4 (44.1 overs)
NV Knight 106*
Warwickshire (4 pts) won by six wickets

Worcestershire lost ground in their battle with Lancashire for the National League title, losing by six wickets to their closest rivals Warwickshire at New Road. Initially, with Graeme Hick stroking 89 and Elliott Wilson 62, things seemed to be going swimmingly for the home side. Hick was off the mark with a boundary first ball, and also struck three fours in one over from Allan Donald – a burst that left the South African fast bowler distinctly unamused. But the mood changed when Nick Knight got going in reply to Worcestershire's 206 for 6, the England one-day opener rattling up 106 not out. At 136 for 4 Worcestershire were still in with a chance, despite Knight's dominance, but Michael Powell then came in to hit an inspired 45 not out and keep Knight company right to the end.

Hampshire endured a miserable day at Canterbury, being shot out for 106 in reply to Kent's 188 for 7. Dean Headley took 4 for 21 after Julian Thompson had exerted another stranglehold on the top order with a new ball spell of 9–1–17–2. During the Hampshire innings Giles White was run out for 0, the decision being given by Terry Bower, the Hampshire dressing room attendant, who was standing as square leg umpire at both ends due to Tony Clarkson being taken ill in mid-match. Earlier Trevor Ward hit 36 and Matthew Fleming finished 34 not out. But, on an eventful afternoon, Kent skipper Fleming pulled a hamstring attempting a bye to the keeper and was unable to take the field when Hampshire batted.

30 August 1999: Division Two
at Derby
Nottinghamshire 286 for 7 (45 overs) JER Gallian 130, P Johnson 68, A Woolley 4 for 61
Derbyshire 148 (30.3 overs) ME Cassar 66
Nottinghamshire (4 pts) won by 138 runs

at Northampton
Northamptonshire 225 for 7 (45 overs) AJ Swann 60
Durham 198 (45 overs) PD Collingwood 86, GP Swann 4 for 44
Northamptonshire (4 pts) won by 27 runs

Jason Gallian took full advantage of some ragged Derbyshire bowling to score 130 from 138 balls, his highest score in the competition, as Nottinghamshire won handsomely by 138 runs. Paul Johnson hit 68 from 63 deliveries, and Chris Read 40, as Notts piled up 286 for 7 from their 45 overs. Derbyshire, bowled out for 148, had nothing to offer bar Matt Cassar's 66.

Northamptonshire moved into equal second place in the second division table, albeit having played two games more than Somerset, by beating Durham by 27 runs at Northampton. Alec Swann's 60 and Russell Warren's 44 were the mainstays of Northants' 225 for 7, and then Graeme Swann celebrated his England winter tour party inclusion earlier in the day by picking up 4 for 44 with his off-spin. Paul Collingwood, promoted to number three, responded with 86 but Durham could only manage 198.

31 August 1999: Division One
at Edgbaston
Warwickshire 215 for 5 (45 overs) DL Hemp 83*, NV Knight 57
Gloucestershire 181 (41 overs)
Warwickshire (4 pts) won by 34 runs

An 8,000 crowd turned out at Edgbaston for this day-night match, played in balmy late-summer temperatures, and they were rewarded with a home victory as Warwickshire defeated newly-crowned NatWest Trophy winners Gloucestershire by 34 runs. David Hemp's unbeaten 83 was chiefly responsible for taking Warwickshire to 215 for 5, although the in-form Nick Knight also hit 57. Gloucestershire, perhaps still hungover from their Lord's celebrations of two days earlier, found life tough in reply and were eventually bowled out for 181 with four overs still available. Tim Hancock, Ian Harvey and Mark Alleyne all got within sight of a half-century before getting out.

31 August 1999: Division Two
at Lord's
Middlesex 252 for 5 (45 overs) OA Shah 112, PN Weekes 80
Surrey 252 for 9 (45 overs) JD Ratcliffe 59, ARC Fraser 4 for 35
Match tied – 2 pts each

at Taunton
Somerset 257 for 9 (45 overs) M Burns 52, RJ Turner 50
Glamorgan 222 (42 overs)
Somerset (4 pts) won by 35 runs

Somerset made sure of National League first division status in 2000 by out-batting Glamorgan in a day-night fixture at Taunton. The home side bounced back from their NatWest Trophy final defeat by posting a challenging 257 for 9 with Mike Burns (52), Rob Turner (50) and Jamie Cox (42) all playing well. Glamorgan were on track for much of their reply, Jacques Kallis hitting 48 and Michael Powell 44, but then fell away to 222 all out.

Lord's, meanwhile, witnessed a thrilling tie between Middlesex and Surrey as 504 runs were split down the middle. Owais Shah's 114-ball 112 was the highlight of the Middlesex total of 252 for 5, with Paul Weekes's 80 not far behind in the entertainment stakes as the pair put on 152 for the second wicket. But the real fun only began after

Surrey's top order had kept up a determined run chase, with Jason Ratcliffe (59), Adam Hollioake (41), Mark Butcher (31) and Ian Ward (37) all making solid contributions. The last over began with tailender Ian Bishop needing to score 10 off Richard Johnson – and he made it. Angus Fraser, who had taken 4 for 35, looked sick as a dog at the end.

5 September 1999: Division One
at Chelmsford
Worcestershire 211 for 6 (45 overs) EJ Wilson 60
Essex 208 for 9 (45 overs) AP Grayson 66, RJ Rollins 51, GR Haynes 4 for 28, A Sheriyar 4 for 42
Worcestershire (4 pts) won by 3 runs

at Scarborough
Leicestershire 139 (45 overs)
Yorkshire 142 for 3 (32.4 overs)
Yorkshire (4 pts) won by seven wickets

Worcestershire, having announced four days earlier the signing of Australian fast bowler Glenn McGrath for the seasons 2000 and 2002, defeated Essex by just three runs at Chelmsford to keep them on course for the National League title. Skipper Tom Moody, whose stated ambition was to end his nine-summer association with the county by leading them to a trophy, stroked 42 from 51 balls three days after returning from Australia's short one-day series in Sri Lanka. He and Elliott Wilson (60) gave the Royals a good start but Peter Such bowled his off-breaks tidily for 3 for 27 and a total of 211 for 6 was not out of reach. Essex, at one stage, looked to be cruising, Stuart Law hitting 45. But Gavin Haynes dismissed Law, in a spell of 4 for 28 from his nine overs, and although Paul Grayson stayed for 66 and Robert Rollins scored a combative 51 towards the end Essex fell just short. Alamgir Sheriyar bowled the last over with nine runs needed and, although he delivered two wides, finished with 4 for 42.

Leicestershire slipped towards the relegation zone as a result of being thrashed by seven wickets at Scarborough. A sea fret descended on their troubled innings of 139 for 9, which was boosted only by a late assault from Mike Kasprowicz which brought the Australian fast bowler 38 from 43 balls. Chris Silverwood took 3 for 16 and, when Yorkshire replied, Michael Vaughan hit 41 and David Byas an unbeaten 36 as the home side swept to their target with 12.2 overs to spare.

5 September 1999: Division Two
at Derby
Derbyshire 215 for 8 (45 overs) RMS Weston 54
Middlesex 190 (42.2 overs) RA Kettleborough 58, ME Cassar 4 for 31, TM Smith 4 for 41
Derbyshire (4 pts) won by 25 runs

Mark Ramprakash, still seething at his England winter tour omission, smashed 41 on his 30th birthday – but it was not enough to prevent Middlesex slipping to yet another defeat in what for them has been a season to forget. Derbyshire totalled 215 for 8 from their 45 overs, Robin Weston top-scoring with 54 and the lower middle-order all chipping in. Angus Fraser took 3 for 24 from his nine overs, but his efforts were trumped by Trevor Smith (4 for 41) and Matt Cassar (4 for 31). Richard Kettleborough made a

Chris Read played his part in Nottinghamshire's win over their neighbours Derbyshire.
David Munden/Sportsline Photographic

competition-best 58 and Keith Dutch a lower-order 37 but no other Middlesex batsman, bar Ramprakash, got into double figures and eventually the visitors were dismissed for 190 in the 43rd over.

6 September 1999: Division One
at Old Trafford (floodlit)
Hampshire 180 for 8 (45 overs) GW White 51,
A Flintoff 4 for 24
Lancashire 181 for 4 (39.3 overs) MA Atherton 55
Lancashire (4 pts) won by six wickets

Lancashire moved back to the top of the National League table with an efficient six-wicket victory against Hampshire at Old Trafford. Giles White (51) and Robin Smith (36) added 71 for the third wicket, but otherwise Hampshire's batting effort was thin. Andrew Flintoff did much to undermine the visitors with 4 for 24 from nine overs, his best figures in one-day cricket and including a spell of three wickets in five balls. Mike Atherton then played the anchor role to perfection with 55 as several of his teammates, including Flintoff with a run-a-ball 27, laid about them.

6 September 1999: Division Two
at Cardiff (floodlit)
Glamorgan 228 for 4 (45 overs) JH Kallis 104*,
MP Maynard 50
Somerset 215 (44.1 overs) SD Thomas 4 for 33
Glamorgan (4 pts) won by 13 runs

at The Oval (floodlit)
Surrey 217 (45 overs) RJ Kirtley 4 for 48
Sussex 218 for 1 (42.5 overs) RR Montgomerie 80*,
MJ Di Venuto 78
Sussex (4 pts) won by nine wickets

Advance publicity at The Oval billed the first of two successive floodlit matches as 'the perfect party'. Unfortunately Sussex, storming to the top of the second division, became the party-poopers as they easily overhauled Surrey's 217 all out. The home side collapsed from 175 for 3, with Butcher, Thorpe and Brown all getting past 40 but failing to go on. James Kirtley finished with 4 for 48 and Robin Martin-Jenkins bowled tightly. Richard Montgomerie and Michael Di Venuto then set about the Surrey attack, the Tasmanian Di Venuto reaching his sixth National League half-century of the season before falling for 78.

Alec Stewart had a mixed summer for both England and Surrey, but he was amongst the runs under lights against Middlesex.
Brendan Monks/Sportsline Photographic

Glamorgan became only the third side to beat Somerset over 45 overs this season, getting home by 13 runs after totalling 228 for 4. Jacques Kallis delighted Cardiff spectators with 104 not out from 129 balls, while Matthew Maynard thrilled them with 50 from just 45 deliveries. Jamie Cox hit 75 to get Somerset's reply off to a good start, but Darren Thomas' 4 for 33 highlighted a proficient performance in the field by the Welsh county.

7 September 1999: Division One
at Leicester
Gloucestershire 216 for 6 (45 overs) THC Hancock 72,
KJ Barnett 57
Leicestershire 202 for 9 (45 overs) DL Maddy 59
Gloucestershire (4 pts) won by 14 runs

Gloucestershire won a crucial relegation battle against Leicestershire at Grace Road by posting a solid total and then defending it with huge tenacity. It was a familiar pattern, following Gloucestershire's triumphs in the Super Cup and NatWest Trophy, but it was enough to see off Leicestershire by 14 runs. As so often earlier in the summer, Kim Barnett (57) and Tim Hancock (72) got Gloucestershire off to a fine start, and an eventual 216 for 6 was just over par for the conditions. Mike Smith then put in a superb new-ball spell but it was Ian Harvey, surely one of the best 'death' bowlers in the game, who once more put the gloss on an excellent all-round display. Conceding just seven runs from his last two overs, at the end, Harvey finished with 3 for 30 from his nine-over stint and, despite Darren Maddy's 59, Leicestershire found themselves needing 20 from the final over.

7 September 1999: Division Two
at The Oval (floodlit)
Surrey 243 for 5 (45 overs) AJ Stewart 76, GP Thorpe 70
Middlesex 174 (41.2 overs)
Surrey (4 pts) won by 69 runs

Surrey's second floodlit match, on a second successive balmy late summer night, produced some fireworks from the home side at the Oval. Alec Stewart (76) and Graham Thorpe, with 70 from 71 balls, added 122 for the third wicket and Surrey's 243 for 5 was way too much for Middlesex. There were four run-outs and only Owais Shah (42) and David Nash (43) made any impression as they were bowled out for 174.

8 September: Division Two
at Hove (floodlit)
Nottinghamshire 148 for 9 (45 overs) RJ Kirtley 4 for 31
Sussex 149 for 1 (31.5 overs) MJ Di Venuto 94*
Sussex (4 pts) won by nine wickets

12 September 1999: Division One
at Bristol
Gloucestershire 188 for 8 (45 overs)
Essex 191 for 3 (39.4 overs)
N Hussain 86
Essex (4 pts) won by seven wickets

Jamie Cox led Somerset superbly throughout the season.
David Munden/Sportsline Photographic

at Southampton
Worcestershire 236 for 7 (45 overs) GA Hick 76
Hampshire 238 for 6 (43.3 overs) AD Mascarenhas 79
Hampshire (4 pts) won by four wickets

at Old Trafford
Kent 198 for 7 (45 overs)
Lancashire 199 for 5 (43 overs) JP Crawley 85*
Lancashire (4 pts) won by five wickets

at Headingley
Yorkshire 238 for 3 (45 overs) D Byas 67,
MP Vaughan 56
Warwickshire 210 (43.3 overs) DP Ostler 52,
MJ Powell 51, C White 4 for 39
Yorkshire (4 pts) won by 28 runs

Lancashire clinched their eighth one-day title of the 1990's by beating Kent by five wickets at Old Trafford – and then waiting 15 minutes in mounting excitement for the confirmation of Worcestershire's defeat by Hampshire at Southampton.

Kent's 198 for 7 was never going to be enough, even after an opening stand of 68 between Will House (49) and Robert Key (36). John Crawley, however, made sure victory was achieved comfortably, with two overs to spare, by hitting 85 not out from 102 balls. It was a day of triumph for Crawley, in his first season as Lancashire captain: earlier, after Warren Hegg had been hit in the mouth, he took over the wicketkeeper's gloves and brought off three stumpings!

Worcestershire's despair was coupled with the knowledge that their four-wicket defeat at Southampton had denied them a showdown with Lancashire, for the title, on their home patch at New Road on 19 September. The defeat was especially hard for Tom Moody to take: the giant, genial Australian desperately wanted to finish his long reign as captain with a trophy, and he had earlier put in a spell of 9–2–14–1 with the ball. Hampshire, though, had still got past Worcestershire's 236 for 7, of which Graeme Hick made 76 from 87 balls, thanks in the main to a stand of 68 in just nine overs between Dimitri Mascarenhas (79) and Nixon McLean (32 from 24 balls). Mascarenhas thumped three sixes and seven fours.

Gloucestershire wasted a chance to confirm retention of their own first division status, going down by seven wickets to bottom-of-the-table Essex at Bristol. Ricky Anderson and Ronnie Irani bowled well, restricting Gloucestershire to 188 for 8, and then Nasser Hussain eased his way to a classy

John Crawley of Lancashire proudly holds up the CGU National League division one trophy.
David Dawson/Sportsline Photographic

86, off 98 balls, as Essex breezed home with 5.2 overs to spare.

A fine all-round performance by Craig White helped to earn Yorkshire a 28-run win against Warwickshire at Headingley. White hit 43 in Yorkshire's 238 for 3, in which David Byas (67) and Michael Vaughan (56) also impressed, and then took 4 for 39 as Warwickshire were held to 210. Dominic Ostler's 52 and Michael Powell's 51 were the only threats.

12 September 1999: Division Two
at Chester-le-Street
Glamorgan 202 for 8 (45 overs) MM Betts 4 for 46
Durham 189 (42.5 overs)
Glamorgan (4 pts) won by 13 runs

at Northampton
Somerset 209 (44 overs) AL Penberthy 5 for 41
Northamptonshire 190 (42.5 overs) PS Jones 4 for 49
Somerset (4 pts) won by 19 runs

Somerset kept alive their chances of winning the second division title by beating Northamptonshire by 19 runs at Wantage Road. Graham Rose's late 41 boosted Somerset to 209 – although Tony Penberthy finished off the innings in dramatic style by taking a hat-trick at the end of the 44th over. Rose and Andrew Caddick then conceded just 14 runs from the first 10 overs of the Northants innings, and the home side never recovered despite Russell Warren's 45. Steffan Jones ended up with 4 for 49 as the Northants batsmen became ever more frantic.

Glamorgan's late-season return to form included a 13-run win against Durham at the Riverside. Melvyn Betts picked up 4 for 46 but Glamorgan reached 202 for 8 after a stand of 67 for the sixth wicket by Keith Newell and Robert Croft. Former England off-spinner Croft was soon playing an important part with the ball, too, taking 3 for 33 as Durham were dismissed for 189 despite Jon Lewis's unbeaten 41.

19 September 1999: Division One
at Canterbury
Kent 148 for 8 (30 overs)
Gloucestershire 120 for 5 (25 overs)
Gloucestershire (4pts) won by 4 runs
(D/L method used when rain stopped play at 25 overs, at which point Gloucestershire needed to have reached 116 runs)

at Leicester
Leicestershire v. Essex
No play possible – 2 pts each

at Edgbaston
Warwickshire 114 for 5 (11 overs)
Hampshire 76 for 6 (9.1 overs)
Match abandoned – 2 pts each

at Worcester
Worcestershire v. Lancashire
No play possible – 2 pts each

More controversy sullied the final day of the 1999 season – and once again Hampshire and Warwickshire were involved. Warwickshire, indeed, suffered one of the blackest weekends in their history when – 24 hours after missing out on a first division championship place because of what they saw as collusion between Hampshire and Derbyshire – they had what seemed to be certain survival in the National League's top division ripped away.

This time, as rain fell towards the end of a 11-overs-a-side slog at Edgbaston, umpires Alan Whitehead and John Steele decided to abandon the match even though just five more balls were required for a result to stand.

David Hemp, with 42 off 25 deliveries, had spearheaded Warwickshire's drive to 114 for 5, after rain relented in time for play to start at 5pm. By now Warwickshire had learned that Leicestershire's match against Essex at Grace Road had been called off – meaning that a victory would push them up above their Midland rivals and out of the relegation zone.

Hampshire, already down, had all but given up in their chase and were 76 for 6 from 9.1 overs when a shower of rain swept across the ground. To the surprise of spectators, and the dismay of the Warwickshire players, the umpires ruled that conditions were unplayable. Whitehead

The Lancashire Lightning team celebrates winning the CGU division one National League.
David Dawson/Sportsline Photographic

said later that the rain was too heavy and that the officials had to be consistent in their interpretation, despite the situation. When the shower passed, the cut-off time of 6.40pm had also gone and so the match had to be abandoned. If five more balls had been bowled – to get the Hampshire innings up to the minimum ten overs – then a Duckworth-Lewis calculation would have occurred and Warwickshire would have won easily.

Dennis Amiss, the Warwickshire chief executive, was so angry that he called a press conference immediately after the abandonment. 'I am astonished by what the umpires did,' he said. 'They didn't use any common sense. I have seen games finished in much heavier rain and, indeed, I played in one myself for England against Australia.'

Neil Smith, the Warwickshire captain, said he was 'amazed' by the umpires' decision, and Amiss added that Smith would be making 'the strongest possible complaint' in his report.

Elsewhere in division one Gloucestershire benefited from Leicestershire's no result against Essex because it meant they did not need to beat Kent at Canterbury to retain their first division status. But they did anyway, reaching 120 for 5 from 25 overs in reply to a 30-over Kent total of 148 for 8 before accepting an offer to go off for bad light in the knowledge they were four runs ahead on the Duckworth-Lewis system. With Matt Windows going along smoothly on 48, and with Jack Russell also settled in, it was a shame however that the Gloucestershire team did not feel they owed a patient and sizeable crowd a proper finish. Kent had little incentive, though, as they were already assured of third place prize money.

The game between champions Lancashire and runners-up Worcestershire, at Worcester, was another victim of the bad weather.

19 September 1999: Division Two
at Derby
Derbyshire 94 for 4 (10 overs)
Sussex 97 for 3 (9.1 overs)
Sussex (4 pts) won by seven wickets

at Cardiff
Glamorgan 99 (31.2 overs)
Middlesex 100 for 5 (29 overs)
Middlesex (4 pts) won by five wickets

at Trent Bridge
Nottinghamshire 211 for 1 (32 overs) GE Welton 104*, U Afzaal 83*
Durham did not bat
Match abandoned – 2 pts each

at Taunton
Somerset 209 for 9 (25 overs) PCL Holloway 54
Northamptonshire 180 for 8 (23 overs) GP Swann 57
(Northamptonshire had two overs deducted for slow over-rate)
Somerset (4 pts) won by 29 runs

Sussex made sure of the division two trophy, their first title since the 1986 NatWest Trophy, by beating Derbyshire by seven wickets at Derby. The rain stopped just in time for a ten-over game to be staged and, although Phil DeFreitas smashed 34 from 21 balls to help Derbyshire reach 93 for 4, Sussex got home with five balls to spare after Dutchman Bas Zuiderant (24) and Tony Cottey (28 not out) produced telling contributions.

Somerset, who could have taken top spot if Sussex had lost, finished runners-up. Jamie Cox's side beat

Andrew Caddick's Somerset earned promotion to the first division...
David Munden/Sportsline Photographic

Northamptonshire by 29 runs, with Piran Holloway (54 off 25 balls) and Marcus Trescothick (43) mainly responsible for a fine total of 209 for 9 in a match reduced to 25 overs per side. Northants' chances diminished when they were penalised two overs for taking too long in the field. Cox, meanwhile, announced that he was carrying on as Somerset's captain and overseas player for a further two years – subject to Australia not wanting him for the 2001 Ashes tour.

In the other games, Middlesex ended a wretched season by beating Glamorgan by five wickets at Cardiff, easily overhauling the home side's pitiful 99 all out in a match reduced to 34 overs per side. At Trent Bridge, the fixture between Nottinghamshire and Durham was abandoned because of rain after Notts had rattled up 211 for 1 in 32 overs thanks to Guy Welton's maiden one-day hundred and an unbeaten 83 from Usman Afzaal.

DIVISION ONE FINAL TABLE

	M	W	L	Tied	NR	Pts
Lancashire	16	11	2	–	3	50
Worcestershire	16	10	4	–	2	44
Kent	16	8	6	–	2	36
Gloucestershire	16	8	8	–	–	32
Yorkshire	16	8	8	–	–	32
Leicestershire	16	6	8	–	2	28
Warwickshire	16	6	8	–	2	28
Hampshire	16	5	9	–	2	24
Essex	16	3	12	–	1	14

Teams in bold relegated to division two for 2000

DIVISION TWO FINAL TABLE

	M	W	L	Tied	NR	Pts
Sussex	16	13	2	–	1	54
Somerset	16	13	3	–	–	52
Northamptonshire	16	9	5	–	2	40
Glamorgan	16	8	7	1	–	34
Nottinghamshire	16	6	8	–	2	28
Surrey	16	5	9	1	1	24
Middlesex	16	5	10	1	–	22
Derbyshire	16	4	10	1	1	20
Durham	16	3	12	–	1	14

Teams in bold promoted to division one for 2000

...but the England and Essex captain, Nasser Hussain will find himself in division two.
David Munden/Sportsline Photographic

NATIONAL LEAGUE AVERAGES

DERBYSHIRE

Batting	M	Inns	NO	HS	Runs	Av	100	50	ct/st
ID Blackwell	9	9	2	97	262	37.42	-	2	2
ME Cassar	14	14	0	109	377	26.92	2	1	6
RMS Weston	13	12	1	56	277	25.18	-	2	2
MJ Slater	10	10	0	59	232	23.20	-	3	3
GM Roberts	7	5	2	27	68	22.66	-	-	2
PAJ DeFreitas	10	10	0	61	223	22.30	-	1	3
AS Rollins	10	10	1	31	198	22.00	-	-	3
SP Titchard	14	13	1	44*	240	20.00	-	-	1
DG Cork	9	9	1	61*	145	18.12	-	1	3
P Aldred	9	6	2	39*	70	17.50	-	-	-
SD Stubbings	6	6	0	37	98	16.33	-	1	-
KM Krikken	10	10	4	25*	90	15.00	-	-	8/2
TM Smith	6	5	4	8*	13	13.00	-	-	2

Also batted: KJ Dean (4 matches) 10; FA Griffith (1 match) 15; SP Griffiths (5 matches) 8*, 1*, 0, 4ct/2st; AJ Harris (4 matches) 3, 8*, 3*; Kasir Shah (3 matches) 0*, 1 ct; SJ Lacey (3 matches) 0, 15, 4, 1 ct; M Newell (3 matches) 0, 2, 1, 1 ct; JP Pyemont (4 matches) 8, 10, 0, 14, 1 ct; BJ Spendlove (3 matches) 11, 5, 26; AP Woolley (5 matches) 1*, 1, 0
MJ Deane, RL Eagleson & CM Wells (1 ct) played in one match but did not bat

Bowling	Overs	Mds	Runs	Wkts	Av	Best	4/inns
ID Blackwell	59.5	3	250	12	20.83	3-17	-
TM Smith	41	2	259	11	23.54	4-38	2
GM Roberts	52.3	0	239	10	23.90	4-23	1
KJ Dean	29	2	129	5	25.80	4-35	1
MA Cassar	61.4	2	338	11	30.72	4-31	1
P Aldred	61	3	294	9	32.66	2-19	-
AP Woolley	31	1	181	5	36.20	4-61	1
PAJ DeFreitas	81	9	283	7	40.42	2-19	-
DG Cork	55.4	2	294	6	49.00	2-33	-

Also bowled: MJ Deane 9-0-42-3; RL Eagleson 5-0-23-1; FA Griffith 5-0-26-2; AJ Harris 27-2-135-2; Kasir Shah 18-0-113-3; SJ Lacey 27-1-121-3; SP Titchard 9-0-48-1; CM Wells 4-0-7-2

DURHAM

Batting	M	Inns	NO	HS	Runs	Av	100	50	ct/st
JJB Lewis	16	15	3	85	455	37.91	-	1	-
NJ Speak	8	6	1	53	159	31.80	-	1	-
DC Boon	13	12	0	66	334	27.83	-	3	3
JA Daley	12	11	0	90	294	26.72	-	1	3
MP Speight	14	13	1	60	302	25.16	-	1	14/4
PD Collingwood	15	14	1	86	316	24.30	-	1	8
JE Morris	9	9	0	41	175	19.44	-	-	-
MM Betts	12	9	3	15	73	12.16	-	-	2
J Wood	14	9	4	16	60	12.00	-	-	6
NC Phillips	16	14	2	19*	109	9.08	-	-	5
N Killeen	13	8	3	10	39	7.80	-	-	2
R Robinson	9	8	0	33	52	6.5	-	-	2

Also batted: SM Ali (2 matches) 2, 17; SJE Brown (4 matches) 0, 4, 2 ct; S Chapman (1 match) 30, 1 ct; MJ Foster (1 match) 2; MA Gough (3 matches) 0, 16, 1 ct; SJ Harmison (5 matches) 0*, 1, 1*, 1 ct; ID Hunter (4 matches) 3, 4; A Pratt (2 matches) 26, 3; MJ Symington (3 matches) 10, 3

Bowling	Overs	Mds	Runs	Wkts	Av	Best	4/inns
NC Phillips	124.5	1	599	22	27.22	4-13	1
MM Betts	90.3	2	482	15	32.13	4-39	2
J Wood	106	5	487	15	32.46	3-43	-
N Killeen	99.4	14	405	11	36.81	3-38	—

Also bowled: SJE Brown 26-3-138-2; S Chapman 5-0-22-1; PD Collingwood 23-1-131-2; MJ Foster 4-0-33-2; MA Gough 7-0-45-0; SJ Harmison 35-2-176-3; ID Hunter 32.1-1-132-4; R Robinson 42-1-214-4; MJ Symington 26-0-163-2

ESSEX

Batting	M	Inns	NO	HS	Runs	Av	100	50	ct/st
N Hussain	8	8	0	114	375	46.87	1	3	7
DDJ Robinson	9	9	1	74*	260	32.50	-	2	3
SG Law	14	14	1	55	396	30.46	-	1	4
AP Grayson	15	14	2	66	276	23.00	-	1	1

NATIONAL LEAGUE AVERAGES

ESSEX (cont)

Batting (cont)	M	Inns	NO	HS	Runs	Av	100	50	ct/st
BJ Hyam	11	8	2	37	128	21.33	-	-	12/1
PJ Prichard	9	9	0	49	183	20.33	-	-	2
RC Irani	14	14	1	64	223	17.15	-	2	2
DR Law	13	12	0	48	193	16.08	-	-	2
SD Peters	9	8	1	28*	102	14.57	-	-	3
TC Walton	7	7	1	23	75	12.50	-	-	1
PM Such	13	9	7	5*	24	12.00	-	-	5
MC Ilott	9	7	1	17	67	11.16	-	-	-
AP Cowan	14	12	2	27	97	9.70	-	-	7
RSG Anderson	7	5	1	10	25	6.25	-	-	-

Also batted: JE Bishop (1 match) 1; GR Napier (4 matches) 15, 4, 19; T Phillips (1 match) 0, 1 ct; RJ Rolling (4 matches) 87, 12, 51, 39, 4 ct/2 st; DJ Thompson (3 matches) 1*, 1

Bowling	Overs	Mds	Runs	Wkts	Av	Best	4/inns
RC Irani	102.2	13	470	24	19.58	5-33	3
MC Ilott	60.5	2	279	13	21.46	3-36	-
DR Law	21.5	0	129	5	25.80	3-26	-
PM Such	97	3	426	16	26.62	3-26	-
AP Cowan	108.2	13	469	13	36.07	3-17	-
AP Grayson	98	0	525	11	47.72	3-48	-

Also bowled: RSG Anderson 44.2-2-241-4; JE Bishop 3-0-24-0; SG Law 21-0-99-2; T Phillips 8-0-56-2; DJ Thompson 13.3-1-67-2

GLAMORGAN

Batting	M	Inns	NO	HS	Runs	Av	100	50	ct/st
JH Kallis	7	7	2	155*	484	96.80	2	2	2
MP Maynard	11	11	1	79	346	34.60	-	3	4/1
A Dale	15	14	3	74*	365	33.18	-	3	3
AW Evans	13	10	0	108	299	29.90	1	1	7
SP James	16	16	1	91	352	23.46	-	1	3
RDB Croft	14	14	1	53	278	21.38	-	1	7
K Newell	8	8	0	41	138	17.25	-	-	3
MJ Powell	13	11	2	44	145	16.11	-	-	4
SD Thomas	13	13	3	38*	153	15.30	-	-	1
AD Shaw	9	6	1	21	75	15.00	-	-	10/2
DA Cosker	14	9	3	27*	76	12.66	-	-	4
OT Parkin	15	6	1	6	16	3.20	-	-	3
SL Watkin	13	7	3	5	10	2.50	-	-	2

Also batted: AP Davies (3 matches) 1, 0; I Dawood (5 matches) 0, 2, 12, 13, 7ct; SP Jones (1 match) 12*; WL Law (3 matches) 16, 21, 1; MA Wallace (3 matches) 2, 1, 4 ct/2 st

Bowling	Overs	Mds	Runs	Wkts	Av	Best	4/inns
OT Parkin	115	7	520	28	18.57	3-31	-
SL Watkin	103.3	17	401	21	19.09	3-15	-
RDB Croft	115.1	7	474	24	19.75	4-31	1
SD Thomas	80.5	4	418	20	20.90	4-33	1
JH Kallis	39.3	3	151	6	25.16	2-27	-
A Dale	83.3	5	339	9	37.66	3-19	-
DA Cosker	106	3	492	12	41.00	2-37	-

Also bowled: AP Davies 15-0-91-2; SP Jones 7-0-39-1; WL Law- 1-0-6-0; MP Maynard 3-0-13-1; K Newell 2-0-12-0

GLOUCESTERSHIRE

Batting	M	Inns	NO	HS	Runs	Av	100	50	ct/st
RC Russell	16	16	4	91*	409	34.08	-	4	13/6
MW Alleyne	16	16	2	91	407	29.07	-	2	8
IJ Harvey	14	14	1	47	297	22.84	-	-	1
KJ Barnett	15	15	0	57	337	22.46	-	1	7
MGN Windows	16	16	1	48*	325	21.66	-	-	9
THC Hancock	16	16	0	72	331	20.68	-	2	6
RJ Cunliffe	9	8	0	66	159	19.87	-	2	1
JN Snape	16	15	2	56	256	19.69	-	1	7
RI Dawson	7	7	1	39	112	18.66	-	-	1
MJC Ball	13	10	3	23*	71	10.14	-	-	7
J Lewis	8	8	1	12	54	7.71	-	-	2

NATIONAL LEAGUE AVERAGES

GLOUCESTERSHIRE (cont)

Batting (cont)	M	Inns	NO	HS	Runs	Av	100	50	ct/st
MJ Cawdron	8	5	2	11*	23	7.66	-	-	1
AM Smith	14	8	6	8*	13	6.50	-	-	5
JMM Averis	6	5	3	5*	5	2.50	-	-	-

Also batted: DR Hewson (2 matches) 0, 1

Bowling	Overs	Mds	Runs	Wkts	Av	Best	4/inns
IJ Harvey	107.5	10	474	30	15.80	5-41	2
JN Snape	80.5	2	338	17	19.88	4-27	1
MCJ Ball	84.2	3	365	17	21.47	5-42	1
MJ Cawdron	46	2	225	10	22.50	4-17	1
KJ Barnett	28	0	149	6	24.83	4-29	1
MW Alleyne	114	8	457	17	26.88	3-29	-
JMM Averis	38	6	149	5	29.80	3-17	-
AM Smith	118.2	18	409	11	37.18	2-25	-
J Lewis	50.1	4	225	6	37.50	2-42	-

Also bowled: THC Hancock 9.2-1-38-3

HAMPSHIRE

Batting	M	Inns	NO	HS	Runs	Av	100	50	ct/st
SJ Renshaw	13	6	5	27*	66	66.00	-	-	1
JP Stephenson	11	11	2	96	365	40.55	-	2	7
JS Laney	12	12	1	106*	304	27.63	1	1	5
RA Smith	14	14	3	97*	290	26.36	-	1	3
DA Kenway	16	14	0	58	341	24.35	-	2	5
AD Mascarenhas	15	13	1	79	285	23.75	-	3	5
GW White	13	13	0	51	223	17.15	-	1	4
WS Kendall	11	10	2	31	136	17.00	-	-	4
AN Aymes	13	10	3	34	105	15.00	-	-	6/1
PJ Hartley	13	5	4	12*	15	15.00	-	-	-
NAM McLean	14	12	2	32	145	14.50	-	-	2
SD Udal	15	12	2	20	103	10.30	-	-	3

Also batted: SRG Francis (4 matches) 1; M Garaway (1 match) 4, 1 ct; KD James (2 matches) 4*; M Keech (4 matches) 27, 6, 3, 1 ct; AC Morris (3 matches) 5; LR Prittipaul played in 2 matches but did not bat (1 ct)

Bowling	Overs	Mds	Runs	Wkts	Av	Best	4/inns
AD Mascarenhas	99.4	7	446	17	26.23	3-23	-
NAM McLean	101	8	500	18	27.77	3-27	-
PJ Hartley	95.2	5	484	17	28.47	4-29	1
SJ Renshaw	88	7	442	13	34.00	4-40	1
SD Udal	84.4	3	393	11	35.72	2-17	-
JP Stephenson	55.5	1	277	6	46.16	2-26	-

Also bowled: SRG Francis 23 3-93-3; KD James 11-0-71-2; JS Laney 0.3-0-9-0; AC Morris 18-0-104-4

KENT

Batting	M	Inns	NO	HS	Runs	Av	100	50	ct/st
RWT Key	10	10	3	76*	329	47.00	-	2	1
NJ Llong	12	12	3	42*	273	30.33	-	-	6
TR Ward	11	11	0	70	318	28.90	-	2	2
A Symonds	9	9	0	95	248	27.55	-	2	3
MA Ealham	13	12	2	43*	267	26.70	-	-	4
WJ House	10	10	0	49	230	23.00	-	-	1
MV Fleming	15	13	3	39	221	22.10	-	-	1
SA Marsh	14	11	3	21	119	14.87	-	-	14/1
MJ Walker	13	12	0	39	153	12.75	-	-	3
DW Headley	11	5	3	14*	24	12.00	-	-	1
MM Patel	10	6	3	11	27	9.00	-	-	2
ET Smith	8	7	0	34	52	7.42	-	-	-
MJ McCague	7	5	1	7	21	5.25	-	-	-

Also batted: JB Hockley (2 matches) 8, 19, 2 ct; JB DeC Thompson (15 matches) 0*, 0*, 1*, 0*, 2*, 3 ct; AP Wells (2 matches) 18, 23; SC Willis (1 match) 3; DA Scott played in 2 matches but did not bat

KENT (cont)

Bowling	Overs	Mds	Runs	Wkts	Av	Best	4/inns
JB DeC Thompson	107	14	382	18	21.22	3-16	-
DW Headley	81	10	320	14	22.85	5-43	2
MA Ealham	87.1	9	309	13	23.76	3-26	-
MM Patel	76	3	292	12	24.33	3-22	-
MJ McCague	46	2	224	7	32.00	3-29	-
MV Fleming	80.2	1	386	12	32.16	3-15	—

Also bowled: WJ House 1-0-12-0; NJ Llong 22-0-104-2; DA Scott 9-0-57-0; A Symonds 31.1-0-165-2; MJ Walker 6-0-26-0

LANCASHIRE

Batting	M	Inns	NO	HS	Runs	Av	100	50	ct/st
MA Atherton	7	6	2	95*	244	61.00	-	3	1
NH Fairbrother	12	11	5	66*	278	46.33	-	3	2
JP Crawley	14	13	2	85*	483	43.90	-	3	2/3
A Flintoff	11	10	1	143	338	37.55	1	1	7
GD Lloyd	14	11	5	55*	183	30.50	1	1	3
WK Hegg	14	8	3	30*	101	20.20	-	-	14/3
MJ Chilton	7	7	0	44	141	20.14	-	-	1
M Watkinson	11	10	0	49	194	19.40	-	-	3

Also batted: ID Austin (12 matches) 10, 8*, 3; G Chapple (12 matches) 12, 10, 2, 5ct; RJ Green (2 matches) 14, 14*, 1 ct; ME Harvey (1 match) 15, 4 ct; PC McKeown (3 matches) 12, 48, 4; PJ Martin (14 matches) 4, 2, 4, 12, 5 ct; M Muralitharan (7 matches) 13*, 4 ct; CP Schofield (2 matches) 5, 28; MP Smethurst (4 matches) 1, 0; G Yates (7 matches) 22*, 7, 5

Bowling	Overs	Mds	Runs	Wkts	Av	Best	4/inns
A Flintoff	67	5	287	17	16.88	4-24	1
M Muralitharan	56.2	12	188	10	18.80	3-12	-
ID Austin	96.3	18	288	15	19.20	4-15	1
M Watkinson	53	5	187	9	20.77	3-25	-
MP Smethurst	19.2	0	111	5	22.20	2-13	-
PJ Martin	110.4	9	403	18	22.38	5-28	1
G Yates	58	0	232	9	25.77	3-36	-
G Chapple	86.2	4	433	12	36.08	3-34	-

Also bowled: MJ Chilton 11-0-65-4; RJ Green 14-2-57-1; CP Schofield 9-0-32-2

LEICESTERSHIRE

Batting	M	Inns	NO	HS	Runs	Av	100	50	ct/st
BF Smith	12	12	1	74	369	33.54	-	3	3
PA Nixon	15	14	4	96*	325	32.50	-	1	22/2
DI Stevens	10	10	0	82	270	27.00	-	2	2
DL Maddy	14	14	1	89*	349	26.84	-	2	5
CC Lewis	9	9	1	116*	214	26.75	1	-	3
Aftab Habib	13	13	3	42	238	23.80	-	-	4
JM Dakin	15	12	2	41	236	23.60	-	-	3
MS Kasprowicz	13	9	2	38	133	19.00	-	-	-
D Williamson	10	9	1	39	121	15.12	-	-	1
VJ Wells	13	13	0	43	195	15.00	-	-	3
IJ Sutcliffe	9	9	0	40	105	11.66	-	-	1
TJ Mason	10	6	2	21*	30	7.50	-	-	1
J Ormond	8	5	2	11*	22	7.33	-	-	1

Also batted: SAJ Boswell (2 matches) 0*; MT Brimson (4 matches) 2, 0, 0*; DJ Millns (2 matches) 13, 9*; AD Mullally (5 matches) 2*, 0, 9; PE Robinson (1 match) 1

Bowling	Overs	Mds	Runs	Wkts	Av	Best	4/inns
AD Mullally	38.4	6	120	6	20.00	2-12	-
MS Kasprowicz	100.1	10	435	18	24.16	4-30	1
J Ormond	64	3	297	12	24.75	3-30	-
D Williamson	53	1	255	10	25.50	3-28	-
JM Dakin	93.3	5	441	17	25.94	5-30	2
CC Lewis	50.5	5	215	6	35.83	2-22	-
VJ Wells	68.4	3	293	8	36.62	2-19	-
TJ Mason	51	0	265	6	44.16	2-37	-

Also bowled: SAJ Boswell 13-0-57-2; MT Brimson 18-2-69-4; DL Maddy 22.2-0-113-3; DJ Millns 14-2-51-2

NATIONAL LEAGUE AVERAGES

MIDDLESEX

Batting	M	Inns	NO	HS	Runs	Av	100	50	ct/st
MA Robinson	13	13	2	91*	423	38.45	-	5	3
OA Shah	15	14	0	134	487	34.78	2	1	2
JL Langer	11	10	0	84	301	30.10	-	3	1
KP Dutch	15	14	3	57	290	26.36	-	1	5
MR Ramprakash	12	11	1	57	255	25.50	-	1	6
DC Nash	16	12	4	43	187	23.37	-	-	17/4
ARC Fraser	15	7	4	31	66	22.00	-	-	6
PN Weekes	16	15	1	80	299	21.35	-	1	9
BL Hutton	8	6	1	24	75	15.00	-	-	7
JP Hewitt	9	5	2	13	40	13.33	-	-	3
AJ Strauss	6	5	2	19	33	11.00	-	-	1
SJ Cook	16	12	2	20	100	10.00	-	-	2

Also batted: D Alleyne (1 match) 13, 2 ct/1 st; CJ Batt (2 matches) 8*; IN Blanchett (1 match) 1;
TF Bloomfield (7 matches) 10, 1*, 2 ct; DJ Goodchild (2 matches) 7, 1 ct; RL Johnson (5 matches)
0, 8*, 0, 10; EC Joyce (1 match) 20; RA Kettleborough (4 matches) 1, 58, 3;
PCR Tufnell (1 match) 1*, 1 ct

Bowling	Overs	Mds	Runs	Wkts	Av	Best	4/inns
KP Dutch	76.1	2	342	23	14.86	5-35	1
ARC Fraser	123.5	21	424	21	20.19	4-35	1
SJ Cook	124.2	11	576	24	24.00	3-16	-
JP Hewitt	51	1	250	9	27.77	2-23	-
PN Weekes	114	4	564	18	31.33	4-43	1
TF Bloomfield	57	0	288	6	48.00	2-45	-

Also bowled: CJ Batt 17-0-64-3; IN Blanchett 4-0-34-2; BL Hutton 6-0-62-1;
RL Johnson 36.2-0-177-1; RA Kettleborough 4-0-28-0; JL Langer 10.5-0-74-2;
MR Ramprakash 11-0-50-1; OA Shah 9-0-54-0; PCR Tufnell 4-1-29-1

NORTHAMPTONSHIRE

Batting	M	Inns	NO	HS	Runs	Av	100	50	ct/st
AL Penberthy	14	14	4	64*	379	37.90	-	2	6
RJ Warren	14	14	1	61	389	29.92	-	1	11
ML Hayden	8	8	0	86	228	28.50	-	1	3
GP Swann	14	13	1	63	295	24.58	-	2	3
JP Taylor	13	6	4	19*	49	24.50	-	-	4
RJ Bailey	6	5	0	43	117	23.40	-	-	1
AJ Swann	8	8	0	60	180	22.50	-	1	2
D Ripley	10	6	3	33	65	21.66	-	-	10/2
KJ Innes	10	8	3	27	104	20.80	-	-	4
DJG Sales	14	14	0	54	288	20.57	-	1	8
KM Curran	14	14	5	36	165	18.33	-	-	6
MB Loye	9	9	0	55	164	18.22	-	1	3
DE Malcolm	13	5	1	2	3	0.75	-	-	2

Also batted: TMB Bailey (3 matches) 10, 2 ct; RJ Logan (4 matches) 8, 2 ct

Bowling	Overs	Mds	Runs	Wkts	Av	Best	4/inns
AL Penberthy	108	3	504	27	18.66	5-41	1
KJ Innes	52.2	1	286	15	19.06	4-37	1
DE Malcolm	86	6	385	20	19.25	3-16	-
GP Swann	89	1	413	17	24.29	5-35	2
JP Taylor	89.5	6	421	15	28.06	4-41	1
KM Curran	97	14	380	11	34.54	3-12	-

Also bowled: RJ Bailey 3-0-20-0; RJ Logan 17-0-101-3

NOTTINGHAMSHIRE

Batting	M	Inns	NO	HS	Runs	Av	100	50	ct/st
U Afzaal	5	5	1	83*	186	46.50	-	2	2
AG Wharf	14	11	7	38*	175	43.75	-	-	3
GF Archer	12	12	3	75*	346	38.44	-	3	5
JER Gallian	15	15	1	130	490	35.00	2	1	5
CMW Read	14	13	0	62	374	28.76	-	1	18/1
GE Welton	9	9	1	104*	201	25.12	1	-	2
RD Stemp	14	5	3	29*	49	24.50	-	-	4
P Johnson	13	13	0	68	291	22.38	-	2	1
MP Dowman	8	8	1	52	134	19.14	-	1	1
VC Drakes	15	12	2	40	181	18.10	-	-	4

NATIONAL LEAGUE AVERAGES

NOTTINGHAMSHIRE (cont)

Batting (cont)	M	Inns	NO	HS	Runs	Av	100	50	ct/st
CM Tolley	9	7	1	39	96	16.00	-	-	-
RT Robinson	6	6	0	29	92	15.33	-	-	-
PJ Franks	15	13	3	40	131	13.10	-	-	-

Also batted: MN Bowen (8 matches) 22*, 1, 1, 2ct; NA Gie (2 matches) 1, 28;
DS Lucas (4 matches) 19*, 1 ct; RT Bates and WM Noon played in 1 match but did not bat

Bowling	Overs	Mds	Runs	Wkts	Av	Best	4/inns
CM Tolley	52	1	223	11	20.27	4-34	2
VC Drakes	112.4	13	511	24	21.29	5-31	2
PJ Franks	107.5	4	512	16	32.00	5-27	1
RD Stemp	108	4	490	13	38.69	3-15	-
MN Bowen	51.5	0	293	7	41.85	4-46	1
AG Wharf	95.4	3	489	8	61.12	3-26	-

Also bowled: U Afzaal 0.5-0-4-0; RJ Bates 5-0-29-0; MP Dowman 16-0-92-2;
JER Gallian 7-0-52-0; DS Lucas 19-0-117-4

SOMERSET

Batting	M	Inns	NO	HS	Runs	Av	100	50	ct/st
PCL Holloway	15	15	4	101*	645	58.63	1	6	4
J Cox	14	14	0	101	593	42.35	1	3	6
ME Trescothick	13	13	2	110	351	39.00	1	-	5
PD Bowler	11	10	0	86	356	35.60	-	4	3
KA Parsons	16	14	4	45*	270	27.00	-	-	8
RJ Turner	16	15	3	63	297	24.75	-	2	19/1
M Burns	16	16	1	52	318	21.20	-	2	5
GD Rose	10	6	0	41	101	16.83	-	-	2
JID Kerr	15	10	1	56	151	16.77	-	1	4
AR Caddick	13	7	3	13*	32	8.00	-	-	1
PS Jones	15	8	2	12	28	4.66	-	-	4

Also batted: MPL Bulbeck (7 matches) 1, 5, 1 ct; PW Jarvis (11 matches) 20*, 4*, 4, 6*, 4ct;
I Jones (1 match) 5*; ARK Pierson (2 matches) 1*, 0*, 1 ct
GJ Kennis played 1 match but did not bat

Bowling	Overs	Mds	Runs	Wkts	Av	Best	4/inns
M Burns	33.2	0	183	8	22.87	2-14	-
PS Jones	113.5	6	653	26	25.11	4-49	1
JID Kerr	86	1	434	17	25.52	2-22	-
AR Caddick	105	19	325	12	27.08	3-16	-
PW Jarvis	84	0	475	16	29.68	4-28	1
GD Rose	70	7	311	9	34.55	2-26	-
KA Parsons	84	4	422	12	35.16	3-21	—

Also bowled: MPL Bulbeck 38-3-195-4; J Cox 7-0-28-3; I Jones 7.1-0-53-1;
ARK Pierson 15-0-77-2; ME Trescothick 4-0-19-1

SURREY

Batting	M	Inns	NO	HS	Runs	Av	100	50	ct/st
GP Thorpe	8	8	-	84	364	45.50	-	3	2
GP Butcher	6	6	2	34*	119	29.75	-	-	1
AJ Stewart	8	8	-	76	231	28.87	-	1	4/1
MA Butcher	12	12	-	44	323	26.91	-	-	4
AD Brown	15	15	-	105	403	26.86	1	-	7
IJ Ward	15	15	2	80	332	25.53	-	1	3
IE Bishop	8	6	5	15*	23	23.00	-	-	-
BC Hollioake	11	n	-	48	244	22.18	-	-	3
DJ Bicknell	6	6	-	62	123	20.50	-	1	-
JD Ratcliffe	9	9	1	59	159	19.87	-	1	-
AJ Hollioake	12	12	-	45	226	18.83	-	-	1
AJ Tudor	6	6	1	28	55	11.00	-	-	-
JN Batty	11	9	1	19	72	9.00	-	-	13/1
GJ Batty	5	5	1	23	34	8.50	-	-	1
MP Bicknell	9	9	4	16	33	6.60	-	-	-
IDK Salisbury	10	9	-	19	57	6.33	-	-	2

Also batted: JE Benjamin (5 matches) 16*, 3, 0* (1 ct); DM Cousins (3 matches) 1, 1* (1 ct);
CG Greenidge, Jr (2 matches) 2* (1 ct); Saqlain Mushtaq (3 matches) 3, 5*, 1 (1 ct);
N Shahid (1 match) 24 (1 ct)

NATIONAL LEAGUE AVERAGES

SURREY (cont)

Bowling	Overs	Mds	Runs	Wkts	Av	Best	4/inns
MP Bicknell	68	7	304	15	20.26	7-30	1
JE Benjamin	32	3	154	7	22.00	2-33	-
IE Bishop	65.1	7	243	11	22.09	4-34	1
BC Hollioake	66	4	293	12	24.41	3-31	-
AJ Hollioake	53.2	5	300	11	27.27	3-47	-
AJ Tudor	43.2		222	8	27.75	2-26	-

Also bowled: GJ Batty 32-1-162-2; AD Brown 25.5-0-141-3; GP Butcher 13.3-0-103-1;
MA Butcher 30-3-142-2; DM Cousins 27-0-125-4; CG Greenidge, Jr 11-0-71-0;
JD Ratcliffe 39-0-169-3; IDK Salisbury 58.2-0-297-3; Saqlain Mushtaq 23-3-80-4;
N Shahid 1-0-9-0; IJ Ward 3-0-18-0

SUSSEX

Batting	M	Inns	NO	HS	Runs	Av	100	50	ct/st
CJ Adams	15	15	5	163	798	79.80	2	5	9
MJ Di Venuto	14	14	4	94*	596	59.60	-	6	6
PA Cottey	15	12	6	62*	289	48.16	-	2	3
RR Montgomerie	13	13	2	80*	393	35.72	-	3	3
JR Carpenter	14	9	3	64*	183	30.50	-	2	4
GR Haywood	7	5	0	24	50	10.00	-	-	4
UBA Rashid	15	6	1	26	39	7.80			10

Also batted: JJ Bates (1 match) 2, 1 ct; K Greenfield (1 match) 16*; S Humphries (13 matches) 8,
5, 3, 2, 8 ct/6 st; R J Kirtley (13 matches) 4*, 4*, 0*, 17*, 7 ct; JD Lewry (1 match) 0; RSC Martin-
Jenkins (12 matches) 2, 1, 6, 26, 5 ct; RK Rao (2 matches) 9; MA Robinson (14 matches) 1, 0;
BV Taylor (9 matches) 21*, 1*, 1 ct; NJ Wilton (2 matches) 7, 2ct; B Zuiderent (2 matches) 0, 24, 2 ct;
AD Edwards (2 ct) played in 2 matches but did not bat

Bowling	Overs	Mds	Runs	Wkts	Av	Best	4/inns
RJ Kirtley	91.2	7	379	26	14.57	4-31	2
CJ Adams	44.2	3	202	12	16.83	3-22	-
UBA Rashid	115.4	9	457	27	16.92	5-24	2
MA Robinson	121	5	468	17	27.52	4-34	1
BV Taylor	61	4	312	11	28.36	3-22	-
RSC Martin-Jenkins	95	16	297	10	29.70	3-27	—

Also bowled: JJ Bates 8-0-24-0; AD Edwards 13-0-69-0; GR Haywood 42.1-0-208-4;
JD Lewry 7-0-55-1

WARWICKSHIRE

Batting	M	Inns	NO	HS	Runs	Av	100	50	ct/st
MJ Powell	7	5	2	51	157	52.33	-	1	1
NV Knight	14	14	2	106*	412	34.33	2	2	14
DL Hemp	13	13	2	83*	336	30.54	-	2	6
DP Ostler	9	9	1	53	232	29.00	-	2	2
A Singh	9	9	1	76	215	26.87	-	2	3
G Welch	12	11	3	71	208	26.00	-	1	3
TL Penney	11	11	3	55	189	23.62	-	1	3
T Frost	11	5	1	22*	67	16.75	-	-	6/2
AF Giles	15	10	1	35	122	13.55	-	-	4
NMK Smith	14	14	0	61	174	12.42	-	1	6
DR Brown	16	13	2	26	106	9.63	-	-	4
TA Munton	9	5	3	6*	13	6.50	-	-	4

Also batted: MD Edmond (2 matches) 15*, 0*; ESH Giddins (11 matches) 1, 4, 1*, 1 ct;
KJ Piper (5 matches) 0, 38*, 6 ct; A Richardson (2 matches) 11*; M Sheikh (3 matches) 0, 2 ct;
GC Small (6 matches) 5, 4, 1 ct; MA Wagh (3 matches) 6, 5, 27; AA Donald (2 ct) played in 4
matches but did not bat

Bowling	Overs	Mds	Runs	Wkts	Av	Best	4/inns
AA Donald	25	1	132	6	22.00	3-45	-
DR Brown	82	3	400	17	23.52	3-34	-
AF Giles	113	6	488	19	25.68	4-29	1
NMK Smith	76	8	340	12	28.33	3-27	-
TA Munton	62	6	286	10	28.60	2-14	-
GC Small	44	3	211	7	30.14	2-16	-
ESH Giddins	87	7	366	11	33.27	2-36	-
G Welch	75.4	8	379	11	34.45	2-15	—

Also bowled: MD Edmond 2-0-17-1; MJ Powell 3-0-23-0; A Richardson 12.1-0-44-3; M Sheikh
22-1-90-4

NATIONAL LEAGUE AVERAGES

WORCESTERSHIRE

Batting	M	Inns	NO	HS	Runs	Av	100	50	ct/st
GA Hick	11	10	2	110*	480	60.00	1	3	8
SR Lampitt	11	6	5	30*	58	58.00	-	-	3
PR Pollard	7	7	1	70	266	44.33	-	3	2
TM Moody	6	5	0	56	188	37.60	-	2	-
EJ Wilson	7	7	0	62	227	32.42	-	2	5
VS Solanki	15	14	2	63	368	30.66	-	2	8
DA Leatherdale	14	12	3	70*	260	28.88	-	2	7
WPC Weston	8	7	0	125	184	26.28	1	-	1
SJ Rhodes	15	10	5	25*	101	20.20	-	-	16/8
RK Illingworth	15	5	3	15*	38	19.00	-	-	5
GR Haynes	14	11	1	66	158	15.80	-	1	6

Also batted: Abdul Hafeez (1 match) 8*, 1 ct; CWJ Athey (1 match) 22*;
DN Catterall (4 matches) 0; RC Driver (1 match) 3; MJ Rawnsley (10 matches) 2, 4, 3 ct;
A Sheriyar (15 matches) 3, 0, 2 ct; KR Spiring (4 matches) 56, 10, 21, 34, 1 ct;
PJ Newport played in 6 matches but did not bat (1 ct)

	Overs	Mds	Runs	Wkts	Av	Best	4/inns
SR Lampitt	72.4	6	286	17	16.82	4-18	1
DA Leatherdale	36.3	1	176	10	17.60	4-23	1
RK Illingworth	102.1	6	402	22	18.27	4-49	1
MJ Rawnsley	49.3	3	225	12	18.75	5-26	2
GR Haynes	92	9	383	20	19.15	4-28	2
A Sheriyar	104.5	6	540	26	20.76	4-42	1
PJ Newport	42	5	179	5	35.80	2-36	-

Also bowled: Abdul Haffez 8-0-29-0; DN Catterall 30-2-125-2; GA Hick 11.1-55-1;
TM Moody 39-6-124-4

YORKSHIRE

Batting	M	Inns	NO	HS	Runs	Av	100	50	ct/st
A McGrath	15	14	2	75	450	37.50	-	3	5
D Byas	16	16	2	87	^7	^.-^	-	2	9
MP Vaughan	16	16	1	72	425	28.33	-	2	10
RJ Blakey	16	15	6	30	226	25.11	-	-	26/6
MJ Wood	7	4	1	48*	73	24.33	-	-	2
C White	15	15	-	67	318	21.20	-	1	1
GM Fellows	14	10	2	36	147	18.37	-	-	2
RJ Harden	11	9	1	42	131	16.37	-	-	1
GS Blewett	11	11	-	48	178	16.18	-	-	6
GM Hamilton	9	9	1	27*	116	14.50	-	-	1
CEW Silverwood	12	9	6	11*	34	11.33	-	-	1
RJ Sidebottom	16	7	2	24*	41	8.20	-	-	1

Also batted: TD Fisher (7 matches) 9, 5, 11* (2 ct); D Gough (3 matches) 15, 0;
MJ Hoggard (3 matches) 2*, 1*; PM Hutchison (3 matches) 2*; B Parker (2 matches)
3, 5 (1 ct)

Bowling	Overs	Mds	Runs	Wkts	Av	Best	4/inns
CEW Silverwood	101.5	13	361	24	15.04	4-44	1
C White	114.1	18	437	26	16.80	4-25	2
PM Hutchison	25.3	6	96	5	19.20	3-30	-
MP Vaughan	97.3	3	420	17	24.70	4-31	1
RJ Sidebottom	134	14	541	20	27.05	3-14	-
GM Hamilton	56.3	5	306	6	51.00	4-33	1

Also bowled: GS Blewett 25.1-0-116-4; GM Fellows 6-0-43-0; ID Fisher 36-1-173-3;
D Gough 23.1-2-80-2; MJ Hoggard 23-2-117-4; A McGrath 27-3-105-3

BENSON AND HEDGES SUPER CUP

QUARTER FINALS

25 June 1999 at Old Trafford
Lancashire 181 for 8 (50 overs)
Sussex 182 for 6 (45 overs) CJ Adams 73*
Sussex won by four wickets
Gold Award Winner: CJ Adams

25 June 1999 at Headingley
Hampshire 187 for 9 (50 overs)
Yorkshire 188 for 1 (38.4 overs) D Byas 104*,
GS Blewett 71
Yorkshire won by nine wickets
Gold Award Winner: D Byas

Yorkshire gave Hampshire a nine-wicket hiding at
Headingley, while Sussex also eased themselves into
the last four with a fine win against Lancashire at
Old Trafford.

A five-man pace attack, augmented by Michael
Vaughan's fast-improving off-breaks, proved too
potent for Hampshire. Jason Laney made 41 and
John Stephenson an undefeated 39, but a 50-over
total of 187 for 9 was easily overhauled with Greg
Blewett scoring 71 but being totally outshone by his
captain, David Byas. With some magnificent driving,
off both front and back foot, he raced to 104 not
out at a run a ball.

Chris Adams guided his Sussex side home with 73
not out from 105 balls, a disciplined innings on a
slow, low pitch ill-suited to one-day cricket.
Lancashire's innings never got going, although
Graham Lloyd reached 45 not out to push the total
up to 181 for 8. Michael Di Venuto hit a quick 41
before being stumped off Muttiah Muralitharan.
The Sri Lankan took 1 for 14 from ten beautifully
varied overs, but Adams was helped by Robin
Martin-Jenkins in a sixth-wicket stand of 35 that all
but clinched the result.

26 June 1999 at Leicester
Warwickshire 229 for 5 (50 overs) NV Knight 96,
DL Hemp 56
Leicestershire 195 (47.1 overs) DL Maddy 84,
ESH Giddins 5 for 21
Warwickshire won by 34 runs
Gold Award Winner: ESH Giddins

Ed Giddins took 5 for 21 to inspire Warwickshire to
a 34-run victory over Leicestershire, with only
Darren Maddy standing firm with 84 as the home
side tried to reach a target of 230. Nick Knight (96)
and David Hemp (56) added 138 in Warwickshire's
total of 229 for 5.

**Matt Windows just fails to hang onto a great catch offered
by Craig White, Benson and Hedges Super Cup Final.**
David Munden/Sportsline Photographic

27 June 1999 at Bristol
Surrey 220 for 9 (50 overs) GP Thorpe 84,
IJ Harvey 4 for 42
Gloucestershire 222 for 3 (48 overs) KJ Barnett 65,
RC Russell 50*
Gloucestershire won by seven wickets
Gold Award Winner: RC Russell

Surrey's seven-wicket demise at Bristol was the
shock of the round, but a sign of Gloucestershire's
growing prowess as a one-day side. Graham
Thorpe made 84, but Ian Harvey kept Surrey
in check with his skilful seamers, picking up 4
for 42, and Gloucestershire then cruised past a
221 target with two overs to spare. Kim Barnett
made 64 and Jack Russell was there at the end
with 50 not out.

SEMI-FINALS

11 July 1999 at Bristol
Gloucestershire 241 (49.5 overs) JN Snape 50
Sussex 217 (48.1 overs) CJ Adams 88, MJ Di Venuto 62
Gloucestershire won by 24 runs
Gold Award Winner: JN Snape

11 July 1999 at Edgbaston
Yorkshire 219 for 8 (50 overs) C White 55
Warwickshire 163 (40.5 overs)
Yorkshire won by 56 runs
Gold Award Winner: C White

**Martyn Ball celebrates catching Greg Blewett, Benson and
Hedges Super Cup Final.**
David Munden/Sportsline Photographic

Tim Hancock is out, bowled by Craig White for 35, Benson and Hedges Super Cup Final.
David Munden/Sportsline Photographic

Yorkshire were the Saturday winners and Gloucestershire the Sunday best as Warwickshire and Sussex, respectively, experienced the massive disappointment of being beaten in a semi-final and losing out on a Lord's day-out.

Craig White's 55 was the basis of Yorkshire's 50-over total of 219 for 8 at Edgbaston, but Richard Harden and Gary Fellows also contributed valuable 30s. Ashley Giles took 3 for 35 but Warwickshire's reply was a tame effort after Nick Knight (45) and Dougie Brown (49) had added 80 for the second wicket.

At Bristol 24 hours later, former England wicketkeeper Jack Russell was clearly overcome by cup fever as he jumped around like a teenager following the 24-run victory against Sussex. Russell said afterwards that his joy reflected the emotion of reaching a Lord's cup final for the first time in his 18-year county career. Gloucestershire batted consistently down their order, but were indebted to 50 from 41 balls by Jeremy Snape at the end as they reached 241. In reply Chris Adams and Michael Di Venuto seemed to be making mincemeat of the victory target, in a second-wicket stand of 93, until Di Venuto fell for 62. James Carpenter, though, increased Sussex hopes with a hard-hit 45 while Adams continued to cruise along. Jon Lewis, recalled into the attack, then induced an edge from left-hander Carpenter and suddenly the Sussex batting began to fall away. Adams was soon left needing to make the bulk of the 25 needed from two overs and, although he had just hit Cawdron for his second six, he holed out for 88 attempting another and Gloucestershire were celebrating.

FINAL
1 August 1999 at Lord's

A near-full Lord's mocked those who claimed this was an unwanted extra competition in World Cup year – and the celebrations of the Gloucestershire players certainly revealed how much the trophy meant to them. This was a day, though, when an emerging Gloucestershire side came of age under the quiet but inspired leadership of Mark Alleyne, and when veterans like Jack Russell and Kim Barnett jumped for joy alongside developing youngsters like Tim Hancock, Rob Cunliffe and Jon Lewis. Alleyne truly led the way on the field with a magnificent 112 from only 91 balls. It was one of the finest innings seen at a showpiece domestic final, and included two sixes and 11 fours. Cunliffe played the major support act with a cultured 61 from 81 deliveries and Yorkshire's bowling fell apart under the strain. The Gloucestershire total of 291 for 9 was intimidating, and Yorkshire got nowhere near it. Lewis picked up 3 for 32 and off-spinner Martyn Ball 3 for 39 from his ten overs as Yorkshire fell away to 167 all out.

Man of the Match and Gloucestershire captain Mark Alleyne celebrates reaching 100 in the Benson and Hedges Super Cup Final.
David Munden/Sportsline Photographic

FINAL – GLOUCESTERSHIRE v. YORKSHIRE
1 August 1999 at Lord's, London

GLOUCESTERSHIRE

Batting				Bowling	O	M	R	W
KJ Barnett	b Hutchison		28	Silverwood	10	0	47	1
THC Hancock	b White		35	Hamilton	6	0	55	0
RJ Cunliffe	b White		61	Hutchison	5	0	30	3
MW Alleyne (capt)	b White		112	Sidebottom	10	0	54	0
IJ Harvey	c Vaughan, b Hutchison		13	White	10	0	51	4
JN Snape	c White, b Hutchison		3	Vaughan	6	0	24	0
*RC Russell	$ run out		1	Blewett	3	0	23	0
	(Harden/Silverwood)							
MGN Windows	not out		18	**Fall of Wickets**				
MCJ Ball	b Silverwood		2	1–66, 2–75, 3–232, 4–255, 5–267,				
J Lewis	b White		2	6–267, 7–270, 8–283, 9–286				
AM Smith	not out		1					
	lb 7, w 8		15					
	50 overs (for 9 wickets)		**291**					

YORKSHIRE

Batting				Bowling	O	M	R	W
C White	b Lewis		38	Smith	8	0	28	1
GS Blewett	$$ c Ball, b Harvey		9	Harvey	5	0	25	1
D Byas (capt)	c and b Smith		13	Lewis	5	0	32	3
MP Vaughan	b Bell		24	Alleyne	6	1	17	0
A McGrath	run out (Windows)		20	Ball	10	1	39	3
RJ Harden	c Cunliffe, b Ball		8	Snape	6	0	20	1
GM Hamilton	$ st Russell, b Lewis		25					
*RJ Blakey	b Ball		14					
CEW Silverwood	b Lewis		4	**Fall of Wickets**				
RJ Sidebottom	c and b Snape		0	1–14, 2–45, 3–78, 4–99, 5–115,				
PM Hutchison	not out		2	6–122, 7–156, 8–161, 9–165				
	b 1, lb 5, w 4		10					
	40 overs		**167**					

$ TV decision
Umpires: R Julian & P Willey
Gold Award Winner: MW Alleyne

Gloucestershire won by 124 runs

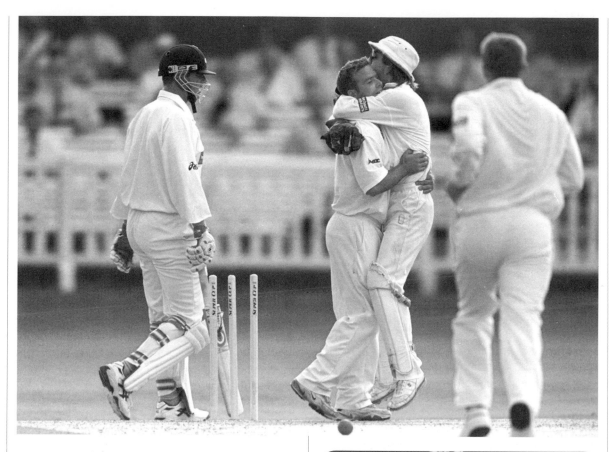

Above: Jack Russell celebrates with Matt Windows after Windows' direct hit ran out Anthony McGrath, Benson and Hedges Super Cup Final.
David Munden/Sportsline Photographic

Right: Jack Russell celebrates winning the Benson and Hedges Super Cup for Gloucestershire.
David Munden/Sportsline Photographic

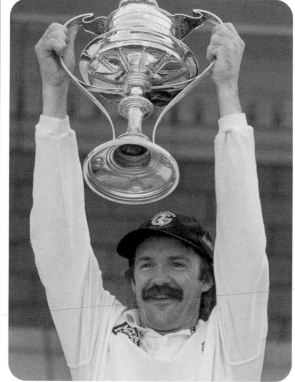

NATWEST TROPHY

FIRST ROUND
4 May 1999

at Luton
Huntingdonshire 222 for 8 (50 overs) S Pope 69,
AR Roberts 5 for 28
Bedfordshire 223 for 3 (45 overs) W Larkins 59
Bedfordshire won by seven wickets
Man of the Match: AR Roberts (Bedfordshire)

at Reading
Warwickshire Cricket Board XI 149 (48 overs)
Berkshire 150 for 4 (45.3 overs) GE Loveday 56
Berkshire won by six wickets
Man of the Match: W Stelling (Berkshire)

at Netherfield, Kendal
Cumberland 314 for 9 (50 overs) AA Metcalfe 138
Cornwall 177 (44.2 overs)
Cumberland won by 137 runs
Man of the Match: AA Metcalfe (Cumberland)

at Hartlepool
Oxfordshire 224 for 7 (50 overs) SV Laudat 58
Durham Cricket Board XI 226 for 8 (48.2 overs)
AJ Hall 78
Durham Cricket Board XI won by two wickets
Man of the Match: AJ Hall (Durham Cricket Board XI)

at Cheltenham
Yorkshire Cricket Board XI 145 (40 overs) J White
4 for 14
Gloucestershire Cricket Board XI 138 (49 overs)
A Bressington 54, S Foster 5 for 26
Yorkshire Cricket Board XI won by 7 runs
Man of the Match: S Foster (Yorkshire Cricket Board XI)

at Radlett
Hertfordshire 323 for 7 (50 overs) AD Griffin 121,
K Jahangir 92
Leicestershire Cricket Board XI 209 for 9 (50 overs)
AS Wright 63
Hertfordshire won by 114 runs
Man of the Match: AD Griffin (Hertfordshire)

at Deventer
Cambridgeshire 215 for 9 (50 overs)
Holland 219 for 2 (43.2 overs) KC Jackson 88*,
RRAF Bradley 78
Holland won by eight wickets
Man of the Match: RRAF Bradley (Holland)

at Maidstone
Kent Cricket Board XI 227 for 8 (50 overs)
MR Featherstone 104*
Denmark 169 for 9 (50 overs)
Kent Cricket Board XI won by 58 runs
Man of the Match: MR Featherstone (Kent Cricket Board XI)

at Sleaford
Lincolnshire 232 for 9 (50 overs) SG Plumb 52
Wales 236 for 6 (47.3 overs) RM Sylvester 69,
JH Langworth 67*
Wales won by four wickets
Man of the Match: JH Langworth (Wales)

at Northampton
Northamptonshire Cricket Board XI 282 for 5
(50 overs) JW Cook 130
Wiltshire 283 for 8 (48.4 overs) RJ Silence 82
Wiltshire won by two wickets
Man of the Match: JW Cook (Northamptonshire Cricket Board XI)

at Jesmond
Northumberland 253 for 8 (50 overs) W Falla 80,
OS Youll 65, RD McGerrigle 5 for 66
Ireland 255 for 5 (47.5 overs) N Carson 58
Ireland won by five wickets
Man of the Match: RD McGerrigle (Ireland)

at Linlithgow
Nottinghamshire Cricket Board XI 212 (50 overs)
S Brogen 61, A Jackman 52, CM Wright 4 for 30
Scotland 215 for 1 (41.4 overs) ST Crawley 109*,
BG Lockie 55
Scotland won by nine wickets
Man of the Match: ST Crawley (Scotland)

at Bury St Edmunds
Suffolk 284 for 8 (50 overs) KM Wijesuriya 109*,
D Callaghan 59
Hampshire Cricket Board XI 290 for 3 (47.1 overs)
M Compton 105*, C Nevin 88
Hampshire Cricket Board XI won by seven wickets
Man of the Match: M Compton (Hampshire Cricket Board XI)

at Cheam
Surrey Cricket Board XI 264 for 8 (50 overs) J Fry 90
Norfolk 241 for 6 (50 overs) C Amos 76,
DR Thomas 70*
Surrey Cricket Board XI won by 23 runs
Man of the Match: J Fry (Surrey Cricket Board XI)

SECOND ROUND
19 May 1999

at Dunstall
Wales 250 for 9 (50 overs) P Camm
4 for 52
Derbyshire Cricket Board XI 198
(49.5 overs)
Wales won by 52 runs
Man of the Match: AJL Barr (Wales)

at Torquay
Devon 267 for 6 (50 overs) ND Hancock 113*,
AM Small 52
Berkshire 199 (44.3 overs) W Stelling 76*
Devon won by 68 runs
Man of the Match: ND Hancock (Devon)

at Gateshead Fell
Staffordshire 256 for 8 (50 overs)
RP Harvey 66
Durham Cricket Board XI 257 for 6 (48.4 overs)
SD Birbeck 88, AJ Hall 78
Durham Cricket Board XI won by four wickets
Man of the Match: SD Birbeck (Durham
Cricket Board XI)

at Brockhampton
Herefordshire 211 for 9 (50 overs)
CW Boroughs 50
Wiltshire 131 (37.5 overs)
Herefordshire won by 80 runs
Man of the Match: K Pearson
(Herefordshire)

at Hertford
Sussex Cricket Board XI 209 for 9 (50 overs)
M Newell 92
Hertfordshire 213 for 3 (42.2 overs) DM Ward 83*,
AD Griffin 60*
Hertfordshire won by seven wickets
Man of the Match: DM Ward (Hertfordshire)

at Belfast
Essex Cricket Board XI 196 for 9 (50 overs)
A Richards 60
Ireland 200 for 8 (47.3 overs) G Dros 51
Ireland won by two wickets
Man of the Match: G Cooke (Ireland)

at Maidstone
Kent Cricket Board XI 250 for 3 (50 overs)
MW Alexander 107*, MR Featherstone 64

Worcestershire Cricket Board XI 245 for 7
(50 overs)
Kent Cricket Board XI won by 5 runs
Man of the Match: MW Alexander (Kent Cricket
Board XI)

at Liverpool
Lancashire Cricket Board XI 122
(49.2 overs)
Holland 126 for 0 (31.2 overs)
RRAF Bradley 63*
Holland won by ten wickets
Man of the Match: F Kloppenburg (Holland)

at Southgate
Cumberland 207 for 9 (50 overs)
Middlesex Cricket Board XI 114 (42.2 overs)
Cumberland won by 93 runs
Man of the Match: ST Knox (Cumberland)

at Glasgow
Scotland 245 for 7 (50 overs) CJ Richards 70
Dorset 169 (47 overs)
Scotland won by 76 runs
Man of the Match: CM Wright (Scotland)

at Wellington
Hampshire Cricket Board XI 217 (49.4 overs)
M Compton 59
Shropshire 216 (50 overs) JT Ralph 89
Hampshire Cricket Board XI won by 1 run
Man of the Match: JT Ralph (Shropshire)

at Taunton
Somerset Cricket Board XI 200 (50 overs)
KA Parsons 65
Bedfordshire 201 for 6 (43.1 overs)
RN Dalton 56
Bedfordshire won by four wickets
Man of the Match: RN Dalton (Bedfordshire)

at Wimbledon
Cheshire 171 for 9 (50 overs)
Surrey Cricket Board XI 162 (45 overs)
Cheshire won by 9 runs
Man of the Match: ND Cross (Cheshire)

at Sheffield
Yorkshire Cricket Board XI 91 (40.5 overs)
Buckinghamshire 92 for 3 (20.4 overs)
Buckinghamshire won by seven wickets
Man of the Match: JNB Bovill
(Buckinghamshire)

THIRD ROUND
23 June 1999

at Luton
Bedfordshire 187 for 9 (50 overs)
Derbyshire 190 for 4 (40 overs) AS Rollins 80,
MA Cassar 57
Derbyshire won by six wickets
Man of the Match: AJ Harris (Derbyshire)

at Marlow
Warwickshire 249 for 7 (50 overs) DL Hemp 110*
Buckinghamshire 136 (40 overs)
Warwickshire won by 113 runs
Man of the Match: DL Hemp (Warwickshire)

at Netherfield, Kendal
Cumberland 214 for 8 (50 overs) T Hunte 82
Sussex 216 for 4 (31.4 overs) MJ Di Venuto 72,
RR Montgomerie 56*, CJ Adams 51
Sussex won by six wickets
Man of the Match: T Hunte (Cumberland)

at Bowden
Kent 312 for 7 (50 overs) NJ Llong 123,
MV Fleming 117*
Cheshire 204 for 9 (50 overs) ND Cross 57,
RJ Hignett 50
Kent won by 108 runs
Man of the Match: MV Fleming (Kent)

at Exmouth
Worcestershire 256 for 8 (50 overs) KR Spiring 57
Devon 211 for 8 (50 overs) AJ Pugh 54
Worcestershire won by 45 runs
Man of the Match: AJ Pugh (Devon)

at Chester-le-Street
Gloucestershire 271 for 8 (50 overs)
THC Hancock 59
Durham Cricket Board XI 109 (34 overs) IJ Harvey
4 for 29, MJ Cawdron 4 for 34
Gloucestershire won by 162 runs
Man of the Match: IJ Harvey (Gloucestershire)

at Southampton
Glamorgan 245 for 8 (50 overs) SP James 87,
AW Evans 52
Hampshire Cricket Board XI 177 (47 overs)
C Nevin 56
Glamorgan won by 68 runs
Man of the Match: C van der Gucht
(Hampshire Cricket Board XI)

at Kingston
Yorkshire 275 for 8 (50 overs) GS Blewett 77,
A McGrath 70, C White 50
Herefordshire 124 for 5 (50 overs)
Yorkshire won by 151 runs
Man of the Match: A McGrath (Yorkshire)

at Radlett
Lancashire 381 for 3 (50 overs) M Watkinson 130,
JP Crawley 85, A Flintoff 57*, MJ Chilton 50
Hertfordshire 213 for 6 (50 overs)
Lancashire won by 168 runs
Man of the Match: M Watkinson (Lancashire)

at Amstelveen
Durham 194 (50 overs) MP Speight 60, BC Boon 51,
F Kloppenburg 4 for 25
Holland 195 for 5 (47 overs) F Kloppenburg 61,
L van Troost 59*
Holland won by five wickets
Man of the Match: F Kloppenburg (Holland)

at Dublin
Leicestershire 287 (49.5 overs) DL Maddy 89,
PA Nixon 51, RL Eagleson 4 for 59
Ireland 151 (48.4 overs)
Leicestershire won by 136 runs
Man of the Match: DL Maddy
(Leicestershire)

at Canterbury
Hampshire 262 for 7 (50 overs) RA Smith 68,
JS Laney 53
Kent Cricket Board XI 132 (41 overs)
Hampshire won by 130 runs
Man of the Match: JM Golding (Kent Cricket
Board XI)

at Northampton
Essex 281 for 6 (50 overs) RC Irani 88,
AP Grayson 74
Northamptonshire 282 for 5 (48 overs)
ML Hayden 107, DJG Sales 53
Northamptonshire won by five wickets
Man of the Match: ML Hayden
(Northamptonshire)

at Trent Bridge
Nottinghamshire 229 for 8 (50 overs)
P Johnson 50
Middlesex 150 (43 overs)
Nottinghamshire won by 79 runs
Man of the Match: PJ Franks (Nottinghamshire)

at Edinburgh
Scotland 147 (48 overs) Saqlain Mushtaq
4 for 17
Surrey 148 for 3 (37.3 overs) AJ Stewart 64
Surrey won by seven wickets
Man of the Match: Saqlain Mushtaq (Surrey)

at Swansea
Somerset 267 for 5 (50 overs) M Burns 52*,
RJ Turner 52
Wales 129 (39.2 overs)
Somerset won by 138 runs
Man of the Match: AR Caddick (Somerset)

FOURTH ROUND
7 July 1999

at Cardiff
Glamorgan 254 for 5 (50 overs) SP James 118*
Warwickshire 238 (49.4 overs) DL Hemp 55
Glamorgan won by 16 runs
Man of the Match: SP James

at Bristol
Derbyshire 112 (41.4 overs) MW Alleyne 4 for 14
Gloucestershire 116 for 2 (32.1 overs)
THC Hancock 54
Gloucestershire won by eight wickets
Man of the Match: MW Alleyne (Gloucestershire)

at Southampton
Hampshire 239 for 8 (50 overs) JS Laney 95,
DA Kenway 53, MP Smethurst 4 for 46
Lancashire 243 for 9 (49.3 overs)
Lancashire won by one wicket
Man of the Match: MP Smethurst (Lancashire)

at Amstelveen
Kent 229 (48.5 overs) RWT Key 67, A Symonds 52,
RP Lefebvre 5 for 26
Holland 167 (47.5 overs)
Kent won by 62 runs
Man of the Match: RP Lefebvre (Holland)

at Northampton
Northamptonshire 281 for 6 (50 overs) AJ Swann 74,
RJ Warren 53
Nottinghamshire 177 (40.5 overs) P Johnson 51,
KM Curran 4 for 29
Northamptonshire won by 104 runs
*Man of the Match: KM Curran
(Northamptonshire)*

at Hove
Sussex 192 for 8 (50 overs) RK Rao 67, JR Carpenter
55, PS Jones 4 for 25
Somerset 195 for 5 (46.2 overs) PCL Holloway 79
Somerset won by five wickets
Man of the Match: PCL Holloway (Somerset)

at Worcester
Worcestershire 204 for 9 (50 overs) GA Hick 66
Surrey 206 for 5 (46.5 overs) GP Thorpe 91*,
MA Butcher 54
Surrey won by five wickets
Man of the Match: GP Thorpe (Surrey)

at Headingley
Leicestershire 229 for 9 (50 overs) VJ Wells 84
Yorkshire 233 for 6 (48.3 overs) MP Vaughan 85,
A McGrath 84, AD Mullally 4 for 23
Yorkshire won by four wickets
Man of the Match: MP Vaughan (Yorkshire)

The most crushing victory came at Bristol where Gloucestershire, who can do no wrong in one-day cricket, overwhelmed Derbyshire by eight wickets after dismissing them for 112 – Mark Alleyne taking 4 for 14.

Kent managed to end Holland's fine run in the competition, despite Roland Lefebvre's 5 for 26 at Amstelveen, while an outstanding unbeaten 118 by Steve James underpinned Glamorgan's 16-run victory against Warwickshire at Cardiff.

Lancashire won a thrilling, one-wicket victory against Hampshire at Southampton – with just three balls to spare – after the home side had failed to build substantially on Jason Laney's 95.

Northamptonshire overwhelmed opponents Nottinghamshire, running up 281 for 6 and then seeing veteran Kevin Curran undermine the Notts reply with 4 for 29.

Steffan Jones, one of the more unsung members of a combative Somerset outfit, took 4 for 25 as Sussex were held to 192 for 8 at Hove. Piran Holloway then scored 79 as Somerset completed a thoroughly professional job with a five-wicket winning margin.

Graham Thorpe's unbeaten 91 proved too much for Worcestershire at New Road, despite Graeme Hick hitting 66 earlier in the day, and there was a similar story at Headingley where Leicestershire posted a defendable total but then saw Yorkshire power past it by four wickets with something to spare. Michael Vaughan (85) and Anthony McGrath (84) were the Yorkshire batsmen in form.

QUARTER-FINALS
28 July 1999

at Cardiff
Gloucestershire 274 for 6 (50 overs) THC Hancock 90,
KJ Barnett 68, RDB Croft 4 for 47
Glamorgan 138 (41.1 overs)
Gloucestershire won by 136 runs
Man of the Match: THC Hancock (Gloucestershire)

at Old Trafford
Yorkshire 263 for 7 (50 overs) D Byas 72,
A McGrath 60
Lancashire 208 (45.4 overs) MA Atherton 61,
NH Fairbrother 54, GS Blewett 4 for 18
Yorkshire won by 55 runs
Man of the Match: C White (Yorkshire)

at Northampton
Northamptonshire 152 (35.5 overs)
Saqlain Mushtaq 4 for 28
Surrey 156 for 3 (35.3 overs)
Surrey won by seven wickets
Man of the Match: Saqlain Mushtaq (Surrey)

at Taunton
Kent 264 for 5 (50 overs) MJ Walker 73, RWT Key 66
Somerset 266 for 4 (46.2 overs) PCL Holloway 75*,
J Cox 73
Somerset won by six wickets
Man of the Match: J Cox (Somerset)

Yorkshire came out on top in the Roses battle, and
on enemy ground at Old Trafford, too, in front of a
crowd upwards of 15,000. Lancashire, in fact, had
not been beaten on home soil in this competition for
12 years and 14 matches. But they were thoroughly
outplayed in every department by a Yorkshire side
who thus remained on course for all three domestic
limited-overs titles. Man of the Match was Craig
White, who launched the Yorkshire innings with a
bold 43 from 47 balls and later took 2 for 24 from
eight aggressive overs. Such was White's early
mastery that Greg Blewett, his opening partner,
contributed only two runs to an opening stand of
47. David Byas then set about anchoring the innings,
scoring 72 from 100 balls and putting on 111 in 20
overs for the fourth wicket with Anthony McGrath
(60). Gavin Hamilton provided a flourish at the end
and a total of 263 for 7 was a formidable one.
Lancashire, though, were given a good start and – at
164 for 2 with Mike Atherton and Neil Fairbrother
having already put on 90 – they were poised to

challenge Yorkshire's score. Fairbrother, however,
was undone by a ball from Chris Silverwood that
nipped back off the seam – and no one else could
match the fluency which brought the veteran left-
hander 54 from 55 balls. Byas now threw the ball to
Blewett, and the Australian's medium-pacers proved
inspirational. Blewett's first ball hit Atherton's off-
stump to dismiss the former England captain for 61
and, in the same over, Andrew Flintoff was leg
before for nought as he attempted to pull. Blewett
also ran out Warren Hegg with a direct hit and, in
all, took 4 for 18 from 5.4 overs as he hurried
Yorkshire to a 55-run triumph. The only consolation
for Lancashire was the announcement during the
day that Sri Lankan spinner Muttiah Muralitharan –
surprisingly wicketless and ineffective here – had
signed a new two-year contract as the county's
overseas player.

Gloucestershire, five days before taking on
Yorkshire in the Super Cup final, earned themselves
another meeting with the White Rose county by
beating Glamorgan in emphatic style at Cardiff.
This quarter-final was a one-sided affair from the
moment Tim Hancock and Kim Barnett added
142 for Gloucestershire's first wicket. Hancock
hit an excellent 90 from 108 balls, full of eye-
catching drives and pulls, while the canny Barnett
worked the ball around busily for 68 from
100 balls. A green tinge to the pitch, prompting
Matthew Maynard to bowl first, proved irrelevant –
but, in addition to minimal movement, the
Glamorgan bowlers did not perform well. Matt
Windows belted 43 not out from 31 balls at the
end, and Jeremy Snape helped him to thrash 46
from the last 19 deliveries of the innings. Darren
Thomas conceded 22 from the final over, and a
total of 274 for 6 was well beyond Glamorgan's
capabilities. Mike Smith, bowling his ten-over
stint straight through, had Jacques Kallis caught
at the wicket attempting an expansive drive and
then bowled Maynard to reduce the home side
to 36 for 4. Robert Croft had earlier fallen to Ian
Harvey and Man of the Match Hancock then ran
out Steve James with a direct hit from mid-wicket.
Smith's strikes, in his eighth and ninth overs, meant
no way back.

Somerset's reward for beating Kent, at Taunton,
was another home tie against Surrey, who obliterated
Northamptonshire in the fourth quarter-final. And,
after Kent were seen off by six wickets, there was
immediate talk in the West Country of a first
Somerset-Gloucestershire Lord's final when the
semi-final draw was made at the close of play.

The absences of Dean Headley and Matthew Fleming, to injury and illness respectively, were bitter blows to Kent – but they still underachieved in scoring 264 for 5 on a superb batting pitch. Andrew Caddick removed Ed Smith in his opening spell but perhaps struck the decisive blow by later removing Andrew Symonds for 40 just when the Australian looked capable of really cutting loose. Robert Key made a solid 66, but Kent were only lifted by a rollicking stand of 118 in 15 overs between Matthew Walker (73) and Mark Ealham (46 not out). Headley's cutting edge was badly missed and Jamie Cox cruised to 73 from 85 balls before being yorked by Symonds. Somerset's top order all contributed as the target was reached with 3.4 overs to spare – but Piran Holloway was once again to the fore with an unbeaten 75. The left-hander took his one-day run tally for the season to 736, at an average of 105.

Spinners Saqlain Mushtaq and Ian Salisbury wrecked Northants' hopes at Northampton – 90 for 1 becoming 152 all out, in just 35.5 overs. Saqlain took 4 for 28 from his ten overs, and Salisbury 3 for 29 from his ten. Graeme Swann, with 42, put on 59 with his elder brother Alec (35) for the second wicket – but both then fell to Saqlain, who took his four wickets in his first five overs. Saqlain's arm ball, or wrong 'un, was again a potent weapon, while leg-spinner Salisbury supported the maestro from Lahore with some potent googlies of his own. Surrey had little bother knocking off the runs, with both Graham Thorpe and Alastair Brown enjoying themselves hugely in an unbroken fourth-wicket stand of 76.

Alec Stewart fails in his appeal to stump centurion Jamie Cox, NatWest Trophy semi-final, Somerset v. Surrey.
David Munden/Sportsline Photographic

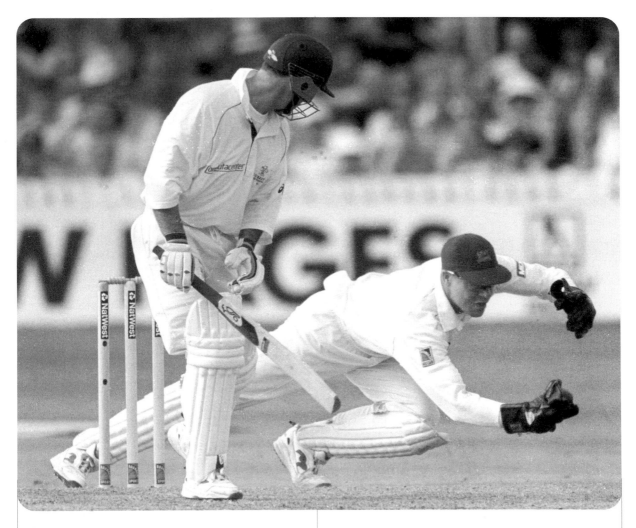

SEMI-FINALS

14 August 1999 at Taunton
Somerset 315 for 8 (50 overs) J Cox 114,
Saqlain Mushtaq 4 for 32
Surrey 195 (43.3 overs) GP Thorpe 62,
KA Parsons 4 for 43
Somerset won by 120 runs
Man of the Match: J Cox (Somerset)

To the unrestrained joy of a capacity Taunton crowd
of 7,500, Somerset thrashed the perceived 'city
slickers' of Surrey by 120 runs to book their first
Lord's final since their last trophy was won in 1983.
Jamie Cox, the Tasmanian who as captain and
opening batsman has transformed the team in his
first year in county cricket, hit 114 from 113 balls to
launch the destruction of the runaway championship

*Rob Turner falls to catch Graham Thorpe, in the NatWest
semi-final, Somerset v. Surrey.*
David Munden/Sportsline Photographic

leaders. Peter Bowler (48) and Piran Holloway (45)
were the major support acts, helping Cox add
135 and 92 respectively for the first two wickets.
Saqlain Mushtaq, the magical Pakistani spinner, was
the only Surrey bowler to escape the carnage – and
Saqlain, with a superb 4 for 32 from his ten overs,
was himself a candidate for Man of the Match,
despite the result. The Hollioake brothers were
taken for 126 runs from their 17 combined overs
and only Graham Thorpe (62) and Alastair Brown
(39) looked like making life uncomfortable for
Somerset when Surrey replied. Keith Parsons
ended with 4 for 43, however, and Surrey fell away
to 195 all out.

Jamie Cox of Somerset batting in the NatWest semi-final. Alec Stewart keeps wicket for Surrey.
David Munden/Sportsline Photographic

15 August 1999 at Bristol
Gloucestershire 240 for 7 (50 overs) KJ Barnett 98
Yorkshire 234 for 6 (50 overs) D Byas 71*,
MP Vaughan 54
Gloucestershire won by 6 runs
Man of the Match: KJ Barnett (Gloucestershire)

In the end the margin of victory for Gloucestershire was just six runs but, in truth, Yorkshire were always second best once Kim Barnett and Tim Hancock, the openers, had ridden their luck against some testing new-ball bowling in the morning. Barnett, using all his vast experience to read the worth of a slow, low pitch early on, played a sensible anchor role for much of his innings, only breaking out to rush to 98 later on. Hancock made 41 and Rob Cunliffe timed the ball better than anyone in the conditions to score a valuable 38 from 36 balls. A total of 240 for 7 was a challenging one, and Yorkshire could not match it despite a fine 54 from Michael Vaughan and a determined 71 not out from David Byas. Only some dramatic late hitting by Gary Fellows, who twice swung Michael Cawdron for six in the penultimate over, got Yorkshire flatteringly close. Gloucestershire's win clinched them a second Lord's final appearance within a month – and the first all-West Country showpiece final, to boot.

NatWest Trophy Final
29 August 1999

The West Country invasion of Lord's ended with Gloucestershire's fans jubilant. After 22 years without a trophy, way back to the days of 'Proctershire', the county was suddenly celebrating a second domestic honour inside a month.

Mark Alleyne's tight-knit, thoroughly competent and always combative unit followed their Super Cup triumph of 1 August by outplaying local rivals Somerset in the first-ever Lord's final between the two clubs. On a warm, muggy day Gloucestershire were given a rousing start by Kim Barnett and Tim Hancock, who put on 125 in 27 overs for the first wicket. Hancock top-scored with 74 and Barnett made 49, but after that the rest of the innings was something of a disappointment. Paul Jarvis, recovering his composure after a wretched first spell, picked up 5 for 55, and only Jack Russell, with 31 not out from 37 balls, managed much late impetus. A total of 230 for 8 seemed well inside Somerset's capabilities but soon, cut down

Jeremy Snape is out, stumped by Turner's throw off Jarvis, NatWest Trophy Final, Gloucestershire v. Somerset.
David Munden/Sportsline Photographic

Above: Somerset batsman Rob Turner plays through the offside.
David Munden/Sportsline Photographic

Below: Somerset skipper Jamie Cox is disappointed after being trapped lbw to Mike Smith.
David Munden/Sportsline Photographic

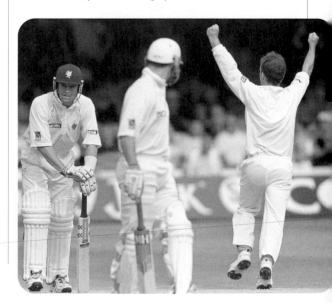

by the testing new ball bowling of Mike Smith and Ian Harvey, they had lost the top half of their much-vaunted batting order with only 52 runs on the board. Rob Turner, batting too low at number seven, did rally things in company with Keith Parsons, and the pair added a sensible 82 for the sixth wicket in 18 overs. But then Turner fell for 52, caught by Russell standing up to the stumps, and when Parsons followed for 42, brilliantly stumped by Russell off Smith's waspish swing, it was all over bar a few defiant hits from Graham Rose. Russell, who also caught Bowler and Trescothick, was a popular choice as Man of the Match. In Somerset's 180 Smith, Harvey and Alleyne all claimed three wickets and – for at least half the crowd – it was a happy journey back home along the M4.

Above: Mark Alleyne lifts the cup for Gloucestershire.
David Munden/Sportsline Photographic

Below: Gloucestershire celebrate victory in the NatWest Trophy Final.
David Munden / Sportsline Photographic

FINAL – GLOUCESTERSHIRE v. SOMERSET
29 August 1999 at Lord's, London

GLOUCESTERSHIRE

Batting		
KJ Barnett	$ run out (Parsons)	49
TC Hancock	lbw, b Jarvis	74
RJ Cunliffe	c Turner, b Rose	3
MW Alleyne (capt)	b Rose	14
*RC Russell	not out	31
MGN Windows	lbw, b Jarvis	12
IJ Harvey	c Holloway, b Jarvis	7
JC Snape	st Turner, b Jarvis	11
MCJ Ball	c Burns, b Jarvis	5
MJ Cawdron	not out	0
AM Smith		
	lb 10, w 10, nb 4	24
	50 overs (for 8 wickets)	**230**

Bowling	O	M	R	W
Caddick	10	1	29	1
Rose	10	3	38	2
Jarvis	10	1	55	5
Kerr	10	0	43	-
Parsons	10	0	55	

Fall of Wickets
1–125, 2–129, 3–161, 4–161, 5–180,
6–193, 7–210, 8–224

SOMERSET

Batting		
PD Bowler	c Russell, b Harvey	1
J Cox (capt)	lbw, b Smith	3
PCL Holloway	c Ball, b Smith	13
M Burns	c Ball, b Alleyne	26
ME Trescothick	$ c Russell, b Alleyne	5
KA Parsons	$ st Russell, b Smith	42
*RJ Turner	c Russell, b Alleyne	51
GD Rose	c Windows, b Harvey	24
JID Kerr	run out (Alleyne)	2
AR Caddick	b Harvey	1
PW Jarvis	not out	3
	lb 4, w 5	9
	45.1 overs	**180**

Bowling	O	M	R	W
Harvey	7.1	0	23	3
Smith	9	0	25	3
Alleyne	10	0	37	3
Cawdron	8	0	38	-
Ball	7	0	33	-
Snape	4	0	20	-

Fall of Wickets
1–5, 2–9, 3–37, 4–51, 5–52, 6–134,
7–166, 8–171, 9–174

$ TV decision
Umpires: NT Plews & DR Shepherd
TV umpire: MJ Kitchen
Toss: Somerset
Man of the Match: RC Russell

Gloucestershire won by 50 runs

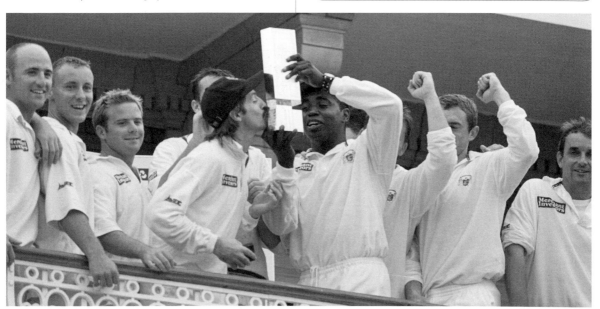

OXFORD AND CAMBRIDGE UNIVERSITIES
By Mark Baldwin

8, 9 and 10 April 1999 at Oxford
Worcestershire 284 for 6 dec. (WPC Weston 84,
DA Leatherdale 71, PR Pollard 60) and 135 for 2 dec.
(VS Solanki 74*)
Oxford University 81 (JM de la Pena 6 for 18)
and 182 (JA Claughton 53, JM de la Pena
4 for 34)
Worcestershire won by 156 runs

8, 9 and 10 April 1999 at Cambridge
Cambridge University 261 for 7 dec. (QJ Hughes 84,
KDM Walker 55) and 197 (GR Loveridge 126,
MP Smethurst 4 for 44)
Lancashire 245 for 1 dec. (MJ Chilton 106*,
PC McKeown 74*) and 216 for 4 (PC McKeown 75,
GD Lloyd 52)
Lancashire won by six wickets

12, 13 and 14 April 1999 at Cambridge
Cambridge University 287 for 8 dec.
(GR Loveridge 87, RG Halsall 76) and
38 for 0 dec.
Nottinghamshire forfeited their first innings;
second innings 212 for 5 (NA Gie 59*,
MP Dowman 52)
Match drawn

14, 15 and 16 April 1999 at Oxford
Hampshire 397 for 5 dec. (JP Stephenson 136,
AN Aymes 69 retired hurt, DA Kenway 56*) and
97 for 0 dec. (AC Morris 58*)
Oxford University 191 (AC Morris 4 for 30) and
30 for 3
Match drawn

15, 16 and 17 April 1999 at Cambridge
Somerset 338 for 1 dec. (PD Bowler 140*, J Cox 139)
and 261 for 3 dec. (RJ Turner 79, PCL Holloway 62
retired hurt)
Cambridge University 247 for 4 dec.
(Imraan Mohammed 110, QJ Hughes 55*)
and 29 for 2
Match drawn

21, 22 and 23 April 1999 at Cambridge
Essex 340 for 3 dec. (DDJ Robinson 111, AP Grayson
83, PJ Prichard 55)
Cambridge University 191 for 7
Match drawn

5, 6 and 7 May 1999 at Oxford
Nottinghamshire 356 for 7 dec. (GF Archer 132,
MP Dowman 67) and 50 for 0
Oxford University 219 for 5 dec. (JA Claughton 85)
Match drawn

9, 10 and 11 May 1999 at Cambridge
Northamptonshire 323 for 4 dec. (AJ Swann 116,
MB Loye 102) and 169 for 2 dec. (RJ Bailey 85*)
Cambridge University 181 for 4 dec. (Imraan
Mohammad 82, JP Pyemont 52) and 251 for 7
(KDM Walker 132)
Match drawn

19, 20 and 21 May 1999 at Oxford
Glamorgan 392 for 5 dec. (AD Shaw 140, MJ Powell
111) and 171 for 7 dec. (I Dawood 58)
Oxford University 289 (OT Parkin 4 for 72) and 106
for 2 (JH Louw 62*)
Match drawn

20, 21 and 22 May 1999 at Cambridge
Kent 368 for 3 dec. (MJ Walker 103*, TR Ward 101,
DP Fulton 99) and 245 for 2 dec. (RWT Key 91,
ET Smith 89)
Cambridge University 102 (MJ McCague 4 for 36) and
160 (MJ Saggers 4 for 26, MM Patel 4 for 58)
Kent won by 351 runs

25, 26 and 27 May 1999 at Oxford
Warwickshire 337 for 2 dec. (MA Wagh 216*,
DL Hemp 94) and 222 for 6 dec. (AF Giles 123*)
Oxford University 158 (AF Giles 5 for 28, CE Dagnall
4 for 20) and 272 (BW Byrne 94, JA Claughton 50,
MA Wagh 4 for 33)
Warwickshire won by 129 runs

15,16 and 17 June 1999 at Chelmsford
Oxford University 158 (BW Byrne 50, DR Law 4 for
32, PM Such 4 for 39) and 268 for 7 (JH Louw 82,
NW Ashley 59, DJ Eadie 52*, PM Such 4 for 80)
Essex 364 (RC Irani 116, DDJ Robinson 53,
IN Flanagan 52)
Match drawn

16, 17 and 18 June 1999 at Cambridge
Cambridge University 247 for 9 dec.
(GR Loveridge 60, JP Hewitt 4 for 43) and
241 for 5 dec. (JP Pyemont 90*)
Middlesex 237 for 7 dec. (OA Shah 103) and 128
(SM Sheikh 4 for 25)
Cambridge University won by 123 runs

Lord's, the venue of the 1999 Varsity Match, which was dominated by the Cambridge batsmen.
David Munden/Sportsline Photographic

Varsity Match

25, 26 and 27 June 1999 at Lord's
Oxford University 259 (NW Ashley 96) and 203 for 6 (TC Hicks 54)
Cambridge University 411 (QJ Hughes 101, JP Pyemont 90, Imraan Mohammed 87)
Match drawn

Nathan Ashley, a postgraduate and former captain of Australia Under-19s, hit 96 and put on 122 for the fourth wicket with Byron Byrne, another Aussie, as Oxford scored a first innings 259. But this total was soon looking inadequate as Imraan Mohammed, son of Sadiq, and Quentin Hughes put on 99 for the second wicket. After Mohammed fell for a hard-hit 87 Hughes (101) and James Pyemont (90) added a further 137 and by the close of the second day Oxford, on 43 for 1, were still 109 runs adrift. On the final day, aided by the weather, Oxford held out for the draw at 203 for 6.

OXFORD

FIRST-CLASS MATCHES
BATTING

	JH Louw	NG Pirihi	JAG Fulton	BW Byrne	JA Claughton	JJ Bull	DJ Eadie	JPB Barnes	D Kino	TC Hicks	DP Mather	SH Khan	NW Ashley	AF Gofton	R G Smalley	AN Bond	SLJ Conway	Extras	Total	Wkts	Result
v. Warwickshire	0	0	1	12	23	10	6	2	1	9	0*							17	81	10	L
(Oxford) 8–10 April	0	4	30	26	53	5	0	28	14*	10	0							12	182	10	
v. Hampshire	5	7	10	13	8		15	45	5	42	4*	18						19	191	10	D
(Oxford) 14–16 April	4	19	–	0*	3*		4	–	–	–	–	–						–	30	3	
v. Nottinghamshire	0	0		85	37			–		–		–	36	37*	–			24	219	5	D
(Oxford) 5–7 May	–			–														–	–		
v. Glamorgan	7		45	14	49		16	4*	4		31	46	0		6			67	289	10	D
(Oxford) 19–21 May	62*		–	16*	19		–	–			–	0	–					9	106	2	
v. Warwickshire	10		48	19*	20		15	0	1	0	4	2	19					20	158	10	L
(Oxford) 25–27 May	2		94	50	10		8	7	28	10*	34	4	0					25	272	10	
v. Essex	4		7	50	8	7	10	30			4	14	10				0*	14	158	10	D
(Chelmsford) 15–17 June	82	0	5	11rh	7	52*	27				–	59	11					14	268	7	
v. Cambridge University	1		32	5	15	5	3		11	11*	24	96	23					33	259	10	D
(Lord's) 25–27 June	6		49*	23	14	16*	–			54	–	–	7	15				19	203	6	
Matches	7	3	3	6	7	6	4	6	5	6	5	6	5	5	1	1	1				
Innings	13	5	5	11	13	11	8	9	6	8	6	9	8	8		1	1				
Not Out	1	0	0	2	4	0	2	0	2	0	4	0	0	1		0	1				
Runs	82	19	30	94	85	49	52*	45	14*	54	11*	34	96	37*		6	0*				
Highest score	183	30	48	374	318	193	108	174	31	159	25	115	264	115		6	0				
Average	15.25	6	9.6	41.55	35.33	17.54	18	19.33	7.75	19.87	12.5	19.16	29.33	16.42		6					

FIRST-CLASS MATCHES
BOWLING

	D Kino	DJ Eadie	DP Mather	TC Hicks	BW Byrne	SH Khan	AF Gofton	NG Pirihi	AN Bond	SLJ Conway	Overs	Totals	Byes/Leg-byes	Wickets	Run-outs
v. Warwickshire	21-3-74-1	15-4-35-0	19-5-55-2	26-10-61-2	15-1-52-1						97	284	7	6	– A
(Oxford) 8–10 April	10-4-22-1	7-3-15-0	10-2-41-0	12-1-46-1	4-0-11-0						43	135	0	2	–
v. Hampshire	30-10-76-0		30-11-64-2	26-4-105-2	16-4-48-0	23-4-93-1					125	397	11	5	–
(Oxford) 14–16 April	10-2-50-0			3.5-0-24-0		7-2-23-0					20.5	97	0	–	–
v. Nottinghamshire	10-1-46-0		27-2-111-3	20-1-84-1		24-3-74-2	12-3-31-0	1-1-0-1			94	356	10	7	–
(Oxford) 5–7 May			4.2-0-25-0			4-0-25-0					8.2	50	0	–	–
v. Glamorgan	18-1-90-0			17.2-4-76-1	3-0-23-0	18-1-95-1	18-1-73-3		4-0-33-0		78.2	392	2	5	–
(Oxford) 19–21 May	17-1-57-1			3-0-16-0		7-1-17-2	7-0-30-0		13-3-41-2		51	171	4	7	–
v. Warwickshire	16-2-86-1		16-2-51-1	16-0-63-0	11-2-52-0	12-2-52-0	7-0-30-0				78	337	3	2	–
(Oxford) 25–27 May	11-0-84-2		9-1-44-3	6-1-18-0	6-0-26-0	7-2-29-0	2-0-15-0				41	222	6	6	1
v. Essex		20.1-4-57-3			30-11-66-3	21-5-82-0	29-6-95-1			14-1-56-0	114.1	364	8	9	2
(Chelmsford) 15–17 June															
v. Cambridge University		13-3-61-0	27-3-78-1	23-4-94-1	16-0-52-1	24-11-70-3	9.1-2-41-3				112.1	411	15	10	1
(Lord's) 25–27 June															
Overs	143	55.1	142.2	153.1	101	151	84.1	1	17	14					
Maidens	24	14	26	25	18	34	13	1	3	1					
Runs	585	168	469	587	330	579	302	0	74	56					
Wickets	6	3	12	8	5	9	9	1	2	0					
Bowler's average	97.5	56	39.08	73.37	66	64.33	33.55		12						

A   JAG Fulton 1-1-0-0

FIELDING

6 –	JPB Barnes
5 –	JH Louw
4 –	NW Ashley, TC Hicks
3 –	JA Claughton
2 –	SH Khan, NG Pirihi
1 –	AN Bond, BW Byrne, JJ Bull, DJ Eadie, JAG Fulton

CAMBRIDGE

FIRST-CLASS MATCHES

BATTING

	KDM Walker	Imraan Mohammed	QJ Hughes	JP Pyemont	GR Loveridge	RG Halsall	BJ Collins	AR Danson	CR Pimlott	JP Lowe	JS Ross	CA Sayers	MJ Birks	SJW Lewis	Samir Sheikh	RK Sadjeh	RW McDowell	TE Goodyer	Extras	Total	Wkts	Result
v. Lancashire	55	12	84	10	31	27	15	6*	4*	–	–								17	261	7	L
(Cambridge) 8-10 April	0	11	17	0	126	0	0	31	7	0*	0								5	197	10	
v. Nottinghamshire	6	13	30	13	87	76	0	17	18*	–		1*	–						26	287	8	D
(Cambridge) 12-14 April	–	8*	–	–	–	–	–	30*											0	38	–	
v. Somerset	31	110	55*	28	–	–	0	9*	–	–	–	–							14	247	4	D
(Cambridge) 15-17 April	–	18*	1*	5	4	–	0												1	29	2	
v. Essex	10	32	14	22	37	0	–	27*	4*	–	–		8	–					37	191	7	D
(Cambridge) 21-23 April	–	–	–	–	–	–							–						–	–	–	
v. Northamptonshire	–	82	19	52	0*	15*	0	–	–	–	–								13	181	4	D
(Cambridge) 9-11 May	132	21	2	21	0	46	0	–	2*	4*	3*	–							22	251	7	
v. Kent		34		0				14	3			3	3	14	12	0		0	17	102	10	L
(Cambridge) 20-22 May		14		34				6	30		0	1*	7	17	0		2	32	17	160	10	
v. Middlesex	32	30	6	10	60	47	10	0*					8	13	–				31	247	9	W
(Cambridge) 16-18 June	–	36	36	90*	29	7	21*						–	3	–				19	241	5	
v. Oxford University	20	87	101	90	39	0	14	8*					18	15	2				17	411	10	D
(Lord's) 25-27 June	–	–	–	–	–			8*											–	–	–	
Matches	7	8	7	8	6	7	7	6	6	2	2	4	7	4	4	1	1	1				
Innings	8	14	11	13	8	9	11	10	6	1	3	4	5	6	1	2	2	2				
Not Out	0	2	2	1	0	1	2	4	5	1	1	3	1	0	0	0	0	0				
Runs	132	110	101	90*	126	76	46	30*	18*	0*	2*	4*	18	17	2	12	2	32				
Highest score	286	508	365	375	413	157	141	153	41		2	9	39	70	2	12	2	32				
Average	35.75	42.33	40.55	31.25	51.62	19.62	15.66	25.5	41		1	9	9.75	11.66		2	6	1	16			

FIRST-CLASS MATCHES

BOWLING

	RG Halsall	CR Pimlott	JP Lowe	JS Ross	GR Loveridge	KDM Walker	CA Sayers	AR Danson	Samir Sheikh	Imraan Mohammed	Overs	Totals	Byes/Leg-byes	Wickets	Run-outs	
v. Lancashire	12-5-32-0	10-1-42-0	15-5-53-0	9-2-37-0	9-1-19-0	14-1-43-1					69	245	19	1	–	A
(Cambridge) 8-10 April	8-0-40-1	8.2-2-33-0	2-0-10-1		16-1-100-2	6-0-30-0					40.2	216	3	4	–	
v. Nottinghamshire																
(Cambridge) 12-14 April	6-1-20-0	9-3-16-0			15-1-74-0	19-4-65-3	8-2-21-2				57	212	16	5	–	
v. Somerset	7-2-19-0	16-3-43-0			29-4-101-1	23-2-78-0	14-2-47-0	7-0-33-0			96	338	17	1	–	
(Cambridge) 15-17 April	16-1-65-2	10-1-18-0			12-2-37-0	10-1-31-0	17-3-64-0	2.3-0-5-1			72.3	261	14	3	–	BE
v. Essex	18-2-48-0	10-1-43-0			15-1-79-0	16-4-65-1		9-1-31-1	17-2-73-1		85	340	1	3	–	
(Cambridge) 21-23 April																
v. Northamptonshire	27-5-78-1		12-2-51-0			12-2-64-1	15-3-84-0		18-5-37-1		84	323	9	3	–	
(Cambridge) 9-11 May	14-2-34-1		11-2-64-0			3-1-19-1	4-1-21-0		9-2-28-0		41	169	3	2	–	
v. Kent			15-3-62-0				14-1-58-0	22-7-74-1	17.5-3-63-1		90.5	368	11	3	1	ACDFG
(Cambridge) 20-22 May			16-2-30-0				11-1-62-0	2-0-23-0	21-5-58-1		68	245	19	2	1	CF
v. Middlesex	21-6-52-2	7-2-19-0			26-1-84-2	10-4-25-2			17-5-48-1		81	237	9	7	–	
(Cambridge) 16-18 June	6-1-20-1	5-2-10-3			15-3-59-1	6-3-11-1			8.2-1-25-4		40.2	128	3	10	–	
v. Oxford University	19-5-64-3	13-3-40-2			15-2-59-2	6-1-22-0			13.3-1-68-3		66.3	259	6	10	–	E
(Lord's) 25-27 June	14-5-19-0	7-2-19-0			25-8-60-2	17-8-26-2			14-2-59-2	3-0-13-0	81	203	7	6	–	
Overs	168	95.2	40	40	177	142	83	42.3	96.5	41.5						
Maidens	35	20	9	7	24	31	13	8	18	8						
Runs	491	283	178	129	672	479	357	166	338	134						
Wickets	11	5	1	0	10	12	2	3	12	2						
Bowler's average	44.63	56.6	178	–	67.2	39.91	178.5	55.33	28.16	67						

A   JS Ross 9-2-37-0; 15-3-62-0 & 16-2-30-0
B   QJ Hughes 5-0-27-0
C   RK Sadjeh 19-3-77-0 & 18-1-53-0
D   TE Goodyer 3-0-23-0; 1-1-0-0
E   QJ Hughes 5-0-27-0
F   RK Sadjeh 19-13-77-0 & 18-1-53-0
G   TE Goodyear 3-0-23-0

FIELDING

9 – MJ Birks (8 ct/1 st)
5 – GR Loveridge
4 – BJ Collins, RG Halsall
3 – SJW Lewis, JP Pyemont
2 – AR Danson, QJ Hughes, KDM Walker
1 – Imraan Mohammad, CA Sayers, SM Sheikh

MINOR COUNTIES
By Ralph Dellor

Cumberland first competed in the Minor Counties championship in 1955, winning the title in 1986. That was the only championship trophy to make its way to English cricket's north-western boundary until 14 September 1999, when Cumberland beat Dorset by six wickets at Netherfield in Kendall to become the latest in a line of Minor County champions stretching back to 1895.

The victory in the first three-day play-off between the winners of the Eastern and Western Divisions represented a major change of fortune for Cumberland who had finished bottom of their division only 12 months earlier. The final itself also saw a Cumberland revival, for at one stage on the first morning they had been 12 for 3. That was when former Lancashire and Worcestershire batsman, Steve O'Shaughnessy, joined David Pearson in a fourth-wicket partnership worth 157. During his Lancashire days O'Shaughnessy had once scored a century in 35 minutes against Leicestershire to equal the first-class record set by Percy Fender in 1920. He treated the Dorset attack with more respect, his total of 118 coming from 197 balls as his side reached 315 for 7 in their first innings.

Dorset's reply began in promising fashion thanks to Jon Hardy, formerly of Hampshire, Somerset and Gloucestershire, and Andrew Sexton. However, from 86 for 0 at one point, the innings collapsed to 130 all out. Following on, Sexton made amends for his colleagues' failings by scoring 196 – just eight runs short of a new county record. Dorset's hopes of building on Sexton's effort disappeared when the leg spin of Simon Kippax got among the tail and although a target of 212 to win might have been competitive, former Yorkshire and Nottinghamshire batsman Ashley Metcalfe's 115 not out calmly steered Cumberland past the winning post with 20 balls and six wickets in hand.

While Sexton missed out on a new Dorset record, Vyvian Pike took his season's tally of wickets to 68 in the final. This not only represented a new county record, it also beat Andrew Golding's 66 wickets in a season for Suffolk in 1995 as the highest number of wickets in Minor Counties cricket for over 20 years. All those who wonder about the demise of English spin bowlers should consider that Pike is a leg-spinner while Golding was a slow left-armer. A current Suffolk player, Russell Catley has been known to bowl a few leg-breaks and in the match against Bedfordshire in June he was joined in the Suffolk side by his two brothers, Matthew and Tim.

Some batsmen did make their mark in the Minor Counties season. Herefordshire's Rob Hughes scored 226 against Wales, while Nick Folland, who made a reasonable entry into first-class cricket with Somerset before returning to a teaching career and Devon, took full advantage of the opportunity offered by a 'grade' match against Oxfordshire at Torquay. Chasing 498 to win, Folland contributed an unbeaten 249 to Devon's five-wicket victory and established a new county individual record and the highest score in the championship for over 50 years.

While in Devon, it is worth noting that two of the county's greatest servants have retired. Nick Gaywood, for so long Folland's partner in causing misery for opposing attacks when they went down the M5, took up a new teaching post in Worksop and left his Minor Counties record at 7,657 runs from 119 matches. Also leaving at the end of the season was Peter Roebuck. After a distinguished career with Somerset he led Devon to six trophies in his seven years as captain, including four consecutive championship titles from 1994 to 1997.

1999 also marked the retirement of Rupert Evans, the Oxfordshire off-spinner who had graced the Minor Counties scene for 26 seasons, having made his debut in 1973 while still a member of the county's Under-19s side. Renowned as one of the best off-spinners outside the first-class game, he was a regular member of the Minor Counties and England Amateur XI's for a number of years and will continue to serve the game as Oxfordshire's Cricket Development Officer.

One of Evans' former colleagues was Mike Nurton, who established the record of the most Minor Counties championship runs, with 12,713 between 1963 and 1990. There is a new name in second place on the list of highest scorers. Steve Plumb, in his fourth season with Lincolnshire after 18 with Norfolk, has overtaken the 11,553 accumulated by Michael Falcon, who played for Plumb's original county in a remarkable 41-year career spanning both world wars (1906–1946). At the age of 45, it is still possible for Plumb to overtake Nurton's record.

Mention should also be made of Hertfordshire quick bowler Paul O'Reilly. The 36-year-old former Chiltern Radio disc jockey became only the 23rd player in the history of Minor Counties cricket and the first Hertfordshire bowler to take all ten wickets in an innings. He had figures of 10 for 38 in

Staffordshire's first innings at Long Marston. Meanwhile, bowling for Northumberland against Hertfordshire at Shenley Park, paceman Craig Stanley took a hat-trick including the 100th Minor Counties wicket of his career.

The ECB County Cup is no longer an exclusively Minor Counties competition. It now incorporates the Board XI's of the 18 first-class counties, but five of the eight qualifying groups were headed by Minors. However, two of the Board XI's were still in contention by the semi-final stage when Cumberland beat Essex by one wicket, when the last scheduled ball resulted in a run out off a wide before a single came off the extra delivery, and Bedfordshire beat Warwickshire by four wickets. The final, at Lord's, was a clear success for Bedfordshire, who won by eight wickets with their captain Richard Dalton, taking 5 for 21.

MINOR COUNTIES FINAL TABLES

Eastern Division

	TWO INNINGS MATCHES						GRADE RULES		
	P	W	L	D	Bat Pts	Bowl Pts	P	Pts	Total Points
Cumberland	6	3	1	2	13	18	3	38	**105** (a)
Norfolk	6	3	0	3	7	11	3	25	**96** (b)
Hertfordshire	6	2	2	2	13	18	3	28	**96** (c)
Buckinghamshire	6	2	1	3	9	19	3	26	**86**
Lincolnshire	6	0	2	4	8	15	3	51	**79** (b)
Suffolk	6	0	1	5	8	10	3	51	**72** (a/b)
Staffordshire	6	0	1	5	7	12	3	36	**65** (d)
Bedfordshire	6	1	1	4	9	15	3	17	**62** (b)
Cambridgeshire	6	1	1	4	4	18	3	23	**59** (a)
Northumberland	6	0	2	4	4	16	3	38	**58**

Western Division

	TWO INNINGS MATCHES						GRADE RULES		
	P	W	L	D	Bat Pts	Bowl Pts	P	Pts	Total Points
Dorset	6	4	1	1	12	18	3	42	**136**
Devon	6	3	0	3	14	15	3	51	**133** (b)
Cheshire	6	2	2	2	11	11	3	40	**104** (e)
Shropshire	6	1	0	5	8	24	3	49	**97**
Oxfordshire	6	2	0	4	8	11	3	29	**85** (b)
Wiltshire	6	1	4	1	13	13	3	29	**76** (b)
Herefordshire	6	1	2	3	7	12	3	25	**60**
Cornwall	6	0	4	2	8	14	3	32	**59** (b)
Berkshire	6	1	0	5	10	15	3	12	**58** (b)
Wales	6	1	3	2	9	11	3	16	**52**

(a) 2 points deducted for slow over rate
(b) includes 5 points for a No Result match
(c) includes 5 points for defeat in a match reduced to one day
(d) includes 10 points in two No Result matches
(e) includes 10 points for a No Result match and a defeat in a
    match reduced to one day

For some years now Minor Counties cricket has been vilified in some quarters as being a last refuge for retired first-class players who take money out of the game, while this level of cricket contributes nothing to the well-being of English cricket. It is worth noting that Dorset won the Western Division of the championship without paying any of their players, while many Minor Counties players go on to significant careers in first-class cricket. Furthermore, ten England Test players of the past decade appeared for Minor Counties earlier in their careers. The latest additions to the list were Chris Read (Devon) and Aftab Habib (Berkshire) who made their debuts at Edgbaston in the first Test against New Zealand.

It will be interesting to see if a young man who made his Minor Counties debut this season goes on to emulate Read and Habib. Sixteen-year-old Durham schoolboy Gordon Muchall received a last-minute call up for Northumberland against Buckinghamshire in July. Up at the crack of dawn, he caught the 6.12am train from Durham to get to Beaconsfield in time for the 11 o'clock start. There should have been a fairytale ending to his epic journey, but cricket is not like that. He was given out leg before first ball!

Championship Final
12, 13 and 14 September 1999 at Netherfield Cricket Club, Kendal
Cumberland 315 for 7 dec. (SJ O'Shaughnessy 118, DJ Pearson 62) and 214 for 4 (AA Metcalfe 115*)
Dorset 130 and (following on) 396 (AJ Sexton 196, DB Pennet 4 for 106)
Cumberland won by six wickets

ECB County Cup Final
1 September 1999 at Lord's
Cumberland 153 (47.4 overs) RN Dalton 5 for 21
Bedfordshire 154 for 2 (36.1 overs) AR Roberts 80*, DJM Mercer 51*
Bedfordshire won by eight wickets
Man of the Match: RN Dalton

THE WORLD CUP

The organisers spoke of a carnival
of cricket and street parties.
Jonathan Agnew is still searching for them.

The 1999 World Cup was billed as being the biggest, brightest and most lucrative cricket tournament there has ever been: a 'carnival' that would attract swarms of new faces to our county grounds. The organisers, the England and Wales Cricket Board, spoke of their vision of street parties and World Cup theme events in schools as new life was breathed into a sport that is, in this part of the world at least, beginning to flag.

'Dust down your sunhats, dig out your T-shirts and shorts, grab your flip-flops and sun cream and prepare to enjoy the greatest cricket carnival on earth,' we were urged in an offering absolutely typical of the pre-tournament hyperbole. The tournament was staged in mid-May, after all, when the players would have more use for handwarmers than sunhats. Just how ludicrous was the notion that anyone in the crowd might actually attend in shorts is best illustrated by the fact that there was not, to my knowledge, a single streaker at even one of the 42 matches!

There was the obligatory World Cup song: 'Life is a Carnival' by Dave Stewart was a cheery rehash of an old number that did not mention or refer to cricket once. It was finally released the day after England were knocked out. Anneka Rice, a TV personality, was wheeled out to promote the World Cup. Instead, in the course of a cringingly embarrassing press conference, she declared cricket to be a 'dodgy' sport! Midway through the tournament, a story found its way into the national press telling us that Anneka was now so smitten with cricket that she had asked to be invited to The Oval to watch the game between Pakistan and Zimbabwe. Either her request was declined or the story simply was not true. Either way, extensive searches failed to locate Ms Rice at The Oval that day!

For the World Cup to be a success, the standard of cricket had to be high. Ignoring any further hiccups that were inevitable in organising a sporting tournament of this scale, the one serious mistake was the use of the white ball in English early-summer conditions. That decision was taken despite any number of advance warnings from players and pundits alike and the result was that the ball swung and seamed all over the place, as we knew it would. Teams batting second were often quickly reduced to 50 for 4, or worse, killing any prospect of an exciting run chase. It was a great shame and, surely, quite unnecessary. Coloured clothes have their place – and the limited-overs World Cup might very well

be it – but any designer worth their salt could have come up with bright, eye-catching and colourful patterns based on white shirts and white trousers. This would have enabled the use of the red ball and, with it, a more even, entertaining contest between bat and ball.

One great success was the use of a number on the back of each player's shirt. Not only did this hugely assist struggling commentators to identify even the little-known players, and the twelfth man and physiotherapist to boot but, far more important, it was greatly appreciated by the crowds. Logic dictates that the numbers on the shirts should correspond with those on the scorecards and scoreboards – too often this was not the case. The sooner shirt-numbering is introduced to Test cricket, the better.

The concept of the Super Six was sound, but needs to be amended slightly before we all meet again in South Africa. Too many points were carried through by the qualifiers, which very nearly resulted in Zimbabwe reaching the semi-finals despite failing to win a single Super Six match.

It is always easy, in retrospect, to pick faults and, to be fair, I would award this World Cup six and a half marks out of ten. The two classic matches between South Africa and Australia towards the end did much to raise the tempo. Unfortunately, the impact here was minimised because both matches were available only to viewers with access to satellite television. It was a shame that the final, between Australia and Pakistan, was a non-event.

Alec Stewart steers England to victory over Sri Lanka.
David Munden/Sportsline Photographic

The highlight of the World Cup was the enthusiastic support by the Asian community. In fact, it was this that made the tournament, not simply because of the noise and the colour, but because it illustrated what a massive following there is for the game in this country. That support must be encouraged: it must be nurtured and protected.

ASIAN SUPPORTERS ENLIVEN TOURNAMENT

For as long as the England team continues to struggle, it might very well be the Asian community that keeps cricket alive in this country. To this end, I strongly urge the ECB to do all it can to ensure that Pakistan and India return to these shores as often as possible. A Test series between the two here, in England would do untold good for cricket.

The opening ceremony of the Cricket World Cup 1999, Lord's.
David Munden/Sportsline Photographic

GROUP A: ENGLAND V. SRI LANKA

14 May at Lord's
Sri Lanka 204 (48.4 overs) RS Kaluwitharana 57, AD Mullally 4 for 37
England 207 for 2 (46.5 overs) AJ Stewart 88, GA Hick 73*
England won by eight wickets
Man of the Match: AJ Stewart

Much of the success of the World Cup would depend on a healthy run in the tournament by the host nation. The first match, against the defending champions, followed an opening ceremony that gave all the indications of having been hastily cobbled together late the previous evening. The smoke from the fireworks hung over Lord's – and the new media centre – like a thick, choking sea fret, the Prime Minister's microphone did not work and all in all the carnival lurched to a somewhat tentative beginning.

Much had been made of the confrontation between Alec Stewart and Arjuna Ranatunga, his opposite number, who clearly fell out during an ill-tempered one-day international in Adelaide during the winter. In fact this match passed off peacefully and without any obvious rancour.

Sri Lanka, put in, were quickly reduced to 65 for 5 with Allan Mullally claiming Jayasuriya,

| THE TOURNAMENT KICKS OFF |

Mahanama and then de Silva for a duck. Kaluwitharana pulled the innings around with 57 from 66 balls but the holders were bowled out in the 49th over for 204, 30 runs short of a par total.

Hussain, controversially preferred to Knight, made 14 but Stewart with 88 and Hick (73 not out) steered England to within 30 runs of victory. Hick lofted Jayasuriya into the near-empty pavilion apron for six to win the match with 19 balls to spare.

GROUP A: SOUTH AFRICA V. INDIA

15 May at County Ground, Hove
India 253 for 5 (50 overs) SC Ganguly 97, RS Dravid 54
South Africa 254 for 6 (47.2 overs) JH Kallis 96
South Africa won by four wickets
Man of the Match: JH Kallis

South Africa, the tournament favourites, were responsible for the first controversy of the World Cup when an eagle-eyed cameraman spotted flesh-coloured earpieces being worn by Cronje and Donald. These, it transpired, were wired up to the coach, Bob Woolmer who was then able to whisper tactics from the dressing room to his captain and leading bowler while they were in the field. The South Africans had not sought permission from the International Cricket Council and were instructed by the match referee, Talat Ali, to remove them immediately.

None of this deterred Ganguly, who made 97 before becoming the first Jonty Rhodes victim of the World Cup, or Dravid who scored a stylish 54. 253 for 5 was a good effort and when South Africa slipped to 68 for 3, India were in charge.

Kallis, first with Boucher (34) and then Cronje (27) steadied the situation until Kallis was run out for 96. This merely enabled the hustling Rhodes and the hard-hitting Klusener (who hit his first three balls to the boundary) to pull off a tight victory with 14 balls in hand.

Rahul Dravid and Allan Donald, during the South Africa v. India match at Hove.
David Munden/Sportsline Photographic

GROUP A: ZIMBABWE V. KENYA

15 May at County Ground, Taunton
Kenya 229 for 7 (50 overs) A Vadher 54, NC Johnson 4 for 42
Zimbabwe 231 for 5 (41 overs) NC Johnson 59
Zimbabwe won by five wickets
Man of the Match: NC Johnson

This was the third consecutive match to be won by the team batting second, in this case Zimbabwe, whose warm-up matches against Derbyshire and Warwickshire had both ended in defeat. Kenya had a good start, rattling up an opening stand of 62 in the 13th over before Neil Johnson – who was to enjoy an outstanding World Cup – found both swing and seam. Kenya were soon 87 for 4 only for Vadher, with 54, and Odoyo to restore some respectability while Johnson finished with 4 for 42.

Opening the innings, Johnson then scored a solid 59 and with sterling support from Zimbabwe's top order, the Kenyan total was passed with nine overs to spare. 41 wides were bowled in the match: worse, much worse, was to come.

GROUP B: AUSTRALIA V. SCOTLAND

16 May at New Road, Worcester
Scotland 181 for 7 (50 overs)
Australia 182 for 4 (44.5 overs) ME Waugh 67
Australia won by six wickets
Man of the Match: ME Waugh

Australia's cricketers had endured a long season, having embarked on a full tour of the Caribbean immediately after their Ashes series against England, and one or two players appeared to be jaded. That, at least, might partially explain Australia's sluggish start to the World Cup for although they beat Scotland with five overs to spare, this was a far from convincing performance.

| AUSTRALIA'S |
| SLUGGISH START |

Mark Waugh, Dale and Lee all dropped regulation catches as the Scottish batsmen battled for survival under heavy cloud cover and the Australian bowling – usually so accurate – delivered 22 wides and eight no-balls. Gavin Hamilton's late flurry (34 from 42 balls) swelled the total, but was never likely to cause the Australians too much difficulty.

Mark Waugh led the way with 67 and Steve Waugh reacquainted himself with English conditions with an undefeated 49.

GROUP B: PAKISTAN V. WEST INDIES

16 May at County Ground, Bristol
Pakistan 229 for 8 (50 overs)
West Indies 202 (48.5 overs) S Chanderpaul 77
Pakistan won by 27 runs
Man of the Match: Azhar Mahmood

A small steel band braved the elements before the start of play, but it was the green-shirted swarms of Pakistan supporters that were in the best voice throughout the chilly day. Wasim's decision to bat

first surprised everyone and when Pakistan were 42 for 4 in the 19th over, the West Indies pace bowlers were firmly in control. However, worries about the form of his batsmen had forced Brian Lara to go into the game with only four front-line bowlers and the combination of Arthurton, Adams and Powell were dispatched for a total of 83 crucial runs. Wasim scored 43 from only 29 balls while Yousuf Youhana and Azhar Mahmood offered splendid support. Walsh took 3 for 28 and Dillon 3 for 29 while Powell's first and only over in one-day international cricket was dispatched for 16 runs.

Shoaib Akhtar, probably the fastest bowler in the world, then demonstrated exactly how he has earned that title. His first delivery of the World Cup induced a hopelessly late hook shot from Campbell. The ball flicked the top edge and whistled over the third man boundary for six. Little wonder, then, that Campbell was clean bowled in Shoaib's next over. Lara made 11 before falling to a catch off the leading edge and, Chanderpaul apart, the rest of the West Indian batting line-up made little impression. Wasim's controversial policy of batting first in good bowling conditions was to emerge as Pakistan's successful routine throughout the competition.

GROUP B: NEW ZEALAND V. BANGLADESH

17 May at County Ground, Chelmsford
Bangladesh 116 (37.4 overs)
New Zealand 117 for 4 (33 overs)
New Zealand won by six wickets
Man of the Match: GI Allott

New Zealand was the favoured dark horse of many pundits and although the resistance offered by Bangladesh was, on this occasion, feeble in the extreme, New Zealand's bowlers

| NEW ZEALAND |
| SHOW EARLY PROMISE |

performed well in the overcast conditions. Bangladesh's top scorer was Enamul Hoque, who made 19, and Hasibul Hussein hit Harris for six to bring up the hundred for his team but no one could get after Larsen, who took 3 for 19 from ten overs.

New Zealand faltered ever so slightly, slipping to 33 for 2, but victory was secured with 17 overs remaining, much to the disappointment of an enormous and vociferous Bangladeshi crowd.

GROUP A: ZIMBABWE V. INDIA

19 May at Grace Road, Leicester
Zimbabwe 252 for 9 (50 overs) A Flower 69*
India 249 (45 overs) S Ramesh 55
Zimbabwe won by 3 runs
Man of the Match: GW Flower

The first thriller of the tournament with India, needing to score nine runs from two overs with three wickets in hand, being stopped in their tracks by a remarkable final over from Henry Olonga.

The disco-dancing, wild-haired fast bowler claimed wickets with his second, fifth and sixth deliveries to leave a large Indian crowd first stunned, and then angry enough for a small minority to stone the Zimbabwe team bus.

Olonga's effort was the more extraordinary because of his waywardness earlier in the afternoon. He lost his run-up, bowled some enormous wides and then nearly struck Jadeja on the head with an unintentional beamer. Despite this, Zimbabwe's captain, Campbell, demonstrated inexplicable faith in his fast bowler who rose magnificently to the occasion.

India were without Sachin Tendulkar who, sadly, returned home to attend his father's funeral. His absence seemed to have an unsettling effect on the Indian players who fielded poorly and whose bowlers gave away 37 wides and no-balls. They were also docked four overs because of a slow over rate: this proved crucial at the end.

Ramesh, Jadeja, Singh and Mongia all contributed to the Indian cause, despite an excellent spell from Streak and when Srinath clubbed two sixes over long on, India appeared to be home and dry. However, up stepped Olonga for a burst that was to propel Zimbabwe into the Super Sixes.

OLONGA WINS THE DAY

GROUP A: ENGLAND V. KENYA

18 May at St. Lawrence Ground, Canterbury
Kenya 203 (49.4 overs) SO Tikolo 71, D Gough 4 for 34
England 204 for 1 (39 overs) N Hussain 88*, GA Hick 61*
England won by nine wickets
Man of the Match: SO Tikolo

Cold, miserable conditions did little to lift a tedious match; the only salvation was the generosity of the Kenyan captain, Karim, who agreed to restart play in the drizzle at 6pm even though it spelt certain defeat for his team.

Shah and Tikolo put together a spirited second-wicket partnership of exactly 100, but the recall of Gough put paid to any fleeting thoughts of giant-killing. Tikolo's 71 was his second World Cup half-century. He eventually fell to a catch at mid-on allowing Odoyo to attack with startling effect: his 34 runs coming from only 32 balls.

Stewart was England's only casualty in reply, his score of 23 being the highest he was to record in the World Cup from this point on. Hussain's unbeaten 88 was a valuable confidence-booster that would condemn Knight – England's original choice as opener – to the sidelines for the whole competition.

GROUP A: SOUTH AFRICA v. SRI LANKA

19 May at County Ground, Northampton
South Africa 199 for 9 (for 50 overs) L Klusener 52*
Sri Lanka 110 (35.2 overs)
South Africa won by 89 runs
Man of the Match: L Klusener

Two controversial umpiring decisions by the third umpire, Ken Palmer, stung South Africa into producing one of the most awesome displays of the tournament. Put into bat by Ranatunga, the South African batsmen found the conditions extremely difficult, and quickly slipped to 103 for 6. After consulting the slow-motion replay, Palmer then gave

Henry Olonga wins the game for Zimbabwe with three wickets in one over, Zimbabwe v. India at Leicester.
David Munden/Sportsline Photographic

Pollock out, caught and bowled by Muralitharan via Ranatunga's boot. The ball, however, clearly bounced on the way leaving some cynics to suggest that Palmer had simply pressed the wrong button. Shortly afterwards, Palmer was in action again, dispatching Cullinan who was caught by Vaas on the boundary edge. Sensing that he was about to fall over the rope, Vaas deliberately threw the ball back into play. Many interpreted this as Vaas not being in control of the ball while taking the catch, but others, including Palmer, believed Vaas 'had complete control over the further disposal of the ball', as required by the Law.

Cullinan made 49 but the fireworks, once again, came from Klusener who smashed 22 runs from the final over of the innings.

Sri Lanka were soon 14 for 4 and then 66 for 6 as South Africa's mighty seam attack revelled in the conditions. Performances such as this only reinforced South Africa's standing as the tournament favourite.

GROUP B: AUSTRALIA V. NEW ZEALAND

20 May at Sophia Gardens, Cardiff
Australia 213 for 8 (50 overs) DS Lehmann 76,
GI Allott 4 for 37
New Zealand 214 for 5 (45.2 overs) RG Twose 80*,
CL Cairns 60
New Zealand won by five wickets
Man of the Match: RG Twose

It is not often that New Zealand dispose of their arch-rivals quite so emphatically in such an important match and the high turn-out of Kiwi supporters at Sophia Gardens had a field day. That New Zealand were largely indebted to an Englishman – Roger Twose – for their victory did

Roger Twose picks up more runs as New Zealand beat their old rivals, Australia, at Cardiff.

David Munden/Sportsline Photographic

not matter one jot and Australia were left to reflect on another surprisingly lacklustre display.

Geoff Allott, the left-arm swing bowler, continued his impressive start to the World Cup by nipping out both openers – Mark Waugh and Gilchrist. While he rested, Ponting and Lehmann rescued the innings with a stand of 94, and from 172 for 5 Australia ought to have posted 250. But Allott returned to finish with 4 for 37 as Lehmann and even Bevan mistimed the charge in the final overs.

| KIWI'S WIN OVER AUSTRALIA |

However, when New Zealand were faltering at 49 for 4, it was looking increasingly like Australia's game. McGrath was bowling first change – and hardly looking as if he relished the challenge – and Warne looked completely out of touch so Twose and Cairns had an opening. Slowly at first, and then powerfully, they put together a stand of 148 for the fifth wicket as the mood of the Australians – and McGrath in particular – grew blacker by the over.

Cairns was caught with 17 runs required leaving Twose (80*) and Parore to complete the now comfortable task with almost five overs to spare.

GROUP B: PAKISTAN V. SCOTLAND

20 May at Riverside, Chester-le-Street
Pakistan 261 for 6 (50 overs) Yousuf Youhana 81*
Scotland 167 (38.5 overs) GM Hamilton 76
Pakistan won by 94 runs
Man of the Match: Yousuf Youhana

A drab match was not helped by the colossal number of extras. Scotland contributed no fewer than 33 wides and 15 no-balls to Pakistan's total and Pakistan returned a further 17 wides and eight no-balls in reply. All in all, a total of 73 extra deliveries were given away so it was a merciful relief to all concerned that Scotland's innings lasted only 39 overs.

Pakistan – who rarely lift themselves for the small occasion – found themselves at 92 for 5 before Yousuf, with 81 not out, Moin and Wasim set about the Scottish bowling.

At 19 for 5, chasing 262 to win, Scotland's run chase lay in tatters but at least Gavin Hamilton crowned a fine all-round performance with a spirited 76.

GROUP A: SRI LANKA V. ZIMBABWE

22 May at New Road, Worcester
Zimbabwe 197 for 9 (50 overs)
Sri Lanka 198 for 6 (46 overs)
MS Atapattu 54
Sri Lanka won by four wickets
Man of the Match: MS Atapattu

A glorious day at New Road but a largely uneventful match which Sri Lanka had to win to remain in with a chance of qualifying for the Super Sixes. They achieved their victory largely because Zimbabwe's middle order self-destructed. At 77 for 2, Zimbabwe were well placed but a brilliant run-out by Jayasuriya to remove Goodwin started a slide to 94 for 6. In the end, a total of 197 was not a bad effort – Carlisle made 27 – but Zimbabwe knew that they would have to bowl Sri Lanka out in order to claim the points.

Johnson accounted for Jayasuriya for 6, but Atapattu steadied the nerves with a classy 54 in a stand of 62 with Mahanama. Zimbabwe handed over 26 extras in wides and no-balls and although de Silva and Ranatunga both fell cheaply, a determined effort by the middle order – and Jayawardene in particular – guided Sri Lanka to their much-needed victory with four overs in reserve.

GROUP B: WEST INDIES V. BANGLADESH

21 May at Castle Avenue, Dublin
Bangladesh 182 (49.2 overs) Shahriar Hossain 64, CA Walsh 4 for 25
West Indies 183 for 3 (46.3 overs) JC Adams 53*, RD Jacobs 52
West Indies won by seven wickets
Man of the Match: CA Walsh

A bracing wind and freezing temperatures reduced the West Indies manager, Clive Lloyd, to watching the match swathed head to toe in blankets. The players were served hot soup during the drinks breaks and the numbing cold severely affected the fielding of both teams.

Phil Simmons, usually so reliable, dropped three chances as Bangladesh, with the now obligatory hand-out of wides, mustered 182. Courtney Walsh took 4 for 25 while the opener Mehrab Hussein completed a fifty.

Bangladesh attempted to defend their total with enormous enthusiasm but the West Indies completed a workmanlike performance with 21 deliveries to spare.

GROUP B: ENGLAND V. SOUTH AFRICA

22 May at The Oval
South Africa 225 for 7 (50 overs) HH Gibbs 60
England 103 (41 overs) AA Donald 4 for 17
South Africa won by 122 runs
Man of the Match: L Klusener

South Africa's fast-bowling machine pulverised England to the extent that the home team only narrowly avoided their lowest ever World Cup score. Dismissed within 41 overs, England lurched from crisis to crisis: 6 for 2, 45 for 5, 78 for 7. It was a huge disappointment for those optimists who really believed that England had a chance of winning the World Cup. This match ruthlessly put that ambition into its true perspective.

At lunch, it did not look so bad for England. South Africa, put in, had slumped from 111 without loss to 127 for 4 as Mullally and Ealham restored some control. Once again, the explosive batting of Klusener – who bludgeoned crucial runs at the end (48 not out from 40 balls in this case) – had a psychological impact on both teams. The importance of this cannot be underestimated. Even so, despite Klusener's effort, Hansie Cronje admitted later that he felt South Africa were 25 runs light. He need not have worried.

Hussain and Stewart both fell to the much improved swing bowling of Kallis – Stewart, rather unluckily, leg before first ball. There cannot ever have been any better second-change fast bowler in world cricket than Allan Donald. He ripped out the middle order, seizing 4 for 17 from eight high-class overs to ensure that England did not even suggest that they were ever going to make a match of it.

Herschell Gibbs goes on the attack against Robert Croft, England v. South Africa at The Oval.
David Munden/Sportsline Photographic

GROUP A: INDIA V. KENYA

23 May at County Ground, Bristol
India 329 for 2 (50 overs)
SR Tendulkar 140*, RS Dravid 104*
Kenya 235 for 7 (50 overs) SO Tikolo 58,
K Otieno 56, DS Mohanty 4 for 56
India won by 94 runs
Man of the Match: SR Tendulkar

A quite spectacular innings of 140 not out from only 101 balls by Sachin Tendulkar was made all the more remarkable by the circumstances. He had returned from his father's funeral in India only the day before. His innings grew in momentum with each passing landmark and Kenya's willing bowlers simply did not have an answer: there was no shame in that. As the crowd bayed, Tendulkar disdainfully flicked the final ball of the innings over mid-wicket for six and marched off the ground with Dravid, with whom he had just registered the highest

> TENDULKAR
> **140** NOT OUT

partnership in World Cup history. Dravid is one of the most stylish batsmen in international cricket; his undefeated 104 came at a run a ball.

Otieno and Tikolo both passed 50 for Kenya and, under the circumstances, their score of 235 was a good effort. However, thanks to the combined brilliance of Tendulkar and Dravid, that commendable total was still 95 runs away from their target.

GROUP B: PAKISTAN V. AUSTRALIA

23 May at Headingley, Leeds
Pakistan 275 for 8 (50 overs) Inzamam-ul-Haq 81,
Abdur Razzaq 60
Australia 265 (49.5 overs) MG Bevan 61, Wasim Akram
4 for 40
Pakistan won by 10 runs
Man of the Match: Inzamam-ul-Haq

Finally, after 15 matches, this was the first to go into
the final over. It was a cracking game played in front
of a packed crowd of, mainly, jubilant Pakistani
supporters who witnessed high tension, aggression
and even some humour.

The comedy was provided by the unlikely figure of
Inzamam-ul-Haq who, in the company of the highly
promising young all-rounder, Abdur Razzaq, pulled the
innings round from the potential difficulty of 46 for 3.
Razzaq scored a very good 60 and Yousuf 29 but the
problem came when Wasim came out to join the burly
– and now tiring – Inzamam. On 81, Inzamam was
struck flush on the foot by a Fleming yorker. Horrified
to see his captain charging down the pitch for a quick
single, Inzamam hobbled a fateful couple of yards out
of his crease, only to sink, slowly to the ground, like a
tranquillised bull elephant. Wasim simply ran straight
past the floundering Inzamam, condemning Inzy to a
painful walk back to the pavilion.

This brought Moin to the crease and his typically
outrageous 31 from 12 balls proved to be the
difference between the two teams.

Wasim bowled Gilchrist third ball, but Mark
Waugh and Ponting put on 91 for the second wicket.
Waugh fell to Razzaq and when Saqlain then nipped
out Ponting and Lehmann within three balls,
Pakistan were back in charge. Bevan and Steve
Waugh calmly added 113 until Bevan chipped
Wasim to Ijaz at point and, in fading light, Pakistan's
fast bowlers (who had maintained a tortuously slow
over rate) became increasingly difficult to see. 13
were required from Wasim's final over. With the fifth
delivery, he knocked over McGrath at which point
the Western terrace broke out into a delirious conga.

GROUP B: NEW ZEALAND V. WEST INDIES

24 May at County Ground, Southampton
New Zealand 156 (48.1 overs) M Dillon 4 for 46
West Indies 158 for 3 (44.2 overs) RD Jacobs 80*
West Indies won by seven wickets
Man of the Match: RD Jacobs

An important match for the
West Indies who had been
strongly criticised by their
former captain, Viv Richards,
for their drab effort in Dublin.
Richards, in fact, was soon
to take charge of the team following Malcolm
Marshall's withdrawal through illness, and his
words seemed to have the desired effect on the
bowlers, at least.

The white ball moved extravagantly under
cloudy skies and, with Reon King working up
a head of steam, New Zealand subsided to 75
for 6. Harris made 30 and Larsen a handy 14
but, in truth, this was another case of a game
being wrecked by the combination of the conditions
and the white ball.

West Indies recovered from 49 for 2, with opener
Ridley Jacobs standing firm to finish with an
unbeaten 80. Lara played the best strokes of the day
to score 36 from 54 balls, but that was it as far as
entertainment was concerned.

GROUP B: SCOTLAND V. BANGLADESH

24 May at Raeburn Place, Edinburgh
Bangladesh 185 for 9 (50 overs) Minhazul Abedin 68*,
JAR Blain 4 for 37
Scotland 163 (46.2 overs) GM Hamilton 63
Bangladesh won by 22 runs
Man of the Match: Minhazul Abedin

Scotland's best chance of a victory in the
World Cup appeared to be guaranteed when
Bangladesh, put in to bat, were reduced to 26
for 5. Butt and Blain shared the wickets but as
Scotland, once again, were hugely profligate
with their wides and no-balls, Minhazul Abedin,
who was dropped on 3, and Naimur Rahman
restored some respectability.
Rahman made 36 from 58 balls
leaving Minhazul (68*) and
Enamul Hoque to post a
defendable total.

| SCOTLAND'S EXTRAS |
| COST THEM GAME |

At 8 for 3, Scotland were soon in trouble. At 49
for 5, defeat beckoned, only for another mature
innings from Hamilton to give them a glimpse of
victory. He was cruelly run out, backing up, for 63
and although wicketkeeper Davies scored 32,
Scotland fell 22 runs short and left rueing the
28 wides and 11 no-balls they had given away
earlier in the day.

GROUP A: ENGLAND V. ZIMBABWE

25 May at Trent Bridge, Nottingham
Zimbabwe 167 for 8 (50 overs)
England 168 for 3 (38.3 overs) GP Thorpe 62,
N Hussain 57*
England won by seven wickets
Man of the Match: AD Mullally

'A dog of a match', was how the new cricket correspondent of the *Daily Telegraph* described this encounter, and how right he was. Devoid of any excitement, it was remarkable, on this showing, that Zimbabwe went on to qualify for the Super Sixes and England did not, for England completely dominated the game.

Mullally bowled expertly in helpful conditions to claim 2 for 16 and the only time the Zimbabwean batsmen looked like taking control was during the 'change' overs from Adam Hollioake and Flintoff which yielded 49 runs.

A target of 168 was never likely to test England and although Stewart and Hick both failed, Hussain and an increasingly confident Thorpe found the afternoon conditions to their liking. Thorpe made 62, falling to a brilliant catch with 20 runs required for victory, and how England were to regret sending

Graham Thorpe sweeps and Andy Flower watches, England v. Zimbabwe at Trent Bridge.
David Munden/Sportsline Photographic

Fairbrother out 'for a net'. With no thought at all given to the run-rate – and its importance later in the tournament – Hussain and Fairbrother prodded about, taking five overs to score the last nine runs. David Lloyd, the coach, might have smiled on the day having gained sweet revenge over his chief tormentor of the past, but his decision at the end helped Zimbabwe qualify – at England's expense.

GROUP A: INDIA V. SRI LANKA

26 May at County Ground, Taunton
India 373 for 6 (50 overs) SC Ganguly 183,
RS Dravid 145
Sri Lanka 216 (42.3 overs) PA de Silva 56, RR Singh
5 for 31
India won by 157 runs
Man of the Match: SC Ganguly

Sri Lanka's batsmen dominated the previous World Cup, but on a flat pitch at Taunton, the holders were effectively blown out of the competition by a whirlwind partnership of 318 between Ganguly and Dravid. It was a record for any wicket in a one-day international and had anyone bothered to keep a note of the number of balls that were hoisted out of the ground that would, more than likely, have been a record, too.

When Ramesh was bowled by Vaas early on, there was no sign of what was to follow. Dravid set the pace, scoring his first fifty from only 43 balls and such was the carnage that followed that by the 30-overs mark, a despairing Ranatunga had already tried seven bowlers; although, wisely, not himself.

GANGULY AND DRAVID'S RECORD PARTNERSHIP

This was Dravid's second successive century in the World Cup and the level of entertainment was such that Tendulkar's dismissal for 2 did not disappoint in the least.

Sri Lanka could not make the slightest impression on their enormous target. De Silva, at least, returned to form and made an obvious gesture to his critics in the small press box on passing 50. However, Robin Singh plugged away effectively taking 5 for 31 to seal a handsome victory for India.

GROUP A: SOUTH AFRICA V. KENYA

26 May at Amstelveen, Amsterdam
Kenya 153 (44.3 overs) R Shah 50, L Klusener 5 for 21
South Africa 153 for 3 (41 overs)
South Africa won by seven wickets
Man of the Match: L Klusener

Five and a half thousand people watched the first international match to be staged on Dutch soil and although the contest itself was hardly riveting, the venture was, clearly, a worthwhile exercise.

Otieno and Shah surprised possibly even themselves by mounting an opening stand of 66 before South Africa's star-studded pace attack woke up and rediscovered their length. Klusener who, up to now, had been the tournament's most destructive lower-order batsman, reminded us all that his principal skill is as a seam bowler, and he cleaned up the Kenyans, taking 5 for 21 from 8.3 overs.

Chasing only 153 to win, South Africa cruised home with nine overs in hand.

GROUP B: SCOTLAND V. WEST INDIES

27 May at Grace Road, Leicester
Scotland 68 (31.3 overs)
West Indies 70 for 2 (10.1 overs)
West Indies won by eight wickets
Man of the Match: CA Walsh

The match took three hours to complete and became the shortest one-day international ever played. Scotland won the toss and the rout began immediately. At 29 for 7, the Scots were humiliated but, not for the first time, Gavin Hamilton stood firm amongst the wreckage, and scored a respectable 24 not out. Walsh claimed 3 for 7 from seven overs as Scotland were dismissed for 68 in only 31 overs.

West Indies, noting the opportunity to boost their run-rate, roared home in only ten overs leaving George Salmond, the captain of Scotland, to reflect on the day's events. 'I thought if we got a few runs on the board, we could give them a game', he said.

Man of the Match Courtney Walsh celebrates his dismissal of Alec Davies, West Indies v. Scotland.
David Munden/Sportsline Photographic

GROUP B: AUSTRALIA V. BANGLADESH

27 May at Riverside, Chester-le-Street
Bangladesh 178 for 7 (50 overs) Minhazul Abedin 53*
Australia 181 for 3 (19.5 overs) AC Gilchrist 63,
TM Moody 56*
Australia won by seven wickets
Man of the Match: TM Moody

Australia failed to dismiss Bangladesh in their 50
overs, confirming that the bowlers were still well
below their best. Minhazul Abedin scored an
unbeaten fifty, Mehrab 42 and, all in all, Bangladesh
will have been satisfied with their total. However, as
news filtered through of West Indies' comfortable win
over Scotland, Australia recognised the need to hoist
their run-rate and the resulting onslaught rushed them
to victory in less than 20 overs. Tom Moody made 56
from 29 balls – poor Khaled Mahmud suffering as
badly as anyone (his 17 deliveries cost 39 runs) – and
Australia duly raised their run-rate to 0.77.

GROUP B: PAKISTAN V. NEW ZEALAND

27 May at County Ground, Derby
Pakistan 269 for 8 (50 overs)
Inzamam-ul-Haq 73*, Ijaz Ahmed
51, GI Allot 4 for 64
New Zealand 207 for 8
(50 overs) SP Fleming 69
Pakistan won by 62 runs
Man of the Match: Inzamam-ul-Haq

The tournament was crying out
for a close contest but, again,
this was a one-sided affair on a
dismally slow pitch. Inzamam
defied both that and the dribbly
New Zealand bowlers in his
unbeaten 61-ball 73 not out.
Inzamam clubbed seven
boundaries and while Ijaz found
the conditions more restrictive,
the pair ensured that Pakistan
had something to bowl at.

That method was fast becoming Pakistan's
winning formula and once again, Shoaib struck
with the new ball to make the run chase even
more difficult. New Zealand were quickly 35
for 3 and when they slipped to 71 for 6, the
contest was over. However, Fleming and Harris
recognised the importance of not being bowled
out within their 50 overs and their patient 82-run
stand was to prove crucial to New Zealand's
qualification when, later in the tournament,
Australia beat West Indies.

GROUP A: ENGLAND V. INDIA

29 and 30 May at Edgbaston, Birmingham
India 232 for 8 (50 overs) RS Dravid 53
England 169 (45.2 overs)
India won by 63 runs
Man of the Match: SC Ganguly

The game, in front of massive Indian support,
began with England's progression into the Super
Sixes apparently guaranteed. However, during
the day, the news of Zimbabwe's astonishing win
over South Africa filtered through from Chelmsford
and, suddenly, England had to win to stay in the

World Cup. That they failed to do so merely underlined, once again, their hopelessness at chasing runs under pressure.

Stewart won the toss for the fifth successive time and, despite the unsettled forecast, put India in to bat. With no pace in the pitch, run-scoring was never easy but England, with a little fortune, did well to restrict India to 232 for 8. Ganguly made a stylish 40 before he was unluckily run out backing up during a tight spell from Ealham but,

ENGLAND'S DESPAIR

all the while, the cloud cover began to build.

Shortly, the conditions were ideal for swing bowling and 22-year-old Debashish Mohanty had a field day. From the sort of unlikely looking open-chested action that would have Fred Trueman chewing his pipe, Mohanty actually managed to swing the ball away from the bat. Stewart felt for an outswinger and edged, firm-footed, to slip. Two balls later, Hick was comprehensively bowled playing exactly the tentative, nervous prod that so exasperates his supporters. 13 for 2 was a dreadful start and the light was deteriorating fast. The umpires conferred, then decided to carry on and immediately a furious Hussain was bowled by Ganguly for 33. It then threw it down with rain.

The force appeared to be with India when the players returned the following morning to complete the match. Srinath struck quickly, dismissing Thorpe leg before for 36, but had umpire Akhtar's decision not been as ghastly as the several howlers he had committed the previous summer at Headingley, he might have been forgiven. Quite how he imagined that this delivery might, conceivably, have hit the stumps was beyond everyone bar Mr Akhtar himself, and the thunderous look Thorpe gave him as he walked past will remain one of the less savoury memories of the World Cup.

Flintoff hit a six but fell to Kumble and as Fairbrother stood helpless at the other end, Hollioake swiped across the line and the match was all but over.

Alec Stewart choked back the tears as he contemplated England's early departure from the competition and David Lloyd, the coach, headed for a quieter life in the commentary box. The following day, Dave Stewart released the official World Cup song: 'Life is a Carnival'. Oh really? There was not much singing in the offices of the ECB as the authorities contemplated a World Cup without England.

GROUP A: SOUTH AFRICA V. ZIMBABWE

29 May at County Ground, Chelmsford
Zimbabwe 233 for 6 (50 overs) NC Johnson 76
South Africa 185 (47.2 overs) L Klusener 52*, SM Pollock 52
Zimbabwe won by 48 runs
Man of the Match: NC Johnson

The first upset of the World Cup – and what an upset! South Africa had breezed through the qualifying stage to this point with barely a hair out of place while the manner in which Zimbabwe were completely outplayed by England at Trent Bridge rather summed up their tournament to date. But how they bounced back here, and what final and terrible retribution for David Lloyd's infamous comments about having 'flipping murdered 'em' in Zimbabwe two years before.

The match was a triumph for Neil Johnson, Zimbabwean born, but who had represented South Africa 'A' before returning north seven months before the World Cup. Very obviously ostracised by South Africa's fielders, Johnson responded by scoring an excellent 76. This was the platform Zimbabwe needed and with contributions from Goodwin and Andy Flower, they reached 233 for 6.

It was with a mixture of horror and sheer that England's cricketers – 100 miles away in their Edgbaston dressing room – tuned in to Teletext: South Africa were 40 for 6 with Johnson nabbing three wickets. Was this some sort of a joke?

Graham Thorpe is disappointed to be given out by umpire Akhtar, England v. India. *David Munden/Sportsline Photographic*

Sadly not! Pollock and Klusener battled away, but not even the mighty Klusener could swing this match his way. Johnson finished with 3 for 27 and the admirable Streak 3 for 35. Having beaten India and South Africa – both fellow qualifiers – Zimbabwe romped to the top of Group A and took four points through to the Super Sixes. Crazily, this meant they were just one win away from the semi-finals.

GROUP A: SRI LANKA V. KENYA

30 May at County Ground, Southampton
Sri Lanka 275 for 8 (50 overs) MS Atapattu 52, A Ranatunga 50
Kenya 230 for 6 (50 overs) MO Odumbe 82, A Vadher 73*
Sri Lanka won by 45 runs
Man of the Match: MO Odumbe

Sri Lanka's undistinguished defence of the World Cup crown ended in victory on a bitterly cold, damp afternoon and with the cricketing world focusing on events at Edgbaston. Jayasuriya finally found some touch in scoring 39 – his highest score in what was, for him, a hugely disappointing tournament. Atapattu stroked 52 from 67 deliveries and our final glimpse of the controversial Ranatunga was of him being run out for exactly 50.

Chasing 276, Kenya were quickly reduced to 52 for 5 and the contest was over. There was, however, the chance for Odumbe to show his class, and he scored a delightful 82 from 95 balls. He and Vadher put on 161 – Vadher making 73 not out before both teams packed their bags and headed for home.

GROUP B: AUSTRALIA V. WEST INDIES

30 May Old Trafford, Manchester
West Indies 110 (46.4 overs) GD McGrath 5 for 14
Australia 111 for 4 (40.4 overs)
Australia won by six wickets
Man of the Match: GD McGrath

One of the much-trumpeted features of this World Cup was the concept of carrying points earned from fellow qualifiers into the Super Six stage. This was to make every match important and to reward teams in the second phase for consistent performances in the first. However, the plan was not thought through carefully enough and was ruthlessly exposed before a bemused crowd of 20,000, half of whom left well before the end of the game.

It was in Australia's interest for West Indies to qualify rather than New Zealand, who would take through two points from their win over Australia earlier in the tournament. So, when victory was assured, Steve Waugh and Michael Bevan took as long as they could over scoring the winning runs. This was designed to bolster the West Indian run-rate and although collusion between Messrs Lara and Waugh was hotly denied, it was a dismal spectacle made worse by the lack of any explanation to the crowd, other than by radio coverage by *Test Match Special*.

The day began extremely competitively with a rejuvenated McGrath bowling spectacularly with the new ball. He accounted for Campbell, Adams and then, with the 'ball of the tournament so far', he bowled Lara neck and crop for 9. Only two West Indians made double figures – Jacobs who carried his bat for 49 not out, and Chanderpaul with 16 – but the West Indies had to bat their full 50 overs if they possibly could, so their total of 110 was compiled tortuously slowly.

Ambrose quickly accounted for Mark Waugh to raise the West Indies' hopes but after 30 overs, Australia had reached 92 for 4 and victory was only 19 runs away. Steve Waugh and Bevan – both the nimblest of one-day batsmen – dragged out proceedings for a further 11 overs and a match which at the start of the tournament promised to provide a true carnival of cricket ended in a chorus of boos.

GROUP B: BANGLADESH V. PAKISTAN

31 May at County Ground, Northampton
Bangladesh 223 for 9 (50 overs) Saqlain Mushtaq 5 for 35
Pakistan 161 (44.3 overs)
Bangladesh won by 62 runs
Man of the Match: Khaled Mahmud

The last time, it was the Kenyans who provided the shock of the tournament. Now it was the turn of Bangladesh to register their first victory of real significance. Pakistan, assured of a place in the Super Sixes and with no points to play for, were clearly unmotivated. Bangladesh, with political points on offer, lifted themselves magnificently in front of 7,000 cheering supporters.

The Bangladeshi top order all contributed solidly, Akram Khan reaching 42 before becoming a rare Waqar Younis victim, but a target of 224 seemed well within Pakistan's range.

At 42 for 5, a shock was clearly on the cards. Mahmud struck three times removing Afridi, Inzamam and Malik to leave Azhar Mahmood and Wasim Akram with the task of avoiding embarrassment. Both scored 29 and when Shahriar clung on to a catch to dismiss Akram, it was as though Bangladesh had just won the World Cup.

The news was greeted rapturously at home, but made the decision to sack the coach, Gordon Greenidge, before the game appear a little hasty.

Pakistan supporters cheer their team during the match against Bangladesh at Northampton.
David Munden/Sportsline Photographic

GROUP B: NEW ZEALAND V. SCOTLAND

31 May at Raeburn Place, Edinburgh
Scotland 121 (42.1 overs) CZ Harris 4 for 7
New Zealand 123 for 4 (17.5 overs) RG Twose 54*
New Zealand won by six wickets
Man of the Match: GI Allott

Following the shenanigans at Old Trafford between Australia and West Indies, New Zealand had to win this match at a canter: within 21.2 overs, in fact. This they achieved with 27 balls to spare, much to the relief of those who hold fair play dear.

Scotland's batting was poor once again. Hamilton and Stanger put on 54 for the fourth wicket, but at 68 for 6, the home team was going nowhere.

New Zealand knew their target and led by Roger Twose, whose unbeaten 54 came off only 49 balls, they got there in only 17.5 overs.

SCOTLAND LOSE AGAIN

WORLD CUP FINALS TABLES

GROUP A	P	W	L	NR	Pts	NRR
South Africa	5	4	1	0	8	+0.86
India	5	3	2	0	6	+1.28
Zimbabwe	5	3	2	0	6	+0.02
England	5	3	2	0	6	−0.33
Sri Lanka	5	2	3	0	4	−0.81
Kenya	5	0	5	0	0	−1.20

GROUP B	P	W	L	NR	Pts	NRR
Pakistan	5	4	1	0	8	+0.53
Australia	5	3	2	0	6	+0.73
New Zealand	5	3	2	0	6	+0.58
West Indies	5	3	2	0	6	+0.50
Bangladesh	5	2	3	0	4	−0.54
Scotland	5	0	5	0	0	−1.93

The teams in bold qualify for the Super Six stage of the tournament.

SUPER SIXES

AUSTRALIA V. INDIA

4 June at The Oval, London
Australia won by 77 runs
Man of the Match: GD McGrath

Neither team carried through any points from the qualifying round so this encounter was, more or less, a sudden-death play-off. Much was made before the game of Sachin Tendulkar's position in the batting order and, under enormous pressure from the Indian media, the Indian management relented, and restored Tendulkar to the top of the order. Once this became public knowledge, the inevitable contest between Tendulkar and Glenn McGrath was the potential high-point of the game.

In fact, it lasted only four balls as McGrath confirmed his return to form that killed the match as a spectacle in mid-afternoon.

The morning was overcast and Azharuddin's decision to put Australia in to bat reflected his belief that the ball would misbehave. In fact, Australia's opening batsmen, led by Mark Waugh, feasted on a wayward opening spell by Mohanty to reach 71 without loss from the first 15 overs.

Waugh was eventually caught at long leg for a 99-ball 83 and Ponting played on three balls later, but this did not affect Australia's progress in the least. Solid contributions all the way down the list posted a total that had never been overhauled in a 50 overs one-day international in England.

McGrath saw to it that India's challenge was non-existent. Tendulkar edged a lovely delivery that bounced and left him. The hush that accompanied him from the field was in sharp contrast to the Australian celebrations in the middle – Tendulkar's last three innings against Australia had all been centuries. Before long, Ganguly, Dravid and Azharuddin had all joined him in the pavilion and India were out of the game at 17 for 4.

> **AUSTRALIA WIN BY 77 RUNS**

Jadeja and Singh had little option but to play for India's flagging run-rate and this was the cue for most of the crowd to fall asleep. Singh excited them briefly when he dispatched Warne for two sixes in an over and Jadeja had the satisfaction of reaching his century before Mohanty was run out to complete Australia's well-deserved victory.

AUSTRALIA v. INDIA
4 June at The Oval, London

AUSTRALIA

Batting			Bowling	O	M	R	W
ME Waugh	c Prasad, b Singh	83	Srinath	10	2	34	0
*AC Gilchrist	c Mohanty, b Ganguly	31	Mohanty	7	0	47	1
RT Ponting	b Singh	23	Prasad	10	0	60	1
DS Lehmann	run out (Jadeja)	26	Kumble	10	0	49	0
SR Waugh (capt)	c Kumble, b Mohanty	36	Ganguly	5	0	31	1
MG Bevan	c Mongia, b Prasad	22	Singh	7	0	43	1
TM Moody	not out	26	Tendulkar	1	0	4	0
SK Warne	not out	0					
PR Reiffel							
DW Fleming			**Fall of Wickets**				
GD McGrath			1–97, 2–157, 3–158, 4–218, 5–231,				
	lb 14, w 10, nb 11	35	6–275				
	50 overs (for 6 wickets)	**282**					

INDIA

Batting			Bowling	O	M	R	W
SC Ganguly	b Fleming	8	McGrath	10	1	34	3
SR Tendulkar	c Gilchrist, b McGrath	0	Fleming	9	1	33	2
RS Dravid	c Gilchrist, b McGrath	2	Reiffel	10	1	30	0
AD Jadeja	not out	100	Moody	10	0	41	1
M Azharuddin (capt)	c SR Waugh, b McGrath	3	ME Waugh	1	0	7	0
RR Singh	c Reiffel, b Moody	75	Warne	6.2	0	49	0
*NR Mongia	run out (Bevan)	2	SR Waugh	2	0	8	2
J Srinath	c Gilchrist, b SR Waugh	0					
A Kumble	c Gilchrist, b SR Waugh	3	**Fall of Wickets**				
BKV Prasad	lbw, b Fleming	2	1–1, 2–10, 3–12, 4–17, 5–158, 6–180,				
DS Mohanty	run out (Warne/Gilchrist)	0	7–186, 8–192, 9–204				
	lb 3, w 4, nb 3	10					
	48.2 overs	**205**					

Umpires: SA Bucknor & P Willey
Man of the Match: GD McGrath

Australia won by 77 runs

SOUTH AFRICA V. PAKISTAN

June 5 at Trent Bridge, Nottingham
South Africa won by three wickets
Man of the Match: L Klusener

Although Australia were running into form and starting to look dangerous, in the minds of most punters this contest remained a likely forerunner to the final. It lived up to its billing, too: this really was a great match.

The early-morning dampness did not help Pakistan's batsmen after Wasim had, once again, followed his favoured tactic of batting first, regardless of the conditions. After 40 overs, Pakistan had laboured their way to 139 for 5, Inzamam having, once again, run himself out. The promising Yousuf Youhana suffered a recurrence of a

PAKISTAN v. SOUTH AFRICA
5 June at Trent Bridge, Nottingham

PAKISTAN

Batting		
Saeed Anwar	c Boucher, b Elworthy	23
Wajahatullah Wasti	c Boucher, b Donald	17
Abdur Razzaq	c Kirsten, b Elworthy	30
Ijaz Ahmed	c Cullinan, b Klusener	23
Inzamam-ul-Haq	run out (Rhodes)	4
Yousuf Youhana	run out (Klusener)	17
*Moin Khan	run out (Cronje/Boucher)	63
Azhar Mahmood	not out	15
Wasim Akram (capt)	not out	5
Saqlain Mushtaq		
Shoaib Akhtar		
	b 4, lb 8, w 11	23
	50 overs (for 7 wickets)	**220**

Bowling	O	M	R	W
Pollock	10	1	42	0
Kallis	10	0	47	0
Donald	10	2	49	1
Elworthy	10	2	23	2
Klusener	9	0	41	1
Cronje	1	0	6	0

Fall of Wickets
1-41, 2-58, 3-102, 4-111, 5-118,
6-150, 7-206

SOUTH AFRICA

Batting		
G Kirsten	lbw, b Wasim Akram	19
HH Gibbs	c Ijaz, b Shoaib Akhtar	0
WJ Cronje (capt)	c Saqlain, b Shoaib	4
DJ Cullinan	c Saeed Anwar, b Azhar	18
JH Kallis	c Moin, b Saqlain Mushtaq	54
JN Rhodes	lbw, b Azhar Mahmood	0
SM Pollock	c Inzamam, b Azhar	30
L Klusener	not out	46
*MV Boucher	not out	12
S Elworthy		
AA Donald		
	lb 11, w 14, nb 13	38
	49 overs (for 7 wickets)	**221**

Bowling	O	M	R	W
Wasim Akram	10	0	44	1
Shoaib Akhtar	9	1	51	2
Azhar Mahmood	10	1	24	3
Abdur Razzaq	10	1	40	0
Saqlain Mushtaq	10	0	51	1

Fall of Wickets
1-7, 2-19, 3-39, 4-55, 5-58, 6-135,
7-176

Umpires: DB Hair & DR Shepherd
Man of the Match: L Klusener

South Africa won by three wickets

was the plan, anyway, and Pollock seemed to follow it precisely when he gave way to Klusener in the 37th over for 30.

So, with 41 runs needed from 26 balls, the stage was set, and Klusener – as he had throughout the tournament – produced an awesome display of massive hitting. He had moments of fortune – an edged four over the 'keeper's head, for example – but his detection and then disposing of an Akram slower ball (clumped through mid-wicket) was classic.

As Pakistan's fielding began to buckle, the winning runs were registered in farcical circumstances: a skyer offered by Klusener to Saeed Anwar was put down, allowing the South Africans to scamper home with an over to spare.

Lance Klusener hits out to win the game for South Africa against Pakistan Super Six stage at Trent Bridge.
David Munden/Sportsline Photographic

hamstring strain with the inevitable consequence that he, too, was run out by his runner!

Enter Moin Khan to play one of those delightful cameos that he produces so often in the final overs of a one-day innings. His 63 came from only 56 deliveries, including 17 from the 47th over, bowled by the increasingly grumpy Allan Donald.

SHOAIB AKHTAR BOWLS AT 95MPH

To spectacular celebrations amongst the 15,000 crowd, Shoaib reduced South Africa to 19 for 2, registering 95mph on the Speedster and when Azhar Mahmood nipped out Jonty Rhodes for a duck, South Africa were 58 for 5.

However, there was plenty of time in which to resurrect the innings and Kallis – with help from Pollock – inched South Africa towards a position from which Klusener could launch an attack. That

ZIMBABWE V. NEW ZEALAND

6 and 7 June at Headingley, Leeds
No result

Remarkably, this was the only wash-out of the World Cup which dealt a cruel blow to New Zealand's hopes of reaching the semi-finals. The weather deteriorated throughout the first day to the extent that Zimbabwe's innings was not completed until 5.45pm. Geoff Allott, in capturing his 18th victim, equalled the record for most wickets in the World Cup, and apart from a stand of 91 between Campbell and Goodwin for the fourth wicket, Zimbabwe's batting was uninspired.

New Zealand, mindful of the poor forecast, set off at a rate of knots to reach 70 for 3 after 15 overs. At this point, the rain became heavier and did not abate at all the following day. Both teams took away a consolation one point each.

INDIA V. PAKISTAN

8 June at Old Trafford, Manchester
India won by 47 runs
Man of the Match: BKV Prasad

Less than a fortnight after the Indian airforce had struck in the hotly disputed territory of Kashmir, the complicated – and combustible – business of

Rain eventually prevented a result in this game, New Zealand v. Zimbabwe at Headingley.
David Munden/Sportsline Photographic

subcontinental politics threatened to overshadow a meeting that is always one of the most eagerly anticipated in international cricket. In fact, those who happily wrote up the prospect of a mass riot at Old Trafford clearly misunderstand that the talk of aggression and hatred between India and Pakistan belongs to the politicians. The players, and also the asian cricket lovers based here, know and respect each other well enough to understand that while there is always a lot at stake when India and Pakistan play cricket, at the end of the day it is simply a game. Pakistani flags fluttered amongst those from India. A Mexican wave mid-afternoon united everyone on the terraces and if there ever was a true carnival of cricket in the World Cup, then this was it. Hopefully this was only the first of many more matches – even Tests? – between India and Pakistan to be played in England.

Tendulkar made his highest score of the tournament against serious opposition before precisely picking out Saqlain at longoff and Dravid completed another fifty before being

RIOT FEARS PROVE GROUNDLESS

NEW ZEALAND v. ZIMBABWE
6 and 7 June at Headingley, Leeds

ZIMBABWE

Batting				Bowling	O	M	R	W
NC Johnson	b Allott	25		Allott	10	1	24	3
GW Flower	run out (Home)	1		Nash	10	2	48	0
MW Goodwin	c Parore, b Harris	57		Larsen	10	0	27	1
*A Flower	c McMillan, b Allott	0		Cairns	6.3	2	24	3
ADR Campbell (capt)	c Nash, b Larsen	40		Harris	4	0	12	1
GJ Whittall	c Astle, b Allott	21		Astle	9	0	25	1
SV Carlisle	c McMillan, b Astle	2						
HH Streak	b Cairns	4		**Fall of Wickets**				
AR Whittall	c Astle, b Cairns	3		1–10, 2–35, 3–45, 4–136, 5–148,				
AG Huckle	c Twose, b Cairns	0		6–154, 7–163, 8–174, 9–174				
HK Olonga	not out	1						
	b 4, lb 11, w 3, nb 3	21						
	49.3 overs	**175**						

NEW ZEALAND

Batting				Bowling	O	M	R	W
MJ Horne	lbw, b GJ Whittall	35		Johnson	3	0	21	0
NJ Astle	c Streak, b Olonga	20		Streak	5	0	25	1
CD McMillan	lbw, b Streak	1		G J Whittall	3	0	9	1
SP Fleming (capt)	not out	9		Olonga	4	1	14	1
RG Twose	not out	0						
CL Cairns								
*AC Parore				**Fall of Wickets**				
CZ Harris				1–58, 2–59, 3–65				
DJ Nash								
GR Larsen								
GI Allott								
	lb 1, nb 4	5						
	15 overs (for 3 wickets)	**70**						

Umpires: DL Orchard & S Venkataraghavan
Man of the Match: nil

Match abandoned

INDIA v. PAKISTAN
8 June at Old Trafford, Manchester

INDIA

Batting				Bowling	O	M	R	W
SR Tendulkar	c Saqlain, b Azhar	45		Wasim Akram	10	0	27	2
S Ramesh	b Abdur Razzaq	20		Shoaib Akhtar	10	0	55	1
RS Dravid	c Shahid Afridi, b Wasim	61		Abdur Razzaq	10	0	41	1
AD Jadeja	c Inzamam, b Azhar	6		Azhar Mahmood	10	0	34	2
M Azharuddin (capt)	c Ijaz Ahmed, b Wasim	59		Saqlain Mushtaq	10	0	67	0
RR Singh	c Wasim, b Shoaib Akhtar	16						
*NR Mongia	not out	6		**Fall of Wickets**				
A Kumble				1–37, 2–95, 3–107, 4–158, 5–218,				
J Srinath				6–227				
BKV Prasad								
DS Mohanty								
	b 1, lb 3, w 8, nb 2	14						
	50 overs (for 6 wickets) 227							

PAKISTAN

Batting				Bowling	O	M	R	W
Saeed Anwar	c Azharuddin, b Prasad	36		Srinath	8	1	37	3
Shahid Afridi	c Kumble, b Srinath	6		Mohanty	10	2	31	0
Ijaz Ahmed	c Azharuddin, b Srinath	11		Prasad	9.3	2	27	5
Salim Malik	lbw, b Prasad	6		Kumble	10	0	43	2
Inzamam-ul-Haq	lbw, b Prasad	41		Singh	8	1	31	0
Azhar Mahmood	c Mongia, b Kumble	10						
*Moin Khan	c Tendulkar, b Prasad	33		**Fall of Wickets**				
Abdur Razzaq	b Srinath	11		1–19, 2–44, 3–52, 4–65, 5–78, 6–124,				
Wasim Akram (capt)	c Kumble, b Prasad	12		7–146, 8–175, 9–176				
Saqlain Mushtaq	lbw, b Kumble	0						
Shoaib Akhtar	not out	0						
	lb 12, w 2	14						
	45.3 overs	**180**						

Umpires: SA Bucknor & DR Shepherd
Man of the Match: BKV Prasad

India won by 47 runs

deceived by Wasim's slower ball. With his captaincy on the line – not to mention the threat of a hostile reception back home – Azharuddin took an age to get going. Finally, he was unshackled by a wild mow through mid-wicket and he reached 59 from 77 balls. India's 227 for 6 was only par but, bearing in mind the importance of the contest, they had the runs on the board.

INDIA REACH SEMI-FINALS

Pakistan set off with a flurry of fours, losing Afridi on their way to 34 for 1 in only five overs. But that quickly became 78 for 5, leaving Inzamam – who had an injured hand – and Moin to swing it around.

Moin made a rapid 34 before he was surprised by a swift bouncer from Prasad – his fourth wicket – and when the same bowler nipped out Wasim Akram for 12, fireworks exploded in the terraces.

AUSTRALIA V. ZIMBABWE

9 June at Lord's, London
Australia won by 44 runs
Man of the Match: NC Johnson

An astonishing all-round performance by Neil Johnson – fresh from his giant-killing activities against South Africa – threatened to overhaul Australia 16 years to the day since Zimbabwe first beat them in the 1983 World Cup.
At 153 for 1 after 28 overs, chasing – for Lord's – an unlikely 304 to win, Zimbabwe were wonderfully poised. Johnson, left-handed, was playing serenely – until cramp set in, that is – and Warne had been dispatched all over

headquarters. In the absence of England, the full house was firmly behind Zimbabwe to deal with the Aussies on their behalf, but Paul Reiffel returned to shoot down Zimbabwe's middle order and leave the admirable Johnson stranded on 132 not out.

Mark Waugh set the pace on a sunny morning with his fourth World Cup century – the first batsman to achieve that landmark. Ponting scored 36 at a run a ball and when the Waugh twins were together, the batting was electrifying: Mark straight-driving Strang with such power that the ball hit his brother flush on the helmet. Bevan and Moody both struck the ball cleanly at the end – Olonga conceded 62 runs from only seven overs – to leave Zimbabwe with an unlikely run chase.

> JOHNSON THE GIANT-KILLER THREATENS AUSSIE CHANCES

SOUTH AFRICA v. NEW ZEALAND

10 June at Edgbaston, Birmingham
South Africa won by 74 runs
Man of the Match: JH Kallis

One of the best pitches of the tournament produced the second-highest partnership in any World Cup. Kirsten and Gibbs put on 176 to give South Africa a wonderful launch pad. Klusener, with the small matter of 400 one-day runs behind him without having been dismissed, was duly promoted to number three to create absolute mayhem. However, he was undone by the nagging Gavin Larsen – bowled for 4 – and South Africa were left to rely on Kallis and Cronje to drive home the advantage.

AUSTRALIA v. ZIMBABWE
9 June at Lord's, London

AUSTRALIA

Batting				Bowling	O	M	R	W
*AC Gilchrist	lbw, b Johnson	10		Johnson	8	0	43	2
ME Waugh	c Goodwin, b Johnson	104		Streak	10	0	50	0
RT Ponting	b Olonga	36		Olonga	7	0	62	1
DS Lehmann	retired hurt	6		GJ Whittall	4	0	24	1
SR Waugh (capt)	b GJ Whittall	62		Strang	10	1	47	0
MG Bevan	not out	37		AR Whittall	8	1	51	0
TM Moody	not out	20		GW Flower	3	0	20	0
SK Warne								
DW Fleming								
PR Reiffel				**Fall of Wickets**				
GD McGrath				1–18, 2–74, 3–226, 4–248				
	lb 6, w 13, nb 9	28						
	50 overs (for 4 wickets) 303							

ZIMBABWE

Batting				Bowling	O	M	R	W
NC Johnson	not out	132		McGrath	10	1	33	1
GW Flower	lbw, b McGrath	21		Fleming	10	0	46	0
MW Goodwin	c Moody, b Bevan	47		Warne	9	0	55	1
*A Flower	c Gilchrist, b Reiffel	0		Reiffel	10	0	55	3
ADR Campbell (capt)	c Fleming, b Reiffel	17		Moody	6	0	38	0
GJ Whittall	c ME Waugh, b Reiffel	0		Bevan	5	1	26	1
DP Viljoen	st Gilchrist, b Warne	5						
HH Streak	not out	18						
PA Strang				**Fall of Wickets**				
AR Whittall				1–39, 2–153, 3–154, 4–188, 5–189,				
HK Olonga				6–200				
	lb 6, w 13	19						
	50 overs (for 6 wickets) 259							

Umpires: DB Cowie & RE Koertzen
Man of the Match: NC Johnson

Australia won by 44 runs

NEW ZEALAND v. SOUTH AFRICA
10 June at Edgbaston, Birmingham

SOUTH AFRICA

Batting				Bowling	O	M	R	W
G Kirsten	c Nash, b Astle	82		Allott	10	0	42	1
HH Gibbs	b Allott	91		Nash	8	0	44	0
L Klusener	b Larsen	4		Cairns	7	0	55	1
JH Kallis	not out	53		Larsen	9	0	47	1
DJ Cullinan	c and b Cairns	0		Harris	10	0	59	0
WJ Cronje (Capt)	run out (Nash)	39		Astle	6	0	29	1
JN Rhodes	not out	0						
SM Pollock								
*MV Boucher				**Fall of Wickets**				
S Elworthy				1–176, 2–187, 3–228, 4–229, 5–283				
AA Donald								
	lb 11, w 3, nb 4	18						
	50 overs (for 5 wickets) 287							

NEW ZEALAND

Batting				Bowling	O	M	R	W
MJ Home	c Pollock, b Kallis	12		Pollock	10	1	29	1
NJ Astle	c Cullinan, b Kallis	9		Kallis	6	2	15	2
CD McMillan	c Gibbs, b Cronje	23		Elworthy	8	0	35	0
SP Fleming (Capt)	c Pollock, b Cronje	42		Donald	10	0	42	0
RG Twose	c Cronje, b Klusener	35		Klusener	9	0	46	2
CL Cairns	b Klusener	17		Cronje	7	0	37	2
AC Parore	run out (Kirsten/Boucher)	3						
CZ Harris	not out	27						
DJ Nash	b Pollock	9		**Fall of Wickets**				
GR Larsen	not out	13		1–20, 2–34, 3–93, 4–107, 5–144,				
GI Allott				6–148, 7–171, 8–194				
	lb 9, w 11, nb 3	23						
	50 overs (for 8 wickets) 213							

Umpires: ID Robinson & S Venkataraghavan
Man of the Match: JH Kallis

South Africa won by 74 runs

Gary Kirsten and Herschell Gibbs made an opening partnership of 176 for South Africa against New Zealand at Edgbaston.

David Munden/Sportsline Photographic

ZIMBABWE v. PAKISTAN

11 June at The Oval, London
Pakistan won by 148 runs
Man of the Match: Saeed Anwar

The size of Zimbabwe's defeat really put their ability into context. Their wins over a demotivated South Africa and an erratic India in the qualifying stage had rewarded them with four points in the Super Sixes and, clearly, this was an absurdity. They were unfortunate in this contest in that only four of their players were fit enough to practise the day before, and Neil Johnson was unable to bowl in the match. He was missed, dreadfully, as the left-handed Saeed Anwar found his form in the most delightful manner. His 103 came from 144 balls and contained 11 wristy boundaries.

PAKISTAN v. ZIMBABWE
11 June at The Oval, London

PAKISTAN

Batting				Bowling	O	M	R	W
Saeed Anwar	c A Flower, b Olonga	103		Streak	10	0	63	2
Wajahatullah Wasti	c Huckle, b Whittall	40		Mbangwa	8	0	28	0
Ijaz Ahmed	run out (Goodwin/A Flower)	5		Whittall	8	1	39	1
Inzamam-ul-Haq	st A Flower, b Strang	21		Olonga	5	0	38	2
Wasim Akram (capt)	lbw, b Huckle	0		Huckle	10	0	43	1
*Moin Khan	run out (GW Flower)	13		GW Flower	2	0	13	0
Shahid Afridi	c Johnson, b Olonga	37		Strang	7	0	38	1
Azhar Mahmood	c A Flower, b Streak	2						
Abdur Razzaq	b Streak	0						
Saqlain Mushtaq	not out	17		**Fall of Wickets**				
Shoaib Akhtar	not out	1		1–95, 2–116, 3–183, 4–194, 5–195,				
	b 6, lb 3, w 20, nb 3	32		6–228, 7–231, 8–231, 9–260				

50 overs (for 9 wickets) 271

ZIMBABWE

Batting				Bowling	O	M	R	W
NC Johnson	lbw, b Azhar Mahmood	54		Wasim Akram	6	1	23	0
GW Flower	b Shoaib Akhtar	2		Shoaib Akhtar	7	1	22	2
MW Goodwin	c Shahid Afridi, b Azhar	4		Abdur Razzaq	9	1	25	3
*A Flower	b Abdur Razzaq	4		Saqlain Mushtaq	6.3	2	16	3
ADR Campbell (capt)	c Wasim, b Abdur Razzaq	3		Shahid Afridi	4	0	20	0
GJ Whittall	c Shahid Afridi, b Azhar	16		Azhar Mahmood	8	1	14	2
HH Streak	not out	16						
PA Strang	c Azhar, b Shoaib Akhtar	5						
HK Olonga	st Moin, b Saqlain Mushtaq	5		**Fall of Wickets**				
AG Huckle	st Moin, b Saqlain Mushtaq	0		1–12, 2–28, 3–46, 4–50, 5–83, 6–95,				
M Mbangwa	lbw, b Saqlain Mushtaq	0		7–110, 8–123, 9–123				
	lb 3, w 7, nb 4	14						

40.3 overs 123

Umpires: SA Bucknor & DL Orchard
Man of the Match: Saeed Anwar

Pakistan won by 148 runs

Kallis then took the new ball, underlining the progress he has made in the past year, and accounted for both New Zealand openers within the first 12 overs. With Klusener coming on to bowl third change, South Africa's attack had remarkable depth and New Zealand's batsmen simply could not impose themselves. Fleming made a stylish 42 and Twose 35 but only one New Zealander will look back on the game with any affection: Geoff Allott. When he bowled Herschelle Gibbs for 91, he claimed his 19th wicket of the tournament, a new World Cup record.

> **KIRSTEN AND GIBBS PUT ON 176**

INDIA v. NEW ZEALAND
12 June at Trent Bridge, Nottingham

INDIA

Batting				Bowling	O	M	R	W
SR Tendulkar	b Nash		16	Allott	10	1	33	1
SC Ganguly	b Allott		29	Nash	10	1	57	1
RS Dravid	c Fleming, b Cairns		29	Cairns	10	0	44	2
AD Jadeja	c Parore, b Cairns		76	Larsen	10	0	40	1
M Azharuddin (capt)	c Parore, b Larsen		30	Astle	7	0	49	0
RR Singh	run out (Fleming/Cairns)		27	Harris	3	0	16	0
J Srinath	not out		6					
*NR Mongia	not out		3	**Fall of Wickets**				
A Kumble				1–26, 2–71, 3–97, 4–187, 5–241,				
BKV Prasad				6–243				
DS Mohanty								
	b 4, lb 8, w 13, nb 10		35					
	50 overs (for 6 wickets)		**251**					

NEW ZEALAND

Batting				Bowling	O	M	R	W
MJ Horne	run out (sub N Chopra)		74	Srinath	10	1	49	1
NJ Astle	c Dravid, b Mohanty		26	Mohanty	10	0	41	2
CD McMillan	c Dravid, b Srinath		6	Prasad	10	0	44	0
SP Fleming (capt)	c Mongia, b Mohanty		15	Singh	4	0	27	1
RG Twose	not out		60	Ganguly	2	0	15	0
CL Cairns	c Kumble, b Singh		11	Kumble	9.2	0	48	0
*AC Parore	not out		26	Tendulkar	3	0	14	0
CZ Harris								
DJ Nash				**Fall of Wickets**				
GR Larsen				1–45, 2–60, 3–90, 4–173, 5–218				
GI Allott								
	b 4, lb 11, w 16, nb 4		35					
	48.2 overs (for 5 wickets)		**253**					

Umpires: DB Hair & DR Shepherd
Man of the Match: RG Twose

New Zealand won by five wickets

Zimbabwe's bowlers found some control in mid-innings as Ijaz, Wasim and Moin departed cheaply, but Afridi launched a blistering counter-attack. One of his two sixes sailed over the unlikely position of extra cover (a huge hit at The Oval). Heath Streak, playing in his 81st one-day international, bowled Razzaq for a duck to claim his 100th wicket, but Zimbabwe's celebrations were muted: they knew they had a stiff target to chase in order to stay in the World Cup.

Shoaib tore in from the Vauxhall End, smashing Johnson's helmet and then demolishing Grant Flower's stumps. Razzaq claimed three cheap wickets; Zimbabwe were suddenly 50 for 4 and out of the contest.

Just as Zimbabwe's lower order threatened to bore everyone rigid by batting to preserve their run-rate, Saqlain nipped out Olonga, Huckle and Mbangwa with successive deliveries. The hat-trick ended the match and Pakistan marched imperiously into the semi-finals.

INDIA v. NEW ZEALAND

12 June at Trent Bridge, Nottingham
New Zealand won by five wickets
Man of the Match: RG Twose

New Zealand had been widely tipped before the tournament as a likely 'dark horse'. Not everyone agreed with this: the England coach, David Lloyd, now restored to his previous existence in a commentary box, observed sagely that 'if Nathan Astle's a bowler, my backside's a fire engine!' It was a curious statement, but one that possibly underlined the general feeling that New Zealand were dangerously underrated.

The Australians certainly did not feel comfortable with that assessment. New Zealand's victory against an Indian team that was playing merely in order to try to appease the hostile mob that was already awaiting their return to Delhi Airport meant that Australia would be knocked out if they lost to South Africa the following day.

The pitch was good and the ground packed with Indian supporters who, much to the chagrin of the public-address announcer, made a lot of noise and enjoyed themselves. India batted solidly, bolstered by an attractive 76 from Jadeja, 30 from Azharuddin and a lively 27 from Robin Singh: 251 for 6 was competitive.

At 90 for 3, and with Astle, McMillan and Fleming all dismissed, the noise of banging drums inside Trent Bridge was deafening. However, Horne was joined by that most obdurate of characters, Roger Twose, and the pair, with a stand of 83, set about wrecking India's party. Horne was eventually run out by the substitute, Chopra, and when Cairns was caught for 11, India still had hope. However, Parore scampered 26 from 14 balls to take New Zealand into the semi-finals with five wickets and eight deliveries to spare.

NEW ZEALAND STORM INTO THE SEMIS

SOUTH AFRICA v. AUSTRALIA

13 June at Headingley, Leeds
Australia won by five wickets
Man of the Match: SR Waugh

Steve Waugh is a man who revels in the direst of dire situations. How many times has he performed a heroic rescue act when his team most needed it?

Adam Parore is lifted by Roger Twose to celebrate the Kiwi win, New Zealand v. India at Trent Bridge.
David Munden/Sportsline Photographic

Steve Waugh jumps for joy at the end of the game. Waugh was Man of the Match with an innings of 120. Australia v. South Africa at Headingley.

David Munden/Sportsline Photographic

And yet, this innings would have to rank in his top five most notable achievements, not least because his team would have been knocked out of the World Cup without it.

Australia were chasing a sizeable target: 272 to win. Herschelle Gibbs probably had his eye on the Man of the Match award (he made a very good 101) when Steve Waugh strode out to bat with Australia floundering on 48 for 3. Mark Waugh had been run out by Boje for 5, Gilchrist was defeated by Elworthy and Damien Martyn strolled

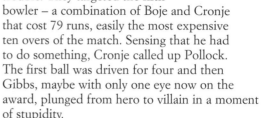

past the incoming captain having made only 11. South Africa were ecstatic.

However, Waugh and Ponting decided to slog their way out of trouble. They targeted the fifth bowler – a combination of Boje and Cronje that cost 79 runs, easily the most expensive ten overs of the match. Sensing that he had to do something, Cronje called up Pollock. The first ball was driven for four and then Gibbs, maybe with only one eye now on the award, plunged from hero to villain in a moment of stupidity.

Waugh, on 58, clipped a straightforward offering to Gibbs at mid-wicket who caught the ball, but in trying to hurl it skywards in celebration, let it slip through his fingers. The catch had not been

AUSTRALIA v. SOUTH AFRICA
13 June at Headingley, Leeds

SOUTH AFRICA

Batting				Bowling	O	M	R	W
G Kirsten	c Ponting, b Reiffel		21	McGrath	10	0	49	1
HH Gibbs	b McGrath		101	Fleming	10	0	57	3
DJ Cullinan	b Warne		50	Reiffel	9	0	47	1
WJ Cronje (capt)	lbw, b Warne		0	Moody	8	1	56	0
JN Rhodes	c M E Waugh, b Fleming		39	Warne	10	1	33	2
L Klusener	c Warne, b Fleming		36	Bevan	3	0	22	0
SM Pollock	b Fleming		3					
*MV Boucher	not out		0	Fall of Wickets				
N Boje				1-45, 2-140, 3-141, 4-219, 5-250,				
S Elworthy				6-271, 7-271				
AA Donald								
	lb 7, w 8, nb 6		21					
	50 overs (for 7 wickets)		271					

AUSTRALIA

Batting				Bowling	O	M	R	W
ME Waugh	run out (Boje/Boucher)		5	Pollock	9.4	0	45	0
*AC Gilchrist	b Elworthy		5	Elworthy	10	1	46	2
RT Ponting	c Donald, b Klusener		69	Donald	10	0	43	0
DR Martyn	c Boje, b Elworthy		11	Klusener	10	0	53	1
SR Waugh (capt)	not out		120	Cronje	7	0	50	1
MG Bevan	c Cullinan, b Cronje		27	Boje	3	0	29	0
TM Moody	not out		15					
SK Warne				Fall of Wickets				
PR Reiffel				1-6, 2-20, 3-48, 4-174, 5-247				
DW Fleming								
GD McGrath								
	lb 6, w 7, nb 7		20					
	49.4 overs (for 5 wickets)		272					

Umpires: S Venkataraghavan & P Willey
Man of the Match: SR Waugh

Australia won by five wickets

controlled and Waugh earned a reprieve that was to win Australia the match. Ponting fell for 69 but Bevan and Moody sustained the momentum. Waugh hit the winning run to remain undefeated on 120 from only 110 balls.

SUPER SIX TABLE

	P	W	L	NR	Pts	NRR
Pakistan	5	3	2	0	6	+0.65
Australia	5	3	2	0	6	+0.37
South Africa	5	3	2	0	6	+0.17
New Zealand	5	2	2	1	5	−0.52
Zimbabwe	5	2	2	1	5	−0.79
India	5	1	4	0	2	−0.15

The top four teams qualify for the semi-finals.

Shoaib Akhtar celebrates taking the wicket of Nathan Astle, Pakistan v. New Zealand semi-final at Old Trafford.
David Munden/Sportsline Photographic

SEMI-FINALS

PAKISTAN V. NEW ZEALAND

16 June at Old Trafford, Manchester
Pakistan won by nine wickets
Man of the Match: Shoaib Akhtar

New Zealand's captain, Stephen Fleming, could hardly believe his luck when he won the toss. Wasim Akram's game-plan throughout the tournament had been to bat first, and then unleash his pacemen. On the two previous occasions that Pakistan had batted second and exposed themselves to the pressures of chasing runs, they had lost. So it was an absolute certainty that New Zealand would bat first, and they threatened to make a reasonable fist of it. In fact, just one man came between New Zealand and a large total: the most glamourous figure in the World Cup, Shoaib Akhtar.

He charged in, hair flopping, like a man possessed. There is absolutely nothing subtle about his run-up, he simply gets his head down and sprints the 35 metres, or so, as fast as he possibly can. When

NEW ZEALAND v. PAKISTAN
16 June at Old Trafford, Manchester

PAKISTAN

Batting				Bowling	O	M	R	W
Saeed Anwar	not out		113	Wasim Akram	10	0	45	2
Wajahatullah Wasti	c Fleming, b Cairns		84	Shoaib Akhtar	10	0	55	3
Ijaz Ahmed	not out		28	Abdur Razzaq	10	0	28	2
Inzamam-ul-Haq				Azhar Mahmood	8	0	32	0
Abdur Razzaq				Saqlain Mushtaq	8	0	36	0
*Moin Khan				Shahid Afridi	5	0	27	0
Wasim Akram (capt)								
Azhar Mahmood				Fall of Wickets				
Saqlain Mushtaq				1–20, 2–38, 3–58, 4–152, 5–176,				
Shahid Afridi				6–209, 7–211				
Shoaib Akhtar	lb 3, w 7, nb 7		17					
	47.1 overs (for 1 wicket)		242					

NEW ZEALAND

Batting				Bowling	O	M	R	W
MJ Home	b Abdur Razzaq		35	Allott	9	0	41	0
NJ Astle	b Shoaib Akhtar		3	Nash	5	0	34	0
CD McMillan	c Moin Khan, b Wasim		3	Larsen	10	0	40	0
SP Fleming (capt)	b Shoaib Akhtar		41	Cairns	8	0	33	1
RG Twose	c Ijaz, b Abdur Razzaq		46	Harris	6	0	31	0
CL Cairns	not out		44	Astle	7.3	0	41	0
CZ Harris	b Shoaib Akhtar		16	McMillan	2	0	19	0
*AC Parore	b Wasim Akram		0					
DJ Nash	not out		6	Fall of Wickets				
GR Larsen				1–194				
GI Allott								
	b 4, lb 14, w 17, nb 12		47					
	50 overs (for 7 wickets)		241					

Umpires: DB Hair & P Willey
Man of the Match: Shoaib Akhtar

Pakistan won by nine wickets

AUSTRALIA v. SOUTH AFRICA
17 June at Edgbaston, Birmingham

AUSTRALIA

Batting			Bowling	O	M	R	W
*AC Gilchrist	c Donald, b Kallis	20	Pollock	9.2	1	36	5
ME Waugh	c Boucher, b Pollock	0	Elworthy	10	0	59	0
RT Ponting	c Kirsten, b Donald	37	Kallis	10	2	27	1
DS Lehmann	c Boucher, b Donald	1	Donald	10	1	32	4
SR Waugh (capt)	c Boucher, b Pollock	56	Klusener	9	1	50	0
MG Bevan	c Boucher, b Pollock	65	Cronje	1	0	2	0
TM Moody	lbw, b Pollock	0					
SK Warne	c Cronje, b Pollock	18	Fall of Wickets				
PR Reiffel	b Donald	0	1–3, 2–54, 3–58, 4–68, 5–158, 6–158,				
DW Fleming	b Donald	0	7–207, 8–207, 9–207				
GD McGrath	not out	0					
	b 1, lb 6, w 3, nb 6	16					
	49.2 overs	213					

SOUTH AFRICA

Batting			Bowling	O	M	R	W
G Kirsten	b Warne	18	McGrath	10	0	51	1
HH Gibbs	b Warne	30	Fleming	8.4	1	40	1
DJ Cullinan	run out (Bevan)	6	Reiffel	8	0	28	1
WJ Cronje (capt)	c ME Waugh, b Warne	0	Warne	10	4	29	4
JH Kallis	c SR Waugh, b Warne	53	ME Waugh	8	0	37	0
JN Rhodes	c Bevan b Reiffel	43	Moody	5	0	27	0
SM Pollock	b Fleming	20					
L Klusener	not out	31	Fall of Wickets				
*MV Boucher	b McGrath	5	1–48, 2–53, 3–53, 4–61, 5–145,				
S Elworthy	run out (Reiffel/McGrath)	1	6–175, 7–183, 8–196, 9–198				
AA Donald	run out (ME Waugh/	0					
	Fleming/ Gilchrist)						
	lb 1, w 5	6					
	49.4 overs	213					

Umpires: DR Shepherd & S Venkataraghavan
Man of the Match: SK Warne

Match tied

he gets his yorkers right – as he did on this occasion – the result is a spectacular shattering of timber.

Nathan Astle was the first to have his stumps ripped out of the ground. Then Fleming, who had made a cultured 41, was cleaned up by a 92mph thunderbolt from round the wicket. Chris Harris was the third victim; blown away as he was quietly adding precious runs towards the end of the innings.

Pakistan's target seemed unlikely to stretch them, unless they messed up batting second for the third time. It did not happen. Saeed Anwar became only the third batsman to score back-to-back centuries in a World Cup; he and the stylish Wasti put on 194 for the first wicket to ensure that Pakistan's progress to the final was both serene and clinical.

SAEED ANWAR
HITS 3RD CENTURY

All that marred the occasion was another mindless pitch invasion towards the end.

AUSTRALIA V. SOUTH AFRICA

17 June at Edgbaston, Birmingham
Match tied (Australia reach final)
Man of the Match: SK Warne

Has there ever been a greater one-day match than this? Steve Waugh should know: he has played in more than 260 of them. 'It was the best game of cricket I ever played', he said afterwards. It should be noted that Australia had squeezed into the final on run-rate, and we will never know if Waugh's observation would have been quite so generous had it been South Africa who had squeezed through in the same heart-stopping manner.

South Africa had the match in the bag: no question. It had

With the scores level and three balls remaining Allan Donald is run out after a huge misunderstanding with Lance Klusener. Keeper Adam Gilchrist leads the celebrations joined by McGrath and Moody. Australia v. South Africa semi-final at Edgbaston.
David Munden/Sportsline Photographic

required some typically bruising Klusener blows to get them into that position, but the fact remained that with four balls of the match remaining – Klusener having hit the first two deliveries of the final over for fours – South Africa needed only one more run to win.

The third ball from Fleming cramped Klusener for room and as Donald, at the non-striker's end, backed up too far, Lehmann very nearly ran him out from mid-on. This seemed to unsettle Donald, for when Klusener toe-ended the next ball between bowler and mid-off, Donald turned and scuttled back into his crease, unaware that Klusener, head down, was charging down the pitch towards him. In the mayhem, Donald dropped his bat as Mark Waugh tossed the ball to Fleming. The bowler had to get the ball to the other end and

CRAZY RUN-OUT COSTS SOUTH AFRICA PLACE IN FINAL

to add to the terrible drama of it all, he pea-rolled the ball down the pitch. At some point, the ball rolled past the despairing Donald, who was desperately trying to scramble the winning run, and into Gilchrist's gloves. Donald was run out by ten yards.

Amidst the excitement of it all, it was impossible not to feel great pity for the dejected figure of Klusener, the man of the tournament, who had so nearly – in such spectacular style – rescued his team once again. This time, it was not to be.

Shane Warne was the difference between the two teams on this occasion. Defending 213 was not going to be straightforward, but his delivery to Gibbs, which spat from outside leg stump to hit the top of the off, was astonishing and, from that moment, the South Africans treated every delivery as if it were a hand grenade. Cricket can be a dreadfully cruel game at times, but also the most dramatic and gut-wrenching sport of all. This was a classic, but viewed by very few in the United Kingdom because of the short-sighted decision by the authorities to screen it exclusively on satellite television.

Adam Gilchrist starts to celebrate after Ijaz Ahmed is out, bowled by Shane Warne for 22. World Cup final at Lord's.

David Munden/Sportsline Photographic

WORLD CUP FINAL

AUSTRALIA V. PAKISTAN

20th June at Lord's, London
Australia won by nine wickets
Man of the Match: SK Warne

After the dizzy excitement created by the semi-final at Edgbaston, it was, perhaps, inevitable that the final would fail to live up to expectation. But what a crushing anticlimax it proved to be.

This is to take nothing away from Australia who confounded the critics by reaching the Super Six stage, let alone the final of the World Cup. All the investigations into the behaviour of the Pakistan players before the match were as irrelevant as they were crass and insulting. It is beyond me how anyone could believe that this match – and indeed the entire tournament – was not of absolute

Dejection on the faces of Pakistan players: Salim Malik, Moin Khan, and Wasim Akram after Pakistan failed to compete in the final.
David Munden/Sportsline Photographic

importance to each and every one of Wasim's team. As was the case in 1992, victory in the World Cup would have resulted in the players being rewarded far more handsomely by the government than any backstreet Bombay bookmaker could ever manage.

Australia were on a roll; riding the crest of a wave that could never break. Mark Waugh started the rot with a scintillating, diving catch to his right at slip to dismiss Wasti. Saeed Anwar followed immediately, dragging Fleming into his stumps and although Razzaq saw off McGrath, he soon drove a catch into the covers. On came Warne, and he captured the wickets that really mattered: Ijaz bowled on the back foot, Moin caught behind off a beauty, Afridi leg before sweeping and, finally, a dejected Wasim caught just inside the circle on the leg side. Warne took 4 for 33 and Pakistan were dismissed for 132 in only 39 overs. Lord's fell silent.

The Australian reply was ruthlessly efficient. Gilchrist saved his best 'till last, racing to 54 from only 36 balls as Shoaib recorded 96mph on the Speedster for the first time, and although Wasim nipped out Ponting, the

Shane Warne celebrates taking the wicket of Wasim Akram in the World Cup Final at Lord's.
David Munden/Sportsline Photographic

Aussies were unstoppable. Pakistan were overwhelmed in only the 21st over and Australia's celebrations began.

Theirs was a remarkable triumph, built on the return to form of two key performers, Glenn McGrath and Shane Warne who, by the end, was looking as dangerous as in his pre-operation days. Steve Waugh's leadership was as inspirational as it was uncompromising and Australia flew home in the knowledge that they are, unquestionably, the best team in the world in both one-day and Test cricket.

| AUSTRALIA'S TRIUMPH |

For the organisers, the World Cup had its moments. It was never going to be a 'carnival' – that was a silly concept dreamed up by marketing people who chose to ignore well-meaning advice on the likely cricketing conditions in May and early June. Had the final been a thriller, the tournament might have been viewed as a success. However, coupled with the disappointment of England's premature demise, then yes: six and a half out of ten would be a fair assessment.

AUSTRALIA v. PAKISTAN
19 June at Lord's, London

PAKISTAN

Batting

Saeed Anwar	b Fleming	15
Wajahatullah Wasti	c ME Waugh, b McGrath	1
Abdur Razzaq	c SR Waugh, b Moody	17
Ijaz Ahmed	b Warne	22
Inzamam-ul-Haq	c Gilchrist, b Reiffel	15
*Moin Khan	c Gilchrist, b Warne	6
Shahid Afridi	lbw, b Warne	13
Azhar Mahmood	c and b Moody	8
Wasim Akram (capt)	c SR Waugh, b Warne	8
Saqlain Mushtaq	c Ponting, b McGrath	0
Shoaib Akhtar	not out	2
	lb 10, w 13, nb 2	25
	39 overs	**132**

Bowling

	O	M	R	W
McGrath	9	3	13	2
Fleming	6	0	30	1
Reiffel	10	1	29	1
Moody	5	0	17	2
Warne	9	1	33	4

Fall of Wickets

1–21, 2–21, 3–68, 4–77, 5–91, 6–104, 7–113, 8–129, 9–129

AUSTRALIA

Batting

ME Waugh	not out	37
*AC Gilchrist	c Inzamam-ul-Haq, b Saqlain Mushtaq	54
RT Ponting	c Moin Khan, b Wasim Akram	24
DS Lehmann	not out	13
SR Waugh (capt)		
MG Bevan		
TM Moody		
SK Warne		
PR Reiffel		
DW Fleming		
GD McGrath		
	lb 1, w 1, nb 3	5
	20.1 overs (for 2 wickets)	**133**

Bowling

	O	M	R	W
Wasim Akram	8	1	41	1
Shoaib Akhtar	4	0	37	0
Abdur Razzaq	2	0	13	0
Azhar Mahmood	2	0	20	0
Saqlain Mushtaq	4.1	0	21	1

Fall of Wickets

1–75, 2–112

Umpires: SA Bucknor & DR Shepherd
Man of the Match: SK Warne

Australia won by eight wickets

Player of the Tournament: L Klusener (South Africa)

Shane Warne celebrates with the World Cup.
David Munden/Sportsline Photographic

SOUTH AFRICA

West Indies in South Africa
Supersport Series
South Africa Domestic One-Day Season
First-Class Averages

WEST INDIES IN SOUTH AFRICA
By Tony Cozier

It was supposed to be an event filled with social and political significance well beyond the boundary. Instead, West Indies' first full tour of South Africa ended in the most severe thrashing they had known and the embarrassment of betraying not only their own people's expectations but also those of the black townships and villages of their hosts.

The clinically efficient South Africans inflicted on them the kind of five-nil drubbing that was such a West Indian speciality in the heady days of the 1980s, the so-called 'blackwashes', and followed it with a six-one dominance in the one-day internationals.

'In the townships, where West Indian cricketers are considered heroes, there is great pain,' was the lament of Sir Conrad Hunte, the former West Indies opener who had spent seven years coaching in South Africa. 'Our friends feel very much let down.'

The tour was cursed from the start. Indeed, there was almost no start at all as West Indies cricket first had to sort out its most threatening crisis since the Kerry Packer affair.

For over a week, the disgruntled West Indies players remained encamped at a hotel at London's Heathrow Airport. Those en route from the Caribbean were joined by others who were in Bangladesh for the Wills International Cup and they refused to budge until the West Indies Cricket Board (WICB) sent its president, Pat Rousseau, to hear their grievances over pay and conditions.

The WICB's immediate reaction was to sack captain Brian Lara and vice-captain Carl Hooper and fine the others. It needed a personal plea from President Nelson Mandela himself, several days of negotiation with Rousseau and the reinstatement of Lara, Hooper and the rest before the tour finally, and belatedly, got underway.

The delay was the origin of the West Indian misery that was to follow. It meant that a preparatory training camp in Johannesburg had to be cancelled, a distinct setback. While West Indies were bickering in the chill of London, the South Africans were diligently getting ready for the challenge with a week's grounding in sunny Bloemfontein and planning appropriate strategy for their opponents, collectively and individually.

South Africa's impressive captain Hansie Cronje credited his team's efficient performance to such preparation. West Indies, on the other hand, were patently not ready, either mentally or physically.

They were also seriously inhibited by injuries. They had to replace the experienced Jimmy Adams and the leg-spinner Dinanath Ramnarine even before the series began and not a match went by for which a fully fit complement of 16 was available. Eventually, Barbados all-rounder Ottis Gibson had to be drafted in from his contract with provincial team, Griqualand West, for the fourth Test.

The contrast between the supremely fit, committed and fiercely competitive South Africans and their slack opponents was stark in every department with the exception of wicketkeeping where Ridley Jacobs, in his debut series, aged 31, stood out like a beacon from the West Indian gloom.

Even the heated media debate sparked by the assertion of sports minister, Steve Tshwete, that the continuation of a basically all-white national team was inappropriate almost a decade after the dismantling of apartheid, could not distract the South Africans.

Throughout, especially on the untrustworthy pitches of the first two Tests, they batted with the application and patience so blatantly lacking on the other side. Their lower order repeatedly provided them with valuable runs while the West Indies showed no interest in batting.

South Africa possessed critical all-round depth, most vividly typified by Jacques Kallis who compiled his 485 runs at an average of 69.28 and took his 17 wickets with lively pace at less than 18 each. In Allan Donald and Shaun Pollock they had two fast bowlers the equal of any in world cricket.

For the first time in their history, no West Indian managed a century in a full Test series. They were bowled out in all ten innings and never once passed 300, placing such strain on their bowlers that Curtly Ambrose and Courtney Walsh, their two great stalwarts, broke down more than once.

The performance went from bad to worse and the recriminations were immediate and inevitable on their return home, particularly directed at the beleaguered captain, Lara.

West Indies v. Nicky Oppenheimer's XI
10 November 1998 at Randjesfontein
Match cancelled

The usual tour opener was a victim of the West Indies players' strike in London, prompting a moan from the wealthy sponsor – hopefully, tongue in cheek – about the quantities of prawns, lobsters and strawberries that went to waste.

Gauteng Invitation XI v. West Indies
11 November 1998 at Elkah Oval, Soweto
West Indies 258 for 7
Gauteng Invitation XI did not bat
Match abandoned because of rain

Less than 24 hours after their controversially delayed arrival, the West Indies strutted their stuff on the solitary ground of South Africa's most infamous township against opponents including several graduates from the UCBSA's development programme. Lara and Hooper enjoyed themselves before rain came to spoil the party.

Griqualand West v. West Indies
14, 15, 16 and 17 November 1998 at De Beers Diamond Oval, Kimberley
Griqualand West 271 and 435 for 9
West Indies 466
Match drawn

There were early hints of the indifference that was to become an unpleasant feature of the West Indies throughout their tour. Centuries by Lara and Hooper and a promising start by Ganga earned them a lead of 195 and the match was theirs when Griquas began the final day 123 for 5, still trailing by 72. Their carelessness, and the absence of Walsh who turned his ankle in the first innings, allowed left-hander Brooker and wicketkeeper Bossinger to score maiden first-class hundreds, Symcox to blast 50 off 30 balls and the home team to earn a draw.

West Indies v. Free State
20, 21, 22 and 23 November 1998 at Springbok Park, Bloemfontein
West Indies 316 and 188
Free State 67 and 438 for 8
Free State won by two wickets

Free State won by two wickets, compiling the second-highest winning total in South African first-class cricket. They had been routed for 67 in their first innings by the speed and hostility of McLean whose 7 for 28 was his career-best. Cronje struck six sixes and 15 fours and an early psychological blow for the Tests to follow with an unbeaten 157 in a Free State record ninth-wicket stand of 135 with van der Wath. West Indies seemed unconcerned. While the labouring leg-spinner Ramnarine sent down 29 successive and ineffective overs with a dodgy shoulder, Ambrose and McLean were limited to the same number between them.

First Test
26, 27, 28, 29 and 30 November 1998 at Johannesburg

An even, engrossing contest, dominated by the high-quality fast bowlers on either side, proved a misleading preview to the remainder of the series. There were only seven runs in it on first innings but the type of top-order failure that was to become the norm undermined West Indies in their second and opened the way to South Africa's critical, if hard-fought, victory. It would become progressively easier for them.

A straw-coloured pitch they reckoned would progressively favour spin influenced West Indies into including the leg-spinner, Lewis – who arrived from the 'A' team tour of India two hours before the start as a replacement for Ramnarine – and into batting on winning the toss. Neither decision was vindicated for Pollock soon removed Lambert, Wallace and Lara within the first hour and Lewis only managed a solitary wicket from his 40.5 overs in the match.

After the initial fireworks that brought 53 runs, nine fours, three wickets and two dropped catches in the opening hour, the remainder of the match developed into more measured fare as batsmen battled for survival on a surface of unreliable bounce. Chanderpaul's first-day 74 was the match top score and, spread over four and a half hours, its longest stay but no one played better than Kallis for his two half-centuries.

Chanderpaul, as usual, thrived in the early crisis and steadied the West Indies in a partnership of contrasting styles and 91 runs with Hooper, using a runner after straining his groin while in single figures. The injury kept Hooper off the field throughout the South African first innings and demoted him to number seven second time round. It was a critical handicap for the tourists.

When Hooper went for 44 to a characteristic concentration lapse and Chanderpaul was becalmed after passing 50, Williams took the lead in a further stand of 45. But the patient South Africans snared all three before the total reached 200 and it was left to the lower order to get it up to 261. Fast and probing, Pollock and Donald deservedly shared eight wickets.

By the end of the second day, shortened by murky light, the West Indies total didn't seem so bad after all. The indomitable Walsh inspired a spirited performance that left South Africa 217 for 6 and the match in the balance. He claimed four crucial

wickets and his second, Kallis to Williams'
breathtaking slip catch, carried him past watching
coach Malcolm Marshall's West Indies record of
376 wickets in his 103rd Test.

Walsh kept going for 19.4 overs, oblivious to
either the humid heat or the tendinitis in his 36-
year-old right knee that had put his place in the
match in jeopardy. He conjured up a special for
Bacher in his second over but West Indies had
to wait another 33 overs, while the left-handed
Kirsten and Kallis added 92, before Walsh
intervened with his record-breaking wicket. It
was soon followed by another, as the tumbling
Jacobs snared Cullinan down the leg side.

Once through, West Indies kept eating away at
the South African order and it was left to Symcox to
distract them with his bold hitting and irritating
kidology and secure the narrow lead before lunch on
the third morning. Lambert and Wallace erased the
deficit before a seasonal high veldt storm arrived to
halt their progress.

It was now a second-innings contest and its
outcome was virtually settled on the fourth day
when the West Indies could raise only 170. This left
South Africa a mere 164 to take the lead in the
series but, before they could set out on their quest,
more thunder, lightning and rain sent them into the
final morning.

For West Indies, it was an opportunity
squandered. With the prospect of bowling on a last-
day pitch of deteriorating quality, 250 should have
been sufficient. They never looked like getting close
and the lively sound of the visiting Starlift steelband
from Trinidad seemed increasingly incongruous as
wickets fell at regular intervals.

They were choked by the penetration of Pollock
and Donald, which accounted for Wallace, Lara and
Chanderpaul for 38 inside the first 50 minutes, and
were never allowed to break free.

The pressure exerted by the disciplined South
Africans was reflected in the pedestrian progress of
normally free-scoring batsmen. Lambert needed
nearly three hours over 33 and then edged Symcox's
prodigious off-break to the keeper. The restricted
Hooper, again with a runner, spent two hours and
90 balls over 34 before Kallis had him leg before.
Jacobs was almost three hours compiling his resolute
top-score 42, only to fall to a slog off Symcox.

There was no wag in the tail this time, the last
three wickets tumbling in four balls. Two were to
Pollock who joined his father, Peter, now chief
selector, as the sixth South African with more than
100 Test wickets.

Jacques Kallis on the go in his undefeated innings of 57, in
the first Test. The non-striker is Shaun Pollock.
Gordon Brooks/Sportsline Photographic

Delayed by the weather, South Africa's batsmen
returned the next day to accumulate the modest 164
runs they needed. It took them almost four and a
half hours and West Indies made them fight all
the way. But they reached their goal five minutes
before tea.

Setting out on a hot, sunny day, the South
Africans needed nerves of steel and precise
judgement to overcome the threat of Walsh and
Ambrose on a troublesome pitch. Early problems
materialised when the openers fell in the first 40
minutes but once the two ageing fast bowlers were

FIRST TEST – SOUTH AFRICA v. WEST INDIES
26, 27, 28, 29 and 30 November 1998 at The Wanderers, Johannesburg

WEST INDIES

	First Innings		Second Innings	
CB Lambert	c Boucher, b Pollock	8	c Boucher, b Symcox	33
PA Wallace	b Pollock	16	b Pollock	14
BC Lara (capt)	b Pollock	11	lbw, b Donald	7
S Chanderpaul	lbw, b Donald	74	lbw, b Pollock	1
CL Hooper	c Cullinan, b Donald	44	(7) lbw, b Kallis	34
SC Williams	c Cronje, b Terbrugge	35	(5) c Kallis, b Terbrugge	12
*RD Jacobs	c Cronje, b Kallis	14	(6) c Terbrugge, b Symcox	42
NAM McLean	c Boucher, b Pollock	28	(9) c Cullinan, b Symcox	11
RN Lewis	c Terbrugge, b Donald	12	(8) lbw, b Pollock	10
CEL Ambrose	c Boucher, b Pollock	0	not out	0
CA Walsh	not out	5	lbw, b Pollock	0
	lb 7, w 2, nb 5	14	b 1, nb 5	6
		261		**170**

	First Innings				Second Innings			
	O	M	R	W	O	M	R	W
Donald	23	4	91	3	15	6	28	1
Pollock	23	4	54	5	20.3	4	49	4
Kallis	15	5	37	1	14	5	26	1
Terbrugge	16	5	32	1	14	5	23	1
Cronje	1	0	3	–				
Symcox	19	5	37	–	18	9	43	3

Fall of Wickets
1–17, 2–24, 3–41, 4–132, 5–177, 6–198, 7–235, 8–255, 9–255
1–24, 2–33, 3–38, 4–53, 5–80, 6–148, 7–148, 8–170, 9–170

SOUTH AFRICA

	First Innings		Second Innings	
G Kirsten	b McLean	62	c Jacobs, b Ambrose	7
AM Bacher	c Jacobs, b Walsh	1	c Wallace, b Walsh	6
JH Kallis	c Williams, b Walsh	53	not out	57
DJ Cullinan	c Jacobs, b Walsh	8	c Williams, b McLean	35
WJ Cronje (capt)	b Ambrose	41	c McLean, b Walsh	31
JN Rhodes	lbw, b McLean	17	c Jacobs, b Walsh	9
SM Pollock	b Walsh	11	c Chanderpaul, b Ambrose	9
*MV Boucher	c Lara, b Lewis	12	not out	1
PL Symcox	run out (Walsh)	25		
AA Donald	c Jacobs, b Ambrose	7		
DJ Terbrugge	not out	3		
	b 1, lb 5, w 1, nb 21	28	lb 2, nb 7	9
		268	(for 6 wickets)	**164**

	First Innings				Second Innings			
	O	M	R	W	O	M	R	W
Ambrose	28	5	63	2	15.4	3	42	2
Walsh	25	5	66	4	21	9	45	3
McLean	17	1	66	2	5	0	17	1
Lewis	23.5	4	67	1	17	4	45	–
Hooper					4	0	13	–

Fall of Wickets
1–10, 2–102, 3–111, 4–154, 5–185, 6–209, 7–229, 8–230, 9–243
1–14, 2–14, 3–58, 4–124, 5–146, 6–163

Umpires: CJ Mitchley & DR Shepherd
Toss: West Indies

South Africa won by four wickets

rested, Kallis held the effort together, remaining to the end while his partners sought to assert themselves.

Cullinan's aggression was ended by Williams' acrobatic mid-wicket catch and, at 58 for 3, South Africa needed captain Cronje's positive influence to counteract Lara's run-choking field-placing. Caught at silly mid-on when 17 off Ambrose's no-ball at 96 for 3, he eventually fell to a top-edged hook off the preserving Walsh but, by then, victory was only 40 runs distant.

Shaun Pollock is congratulated by Allan Donald on claiming his 100th Test wicket in the first Test.
Gordon Brooks/Sportsline Photographic

Even though Rhodes fell to Walsh and Pollock to Ambrose with score level, South Africa still had plenty in hand when Boucher formalised the result with a cut off Ambrose. The West Indies would not come so close again.

Border v. West Indies
4, 5 and 6 December 1998 at Buffalo Park, East London
Border 282 for 9 dec. and 340 for 8 dec.
West Indies 356
Match drawn

Lara went in number seven, Rose damaged his right shoulder so was unable to bowl or field during Border's second innings when Lambert and Chanderpaul shared 25 overs and the substitute Murray was allowed to keep wicket. It was certainly not the best preparation for 'don't-carish' West Indies on the eve of the second Test. Chanderpaul and Wallace had meaningful knocks and Dillon carned his Test place but those who enjoyed themselves most were on the other side – the opener Sugden, with 76 and 84, and the heavy-set Wiblin, with a robust, unbeaten, run-a-ball hundred in the second innings.

SECOND TEST
10, 11 and 12 December 1998 at Port Elizabeth

As the one-sided match hurtled towards its conclusion 35 minutes before tea on the third day, the resident brass band included an appropriate item in its repertoire. It chose the theme from 'Titanic' as, for the second time in the match, the West Indies were sunk without trace. The techniques and temperaments of their batsmen were exposed by the speed, movement and direction of Donald, Pollock, Terbrugge and Kallis on a well-grassed pitched and supported by unerring catching and sharp fielding.

Ambrose and Walsh replied in kind, sharing 15 of the 20 wickets, but McLean and Dillon could not provide what Terbrugge and Kallis did for Donald and Pollock. South Africa were twice on the ropes, at 142 for 7 on the first day, 53 for 5 on the second, but rallied each time as the overworked Ambrose and Walsh tired. West Indies were never allowed such a luxury.

Unlucky to lose Wallace who came down with glandular fever on the morning of the match, the West Indies had to further adjust their second-innings order when Williams wasn't well enough to

open. It was vital in the crisis for Lara to step forward to lead from the front. Instead, he dropped from number three to number five, by which time he could do nothing but flail around him for an electrifying, but meaningless, 39.

Stung by their shocking performance, manager Clive Lloyd summoned his players for an immediate post-mortem behind the doors of the dressing room that remained closed for two and a half hours. It wasn't difficult to imagine what was said.

Yet the West Indies started promisingly. Buoyed by the luck of the toss in overcast weather and on a pitch more identifiable as Headingley than Port Elizabeth, the perennial Walsh dispatched the new opener Gibbs, Kirsten and Kallis in his opening spell and Dillon yorked Cullinan so that South Africa lunched at 86 for 4. Ambrose had endured seven luckless overs in the morning but returned to remove the dangerous Rhodes to a slip catch sixth ball into the second session.

The depth of South Africa's batting now materialised. Pollock compiled 28 with more flair and assurance than anyone, dominating a stand of 49 with Cronje, but the revival seemed wasted when they were out within four runs of each other in mid-afternoon. At 142 for 7, Symcox, Test cricket's oldest, most talkative, combative and underestimated player, entered the type of situation he relishes.

It became more critical when Boucher fended a lifter from McLean to slip, but Symcox and Donald saw out the day at 223 for 8, carrying their ninth-wicket stand to 66 the next morning. Donald's highest Test score, 34, was a show of bravado sufficient to invigorate any dressing room and, by the close, South Africa had taken complete command.

Observing the full length and direct line required by a green, ball-marked surface, Pollock, Donald and Terbrugge dispatched West Indies in 37.3 overs for their lowest Test total since their 100 against New Zealand in Christchurch in 1987. The resultant lead was 124 and, in spite of the efforts of Ambrose and Walsh, it had been extended to 247 with half the second-innings wickets intact when fading light ended play with 11 overs remaining. Rhodes and Pollock were together in the highest partnership of the match after 17 wickets tumbled for 196 on the second day.

The left-handed Lambert set the tone for West Indies' demise with a loose drive to mid-off from Pollock's fifth ball. Donald again got Lara cheaply with a sharp, chest-high lifter parried to second slip, and when Terbrugge bowled Williams, Hooper and Jacobs, and Pollock claimed Chanderpaul leg before

SECOND TEST – SOUTH AFRICA v. WEST INDIES
10, 11 and 12 December at St George's Park, Port Elizabeth

SOUTH AFRICA

	First Innings		Second Innings	
G Kirsten	c Jacobs, b Walsh	29	c Jacobs, b Walsh	2
HH Gibbs	b Walsh	2	c Lambert, b Ambrose	4
JH Kallis	c Hooper, b Walsh	30	c Jacobs, b Ambrose	3
DJ Cullinan	b Dillon	4	c Lambert, b Walsh	10
WJ Cronje (capt)	run out (Reifer)	21	run out (Chanderpaul)	24
JN Rhodes	c Hooper, b Ambrose	17	b Ambrose	64
SM Pollock	c Williams, b Ambrose	28	c Dillon, b Ambrose	42
*MV Boucher	c Hooper, b McLean	17	c Hooper, b Ambrose	1
PL Symcox	b McLean	36	c Lambert, b Ambrose	16
AA Donald	c Hooper, b Walsh	33	b Walsh	11
DJ Terbrugge	not out	2	not out	3
	b 4, lb 7, w 1, nb 14	26	b 1, lb 5, nb 9	15
		245		**195**

	First Innings				Second Innings			
	O	M	R	W	O	M	R	W
Ambrose	17	6	28	2	19	4	51	6
Walsh	23.4	0	86	4	23.5	5	58	3
McLean	19	4	66	2	5	0	19	-
Dillon	11	1	54	1	9	2	26	-
Hooper					7	0	35	-

Fall of Wickets
1–6, 2–52, 3–67, 4–67, 5–89, 6–138, 7–142, 8–175, 9–241
1–5, 2–9, 3–11, 4–47, 5–53, 6–145, 7–151, 8–173, 9–183

WEST INDIES

	First Innings		Second Innings	
SC Williams	b Terbrugge	37	(8) lbw, b Donald	8
CB Lambert	c Cronje, b Pollock	0	(1) c Boucher, b Donald	2
BC Lara (capt)	c Cullinan, b Donald	4	(5) c Kirsten, b Donald	39
CL Hooper	b Terbrugge	15	run out (Cronje)	8
S Chanderpaul	lbw, b Pollock	4	(2) c Kallis, b Pollock	16
*RD Jacobs	b Terbrugge	1	(3) lbw, b Kallis	22
FL Reifer	c Boucher, b Pollock	0	(6) c Cullinan, b Donald	9
NAM McLean	c Cronje, b Donald	31	(7) run out (Cronje/Boucher)	1
CEL Ambrose	b Pollock	12	c Pollock, b Donald	16
MV Dillon	c Rhodes, b Pollock	9	b Pollock	9
CA Walsh	not out	2	not out	0
	lb 1, nb 5	6	lb 2, nb 9	11
		121		**141**

	First Innings				Second Innings			
	O	M	R	W	O	M	R	W
Donald	10	1	33	2	14.2	5	49	5
Pollock	13.3	2	43	5	13	1	46	2
Terbrugge	9	4	27	3	5	1	27	-
Kallis	3	1	8	-	6	2	17	1
Symcox	2	0	9	-				

Fall of Wickets
1–0, 2–31, 3–58, 4–63, 5–64, 6–67, 7–75, 8–103, 9–112
1–3, 2–39, 3–53, 4–57, 5–68, 6–69, 7–77, 8–132, 9–141

Umpires: RE Koertzen & DR Shepherd
Toss: West Indies

South Africa won by 178 runs

Allan Donald celebrates the dismissal of Stuart Williams leg before on 8, in the second Test.
Gordon Brooks/Sportsline Photographic

on the back foot, four wickets had fallen for nine, it was 67 for 6 and there was no way back.

The giant left-handed McLean hit with the force, and style, of a lumberjack, hoisting four long sixes in 31 off 12 balls, but it was a brief interlude and Pollock took care of the tail to finish with five wickets in a Test innings for the seventh time.

Ambrose and Walsh immediately struck back, removing Gibbs, Kirsten and Kallis for 11. Cullinan and Cronje steadied things for a while until Cullinan popped a close catch off Walsh and Cronje was run out for the second time in the match. West Indies could see a glimmer of hope but Rhodes and Pollock snuffed it out as their support bowling staff was found wanting.

It was only when the two stalwarts returned refreshed on the third morning that wickets fell again, the last five for 52. Ambrose added four to his previous two, the 21st time in his great career he

Pat Symcox top edges Nixon McLean in his first innings of 36, second Test.
Gordon Brooks/Sportsline Photographic

had accounted for more than half the opposition. In the process, he also lit a fire in Donald, pole-axing him for a few anxious moments with a bouncer that cracked him on the side of the head.

Treated with an ice pack and recovered from his blow, Donald remained to be last out. He then returned to deliver several explosive blasts of his own as West Indies capitulated, fittingly completing the victory with his fifth wicket, a vengeful bouncer that Ambrose could only fend off into the slips.

Only Chanderpaul, shifted upwards to open in Williams' absence, lasted more than 50 balls as Donald, Pollock and Kallis sliced through the butter-soft batting. The schoolboyish run-outs of

Hooper and McLean accelerated the end and heightened the embarrassment.

It meant that Lara was stranded with only Ambrose, Dillon and Walsh as partners and, after restricting himself to a single off his first 22 balls, he unleashed a volley of strokes that brought him 38 off his next 27, among them a six and six fours, most off Donald. It was only the flailing of a dying innings and, once Lara's miscued pull provided Donald with another wicket, the tail-enders did not unduly delay South African celebrations – and West Indian recriminations.

West Indies v. Eastern Province
2 December 1998 at Dan Qeqe Stadium, Zwide
West Indies 239 for 8 (46 overs)
Eastern Province 209 for 6 (38.1 overs)
Eastern Province won on a faster scoring rate

Even though the result was decided by the calculator, this was another embarrassment for West Indies in the second of their township matches. The left-handed Reifer, the replacement for Adams, top scored in his first innings on tour and Wallace cracked a half-century but the remainder of the batting was disappointing. Grace and Kemp, the province's two young batsmen, added 118 for the third wicket that was the basis for the combined team's win.

KwaZulu-Natal v. West Indies
17 December at Chatsworth Oval
KwaZulu-Natal 120 (39.4 overs)
West Indies 123 for 2 (25.3 overs)
West Indies won by eight wickets

West Indies' first victory of the tour was comfortably achieved before a crowd of 10,000 that filled every vantage point of the ground in the mainly Indian district of Durban. Only Hudson, the former Test opener, batted with any assurance for the home side on a tricky pitch. Lambert and Murray virtually settled the issue by adding 100 for the first wicket.

South Africa 'A' v. West Indies
19, 20, 21 and 22 December 1998 at Alexandra Oval, Pietermartizburg
West Indies 375 and 95 for 3
South Africa 'A' 293
Match drawn

Only Chanderpaul got any satisfaction from an unsatisfactory match at the beautiful old Alexandra Park ground. His 182 occupied six hours and 20 minutes over the first three days as rain, poor light and overcautious umpires restricted play. In keeping with tradition, Chanderpaul planted a tree in the park, as all visiting century-makers have done through the years. Klusener went through his first major match since foot surgery with no ill effects.

THIRD TEST
26, 27, 28, 29 December 1998 at Durban

West Indies adopted desperate measures for their desperate situation. They rung five changes but these made no difference. South Africa, confident and settled, secured the series midway through the fourth day with their eleven from Port Elizabeth.

Once again, the decisive factor was West Indies' flimsy batting that twice blew promising positions.

Brian Lara drives Terbrugge in his innings of 51, third Test.
Gordon Brooks/Sportsline Photographic

In spite of an encouraging start from Wallace and Murray, their ninth opening pair in two years, and a half-century from Lara, they could only muster 198 after being sent in on a dank, overcast opening day. After Rose's seven wickets and spectacular run-out of Cullinan limited South Africa's lead to 114, Chanderpaul and Lara were building a challenging lead in a second-innings stand of 160 when the first of two breathtaking catches by Gibbs removed Lara and triggered a familiar slide.

Donald and Pollock swept aside the last eight wickets for 58 and left their opponents so broken they simply went through the motions as South Africa comfortably accumulated 147 to win the match. West Indian misery was compounded by the sight of Walsh, their oldest and most faithful campaigner, stretchered off the field in the closing stages after tearing his left hamstring.

The course of the match was established when both openers and the promoted Chanderpaul fell for seven runs after Wallace and Murray had occupied the first hour adding 50. There was no significant recovery and, even though the floodlights were

Franklyn Rose celebrates the dismissal of Allan Donald to give him career-best figures of 7 for 84, in the third Test.
Gordon Brooks/Sportsline Photographic

THIRD TEST – SOUTH AFRICA v. WEST INDIES
26, 27, 28 and 29 December at Kingsmead, Durban

WEST INDIES

	First Innings		Second Innings	
PA Wallace	c Cullinan, b Kallis	21	c Boucher, b Donald	1
JR Murray	lbw, b Terbrugge	29	c Gibbs, b Kallis	29
S Chanderpaul	c Boucher, b Kallis	4	c and b Pollock	75
BC Lara (capt)	c Cronje, b Terbrugge	51	c Gibbs, b Terbrugge	79
CL Hooper	c Cullinan, b Kallis	10	c Boucher, b Pollock	2
D Ganga	b Pollock	28	c Gibbs, b Pollock	5
*RD Jacobs	b Cronje	39	not out	15
RN Lewis	c Cullinan, b Cronje	0	c Boucher, b Donald	0
FA Rose	c Kallis, b Cronje	6	c Gibbs, b Pollock	22
CEL Ambrose	run out (Rhodes)	0	c Cronje, b Pollock	5
CA Walsh	not out	0	b Donald	3
	lb 5, nb 5	10	lb 12, w 2, nb 9	23
		198		**259**

	First Innings				Second Innings			
	O	M	R	W	O	M	R	W
Donald	13.4	1	55	–	20.2	4	62	3
Pollock	23.2	8	45	1	27	6	83	5
Terbrugge	12	2	39	2	13	4	28	1
Kallis	10	3	18	3	10	1	31	1
Symcox	8	1	17	–	12	3	43	–
Cronje	4.1	0	19	3				

Fall of Wickets
1–50, 2–52, 3–57, 4–105, 5–133, 6–178, 7–179, 8–185, 9–186
1–17, 2–41, 3–201, 4–201, 5–204, 6–213, 7–214, 8–245, 9–252

SOUTH AFRICA

	First Innings		Second Innings	
G Kirsten	c Hooper, b Rose	26	not out	71
HH Gibbs	c Wallace, b Rose	35	lbw, b Hooper	49
JH Kallis	c Jacobs, b Rose	11	not out	23
DJ Cullinan	run out (Rose/Jacobs)	40		
WJ Cronje (capt)	b Walsh	30		
JN Rhodes	c and b Walsh	87		
SM Pollock	c Hooper, b Rose	30		
*MV Boucher	b Rose	0		
PL Symcox	b Rose	12		
AA Donald	b Rose	13		
DJ Terbrugge	not out	2		
	b 4, lb 8, w 1, nb 13	26	lb 1, nb 3	4
		312		**147**

	First Innings				Second Innings			
	O	M	R	W	O	M	R	W
Ambrose	17	1	60	–	4	0	16	–
Walsh	29	6	68	2	4	1	6	–
Rose	28	6	84	7	9	0	31	–
Lewis	20	2	70	–	12.4	0	43	–
Hooker	4	0	18	–	19	4	50	1

Fall of Wickets
1–57, 2–79, 3–80, 4–140, 5–182, 6–262, 7–262, 8–284, 9–295
1–97

Umpires: DL Orchard & RB Tiffin
Toss: South Africa

South Africa won by nine wickets

activated just after tea so play could continue, the late-order West Indians still seemed lost in darkness.

Lara was more recognisable as Lara than in the earlier Tests, stroking a six and eight fours in 51, until the pull shot that was always likely to prove his undoing presented a catch to mid-on off Terbrugge. Ganga, on debut, batted with more aplomb than anyone for nearly two hours and he and the level-headed Jacobs added 45 before the fragile tail was exposed.

The depth of South Africa's resources was revealed by the spread of their wicket-takers. Donald and Pollock, who shared 27 of the 40 wickets in the first two Tests, had only one between them. The support cast of Kallis and Cronje, with three each, and Terbrugge, with two, took care of things.

Inevitably, there were several of the same reckless dismissals of the earlier Tests. No one was more culpable that Hooper who somehow managed to edge an out-swinger from Kallis that was barely in the precincts of Durban.

The familiar batting failure unfairly placed the onus on the bowlers once more. This time Rose, one of the forgotten men of West Indies cricket, responded with fast, accurate, out-swing bowling under leaden skies and all but single-handedly kept the West Indies in the game.

He set South Africa back with the first three wickets in 11 consecutive overs at the start of the second day. When Rhodes was directing South Africa towards a match-winning advantage in stands with Cullinan and Pollock, Rose repeatedly stepped in to check the advance with his work in the field and with three more wickets with the second new ball.

The hyperactive Rhodes entered with the innings at the crossroads of 140 for 4 half an hour after lunch. He was a chanceless and unbeaten 85 off 143 balls with eight fours and a couple of sixes off Ambrose when play was called 12.4 overs early, in spite of the lights that had been on since 25 minutes after lunch. He led successive partnerships of 42 with Cullinan and 80 with Pollock, both of whom were victims of outstanding West Indian fielding. Attempting a second run, Cullinan was beaten by inches by Rose's flat, accurate throw to Jacobs from third man. Pollock was gathered in by the tumbling Hooper's elastic right hand at second slip.

South Africa had a healthy, but not overwhelming, lead by the time Rhodes and Donald were dismissed early on the third morning. Then, for just over three hours, they encountered their first genuine batting resistance of the series as Chanderpaul and Lara, in their differing left-handed styles, engaged in their spirited counter-attack.

Between them, they stroked 28 boundaries and, by tea, had earned a lead of 79 with eight wickets intact. But the illusion of a West Indian revival proved misleading. Within ten minutes of the resumption, both were gone in successive overs, at the same score, and the fightback promptly ended.

South Africa were inspired by two incredible catches by the flying Gibbs. The first, right-handed at square leg, snared Lara's fierce pull; the second, running back to gather in a top-edged hook, accounted for Ganga. Pollock also claimed a sharp,

Courtney Walsh is carried off by manager Clive Lloyd and physio Denis Waight after straining his hamstring in the third Test.
Gordon Brooks/Sportsline Photographic

shin-high return to dislodge Chanderpaul but wicketkeeper Boucher's claim off Hooper was of dubious authenticity as television replays hinted the ball had touched down before entering the gloves.

By the time the umpires again deemed the artificially boosted light too dim to continue, West Indies had declined from the optimism of 201 for 2 with Chanderpaul and Lara together to the hopelessness of 246 for 8 with only Ambrose and Walsh left with the dogged Jacobs.

On the other side of the Pacific, England were simultaneously completing their remarkable fightback victory over Australia at the MCG, the progress of which was relayed by the ground announcer. It was of no motivational value to the West Indies as they meekly accepted the inevitable.

South Africa were setting out after their straightforward target after 35 minutes and they reached it an hour into the second session for the solitary loss of Gibbs.

FOURTH TEST
2, 3, 4, 5 and 6 January 1998 at Cape Town

By now utterly disorganised and dispirited, West Indies were again thoroughly outplayed. Injury robbed them of Walsh and Rose, their champion at Kingsmead, so that they had to go outside the touring squad to recruit Gibson, the Barbadian all-rounder, from his contract with Griqualand West. They were further handicapped by the hamstring strain that ended Ambrose's bowling involvement in the second over after lunch on the second day.

At least they were able to stretch the match into the final day when, on the truest pitch of the series, their lower order provided unexpected entertainment for a crowd of over 7,000 by adding 178. There were three mighty sixes by McLean, one landing on the tracks of the adjoining train station, and 23 fours as they went down with guns blazing.

They had also come out smoking as Ambrose dismissed Kirsten with the first ball of the match, a gloved leg-side deflection that earned the beanpole fast bowler his 350th Test wicket. Between then and the final volley, all the most telling shots were South African.

Curtly Ambrose celebrates his 350th Test wicket, with captain Brian Lara and Ridley Jacobs. He had Kary Kirsten caught by Jacobs for a first ball duck in the fourth Test match.
Gordon Brooks/Sportsline Photographic

Kallis was South Africa's talisman. Entering to face the second ball of the match, he shared a third-wicket partnership of 235 with Cullinan, both amassing the first hundreds of the series. He returned with an unbeaten 88 in the second innings and, using the new ball in the absence of the injured Donald, finished off the job with five wickets as the West Indies went down to their fourth successive defeat. Only eight others had ever had such a profound all-round effect on a Test match.

South Africa's dominance was first established by Kallis and Cullinan. The free-stroking Cullinan gave the more deliberate Kallis a head start of nearly two hours and 28 runs but passed him well before the end of the opening day to register his sixth Test century. Kallis arrived at his third in the last quarter of an hour to the delight of his home town crowd of 18,000, basking in a day of crystal clear sunshine.

The pitch offered the bowlers nothing but heartache and the lack of quality and experience among Ambrose's support bowlers was exposed by the assured South Africans. While his 18 overs on the day went for only 35, the other three fast men were carted around at more than three an over.

The West Indies regrouped overnight and, for the first four hours of the second day, were identifiable as a genuine, competitive Test team. It took Donald five overs to transform them back into their more familiar guise and commit them to another frantic fight for survival.

Their bowlers, supported by sharp ground fielding, responded to Ambrose's enforced exit with a purpose rarely shown in the series. It converted South Africa's overnight 282 for 2 to 406 for 8 when Cronje perversely declared the ball before tea.

Throughout the first two sessions, South Africa lost six wickets in adding 124 from 56.5 overs. Kallis, caught behind off Gibson's perfect out-swinger, made only nine more and Cullinan, bounced out by McLean, could not repeat his momentum of the previous day, spending three hours over an additional 46 and managing only two boundaries.

Although South Africa's total effectively put West Indies out of the match, Lara and his batsmen should have also enjoyed the ideal batting conditions. Donald quickly dispelled the hope.

Fast and hostile, he removed Murray with his fifth ball, Wallace in his fourth over and, prize of prizes, forced Lara to step back into his leg stump in his fifth. He immediately left the field for treatment of a delicate hamstring that could have been done no good by his leaping celebration of Lara's dismissal.

Jacques Kallis is all smiles after bowling Carl Hooper for 20, in the fourth Test. He finished with 5 for 90.
Gordon Brooks/Sportsline Photographic

FOURTH TEST – SOUTH AFRICA v. WEST INDIES

2, 3, 4, 5 and 6 January 1999 at Newlands, Cape Town

SOUTH AFRICA

	First Innings		Second Innings	
G Kirsten	c Jacobs, b Ambrose	0	c Murray, b McLean	5
HH Gibbs	c Wallace, b Dillon	42	c Jacobs, b Dillon	25
JH Kallis	c Jacobs, b Gibson	110	not out	88
DJ Cullinan	c Jacobs, b McLean	168	lbw, b McLean	0
WJ Cronje (capt)	c Jacobs, b McLean	0	c Hooper, b Dillon	54
JN Rhodes	b Hooper	34	lbw, b Hooper	23
SM Pollock	c Lara, b Dillon	9	c Lara, b Hooper	3
*MV Boucher	not out	15	c and b McLean	22
AA Donald	c Wallace, b Dillon	0	not out	0
DJ Terbrugge	not out	4		
PR Adams				
	lb 3, w 1, nb 20	24	lb 4, w 1, nb 1	6
	(for 8 wickets, dec.)	406	(for 7 wickets, dec.)	226

	First Innings				Second Innings			
	O	M	R	W	O	M	R	W
Ambrose	24.1	7	49	1				
McLean	25.5	7	76	2	16	1	53	3
Gibson	30	4	92	1	14.4	2	51	–
Dillon	33.5	6	99	3	17	2	37	2
Hooper	27	6	60	1	28	8	52	2
Chanderpaul	6	0	27	–	12	1	29	–

Fall of Wickets
1-0, 2-74, 3-309, 4-312, 5-376, 6-380, 7-397, 8-397
1-31, 2-31, 3-31, 4-125, 5-174, 6-190, 7-222

WEST INDIES

	First Innings		Second Innings	
PA Wallace	c Cullinan, b Donald	8	c Gibbs, b Pollock	0
JR Murray	c Boucher, b Donald	0	lbw, b Kallis	7
S Chanderpaul	c Rhodes, b Terbrugge	6	c Cullinan, b Kallis	5
BC Lara (capt)	hit wicket, b Donald	4	c and b Adams	33
CL Hooper	run out		b Kallis	20
	(Cronje/Terbrugge)	86		
D Ganga	c Kirsten, b Pollock	17	lbw, b Pollock	16
*RD Jacobs	c Kallis, b Pollock	29	not out	69
OD Gibson	c Kirsten, b Kallis	37	run out (Rhodes)	13
NAM McLean	c Cronje, b Adams	14	c Adams, b Kallis	39
CEL Ambrose	not out	4	c Kirsten, b Adams	19
MV Dillon	c Boucher, b Kallis	0	c Cronje, b Kallis	36
	lb 2, w 2, nb 3	7	lb 2, nb 12	14
		212		271

	First Innings				Second Innings			
	O	M	R	W	O	M	R	W
Donald	6	1	20	3				
Pollock	22	9	35	2	25	4	49	2
Terbrugge	20	8	37	1	11	4	40	–
Kallis	15	5	34	2	27.4	4	90	5
Adams	16	2	61	1	23	5	80	2
Cronje	6	1	23	–	1	1	–	–
Cullinan					4	1	10	–

Fall of Wickets
1-1, 2-10, 3-14, 4-34, 5-108, 6-146, 7-164, 8-199, 9-210
1-2, 2-7, 3-15, 4-47, 5-87, 6-87, 7-108, 8-173, 9-207

Umpires: DL Orchard & S Venkataraghavan
Toss: South Africa

South Africa won by 149 runs

Captain Brian Lara and manager Clive Lloyd face the press after South Africa's victory in fourth Test.
Gordon Brooks/Sportsline Photographic

In Donald's absence, Terbrugge claimed Chanderpaul as well before Hooper and Ganga halted the slide over the last 50 minutes to stumps, adding 55. Next day, only unusual South African generosity in the field allowed the West Indies to scramble their way out of a possible follow-on.

Rhodes dropped a chance at cover point off Cronje in the first over when Hooper was 55. He proceeded to 86, the highest West Indian score of the series, before a typical piece of cricketing nonchalance caused his run-out as he cantered through for a third run. Adams let a skyer off Terbrugge through his lunging grasp at deep mid-on and Jacobs advanced from 13 to 29 as a result. Boucher watched a catchable outside edge off Terbrugge fly past his right, allowing Gibson to move from 4 to 37. Substitute Prince put down McLean's steepler at long off, the least costly of the errors yielding only two more.

All these lapses occurred before West Indies reached their goal of 207 but, since Cronje would be without Donald in the second innings, he might have been relieved not to have to make the decision whether to enforce the follow-on. Even with the loss of the first three wickets at 31, South Africa extended their lead to 287 by close and, with two

days remaining, had ample time to complete the task. Within 24 hours, they were on the verge of yet another victory, as crushing as the previous two.

Their batsmen dawdled to such an extent over the first half of the fourth day that their 137 additional runs took them 49.4 overs and cost four wickets. Kallis' inactivity over four and a quarter hours left him 12 short of his second century of the match when Cronje declared. The winning target of 421 set the West Indies was clearly out of reach but there was still pride to play for. It had all but gone when they stumbled to close at 93 for 6, Lara scooping a return catch to the jubilant, and reinstated, Adams in the final over.

Donald took the field but did not bowl the next morning. Without him, Pollock and Kallis did the business, the former achieving his stated ambition by passing the 116 wickets of his father, Peter. There appeared little left to do on the final day but a sizeable crowd turned up all the same, taking advantage of an entrance fee reduced to 5 Rand. Neither their money, nor their time, was wasted as the West Indies tail wagged merrily, if in vain.

Western Province v. West Indies
9 January 1999 at Langa CC, Cape Town
West Indies 231 for 6 (50 overs)
Western Province 198 (48.4 overs)
West Indies won by 33 runs

A lively crowd turned out for the match at the open ground in one of Cape Town's black townships. Tsolekile and Nkomo, two locals boys in South Africa's under-19 team that left for Pakistan later in the month, were in the provincial side. Nkomo and Simelela, another product of the development programme, bowled with pace and promise but batting was not easy on an uneven pitch.

West Indies v. Boland
10, 11 and 12 January 1999 at Boland PKS Park, Paarl
West Indies 220 and 307
Boland 135 and 123 for 5
Match drawn

The weakest of the first-class provinces, Boland struggled to keep in touch even though West Indies were inconsistent and apathetic. Well placed to press their advantage after Boland's first three second-innings wickets fell to McLean for 10, West Indies relaxed as Lara turned to gentler stuff. He and Ganga took a wicket each as the match drifted to a draw.

FIFTH TEST
15, 16, 17 and 18 January 1999 at Centurion

Mark Boucher cutting en route to his century in the fifth Test.
Gordon Brooks/Sportsline Photographic

South Africa's first series clean sweep in their history was inevitable against opponents, as Lara acknowledged, disunited, mentally weak and keen to end their troubled tour.

The method of another one-sided contest was similar to the others. The West Indies bowlers made early inroads into South Africa's batting but then ran out of steam and ideas. Kallis, as solid as he was at Cape Town, restored the balance and the wicketkeeper, Boucher, at number seven, shifted it with an even, aggressive hundred, his first in Tests, that carried the total past 300.

Lara responded with another brilliant cameo, 68 off 77 balls, that included an unforgettable confrontation with Donald. Once Donald had the final say and ended a partnership of 97 with Chanderpaul, the bottom fell out of the innings, the last eight wickets could only muster 42 and that was just about that.

Kirsten, out to the second ball of the match exactly as he had been to the first at Cape Town, then ended a disappointing series with his sixth Test hundred, a laboured 134 off 305 balls, but West Indies' misery was more ruthlessly compounded by Rhodes. He was all action in a thunderous unbeaten 103, off 104 balls, during which he belted eight fours and six sixes, the last of which carried him past three figures for the third time in Tests. No South African had got to a Test hundred as fast.

Cronje promptly declared and was celebrating his team's momentous achievement 15 minutes after tea the following day.

FIFTH TEST – SOUTH AFRICA v. WEST INDIES
15, 16, 17 and 18 January 1999 at Centurion Park, Centurion

SOUTH AFRICA

	First Innings		Second Innings	
G Kirsten	c Jacobs, b Walsh	0	c Ganga, b Hooper	134
HH Gibbs	c Reifer, b Walsh	2	c Wallace, b Hooper	51
JH Kallis	c Chanderpaul, b Hooper	83	c Jacobs, b Hooper	27
DJ Cullinan	c Wallace, b McLean	9	c Ganga, b Dillon	4
WJ Cronje (capt)	c Jacobs, b Dillon	25	c Ganga, b McLean	58
JN Rhodes	c King, b Dillon	24	not out	103
SM Pollock	c Lara, b Walsh	13	not out	3
*MV Boucher	c Lara, b Walsh	100		
L Klusener	c Jacobs, b Walsh	12		
AA Donald	not out	12		
PR Adams	c Jacobs, b Walsh	7		
	b 4, lb 3, nb 19	26	b 3, lb 2, w 1, nb 13	19
		313	(for 5 wickets dec.)	399

	First Innings				Second Innings			
	O	M	R	W	O	M	R	W
Walsh	24.5	6	80	6	7.3	4	6	-
McLean	18	1	71	1	23.3	3	89	1
King	11	1	50	-	17	1	80	-
Dillon	17	2	62	2	23	0	79	1
Hooper	17	5	27	1	36.2	4	117	3
Chanderpaul	5	1	16	-	8	1	23	-

Fall of Wickets
1–0, 2–5, 3–18, 4–65, 5–98, 6–123, 7–215, 8–270, 9–302
1–82, 2–140, 3–149, 4–256, 5–375

WEST INDIES

	First Innings		Second Innings	
PA Wallace	b Donald	4	c Boucher, b Donald	4
D Ganga	c Kallis, b Pollock	0	c Rhodes, b Pollock	9
S Chanderpaul	c Donald, b Klusener	38	c Cronje, b Kallis	43
BC Lara (capt)	c Kallis, b Donald	68	lbw, b Kallis	14
CL Hooper	b Klusener	8	lbw, b Klusener	10
FL Reifer	c Rhodes, b Pollock	0	c Kallis, b Adams	6
*RD Jacobs	not out	8	c Boucher, b Kallis	78
NAM McLean	c Cronje, b Donald	8	b Adams	33
MV Dillon	c Adams, b Donald	0	b Cullinan	5
RD King	lbw, b Donald	0	not out	2
CA Walsh	lbw, b Kallis	2	b Adams	0
	lb 1, nb 7	8	lb 5, nb 8	13
		144		217

	First Innings				Second Innings			
	O	M	R	W	O	M	R	W
Donald	13	2	49	5	2	0	8	1
Pollock	14	2	41	2	16	5	38	1
Klusener	13	3	27	2	16	4	50	1
Kallis	7.1	1	26	1	8	5	12	2
Adams					21.2	6	64	4
Cronje					5	3	8	-
Cullinan					7	1	32	1

Fall of Wickets
1–1, 2–5, 3–102, 4–122, 5–125 6–126, 7–140, 8–140, 9–140
1–4, 2–46, 3–68, 4–86, 5–86, 6–117, 7–198, 8–209, 9–216

Umpires: RE Koertzen & S Venkataraghavan
Toss: West Indies

South Africa won by 351 runs

Jonty Rhodes pulls for six to bring up his century in the fifth Test. The wicketkeeper is Ridley Jacobs.

Gordon Brooks/Sportsline Photographic

South Africa's substantial depth of batting and sheer resolve again carried them from strife to strength on the opening day. Boucher, whose previous highest score in the series was 22, was their standard-bearer. He entered half an hour after lunch when things were faltering at 123 for 6 and was only dismissed quarter of an hour before close to a low first-slip catch off the persevering Walsh. South Africa ended with the highest return for any day in the series, 311 for 9.

Boucher had two vital partnerships. He added 92 with Kallis and 55 with the left-handed Klusener, playing his first Test of the series for the injured Terbrugge. In Ambrose's enforced absence, Walsh soldiered on for 23 overs in spite of various aches and pains that obliged him to seek intermittent attention in the dressing room. He claimed five wickets on the day for 78. Between them, the younger fast bowlers, McLean, Dillon and King, in his debut Test 24 hours after arriving from the Caribbean, conceded 183 runs from their 46 overs. They took only three wickets and, together, had a six and 26 fours taken off them.

Walsh added a sixth wicket to complete South Africa's innings early on the second day. Once the West Indies openers were again summarily dismissed, two hours of breathtaking cricket followed as Lara and Donald, two of the great cricketers of their time, engaged in their head-to-head confrontation. In two distinct and separate periods either side of lunch, they went after each other with the intense ferocity of two champion heavyweight boxers.

Lara immediately set about Donald on entering, plundering 26 off 13 balls with pulls, cuts and drives. Cronje cut the conflict short by removing Donald from the firing line for later use as Lara completed his 50 off 38 balls with 12 fours. When Cronje reintroduced his ace fast bowler immediately after lunch, Donald changed tactics, going round the wicket for a clinical bodyline assault at menacing speed.

Lara took a stinging blow on the forearm from one ball and, in desperate self-preservation against another throat-seeking missile, fended a catch into the gully to end the ferment. In contrast to his early assault, he had added only one boundary, and six runs, off the 13 balls from Donald second time round.

It was a brief, exhilarating interlude. Once over, the main contest returned to type. The West Indies collapsed like a pricked balloon and their last eight wickets raised a mere 42. The deficit was 165 and South Africa had readily increased that by 100, for the loss of Gibbs, by close. West Indian woes were heightened when Walsh, his left knee swollen and in pain, pulled up in the day's final over and limped off the ground.

The forlorn visitors had nothing left to give but the South Africans spared them no mercy. Restricting themselves to 74 off the 34 overs before lunch, losing Kallis and Cullinan, they scored another 229 off the remaining 46.3 overs to the declaration.

Cronje himself furnished the initial acceleration with a huge six off Hooper that kick-started his 58. Rhodes bounded out to replace him, hooked a McLean no-ball for six as his fourth scoring shot and outscored his two partners, Kirsten and Pollock, 103 to 32 before Cronje closed with a superfluous lead of 568.

It left his bowlers ten overs and two days to finish things off. It was more than ample time. Wallace touched his fourth ball to the keeper down the leg side, Donald's 23rd and, as it proved, last wicket of the series. Resting his strained hamstring, he did not take the field again but, as at Cape Town, his absence was hardly noticed as all the other bowlers claimed wickets. There were four for Adams, including Lara leg before, sweeping, and even one for Cullinan as Dillon was bowled attempting a ridiculous reverse sweep.

It was left, yet again, to Jacobs to save West Indies even further shame. He batted, with the common sense and confidence that were his hallmarks all series, for 78. He and McLean put on an entertaining, but meaningless, 81 in just under an hour while Adams and Cullinan were operating together. It simply delayed the unavoidable.

One of many signs in the Test series that depicted West Indies weaknesses.

Gordon Brooks/Sportsline Photographic

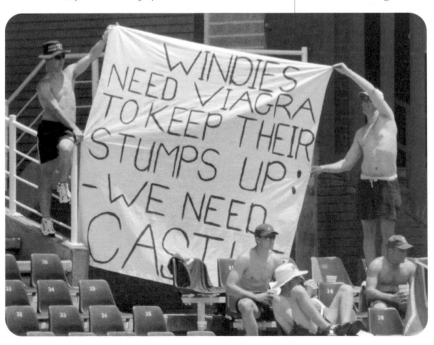

TEST MATCH AVERAGES
South Africa v. West Indies

SOUTH AFRICA

Batting	M	Inns	NO	HS	Runs	Av	100	50
JH Kallis	5	10	3	110	485	69.28	1	4
JN Rhodes	5	9	1	103*	378	47.25	1	2
PN Kirsten	5	10	1	134	336	37.33	1	2
WJ Cronje	5	9	-	58	284	31.55	-	2
DJ Cullinan	5	9	-	168	278	30.88	1	-
MV Boucher	5	8	2	100	168	28.00	1	-
HH Gibbs	4	8	-	51	210	26.25	-	1
PL Symcox	3	4	-	36	89	22.25	-	-
SM Pollock	5	9	1	42	148	18.50	-	-
AA Donald	5	7	2	33	76	15.20	-	-

Played in four Tests: DJ Terbrugge 3*, 2*, 3*, 2* & 4*
Played in two Tests: PR Adams 7
Played in one Test: AM Bacher 1 & 6; L Klusener 12

Bowling	Overs	Mds	Runs	Wkts	Av	Best	10/m	5/inns
SM Pollock	197.2	45	483	29	16.65	5-43	-	3
AA Donald	117.2	24	395	23	17.17	5-49	-	2
JH Kallis	115.5	32	299	17	17.58	5-90	-	1
DJ Terbrugge	100	33	253	9	28.11	3-27	-	-
PR Adams	60.2	13	205	7	29.28	4-64	-	-

Also bowled: WJ Cronje 17.1-5-53-3; DJ Cullinan 11-2-42-1; L Klusener 29-7-77-3;
PL Symcox 59-18-149 -3

Fielding Figures
14 – MV Boucher; 10 – WJ Cronje; 9 – DJ Cullinan; 7 – JH Kallis; 5 – HH Gibbs; 4 – G Kirsten,
JN Rhodes; 3 – PR Adams; 2 – SM Pollock, DJ Terbrugge; 1 – AA Donald

WEST INDIES

Batting	M	Inns	NO	HS	Runs	Av	100	50
RD Jacobs	5	10	3	78	317	45.28	-	2
BC Lara	5	10	-	79	310	31.00	-	3
S Chanderpaul	5	10	-	75	266	26.60	-	2
CL Hooper	5	10	-	86	237	23.70	-	1
SC Williams	2	4	-	37	92	23.00	-	-
NAM McLean	4	8	-	39	165	20.62	-	-
JR Murray	2	4	-	29	65	16.25	-	-
D Ganga	3	6	-	28	75	12.50	-	-
CB Lambert	2	4	-	33	43	10.75	-	-
M Dillon	3	6	-	36	59	9.83	-	-
CEL Ambrose	4	8	2	19	56	9.33	-	-
PA Wallace	4	8	-	21	68	8.50	-	-
RN Lewis	2	4	-	12	22	5.50	-	-
FL Reifer	2	4	-	9	15	3.75	-	-
CA Walsh	4	8	4	5*	12	3.00	-	-

Played in one Test: OD Gibson 37 & 13; RD King 0 & 2*; FA Rose 6 & 22

Bowling	Overs	Mds	Runs	Wkts	Av	Best	10/m	5/inns
F A Rose	37	6	115	7	16.42	7-84	-	1
C A Walsh	158.5	36	415	22	18.86	6-80	-	1
C E L Ambrose	124.5	26	309	13	23.76	6-51	-	1
N A M McLean	129.2	12	457	12	38.08	3-53	-	-
M Dillon	110.5	13	357	9	39.66	3-99	-	-
C L Hooper	142.2	27	372	8	46.50	3-117	—	-

Also bowled: S Chanderpaul 31-3-95-0; OD Gibson 44.4-6-143-1; RD King 28-2-130-0;
RN Lewis 73.3-10-225-1

Fielding Figures
19 – RD Jacobs; 8 – CL Hooper; 6 – PA Wallace; 5 – BC Lara; 3 – D Ganga, CB Lambert,
SC Williams; 2 – S Chanderpaul, NAM McLean; 1 – M Dillon, RD King, JR Murray, FL Reifer,
CA Walsh

ONE-DAY INTERNATIONALS

The force had long been with South Africa and, even with the injured Donald confined to the final match, they completed the humiliation of West Indies with an unprecedented six-one triumph in the limited-overs series.

The West Indies actually won the second match, their only major victory on tour, as Chanderpaul (150) and Hooper (108) brilliantly accumulated the highest West Indies partnership in the shorter form of the game, 226. They would have won the rain-shortened first as well but for strange tactics and their self-doubt that allowed South Africa to sneak in with a last-ball leg-bye.

They could maintain neither their form nor their commitment and were no match for the South Africans over the remaining five matches in which they did not bat longer than 45 overs or total more than 219. The margins of defeat were between 50 and 114 runs.

West Indies were hampered as much by their selection as by the loss of all seven tosses. There was no place for four of the team that had reached the final of the Wills International Trophy in Bangladesh

Lance Klusener hits Carl Hooper for four in his knock of 64 in the third one-day international at Kingsmead, Durban.
Gordon Brooks/Sportsline Photographic

Shivnerine Chanderpaul pulling for four in the fourth one-day international at St. George's Park, Port Elizabeth. He was West Indies highest scorer with 328 runs.
Gordon Brooks/Sportsline Photographic

a few months earlier (Dillon, Lambert, Simmons and Williams), both wicketkeepers were included and Ganga retained for a form of the game to which his style was clearly not suited.

Cronje's luck with the toss meant the West Indies had to bat under the lights at Durban and Cape Town after dew had freshened the pitch. At Durban, Elworthy and Kallis peppered them with short-pitched bowling that inflicted a hairline fracture on Lara's right wrist, ending his tour, delivered a blow to Murray's helmet and initiated a collapse after a flying start of 88 in 11 overs between Chanderpaul and Murray.

There was an irony in manager Clive Lloyd's complaint to the match referee for, under his captaincy, West Indies had perfected such tactics. He was quick to explain he was simply concerned about it getting out of hand and there was no recurrence.

With the World Cup less than four months away, the series was a timely chance for preparation. South Africa made full use of it. For West Indies, it was meaningless.

Klusener gave an imposing preview of what was to follow, clubbing 229 runs at an average of 70 and a strike rate of 112 and picking up 11 wickets. Gibbs, brought back as an opener in the Tests, emphasised his growing confidence with his first hundred for South Africa, 125 at Port Elizabeth. Benkenstein, who did not appear in the Tests, asserted himself as an inventive middle-order batsman and a fielder who enhanced the already high-calibre fielding. All those South Africa eventually carried to the World Cup appeared in the series. Only six West Indians survived.

South Africa satisfied the political pressure for a more racially representative composition by giving the fast bowlers Williams and Mpitsang a match each. Williams was 32 but, at 18 years, 314 days, Mpitsang became South Africa's youngest international cricketer before his home crowd in Bloemfontein.

Match One
22 January 1999 at Wanderers Stadium, Johannesburg
West Indies 154 for 4 (28 overs) CL Hooper 66*
South Africa 160 for 8 (27 overs)
South Africa won by two wickets (D/L Method)
Man of the Match: CL Hooper

Match Two
24 January 1999 at Buffalo Park, East London
West Indies 292 for 9 (50 overs) S Chanderpaul 150,
CL Hooper 108, SM Pollock 6 for 35
South Africa 249 (46.5 overs) JH Kallis 51, MV Boucher 51
West Indies won by 43 runs
Man of the Match: S Chanderpaul

Match Three
27 January 1999 at Kingsmead, Durban
South Africa 274 for 9 (50 overs) WJ Cronje 58,
CL Hooper 4 for 52
West Indies 219 (43.1 overs) S Chanderpaul 52
South Africa won by 55 runs
Man of the Match: WJ Cronje

Match Four
30 January 1999 at St George's Park, Port Elizabeth
South Africa 278 for 6 (50 overs) HH Gibbs 125,
WJ Cronje 74, KLT Arthurton 4 for 56
West Indies 179 (43.1 overs) CL Hooper 57
South Africa won by 99 runs
Man of the Match: HH Gibbs

Match Five
2 February 1999 at Newlands, Cape Town
South Africa 221 for 8 (50 overs) DM Benkenstein 69,
L Klusener 54*
West Indies 132 (42.4 overs)
South Africa won by 89 runs
Man of the Match: L Klusener

Match Six
5 February 1999 at Springbok Park, Bloemfontein
South Africa 273 (49.5 overs) WJ Cronje 82,
KLT Arthurton 4 for 44
West Indies 159 (40.3 overs)
South Africa won by 114 runs
Man of the Match: WJ Cronje

Match Seven
7 February 1999 at Centurion Park, Centurion
South Africa 226 for 8 (50 overs) JH Kallis 66
West Indies 176 (44.5 overs) JR Murray 57
South Africa won by 50 runs
Man of the Match: L Klusener

SUPERSPORT SERIES
By Telford Vice

It was Border's season, and yet it wasn't. The men from the impoverished eastern half of the Eastern Cape, an economically ailing province low in the South African pecking order, won five of their eight matches, losing one, and seemed unstoppable going into the final.

They proved anything but as Western Province recovered from a perilous 32 for 5 on the first morning to win by 163 runs 20 minutes before tea on the fifth day, in the process recording their 19th championship with three of them shared.

In a country torn by fierce provincialism the pangs of sympathy for Border's crash at the final hurdle were widespread. After 103 years of trying they were still without a trophy, and it did not ease their disappointment that the rare though not unprecedented provision of a final effectively robbed them of the title.

Border led the standings by five points after the single round of league matches, which in past seasons would have seen them declared champions.

Brian McMillan of Western Province.
David Munden/Sportsline Photographic

But the Supersport Series – the modern version of the Currie Cup – is sponsored by a pay-TV company, so a final between the top two teams was inevitable.

It didn't help that only three weeks after the first-class final, Border lost the limited-overs version to Free State.

However, for all the gloom that descended on Border's East London headquarters, Buffalo Park, nothing could disguise the fact that they had a remarkable season. And this for a province which had little besides their bootstraps with which to pull themselves up when they were elevated to the 'A' section before the 1991–92 season.

Border were the Durham of South African cricket, minnows in a pond brimming with ruthlessness. That they have grown immeasurably is due in large part to the contribution of Peter Kirsten from 1990–91 until the end of his playing career in 1996–97.

But even Kirsten could not take Border to the top of the table. That honour belongs to senior cricket manager Stephen Jones, the coach until last season, current coach Richard Pybus (a Geordie, no less!) and Pieter Strydom, one of South Africa's most innovative provincial captains.

Add Vasbert Drakes' roaring success – a Border record 56 wickets at 14.64 – and the blossoming of Tyron Henderson from a fast-medium nobody into the pick of South Africa's young quick bowlers, and the rest virtually falls into place.

Drakes was signed by Border before the 1996–97 season with little to recommend him except the five one-day internationals he had played for West Indies and a steady record for Barbados. Four summers ago Henderson could not secure a place in the Natal 'B' team.

After three South African campaigns Drakes has taken 103 wickets at 19.07, while Henderson claimed 34 at 21.85 in 1998–99. Jones, and Pybus to a degree, can claim much of the credit for their development.

But Western Province nevertheless deserved their championship. As one of the hardest hit provinces in terms of sacrifices to the national team with seven of their players involved at a higher level, Province showed remarkable depth of talent to achieve a record identical to Border.

Gary Kirsten and Jacques Kallis, Province's major batsmen, played only three and two matches respectively, which left the bulk of the run-scoring to be done by Brian McMillan, who responded to the challenge by scoring 465 at 42.27 with five half-centuries.

Vasbert Drakes of Border.
David Munden/Sportsline Photographic

For wickets, the Capetonians looked to Eric Simons, who at 37 bowled like a man in his prime to take 36 at 14.16 before announcing his retirement from first-class cricket. However, he is expected to be available for one-day matches next season.

Northerns, the new name for Northern Transvaal, were the other team with five wins in a season that saw the top five sides separated by a slim ten points on the final log.

For the first half of the summer it was all Border as they reeled off victories in their first four matches.

Thus Buffalo Park hosted its first final, and after losing the toss Border exploited the early humidity to send Province crashing to 48 for 5 at lunch. Henderson's opening spell of 3 for 11 in 6 overs was the attack's sharp edge.

Conditions eased after lunch but Province were to dwindle to 84 for 7 before Simons and Dawson, batting with a cracked thumb, ground out 70 runs with solid, unflashy batting.

Province were 180 for 8 at the close, but Dawson's maiden first-class century of 143 in five and a half hours – the highest score by a number nine batsman in South African first-class cricket – was to see them dismissed for 302 almost an hour after lunch on the second day. Dawson and debutant Ryan Joffe set a Province last-wicket partnership record of 89.

Border began the third day on 56 for 1, but threw away six wickets for 14 runs and the last four for 25 on their way to a total of 191. By the close, Province were 198 ahead with nine wickets in hand.

Drakes took 5 for 48 as Province were dismissed for 249, leaving Border to score 361 for victory. The fourth day ended with Border having forged to 96 for one – 265 runs away.

A still sound surface meant the match remained in the balance going into final day, but when Border lost three wickets in eight balls in the ninth and tenth overs of the morning (two of them to the evergreen Simons) the contest was effectively over.

The match was a memorable climax to the domestic season, but it was a summer that will also be remembered for internal strife at Gauteng – the old Transvaal – and as the season in which on-field comments of a racial nature were officially forbidden.

Ray Jennings was sacked as Gauteng cricket manager not for lack of performance, but for reportedly holding opinions which clashed with the Gauteng Cricket Board's view of the new South Africa. The ramifications included players leaving for less troubled waters.

McMillan's image as the Oscar Wilde of the slip cordon took a dive when he suggested, loudly, to team-mate Claude Henderson that he bowl a 'coolie creeper' to Natal batsman Ashraf Mall, who is of Asian descent.

The United Cricket Board of South Africa (UCB) reprimanded McMillan and ordered him to apologise publicly, which he had earlier refused to do. He did so, smirkingly.

Eastern Province 'B' captain Alan Badenhorst was banned for two years from playing any match under the auspices of the UCB after a disciplinary committee found him guilty of calling Griqualand West B batsman Mario Arthur a 'half-bred kaffir'. Badenhorst enlisted lawyers for his appeal and was exonerated due to lack of evidence. 'The death of cricket's innocence,' was how one newspaper saw it. And about time, too.

SOUTH AFRICA DOMESTIC ONE-DAY SEASON
By Telford Vice

Northerns won their second league title in three years, and Griqualand West and Border – who between them had not claimed a trophy this century – contested the final in the knockout competition.

Perhaps that is a consequence of the limited-overs game's classless society, which pays scant respect to the qualities required for first-class success. More likely it is an indication of a shift in South African cricket's flavours-of-the-season for summers hence, especially as it is one-day cricket and not the first-class game that nurtures such change.

Northerns – formerly Northern Transvaal – are one of the most affluent unions in the country and their Centurion Park base – which in a previous political era was called Verwoerdburg – is rapidly gaining a reputation among players and spectators alike as South Africa's modern cricket arena of choice. Yet before the 1996–97 season their trophy cabinet was bare except for the cobwebs.

Griquas beat Border in the knockout final, but the last time they won anything – in 1891 when, as Kimberley, they triumphed in the second Currie Cup – the Jameson Raid was still four years away.

Pity poor Border who, after 103 years, are still seeking that first title. Their disappointment was doubled when Griquas won, because three weeks earlier Western Province had beaten them in the first-class final.

The limited-overs season encompassed two related competitions. The Standard Bank League comprised a single round of 45-overs-a-side matches contested by all 11 affiliates of the United Cricket Board of South Africa. That was followed by the Standard Bank Cup, a knockout involving the top five teams in the league and a side from the nether regions of the log who emerged after a series of play-off matches.

Northerns were good value for their league title, winning seven and losing two of their ten matches. They did not play the most exciting cricket, but stuck instead to percentage tactics of solid top-order batting and tight bowling.

Their runs came mainly from veteran Roy Pienaar – who, at 38, has the knees of a geriatric – and Gerald Dros. Pienaar had a century and three half-centuries in scoring 411 runs at 45.66 in the league and cup combined, while Dros scored 320 at 55.33 with three half-centuries.

However, sentiment holds no respect for facts and figures and most South Africans, whatever their provincial allegiances, had a place in their hearts for Griquas.

In Kepler Wessels and Pat Symcox – the former signed following acrimony with Eastern Province and the latter returning to his roots after spending all but one of the preceding 14 seasons in Natal – they were represented by two of South African cricket's most enduring characters. Symcox will be back again, but by the end of the season Wessels, now 42, was leaning towards retirement.

West Indies fast bowler Ottis Gibson completed the trio of high-quality players Griquas were able to call on in the numerous tight spots they faced.

Symcox hit 82 runs off 63 balls to lead Griquas to an unlikely five-wicket win over Eastern Province early in the campaign, and in the semi-final against Gauteng, Gibson smashed 76 off 52.

Wessels was the second highest run-scorer in the competition with 509 at 50.90, and as captain his experience was plain in everything Griquas did.

Eddie Barlow might have been part of it all as coach, but before the halfway point in the season he resigned after a selection dispute. 'So long, it's been fun. Enjoy the rest of the season, Eddie,' is about as curt as resignation letters get.

The final was one-sided with Border restricted to 199 for 6 and Griquas cruising to victory by six wickets in 40.2 overs. For once, though, not all that gleamed in Kimberley came out of the Big Hole.

FIRST-CLASS AVERAGES

BATTING

	M	Inns	NO	HS	Runs	Av	10	50
JH Kallis	7	13	3	110	646	64.60	1	6
N Boje	5	10	2	116	500	62.50	1	5
KR Rutherford	8	15	2	160*	810	62.30	3	4
Shakeel Ahmed	6	12	1	132	679	61.72	3	2
HH Dippenaar	11	21	3	147	1070	59.44	4	6
PH Barnard	9	17	3	250	831	59.35	2	5
G Kirsten	8	15	2	194	758	58.30	2	4
N Pothas	9	13	4	165	515	57.22	2	-
C Light	6	8	0	101	424	53.00	1	3
CC Bradfield	8	15	1	143*	661	47.21	2	3
HM de Vos	6	10	2	96	377	47.12	-	3
SG Koenig	10	18	1	96	794	46.70	-	6
DJ Cullinan	8	15	3	168	555	46.25	1	3
FC Brooker	10	19	2	111	738	43.41	1	6
S Chanderpaul	9	15	0	182	642	42.80	1	3
PJ de Bruyn	7	11	1	202	428	42.80	1	1
ELR Stewart	8	14	0	177	594	42.42	1	3
BM McMillan	7	13	2	75	465	42.27	-	5
JN Rhodes	9	16	1	103*	633	42.20	1	3
MA Alexander	6	12	1	143*	456	41.45	2	1
M Strydom	6	11	2	69*	373	41.44	-	3
WJ Cronje	8	15	1	158*	575	41.07	2	2
M van Jaarsfeld	11	18	1	147	686	40.35	3	2
AJ Hall	8	10	1	119	353	39.22	1	3
SJ Palframan	10	18	2	147	627	39.18	2	2
Q Still	8	12	1	85	418	38.00	-	4
W Bossenger	9	12	4	102	303	37.87	1	1
AJ Seymore	4	8	0	124	303	37.87	1	1
AM Bacher	10	19	0	135	715	37.63	1	5
RD Jacobs	7	13	3	78	376	37.60	-	2
G Rowley	5	10	1	108	337	37.44	1	2
WM Dry	9	16	4	74*	444	37.00	-	5
BM White	10	20	1	120	695	36.57	1	5
W Wiblin	10	19	2	112	611	35.94	2	3
ND McKenzie	6	11	2	99	322	35.77	-	3
LD Ferreira	10	17	0	121	608	35.76	2	2
MV Boucher	10	18	3	100*	535	35.66	2	2
DJ Callaghan	7	13	1	79	427	35.58	-	5
AC Hudson	7	12	0	108	422	35.16	1	2
MJR Rindel	8	14	1	117	457	35.15	2	2
PJR Steyn	7	13	1	132	412	34.33	1	-
JF Venter	9	18	1	142*	583	34.29	1	3
AG Prince	10	17	1	133	541	33.81	1	3
DJ Watson	8	14	0	155	473	33.78	1	2

FIRST-CLASS AVERAGES

BATTING

	M	Inns	NO	HS	Runs	Av	10	50
H Pangarker	7	12	1	122*	371	33.72	2	1
CL Hooper	9	16	0	109	538	33.62	1	3
ML Bruyns	9	16	0	140	530	33.12	2	2
D Jordaan	8	14	2	73	390	32.50	-	3
CB Sugden	10	20	0	84	647	32.35	-	5
AC Botha	7	14	2	64	388	32.33	-	4
BC Lara	9	16	0	101	515	32.18	1	4
DJJ de Vos	10	16	5	105*	351	31.90	1	2
SC Pope	9	17	2	61	470	31.33	-	2
KC Wessels	6	10	0	67	311	31.10	-	3
JM Arthur	13	25	1	148	727	30.29	2	2
R Munnik	10	16	0	138	484	30.25	1	2
D Moffat	6	12	1	67	326	29.63	-	4
LJ Koen	8	15	0	87	443	29.53	-	3
DN Crookes	9	16	2	69	405	28.92	-	2
A Badenhorst	6	10	2	56	227	28.37	-	1
JDC Bryant	7	14	2	88	337	28.08	-	1
KC Jackson	10	18	0	82	501	27.83	-	3
PC Strydom	10	20	2	92*	496	27.55	-	3
JM Kemp	10	18	2	61*	432	27.00	-	3
S Abrahams	10	16	3	66	350	26.92	-	2
MI Gidley	9	17	0	92	454	26.70	-	2
PPJ Koortzen	5	10	1	63	240	26.66	-	1
I Mitchell	5	8	1	96	179	25..57	-	1
GA Pollock	6	10	1	91	229	25.44	-	2
MW Rushmere	7	13	1	117*	305	25.41	1	1
PJ Botha	10	19	2	74	427	25.11	-	2
MN van Wyk	8	16	2	55	347	24.78	-	1
AG Lawson	6	11	2	36	217	24.11	-	-
M Creed	6	10	1	72	216	24.00	-	2
CB Lambert	7	12	0	67	286	23.83	-	2
MLG Pedi	6	10	1	41	214	23.77	-	-
JM Henderson	9	16	1	117*	353	23.53	1	-
GV Grace	9	17	0	104	400	23.52	1	-
J-P Schoeman	5	10	0	90	232	23.20	-	1
HH Gibbs	8	14	0	51	320	22.85	-	1
CR Norris	6	12	1	36	251	22.81	-	-
M Badat	6	12	2	77	227	22.70	-	1
G Morgan	10	15	3	58	272	22.66	-	1
LL Bosman	7	13	1	62*	271	22.58	-	1
SM Pollock	7	13	1	92	269	22.41	-	1
CR Matthews	8	10	2	76	179	22.37	-	1
LJ Wilkinson	6	12	1	80	244	22.18	-	2
OD Gibson	9	12	0	37	266	22.16	-	-

FIRST-CLASS AVERAGES

BATTING

	M	Inns	NO	HS	Runs	Av	10	50
EJ Ferreira	10	18	0	63	397	22.05	-	3
PL Symcox	8	12	0	50	261	21.75	-	1
EO Simons	7	11	2	75	193	21.44	-	1
HD Ackerman	9	16	1	98*	317	21.13	-	2
GJF Liebenberg	9	18	0	116	380	21.11	1	-
PA Wallace	8	14	0	68	295	21.07	-	2
DR Gain	10	18	0	79	375	20.83	-	3
SC Williams	7	12	0	55	250	20.83	-	2
T Henderson	10	15	3	45	241	20.08	-	-
JL Ontong	7	12	1	46	220	20.00	-	-
AP McLaren	6	12	0	67	235	19.58	-	1
S Ackerman	5	10	1	43	175	19.44	-	-
D Ganga	7	12	0	50	227	18.91	-	1
MG Brouwers	5	9	0	52	170	18.88	-	1
F Davids	6	10	0	37	188	18.80	-	-
G Dros	9	16	3	48*	244	18.76	-	-
GW Myburgh	4	8	0	41	147	18.37	-	-
NAM McLean	8	14	0	46	257	18.35	-	-
ZA Abrahim	6	11	2	67	165	18.33	-	1
EAE Baptiste	8	14	2	66	218	18.16	-	1
DK Dobson	6	12	0	35	216	18.00	-	-
CW Henderson	9	13	3	33	170	17.00	-	-
WR Wingfield	7	13	1	73	203	16.91	-	1
J Beukes	8	16	0	49	268	16.75	-	-
VC Drakes	9	15	0	61	246	16.40	-	1
MW Pringle	8	13	1	37	182	15.16	-	-
B van Beuge	6	9	0	61	131	14.55	-	1
AG Botha	7	11	1	47	141	14.10	-	-
M Dillon	8	13	2	44	153	13.90	-	-
DM Koch	10	16	4	28	165	13.75	-	-
DW Murray	6	10	2	27*	109	13.62	-	-
L Masikazana	9	14	4	24*	134	13.40	-	-
HS Bakkes	8	16	1	29	176	11.73	-	-
FL Reifer	5	9	1	36	92	11.50	-	-
MJG Davis	6	8	0	41	91	11.37	-	-
GA de Kock	6	10	1	29	102	11.33	-	-
RE Bryson	6	8	0	57	81	10.12	-	-

Qualification: 8 completed innings, average 10.00

BOWLING

	Overs	Mds	Runs	Wkts	Av	Best	10/m	5/inns
DJ Pryke	122.2	40	240	18	13.33	5-41	-	1
EO Simons	253	94	510	36	14.16	5-14	1	4
VC Drakes	342.3	93	820	56	14.64	5-35	-	5
LCR Jordaan	209.1	67	441	30	14.70	6-30	-	2
MJG Davis	171.2	60	328	21	15.61	5-39	-	1
DH Townsend	320.5	80	903	50	18.06	6-36	1	4
DG Payne	128.3	31	308	17	18.11	3-25	-	-
SM Pollock	268.2	72	625	34	18.38	5-43	-	3
JH Kallis	203	63	479	26	18.42	5-90	-	1
Q Ferreira	152	40	379	20	18.95	3-39	-	-
BT Player	196	42	494	26	19.00	5-28	-	1
M Strydom	126.3	29	424	22	19.27	4-55	-	-
L Klusener	179.5	48	482	25	19.28	5-42	1	2
RE Bryson	115.2	24	283	14	20.21	4-40	-	-
CA Walsh	173.1	39	470	23	20.43	6-80	-	1
DJ Terbrugge	286.2	83	672	32	21.00	5-32	-	1
MW Pringle	281	61	746	35	21.31	4-46	-	-
G Kruger	124.3	30	386	18	21.44	4-23	-	-
AC Dawson	180.1	53	452	21	21.52	6-79	-	1
CR Douglas	142.1	37	378	17	22.23	5-60	-	1
EAE Baptiste	252.1	95	490	22	22.27	3-46	-	-
S Elworthy	154.2	41	431	19	22.68	5-33	-	1
T Henderson	291.1	73	772	34	22.70	5-51	-	1
AA Donald	175.2	29	583	25	23.32	5-49	-	2
M Hayward	218.1	41	688	29	23.72	5-56	-	1
NG Brouwers	166.4	49	336	14	24.00	6-57	-	1
SM Adam	114.3	34	288	12	24.00	4-63	-	-
CEL Ambrose	149.5	36	363	15	24.20	6-51	-	1

FIRST-CLASS AVERAGES

BOWLING

	Overs	Mds	Runs	Wkts	Av	Best	10/m	5/inns
NAM McLean	213	26	729	30	24.30	7-28	-	1
PJ de Bruyn	72.3	10	243	10	24.30	6-56	-	1
S Abrahams	303.5	80	688	28	24.57	5-58	1	2
RT Coetzee	194.5	43	557	22	25.31	4-50	-	-
D Pretorius	210.1	33	611	24	25.45	5-50	-	1
R Joffe	145.4	49	371	14	26.50	4-40	-	-
JE Bastow	154.1	29	482	18	26.77	4-42	-	-
OD Gibson	361.4	71	1048	39	26.87	5-37	-	2
A Badenhorst	187.5	49	486	18	27.00	4-50	-	-
CR Matthews	181	49	433	16	27.06	4-15	-	-
CE Eksteen	407.2	146	929	34	27.32	7-52	-	2
CM Willoughby	377.3	90	999	36	27.75	5-60	-	1
AJ Hall	256	58	736	26	28.30	5-23	-	1
CW Henderson	463	141	1035	36	28.75	5-57	-	1
PJ Botha	186	39	547	19	28.78	6-75	-	1
JM Henderson	128.5	39	350	12	29.16	3-13	-	-
MJ Lavine	156.2	38	441	15	29.40	3-54	-	-
GT Love	156.2	25	420	14	30.00	5-72	-	1
KG Storey	218.3	63	517	17	30.41	3-34	-	-
GJ Kruis	360.2	79	978	32	30.56	6-84	-	1
ZA Abrahim	174	35	552	18	30.66	3-53	-	-
JM Kemp	223	57	633	20	31.65	3-40	-	-
CT Enslin	90.3	21	323	10	32.30	2-14	-	-
GJ Smith	221.1	65	584	18	32.44	4-33	-	-
PR Adams	231	47	714	22	32.45	4-64	-	-
HC Bakkes	238	54	620	19	32.63	5-57	-	1
PC Strydom	215	54	523	16	32.68	4-12	-	-
M Creed	110.3	20	332	10	33.20	4-30	-	-
R Munnik	193	34	671	20	33.55	3-30	-	-
GM Gilder	207	60	611	18	33.94	4-39	-	-
DM Koch	347.4	92	899	26	34.57	5-128	-	1
PL Symcox	345.1	80	869	25	34.76	4-45	-	-
M Ntini	171.5	38	630	18	35.00	3-51	-	-
AC Botha	147	35	426	12	35.50	4-52	-	-
MV Dillon	237.1	39	771	21	36.71	4-56	-	-
DN Crookes	283.3	57	890	24	37.08	6-59	-	1
RB MacQueen	194.1	49	600	16	37.50	4-54	-	-
GA Roe	224.1	63	491	13	37.76	3-58	-	-
CL Hooper	263.4	52	716	18	39.77	3-117	-	-
HS Williams	275.4	64	679	17	39.94	3-36	-	-
JF Venter	341.2	81	1009	25	40.36	3-55	-	-
JN Dreyer	247.5	49	851	21	40.52	4-72	-	-
AG Botha	207.4	58	532	12	44.33	3-37	-	-
RN Lewis	198	36	592	12	49.33	4-45	-	-
PV Mpitsang	154	27	505	10	50.50	4-37	-	-
AJ Swanepoel	228	61	532	10	53.20	3-68	-	-
CR Tatton	247.1	65	781	12	65.08	5-82	-	1

Qualification: 10 wickets in 8 innings

The following players took 10 wickets in fewer than 8 innings:

	Overs	Mds	Runs	Wkts	Av	Best	10/m	5/inns
RA de Vry	75.2	18	193	12	16.08	4-19	-	-
JJ van der Wath	81.3	21	226	14	16.14	5-26	-	2
C Copeland	87.1	18	287	16	17.93	6-77	-	2
MJ Hoggard	160.1	53	311	17	18.29	5-60	-	1
DA Cosker	102.1	22	248	13	19.07	5-57	-	1
GP Swann	98.4	20	246	12	20.50	5-77	-	1
C Kruger	142.1	37	378	17	22.23	5-60	-	1
RE Veenstra	144	31	473	10	47.30	2-57	-	-

Leading Fielders

43 – G Morgan (38 ct/5 st); 39 – JA Palframan (36 ct/3 st); 38 – W Bossenger (35 ct/3 st); 34 – L Masikazana (32 ct/2 st); 33 – MV Boucher; 27 – ELR Stewart (26 ct/l st); 24 – RD Jacobs (23 ct/1 st); 22 – B van Beuge (18 ct/4 st); 21 – EG Poole (16 ct/5 st); 20 – N Pothas (17 ct/3 st); 18 – PN Kirsten (17 ct/1 st); 17 – I Mitchell (16 ct/1 st), BK Hughes, MN van Wyk; 16 – AP McLaren (15 ct/1 st), LJ Koen; 15 – DW Murray (13 ct/2 st); 13 – AM Bacher, DN Crookes, DJ Cullinan; 12 – HH Gibbs, BM McMillan, R Munnik; 11 – I Pistorius (9 ct/2 st), WJ Cronje, CB Lambert, KLR Rutherford, PA Wallace, W Wiblin; 10 – MLG Pedi (8 ct/2 st), S Abrahams, CL Hooper, KC Jackson, PC Strydom, M van Jaarsfeld, BM White

ASIAN TEST CHAMPIONSHIP

By Qamar Ahmed

The popularity of one-day cricket, declining crowd appeal of Test cricket and a growing demand to stage a World Championship of Test cricket had certainly given the Asian Cricket Council (ACC) the idea of staging an Asian Test Championship between Pakistan, India and Sri Lanka. But this had come at the expense of Pakistan's Test tour of three matches in India, which was curtailed to two Tests to launch the championship.

Launching the competition officially at Calcutta in February the President of the ACC Mr Thimanga Sumathipala said, 'We have taken the lead to stage the championship which will determine the champion nation in Test cricket in Asia.'

The International Cricket Council (ICC) president Mr Jagmohan Dalmiya, endorsing the comments, approved the idea and added, 'The championship that will determine the best Test nation in the world is still on the drawing board. But we have already instituted the Asian championship.'

Neutral umpires officiated the four matches in the competition, which were played at Calcutta, Colombo, Lahore and Dhaka. Pakistan won, beating Sri Lanka in the final to bag US$100,000 prize money. Bonus points were also introduced in Test cricket. For a win 12 points, for a draw no points except for batting and bowling in the first 100 overs of the first innings. Sri Lanka and Pakistan accumulated the highest and the second-highest points to reach the final.

The highlights of the tournament included two hat-tricks by the Pakistan captain Wasim Akram in successive Tests – at Lahore and at Dhaka, in the final against Sri Lanka. Saeed Anwar carried his bat through an innings in the first Test at Calcutta to score an unbeaten 188, emulating his Pakistan predecessors Nazar Mohammad and Muddasar. A century in each innings by Wajahatullah Wasti against Sri Lanka at Lahore, and a double century each by Ijaz Ahmed and Inzamam-ul-Haq in the final at Dhaka also determined Pakistan's domination of the competition.

The championship was launched with a high hopes, but in the end it was debatable whether it met its desired aims. The Calcutta match was marred by crowd trouble and in terms of spectator response, except in Calcutta where nearly 400,000 turned up, the championship failed to catch the imagination of the fanatic fans of the subcontinent. There were dull draws at Colombo and Lahore and matches were played in front of near-empty stands. The final at Dhaka finished in an anticlimax as Pakistan won comfortably against Sri Lanka.

Shoaib Akhtar celebrates Rahul Dravid's dismissal on fourth day of the Test match at Eden Gardens, Calcutta.
Mueen ud din Hameed/Sportsline

With India ousted after debatable tactics by Pakistan, who allowed Sri Lanka the required bonus points to reach the finals, the response at Dhaka was mute. India had reasons be unhappy but no recourse to complaint because Pakistan had played within the framework of the guidelines of the championship.

FIRST TEST: INDIA V. PAKISTAN
16, 17, 18, 19 and 20 February 1999 at Calcutta

The inaugural match of the new championship of Tests was won by Pakistan, who beat India by 46 runs. Watched by nearly 400,000 people in four and a half days, the match at the Eden Garden was, however, marred by crowd trouble on the fourth afternoon and on the final day. Sachin Tendulkar's run-out in the second over after he had collided with the fielder, Shoaib Akhtar, had sparked the first incident as India chased 279 runs to win the Test. And on the last day Pakistan's victory was delayed for nearly three and half hours after India lost three wickets for 17 runs to slump to 231 for 9.

A group of people in the stand, hurt at the prospect of India's inevitable defeat set heaps of newspapers on fire and hurled plastic bottles at the players to stop the match, very much reminiscent of the 1996 World Cup game between Sri Lanka and India. Nearly 80,000 people were then evacuated from the ground to allow Pakistan to take the last Indian wicket and win the match. Pakistan did this within ten balls and in front of deserted stands. Only the media, officials of the match and police remained in the ground.

Considering the fact that Pakistan were reduced to 26 for 6 on the first day after choosing to bat, it was commendable that they came back into the game to win it. Shoaib Akhtar's venomous pace and an unbeaten 188 by Saeed Anwar, who carried his bat through the completed second, were the major factors in Pakistan success. Moin Khan's fighting 70 had salvaged the first innings. He added 84 with Salim Malik for the seventh wicket and 63 with Wasim Akram for the eighth to enable Pakistan to make 185 in their first innings. Javagal Srinath, with 4 for 3, and Venkatesh Prasad, with 2 for 7 in 177 balls, had done the early damage.

India's reply of 223 on the second day was aided by Sadagopan Ramesh who made 79 with nine fours, adding 56 with Rahul Dravid for the third wicket. He and Sachin Tendulkar were later yorked on successive balls by Shoaib Akhtar's

---

FIRST TEST – INDIA v. PAKISTAN
16, 17, 18, 19 and 20 February 1999 at Eden Gardens, Calcutta

PAKISTAN

	First Innings		Second Innings	
Saeed Anwar	b Prasad	0	not out	188
Shahid Afridi	c Mongia, b Srinath	8	(6) c Laxman, b Srinath	0
Ijaz Ahmed	lbw, b Prasad	1	(4) c Mongia, b Srinath	11
Wajahatullah Wasti	c Mongia, b Prasad	6	(2) c Mongia, b Srinath	9
Yousuf Youhana	c Azharuddin, b Srinath	2	c Dravid, b Srinath	56
Salim Malik	c Mongia, b Srinath	32	(7) lbw, b Srinath	9
Azhar Mahmood	b Srinath	0	(9) lbw, b Srinath	0
*Moin Khan	c Laxman, b Tendulkar	70	c Mongia, b Prasad	8
Wasim Akram (capt)	c sub (HH Kanitkar), b Harbhajan Singh	38	(10) c Mongia b Srinath	1
Shoaib Akhtar	lbw, b Kumble	4	(11) b Srinath	1
Saqlain Mushtaq	not out	4	(3) c Mongia, b Harbhajan Singh	21
	lb 11, w 1, nb 8	20	lb 3, w 5, nb 4	12
		185		316

	First Innings				Second Innings			
	O	M	R	W	O	M	R	W
Srinath	19	4	46	5	27	6	86	8
Prasad	18	6	27	2	24	5	61	1
Ganguly	5	2	9	–				
Kumble	19.2	8	48	1	27	4	91	–
Harbhajan Singh	12	2	36	1	16	1	56	1
Tendulkar	3	1	8	–	2	0	10	–
Laxman					2	0	4	0
Ramesh					1	0	5	–

Fall of Wickets
1-15, 2-17, 3-19, 4-23, 5-25, 6-26, 7-110, 8-173, 9-177
1-26, 2-94, 3-147, 4-262, 5-262, 6-284, 7-301, 8-302, 9-304

INDIA

	First Innings		Second Innings	
S Ramesh	lbw, b Wasim Akram	79	lbw, b Saqlain Mushtaq	40
VVS Laxman	b Shoaib Akhtar	5	c Yousuf Youhana, b Saqlain Mushtaq	67
A Kumble	c Moin, b Azhar Mahmood	18	(8) c Shahid Afridi, b Shoaib	16
RS Dravid	b Shoaib Akhtar	24	(3) c Moin, b Shoaib Akhtar	13
SR Tendulkar	b Shoaib Akhtar	0	(4) run out (sub: Nadeem Khan)	9
M Azharuddin (capt)	c Saqlain Mushtaq, b Wasim Akram	23	(5) c Yousuf Youhana, b Saqlain Mushtaq	20
SC Ganguly	c Wasim Akram, b Saqlain Mushtaq	17	(6) c Azhar Mahmood, b Wasim Akram	24
*NR Mongia	run out (Moin Khan)	5	(7) lbw, b Shoaib Akhtar	1
J Srinath	c Moin Khan, b Wasim Akram	3	c Moin Khan, b Wasim Akram	3
BKV Prasad	b Shoaib Akhtar	0	b Shoaib Akhtar	2
Harbhajan Singh	not out	8	not out	0
	lb 9, nb 32	41	b 10, lb 9, nb 18	37
		223		232

	First Innings				Second Innings			
	O	M	R	W	O	M	R	W
Wasim Akram	24	5	65	3	24	4	64	2
Shoaib Akhtar	19.2	1	71	4	20.1	5	47	4
Azhar Mahmood	18	5	40	1	6	0	23	–
Saqlain Mushtaq	13	3	31	1	25	5	69	3
Shahid Afridi	2	0	7	–	4	1	10	–

Fall of Wickets
1-26, 2-91, 3-147, 4-147, 5-164, 6-205, 7-205, 8-211, 9-212
1-108, 2-134, 3-145, 4-149, 5-183, 6-190, 7-219, 8-224, 9-231

Umpires: DL Orchard & SA Bucknor
Toss: Pakistan

Pakistan won by 46 runs

fiery pace. Pakistan in their second innings made 316 losing their last five wickets for 32, thus setting India a target of 279 to win on the third evening. Saeed Anwar had added 68 for the second wicket with nightwatchman Saqlain Mushtaq, 53 with Ijaz Ahmed for the third wicket and 115 with Yousuf Youhana for the fourth-wicket stand as he carried his bat through for 188, his highest score in a Test. He batted for 452 minutes to hit 23 fours and a six. Srinath had 8 for 86, his best in a Test, to finish with 12 for 132, his first ten-wicket haul.

India managed 214 for 6 on the fourth day. Tendulkar was run out off a direct throw from deep mid-wicket by substitute Nadeem Khan. Taking the third run, Tendulkar had collided with fielder Shoaib Akhtar and failed to land his bat in the crease. His dismissal sparked crowd trouble. Later Tendulkar himself and the ICC president Mr Jagmohan Dalmiya had to appeal to the crowd to calm down. Shoaib's obstruction was not deliberate.

On the final day India, with four wickets intact required a further 65 runs to win. However, Wasim and Shoaib were in no mood for generosity and wrapped up the match by 46 runs.

Saeed Anwar remained unbeaten in Pakistan's second innings of the Asian Test Championship match in Calcutta.
Mueen ud din Hameed/Sportsline

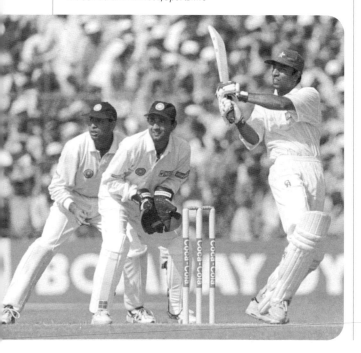

SECOND TEST: SRI LANKA V. INDIA
24, 25, 26, 27 and 28 February 1999 at Colombo

On a flat pitch both Sri Lanka and India scored heavily as the match petered out in a tame draw, a result which assured Pakistan a place in the final. India ended with five bonus points and Sri Lanka four. In a match in which over 1,300 runs were scored, three Indian batsmen – Sadagopan Ramesh (143) Rahul Dravid (107) and Sachin Tendulkar (124) – hammered the Sri Lankan bowlers to their heart's content. For Sri Lanka Mahela Jayawardene scored 242.

Arjuna Ranatunga's dream of bowling India out after asking them in had backfired as opener Ramesh and Dravid put on 232 record runs for the second wicket for India against Sri Lanka. Dravid made 107 with 12 fours in 314 minutes batting, his fifth Test century; Ramesh's maiden Test hundred 143 contained 18 fours in 317 minutes' stay. India declared after tea on the second day at 518 for 7 but not before Sachin Tendulkar hit 53 with ten fours, and Mohammad Azharuddin and Saurav Ganguly had made 87 and 56 respectively.

Sri Lanka made a fitting reply with the help of Jayawardene who notched up 242, his highest score in seven Tests. Dropped four times, he batted with gusto, hitting 30 fours and two sixes. Anil Kumble's 4 for 134 was a just reward as he caught Jayawardene off his own bowling on the fourth day. Upashantha had denied him the hat-trick after he had dismissed Vaas and Ranatunga with successive deliveries. With no result in sight India batted through the fourth afternoon and on the final day. Five men close to the bat did not much affect Tendulkar and Ganguly, who put on 139 for the third wicket after India had lost two for 74. Tendulkar's 124 in the second innings was his 19th Test century and contained ten fours and a six in 304 minutes' batting, and Ganguly's 78 had eight crisp fours.

THIRD TEST: PAKISTAN V. SRI LANKA
4, 5, 6,7 and 8 March 1999 at Lahore

Sri Lanka assured themselves a place in the final with another drawn game, which earned them the required bonus points to oust India from the finals. That they were able to achieve a draw was itself creditable considering that their main performers Arjuna Ranatunga, Aravinda de Silva, Sanath Jayasuriya and Muttiah Muralitharan were unavailable due to injury. They needed to

SECOND TEST – SRI LANKA v. INDIA
24, 25, 26, 27 and 28 February 1999 at Sinhalese Sports Club, Colombo

INDIA

	First Innings		Second Innings	
S Ramesh	c Ranatunga, b Jayawardene	143	c Tillekeratne, b Upashantha	30
VVS Laxman	c de Silva, b Perera	11	lbw, b Upashantha	25
RS Dravid	c Ranatunga, b Hathurasinghe	107		
SR Tendulkar	c Kaluwitharana,		(4) not out	124
	b Hathurasinghe	53		
M Azharuddin (capt)	c Hathurasinghe, b Arnold	87	c Arnold, b de Silva	15
SC Ganguly	c sub (RS Kalpage),		(3) st Kaluwitharana,	
	b Upashantha	56	b de Silva	78
*NR Mongia	c de Silva, b Arnold	25		
A Kumble	not out	10	(6) c Vaas, b Arnold	10
BKV Prasad			(7) not out	9
Harbhajan Singh				
A Nehra				
	b 5, lb 6, w 3, nb 12	26	b 1, lb 3, w 2, nb 9	15
	(for 7 wickets dec.)	518	(for 5 wickets)	306

	First Innings				Second Innings			
	O	M	R	W	O	M	R	W
Vaas	31	5	108	1	18	3	58	-
Perera	30	4	125	1	14	2	60	-
Upashantha	28	3	94	1	15	2	41	2
Hathurasinghe	18	3	51	1				
Arnold	24.5	2	94	2	23.4	4	54	1
Jayawardene	11	3	35	1	14	1	30	-
de Silva					18.2	2	59	2
Tillekeratne					1	1	-	-

Fall of Wickets
1–20, 2–252, 3–288, 4–351, 5–463, 6–491, 7–518
1–50, 2–73, 3–213, 4–253, 5–283

SRI LANKA

	First Innings	
MS Atapattu	lbw, b Nehra	6
RP Arnold	run out (Dravid)	34
DPM Jayawardene	c and b Kumble	242
UC Hathurasinghe	lbw, b Prasad	14
PA de Silva	b Harbhajan Singh	23
A Ranatunga (capt)	c sub (HH Kanitkar), b Kumble	66
HP Tillekeratne	st Mongia,	
	b Harbhajan Singh	14
*RS Kaluwitharana	b Harbhajan Singh	23
WPUJC Vaas	c Laxman b Kumble	23
KEA Upashantha	lbw, b Kumble	6
RL Perera	not out	1
	b 1, lb 19, w 4, nb 9	33
		485

	First Innings			
	O	M	R	W
Prasad	31	6	94	1
Nehra	28	4	94	1
Kumble	54.1	10	134	4
Harbhajan Singh	40	9	127	3
Tendulkar	5	0	16	-
Ganguly	1	1	-	-

Fall of Wickets
1–18, 2–93, 3–129, 4–178, 5–354, 6–390, 7–466, 8–466, 9–484

Umpires: RE Koertzen & RB Tiffin
Toss: Sri Lanka

Match drawn

Rahul Dravid.
David Munden/Sportsline

pass 300 runs within 100 overs in reply to Pakistan's 398 in the first innings to gain the required bonus points to be in the final. They succeeded.

Any suggestion that Pakistan allowed Sri Lanka the freedom of the field and enabled them to score with ease was strongly denied by the Pakistan captain Wasim Akram who had the distinction of taking a hat-trick in a Test, the first by a Pakistan bowler. Wajahatullah Wasti, in only his second Test, scored a hundred in each innings to join Hanif Mohammad and Javed Miandad who had done so before him for their country against England at Dhaka in 1961–62 and at Hyderabad in 1984–85.

Wasti, dropped at 9 off Wickremasinghe, made 133 in the first innings with 18 fours and two sixes in 335 minutes' batting. Yousuf Youhana scored 83 with one four. Imran Nazir, the 17-year-old debutant, batted comfortably for his 64.

In reply Russel Arnold notched up 123 in Sri Lanka's 328. Arnold hit 20 fours in his maiden Test hundred. He put on 84 with Avishka Gunawardene for the first wicket and 143 for the fifth wicket with Rumesh Kaluwitharana, who made exactly 100. Pakistan took a lead of 70 runs but not before Wasim Akram had Kaluwitharana caught at the wicket, and Bandaratilleke and Wickremasinghe bowled, to take a hat-trick in his 87th Test.

Pakistan declared at 318 for 8 on the fourth day. Afridi's 84 was eclipsed by another century, 121 by Wasti who hit 12 fours in 425 minutes' batting and added 156 with Afridi for the first wicket. Sri Lanka, requiring 385 to win on the final day, were restricted to 164 for 2 before rain and bad light halted the proceedings.

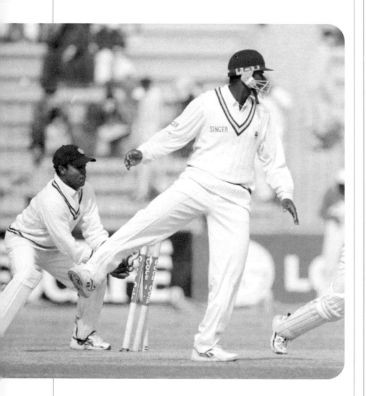

Imran Nazir of Pakistan is bowled by Bandarathilleke on the 4th day of Lahore test.
Mueen ud din Hameed/Sportsline

THIRD TEST – PAKISTAN v. SRI LANKA
4, 5, 6, 7 and 8 March 1999 at Gaddafi Stadium, Lahore

PAKISTAN

	First Innings		Second Innings	
Saeed Anwar	b Wickremasinghe	0	(4) run out (de Silva)	45
Wajahatullah Wasti	run out (Atapattu)	133	(1) not out	121
Imran Nazir	c de Silva, b Wickremasinghe	64	(5) b Bandaratilleke	13
Inzamam-ul-Haq	b Wickremasinghe	0	(3) lbw, b de Silva	4
Yousuf Youhana	c and b Kalpage	83	(6) st Kaluwitharana, b Bandaratilleke	0
Shahid Afridi	c Gunawardene, b Kalpage	0	(2) c Kaluwitharana, b de Silva	4
*Moin Khan	lbw, b Wickremasinghe	57	(8) run out (sub: UDU Chandana)	2
Saqlain Mushtaq	c de Silva, b Bandaratilleke	15	(9) st Kaluwitharana, b Kalpage	9
Wasim Akram (capt)	c Arnold, b Wickremasinghe	4	(7) b Kalpage	17
Shahid Nazir	c Atapattu, b Wickremasinghe	10		
Fazl-e-Akbar	not out	15		
	b 2, lb 11, nb 4	17	b 3, lb 7, nb 9	19
		398	(for 8 wickets dec.)	**314**

	First Innings				Second Innings			
	O	M	R	W	O	M	R	W
Wickremasinghe	29.1	7	103	6	9	1	27	–
de Silva	14	0	88	–	29	5	90	2
Hathurasinghe	12	3	29	–	13	2	41	–
Bandaratilleke	31	8	90	1	25	12	54	2
Kalpage	16	2	75	2	20.5	0	92	2

Fall of Wickets
1–0, 2–105, 3–105, 4–283, 5–283, 6–302, 7–323, 8–339, 9–373
1–156, 2–161, 3–226, 4–250, 5–254, 6–288, 7–297, 8–314

SRI LANKA

	First Innings		Second Innings	
RP Arnold	b Saqlain Mushtaq	123	not out	56
DA Gunawardene	c Shahid Nazir, b Fazl-e-Akbar	43	lbw, b Shahid Nazir	37
DPM Jayawardene	b Saqlain Mushtaq	4	c Moin Khan, b Wasim Akram	50
MS Atapattu	c Yousuf, b Saqlain Mushtaq	23	not out	6
HP Tillekeratne (capt)	b Saqlain Mushtaq	9		
*RS Kaluwitharana	c Moin Khan, b Wasim Akram	100		
UC Hathurasinghe	lbw, b Shahid Afridi	0		
RS Kalpage	not out	2		
MRCN Bandaratilleke	b Wasim Akram	0		
GP Wickremasinghe	b Wasim Akram	0		
KSC de Silva	b Wasim Akram	8		
	lb 8, nb 8	16	lb 11, nb 5	16
		328	(for 2 wickets)	**165**

	First Innings				Second Innings			
	O	M	R	W	O	M	R	W
Wasim Akram	9.2	2	30	4	13	2	39	1
Fazl-e-Akbar	19	4	92	1	8	1	27	–
Shahid Nazir	11	1	45	–	8	0	27	1
Saqlain Mushtaq	25	6	82	4	21.1	8	53	–
Shahid Afridi	20	4	71	1				
Wajahatullah Wasti					1	0	8	–

Fall of Wickets
1–84, 2–91, 3–146, 4–156, 5–299, 6–308, 7–320, 8–320, 9–320
1–64, 2–158

Umpires: RE Koertzen & DR Shepherd
Toss: Pakistan

<u>Match drawn</u>

ASIAN TEST CHAMPIONSHIP FINAL
Pakistan v. Sri Lanka
12, 13, 14 and 15 March 1999 at Dhaka

Wajahatullah Wasti made a century for Pakistan in each innings during the Lahore Test against Sri Lanka.
Mueen ud din Hameed/Sportsline

There was little by way of quality and excitement in the first ever final of the Asian Test Championship. Pakistan inflicted a heavy defeat on Sri Lanka to win the match by an innings and 175 runs to become the Asian Test champions. The Pakistan captain Wasim Akram was elated not only because his team had won but also because he had achieved yet another hat-trick: his second in successive Tests to join Trumble and Matthews of Australia who had performed the feat twice before him.

A double century each by Ijaz Ahmed and Inzamam-ul-Haq provided lustre to a match that was rather dull and one-sided from the moment Sri Lanka won the toss, decided to bat and failed to capitalise on it. Of the injured four – Arjuna Ranatunga, Aravinda de Silva, Sanath Jayasuriya and Muttiah Muralitharan – only de Silva could make it to the final, which left Sri Lanka's batting rather fragile and exposed. They were bowled out for 231 in their first innings as off-spinner Arshad Khan took 5 for 38 after Wasim Akram, Shoaib Akhtar and Saqlain Mushtaq had dented the early batting. De Silva's 72 with ten fours was a lone effort.

When Pakistan batted, Saeed Anwar made 57 and later Ijaz Ahmed and Inzamam-ul-Haq piled on the agony for the Sri Lankan bowlers, who toiled aimlessly as the two batsmen hammered them. Ijaz made 211 and Inzamam 200 adding 352 for the third wicket. For both batsmen it was their first double century in a Test. Ijaz's innings contained 23 fours and a six and Inzamam's innings had as many fours and two sixes. Ijaz's career-best also took him past 3,000 runs in Tests. Upal Chandana, the right-arm leg-spinner had the consolation of 6 for 179 on his debut.

Sri Lanka, trailing by 363 on the first innings, were all out for 188 in their second innings. Wasim Akram took a hat-trick by removing Avishka Gunawardene, Chaminda Vaas and Mahela Jayawardene off his fifth and sixth deliveries of his first over and the first of his second over to finish with 3 for 33. Saqlain Mushtaq, Shahid Afridi and Arshad Khan with 3 for 46, 2 for 31, and 1 for 41, had also played their part in Pakistan's historic victory.

Wasim Akram captained the winning Pakistan side during the fourth Test in Dhaka.

David Munden/Sportsline

FOURTH TEST – PAKISTAN v. SRI LANKA
12, 13, 14 and 15 March 1999 at Bangabandhu National Stadium, Dhaka

SRI LANKA

	First Innings		Second Innings	
RP Arnold	b Shoaib Akhtar	10	c Wasim Akram, b Arshad Khan	30
DA Gunawardene	c Wajahatullah Wasti, b Wasim Akram	4	c Shahid Afridi, b Wasim Akram	0
DPM Jayawardene	lbw, b Wasim Akram	0	(4) c Wajahatullah Wasti, b Wasim Akram	1
MS Atapattu	lbw, b Saqlain Mushtaq	36	(5) run out (Wasim Akram)	22
PA de Silva (capt)	lbw, b Arshad Khan	72	(6) c Wajahatullah, b Saqlain	6
HP Tillekeratne	c Wajahatullah, b Arshad Khan	15	(7) not out	55
*RS Kaluwitharana	c Yousuf, b Arshad Khan	9	(8) lbw, b Shahid Afridi	0
UDU Chandana	c Moin Khan, b Shoaib Akhtar	15	(9) lbw, b Shahid Afridi	28
WPUJC Vaas	not out	20	(3) b Wasim Akram	0
GP Wickremasinghe	c Wajahatullah, b Arshad Khan	2	b Shahid Afridi	7
KSC de Silva	c Moin Khan, b Arshad Khan	11	b Saqlain Mushtaq	27
	b 12, lb 9, nb 16	37	b 4, lb 7, nb 1	12
		231		**188**

	First Innings				Second Innings			
	O	M	R	W	O	M	R	W
Wasim Akram	14	2	45	2	7	0	33	3
Shoaib Akhtar	13	3	36	2	10.4	3	26	–
Saqlain Mushtaq	29	6	76	1	28.5	15	46	3
Shahid Afridi	2	0	15	–	7	1	31	2
Arshad Khan	20	5	38	5	12	3	41	1

Fall of Wickets
1–16, 2–16, 3–19, 4–84, 5–119, 6–135, 7–177, 8–201, 9–208
1–5, 2–5, 3–9, 4–48, 5–59, 6–59, 7–61, 8–101, 9–115

PAKISTAN

	First Innings	
Saeed Anwar	c and b Arnold	57
Wajahatullah Wasti	c Jayawardene, KSC b de Silva	22
Ijaz Ahmed	st Tillekeratne, b Chandana	211
Inzamam-ul-Haq	not out	200
Yousuf Youhana	c sub (UC Hathurasinghe), b Chandana	19
Shahid Afridi	c and b Chandana	21
*Moin Khan	c KSC de Silva, b Arnold	10
Wasim Akram (capt)	c Vaas, b Chandana	8
Saqlain Mushtaq	run out (Tillekeratne/ Gunawardene)	4
Arshad Khan	c Tillekeratne, b Chandana	3
Shoaib Akhtar	st Tillekeratne, b Chandana	4
	b 15, lb 12, nb 8	35
		594

	First Innings			
	O	M	R	W
Vaas	32	4	101	–
Wickremasinghe	20	4	53	–
K S C de Silva	25.4	3	75	1
Chandana	47.4	8	179	6
P A de Silva	12	0	44	–
Arnold	37.2	2	80	2
Jayawardene	10	0	35	–

Fall of Wickets
1–75, 2–117, 3–483, 4–515, 5–518, 6–534, 7–542, 8–555, 9–560

Umpires: DB Cowie & DR Shepherd
Toss: Sri Lanka

Pakistan won by an innings and 175 runs

AUSTRALIA

England Tour of Australia
Carlton and United One-day Series
Sheffield Shield
Mercantile Mutual Cup

ENGLAND TOUR OF AUSTRALIA
By Jonathan Agnew

Reporting on Test matches between England and Australia in the 1990s has been a chastening experience. As Alec Stewart mustered his troops for what would be his third Ashes tour, he needed no reminding of the grisly details: since England last won the Ashes in 1987, they had won just four of the 29 tests played between the two countries and had lost a staggering 17. Stewart, himself, faced the prospect of an exhausting trip. Saddled with the responsibility of the captaincy, he was to open the batting and keep wicket, too. 'The Gaffer' is never less than massively enthusiastic about just about anything you care to mention, but these were quite unrealistic demands.

Only a supreme patriot could really have envisaged Stewart's men returning with the urn this time, and this despite their narrow victory over South Africa during the summer. True, that had done wonders for morale – as well as cementing Stewart's position as England's leader – but the outcome of that series had depended too much on umpiring mistakes in the last two Tests. One could always choose to overlook that not insignificant detail if it suited, but the fact is that it tempered even the usually extravagant forecasts of that most eternal of all optimists, the coach David Lloyd. That – and, no doubt, the very public dressing down he received from his employers at the end of the summer for raising doubts about the legality of Muttiah Muralitharan's bowling action. Lloyd embarked on the trip of Australia knowing that he had picked up his final yellow card.

As is customary, England's selection caused the usual quota of raised eyebrows amongst the pundits. Two off spinners – Robert Croft and Peter Such – were preferred to the more logical balance of one off spinner and Ashley Giles, the left-arm spinner. Graeme Hick was left out of the party, despite having scored 107 against Sri Lanka. John Crawley, who made an unbeaten 156 in the same game to cap a terrific summer, was preferred while Warren Hegg won the vote ahead of Paul Nixon for the reserve wicketkeeper's spot. The most interesting – not to mention imaginative – selection of all was that of 21-year-old Alex Tudor. The young fast bowler had taken just 29 first-class wickets for Surrey in the 1998 season, and fitness had been a perpetual problem ever since his raw pace and good action had earmarked him as being a genuine prospect. His brief for the tour was to look and learn.

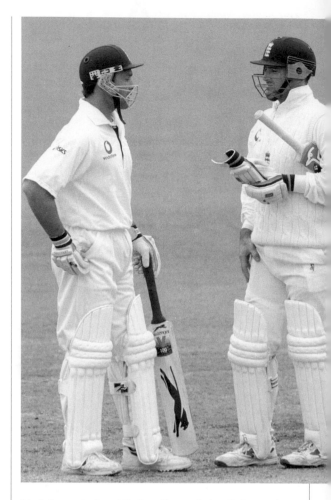

Mark Ramprakash and Graham Thorpe during their record-breaking stand against South Australia at Adelaide.
David Munden/Sportsline Photographic

England's departure for Perth coincided with Australia's successful tour of Pakistan that confirmed their status as the leading and most ruthless all-round Test team in world cricket. Even without Shane Warne, who was making noises about returning to the fray at the Boxing Day Test in Melbourne, Australia revelled in the subcontinental conditions. This was largely due to the efforts of Stuart MacGill, Warne's replacement, who immediately made his mark and ensured that any relief England might have felt at Warne's absence would be short-lived. In fact, MacGill was to claim 27 victims in the Ashes series including a haul of 12 wickets in the final Test in Sydney while Warne, operating at the other end in that match, took just two.

ACB Chairman's XI v. England
29 October 1998 at Lilac Hill
England 297 for 5 (50 overs) MA Atherton 88,
AJ Stewart 74, JP Crawley 64
ACB Chairman's XI 296 (50 overs) RJ Campbell
England won by 1 run

Eleven thousand people turned up to witness
Dennis Lillee's annual outing. He was joined,
from the veteran's department, by Bruce Reid
and Graeme Wood for Western Australia's
equivalent of Arundel – if a little more raucous.

For England, Mike Atherton's 88 came from 108
balls, including 13 fours while Lillee's six overs
conceded only 22 runs – the most economical
analysis of the day. Stewart injured his back; an
injury that kept him out of England's opening first-
class match, and Ben Hollioake's groin strain
prevented him from playing until 5 December.

The ACB Chairman's XI were always in the hunt,
Ryan Campbell's 74 was scored from 60 balls and
only a crazy run-out gave England victory off the
last ball of the day by the narrowest of margins.

The post-match press conference was conducted
in a beer tent.

Western Australia v. England
31 October, 1, 2 and 3 November at Perth
Western Australia 334 for 8 dec. (SM Katich 106,
JL Langer 85, MJ Nicholson 58*, D Gough 4 for 74) and
268 for 3 dec.
England 321 (N Hussain 118, MR Ramprakash 81,
MJ Nicholson 7 for 77) and 192 for 4 (JP Crawley 65,
GP Thorpe 64*)
Match drawn

A horrible injury to Mark Butcher, who was hit above
the right eye by a delivery from Matthew Nicholson,
reminded England of the unique requirements of
batting on the fastest cricket pitch in the world.
Butcher required ten stitches and was unable to bat
in the second innings, joining Atherton, Stewart and
Hollioake on the physio's table.

In blistering heat on the first day, England's
fielders dropped their first of six important catches
– a habit that was to plague them throughout the
tour. Langer profited twice and Nicholson once in
his breezy tail-ender's knock of 58 not out, but
Western Australia's first innings was built around
Simon Katich's six-hour marathon.

The unfortunate Butcher having been lead away,
Nasser Hussain emerged to score a memorable
century in his first first-class match in Australia. He

Western Warriors v. England at Perth. Mark Butcher is
tended to by Wayne Morton after being hit on the head
by a ball from Nicholson.
David Munden/Sportsline Photographic

was finally caught at second slip off the second
new ball as Nicholson, operating at high pace,
ran through the England line-up. Only Mark
Ramprakash, who batted for four and a half hours,
stood firm although Allan Mullally startled a few by
scoring an unbeaten 25.

Poor Angus Fraser got his first taste of difficult
times to come when Campbell bludgeoned him for
four consecutive fours – Campbell hit 23 boundaries
in all. In fact, both Fraser and Dominic Cork were
well below their best allowing Langer to set England
a target of 282 in 63 overs to win.

At tea on the final day, England needed a further
162 off 28 overs with eight wickets in hand. Crawley
was caught at cover almost immediately after the
break for a fluent 65 but despite the fact that
Graham Thorpe was also in good touch, the shutters
came down on England's run chase. Afterwards,
Langer supplied the English tabloids with plenty of
material when he criticised the tourists for their
'negative' approach.

South Australia v. England
7, 8, 9 and 10 November 1998 at Adelaide
England 187 (N Hussain 57, DG Cork 51) and 457 for 4
(GP Thorpe 223*, MR Ramprakash 140*, MA Atherton 53)
South Australia 325 (GS Blewett 143, JM Vaughan 58,
DG Cork 4 for 45)
Match drawn

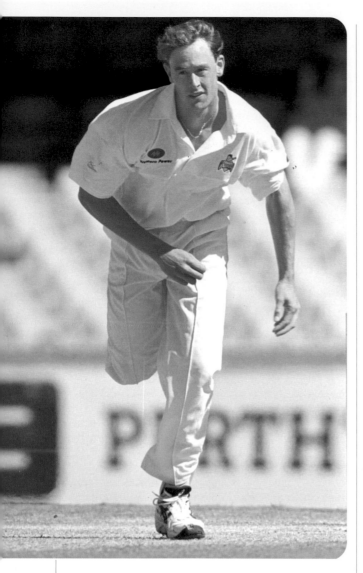

Matthew Nicholson of Western Australia.
David Munden/Sportsline Photographic

An astonishing unbeaten partnership of 377 between Ramprakash and Thorpe denied South Australia what had appeared to be a certain victory. The stand, which lasted throughout the final day, is the highest record for any touring team to Australia and was immediately offered as evidence of the new, hardened approach that England were keen to display in the Test series. Thorpe's effort was all the more remarkable because he was reported to have been ill before the start of the final morning and there was real doubt about his being able to bat. In

fact, he scored the small matter of 223 not out, 125 of them between lunch and tea as the pair added 194 runs in the session. In mitigation, it must be noted that both of South Australia's spinners were making their first-class debuts and their inexperience was ruthlessly exposed.

England's first-innings total was a feeble performance with only Atherton being able to claim that his dismissal was unlucky. Stewart, Butcher, Thorpe and, eventually, Hussain all fell to cavalier strokes and had it not been for a stand of 59 between Cork and Alex Tudor, who rescued England from 97 for 6, the tourists' predicament would have been even worse.

Greg Blewett quickly put all of that into perspective with a brilliant hundred, but from 214 for 2, South Australia collapsed to Cork and Fraser to restrict their lead to 138.

Atherton made a solid 53 before being run out, backing up at the non-striker's end, but Stewart bagged a pair as England quickly slipped to 80 for 4 in reply. By the close of the third day, England were only 11 runs in front. However, that merely set the stage for Ramprakash's and Thorpe's heroics. For the record, Thorpe's 223 not out came in 303 minutes and included 23 fours and four sixes. Ramprakash faced 292 balls and hit 18 boundaries.

Queensland v. England
13, 14 and 15 November at Cairns
Queensland 209 (DI Foley 71, IA Healy 57) and 124 (JP Mahler 56)
England 192 (AJ Stewart 52, AC Dale 7 for 33) and 142 for 9 (MS Kasprowicz 6 for 31)
England won by one wicket

A new venue for many of us, and a Queensland team bristling with fine players. However, the start of the match was a curious affair. Heavy overnight rain had found its way under the covers and the second delivery of the game, bowled by Darren Gough, climbed from a good length to break Matthew Hayden's finger. There was a further delay when Gough then called for some sawdust only for the groundsman to discover that he had forgotten to order any from the local sawmill. A local was dispatched in his pick-up and, 20 minutes later, he finally returned with copious amounts of sawdust, thereby allowing the match to continue.

Scoring was never easy in the damp conditions, and Gough, Mullally and Dean Headley all swung the ball. The exception was Cork who, again, looked out of sorts, although he did have Ian Healy, on 7, dropped by Stewart. Healy and Geoff Foley then put together a stand of 90 for the fifth wicket to give Queensland a competitive total.

Butcher failed again as England slipped to 4 for 2, but Stewart found his form, scoring 52 in a stand of 100 with Hussain for the third wicket. Adam Dale – later to appear in the one-day series – relished the heavy atmosphere to claim 7 for 33 and give his team a slender lead of 17.

Gough, with 3 for 41, and Robert Croft, 3 for 56, kept England in the low-scoring match and when Queensland were bowled out for 124, England needed 142 to win.

Butcher's second-ball 0, giving him an aggregate of nine runs in five first-class innings, got England away to a terrible start. Soon they were 51 for 4 and 100 for 7. At 106 for 9, England's last pair of Croft and Mullally needed to score a further 36 to win. Painstakingly – and with Mullally wisely restraining himself – they chipped away and, after 78 nervous minutes, saw England to a morale-boosting victory.

Mullally's effort successfully conned the Australian public into believing that he could hold a bat and, after two memorable fighting performances, we were all left wondering if this team really was about to make a fight of the Ashes series after all.

First Test
20, 21, 22, 23 and 24 November 1998 at Brisbane

If ever there were a Test match in recent years that England's cricketers were determined not to lose, this was it. The opening Tests of the past two tours – both staged at the 'Gabba – had ended in overwhelming victories for Australia. They were results that set the tone for the remainder of both series and England, with their new-found – and much vaunted – 'mental toughness' knew they had to emerge from this encounter unscathed. That, eventually, they managed to do so was almost entirely due to a cataclysmic tropical storm that arrived bang on cue midway through the final afternoon, just as England were in danger of being overrun, to transform the lush 'Gabba outfield into a large boating pond.

At the height of the storm, it was impossible to see one end of the ground from the other. Lightning bolts struck all around Brisbane, including a direct hit on the Channel 9 control van that resulted in Richie and co. being blacked out. Meanwhile, on BBC Radio, Henry Blofeld's vivid description, interspersed with deafening cracks of thunder, was a startling beginning of the day for drowsy *Test Match Special* listeners in England, many of whom then lay in bed mesmerised by the dramatic sound effects. It was an awesome and violent act of nature.

When the heavens opened, England were still 168 runs adrift and, with only four second-innings wickets remaining on a pitch that was now allowing sharp spin, had little prospect of surviving the 30 overs that were still to be bowled. As members of the Barmy Army enjoyed themselves on the grassy bank beneath the scoreboard, which was, by now, a water slide of theme-park proportions, an argument that had briefly raised its head at the start of the tour was prompting angry debate in the post-match press conference. The Australian authorities had offered England the option of switching on the floodlights in cases of poor light so playing time would not be lost. England had declined, arguing, with some justification, that they had never played cricket under those artificial conditions with a red ball before. Had the Australians suggested that one of the early tour matches start and end two hours later each day, with the floodlights being used in the

Damien Fleming plays a ball through the on-side during his innings of 71 not out, second day of the first Test at Brisbane.
David Munden/Sportsline Photographic

final session, England might have agreed to the experiment. But by now it was too late.

This did not appease the Australians who felt deprived of victory. However, the argument that the floodlights could have been used on the last afternoon before the storm finally arrived simply did not make sense. True, the gloom might certainly have been lifted sufficiently long for Stuart MacGill and Glenn McGrath to finish off England's tail. However, the flashes of lightning that preceded the storm would have driven the players from the field only a matter of minutes after the batsmen gratefully accepted the original offer of bad light from the umpires. No. The weather would not be denied that day, either way.

It was good sport for the Australian newspapers, however, which, after the first day's play, had been rocked a little uncomfortably on to the back foot. Australia were 246 for 5 at the close, having been reduced to 178 for 5, and, fleetingly, it seemed that, contrary to public opinion, the battle for the Ashes might prove to be a contest after all. Steve Waugh and Ian Healy were still at the crease and, crucially, both batsmen had already been dropped.

For England, those missed chances were nothing short of calamitous. Angus Fraser was the first culprit at third man, putting down a steepling mis-pull off Gough when Healy had scored 36. Waugh should have been run out on 29 when Allan Mullally, the bowler, suffered a brainstorm and stopped a potentially accurate throw by Alec Stewart from hitting the stumps. Waugh was then dropped by Nasser Hussain at slip off the persevering Gough when he had 68.

Both batsmen have, for years, been aggravating thorns in England's side. After so many missed opportunities, it was inconceivable that they would do anything other than make the tourists pay dearly. Their partnership of 187 for the sixth wicket ended 20 minutes after lunch on the second day and even the construction workers in their hard hats, who were noisily transforming a previously attractive and charming cricket ground into yet another hideous concrete bowl, paused to watch.

To add further insult, Damien Fleming – a lusty hitter at number nine – thrashed an uncompromising 71 not out from 107 balls and, between them, the last five Australian wickets added 307 runs. Mullally recorded his first five-wicket haul in Test cricket while Gough was wretchedly unlucky. The field placements for the solitary spinner, Robert Croft, were baffling beyond belief.

For the tenth time in 14 innings, McGrath dealt with Mike Atherton, this time taken at slip for a

FIRST TEST – AUSTRALIA v. ENGLAND
20, 21, 22, 23 and 24 November at Woolloongabba, Brisbane

AUSTRALIA

	First Innings		Second Innings	
MA Taylor (capt)	c Hussain, b Cork	46	(2) b Cork	0
MJ Slater	c Butcher, b Mullally	16	(1) c & b Fraser	113
JL Langer	lbw, b Gough	8	c Mullally, b Croft	74
ME Waugh	c Stewart, b Mullally	31	not out	27
SR Waugh	c Stewart, b Mullally	112	not out	16
RT Ponting	c Butcher, b Cork	21		
*IA Healy	c Mullally, b Fraser	134		
MS Kasprowicz	c Stewart, b Mullally	0		
DW Fleming	not out	71		
SCG MacGill	c Stewart, b Mullally	20		
GD McGrath	c Atherton, b Croft	5		
	lb 14, w 1, nb 6	21	b 1, lb 1, nb 5	7
		485	(for 3 wickets, dec.)	**237**

	First Innings				Second Innings			
	O	M	R	W	O	M	R	W
Gough	34	4	135	1	6	0	50	–
Cork	31	6	98	2	5	0	18	1
Mullally	40	10	105	5	14	4	38	–
Croft	23	6	55	1	20	2	71	1
Fraser	28	7	76	1	15	1	52	1
Ramprakash	2	1	2	–	2	0	6	–

Fall of Wickets
1-30, 2-59, 3-106, 4-106, 5-178, 6-365, 7-365, 8-420, 9-445
1-20, 2-182, 3-199

ENGLAND

	First Innings		Second Innings	
MA Butcher	c & b ME Waugh	116	lbw, b MacGill	40
MA Atherton	c ME Waugh, b McGrath	0	c Fleming, b McGrath	28
N Hussain	c Healy, b Kasprowicz	59	b MacGill	47
*AJ Stewart (capt)	c Kasprowicz, b MacGill	8	c Ponting, b ME Waugh	3
GP Thorpe	c Langer, b McGrath	77	c Langer, b ME Waugh	9
MR Ramprakash	not out	69	st Healy, b MacGill	14
DG Cork	c MacGill, b McGrath	0	not out	21
RDB Croft	b Kasprowicz	23	not out	4
D Gough	lbw, b McGrath	0		
AD Mullally	c Kasprowicz, b McGrath	0		
ARC Fraser	c ME Waugh, b McGrath	1		
	b 1, lb 9, nb 12	22	lb 3, w 1, nb 9	13
		375	(for 6 wickets)	**179**

	First Innings				Second Innings			
	O	M	R	W	O	M	R	W
McGrath	34.2	11	85	6	16	6	30	1
Fleming	27	5	83	–	7	2	12	–
Kasprowicz	29	7	82	2	8	3	28	–
MacGill	24	4	70	1	22	3	51	3
SR Waugh	3	0	17	–				
Ponting	3	0	10	–	1	1	–	–
ME Waugh	8	1	18	1	14	0	55	2

Fall of Wickets
1-11, 2-145, 3-168, 4-240, 5-315, 6-319, 7-360, 8-373, 9-373
1-46, 2-96, 3-103, 4-133, 5-148, 6-161

Umpires: DB Hair & KT Francis
Toss: Australia

Match drawn

Last day at the first Test: lightning strikes around the scoreboard showing England in trouble trying to save the game at 179 for 6 wickets.

David Munden/Sportsline Photographic

duck; but with Butcher – supported by Hussain and Thorpe – playing with admirable fluency, England appeared to be making a decent fist of their reply. However, 314 for 4 quickly became 375 all out as McGrath took 5 for 9 in 35 balls and, with the ball beginning to spin, Australia's lead was 110.

Now the confidence of a team accustomed to winning shone through. Michael Slater and Justin Langer set about the bowling in order to set up a declaration. Slater's century was a typically busy, jaunty effort while Langer, who was playing for his place, batted without a trace of selfishness. Their partnership of 182 was scored in only 42 overs enabling Mark Taylor, in his 100th Test, to put England back into bat on the fourth evening needing to score 348 in 98 overs. How many other captains, I wonder, would dare to be quite so generous in the first Test of a five-match series?

Realistically, an England victory was highly improbable, but they could certainly survive and earn their precious draw. At 96 for 1, Stuart MacGill fooled Butcher into playing no stroke. Moments later Stewart was taken at silly point and Thorpe prodded to short leg. The slide had begun, and England's eyes began, nervously, to look towards the skies. Hussain, who was bowled, cutting a googly and Ramprakash – uncharacteristically stumped – were both hopelessly undone by MacGill, leaving Croft and Cork to hang on grimly until the storm made its spectacular arrival.

England had their draw, but after an encouraging start their survival was far from convincing.

SECOND TEST
28, 29 and 30 November 1998 at Perth

The match was over by mid-afternoon on the third day with Australia taking a one-nil lead in the series. Therefore, in order for England to regain the Ashes, they would have to win two of the remaining three matches.

The winning hit was watched by hundreds of schoolchildren. They were bussed in, free of charge, by the local authorities in the hope that the moment of victory over the old enemy would leave an indelible mark on many of them. Throughout the truncated proceedings, 'Go, Aussie, Go!', the superb promotional video, played loudly on the huge, colour screen. It was a sobering thought for those of us who have yet to witness a successful England tour of Australia, that the future of the game in that corner of the planet is secure for at least another generation.

What a contrast to the complacency of the West Indies Cricket Board when their team ruled the world in the 1980s. That irresponsibility has been graphically underlined by the dramatic collapse that now threatens cricket in the Caribbean. Nothing was done to market and promote the winning team throughout a region that finds itself bombarded by American sports on satellite television. It is a lesson for cricket authorities throughout the world: periods of success must be promoted for all they are worth, with sensible ticket-pricing at the grounds and access guaranteed to the widest possible television audience.

After that well-deserved pat on the back for the Australian Cricket Board, there has to be a moan! The journey from Brisbane to Perth, via Melbourne, took all day, with a time change to boot. The Test match started just three days later. Back-to-back Tests are no bad thing, but the players have to be in a position to give of their best. Sadly, Graham Thorpe's dodgy back could not stand the hours spent cooped up in the back of an aeroplane. His withdrawal threw an unlikely lifeline to Graeme Hick, who had been flown out to act as standby for Atherton in Brisbane, and who had yet to face a ball in anger. One look at the rock-hard surface and generous grass cover was enough to condemn Croft to the sidelines as England preferred the extra batsman, John Crawley, and, commendably, Tudor was called in to replace Fraser.

Australia had so many talented players to choose from that the national selectors were sticking to, what they termed, a policy of 'horses for courses'. In this case, it meant no place for MacGill, who was replaced by Colin Miller, a journeyman all-rounder, currently playing for Tasmania. One Australian newspaper revealed the startling information that Miller not only bowled medium pace and off-breaks with his right arm, but that he bowled with his left arm as well! Fortunately for England, there was no sign of his alleged ambidexterity during the match but Miller's was a shrewd selection in that he was an ideal man to make use of the afternoon sea breeze, the Freemantle Doctor. Jason Gillespie, omitted at Brisbane, replaced the wholehearted Mike Kasprowicz.

Local knowledge favoured batting first on what promised to be a fast, bouncy pitch. Rumour had it that England would have chosen to do so had Alec Stewart not lost the toss again only for Taylor to surprise everyone, and put England in. It was only the fourth time in his 46 Tests as captain that Taylor had inserted the opposition.

It proved to be an inspired decision. Only two top-order batsmen reached double figures as England collapsed to 76 for 6 at lunch. Tudor, in his first Test, showed promise and bravery at number nine, but the reality was that England were undone by a combination of superb swing bowling by Fleming and poor technique. That was a particularly galling fact given that England had specifically chosen to begin their tour in Perth in order to practise in the unique conditions.

By the close of the first day, Australia already had a lead of 38 with seven wickets in hand. Nervous tour operators were busily planning trips to the Margaret River and Rottnest Island for the several hundred England supporters who were also beginning to realise that this match would not go the distance.

Australia's lead was extended to 82 at lunch which heralded a most spectacular and unexpected collapse that helped to hasten the end of the game. Tudor, who, with the second new ball, accounted for the Waugh twins and Ricky Ponting, began the clatter of wickets as six fell for 31 runs in 39 balls. It was hectic stuff as Gough took two in two deliveries. Nevertheless, Australia were still handily placed with a 128-run advantage.

There was so much time remaining that England could not even contemplate saving the match as they began their second innings. Their objective had to be to score enough runs to overhaul Australia and win it. However, by the ninth over they were already 15 for 3 – Butcher, Hussain and Stewart all falling to Fleming – and by the close of what was still only the second day, England were two runs behind with only five wickets still to fall.

The one bright feature of the innings was a breezy 68 from Hick. Having recorded a second-ball duck on the first day (they were, after all, the first two balls he had faced on the trip!) he made 68, including two enormous pulled sixes off Gillespie before the South Australian gained his revenge, via a catch at third slip.

Suddenly, there was pandemonium once again. England lost their final four wickets in two overs as Gillespie, who had been expensive up to this point, took all four in just six balls. Mullally registered his third consecutive duck, missing a furious swipe, and as the Australian fielders surveyed the wreckage of his shattered stumps, they knew they needed to score only 64 to win.

Three wickets were lost on the way but the result was never in doubt.

Alex Tudor bowling during the second Test.
David Munden/Sportsline Photographic

SECOND TEST – AUSTRALIA v. ENGLAND
28, 29 and 30 November 1998 at WACA Ground, Perth

ENGLAND

	First Innings		Second Innings	
MA Butcher	c Healy, b Fleming	0	c Ponting, b Fleming	1
MA Atherton	c Healy, b McGrath	1	c Taylor, b Fleming	35
N Hussain	c Healy, b McGrath	6	lbw, b Fleming	1
*AJ Stewart (capt)	b McGrath	38	c Taylor, b Fleming	0
MR Ramprakash	c Taylor, b Fleming	26	not out	47
JP Crawley	c ME Waugh, b Gillespie	4	c Langer, b Miller	15
GA Hick	c Healy, b Gillespie	0	c Ponting, b Gillespie	68
DG Cork	c Taylor, b Fleming	2	lbw, b Gillespie	16
AJ Tudor	not out	18	c Healy, b Gillespie	0
D Gough	c ME Waugh, b Fleming	11	lbw, b Gillespie	0
AD Mullally	c Healy, b Fleming	0	b Gillespie	0
	lb 2, w 2, nb 2	6	nb 8	8
		112		**191**

	First Innings				Second Innings			
	O	M	R	W	O	M	R	W
McGrath	16	4	37	3	26	10	47	–
Fleming	14	3	46	5	19	7	45	4
Gillespie	7	0	23	2	15.2	2	88	5
Miller	2	0	4	–	10	4	11	1

Fall of Wickets
1–2, 2–4, 3–19, 4–62, 5–74, 6–74, 7–81, 8–90, 9–108
1–5, 2–11, 3–15, 4–40, 5–67, 6–158, 7–189, 8–189, 9–189

AUSTRALIA

	First Innings		Second Innings	
MA Taylor (capt)	c Stewart, b Cork	61	(2) c Hick, b Mullally	3
MJ Slater	c Butcher, b Gough	34	(1) c & b Gough	17
JL Langer	c Crawley, b Ramprakash	15	c Atherton, b Tudor	7
ME Waugh	c Butcher, b Tudor	36	not out	17
JN Gillespie	c Stewart, b Mullally	11		
SR Waugh	b Tudor	33	(5) not out	15
RT Ponting	c Stewart, b Tudor	11		
*IA Healy	lbw, b Gough	12		
DW Fleming	c Hick, b Gough	0		
CR Miller	not out	3		
GD McGrath	c Cork, b Tudor	0		
	b 1, lb 10, nb 13	24	lb 3, nb 2	5
		240	(for 3 wickets)	**64**

	First Innings				Second Innings			
	O	M	R	W	O	M	R	W
Gough	25	9	43	3	9	5	18	1
Cork	21	5	49	1				
Tudor	20.2	5	89	4	5	0	19	1
Mullally	21	10	36	1	9	0	24	1
Ramprakash	2	0	12	1				

Fall of Wickets
1–81, 2–115, 3–138, 4–165, 5–209, 6–214, 7–228, 8–228, 9–239
1–16, 2–24, 3–36

Umpires: DJ Harper & S Venkataraghavan
Toss: Australia

Australia won by seven wickets

Nasser Hussain is out leg before to Damien Fleming in the second Test.
David Munden/Sportsline Photographic

Victoria v. England at Melbourne
5, 6, 7 and 8 December 1998
England 373 (AJ Stewart 126, MR Ramprakash 78, GA Hick 67) and 207 for 5 dec. (JP Crawley 68)
Victoria 300 (SAJ Craig 83*, PJ Roach 80, DW Headley 5 for 58) and 245 for 8 (GR Vimpani 72, BJ Hodge 50)
Match drawn

This was a forgettable draw, of interest only in that it marked the end of Graham Thorpe's tour. Thorpe had struggled ever since the flight from Brisbane to Perth and this match was make or break. Forced to retire hurt after scoring only a single, Thorpe had to concede that it was over and promptly flew home.

Victoria rested virtually every recognisable player, including Shane Warne, through some spurious injury or other. Stewart, Hick, Ramprakash and, in the second innings, Crawley all enjoyed themselves against the weakened attack, but things became

It was Langer's determination – he batted for more than eight hours – that drove Australia on to a sizeable total on a flat Adelaide track and before long England were 84 for 3. This included the wicket of Mike Atherton who was given out by the third umpire for a low catch by Taylor at slip. It is possible that the ball carried, fractionally, but the umpire involved, Paul Angley, allowed his inexperience to show by failing to give the batsman the benefit of the doubt. Angley had stood in only three first-class matches prior to the Test, but decisions made by the third umpire are as crucial as those made by his colleagues in the middle – and are, often, scrutinised more closely. It was a thoroughly irresponsible appointment.

Atherton departed, muttering darkly, and although Hussain and Ramprakash gave England's innings some backbone, the inevitable collapse was just around the corner. The last five wickets fell from only 21 balls as 210 for 5 became 227 all out, handing Australia a first-innings lead of 164.

As was the case in Brisbane, Australia's push for a second-innings declaration came from Michael Slater. An enormous straight six – no mean feat at Adelaide – sticks in the mind and while Mark

Alan Mullally after being dismissed by Damien Fleming in the third Test in Adelaide.

David Munden/Sportsline Photographic

Waugh was being roundly applauded for scoring an unbeaten half-century, Taylor declared. England needed to survive for 140 overs.

By the close of play on the fourth day, the match was all but over. England were 122 for 4, with Colin Miller having claimed three wickets. Ramprakash was spectacularly bowled in the 16th over of the final morning and, as in the first innings, England's tail collapsed in the most feeble of heaps. This time it was five wickets for 16 runs in 29 balls. Mullally broke his sequence of ducks with an edged boundary through the slips, but this was no time for smiling. England's demise was spineless and with it came a chorus of thoroughly deserved condemnation. Even the future of the Ashes was questioned, not least because this was, by 13 days, the earliest the Ashes had ever been settled in Australia. True, the revised itinerary had something to do with that but, even so, the milestone did not go unnoticed.

FOURTH TEST
26, 27, 28 and 29 December 1998 at Melbourne

This was as fine a Test match as you could ever wish to see. Bursting with drama, excitement, controversy and, of course, some terrific cricket, a cold and windy Melbourne Cricket Ground became the scene of one of England's most remarkable triumphs in recent years.

It is quite impossible to explain the turnaround in England's fortunes since the Adelaide debacle of barely a fortnight before. One could offer the barely plausible excuse that Australia's players, the Ashes having been secured, were not trying very hard. Or, similarly, that England relaxed to produce the superior cricket that, frustratingly, they are more than capable of playing.

Neither offering is adequate. Besides, anything that diminishes the pride and passion felt by every Englishman on the ground at the moment of victory simply will not do. Darren Gough, Viking-like, raised his clenched fists and brandished an uprooted stump like a spear to salute England's triumph that came eight hours and three minutes after the start of play. It was the longest – and perhaps the most exhausting – day in Test history.

The reason for the extended hours of play is a new regulation that, surely, was not given proper consideration before being implemented. Logically, it makes great sense to add any time lost on to the start and end of play the following day – at least it does to anyone who has never stepped on to a cricket field before. Any Test player will tell you that it is lunacy.

Due in no small part to their desultory over rate earlier in the day, that regulation – in which half an hour's play was added to both the start and close of play – explains why England were still on the field three and three-quarter hours after the tea break. In mitigation, it must be said that England knew they were in for a long day and, in a low-scoring match dominated by seam bowling, it is hardly surprising that the bowlers took their time. The over rates issue is entirely separate from this act of madness by the administrators which, if anything, will slow the over rates down still further. While cricket remains an outdoor pursuit, it will always be affected by the elements and no amount of ill-conceived legislation can do anything about it.

Mark Taylor won the toss for the fourth successive time in the series and England's batsmen soon found themselves battling under slate-grey skies. Glenn McGrath dismissed Atherton and Butcher for ducks but Alec Stewart who, in desperation, had promoted himself to open the innings, cut and drove his way to his first century in 23 Tests against Australia. It was the first time since his appointment as captain that he was not saddled with the onerous additional task of wicketkeeping. However, this also gave ammunition to those critics (and I am one) who have never understood why in the past, when England batted first, Stewart did not open the batting, whether he was wicketkeeper, or not.

Stewart and Mark Ramprakash added 119 for the fourth wicket before Stewart was bowled behind his legs as he aimed to sweep MacGill. In the next over, Ramprakash holed out at mid-on off the bowling of Steve Waugh and, apart from a breezy contribution from Graeme Hick, the lower order was brushed aside once again. England lost seven wickets for 70 and MacGill took the last three for no runs off eight balls including Mullally for his fifth duck in six innings.

Throughout the series, Darren Gough had bowled with no luck at all. He had watched in mounting despair as catch after catch went to ground off his bowling; but now was pay-back time. He grabbed four of the first five wickets to fall only for memories of Brisbane to come flooding back as Steve Waugh and Ian Healy embarked on one of their famous rescue acts.

It ended after a stand of 58 when Healy – whose contribution was 36 – pulled Fraser to long leg. Australia were still 61 runs behind and neither Fleming nor Matthew Nicholson, in his first Test,

England captain Alec Stewart pulls Nicholson for four on his way to a century at the Melbourne Test.
Brendan Monks/Sportsline Photographic

lasted long. But Steve Waugh suddenly emerged to play a superbly spirited innings that, in company with MacGill, swept Australia into the lead. The pair added 88 for the ninth wicket and when MacGill and McGrath fell to Mullally, Waugh remained undefeated on 122 made in five and a half hours. At the close of the third day, England were still 211 in arrears having lost Atherton for his second duck in the match and Butcher for 14.

And so began the momentous fourth and final day in which 18 wickets fell and the nerve of player and spectator alike was constantly tested. The nightwatchman, Headley, fell in the third over, and within 20 minutes Stewart had followed him via a catch by silly point. Ramprakash was bowled by a very good delivery from Nicholson but Hussain and Hick then combined to lift English hearts with a stand of 51. As the customary late-order collapse began, Hick opened his shoulders and brought the Barmy Army – now several thousand strong – to its feet as he punished McGrath, who became increasingly grumpy.

Taylor, Fraser then plundered the Australia captain's seldom seen dobbers for 16 off the final over of England's innings. This turned out to be the margin of victory.

Australian XI v. England
19, 20, 21 and 22 December 1998 in Hobart
England 469 for 6 dec. (MA Atherton 210*, GA Hick, MR Ramprakash 65) and 199 for 3 dec. (MA Butcher 103*, JP Crawley 63)
Australian XI 293 for 4 dec. (GS Blewett 169*, MTG Elliott 81) and 376 for 1 (GS Blewett 213*, CJ Richards 138*)
Australian XI won by nine wickets

An astonishing assault on England's bowling brought the Australians victory on the final afternoon. Set 376 to win in 78 overs on a pitch that had claimed only 13 wickets in three innings, the home team roared in with a staggering 22 overs to spare and nine wickets in hand! Blewett (213 not out) scored his fourth consecutive first-class century and added the small matter of 345 with Richards (138 not out) for the second wicket. All in all a miserable return to the helm for Atherton who scored his first double century against a depleted attack, but who had agreed to lead England in the absence of Stewart and Hussain. Such was the shambles on the final day that, surely, the next time the invitation comes Atherton's way, he will politely decline. Gooch publicly savaged the England bowlers afterwards and Cork did not play again on the tour.

FIFTH TEST
2, 3, 4 and 5 January 1999 at Sydney

The first Test of the New Year was a mouth-watering prospect. Following on, back-to-back, from England's victory in Melbourne, the realisation that the tourists – who had spent much of the tour being ridiculed at every turn – might actually square the series had sneaked up to surprise everyone. In truth, it would not have been a fair reflection of the winter's cricket had that been the case. Besides, Stuart MacGill returned match figures of 12 for 107 to condemn England to defeat inside four days.

MacGill's outstanding contribution was made all the more impressive by the return to the Australian ranks of one SK Warne. It had been a long road back to full fitness for the bowler widely regarded as the best of his generation and, in the

Michael Slater hits a four past Darren Gough in the fifth Test in Sydney.
David Munden/Sportsline Photographic

meantime, MacGill had performed more than adequately. How could Australia accommodate the pair of them? It was an intriguing sub-plot to the main event.

Bubbling away in the background, the cynical observations about the value of the Ashes as a true contest were continuing unabated despite England's victory in Melbourne. In fact, the matter was being so widely discussed that the leaders of the respective cricket boards, Lord MacLaurin of the ECB and Denis Rogers of the ACB got together over dinner and vowed to continue the tradition of a five-Test series every two years. This will inevitably be complicated by the forthcoming championship of Test cricket which will make it extremely difficult to have five-Test series against anybody as regularly as that. However, the statement was aimed more at silencing the cynical voices in the Australian press than anything else.

In fact – as is so often the case – the game of cricket did the talking for itself. Everybody who was lucky enough to be at the Sydney Cricket Ground revelled in an experience they are unlikely ever to forget, such was the atmosphere of tension and sheer enjoyment provided by the huge crowds in glorious sunshine.

England's selection was, at best, curious and devoid of logic. At worst it was irresponsible,

brainless and nothing short of an insult to Allan
Mullally. The left-armer had bowled his boots off
with little credit in Melbourne and his accuracy
throughout the tour had made him England's most
economical bowler. Yet on a traditional Sydney pitch
that demanded rigid discipline and accuracy from
the seamers, England chose to omit Mullally in
favour of the promising young tearaway, Alex Tudor.
To make matters worse, they did not even give
Tudor the new ball. Instead, he was asked to
perform the duties of a line-and-length merchant
at first change. How I would love, one day, to
hear a sensible explanation of these utterly
bewildering tactics.

England had, at least, recognised that spin
bowlers were likely to flourish in the dry conditions
and they called into their squad the Warwickshire
left-arm spinner, Ashley Giles. As it turned out,
only the patient and persevering Peter Such made
it into the final eleven. In MacGill, Warne and
Colin Miller, Australia seemed to possess the
heavy artillery and the odds were stacked firmly in
Australia's favour when, for the fifth time in the

series, Mark Taylor won the toss. We did not
know it then, but this was to be Taylor's last
Test for Australia.

Taylor's contribution with the bat – four runs
in the whole match – was a disappointment but,
throughout, his fellow New South Welshmen
capitalised on their home ground. On the opening
day, the Waugh twins added 190 runs for the
fourth wicket but Australia's first innings was
cut dramatically short by a hat-trick from Darren
Gough. First, Ian Healy edged to Warren Hegg.
MacGill was then comprehensively bowled first
ball and, with the final delivery of the over,
Gough produced a snorter which spectacularly
defeated the groping Miller. On the hill – or, at
least, the concrete jungle that now passes for the
hill – the massed ranks of the Barmy Army bellowed
and cheered. It was, indeed, rousing stuff and

**Ian Healy and Michael Slater start to celebrate the freak
caught and bowled wicket of Peter Such by Stuart MacGill,
which ended the Ashes series in Australia's favour.**
David Munden/Sportsline Photographic

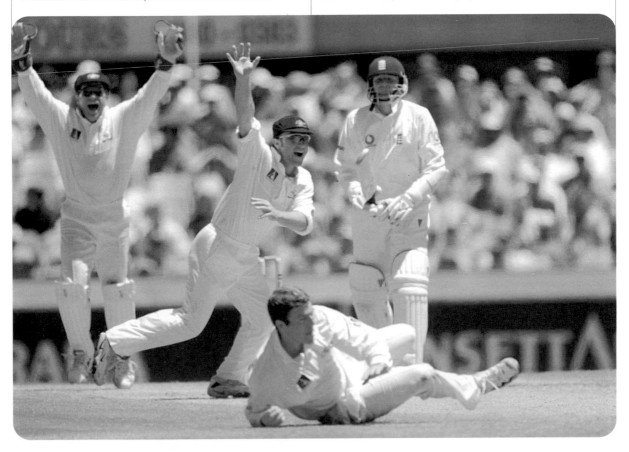

FIFTH TEST – AUSTRALIA v. ENGLAND
2, 3, 4 and 5 January 1999 at Sydney Cricket Ground

AUSTRALIA

	First Innings		Second Innings	
MA Taylor (capt)	c Hick, b Headley	2	(1) c Stewart, b Gough	2
MJ Slater	c Hegg, b Headley	18	(2) c Hegg, b Headley	123
JL Langer	c Ramprakash, b Tudor	26	lbw, b Headley	1
ME Waugh	c Hegg, b Headley	121	c Ramprakash, b Headley	24
SR Waugh	b Such	96	(7) b Headley	8
DS Lehmann	c Hussain, b Tudor	32	(5) c Crawley, b Such	0
*IA Healy	c Hegg, b Gough	14	(6) c Crawley, b Such	5
SK Warne	not out	2	c Ramprakash, b Such	8
SCG MacGill	b Gough	0	c Butcher, b Such	6
CR Miller	b Gough	0	not out	3
GD McGrath	c Hick, b Headley	0	c Stewart, b Such	0
	lb 2, nb 9	11	b 3, lb 1	4
		322		**184**

	First Innings				Second Innings			
	O	M	R	W	O	M	R	W
Gough	17	4	61	3	15	3	51	1
Headley	19.3	3	62	4	19	7	40	4
Tudor	12	1	64	2	5	2	8	–
Such	24	6	77	1	25.5	5	81	5
Ramprakash	15	0	56	–				

Fall of Wickets
1–4, 2–52, 3–52, 4–242, 5–284, 6–319, 7–321, 8–321, 9–321
1–16, 2–25, 3–64, 4–73, 5–91, 6–110, 7–141, 8–180, 9–184

ENGLAND

	First Innings		Second Innings	
MA Butcher	lbw, b Warne	36	st Healy, b Warne	27
AJ Stewart (capt)	c Warne, b McGrath	3	st Healy, b MacGill	42
N Hussain	c ME Waugh, b Miller	42	c & b MacGill	53
MR Ramprakash	c MacGill, b McGrath	23	c Taylor, b McGrath	14
GA Hick	c Warne, b MacGill	23	b MacGill	7
JP Crawley	c Taylor, b MacGill	44	lbw, b Miller	5
*WK Hegg	b Miller	15	c Healy, b MacGill	3
AJ Tudor	b MacGill	14	b MacGill	3
DW Headley	c McGrath, b MacGill	8	c Healy, b MacGill	16
D Gough	lbw, b MacGill	0	not out	7
PM Such	not out	0	c & b MacGill	2
	b 8, lb 8, w 1, nb 4	21	lb 5, w 1, nb 3	9
		220		**188**

	First Innings				Second Innings			
	O	M	R	W	O	M	R	W
McGrath	17	7	35	2	10	0	40	1
Miller	23	6	45	2	17	1	50	1
MacGill	20.1	2	57	5	20.1	4	50	7
Warne	20	4	67	1	29	3	43	1

Fall of Wickets
1–18, 2–56, 3–88, 4–137, 5–139, 6–171, 7–204, 8–213, 9–213
1–57, 2–77, 3–110, 4–131, 5–150, 6–157, 7–162, 8–175, 9–180

Umpires: DB Hair & RS Dunne
Toss: Australia

Australia won by 98 runs

TEST MATCH AVERAGES
Australia v. England

AUSTRALIA

Batting	M	Inns	NO	HS	Runs	Av	100	50
SR Waugh	5	10	4	122*	498	83.00	2	2
ME Waugh	5	10	3	121	393	56.14	1	1
JL Langer	5	10	1	179*	436	48.44	1	2
MJ Slater	5	10	–	123	460	46.00	3	–
IA Healy	5	8	1	134	221	31.57	1	–
DW Fleming	4	5	1	71*	95	23.75	–	1
MA Taylor	5	10	–	61	228	22.80	–	2
DS Lehmann	2	4	–	32	49	12.25	–	–
RT Ponting	3	4	–	21	47	11.75	–	–
SCG MacGill	4	6	–	43	69	11.50	–	–
CR Miller	3	4	2	11	17	8.50	–	–
GD McGrath	5	7	–	10	15	2.14	–	–

Played in one Test: JN Gillespie 11; MS Kasprowicz 0; MJ Nicholson 5 & 9; SK Warne 2* & 8

Bowling	Overs	Mds	Runs	Wkts	Av	Best	10/m	5/inn
JN Gillespie	22.2	2	111	7	15.85	5–88	–	1
SCG MacGill	185.2	32	478	27	17.70	7–50	1	2
GD McGrath	196.4	53	492	24	20.50	6–85	–	1
DW Fleming	134.5	29	392	16	24.50	5–46	–	1
CR Miller	99	18	238	9	26.44	3–57	–	–

Also bowled: MS Kasprowicz 37–10–110–2; MJ Nicholson 25–4–115–4; RT Ponting 4–1–10–0; SK Warne 39–7–110–2; ME Waugh 26–2–90–3; SR Waugh 11–3–28–2

Fielding
19 – IA Healy (16 ct/3 st); 10 – ME Waugh; 9 – MA Taylor; 5 – SCG MacGill, MJ Slater; 4 – JL Langer, RT Ponting; 3 – GD McGrath; 2 – DW Fleming, MS Kasprowicz, SK Warne

ENGLAND

Batting	M	Inns	NO	HS	Runs	Av	100	50
MR Ramprakash	5	10	2	69*	379	47.37	–	4
N Hussain	5	10	1	89*	407	45.22	–	4
AJ Stewart	5	10	1	107	316	35.11	1	2
MA Butcher	5	10	–	116	259	25.90	1	–
GA Hick	4	8	–	68	205	25.62	–	2
JP Crawley	3	6	–	44	86	14.33	–	–
MA Atherton	4	8	–	41	110	13.75	–	–
DG Cork	2	4	1	21*	39	13.00	–	–
AJ Tudor	2	4	1	18*	35	11.66	–	–
WK Hegg	2	4	–	15	30	7.50	–	–
DW Headley	3	6	–	16	41	6.83	–	–
D Gough	5	9	1	11	43	5.37	–	–
AD Mullally	4	7	–	16	20	2.85	–	–
PM Such	2	4	1	2	2	0.66	–	–

Played in two Tests: ARC Fraser 1, 0* & 7
Played in one Test: RDB Croft 23 & 4*; GP Thorpe 77 & 9

Bowling	Overs	Mds	Runs	Wkts	Av	Best	10/m	5/inn
DW Headley	121.3	20	423	19	22.26	6–60	–	1
AJ Tudor	42.2	8	180	7	25.71	4–89	–	–
PM Such	116.5	24	323	11	29.36	5–81	–	1
AD Mullally	157.3	44	364	12	30.33	5–105	–	1
D Gough	201.3	39	687	21	32.71	5–96	–	1

Also bowled: DG Cork 57–11–165–4; RDB Croft 43–8–126–2; ARC Fraser 69–8–229–4; GA Hick 1–0–1–0; MR Ramprakash 44–3–136–1

Fielding
11 – AJ Stewart, GA Hick; 8 – WK Hegg; 5 – MA Butcher, MR Ramprakash; 4 – N Hussain; 3 – JP Crawley; 2 – MA Atherton, DW Headley, AD Mullally; 1 – DG Cork, ARC Fraser, D Gough, PM Such

Australia were now restricted to a first-innings score of 322. The ball, however, was already spinning menacingly.

Warne captured a wicket – Butcher leg before – with his fourth delivery of his comeback match (well, he would wouldn't he!) but MacGill, who took 4 for 1 to finish with 5 for 57, stole the show. Batting was not easy but, once again, England's batsmen simply could not cope with wrist spin bowling. There might very well be an element of truth in Taylor's observation after the match that England do not tour the subcontinent frequently enough to gain the necessary experience. Indeed, England have played only four Tests in that part of the world (three against India and one against Sri Lanka) in the last 12 years.

Australia's second-innings scorecard makes for extraordinary reading. Michael Slater's 123 constituted 66.84% of his team's total; the highest percentage since Bannerman's effort in the first Test of 1876. Only Mark Waugh reached double figures. It must be recorded that Slater was extremely fortunate to survive a run-out appeal on 35. The third umpire awarded Slater the benefit of the doubt in yet another example of the technology failing to provide sufficient evidence. Slater was probably out. However, better for the batsman to receive the benefit of the doubt rather than be dismissed – such as Atherton was in Adelaide. Nothing should detract from Slater's remarkable – and typically jaunty – performance. It was his third opportunity of the series to kiss the Australian emblem on his baggy green cap and, in front of his home supporters, he did so with a real flourish.

Slater was eighth out, and Such then claimed the last three wickets to finish with 5 for 81. England needed an apparently tempting 287 to win.

After much digging through records, this was quickly put into its true perspective. Only one Test team batting last had ever successfully chased more than 200 to win at the SCG. Although Stewart and his brother-in-law Butcher scampered to 57 for the first wicket, England lost eight wickets for 78 runs as MacGill ran amok. His 7 for 50 (Warne finished with 1 for 43) meant that Australia took the series by three Tests to one. It was a deserved margin of victory.

After the match, Stewart singled out David Lloyd for a particularly glowing tribute. The coach had become increasingly marginalised during the tour and Stewart added the hope that Lloyd would continue in the post for some time to come. In fact this was Lloyd's final Test match.

CARLTON AND UNITED ONE-DAY SERIES
By Jonathan Agnew

There is nothing an international cricketer looks forward to more after a full Test series in Australia than the inevitable World Series one-day tournament! It would be a tiring enough exercise if Australia were the size of Rutland. That flying from Sydney to Perth is the equivalent of travelling from London to Moscow makes it a trying business. This particular competition required no fewer than 14 matches to whittle three teams – Australia, England and Sri Lanka – down to two. However, huge crowds thoroughly enjoyed the spectacle that provided drama, controversy and several nail-biting finishes. And that, let us face it, is what the one-day game is all about.

Both England and Australia made significant changes to their squads to distinguish between the two forms of the game. The Carlton and United Series had gained added importance because of the impending World Cup, and all three participants were keen to use the tournament as fine-tuning. England called up men they regarded as one-day specialists: Mark Alleyne, Ashley Giles, Vince Wells, Mark Ealham, Nick Knight, Adam Hollioake and Neil Fairbrother. Australia continued the controversial policy that had been pioneered by England a year before: namely, dropping the regular captain. In this case, Steve Waugh was to have replaced Mark Taylor only to then rule himself out through injury. So, despite the hullabaloo over the match-fixing allegations, Shane Warne was promoted, and he did a magnificent job.

England still had many unanswered questions about their final choices for the World Cup. In the back of the minds of the selectors was the lurking suspicion about the impact of using a white ball in England in mid-May. White balls swing and seam more prodigiously than their red counterparts and, with five months still to go before the World Cup, there were real fears that the tournament could be blighted by low scores. All of this made it difficult to put the final preparations for the World Cup in place. After all, day/night matches on balmy evenings in Australia bear absolutely no resemblance to May mornings in Manchester – or Lord's for that matter. As it turned out, the Carlton and United Series, for all its excitement, did little to enlighten England's World Cup selectors. The following month, they announced their preliminary squad. Rather surprisingly, this contained both Mike Atherton and Angus Fraser, neither of whom had

Alan Mullally celebrates another wicket.
David Munden/Sportsline Photographic

taken part in the one-day series in Australia. Atherton was later to withdraw with a recurrence of his back injury.

To add to the intrigue of this particular series, it was to be the first appearance of Muttiah Muralitharan in Australia since he was called for throwing by umpire Darryl Hair in the Melbourne test of 1995–96. Hair, with rather clumsy timing, had just published a book about his umpiring exploits in which he referred to Murali's action as 'diabolical'. For a while, Hair's future was uncertain but the sensible compromise was reached in which he was deliberately kept away from matches

involving Sri Lanka. It had already been noted that a certain Ross Emerson, who had also called Murali for throwing before, was due to stand in a match involving Sri Lanka and England midway through the tournament in Adelaide.

It all kicked off in Brisbane where the one plus point of all the building works is that there are now floodlights at the 'Gabba. England beat both Australia and Sri Lanka in low-scoring matches. Fairbrother gave an early reminder of his outstanding value as a play-maker in the middle order of a one-day game. Scoring at a run a ball, he made 47 and 67 not out to steer England home on each occasion. Allan Mullally took 4 for 18 against Australia to ensure that their chase for 179 – later reduced, because of a storm, to 153 in 16 overs – never got off the ground.

Nasser Hussain replaced Alleyne in the next encounter with Australia, this time in Melbourne, and he played rather well. After a short-lived (one match) experiment employing Ealham as a pinch hitter, Hussain made 47 – England's top score in a paltry total of 178. The result was a rout and Australia romped home by nine wickets with ten overs to spare in front of 83,000 noisy but ultimately bored spectators.

Up to Sydney we sloped and witnessed some revenge for England who beat Australia in a last-over thriller. Hick made a century ('Did this innings exorcise any demons Graeme?' 'No! Not really.') and Hussain 93 (his first one-day international half-century in 20 matches spanning nine years) to set Australia 283 to win on a turning pitch. They got very close, thanks to Mark Waugh and Lehmann. At this stage the table had England on top with three wins, Australia second with two and Sri Lanka, who had also been trounced by Australia, not yet off the mark.

Sri Lanka's dismal opening continued when, three days later, they were overwhelmed by England in Melbourne. England was now playing some excellent cricket and with Gough at full cry (4 for 28) and more runs from Hick (66 not out) England won by seven wickets.

It was now time for umpire Emerson's date with Muralitharan. The setting was the gorgeous Adelaide Oval and when Emerson called the bowler for throwing, Sri Lanka's captain, Arjuna Ranatunga, led his players to the boundary in a protest that lasted for 15 minutes. Emerson was also involved in a bad run-out decision as the players' tempers became frayed. However, for all the protests by some pundits on the day, the fact is that the umpire is obliged to call 'no ball' if in *his* opinion the bowler's action is illegal. To suggest, as some did, that the ACB should not have appointed Emerson for fear that he might call Muralitharan is absurd. Murali's action is extremely complicated and provokes more interest and informed debate in world cricket today than any other. It is inevitable that, in the opinion of some, 'the process of straightening the arm, whether partial or complete' occurs, and to suggest that any umpire who might fall into that category should be stood down as a result is quite ridiculous.

Ranatunga's outburst was completely out of order, as Stewart informed him in no uncertain terms: 'Your behaviour has been appalling for a country's captain.' Sri Lanka won what was just about as ill-tempered a match as there has been in recent years and Ranatunga was hauled before the match referee, Peter van der Merwe. Once again, the ineffectiveness of the ICC's code of conduct was highlighted when Ranatunga's legal team threatened to expose cricket's regulations to the courts of law. Van der Merwe, visibly angry, could do little more than condemn the threat and hand Ranatunga a suspended ban.

Not surprisingly there was great interest the following week in Perth when the two teams met again. Australia had beaten Sri Lanka and, narrowly, England in Adelaide so England needed one more victory to ensure qualification – at Sri Lanka's expense – for the final. This they achieved in a hopelessly one-sided contest by bowling Sri Lanka out for 99. David Graveney, the England manager, admitted that because of the previous week's events, this victory gave him more pleasure than any other England win he had been associated with.

With the finalists now settled, another low-key round remained, in Sydney (again). England, possibly feeling the strain of a long tour, lost both matches. This must have had an effect on the way they went into the finals although, that said, they lost the first by only ten runs. Hussain made 58 but became embroiled in a verbal clash with Warne. When, moments later, Hussain dashed down the pitch and was stumped, age-old questions about his temperament on the big occasion were raised again. It was a dismissal that counted against him in

the original selection for the World Cup. Vince Wells took three wickets and scored 33 as England chased 223. They lost five wickets in the middle order for only six runs and Croft was unable to coax the necessary support from Gough and Mullally at the end.

The second final, played three days later in Melbourne, resulted in England's second-largest margin of defeat in one-day internationals and brought the tour to a shuddering stop. That England managed to reach 110 in reply to Australia's 272 for 5 was only due to two missed catches by Warne and Ponting. At one early stage England were 13 for 4 and the contest, such as it was, had died an early death.

Alec Stewart, with an eye on the World Cup gave his troops a rally-cry: 'Play well and we'll win it.' However, they had just been decisively beaten by the team that was already the punters' favourite to lift the Cup in England on 20 June.

Match One – Australia v. England
10 January 1999 at Woolloongabba, Brisbane
England 178 for 8 (50 overs)
Australia 145 for 9 (36 overs) MG Bevan 56*,
AD Mullally 4 for 18
England won by 8 runs (D/L Method)
Man of the Match: AD Mullally

Match Two – England v. Sri Lanka
11 January 1999 at Woolloongabba, Brisbane
Sri Lanka 207 for 7 (50 overs) RS Kaluwitharana 58,
MS Atapattu 51, HP Tillekeratne 50*
England 208 for 6 (49.3 overs) NH Fairbrother 67*
England won by four wickets
Man of the Match: NH Fairbrother

Match Three – Australia v. Sri Lanka
13 January 1999 at Sydney Cricket Ground
Sri Lanka 259 for 9 (50 overs) HP Tillekeratne 73,
ST Jayasuriya 65
Australia 260 for 2 (46.1 overs) AC Gilchrist 131,
ME Waugh 63
Australia won by eight wickets
Man of the Match: AC Gilchrist

Match Four – Australia v. England
15 January 1999 at Melbourne Cricket Ground
England 178 (43.2 overs) GD McGrath 4 for 54
Australia 182 for 1 (39.2 overs) ME Waugh 83*,
RT Ponting 75*
Australia won by nine wickets
Man of the Match: ME Waugh

MARK TAYLOR RETIRES

Mark Taylor is a good bloke: simple as that. For one of Australia's more exceptional cricket captains, Taylor makes no presumption about being either exceptional or conspicuous. Now that might not be the image that the Sydney Olympic Games organisers are trying to convey by using Taylor as their major promotional face, but it's the image he has created during a distinguished and undemonstrative five-year reign in the most significant leadership role in Australian sport.

BY JIM MAXWELL

Taylor's unpretentious, relaxed and straightforward attitude has won the kind of following that other phlegmatic heroes like Doug Walters and Steve Waugh used to inspire. Australian fans appreciate Taylor's calm, unemotional demeanour. His personality is the antithesis of flamboyant showmen such as Merv Hughes and Dennis Lillee, but he has earned admiration both for his unwavering perseverance and for his attacking approach as the Test captain. He won 11 out of 13 series. Only 11 of 50 matches were drawn. Twenty-six were won, and if the support of two great strike bowlers, Shane Warne and Glenn McGrath, was the linchpin of Taylor's success, crucial too were his tactics – and the best pair of hands at first slip since Bob Simpson. He was decisive, always backing his judgement, with the occasional slice of luck that every captain needs.

His use of Stuart Law's part-time leg spin in the World Cup semi-final in Mohali was a surprise tactic that triggered a crazy West Indies collapse. The decision to bat on a damp pitch at Old Trafford in the 1997 Ashes series was ultimately vindicated when the ball turned victoriously in the final innings. The other remarkable point about Taylor's career was his survival. Kim Hughes' lachrymose abdication in 1984 was an inevitable tragedy that befell a captain bereft of leadership and a team that only knew defeat. When Taylor suffered an alarming loss of form in 1996–97, failing to pass 50 in 20 Test innings, he knew that another failure would be terminal. Throughout this drought the selectors stuck with him, because his captaincy had been outstanding, and Australia had kept on winning. For Taylor there was never a sense of panic as he grappled with this frustrating loss of form. Failure tests character, and in the second innings at Edgbaston, Taylor triumphed over his despair. He made 129. Was he blessed with a fortuitous gift of timing? There were other times when he had needed runs and scored them. As a youth who had moved to Sydney from Wagga Wagga's malthoid-covered concrete pitches, he confronted the irascible speedster Len Pascoe in a club match. Dismissed cheaply in the first innings by a Pascoe snorter, Taylor got the benefit of an umpire's decision in the second, and clouting a Pascoe bouncer over the fence, made a match-winning score. In 1989 Tom Moody and Taylor were rivals for the opener's spot alongside Geoff Marsh in the Ashes series. The 'slender' left-hander won selection, scored 136 at Leeds, and compiled a rousing 839 runs in the series.

And then in his career twilight, in India in 1998, runs dried up again, as Tendulkar pulverised Australia. Playing for pride in Bangalore, after losing the series two-nil, Taylor belted one of his fastest Test hundreds, 102 not out from 193 balls, laced with 17 boundaries, stirring a face-saving win. Later in the memorable Pakistan series, he suffered another slump. Determined not to be distracted by the ongoing corruption inquiry, Taylor wanted a big innings. Dropped twice before reaching 50, he amassed a monumental, Bradman-equalling 334 not out in Peshawar. And with typical altruism he declared, preferring the pursuit of victory to the chance of a world record.

Taylor's batting accomplishments are exemplary. Facing the new ball exposes batting deficiencies and mental doubts more than any other position in the order. Averaging 43.50 puts Taylor in the top ten list of Australian openers, alongside Ponsford, Slater, Lawry, Simpson, Morris and Woodfull. His 7,525 Test runs were made against some of the most potent missile–hurlers in Test history: Curtly Ambrose, Courtney Walsh, Allan

Mark Taylor, opposite page, and above with Steve Waugh.
David Munden/Sportsline Photographic

Donald, Wasim Akram, and Waqar Younis. Like a latter-day John Edrich he knew exactly where his off-stump was, and either leaving or missing the bouncing ball, appeared to be unaffected by long periods without scoring. Some of his best innings were one-session survivals, blunting a Waughpath. Accompanying the effervescent Slater, Taylor was the calming accomplice in one of the most consistent first-wicket duos in memory, making the selectors' decision to split them all the more bewildering.

Team-mates affectionately called him Tubby, and although he never moved like an Olympic athlete, his reflexes at first slip were as swift as Ian Healy's stumpings or Shane Warne's appeals. His deeds may well be superseded by his successor, Steve Waugh. But by any evaluation his contribution has confirmed that dignity and composure are prerequisites to cricket's continuing integrity.

FIRST-CLASS AVERAGES

BATTING

	M	Inns	NO	HS	Runs	Av	100	50
GS Blewett	7	12	2	213*	1187	118.70	6	1
MG Bevan	6	10	4	202*	636	106.00	3	1
GP Thorpe	4	8	3	223*	438	87.60	1	2
MTG Elliott	8	15	2	161	1014	78.00	5	5
SR Waugh	6	12	4	122*	619	77.37	3	2
DS Lehmann	7	12	3	175	592	65.77	2	2
ME Waugh	6	12	3	126	583	64.77	2	2
SM Katich	12	22	5	154*	1039	61.11	5	3
CJ Richards	10	18	3	161	848	56.53	4	3
J Cox	10	17	1	184	863	53.93	4	3
JM Vaughan	8	13	1	157*	642	53.50	2	3
MR Ramprakash	10	19	3	140*	845	52.81	1	7
SAJ Craig	6	10	2	128*	417	52.12	1	1
S Lee	8	14	2	102*	602	50.16	1	6
SG Law	11	17	1	216	781	48.81	3	1
RM Baker	8	13	3	111*	486	48.60	1	3
JP Mahler	12	21	2	208*	897	47.21	1	7
JD Siddons	6	12	2	166	465	46.50	2	1
N Hussain	9	18	1	118	724	42.58	1	5
JL Langer	11	22	2	179*	842	42.10	1	5
BJ Hodge	10	18	1	120	706	41.52	2	5
MJ di Venuto	9	15	1	95	579	41.35	–	7
BA Johnson	11	18	2	122	661	41.31	2	3
ME Hussey	12	22	0	187	907	41.22	1	7
GA Hick	6	11	1	125	412	41.20	1	3
ML Hayden	11	18	1	103	686	40.35	1	5
MJ Slater	8	16	0	123	639	39.93	4	–
AC Gilchrist	8	12	1	125	418	38.00	2	1
GR Parker	7	14	3	117	416	37.81	1	2
DJ Marsh	10	14	1	123	489	37.61	1	3
DA Fitzgerald	8	15	0	167	561	37.40	2	2
GI Foley	12	20	3	122	632	37.17	1	4
DR Martyn	8	14	1	123	477	36.69	2	1
AJ Stewart	8	16	1	126	530	35.33	2	3
IJ Harvey	9	16	1	82	523	34.86	–	3
MS Kasprowicz	8	9	3	52*	200	33.33	–	1
JL Arnberger	11	20	2	125*	599	33.27	1	3
DF Hills	9	15	1	66*	458	32.71	–	5
RJ Campbell	11	20	0	146	651	32.55	1	4
MA Atherton	8	15	1	210*	438	31.28	1	1
A Symonds	11	20	1	113	557	29.31	1	3
BE Young	8	11	2	70	250	27.77	–	1
MP Mott	8	13	0	106	353	27.15	2	–
BP Julian	8	11	2	84	244	27.11	–	2
IA Healy	10	17	2	134	399	26.60	1	2
MA Butcher	9	17	2	116	396	26.40	2	–
ML Love	12	21	0	72	539	25.66	–	4
RJ Davison	5	9	1	54	204	25.50	–	1
S Young	10	16	2	76	356	25.42	–	2
JP Crawley	7	14	0	68	355	25.35	–	3
PA Emery	10	14	2	84*	299	24.91	–	2
TM Moody	7	12	2	109	248	24.80	1	–
GC Rummans	10	17	2	67	368	24.53	–	2
MP Faull	8	14	0	80	330	23.57	–	1
LD Harper	5	9	0	89	201	22.33	–	1
GR Vimpani	7	12	0	72	243	20.25	–	1
DJ Saker	10	14	3	34	221	20.09	–	–
DC Boon	10	15	1	64	260	18.57	–	2
DG Cork	6	10	1	51	164	18.22	–	1
MJ Nicholson	8	13	2	58*	198	18.00	–	1
AJ Sainsbury	4	8	0	72	144	18.00	–	1
BA Swain	7	10	5	36*	90	18.00	–	–
RJ Tucker	5	8	1	41	125	17.85	–	–
MA Taylor	11	19	0	61	339	17.84	–	3
PW Jackson	11	13	4	40*	157	17.44	–	–
DW Fleming	7	9	2	71*	119	17.00	–	1
PR Reiffel	8	10	2	30	126	15.75	–	–
MN Atkinson	10	13	1	33	187	15.58	–	–
DS Berry	10	16	4	31	181	15.08	–	–
TJ Nielsen	11	17	0	51	219	12.88	–	1
JH Dawes	7	10	3	23*	84	12.00	–	–
WA Seccombe	7	11	4	48*	81	11.57	–	–
RT Ponting	6	8	1	21	75	10.71	–	–

FIRST-CLASS AVERAGES

BATTING

	M	Inns	NO	HS	Runs	Av	100	50
J Angel	8	10	4	23	63	10.50	–	–
JM Davison	9	13	2	42	115	10.45	–	–
BJ Oldroyd	8	11	3	26*	82	10.25	–	–
WK Hegg	4	8	2	15	60	10.00	–	–

Qualification: 8 innings, average 10.00.

BOWLING

	Overs	Mds	Runs	Wkts	Av	Best	10/m	5/inn
AC Dale	277.3	109	530	31	17.09	7-33	–	2
A Symonds	156.5	50	417	24	17.37	4-39	–	–
J Angel	296.1	101	638	35	18.22	5-64	–	1
SA Muller	150.1	44	408	22	18.54	5-35	–	1
PR Reiffel	290.5	91	634	32	19.81	4-59	–	–
SCG MacGill	269.2	42	769	38	20.23	7-50	–	2
GD McGrath	196.4	52	492	24	20.50	6-85	–	1
JN Gillespie	175.3	50	476	22	21.63	5-88	–	1
GS Blewett	139	34	371	17	21.82	3-24	–	–
JH Dawes	187.4	52	506	23	22.00	4-28	–	–
AJ Bichel	319.1	78	948	42	22.57	6-54	–	3
GR Robertson	140	38	364	16	22.75	3-23	–	–
DW Headley	213.3	38	665	29	22.93	6-60	–	2
CR Miller	287	76	623	27	23.07	6-87	–	1
DJ Saker	392.4	102	1049	45	23.31	5-28	–	1
MJ Nicholson	293.2	70	888	37	24.00	7-77	–	3
MWH Inness	220.1	67	584	24	24.33	4-25	–	–
GJ Rowell	183.2	54	459	18	25.50	4-44	–	–
DW Fleming	238.5	65	619	24	25.79	5-46	–	1
SR Cary	269.3	68	754	29	26.00	4-9	–	–
BA Swain	247.2	66	702	25	28.08	5-59	–	1
D Gough	266.2	56	873	31	28.16	5-96	–	1
AD Mullally	220.3	61	509	18	28.27	5-105	–	1
TM Moody	162	46	482	17	28.35	4-33	–	–
NW Bracken	157	55	334	11	30.36	3-10	–	–
MA Harrity	295.3	71	871	28	31.10	4-35	–	–
RDB Croft	162	32	488	15	32.53	3-56	–	–
PW Jackson	291.5	91	715	21	34.04	5-65	–	1
GJ Denton	232.4	55	766	22	34.81	4-53	–	–
BJ Oldroyd	286.4	74	736	21	35.04	4-68	–	–
BP Julian	262	65	748	21	35.61	4-15	–	–
MS Kasprowicz	274.5	64	846	23	36.78	6-31	–	1
BA Johnson	183.5	35	558	15	37.20	3-29	–	–
DJ Marsh	240	59	635	17	37.35	3-48	–	–
DG Cork	162.2	35	475	12	39.58	4-45	–	–
S Young	182	57	449	11	40.81	3-55	–	–
BE Young	449.2	105	1237	28	44.17	5-52	–	1
P Wilson	285.3	68	723	16	45.18	5-68	–	1
MP Atkinson	156.4	25	512	10	51.20	3-40	–	–
IJ Harvey	218.4	52	589	11	53.54	2-20	–	–
SK Warne	178.1	33	631	10	63.10	2-80	–	–
JM Davison	317.1	83	961	14	68.64	3-69	–	–

Qualification: 10 wickets in 8 innings

The following bowlers took 10 wickets in fewer than 8 innings:

B Lee	137.3	32	420	14	30.00	5-53	–	1
BS Targett	137.1	47	337	10	33.70	3-43	–	–
MW Ridgway	134	28	403	11	36.63	3-58	–	–
DA Freedman	166.1	38	513	12	42.75	4-93	–	–
PM Such	169.4	33	530	12	44.16	5-81	–	1

LEADING FIELDERS

40 – IA Healy (35 ct/4 st); 38 – DS Berry (36 ct/2 st); 37 – AC Gilchrist (36 ct/1 st); 33 – TJ Nielsen (32 ct/1 st); 28 – WA Seccombe (26 ct/1 st); 27 – MN Atkinson (26 ct/1 st); 21 – RJ Campbell; 19 – PA Emery (16 ct/3 st); 18 – GI Foley; 15 – GA Hick; 14 – AJ Stewart; 13 – MTG Elliott, JL Langer; 12 – MA Taylor; 11 – SG Law, ML Love, DR Martyn; 10 – JL Arnberger, MR Ramprakash, ME Waugh

SHARJAH

Champions' Trophy
Coca Cola Cup

CHAMPIONS' TROPHY
By Qamar Ahmed

The 1998 Champions' Trophy, initiated in 1986 and taking place for the eighth time, was won by India for the first time. In their previous four attempts in the tournament they had failed to make much impression in the presence of Pakistan and West Indies. Neither team played in the 1998 competition – instead Sri Lanka and Zimbabwe were India's opponents.

All the matches played at Sharjah were played under floodlights, and in the absence of Pakistan, India's arch-rivals, the seven matches played during the course of one week were poorly attended. Sri Lanka, the World Cup champions of 1996, failed to win a single match in the tournament, which was a big disappointment for the many thousands of expatriate supporters. Zimbabwe won two matches against Sri Lanka as well as one against India to sound a warning to all that they would not be an easy team to handle in the forthcoming World Cup.

India dominated the seven-match tournament to reach the final, in which they beat Zimbabwe by a huge margin. Having defeated Sri Lanka in the opening game by three wickets, India then raced to victory by seven wickets in their second match, against Zimbabwe. Their win against Sri Lanka by 81 runs assured them a place in the finals.

In the opening match Sri Lanka made an impressive 245 for 7 in 50 overs as Avishka Gunawardene made 52, Marvan Atapattu 64 and Arjuna Ranatunga 42. But India, on a batting wicket, paced its innings well to reach the target in the 50th over. Having lost two wickets for 13, India recovered through a 104-run stand between Nayan Mongia (51) and Mohammad Azharuddin (94) to be on course for victory.

Zimbabwe beat Sri Lanka in the second match by a seven-wicket margin. Having bowled Sri Lanka out for 196, Zimbabwe had no difficulty in reaching the target for the loss of three wickets. Aravinda de Silva's 55 and Roshan Mahanama's 51 were not enough in Sri Lanka's innings as Eddo Brandes and Craig Evans picked up three wickets each. Grant Flower (87) and Murray Goodwin (54) put on 112 runs for the third wicket to seal victory for Zimbabwe.

Zimbabwe, however, lost their next match. India, chasing a target of 197, achieved it in the 41st over with the help of Sachin Tendulkar's unbeaten 118.

Sachin Tendulkar, Man of the Series in the 1998 Champions' Trophy.
David Munden/Sportsline Photographic

Heath Streak batting at number eight made 59, but the rest of the Zimbabwe batting failed to stand the pressure of some accurate bowling by the Indians.

India's third win in the competition by 81 runs against Sri Lanka had a lot to do with some fine bowling by their left-arm spinner Sunil Joshi, who took 3 for 17. Ajit Agarkar took 3 for 35 to damage the Sri Lankan batting and bowl them out for 98 in the 39th over as they chased 180 to win.

Later Zimbabwe won two matches in a row, against Sri Lanka and against India to secure a place in the finals. They beat Sri Lanka by 24 runs and India by 13 runs. Neil Johnson scored 72 and Andy Flower missed his century against Sri Lanka by only five runs as Zimbabwe made 259 for 7 against Sri Lanka. In Sri Lanka's batting disaster, Hashan Tillekeratne made 72. Against India,

Zimbabwe made 205 for 7 with the help of a fine innings by Alistair Campbell, who made 83. They then bowled India out for 192. For once in the tournament Indian batting had failed to come to its full potential as Henry Olonga took 4 for 46.

In a lacklustre final India restricted Zimbabwe to 196 for 9 in 50 overs. Neil Johnson, with 34 early in the innings, and later Paul Strang, with 48, and Eddo Brandes, with 33, gave some respectability to the innings, which had been tottering at 116 for 7. Srinath with 3 for 42 and Anil Kumble with 2 for 29 had done the damage. Indian openers Saurav Ganguly and Sachin Tendulkar wasted no time in knocking off the runs as they put on 197 runs in 30 overs to lift the Trophy. Ganguly made 63 and Tendulkar 124.

For his unbeaten 124 in the final and 118 unbeaten runs earlier on in the league games against Zimbabwe, Sachin Tendulkar was not only the Man of the Match in the final, but also was declared the Man of the Series.

Match One – India v. Sri Lanka

6 November 1998 at Sharjah CA Stadium
Sri Lanka 245 for 7 (50 overs) MS Atapattu 64, DA Gunawardene 52
India 248 for 7 (49.1 overs) M Azharuddin 94, NR Mongia 51
India won by three wickets
Man of the Match: M Azharuddin

Match Two – Sri Lanka v. Zimbabwe

7 November 1998 at Sharjah CA Stadium
Sri Lanka 196 (49.4 overs) PA de Silva 55, RS Mahanama 51
Zimbabwe 197 for 3 (46.1 overs) GW Flower 87*, MW Goodwin 54
Zimbabwe won by seven wickets
Man of the Match: EA Brandes

Match Three – India v. Zimbabwe

8 November 1998 at Sharjah CA Stadium
Zimbabwe 196 (49.5 overs) HH Streak 59
India 197 for 3 (40.4 overs) SR Tendulkar 118*
India won by seven wickets
Man of the Match: SR Tendulkar

Match Four – India v. Sri Lanka

9 November 1998 at Sharjah CA Stadium
India 179 (49.5 overs) AD Jadeja 64
Sri Lanka 98 (39 overs)
India won by 81 runs
Man of the Match: AB Agarkar

Match Five – Sri Lanka v. Zimbabwe

10 November 1998 at Sharjah CA Stadium
Zimbabwe 259 for 7 (50 overs) A Flower 95, NC Johnson 72
Sri Lanka 235 (48.5 overs) HP Tillekeratne 72*, PA Strang 4 for 32
Zimbabwe won by 24 runs
Man of the Match: PA Strang

Match Six – India v. Zimbabwe

11 November 1998 at Sharjah CA Stadium
Zimbabwe 205 for 7 (50 overs) ADR Campbell 83*
India 192 (47.4 overs) HK Olonga 4 for 46
Zimbabwe won by 13 runs
Man of the Match: HK Olonga

FINAL - INDIA v. ZIMBABWE
13 November 1998 at Sharjah CA Stadium

ZIMBABWE

Batting				Bowling	O	M	R	W
ADR Campbell (capt)	c Ganguly, b Agarkar		2	Srinath	10	1	40	3
GW Flower	c Agarkar, b Srinath		18	Agarkar	10	1	36	1
NC Johnson	c and b Chopra		34	Kumble	10	1	29	2
MW Goodwin	lbw, b Srinath		2	Chopra	7	0	32	1
*A Flower	b Kumble		19	Joshi	9	1	36	1
CB Wishart	c Tendulkar, b Joshi		18	Tendulkar	4	0	16	1
HH Streak	lbw, b Kumble		0					
PA Strang	lbw, Srinath		46					
EA Brandes	b Tendulkar		33	**Fall of Wickets**				
AR Whittall	not out		10	1-8, 2-36, 3-44, 4-77, 5-81, 6-81,				
HK Olonga	not out		0	7-116, 8-174, 9-194				
	lb 7, w 4, nb 3		14					
50 overs (for 9 wickets)			**196**					

INDIA

Batting				Bowling	O	M	R	W
SC Ganguly	not out		63	Brandes	2	0	9	0
SR Tendulkar	not out		124	Olonga	6	0	50	0
M Azharuddin (capt)				Johnson	4	0	18	0
AD Jadeja				Strang	5	0	45	0
RR Singh				Streak	4	0	17	0
*NR Mongia				Whittall	6	0	28	0
AB Agarkar				GW Flower	3	0	28	0
N Chopra								
A Kumble								
SB Joshi								
J Srinath								
	lb 2, w 6, nb 2		10					
30 overs (for 0 wicket)			**197**					

Umpires: RS Dunne & DL Orchard
Man of the Match: SR Tendulkar
Man of the Series: SR Tendulkar

India won by ten wickets

COCA COLA CUP
By Jonathan Agnew

Pakistan emerged as the deserved champions of this triangular tournament that also featured England and India. For all three teams, the competition represented an ideal warm-up for the World Cup, to be staged in England the following month. For that reason, there was particular interest in England's squad, which had been hand-picked to perform well in English conditions but, with only one front-line spinner, looked inadequate for the arid atmosphere and slow pitches of Sharjah.

Before a ball had been bowled, England's management team of David Graveney and David Lloyd – who had just announced that he would be standing down as coach after the World Cup – conceded that England were the underdogs. However, they argued – reasonably enough – that it was better for the players to be getting some competitive cricket under their belts as opposed to practising indoors. It is true that had England progressed to the final, their confidence would have been boosted as a result. As it turned out, England won only one match (against Pakistan) which, since the final pairing had already been sorted out, was viewed in many quarters as meaningless. It was, however, the only occasion that England batted first in their four games.

The opening match was played in a temperature of 45°C. This was considered to be unusually excessive for April, even in this part of the world where the day/night matches begin at 3.30pm to combat the heat. Alec Stewart lost the toss as usual,

Indian skipper Ajay Jadega made unbeaten 74 in 67 balls against England, match three in the Coca Cola Cup.
Mueen ud din Hameed/Sportsline Photographic

condemning England to a hot, dusty session in the field. Shahid Afridi scored a bright 41, but the Pakistan innings was dominated by a quite brilliant 137 by Ijaz Ahmed. He scored his runs from only 130 deliveries and, with Inzamam-ul-Haq, added 145 for the third wicket in just 22 overs. Moin Khan hit both the final two deliveries of the innings – bowled by Andrew Flintoff – for six and England needed to score at a rate of six and a half an over from the word go.

When Graham Thorpe was dismissed in the tenth over, England were effectively derailed at 53 for 3. Shoaib Akhtar, the 23-year-old fast bowler, charged in from a full 40 yards and clocked 94 miles per hour, admittedly on a speed-measuring device of uncertain accuracy. He removed Nick Knight, Alec Stewart and Thorpe in a burst of 3 for 29 in five overs to leave only Graeme Hick, with 65, to give England's total a shred of respectability.

A packed house gathered the following day to watch India play Pakistan. Once again, Pakistan's batsmen looked in terrific form as Inzamam clubbed a century. He was well supported by Yousuf Youhana and Ijaz to set India 280 to win. The

Mark Ealham during his 36-run knock in 47 minutes, England v. Pakistan, match five in the Coca Cola Cup.
Mueen ud din Hameed/Sportsline Photographic

response to this challenge can only be described as extraordinary. India gave absolutely no sign of attempting to chase the runs, apparently forgetting that it is not possible to draw a one-day match. After 15 overs, they had mustered 43 runs for the loss of two wickets and, finally, they crawled to the curious total of 163 for 6. It really was impossible to fathom exactly what was going on in the Indian dressing room, which had now welcomed the former Australian coach, Bobby Simpson, as a team adviser.

When India batted first against England – Stewart having lost the toss, again – a repeat performance appeared to be taking place. After 40 overs, India were 159 for 3 with Ramesh labouring over his half-century. Azharuddin added some welcome impetus to proceedings, although he injured a toe in the process, but England's target of 223 to win seemed 30 runs light.

Stewart and Knight fell within three balls of each other with only 25 on the board and although Hick and Thorpe added 55, England were soon 83 for 4. Flintoff and Fairbrother then appeared to be leading England to victory. Flintoff, who made his England debut the previous summer, was clearly more confident now, reaching 32 from 40 balls before he was startled by a nip-backer from Prasad, who also bowled Ealham for 7. With England needing to score 27 runs from four overs and with four wickets in hand, India's acting captain, Ajay Jadeja, brought himself on to bowl the crucial 47th over. He proceeded to take three wickets – including Fairbrother for 57 – for only three runs and the game was won by 20 runs.

The result meant that England had to beat India in their rematch to stand any chance of qualifying for the final. Once again, Stewart lost the toss and India batted first. Angus Fraser was given his first opportunity of the tournament because of an injury to Mullally, and the old campaigner slipped three maidens into his opening spell of eight overs which conceded only 15 runs and included the wicket of Ramesh. Fraser returned later in the innings to finish with 1 for 24: a terrific effort. Dravid made an elegant 63 but the innings of the afternoon was that of Jadeja who was, by now, relishing his captain's role. He scored an unbeaten 74 from only 64 balls and, with Mongia, added 32 from only 23 balls in a final thrash.

When England were 66 for 4 in the 17th over, they seemed to be on their way out. Knight and Thorpe put on 59 together, but England's tactics had, by now, degenerated to such obscurity that Fairbrother emerged to bat at number eight!

Thorpe tried his best, but he was stumped with 21 more runs needed by the last pair from 16 balls with the inevitable consequence that England slipped to their eighth consecutive one-day defeat.

Their demise rendered the final qualifying matches meaningless, but at least England managed to beat Pakistan by 62 runs. Finally, Stewart won the toss and batted first but Shoaib's 4 for 37 restricted England to only 206. Again, it was Fraser who asserted the early command, bowling unchanged to take 3 for 32 from ten overs. It might be that Pakistan's hearts were not in the game, and they lost their last five wickets for only six runs to lose by 62.

The very reason for the existence of a cricket stadium in Sharjah is the demand for the game created by the workforce that is brought in predominately from India and Pakistan. Therefore,

Ramesh of India in the Coca Cola Cup final, India v. Pakistan.
Mueen ud din Hameed/Sportsline Photographic

any match between the two countries is hugely anticipated and the subject of much debate wherever you go. What a shame, then, that this final proved to be such a devastating anticlimax. Wasim Akram seized two wickets in his opening over and in no time India were 46 for 4. That soon became 84 for 7 and although Ganguly scored 50, the innings subsided in a flurry of crazy run-outs.

Once Pakistan's openers, Saeed Anwar and Shahid Afridi had put on 50, the outcome was beyond any doubt. Pakistan cruised home with 22 overs remaining, leaving India's captain Azharuddin to fend off angry and often bizarre questions in the post-match press conference.

It was a triumph for Pakistan, whom I had never seen play either so well or with such obvious relish and team spirit. I told their coach, Javed Miandad, as much. 'Ah!' he replied. 'They are now in the right hands!' Days later, Javed resigned in mysterious circumstances, apparently following a fall-out in the dressing room.

Match One – England v. Pakistan

7 April 1999 at CBFS Stadium, Sharjah
Pakistan 323 for 5 (50 overs) Ijaz Ahmed 137, Inzamam-ul-Haq 59
England 233 (45.5 overs) GA Hick 65, A Flintoff 50
Pakistan won by 90 runs
Man of the Match: Ijaz Ahmed

Match Two – India v. Pakistan

8 April 1999 at CBFS Stadium, Sharjah
Pakistan 279 for 8 (50 overs) Inzamam-ul-Haq 107, Yousuf Youhana 57
India 163 for 6 (50 overs)
Pakistan won by 116 runs
Man of the Match: Inzamam-ul-Haq

Match Three – England v. India

9 April 1999 at CBFS Stadium, Sharjah
India 222 for 5 (50 overs) M Azharuddin 74*, S Ramesh 60
England 202 (47.5 overs) NH Fairbrother 57
India won by 20 runs
Man of the Match: AD Jadeja

Match Four – England v. India

11 April 1999 at CBFS Stadium, Sharjah
India 239 for 6 (50 overs) AD Jadeja 74*, RS Dravid 63
England 230 (48.5 overs) NV Knight 84, GP Thorpe 79
India won by 9 runs
Man of the Match: BKV Prasad

Match Five – England v. Pakistan

12 April 1999 at CBFS Stadium, Sharjah
England 206 (49.1 overs) GP Thorpe 62, Shoaib Akhtar 4 for 37
Pakistan 144 (40.2 overs) MA Ealham 4 for 30
England won by 64 runs
Man of the Match: MA Ealham

Match Six – India v. Pakistan

13 April 1999 at CBFS Stadium, Sharjah
Pakistan 205 for 9 (50 overs) Moin Khan 54, Salim Malik 50
India 206 for 4 (48.1 overs) S Ramesh 82, RS Dravid 81
India won by six wickets
Man of the Match: S Ramesh

FINAL – INDIA v. PAKISTAN
16 April 1999 at CBFS Stadium, Sharjah

INDIA

Batting			Bowling	O	M	R	W
S Ramesh	lbw, b Wasim Akram	0	Wasim Akram	8	3	11	3
SC Ganguly	c Yousuf Youhana, b Arshad Khan	50	Shoaib Akhtar	8	1	31	1
RS Dravid	lbw, b Wasim Akram	0	Azhar Mahmood	10	0	31	2
M Azharuddin (capt)	c Azhar Mahmood, b Shoaib Akhtar	2	Saqlain Mushtaq	7	0	20	0
AD Jadeja	c Saeed Anwar, b Azhar Mahmood	14	Arshad Khan	10	1	24	1
J Srinath	c Moin Khan, b Azhar Mahmood	3	Shahid Afridi	2	0	8	0
RR Singh	run out	15					
*NR Mongia	run out	0	**Fall of Wickets**				
AB Agarkar	b Wasim Akram	20	1-0, 2-0, 3-14, 4-46, 5-50, 6-82,				
A Kumble	run out	7	7-84, 8-104, 9-121				
BKV Prasad	not out	1					
	w 4, nb 9	13					
	45 overs	**125**					

PAKISTAN

Batting			Bowling	O	M	R	W
Saeed Anwar	c and b Kumble	30	Srinath	8	0	31	0
Shahid Afridi	c Ganguly, b Kumble	24	Prasad	6	0	17	0
Ijaz Ahmed	not out	21	Agarkar	5	0	52	0
Inzamam-ul-Haq	not out	39	Kumble	9	1	28	2
Yousuf Youhana							
Azhar Mahmood							
*Moin Khan			**Fall of Wickets**				
Wasim Akram (capt)			1-53, 2-65				
Saqlain Mushtaq							
Arshad Khan							
Shoaib Akhtar							
	lb 1, w 5, nb 9	15					
	28 overs (for 2 wickets) 129						

Umpires: KT Francis & DB Hair
Man of the Match: Wasim Akram
Player of the Series: Shoaib Akhtar

Pakistan won by eight wickets

NEW ZEALAND

India in New Zealand
South Africa in New Zealand
New Zealand Domestic First-Class Season
New Zealand Domestic One-Day Season
First-Class Averages

INDIA IN NEW ZEALAND
By Bryan Waddle

International cricket's unofficial world Test championship was more than enough motivation for New Zealand to perform above itself when the Indian team arrived for its first substantial tour since 1990. Depending on which authority you believe, New Zealand was eighth equal or ninth of the Test-playing countries. By their own determination, the 'Black Caps' deserved to be eighth by virtue of their recent successes over Zimbabwe without ever having lost a Test to that fledgling cricket nation.

India, on the other hand, had a good record in home internationals. With a substantial diet of one-day cricket to back them, they were favourites to beat New Zealand even though they had not won a Test in that country since 1976. The Indians arrived in New Zealand a pace bowler short, with Ajit Agarkar injured prior to leaving home, and his replacement Robin Singh Jnr hardly a household name. Much of the burden of bowling out New Zealand rested with the deceptive spin of Anil Kumble and the experienced seamer Javagal Srinath, who gave early signs of having problems with his fitness.

But they did boast a batting order second to none on world rankings. Four players – Sidhu, Tendulkar, Dravid and Azharuddin – were listed in the top ten with Ganguly rated 11th. The first three have averaged more than 50 over the past two years.

New Zealand was a side searching for international credibility, still carrying a promising re-development tag that should have been discarded long ago. Results in recent Test series had been mixed; Tests were mainly played overseas, with just two against Zimbabwe at home in the previous 12 months. There had, however, been a Test win in a lost three-match series in Sri Lanka, six months previously.

Stephen Fleming was firmly installed as captain and his leading players – Cairns, Doull, Astle, McMillan and Parore – were all becoming more and more experienced. There were real question marks, though, over New Zealand's ability to bowl out international sides. Lacking a genuine quick bowler, there also appeared to be no back-up for the one class spinner in the side, Daniel Vettori. There were major concerns, too, at the top of the order, with no experienced or established opening pair to give the batting a foundation. That was to be highlighted painfully throughout the summer of Tests with India and South Africa.

India hardly made an auspicious start to its tour, losing a three-day match against Central Districts and struggling to come to grips with Wellington in a game that was won but not as convincingly as it should have been. Added to that, the first Test was abandoned without a ball being bowled – only the sixth Test at that stage to be completely ruined by the weather. The abandoned match in Faisalabad between Pakistan and Zimbabwe followed a few days later.

There was a further irony in the Dunedin abandonment, with New Zealand's most experienced umpire Steve Dunne for the second time denied the opportunity to stand in a Test at his home ground. Dunne had been scheduled to officiate in his first ever Test match at Carisbrook, Dunedin in the first Test of the 1988–89 series against Pakistan. Amazingly that too was abandoned without a ball being bowled for the same reason: appalling weather.

Central Districts v. India
7, 8, 9 and 10 December 1998 at McLean Park, Napier
India 103 and 390
Central Districts 336 and 158 for 3
Central Districts won by seven wickets

Four for 177 off 24 overs is hardly the stuff memories are made of, but Central Districts off-spinner, Campbell Furlong, will forever recall the day he captured the wicket of Sachin Tendulkar after a severe mauling on McLean Park.

It will not only be the wicket he remembers, but the fact that Central Districts won the match against India by seven wickets to record only their second victory over a touring side since the association was formed in 1950.

After eight overs Furlong had 2 for 44, after 15 he had 2 for 117 as Tendulkar posted 50 from 33 balls, his hundred from 81 and 150 from 119. But an outfield catch gave Furlong some revenge as Central Districts recorded a meritorious win over the tourists.

Wellington v. India
12, 13, 14 and 15 December 1998 at Basin Reserve, Wellington
Wellington 317 and 124
India 268 and 175 for 2
India won by eight wickets

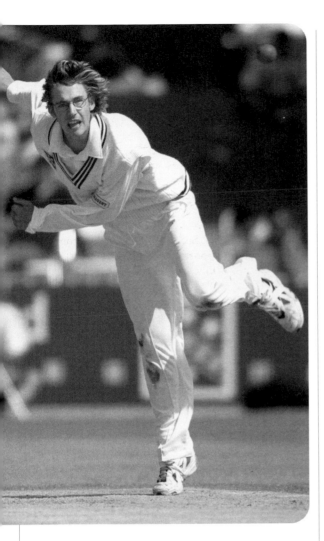

Daniel Vettori, New Zealand's young and talented left-arm spinner.

David Munden/Sportsline Photographic

Roger Twose joined a select band of New Zealand cricketers in becoming only the fifth player to be dismissed on 99 on more than one occasion.

But despite that, his 99 was a significant innings for Wellington on a pitch that gave the seam bowler unusual pace and bounce on the first day.

There was satisfaction for the home side in that they were able to take a first innings lead of 49, although it should have been greater with India at 208 for 7 at one stage in its first innings.

First Test
Match abandoned

Second Test
26, 27, 28, 29 and 30 December 1998 at Wellington

Simon Doull did not have an outstanding domestic season, taking only 13 wickets, but his lack of success was more than offset by his match-winning effort with the ball in the Basin Reserve Test.

Opting to play a Boxing Day Test instead of using the domestic one-day competition as the Christmas/New Year showpiece paid off handsomely for New Zealand cricket.

Doull, the country's leading pace bowler, made a devastating start to the series with career-best 7 for 65. He probably would not have played in the abandoned first Test because of injury and was doubtful for the second until the opening morning of the match.

India might have considered the Basin Reserve pitch was worth batting on after experiencing its nature just prior to Christmas, but while it had pace and bounce it didn't encourage the bowlers to the degree that 16 for 4 after 11 overs might suggest.

New Zealand's attack, spearheaded by Doull, Cairns and Nash, was hardly venomous. However, with some outstanding control of late swing, Doull had all four wickets before Tendulkar and Azharuddin had time to get their pads on.

The dismissal of Tendulkar soon after lunch, brilliantly caught by Bell at square leg was the turning point of the innings and, indeed, the match.

Even though Azharuddin scored an unbeaten hundred, Doull continued to work through innings grabbing the first seven wickets to fall, before Nash, Vettori and McMillan did the mopping up.

As usual, Azharuddin's knock was full of class with crisp on-side shots and 14 boundaries in his 156-ball innings.

New Zealand's 144-run first-innings lead wasn't achieved without some difficulty, losing their seventh wicket with the first-innings scores tied and needing a record eighth-wicket stand between Nash and Vettori to establish dominance. They might have wondered how on earth that was possible considering Vettori's previous Test form. In four innings in Sri Lanka he'd recorded three ducks, which was out of character for man with a top score of 90.

India lost three wickets erasing the deficit, and called on Tendulkar and Azharuddin to give them a defendable target with another important stand of 97. Tendulkar's 17th Test hundred – surprisingly his first against New Zealand – came from a

Stephen Fleming led New Zealand to a memorable victory at Basin Reserve.

Andrew Cornaga/Sportsline Photographic

remarkable 112 balls including two sixes and 11 fours. Srinath and Kumble, so often the key bowling partnership, then ensured they had something to bowl at by plundering 42 for the eighth wicket as India reached 356.

The chase for victory was decidedly shaky even though there was ample time, with four of the top order dismissed before stumps on the fourth day and Astle out after breaking a bone in his left hand from a nasty rearing delivery from Srinath.

With nightwatchman Wiseman out early on the fifth morning, New Zealand had half the side out for 74 and Astle unable to bat. But some positive stroke-play by Cairns and McMillan, arguably New Zealand's most aggressive and innovative batsmen, produced a partnership of 147 which took New Zealand to within two runs of victory when Cairns was dismissed.

The promotion of a Boxing Day Test had proved a bonanza for New Zealand cricket not only in attendance figures but also in giving New Zealand its seventh Test victory against the Indians.

SECOND TEST – NEW ZEALAND v. INDIA
26, 27, 28, 29 and 30 December 1998 at Basin Reserve, Wellington

INDIA

	First Innings		Second Innings	
NS Sidhu	c Fleming, b Doull	0	(2) lbw, b Doull	34
AD Jadeja	lbw, b Doull	10	(1) b Nash	22
RS Dravid	lbw, b Doull	0	b Wiseman	28
SC Ganguly	c Parore, b Doull	5	c Bell, b Wiseman	48
SR Tendulkar	c Bell, b Doull	47	c Fleming, b Nash	113
M Azharuddin (capt)	not out	103	c Parore, b Nash	48
*NR Mongia	c Astle, b Doull	0	c Fleming, b Doull	2
A Kumble	c McMillan, b Doull	11	c Nash, b Vettori	23
J Srinath	c Fleming, b Nash	7	not out	27
BKV Prasad	c Fleming, b Vettori	15	c and b Astle	0
Harbhajan Singh	c Astle, b McMillan	1	c Horne, b McMillan	1
	lb 3, nb 6	9	b 3, lb 1, w 1, nb 5	10
		208		**356**

	First Innings				Second Innings			
	O	M	R	W	O	M	R	W
Doull	24	7	65	7	25	10	49	2
Cairns	17	3	69	–	19	2	68	–
Nash	14	1	46	1	15	9	20	3
Vettori	7	0	20	1	20	6	92	1
Astle	2	0	5	–	7	3	7	1
McMillan	1.4	1	0	1	9.5	2	26	1
Wiseman					19	1	90	2

Fall of Wickets
1–0, 2–2, 3–15, 4–16, 5–99, 6–99, 7–132, 8–149, 9–207
1–41, 2–74, 3–112, 4–200; 5–297, 6–304, 7–304, 8–346, 9–349

NEW ZEALAND

	First Innings		Second Innings	
MD Bell	c Mongia, b Prasad	4	c Dravid, b Srinath	0
MJ Horne	b Kumble	38	lbw, b Kumble	31
SP Fleming (capt)	run out (Jadeja)	42	b Kumble	17
NJ Astle	b Kumble	56	retired hurt	1
CD McMillan	c Dravid, b Srinath	24	not out	74
*AC Parore	lbw, b Kumble	2	run out (Dravid)	1
CL Cairns	c Tendulkar, b Prasad	3	(8) c Jadeja, b Srinath	61
DJ Nash	not out	89	(9) not out	4
DL Vettori	b Tendulkar	57		
PJ Wiseman	b Tendulkar	0	(7) lbw, b Srinath	0
SB Doull	lbw, b Kumble	0		
	b 13, lb 19, nb 5	37	b 9, lb 9, nb 8	26
		352	(for 6 wickets)	**215**

	First Innings				Second Innings			
	O	M	R	W	O	M	R	W
Srinath	36	6	89	1	19.3	1	82	3
Prasad	30	8	67	2	10	3	26	–
Kumble	45.4	18	83	4	23	6	70	2
Harbhajan Singh	25	6	61	–	5	1	11	–
Ganguly	6	0	13	–				
Tendulkar	6	2	7	2	3	0	8	–

Fall of Wickets
1–7, 2–79, 3–112, 4–162, 5–172, 6–179, 7–208, 8–345, 9–349
1–0, 2–42, 3–51, 4–67, 5–74, 6–211

Umpires: EA Watkin & EA Nicholls
Toss: India

New Zealand won by four wickets

THIRD TEST
2, 3, 4, 5 and 6 January 1999 at Hamilton

However, the positive, adventurous spirit that characterised New Zealand's performance in the second Test was strangely missing in the third and deciding Test, as the home side opted to play for a draw and a series victory from the start. It created a philosophical argument surrounding New Zealand's current approach to Test cricket, as to how far a team should go to entertain at the expense of winning Test cricket.

Astle's broken left hand provided the opportunity for Roger Twose to force his way back into international cricket and create a chance for selection for the World Cup. He wasted little time in showing his worth as New Zealand, batting first and two down for no runs in the first over, owed its recovery to the left-hander who stuck it out, doggedly, until the second-last over of the day for a determined 87. He had a share of luck, being dropped at third slip early on by Prasad: it was to be an expensive let-off.

In stark contrast, McMillan produced an innings of sublime skill but his inexperience meant a century in both innings went begging despite scoring his 92 from just 102 balls. He also reached 84 in the second just as effortlessly.

Even though the lower order failed to capitalise on the efforts of Twose, McMillan and the reliable Horne, New Zealand's 366 gave them a position that was defendable and firm enough to push for the draw they desired. But anything that New Zealand could offer was exceeded by the elegant Rahul Dravid, whose chanceless 190 was ample evidence of his emerging class. This was further displayed in the second innings when he became only the third Indian to score centuries in both innings of a Test. The second, though, was somewhat of a gift after New Zealand had put the result beyond doubt, offering the part-time bowling skills of McMillan, Twose and Horne.

India made little effort to reach the 415-run target they had been set and it was evident from early on that New Zealand had only one result in mind: a draw.

Cairns' second Test hundred was vital in achieving that goal, particularly as New Zealand were only 35 in front with the top four dismissed, until McMillan, Parore, Nash and Vettori gave the innings its substance.

Cairns collected the Man of the Match award for that century, four wickets in the first innings and a couple of scalps early in the second before the game became utterly meaningless in the final two sessions.

Individually, India took the statistical honours with five centuries shared between Tendulkar, Azharuddin, Dravid and Ganguly while New Zealand produced just one. However, India suggested once again they do not travel well. Since winning the series against England in 1986, they have won only one Test in the ensuing 15 overseas series.

Simon Doull: 7 for 65 in the second Test against India at Wellington.
David Munden/Sportsline Photographic

THIRD TEST – NEW ZEALAND v. INDIA
2, 3, 4, 5 and 6 January 1999 at Westpac Trust Park, Hamilton

NEW ZEALAND

	First Innings		Second Innings	
MD Bell	c Mongia, b Srinath	0	lbw, b Tendulkar	25
MJ Horne	b Srinath	63	c Mongia, b Srinath	26
SP Fleming (capt)	c Dravid, b Srinath	0	b Prasad	18
RG Twose	c Mongia, b Prasad	87	lbw, b Tendulkar	4
CD McMillan	c Prasad, b Kumble	92	c Mongia, b Harbhajan Singh	84
*AC Parore	c sub (VVS Laxman), b Prasad	21	c Harbhajan Singh, b Kumble	50
PJ Wiseman	c Ganguly, b Harbhajan Singh	13		
CL Cairns	b Harbhajan Singh	2	(7) c Dravid, b Kumble	126
DJ Nash	not out	18	(8) run out (Dravid)	63
DL Vettori	b Srinath	24	(9) not out	43
SB Doull	c Kumble, b Srinath	6		
	b 5, lb 19, w 2, nb 14	40	b 9, lb 7, w 1, nb 8	25
		366	(for 8 wickets, dec.)	**464**

	First Innings				Second Innings			
	O	M	R	W	O	M	R	W
Srinath	32.2	10	95	5	27	6	90	1
Prasad	33	10	61	2	33	8	75	1
Kumble	27	7	64	1	45.5	9	124	2
Harbhajan Singh	21	5	74	2	19	3	102	1
Ganguly	5	3	25	–	6	1	27	–
Tendulkar	3	0	23	–	7	0	30	2

Fall of Wickets
1–0, 2–0, 3–95, 4–255, 5–278, 6–311, 7–314, 8–315, 9–356
1–46, 2–69, 3–76, 4–85, 5–225, 6–225, 7–373, 8–464

INDIA

	First Innings		Second Innings	
NS Sidhu	c Parore, b Cairns	1	(2) b Cairns	13
AD Jadeja	c Nash, b Doull	12	(1) c Parore, b Cairns	21
RS Dravid	c McMillan, b Cairns	190	not out	103
SR Tendulkar	lbw, b Nash	67		
SC Ganguly	c Fleming, b Doull	11	(4) not out	101
M Azharuddin (capt)	c Fleming, b Cairns	4		
*NR Mongia	c Horne, b Nash	7		
A Kumble	c Parore, b Doull	0		
J Srinath	c Twose, b Wiseman	76		
BKV Prasad	not out	30		
Robin Singh	c Fleming, b Cairns	0		
	b 2, lb 4, w 8, nb 4	18	lb 9, nb 2	11
		416	(for 2 wickets)	**249**

	First Innings				Second Innings			
	O	M	R	W	O	M	R	W
Doull	36	15	64	3	4	0	17	–
Cairns	22.3	3	107	4	9	1	30	2
Nash	37	10	98	2				
Vettori	16	2	71	–				
McMillan	4	0	24	–	17	4	59	–
Wiseman	13	2	46	1	12	0	80	–
Twose					9.1	0	50	–
Horne					1	0	4	–

Fall of Wickets
1–17, 2–17, 3–126, 4–164, 5–195, 6–204, 7–211, 8–355, 9–416
1–33, 2–55

Umpires: DB Cowie & RE Koertzen
Toss: India

Match drawn

TEST MATCH AVERAGES
New Zealand v. India

NEW ZEALAND

Batting	M	Inns	NO	HS	Runs	Av	100	50
DJ Nash	2	4	3	89*	174	174.00	–	2
CD McMillan	2	4	1	92	274	91.33	–	3
DL Vettori	2	3	1	57	124	62.00	–	1
CL Cairns	2	4	–	126	192	48.00	1	1
MJ Horne	2	4	–	63	158	39.50	–	1
SP Fleming	2	4	–	42	77	19.25	–	–
AC Parore	2	4	–	50	74	18.50	–	1
MD Bell	2	4	–	25	29	7.25	–	–
PJ Wiseman	2	3	–	13	13	4.33	–	–

Played in two Tests: SB Doull 0 & 6
Played in one Test: NJ Astle 56 & 1*; RG Twose 87 & 4

Bowling	Overs	Mds	Runs	Wkts	Av	Best	10/m	5/inn
SB Doull	89	32	195	12	16.25	7–65	–	1
DJ Nash	66	20	164	6	27.33	3–20	–	–
CL Cairns	67.3	9	274	6	45.66	4–107	–	–

Also bowled: NJ Astle 9–3–12–1; MJ Horne 1–0–4–0; CD McMillan 32.3–7–109–2;
RG Twose 9.1–0–50–0; DL Vettori 43–8–183–2; PJ Wiseman 44–3–216–3

Fielding Figures
8 – SP Fleming; 5 – AC Parore; 3 – NJ Astle; 2 – MD Bell, MJ Horne, CD McMillan, DJ Nash;
1 – RG Twose

INDIA

Batting	M	Inns	NO	HS	Runs	Av	100	50
RS Dravid	2	4	1	190	321	107.00	2	–
M Azharuddin	2	3	1	103*	155	77.50	1	–
SR Tendulkar	2	3	–	113	227	75.66	1	1
SC Ganguly	2	4	1	101*	165	55.00	1	–
J Srinath	2	3	1	76	110	55.00	–	1
BKV Prasad	2	3	1	30*	45	22.50	–	–
AD Jadeja	2	4	–	22	65	16.25	–	–
NS Sidhu	2	4	–	34	48	12.00	–	–
A Kumble	2	3	–	23	34	11.33	–	–
NR Mongia	2	3	–	7	9	3.00	–	–

Played in one Test: Harbhajan Singh 1 & 1; R Singh 0

Bowling	Overs	Mds	Runs	Wkts	Av	Best	10/m	5/inn
J Srinath	114.5	23	356	10	35.60	5–95	–	1
A Kumble	141.3	40	341	9	37.88	4–83	–	–
BKV Prasad	106	29	229	5	45.80	2–61	–	–

Also bowled: SC Ganguly 17–4–65–0; Harbhajan Singh 30–7–72–0; R Singh 40–8–176–3;
SR Tendulkar 19–2–68–4

Fielding Figures
5 – NR Mongia; 4 – RS Dravid; 1 – SC Ganguly, AD Jadeja, A Kumble, BKV Prasad, R Singh,
SR Tendulkar

ONE-DAY INTERNATIONALS

Let there be light! But there wasn't any; at least not for an hour as New Zealand's newest one-day cricket venue in the delightful holiday resort town of Taupo – on New Zealand's volcanic plateau – struggled to cope with the modern game's requirements.

Owen Delany Park is a charming little ground, ideal for domestic cricket; but the 13,000 people who attended the first international between India and New Zealand tested the facilities to the point of blowing a fuse in the electrical supply, plunging the ground into darkness. It may have been a successful ploy by New Zealand's team and management, because the interruption made the ultimate target a little easier, with the help of the confusing Duckworth-Lewis re-calculation system.

When the fuse blew in the 31st over, New Zealand, 168 for 3, had been chasing 258, but that target was altered to 200 off 39 overs, leaving them 8.2 overs to score 32. A bye brought New Zealand success with six balls remaining.

India's total was built upon another sparkling century from Rahul Dravid, who completed his third successive hundred against New Zealand following the two he scored in the third Test of the series.

Dravid dominated the one-day batting as he had done in the two Test series. He scored 309 runs at 77.25 and with a strike rate of 84, but, as in the Tests, it failed to help India win the series. They had to settle for a drawn series after the third game at Wellington was washed out.

While the failure of the floodlights was the talking point in Taupo, some appalling running and calling produced an almost derisive response in the second match in Napier. The five run-outs in the New Zealand innings equalled a world record for that mode of dismissal, while the eight in the match was also a new record.

There could easily have been another, too, with Adam Parore adjudged stumped although he seemed to be setting off for a run after missing a delivery off Tendulkar's bowling that wasn't retrieved initially by wicketkeeper Mongia.

India took a decisive two-one series lead, winning the fourth game after the third at the Basin Reserve had been ruined by rain.

It was an emphatic victory in the last match that squared the series, with Chris Cairns the dominant individual, although his 75-ball century was tinged with controversy. Soon after passing his 50 from 52 balls, it seemed Cairns had been caught at the wicket, and appeared to be about to leave only to be given not out by umpire Chris King. Cairns took advantage of his good fortune to bludgeon the fastest ever one-day hundred in New Zealand. It was his second, the previous one also being against India.

It was an encouraging performance by New Zealand, especially since they were without the services of regular captain Stephen Fleming, who had undergone groin surgery, and top-order batsman Nathan Astle, who had a broken bone in his hand.

New Zealand had enjoyed a home victory in the Test series, but the drawn one-day series was an important confidence-booster in the buildup to the World Cup.

Match One
9 January 1999 at Owen Delany Park, Taupo
India 257 for 5 (50 overs) RS Dravid 123*,
SC Ganguly 60
New Zealand 200 for 5 (38 overs) CD McMillan 73,
MJ Horne 57
New Zealand won by 5 wickets (D/L Method)
Man of the Match: RS Dravid

Match Two
12 January 1999 at McLean Park, Napier
New Zealand 213 (49.3 overs) MJ Horne 61
India 214 for 8 (49.5 overs)
India won by two wickets
Man of the Match: MJ Horne

Match Three
14 January 1999 at Basin Reserve, Wellington
India 208 for 4 (32 overs) RS Dravid 68,
M Azharuddin 52
New Zealand 89 for 2 (12.1 overs) Young 52*
Match abandoned

Match Four
16 January 1999 at Eden Park, Auckland
New Zealand 207 for 7 (50 overs)
India 208 for 5 (43.5 overs) RS Dravid 51, SC Ganguly 50
India won by five wickets
Man of the Match: RS Dravid

Match Five
19 January 1999 at Jade Stadium, Christchurch
New Zealand 300 for 8 (50 overs) CL Cairns 115,
RG Twose 63, BA Young 57
India 230 (45.3 overs) M Azharuddin 63, SC Ganguly 60, CZ Harris 4 for 40
New Zealand won by 70 runs
Man of the Match: CL Cairns

SOUTH AFRICA IN NEW ZEALAND
By Neal Manthorpe

The taste of the Nederburg Cuvée Brut had barely left the mouths of South Africa's cricketers following their six-one demolition of the West Indies in the one-day series before they were on the plane again for the 36-hour journey to New Zealand. There had been little enough time for Hansie Cronje's team to comprehend the five-nil Test whitewash against Brian Lara's unhappy West Indians, never mind to take in the results of the one-dayers that immediately preceded the flight to Auckland.

South Africa's success against the West Indies had been achieved in the face of some discord of their own when the United Cricket Board had ordered the national selectors to pick an enlarged squad of 19 for the one-day series in order to include two players 'of colour', one of whom also made the trip to New Zealand.

David Terbrugge, the fast-medium seamer who played such an important, strangling role during the first four Tests against the West Indies, was ruled out of the New Zealand series with rib and ankle trouble at the eleventh hour and Steve Elworthy, due to turn 34 on tour, was called up.

Also in the squad was 18-year-old Victor Mpitsang, who became South Africa's first 'black African' international with a politically induced debut against the West Indies. He was, according to selection chief Peter Pollock, on tour this time 'to learn as much as possible and to allow some of the front-line bowlers to rest during the non-international matches.'

Hansie Cronje said clearly before the season started that beating the West Indies and winning the World Cup were the major objectives for the season, but he neither disregarded the New Zealand series nor underestimated their strengths.

The home side, of course, was buzzing after a Test series win against India and the drawn one-day series that followed it. But injuries to three key players, Stephen Fleming, Chris Cairns and Craig McMillan, were to play an important role during the second half of their summer and a South African top order, famous for its brittle composition, was to have the tour of its collective life.

Northern Districts v. South Africa
22, 23 and 24 February 1999 at Westpac Trust Park, Hamilton
South Africa 407 for 4 dec. and 200 for 5 dec.
Northern Districts 306 for 8 dec. and 120 for 3
Match drawn

South Africa scored three centuries on the first day (Cullinan 100, Cronje 104 and Rhodes 100 not out) in a declared total of 407 for 4 and still had time to bowl seven overs at the end of it. Victor Mpitsang made his international first-class debut. On the second day the Districts' batsmen looked as outclassed as their bowlers as they flopped to 136 for 8 but a maiden first-class century from Matthew Hart (102 not out) and an unbroken ninth-wicket stand of 170 with Joey Yovich (63 not out) halted the slide. More batting practice of the third day saw Herschelle Gibbs add an attractive 85 to his first innings 57.

Number eleven Geoff Allott had a record-breaking 101-minute duck in the first Test against South Africa.
Andrew Cornaga/Sportsline Photographic

First Test
27 and 28 February, 1, 2 and 3 March 1999 at Auckland

Two mighty, though very different batting records were set on a pitch flat enough to force a draw from a timeless Test. Oddly, talk before the match focused on the grassless, cracked nature of the surface, giving rise to concern that it wouldn't last. The answer was glue. Hundreds of litres were poured into the ground which, when dried, acquired the properties of an indoor net. Effectively, it killed the game.

In the absence of victory, or any prospect of one, the Test will be remembered for Daryll Cullinan's record-breaking 275 not out and for Geoff Allott's bizarre but highly humorous, world-record duck. Cullinan batted for 11 hours, Allott for 101 minutes.

Only in cricket could a man do so little, for so long, and claim to have done as much for his team as a man who did so much, for so much longer.

Dion Nash was vilified for putting South Africa in to bat but, in truth, Hansie Cronje would almost certainly have made the same, embarrassing mistake if he had called correctly. The last time the glue process was used at Eden Park, Javed Miandad, like Cullinan and Gary Kirsten, found it much to his liking. Miandad scored 271 in 1989.

Kirsten equalled Dudley Nourse's South African record of nine Test centuries before falling early on the second day for 128. It was a typical Kirsten innings, full of determined defence but also plenty of cover drives and quick singles. The rest of the innings, though, belonged to Cullinan who removed the great Graeme Pollock from the top of South Africa's list of highest Test scorers.

Curiously, Cronje allowed Cullinan an hour on the third morning to chase Pollock's 274 (scored at Kingsmead against Australia in 1969–70) but when he got there, running a quick two off Craig McMillan's occasional medium pace, the declaration came immediately. Having chased one record, the captain left his team just two runs short of beating the previous highest total by a South African side – the 622 for 9 that featured Pollock's record. He confessed afterwards that he simply wasn't aware of the landmark.

Matt Horne reached 92 by the close of the third day as New Zealand reached an untroubled 205 for 2 but, by tea on the fourth day, the home side had slipped to 317 for 8 and the prospects of following on with almost four full sessions remaining gave South Africa great hope.

FIRST TEST – NEW ZEALAND v. SOUTH AFRICA
27 and 28 February, 1, 2 and 3 March 1999 at Eden Park, Auckland

SOUTH AFRICA

	First Innings		
G Kirsten	c Astle, b Allott	128	
HH Gibbs	b Vettori	34	
JH Kallis	lbw, b Doull	7	
DJ Cullinan	not out	275	
WJ Cronje (capt)	c Allott, b Harris	30	
JN Rhodes	c Twose, b Harris	63	
SM Pollock	not out	69	
*MV Boucher			
L Klusener			
AA Donald			
PR Adams			
	b 4, lb 9, nb 2	15	
	(for 5 wickets, dec.)	621	

	First Innings			
	O	M	R	W
Doull	33	7	90	1
Allott	38	5	153	1
Nash	28	2	97	–
Vettori	42	8	120	1
Harris	45	10	94	2
McMillan	5.1	0	24	–
Astle	9	1	30	–

Fall of Wickets
1–76, 2–97, 3–280, 4–354, 5–495

NEW ZEALAND

	First Innings			Second Innings	
RG Twose	c Boucher, b Donald	31		(3) c Cullinan, b Klusener	65
MJ Horne	b Adams	93		(1) b Adams	60
NJ Astle	c Boucher, b Donald	41		(4) not out	69
CD McMillan	c Boucher, b Cronje	25		(5) not out	22
CZ Harris	not out	68			
*AC Parore	b Pollock	9			
MD Bell	b Klusener	6		(2) c Donald, b Pollock	6
DJ Nash (capt)	c Boucher, b Klusener	1			
DL Vettori	c Cronje, b Adams	32			
SB Doull	c Gibbs, b Adams	17			
GJ Allott	c Pollock, b Kallis	0			
	lb 21, w 2, nb 6	29		b 13, lb 2, w 2, nb 5	22
		352		(for 3 wickets)	244

	First Innings				Second Innings			
	O	M	R	W	O	M	R	W
Donald	27	16	40	2	9	2	20	–
Pollock	28	11	51	1	13	5	21	1
Klusener	27	8	60	2	13	6	26	1
Adams	46	18	103	3	30	11	96	1
Kallis	21.4	10	44	1	13	0	61	–
Cullinan	2	1	8	–				
Cronje	9	2	25	1	6	4	5	–

Fall of Wickets
1–80, 2–170, 3–210, 4–210, 5–224, 6–242, 7–251, 8–294, 9–320
1–15, 2–104, 3–193

Umpires: DB Cowie & DJ Harper
Toss: New Zealand

Match drawn

South Africa tried everything they knew when Allott came to the crease. Bouncers and yorkers from Donald, Pollock, Klusener and Kallis, with tight, 'pressure' fielders. Paul Adams's spinners were stoutly kept out, too.

Allott knew nothing of his impending fame until the stadium announcer revealed that he had passed John Wright's New Zealand record for the longest nought. He seemed puzzled by the applause but when it continued, he sheepishly raised his bat and quickly lowered it again. The minutes ticked by and when Godfrey Evans (97 minutes v. Australia, 1946–47) was finally erased from the record books, Allott was less reticent about the raised bat – although still a little shy. To their great credit Hansie

South Africa's Daryll Cullinan scored a total of 427 runs in the series without being dismissed.
David Munden/Sportsline Photographic

Cronje's players smiled and enjoyed the moment, even though they knew that by batting most of the final session, Allott had virtually saved the game. The following day, half-centuries from Nathan Astle, Roger Twose and Horne again ensured a draw with full honours although the day was spoiled in the day's penultimate over when a Jacques Kallis lifter broke a finger in Craig McMillan's right hand.

New Zealand 'A' v. South Africa
6, 7 and 8 March 1999 at Lincoln Green, Lincoln
South Africa 403 for 6 dec. and 232 for 6 dec.
New Zealand 'A' 276 for 9 dec. and 219 for 8
Match drawn

Gary Kirsten invested five hours in his 137 after South Africa batted first and made 403 for 6 while Jonty Rhodes walloped an unbeaten 101 from 110 balls with 12 fours and three sixes. On the second day, unheralded Canterbury captain Gary Stead made 70 to advance his claims for the Test batting place made available by Craig McMillan's injury.

Rhodes hooked and pulled his way to another unbeaten ton on the third morning after Shayne O'Connor had taken 4 for 27 in an impressive opening burst of ten overs. Chasing an impossible 360 to win in two sessions, the 'A' team were steered to the draw at 219 for 8 by young leg-spinner Brooke Walker's 31 not out from 145 balls.

SECOND TEST
11, 12, 13, 14 and 15 March 1999 at Christchurch

The infamous New Zealand weather finally had its say in this match although, for South Africa, a personal milestone, this time for Herschelle Gibbs, again made the match worthwhile.

Dion Nash's decision to bat first under overcast skies was made to look as awful as the choice to bowl first in Auckland although feeble, ill-disciplined batting from the top order let him down.

A pitch with some grass on it, and no glue, appeared to excite Donald and Pollock to such an extent that they lost control completely in the morning session. Yet Bryan Young (5), Roger Twose (0) and Matt Horne (36) all contrived either to miss a rare straight ball or chase a wide one.

Nathan Astle, having survived a Daryll Cullinan slip 'catch' on 16 (third umpire Steve Dunne over-ruled the fielder's claim), threw his wicket away on 44 when he uppercut a Donald bouncer to third man. Thereafter a much improved Pollock wrapped New Zealand up for 168 and finished with 4 for 34.

On the second day South Africa consolidated their advantage, with Gibbs scoring the most significant and cherished post-isolation century by a South African. His unbeaten 101 led the tourists to 229 for 1 but, for many of his countrymen, the 'who' was more important than the 'what' despite an innings that was, in purely cricketing terms, a monumental effort of self-denial for a player so supremely gifted with attacking, attractive shots.

Gibbs, a Cape coloured, was never suspected of receiving preferential treatment but, given the country's painful, politically created fragility concerning racial composition of national teams, his presence in the side had been under close scrutiny.

Since being promoted to open the innings in the second Test against the West Indies he had promised much with six scores between 20 and 50 in nine innings before natural ebullience and concentration lapses cost him. This time he batted with an intensity of thought that would have made a monk proud. His 50 contained just four boundaries and, in a single moment of decadence, a delicious straight six off Daniel Vettori.

His century was completed, just before the players left the field for bad light, from 268 balls with 11 fours and a six. It took him nearly six and a half hours. Jacques Kallis, Gibbs's Western Province contemporary and good friend, finished the day with an unbeaten 53 in a stand of 102. This followed the South Africans' first century opening stand (127) for 17 Tests between Gibbs and Gary Kirsten (65).

The third day belonged almost entirely to the weather with just 18 further runs added in ten overs. However, on the fourth day records tumbled for the second successive Test as South Africa took their batting aggregate in two innings against New Zealand to 1063 for the loss of six wickets.

Gibbs and Kallis added an unbroken 315 for the second wicket as New Zealand's feeble attack popped away under leaden, misty skies hoping for a declaration to rescue them. It never came, specifically because the weather would have spared their batsmen had they been given a chance. Both batsmen completed personal best scores, amongst other milestones. Their stand was the third-highest for South Africa, four runs behind the 319 scored against England at Trent Bridge in 1947 by Dudley Nourse and Alan Melville and just 26 behind Graeme Pollock and Eddie Barlow's 341 against Australia in Adelaide in 1963–64.

Hansie Cronje bowled, but did not bat in the drawn Christchurch Test.
David Munden/Sportsline Photographic

Gibbs provided further delight for his country's supporters by becoming the ninth South African double centurion (211 not out, 468 balls, 23 fours, three sixes). He finished the day with his country's longest Test innings – 10 hours and 59 minutes beating by one minute the time taken for Daryll Cullinan's marathon 275 not out in the first Test. Kallis, who completed his fourth Test century, finished with 148. The two innings gave the tourists something to smile about on the last day when South Island squalls blew away any small, final chance of victory.

Just as New Zealand had finished the first Test with an injury, South Africa were resigned to playing the third Test without Allan Donald, who tore a stomach muscle.

SECOND TEST – NEW ZEALAND v. SOUTH AFRICA
11, 12, 13, 14 and 15 March 1999 at Lancaster Park, Christchurch

NEW ZEALAND

	First Innings			Second Innings	
MJ Horne	c Kirsten, b Kallis	36		(2) run out	56
				(Adams/Boucher)	
BA Young	b Donald	5		(1) not out	55
RG Twose	c Cullinan, b Pollock	0		not out	6
NJ Astle	c Klusener, b Donald	44			
GR Stead	c Boucher, b Donald	27			
CZ Harris	c Adams, b Pollock	0			
*AC Parore	c sub (DM Benkenstein),	14			
	b Pollock				
DJ Nash (capt)	lbw, b Adams	14			
DL Vettori	lbw, b Adams	18			
SB Doull	c Boucher, b Pollock	0			
GJ Allott	not out	1			
	lb 4, nb 5	9		lb 5, nb 5	10
		168		**(for 1 wicket)**	**127**

	First Innings				Second Innings			
	O	M	R	W	O	M	R	W
Donald	17.5	4	54	3				
Pollock	17	5	34	4	12	4	23	–
Klusener	12	3	37	–	17	4	33	–
Kallis	5	1	21	1	6	2	13	–
Cronje	6.1	4	9	–	4	3	1	–
Adams	5.4	2	9	2	15	0	52	–

Fall of Wickets
1–13, 2–18, 3–60, 4–112, 5–115, 6–115, 7–138, 8–157, 9–157
1–107

SOUTH AFRICA

	First Innings	
G Kirsten	c Astle, b Vettori	65
HH Gibbs	not out	211
JH Kallis	not out	148
DJ Cullinan		
WJ Cronje (capt)		
JN Rhodes		
SM Pollock		
*MV Boucher		
L Klusener		
PR Adams		
AA Donald		
	lb 12, nb 6	18
	(for 1 wicket, dec.)	**442**

	First Innings			
	O	M	R	W
Doull	25.5	9	48	0
Allott	43	11	109	0
Nash	22	5	46	0
Astle	18.1	2	76	0
Vettori	24	6	73	1
Stead	1	0	1	0
Harris	28	9	77	0

Fall of Wickets
1–127

Umpires: DM Quested & KT Francis
Toss: New Zealand

Match drawn

THIRD TEST
18, 19, 20, 21 and 22 March 1999 at Wellington

The cold, wet weather of Christchurch was quickly forgotten in Wellington as the Basin Reserve was bathed in sunshine for the first four days of the Test that would decide the outcome of the series. The cricket, though, was bleaker than the weather.

Lance Klusener made the winning hit – a massive six – at Napier.

David Munden/Sportsline Photographic

Dion Nash won the toss for the third time and, once again, wished he hadn't. In truth, neither captain was sure how the pitch would behave but they did know that the first session, with early moisture, would be important – maybe crucial.

At lunch the home side were 50 for 2, but within six balls of the resumption Steve Elworthy had plunged them to 58 for 4. Nathan Astle was superbly yorked on 20 and Roger Twose, cracked on the elbow two balls earlier, edged to the keeper for a dour 12 from 79 balls.

The rescue act, initially led by Gary Stead, was continued by Chris Harris who survived a bout of vomiting shortly before the close to finish 66 not out. The hot sunshine, so enjoyed by the crowd, gave Harris dehydration.

Stead, the 27-year-old Canterbury captain, survived with tremendous determination despite a fragile technique which allowed him, seemingly, to score only behind the wicket.

Harris played every ball as though his life depended on it and, when the bowling was short, it often looked as though it did. But the two men completed a genuinely brave stand of 145 before Stead (68) perished to Elworthy courtesy of a brilliant slip catch by Shaun Pollock.

On the second day South Africa tightened the noose dramatically with Pollock closing the innings within just 20 balls of quality fast bowling that sent the home side tumbling from 211 for 6 to 222 all out. All four wickets were fast bowlers' classics including Harris (68) who fended a lifter to gully. Pollock's 5 for 33, after starting the day with 1 for 30, was his ninth five-wicket haul in 33 Tests but did not quite match his father Peter's memorable 6 for 47 on the same ground in 1964.

Then the South African batsmen continued the orgy of runs that characterised their tour.

Herschelle Gibbs added a chanceless and brilliant 115 not out to his unbeaten 211 of five days earlier and Daryll Cullinan shared in an unbroken third-wicket stand of 130 as the tourists claimed a 13-run lead before the end of the day.

Gibbs, displaying his rare gift of timing with back-foot cover-drives and effortless flicks through midwicket, reached three figures from 184 balls with 14 boundaries while Cullinan, for once, played second fiddle with 56 from 112 balls with nine boundaries.

The third day, though, belonged yet again to Cullinan who scored 152 to take his aggregate to 427 before his first, and only, dismissal of the series (caught and bowled by Nathan Astle off a fierce drive). It was the second-highest average ever recorded in a Test series and the highest for a three-Test series. England's Wally

South African Coach Bob Woolmer with captain Hansie Cronje.
David Munden/Sportsline Photographic

THIRD TEST – NEW ZEALAND v. SOUTH AFRICA
18, 19, 20, 21 and 22 March 1999 at Basin Reserve, Wellington

NEW ZEALAND

	First Innings				Second Innings			
MJ Horne	c Cullinan, b Pollock			2	(2) lbw, b Elworthy			27
BA Young	c Rhodes, b Kallis			18	(1) c Boucher, b Pollock			2
RG Twose	c Boucher, b Elworthy			12	c Pollock, b Elworthy			5
NJ Astle	b Elworthy			20	b Elworthy			62
GR Stead	c Pollock, b Elworthy			68	lbw, b Elworthy			33
CZ Harris	c Rhodes, b Pollock			68	b Adams			41
DL Vettori	c Kallis, b Elworthy			4	(9) b Pollock			16
*AC Parore	c Cullinan, b Pollock			5	(7) c Rhodes, b Adams			19
DJ Nash (capt)	c Adams, b Pollock			2	(8) c Boucher, b Adams			27
SB Doull	c Boucher, b Pollock			0	not out			38
SB O'Connor	not out			2	c Rhodes, b Adams			2
	lb 18, nb 3			21	b 9, lb 7, nb 3			19
				222				**291**

	First Innings				Second Innings			
	O	M	R	W	O	M	R	W
Pollock	28.3	14	33	5	25	8	54	2
Elworthy	27	10	66	4	28	5	93	4
Kallis	20	5	44	1	19	7	50	0
Klusener	15	7	33	0	11	7	15	0
Adams	7	2	12	0	22.3	6	63	4
Cronje	5	3	16	0				

Fall of Wickets
1–7, 2–32, 3–57, 4–58, 5–203, 6–207, 7–218, 8–219, 9–219
1–8, 2–35, 3–35, 4–100, 5–152, 6–196, 7–199, 8–233, 9–281

SOUTH AFRICA

	First Innings				Second Innings			
G Kirsten	b O'Connor			40	not out			12
HH Gibbs	c O'Connor, b Vettori			120	run out (Horne/Vettori/Harris)			0
JH Kallis	c Horne, b Nash			17	b Vettori			4
DJ Cullinan	c and b Astle			152	not out			0
WJ Cronje (capt)	c Nash, b Vettori			72				
JN Rhodes	c Young, b Vettori			3				
SM Pollock	not out			43				
*MV Boucher	b Vettori			8				
L Klusener	c Parore, b Nash			19				
S Elworthy	not out			3				
PR Adams								
	b 10, lb 6, nb 5			21				
	(for 8 wickets, dec.)			**498**	(for 2 wickets)			**16**

	First Innings				Second Innings			
	O	M	R	W	O	M	R	W
Doull	24	4	77	0				
O'Connor	24	4	89	1	4.1	0	9	0
Nash	25	7	76	2				
Vettori	54	16	153	4	4	0	7	1
Harris	22	0	66	0				
Astle	16	8	21	1				

Fall of Wickets
1–73, 2–105, 3–258, 4–403, 5–415, 6–420, 7–440, 8–489
1–6, 2–14

Umpires: RS Dunne & S Venkataraghavan
Toss: New Zealand

South Africa won by eight wickets

TEST MATCH AVERAGES
New Zealand v. South Africa

NEW ZEALAND

Batting	M	Inns	NO	HS	Runs	Av	100	50
NJ Astle	3	5	1	69*	236	59.00	–	2
CZ Harris	3	4	1	68*	177	59.00	–	2
MJ Horne	3	6	–	93	274	45.66	–	3
GR Stead	2	3	–	68	128	42.66	–	1
BA Young	2	4	1	55*	80	26.66	–	1
RG Twose	3	6	1	65	119	23.80	–	1
SB Doull	3	4	1	38*	55	18.33	–	–
DL Vettori	3	4	–	32	70	17.50	–	–
AC Parore	3	4	–	19	47	11.75	–	–
DJ Nash	3	4	–	27	44	11.00	–	–

Played in two Tests: GI Allott 0 & 1*
Played in one Test: MD Bell 6 & 6; CD McMillan 25 & 22*; SB O'Connor 2* & 2

Bowling	Overs	Mds	Runs	Wkts	Av	Best	10/m	5/inn
DL Vettori	124	30	353	7	50.42	4–153	–	–

Also bowled: GI Allott 81–6–262–1; NJ Astle 43.1–11–127–1; SB Doull 82.5–20–215–1;
CZ Harris 95–19–237–2; CD McMillan 5.1–0–24–0; DJ Nash 75–14–219–2;
SB O'Connor 28.1–4–98–1; GR Stead 1–0–1–0

Fielding Figures
3 – NJ Astle; 1 – GI Allott, MJ Horne, DJ Nash, SB O'Connor, AC Parore, RG Twose, BA Young

SOUTH AFRICA

Batting	M	Inns	NO	HS	Runs	Av	100	50
DJ Cullinan	3	3	2	275*	427	427.00	2	–
HH Gibbs	3	4	1	211*	365	121.66	2	–
G Kirsten	3	4	1	128	245	81.66	1	1
JH Kallis	3	4	1	148*	176	58.66	1	–

Played in three Tests: MV Boucher 8; WJ Cronje 30 & 72; L Klusener 19; SM Pollock 69* & 43*;
JN Rhodes 63 & 3
Played in one Test: S Elworthy 3*
PR Adams (3 Tests) and AA Donald (2 Tests) did not bat

Bowling	Overs	Mds	Runs	Wkts	Av	Best	10/m	5/inn
SM Pollock	123.3	47	216	13	16.61	5–33	–	1
S Elworthy	55	15	159	8	19.87	4–66	–	–
AA Donald	53.5	22	114	5	22.80	3–54	–	–
PR Adams	126.1	39	335	10	33.50	4–63	–	–

Also bowled: WJ Cronje 30.1–16–56–1; DJ Cullinan 2–1–8–0; JH Kallis 84.4–25–233–3;
L Klusener 95–35–204–3

Fielding Figures
10 – MV Boucher; 4 – DJ Cullinan, JN Rhodes; 3 – SM Pollock; 2– PR Adams; 1 – WJ Cronje,
AA Donald, HH Gibbs, JH Kallis, G Kirsten, L Klusener

Hammond averaged 563 for England against New Zealand in a two-Test series in 1932–33.

Cullinan's 427 was also the second-highest number of runs scored without being dismissed in Test cricket after Garfield Sobers who scored 490 runs (365 not out and 125) before being dismissed for West Indies against Pakistan in a three-Test series in 1957–58.

Australian Mark Taylor is third on the list having scored 426 runs (334 not out and 92) before being dismissed against Pakistan in 1998.

On day four, Elworthy and Paul Adams, as contrasting a pair of bowlers as it is possible to find, took South Africa to the verge of victory. Needing 276 to make the tourists bat again, New Zealand finished the day still 59 runs in arrears on 217 for 7.

Elworthy, 34 and playing just his second Test in the injured Allan Donald's place, claimed two important wickets in the 12th over when Roger Twose (5) flapped a bouncer to fine leg from in front of his face and Matt Horne missed a pull shot and was leg before for 27.

Elworthy took the next two wickets as well to finish with 4 for 58, breaking stands of 65 and 52 with fast, ripping off-cutters that trapped Stead leg before for 33 and bowled Astle for a charmed 62 that included three dropped catches.

Left-arm wrist spinner Adams then removed the stubborn Harris (41) with a beauty that fizzed from the rough a foot outside off-stump to hit leg and Adam Parore was brilliantly caught at silly point by Jonty Rhodes.

Simon Doull bashed an unbeaten 38 from 33 balls on the final morning to make South Africa bat again while Elworthy, who took four of the first six wickets in both innings, was again unable to claim a fifth. His consolation was the Man of the Match award for a return of 8 for 159.

A fidgety Gibbs ran himself out for a 22-ball duck when the victory 'chase' began which sent his series average plummeting from 182.5 to 121.6 and Jacques Kallis (4) was bowled off a bottom edge by Daniel Vettori, who finished the series with seven wickets at an average of 50. Only 16 South African wickets were taken in all, the lowest ever in a three-Test series.

Kirsten's 12 not out took him past Bruce Mitchell (3,471) as the leading run-scorer for South Africa with an aggregate of 3,476 while Cullinan nervously protected his record with four dot balls before Kirsten hit the winning runs.

The victory was the 21st – and last – of the Hansie Cronje/Bob Woolmer partnership spanning 44 Tests in five years.

ONE-DAY INTERNATIONALS

Seldom could the result of an entire six-match series have hinged so decisively on a single shot. When Lance Klusener hit the final ball of the fourth match for six, not only did South Africa win a match they seemed destined to lose, but the series swung dramatically the tourists' way. Instead of being three-one down, they drew level at two-two before winning the fifth, and as it transpired final game to triumph three-two.

It all began so differently. The first game in Dunedin saw South Africa out-scrapped by a team that used to have a reputation as soft and selfish. Geoff Allott, who had a brilliant series, struck early and Gavin Larson gently rubbed out the middle order leaving the tourists indebted to Jacques Kallis's fourth one-day century which spared them total oblivion.

There was not an optimist in the house when Allan Donald pushed the reply to 56 for 4 in the 11th over but Nathan Astle (95) found a staunch ally in Matthew Bell (37) and victory was achieved with five balls to spare. The bad news came with the announcement that Chris Cairns would not play again in the summer after rupturing a calf muscle while setting off for a quick single.

Cynics who claimed the win was a one-off appeared to be vindicated at Lancaster Park, Christchurch, two days later.

Roger Twose propped New Zealand up with a slow but important 78 and Adam Parore (47) and Chris Harris (45 not out) did their bit while Allan Donald and Shaun Pollock shared 7 for 79. Gary Kirsten's shocking one-day form – which had seen him reach double figures in just two of his previous ten innings – came to an end with a match-winning 81 not out, and Cronje made a statement by smashing 74 not out from just 69 balls with three sixes. South Africa romped home with seven overs to spare.

Two days later, at Eden Park, it all changed again when New Zealand needed just one more ball to achieve the identical, seven-wicket win. Lance Klusener (103 not out), sent in as a pinch hitter, played an anchoring role while the 'specialist' batsmen all failed.

Astle though, rendered his effort irrelevant with an undefeated century of his own from 126 balls. He nearly did not get there when Pat Symcox deliberately bowled four wides down the leg side with the batsman on 96 and just five runs needed to win. Happily he swept the next ball for four and

Symcox, who conceded 64 runs in 7.1 overs returned home to South Africa and retired from international cricket ten days later. It was a sad way for the 38-year-old veteran to go, and it surprised everyone. He had been included in South Africa's provisional squad of 19 and was all but certain of going to the World Cup.

Once the Test series was over the teams moved on to scenic Napier and the rustic but charming McLean Park. New Zealand were hot favourites to take a three-one lead after batting first and making 257 for 8 in 48 overs but torrential rain, with South Africa 10 for 0 from nine balls, forced a restart at 10.15am the following day.

Reduced again to 40 overs per side, the hosts seemed 30 runs shy of a competitive total when they were dismissed for 191 thanks mainly to Twose's unbeaten 79 from 77 balls and Parore's aggressive 37.

South Africa were coasting at 106 for 2 with 16 overs remaining but Herschelle Gibbs (52) was run out and Daryll Cullinan (61) bowled by Astle; some frail nerves were evident and the game came to life.

Three controversial incidents turned the game back South Africa's way. Pollock was given not out after thick-edging an Astle delivery into Parore's gloves, standing up, and Klusener was twice given not out to run-out appeals because of inconclusive television replays. Human instinct and common sense said he was out both times but third umpire Steve Dunne simply could not press the red light.

Nineteen runs were needed from the last two overs and Klusener hit three boundaries to bring the equation down to six from the last three balls from Nash. Klusener took a single, number ten Steve Elworthy scrambled another to leave Klusener needing a boundary to win. Nash's attempted yorker was a knee-high full toss which flew 100 metres straight back over his head and into the crowd.

Cronje admitted that Klusener's bat, at 3lbs 2oz, is nowhere near normal – 'but then neither is he', he said afterwards.

The teams made a hectic dash to the airport after the match for a chartered flight to Auckland and the mood on the flight was a harbinger of what was to come the following day during Eden Park's first ever day-nighter. The tourists were buzzing and the home side was in shock.

Kirsten's 70 and even Jacques Kallis's second exact century of the series were completely overshadowed by Cullinan's astonishing 56-ball innings of 94 that included seven sixes. Only Shahid Afridi and Sanath Jayasuriya (11 each), Ijaz Ahmed (9) and Gordon Greenidge (8) have cleared the fence more often in a one-day innings. At one stage he hit Daniel Vettori for three successive crowd-pleasers; two over extra cover.

Herschelle Gibbs: a half-century in South Africa's narrow victory in Napier.
David Munden/Sportsline Photographic

New Zealand were shattered for the second successive day and could hardly be blamed for their swift demise. Most memorable in their sorry innings of 147 were the catching hat-tricks performed by both Kallis and Rhodes and the 3 for 26 by Cronje which gave him 101 wickets and the 16th membership ticket to the 'double' club of 1000 runs and 100 wickets.

Match One
14 February 1999 at Carisbrook, Dunedin
South Africa 211 (49.1 overs) JH Kallis 100,
GI Allott 4 for 35
New Zealand 215 for 7 (49.1 overs) NJ Astle 95
New Zealand won by three wickets
Man of the Match: NJ Astle

Match Two
17 February 1999 at Lancaster Park, Christchurch
New Zealand 220 for 9 (50 overs) RG Twose 78,
SM Pollock 4 for 45
South Africa 224 for 3 (43 overs) G Kirsten 81*,
WJ Cronje 74*, JH Kallis 53
South Africa won by seven wickets
Man of the Match: G Kirsten

Match Three
20 February 1999 at Eden Park, Auckland
South Africa 212 for 7 (50 overs) L Klusener 103*
New Zealand 215 for 3 (43.1 overs)
NJ Astle 100*
New Zealand won by seven wickets
Man of the Match: NJ Astle

Match Four
25 March 1999 at McLean Park, Napier
New Zealand 257 for 8 (48 overs)
South Africa 10 for 0 (1.3 overs)
Match abandoned – replayed 26 March

Match Five
26 March 1999 at McLean Park, Napier
New Zealand 191 (38.5 overs) RG Twose 79*
South Africa 194 for 8 (40 overs) DJ Cullinan 61,
HH Gibbs 52
South Africa won by two wickets
Man of the Match: L Klusener

Match Six
27 March 1999 at Eden Park, Auckland
South Africa 290 for 5 (50 overs) JH Kallis
100, DJ Cullinan 94, G Kirsten 70, GI Allott
4 for 47

Shaun Pollock took four wickets as South Africa won comfortably at Christchurch.
David Munden/Sportsline Photographic

New Zealand 147 (36.1 overs)
South Africa won by 143 runs
Man of the Match: DJ Cullinan

Match Seven
30 March 1999 at Basin Reserve, Wellington
South Africa 249 for 4 (48.4 overs) Kallis 54
v. New Zealand
Match abandoned
There was no play possible in the re-scheduled match on 31 March

NEW ZEALAND DOMESTIC FIRST-CLASS SEASON
By Bryan Waddle

Who ever it was that first wrote 'they played in front of a man and his dog' was probably watching New Zealand first-class cricket. Such was the lack of interest in the domestic competition that it almost passed unnoticed as Central Districts comfortably won the five-day final over Otago in less than the allotted time. It was a comment as much on the interest as on the standard of the first-class game with the leading players absent on Test and one-day duty against South Africa and India.

Central recorded their only win in the Shell Trophy although they had won its predecessor, the Plunket Shield, four times. Without any players in the national side, Central was seldom required to test its players' depth and the consistency the team was able to bring to its selections was key to its success. It was also significant that two Central Districts players were leading domestic performers. The captain, Craig Spearman, was second-highest run-scorer behind Test player Matt Horne, while Andrew Penn was equal top wicket-taker with 40 victims without playing a Test.

New Zealand's first-class programme was severely criticised by most followers of the game. For many, there was not a single first-class game until early February, more than three months after the season started.

The Conference series, which ran for its second year, was finally proved to be flawed. Most players wanted two rounds of the Shell Trophy rather than the round-robin series that began the season with three regional teams comprising the best players from the six associations and an invited overseas team, this year Pakistan 'A'.

The tourists had an unfortunate time because their performance lacked the commitment of an international side. They weren't helped by early season conditions with the first match of the series against a Northern selection abandoned soon after tea on the second day after the umpires deemed the pitch at Timaru's Aorangi Park too dangerous. The decision came after deliveries from the left-arm spinner Daniel Vettori had jumped shoulder-high to the alarmed Pakistani batsmen.

To make matters worse, New Zealand opener Bryan Young sustained a hand injury early in the game, while two of the Pakistan team had been hit by awkward rearing deliveries. It was the first of two games featuring the touring side to be curtailed early in extraordinary circumstances.

Towards the end of their development tour, Pakistan became the first side in New Zealand cricket history to forfeit a game. They declined to continue their match against New Zealand 'A' at Westpac Trust Park after some overnight pitch damage.

Despite the presence of gifted all-round cricketers such as Chris Cairns, New Zealand's domestic cricket was played on empty grounds.
David Munden/Sportsline Photographic

Three small holes in the pitch were repaired by groundstaff, but the tourists refused to take the field when the umpires decided the pitch was fit for play.

It wasn't a memorable season for New Zealand cricket with only two players, Matthew Bell and Matthew Sinclair registering double centuries. Shayne O'Connor, who took six wickets in an innings three times, was the only other player to make an impression on the series.

NEW ZEALAND DOMESTIC ONE-DAY SEASON
By Bryan Waddle

Canterbury's success in the provincial one-day competition was hardly a surprise. The 1990s have been good to the 'Red and Blacks' who took their sixth Shell Cup in eight years. It wasn't only that they won the title, but the manner of their success: they weren't the top qualifiers for the play-offs, finishing third behind Wellington and Northern Districts winning a sudden-death minor semi-final to advance.

Having beaten Auckland in that game they then had to dispose of the defending champions Northern Districts in order to qualify for the final.

That performance was every bit as efficient as their victory over a Wellington side that in recent years has earned the 'chokers' tag for their failure to capture any titles.

Canterbury captain Gary Stead set up the title win with an accomplished innings of 84 in his team's total of 217. He arrived at the crease with his side 19 for 2 on a lively Basin Reserve pitch against an attack that was strangely lopsided.

Pace bowler Carl Bulfin did all that was required of him with the new ball but, curiously, Wellington opened up with a left-arm spinner, dispatching their other pace bowler, Heath Davis, to the wilderness. The decision was even more unusual considering Wellington had won the toss. They never got close in pursuit of a modest target, losing by 49 runs and highlighting the inadequacies evident throughout the series.

The lack of consistency from the batsmen and the failure of many top-order players to produce large innings meant the competition hardly lifted itself above mediocrity. Only three players, Craig McMillan, Chris Harris and Roger Twose scored centuries, while in each of the previous two seasons, 13 one-day hundreds had been recorded. The failure of both the Shell Cup and Shell Trophy to capture the public's imagination contributed to the financial struggle all six associations faced, while the internationals were an unqualified success.

Dion Nash: a member of New Zealand's much-improved pace attack.
David Munden/Sportsline Photographic

FIRST-CLASS AVERAGES

BATTING

Batting	M	Inns	NO	HS	Runs	Av	100	50
DJ Cullinan	5	7	2	275*	553	110.60	3	–
RS Dravid	4	8	2	190	483	80.50	2	2
Wajahatullah Wasti	5	6	1	196	401	80.20	1	2
SR Tendulkar	3	5	–	154	386	77.20	2	1
HH Gibbs	5	8	1	211*	532	76.00	2	2
G Kirsten	5	8	2	137	436	72.66	2	1
RT King	5	6	1	130*	347	69.40	1	1
SC Ganguly	4	8	2	101*	390	65.00	1	2
MW Douglas	7	8	3	104	317	63.40	1	1
CL Cairns	5	9	2	126	425	60.71	2	1
JI Englefield	5	8	2	71*	358	59.66	–	4
MS Sinclair	11	17	3	203*	823	58.78	2	5
L Vincent	6	8	–	159	460	57.50	1	3
CZ Harris	8	10	2	159*	437	54.62	1	2
CM Spearman	11	17	1	137	842	52.62	2	4
MJ Horne	10	19	2	132	887	52.17	1	7
JH Kallis	4	6	1	148*	253	50.60	1	–
JPD Oram	7	7	1	155	271	45.16	1	1
CD McMillan	8	14	2	92	526	43.83	–	3
NJ Astle	9	14	3	69*	482	43.81	–	4
GR Stead	6	10	1	86	389	43.22	–	4
GP Sulzberger	6	7	1	103	258	43.00	1	1
MD Bell	10	17	–	219	726	42.70	1	6
SP Fleming	6	10	1	145	380	42.22	1	1
PJB Chandler	4	8	1	150	291	41.57	1	–
DJ Nash	9	13	3	98	406	40.60	–	4
CD Cumming	9	17	1	187	648	40.50	1	4
SB Styris	6	12	3	100*	361	40.11	1	2
BJK Doody	4	8	1	137	280	40.00	1	1
Akhtar Sarfraz	5	6	–	84	229	38.16	–	2
MN Hart	9	13	3	102*	380	38.00	1	1
CJ Nevin	8	12	1	113	396	36.00	1	1
JD Wells	6	9	–	89	314	34.88	–	3
JAH Marshall	7	12	–	122	417	34.75	1	3
RA Lawson	6	11	–	86	379	34.45	–	4
MH Richardson	9	15	1	110	468	33.42	1	1
RG Hart	10	14	2	127*	397	33.08	1	1
GT Donaldson	5	8	1	89	219	31.28	–	1
JAF Yovich	6	7	2	63*	152	30.40	–	1
MD Bailey	9	15	1	128	409	29.21	1	1
RG Twose	10	18	1	99	495	29.11	–	5
MR Jefferson	11	16	1	103*	432	28.80	1	2
MW Priest	9	11	1	78	282	28.20	–	2
DL Vettori	10	12	1	57	306	27.81	–	2
WA Wisneski	7	8	–	77	208	26.00	–	2
Ijaz Mhmood	5	7	1	44	145	24.16	–	–
BA Young	9	16	2	111	334	23.85	1	1
SFM Forde	6	11	1	48	236	23.60	–	–
GJ Hopkins	5	8	1	115	165	23.57	1	–
RG Petrie	5	7	–	48	162	23.14	–	–
BK Walker	8	11	2	52	194	21.55	–	1
TA Boyer	5	8	–	54	172	21.50	–	1
SP Mather	7	12	1	50*	236	21.45	–	1
GE Bradburn	6	10	1	58	192	21.33	–	1
CB Gaffaney	6	11	–	43	226	20.54	–	–
MG Gray	10	15	2	69*	265	20.38	–	1
AD Jadeja	4	8	–	46	162	20.25	–	–
HJH Marshall	6	9	–	49	170	18.88	–	–
NR Mongia	4	6	–	79	112	18.66	–	1
AC Barnes	5	6	–	27	112	18.66	–	–
LG Howell	3	6	1	30	91	18.20	–	–
Mohammad Wasim	5	6	–	57	105	17.50	–	1
BA Pocock	8	12	2	41	171	17.10	–	–
PJ Wiseman	13	18	4	54*	238	17.00	–	1
AJ Penn	9	10	0	74	158	15.80	–	1
SB Doull	8	10	2	38*	126	15.75	–	–
Faisal Iqbal	5	6	1	48	71	14.20	–	–
SJ Pawson	4	6	1	54*	70	14.00	–	1

FIRST-CLASS AVERAGES

BATTING

Batting	M	Inns	NO	HS	Runs	Av	100	50
ME Parlane	8	11	1	25*	138	13.80	–	–
CE Bulfin	4	6	1	19	66	13.20	–	–
CJM Furlong	7	7	2	21	64	12.80	–	–
AC Parore	8	12	–	50	139	11.58	–	1
SB O' Connor	9	10	4	17*	62	10.50	–	–
NS Sidhu	4	7	–	34	71	10.14	–	–

Qualification: 5 completed innings, average 10.00

BOWLING

	Overs	Mds	Runs	Wkts	Av	Best	10/m	5/inn
CJ Drum	171.2	49	431	25	17.24	6–49	–	1
SM Pollock	150.3	49	324	17	19.05	5–33	–	1
AJ Penn	288	76	763	40	19.07	5–51	–	2
CD McMillan	133	32	373	18	20.72	6–71	–	1
DC Blake	145.5	32	435	19	22.89	3–26	–	–
CS Martin	160.2	48	513	22	23.31	4–33	–	–
SB O'Connor	279.2	45	972	40	24.30	6–58	1	4
DG Sewell	204.1	53	624	25	24.96	6–50	–	1
WA Wisneski	205.3	56	593	23	25.78	5–48	–	1
DR Tuffey	205.5	56	542	21	25.80	5–44	–	2
MW Priest	283.4	77	684	23	29.73	5–44	–	1
Mohammad Hussain	210.2	66	508	17	29.88	5–93	–	1
SB Styris	193.3	42	570	17	33.52	5–79	–	1
PR Adams	191.1	56	470	14	33.57	4–63	–	–
SB Doull	195.5	56	475	13	36.53	7–65	–	1
PJ Wiseman	374	77	1110	28	36.94	4–52	–	–
GE Bradburn	207.1	58	484	13	37.23	3–35	–	–
CL Cairns	131.3	27	448	12	37.33	5–44	–	1
DJ Nash	202	49	540	14	38.57	3–20	–	–
TR Anderson	154	31	470	12	39.16	4–76	–	–
DL Vettori	295	76	844	19	44.42	4–40	–	–
MR Jefferson	272.5	47	867	19	45.63	3–81	–	–
CJM Furlong	207	43	715	15	47.66	4–177	–	–
MN Hart	221	47	674	14	48.14	5–164	–	1

Qualification: 10 wickets

The following bowlers took 10 wickets in fewer than 8 innings:

	Overs	Mds	Runs	Wkts	Av	Best	10/m	5/inn
KP Walsmley	99.5	25	277	12	23.08	4–15	–	–
A Kumble	180.3	49	423	17	24.88	5–56	–	1
S Elworthy	127.1	27	431	17	25.35	4–66	–	–
Shahid Nazir	125.5	21	384	15	25.60	7–39	–	1
GR Jones	100.2	30	309	12	25.75	5–62	–	1
MJ Mason	114.5	41	258	10	25.80	2–21	–	–
AR Tait	114	35	289	10	28.90	3–39	–	–
J Srinath	136.5	28	438	12	36.50	5–95	–	1
BKV Prasad	147	37	366	10	36.60	3–100	–	–
Fazl-e-Akbar	177	26	614	16	38.37	6–69	–	1
GI Allott	162	37	558	12	46.50	3–47	–	–

LEADING FIELDERS

31 – MG Croy (30 ct/1 st); 23 – RG Hart (22 ct/1 st); 19 – MA Sigley (18 ct/1 st); 16 – AC Parore; 14 – SP Fleming; 12 CM Spearman; 11 – NR Mongia (10 ct/1 st), GJ Hopkins (10 ct/1 st), MV Boucher, NJ Astle; 10 – Javed Qadir (9 ct/1 st); 9 – SR Mather; 8 – CJ Nevin (7 ct/1 st), CJM Furlong, G Kirsten, BA Young

ZIMBABWE

India in Zimbabwe
Zimbabwe Domestic First-Class Season
Zimbabwe Domestic One-Day Season
First-Class Averages

INDIA IN ZIMBABWE
By Telford Vice

Zimbabwe's first Test victory, over Pakistan in 1994–95, was an event of obvious importance. But their second win, which came in their 31st match, is sure to be remembered at least as fondly.

Against Pakistan the tone was set by Zimbabwe's declaration at 544 for 4. There was no cricket-by-numbers against India, however, as fortunes soared and plummeted with irresistible unpredictability.

The Zimbabweans' satisfaction at their triumph, eventually by 61 runs on the fourth afternoon, was enhanced by the fact that it was shared by only four of the 11 who had beaten Pakistan, namely Andy Flower, Alistair Campbell, Heath Streak and Henry Olonga.

Significantly in a country where the national team draws its players from a mere eight league clubs, Campbell was deprived through injury of the services of Grant Flower and Guy Whittall.

Zimbabwe had been soundly beaten in the first two of the three one-day internationals, and although they won the third the team's image had

Gavin Rennie scored 84 for Zimbabwe in the second innings of the Test against India.
Sportsline Photographic

TEST MATCH – ZIMBABWE v. INDIA
7, 8, 9 and 10 October 1998 at Harare Sports Club, Harare

ZIMBABWE

	First Innings		Second Innings	
GJ Rennie	c sub (DS Mohanty), b Agarkar	47	c RR Singh, b Harbhajan Singh	84
CB Wishart	c Harbhajan Singh, b Ganguly	21	c and b Kumble	63
MW Goodwin	lbw, b Srinath	42	c and b Kumble	44
ADR Campbell (capt)	c Dravid, b Srinath	0	(5) c Azharuddin, b Harbhajan Singh	25
*A Flower	c RR Singh, b Srinath	30	(6) not out	41
NC Johnson	c RR Singh, b Kumble	4	(7) c RR Singh, b Kumble	1
CN Evans	c Mongia, b Harbhajan Singh	11	(8) lbw, b Kumble	4
HH Streak	c RR Singh, b Harbhajan Singh	8	(9) c Dravid, b Agarkar	3
HK Olonga	lbw, b Kumble	5	(4) c Azharuddin, b Harbhajan Singh	5
AG Huckle	not out	28	lbw, b Srinath	1
M Mbangwa	st Mongia, b Kumble	2	b Srinath	0
	lb 1, w 2, nb 20	23	b 1, lb 12, nb 9	22
		221		**293**

	First Innings				Second Innings			
	O	M	R	W	O	M	R	W
Srinath	21	3	59	3	23.3	7	43	2
Agarkar	16	3	40	1	18	2	60	1
Ganguly	5	1	21	1	4	1	10	0
RR Singh	6	2	16	0	4	2	16	0
Harbhajan Singh	15	2	42	2	20	4	64	3
Kumble	17.4	3	42	3	36	4	87	4

Fall of Wickets
1–42, 2–120, 3–120, 4–122, 5–140, 6–163, 7–180, 8–181, 9–214
1–138, 2–209, 3–223, 4–223, 5–246, 6–249, 7–257, 8–288, 9–293

INDIA

	First Innings		Second Innings	
*NR Mongia	b Olonga	1	c Wishart, b Olonga	0
NS Sidhu	c Flower, b Olonga	6	c Johnson, b Streak	0
A Kumble	b Streak	29	(8) c Goodwin, b Johnson	12
RS Dravid	c Johnson, b Mbangwa	118	(3) c Flower, b Mbangwa	44
SR Tendulkar	c Campbell, b Johnson	34	(4) c Flower, b Johnson	7
M Azharuddin (capt)	c Johnson, b Olonga	1	(5) c Campbell, b Streak	7
SC Ganguly	lbw, b Olonga	47	(6) lbw, b Huckle	36
RR Singh	lbw, b Olonga	15	(7) lbw, b Johnson	12
AB Agarkar	c Flower, b Streak	4	c Olonga, b Mbangwa	5
J Srinath	c sub (AR Whittall), b Streak	6	run out (Rennie/Flower)	23
Harbhajan Singh	not out	0	not out	15
	lb 4, w 4, nb 11	19	lb 3, w 1 nb 8	12
		280		**173**

	First Innings				Second Innings			
	O	M	R	W	O	M	R	W
Streak	29	9	62	3	14	2	49	2
Olonga	26	7	70	5	10	1	40	1
Johnson	18	5	64	1	14.5	5	41	3
Huckle	15	2	39	0	6	0	24	1
Mbangwa	14.2	4	28	1	12	6	16	2
Evans	3	0	8	0				
Goodwin	2	0	5	0				

Fall of Wickets
1–2, 2–22, 3–43, 4–124, 5–127, 6–215, 7–259, 8–268, 9–280
1–3, 2–6, 3–29, 4–37, 5–104, 6–112, 7–124, 8–129, 9–133

Umpires: ID Robinson & RE Koertzen
Toss: India

Zimbabwe won by 61 runs

been damaged in a milieu where cricket is still as white as mainstream society is black.

'A lot of people who don't know much about cricket had a lot to say after the two one-day defeats,' Campbell reflected after the Test.

Some of that ignorance would have been wiped out over the course of four exhilarating days at Harare Sports Club, to be replaced if not by enlightenment about one of the most un-African of games then at least by awe at the universally accessible drama it was able to conjure.

It began days before the first ball was bowled with the Zimbabweans' plot to produce a green, seaming pitch on which, they hoped, their superior pace attack might be able to ambush the comparatively heavyweight Indian batting line-up.

Instead, a firm, brown surface of steep but consistent bounce emerged from under the covers on the first morning. Zimbabwe, who lost the toss and with it their gamble, were dismissed for 221.

The match turned on 13 balls delivered 45 minutes after lunch, which claimed the wickets of Murray Goodwin, Campbell and David Rennie.

Half an hour before tea on the second day India were 127 for 5, but Rahul Dravid provided the fulcrum around which the recovery turned with his diligently restrained second Test century. With him for more than two hours in a rescuing partnership of 88 was Sourav Ganguly.

India closed at 248 for 6, and were dismissed with a lead of 59 two balls after the drinks break on the third morning. Olonga revelled in Campbell's instruction to bowl as fast as he could and finished with 5 for 70.

Javagal Srinath and debutant Ajit Agarkar then wasted the new ball for the second time as Gavin Rennie and Craig Wishart shared a partnership of 138 in more than three-and-a-half hours to enable Zimbabwe to take control of the match.

However, it threatened to all come to nought for Zimbabwe as their second innings, which adjourned overnight at 219 for two, was ended 74 runs later. India were left to score a moderate 235 in five sessions to win.

But by the end of the 12th over, Nayan Mongia, Navjot Sidhu, Tendulkar and Azharuddin had gone for just 37 runs between them.

Tendulkar fell to a fine away-swinger from Neil Johnson – the debutant who had hitherto played all his big cricket for South African teams – and the others departed to weary attempted cuts.

Dravid and Ganguly halted Zimbabwe's progress for more than two hours, but relentlessly straight

Craig Wishart.
Sportsline Photographic

bowling paid off when Ganguly went five minutes after Dravid. From there, the only uncertainty was when the pubs would run dry.

Match One
26 September 1998 at Queen's Sports Club, Bulawayo
Zimbabwe 213 (50 overs) ADR Campbell 53
India 216 for 2 (42.2 overs) SR Tendulkar 127*, RS Dravid 64
India won by eight wickets
Man of the Match: SR Tendulkar

Match Two
27 September 1998 at Queen's Sports Club, Bulawayo
Zimbabwe 235 for 7 (45 overs) ADR Campbell 74, MW Goodwin 66
India 236 for 2 (41.5 overs) SC Ganguly 107*, M Azharuddin 72
India won by eight wickets
Man of the Match: SC Ganguly

Match Three
30 September 1998 at Harare Sports Club
Zimbabwe 259 for 5 (50 overs) CB Wishart 102, A Flower 55
India 222 (47.2 overs) RR Singh 57
Zimbabwe won by 37 runs
Man of the Match: CB Wishart

The charismatic Zimbabwean fast bowler, Henry Olonga. *David Munden/Sportsline Photographic*

ZIMBABWE DOMESTIC FIRST-CLASS SEASON
By Telford Vice

Losing a game to rain is an irritation in competitions with lengthy fixture lists, but when the entire domestic first-class programme consists of three matches it is a calamity.

That was the story of the match between Mashonaland and Mashonaland 'A', scheduled to be played at Sunrise Sports Club in Harare in mid-January. Torrents of the calibre of which surely only Africa and Asia are capable condemned this fixture, and the one-day game which was to have followed it, to that dreariest of cricketing fates – abandoned without a ball bowled.

Better news came on the day of the washed-out limited-overs match with the announcement of the Zimbabwe cricket academy's inaugural intake. This will have a direct impact on the Logan Cup as the academy will field a team in the competition next season.

In the other two matches of 1998–99, both played at Bulawayo Athletic Club, Matabeleland and Mashonaland drew an absorbing contest and Matabeleland beat Mashonaland 'A' by seven wickets to claim the championship.

The first match began with Matabeleland captain Andrew Whittall inserting Mashonaland, and the batsmen duly struggled on a spongy surface.

Given the conditions and the fact that Matabeleland were able to call on what amounted to the Zimbabwe attack, the visitors' total of 243 was commendable. That they reached it was due largely to batsmen at opposite ends of the order.

Bespectacled left-handed opener Gavin Rennie, fifth out for 62, displayed ample patience while most of his top- and middle-order colleagues failed to scrape together enough to keep them at the crease for a significant period. Craig Wishart provided Rennie's steadiest support in a second-wicket partnership which endured for more than an hour and realised 51 runs.

However, from there it was steeply downhill for Mashonaland as the home-side spinners, the captain and Adam Huckle, drew the noose ever tighter with a sequence of eight wickets interrupted only by Heath Streak's dismissal of Rennie.

Not for the first time, though, number eight Paul Strang was not about to be dictated to by two of his own ilk and lashed out lustily to hit 70 runs off 90 balls, nine of them dispatched for four and one heaved away for six. Strang arrived at the crease with Mashonaland in imminent danger of cheap

It was a disappointing domestic season for Stuart Carlisle.
David Munden/Sportsline Photographic

dismissal at 150 for 6. The seventh wicket fell two balls later and seven overs after that the visitors were 172 for 9. But a memorable last-ditch effort saw the towering Everton Matambanadzo, who has all the grace of a brontosaurus on Prozac, help Strang add 71 as Mashonaland recovered to respectability. Matambanadzo knew the number 11's role well and faced 37 deliveries for his seven not out.

Matabeleland batted with purpose in the 24 overs they faced before the close, but 68 for 3 was not the score they wanted. The dismissal three balls before the close of the aggressive Neil Johnson, the former Natal all-rounder, was a particularly bitter blow for the home side.

Guy Whittall, 18 not out overnight, had been joined at the wicket by 15-year-old debutant Charles Coventry in that last over and they forged ahead impressively on the second morning.

Coventry showed admirable composure in the face of hostile bowling, and shared 80 runs for the fourth wicket before Whittall lost patience to be caught and bowled by Murray Goodwin for 62. Six overs later Coventry was run out for a 33 that was

121 balls in the making, an innings that brimmed with promise.

The rest of Mashonaland's batting crumpled for 86 runs as Grant Flower ran through the middle order to take three wickets. Strang was a constant threat and finished with 2 for 58 in 35 overs.

By the close Matabeleland were in front by all of 203 runs as the pitch finally dried enough to allow Flower and Goodwin to build a monumental second-wicket stand.

Their partnership stretched to 216 on the final day before Streak dismissed Goodwin for 111. Flower hit just six fours and two sixes in his 163 not out, a performance which confirmed again his class as one of the finest batsmen in the game.

The timing of Alistair Campbell's declaration was always going to be crucial, and at 333 for 2 it seemed to come too late to keep the

match alive: chasing 345 in less than a day was surely few teams' idea of a fair contest.

However, the pitch was at its best for batting and Matabeleland made a fine fist of it in finishing 67 runs short with four wickets standing. The innings was built around Guy Whittall's 131 not out, a fluent display which came off 168 balls and included 16 fours and three sixes.

Ross Craig and Whittall put on 177 for the second wicket to keep the home side's victory hopes alive. But those who followed Craig batted with too little caution to prosper against the canny spin of Flower and Strang, and Matabeleland's momentum drained away until hands were shaken on a truce.

There was no such thickening of the plot in the third match, between Matabeleland and Mashonaland 'A'. At least, not after Matabeleland replied to the visitors' dismal first innings of 102 with 403 for nine declared.

Andrew Whittall again asked the opposition to bat, and they were shot out in 43.1 overs with Streak, Johnson and Mpumolelo Mbangwa sharing seven wickets on a pitch which offered the seamers noticeable assistance.

That said, Mashonaland 'A' were the bigger culprits in their own downfall, as the home side proved when their application at the crease earned them the lead with one wicket down.

Solid top-order partnerships were followed by Guy Whittall and Johnson adding 149 for the fourth, with useful bits and bobs down the order. Gus Mackay kept the fast bowlers interested by taking five for 85.

Mashonaland 'A', labouring in the shadow of a deficit of 301, had little left to play for but reclaimed some of their confidence in avoiding an innings defeat.

Dirk Viljoen, out for 92, and Trevor Penney provided vital stability with a fourth-wicket stand of 143. Jason Oates and Penney then shared 94 for the sixth and Penney, the captain, was 130 not out after more than five-and-a-half hours at the crease.

All of which came to nought as Matabeleland knocked off the 50 runs required in 14.2 overs.

Grant Flower steered Matabeleland to victory over Mashonaland in the Logan Cup.

Sportsline Photographic

ZIMBABWE DOMESTIC ONE-DAY SEASON
By Telford Vice

The rain which hampered the first-class programme also prevented any play in the second of the three Logan Cup limited-overs matches, between Mashonaland and Mashonaland 'A' at Old Hararians.

However, there was a surfeit of one-day cricket to be seen from the touring England 'A', Australian academy and Denmark teams, who between them played 19 such contests against Zimbabwean sides of varying quality.

Matabeleland won the first Logan Cup game, against Mashonaland at Bulawayo Athletic Club, by six wickets. The result was all but inevitable after the visitors were dismissed for a sub-standard 164 in 46 overs – and that after one man, Grant Flower, scored more than half the total with an undefeated 88. Mashonaland failed to come to terms with their opponents' exemplary bowling and fielding and a pitch of variable bounce. Henry Olonga took full advantage of the pressure that built as a consequence to claim 4 for 21. Neil Johnson led Matabeleland's victory charge, achieved in 40 overs at a touch more than four runs to the over, with a slick 84 not out.

A closer encounter unfolded two weeks later when Matabeleland hosted Mashonaland 'A', ostensibly the Shonas' second string, in the third match of the competition also at Bulawayo Athletic Club.

Trevor Penney won the toss and inserted Matabeleland on what looked like another idiosyncratic surface. So it proved as the home side were dismissed for 179 with seven balls of their 50 overs remaining.

Partnerships were ended before they could be fleshed out and what would otherwise have been minor contributions had their value inflated. None more so than captain Andrew Whittall's 13 not out off eight balls – and not a boundary among them – which was received by one half of the pavilion with all the gusto usually reserved for match-winning half-centuries.

The bulk of the runs trickled from Guy Whittall and Heath Streak, with 20 each, and Mark Abrams, eighth out for a carefully crafted 51 in which he showed admirable restraint by not bothering with boundaries – he hit just two of the 71 deliveries he faced for four.

Trevor Penney, captain of the champions, Mashonaland 'A'.
David Munden/Sportsline Photographic

Scoring was easier off the bowling of the attack's supporting cast, but little was given away by the front line. In 29.5 tight overs between them Gus Mackay, Gary Brent and Paul Strang took seven wickets at less than three to the over.

Matabeleland looked to have kept their hand in the match when they reduced Mashonaland 'A' to 62 for 3 in the 14th over and to 105 for 6 in the 31st. However, a steady unbroken stand of 75 between Stuart Carlisle and Penney took the visitors all the way to their four-wicket victory with the winning runs struck in the 47th over.

To Carlisle, the number four, fell the task of rebuilding the innings and his 61 not out off 106 balls with three fours and a six represented a fine effort in that ultimately successful cause. But he could not have done the job without the compact, organised Penney, who stopped the rot at three wickets in five overs and finished unbeaten with 40.

FIRST-CLASS AVERAGES

BATTING

	M	Inns	NO	HS	Runs	Av	100	50
A Flower	4	6	3	194*	469	156.33	2	–
GJ Whittall	4	7	2	131*	311	62.20	1	3
A Flintoff	3	5	1	88	247	61.75	–	3
MB Loye	3	5	0	133	259	51.80	1	1
TL Penney	2	4	1	130*	149	49.66	1	–
MW Goodwin	3	5	0	111	239	47.80	1	–
MP Vaughan	3	5	0	131	230	46.00	1	1
DP Viljoen	5	8	0	92	297	37.12	–	2
AG Huckle	6	9	5	41	148	37.00	–	–
JAR Craig	2	4	0	71	136	34.00	–	1
GJ Rennie	4	8	0	84	239	29.87	–	2
SV Carlisle	3	5	0	47	143	28.60	–	–
NC Johnson	4	7	0	84	180	25.71	–	1
CB Wishart	6	11	0	106	275	25.00	1	1
MA Vermeulen	2	4	0	46	94	23.50	–	–
GP Swann	3	5	0	48	115	23.00	–	–
ADR Campbell	2	4	1	28*	66	22.00	–	–
DA Cosker	3	4	2	28*	42	21.00	–	–
HH Streak	4	7	1	49	122	20.33	–	–
TR Gripper	3	6	0	62	112	18.66	–	1
BC Strang	4	7	0	48	130	18.57	–	–
AM Blignaut	3	4	0	58	72	18.00	–	1
DA Marillier	2	4	0	33	72	18.00	–	–
CMW Read	3	5	1	47	70	17.50	–	–
S Nyakutse	4	6	1	39	86	17.20	–	–
AJ Mackay	3	5	0	44	85	17.00	–	–
NR van Rensburg	2	4	1	33	51	17.00	–	–
TN Madondo	6	10	1	57	142	15.77	–	1
CP Gurr	5	8	3	21	69	13.80	–	–
GB Brent	3	6	0	38	82	13.66	–	–
RWT Key	2	4	0	25	51	12.75	–	–

Qualification: 4 completed innings, average 10.00

FIRST-CLASS AVERAGES

BOWLING

	Overs	Mds	Runs	Wkts	Av	Best	10/m	5/inn
B Lee	36.4	7	91	17	5.35	6–25	–	2
A Kumble	92.1	25	182	17	10.70	5–18	1	2
SD Thomas	54.2	14	127	11	11.54	8–50	–	1
JA Rennie	28	9	80	5	16.00	5–80	–	1
Harbhajan Singh	67	13	204	10	20.40	3–60	–	–
M Mbangwa	96.2	37	191	9	21.22	3–22	–	–
GW Flower	100.2	31	222	10	22.20	3–35	–	–
NC Johnson	73.4	20	225	10	22.50	3–41	–	–
JD Lewry	47	18	129	5	25.80	3–45	–	–
J Srinath	54.3	12	130	5	26.00	3–59	–	–
AR Whittall	138.5	20	437	16	27.31	4–49	–	–
HH Streak	129	27	357	13	27.46	3–62	–	–
PA Strang	62	16	142	5	28.40	3–84	–	–
DA Cosker	101	29	256	9	28.44	4–54	–	–
AJ Mackay	79.3	19	247	8	30.87	5–85	–	1
GP Swann	103.1	23	292	9	32.44	4–52	–	–
HK Olonga	82	17	262	8	32.75	5–70	–	1
BV Strang	136.2	43	427	12	35.58	4–107	–	–
DP Viljoen	81.1	21	225	6	37.50	2–46	–	–
GB Brent	59.5	9	214	5	42.80	2–79	–	–
AG Huckle	211	31	717	12	59.75	4–86	–	–
DJ Peacock	120	55	374	6	62.33	3–66	–	–

Qualification: 5 wickets

LEADING FIELDERS

8 – AR Whittall; 7 – A Flower (6 ct/1 st), CMW Read (6 ct/1 st); 6 – CP Gurr (5 ct/1 st), RR Singh; 5 – RS Dravid, GW Flower, WK Gilmour, NC Johnson, GP Swann, GJ Whittall; 4 – MW Goodwin, VS Solanki, DP Viljoen

WEST INDIES

Australia in West Indies
Busta Cup
Red Stripe Bowl
First-Class Averages

AUSTRALIA IN WEST INDIES
By Tony Cozier

Their latest series in the Caribbean thoroughly lived up to the tradition of competitive and compelling contests long since established by Australia and West Indies. Indeed, it exceeded all expectations.

The teams originally appeared so mismatched that fears of a one-sided embarrassment were well founded. Australia, justifiably regarded as the unofficial champions of Test cricket, arrived directly from another triumphant season at home, in which they had comfortably retained the Ashes over England. The West Indies awaited them in a state of disarray and depression following a humiliating five-nil thrashing in South Africa. Blaming 'weaknesses in leadership' for the shambles, the West Indies Cricket Board (WICB) grudgingly retained Brian Lara as captain amidst widespread calls for his removal but placed him on a two-match probation. In addition, a shoulder injury eliminated the reliable Shivnarine Chanderpaul from the series, his infant son's illness in Australia kept Carl Hooper away for the first two matches.

When Australia bowled West Indies out in 19.1 overs for 51, their lowest total in 71 years of Test cricket, to win the first Test by 312 runs, all the pessimistic predictions seemed justified.

What followed bordered on the incredible. Lara, the egocentric superstar of a dozen different controversies, chose the moment to respond to the intense pressure with two exceptional innings almost mystical in concept and execution.

His 213 in Kingston and his unbeaten last-day 153 in Bridgetown so transformed West Indies' spirit that they won both Tests, the latter by one wicket in a match described by Australian captain, the veteran Steve Waugh, as the best he had ever played in. Lara blazed his way to another century, an even 100 off 84 balls in the final Test, but it was not sufficient to prevent defeat and retrieve the Frank Worrell Trophy that had been in Australia's custody since 1995.

While Lara's feats were dominant and colossal there was more to the series than one man. Steve Waugh, in his first assignment as captain in succession to Mark Taylor, confirmed his status as the game's most reliable batsman. The skill and stamina of the great fast bowlers on either side, the ageing Curtly Ambrose and Courtney Walsh for West Indies and Glenn McGrath for Australia, were remarkable.

Steve Waugh replaced Mark Taylor as captain of Australia for the series against West Indies.
David Munden/Sportsline Photographic

Waugh's hundred in the second Test and 199 in the third should have been enough to guarantee Australia invincibility but for Lara's genius. Instead, they were the Tests Australia lost. Waugh's renewed encounters with Ambrose and Walsh were as fascinating as Lara's with his abrasive adversary, McGrath.

These five were the star turns. The rest simply made up the supporting cast.

Lara totalled 546 runs and averaged 91. No other West Indian reached 200 or averaged better than 30. Waugh's 409 runs were 108 more than the next Australian, the left-handed Justin Langer.

In his 37th year, Walsh still found the energy and enthusiasm to send down more overs than anyone of either side and the penetration to earn 26 wickets. Ambrose, a year Walsh's junior, had 19 wickets and, with a little more luck, would have had more.

Yet McGrath's statistics were even more imposing than those of his West Indian counterparts. His 30 wickets, at just under 17 each, were a new record for a visiting bowler in a Test series in West Indies. In four of the seven innings he claimed half the wickets. Such statistical imbalances left both teams with worries for the immediate future.

Australia's surrounded Shane Warne, the vice-captain and Test cricket's most successful spin bowler, whose effectiveness was so diminished that he took only two late-order wickets in the first three Tests before he was dropped for the last. His problems could be sourced to his premature return to action following major shoulder surgery less than a year before. His encouraging form in the subsequent one-day internationals suggested it was only a matter of time before he would return to his best. But his omission was a morale-shattering decision, taken against his wishes.

While West Indies' resurgence centred around Lara, Ambrose and Walsh, Jimmy Adams and Sherwin Campbell, both missing for almost a year, made significant contributions in the two victorious Tests. Still, the prolonged search for a reliable opening pair continued, the stability of Chanderpaul was badly missed and no new middle-order batsman was uncovered, a predicament accentuated by the sudden retirement of Hooper prior to the last one-day international.

Where West Indies gained most was in the restoration of team spirit and commitment, glaringly absent in South Africa. In the end, they would have been happy with the outcome. Australia would have been relieved. The two-two balance was just about right.

West Indies Cricket Board XI v. Australia
22, 23 and 24 February 1999 at Antigua Recreation Ground, St John's
Australia 156 and 209 for 4 dec.
West Indies Cricket Board XI 55 and 121 for 4
Match drawn

The Australians' rustiness was reflected in a weak first-day batting performance against a young, inexperienced team for whom left-arm spinner Ryan Hinds, 18, was the most successful bowler. The Board XI, losing their first three wickets without a run scored, were then routed for 55 by Dale's each-way swing. A last-wicket stand of 21 avoided an even lower total. Griffith's unbeaten 39 stretched over 59 overs on a rain-interrupted final day to claim a draw.

WICB President's XI v. Australia
27 and 28 February and 1 March 1999 at Guaracara Park, Pointe-a–Pierre, Trinidad
WICB President's XI 177 and 185
Australia 368
Australia won by an innings and 6 runs

The Test hopefuls in the home team were mesmerised by MacGill's sharp each-way spin that earned him 13 wickets in the match and his career-best figures, 7 for 29, in the second innings. Half-centuries by Joseph and Ragoonath were enough to gain them debuts in the first Test a few days later but not enough to stave off a heavy defeat. Mark Waugh's first hundred of the tour was made from 129 balls with a six and 14 fours.

Mark Waugh made 106 against the WICB President's XI.
David Munden/Sportsline Photographic

FIRST TEST
5, 6, 7 and 8 March 1999 at Port-of-Spain

After their disastrous tour of South Africa, it was inconceivable that things could get worse for West Indies. A month later, in front of their own despairing crowds, they did.

Folding to their sixth successive defeat, by 312 runs, their depleted batting was dispatched in their second innings for 51, the lowest West Indies total in their 71 years of Test cricket. It was two fewer than the 53 against Pakistan in 1986 when they were bundled out by Imran and Abdul Qadir on a worn Karachi pitch. Never before had they been bowled out for under 100 in a home Test.

On the same ground where they themselves had routed England for 46 for a stunning victory five years earlier, West Indies managed to hold out for only the same 19.1 overs their opponents did then. Had it not been for four byes from a high McGrath bouncer and two sets of overthrows that reached the boundary that figure would not have been passed.

They were clearly disadvantaged by the absence of two main batsmen, Chanderpaul, whose shoulder

Glen McGrath bowls Mervyn Dillon for 0, to end West Indies first innings and claim 5 for 50, in the first Test at Queen's Park Oval.

Gordon Brooks/Sportsline Photographic

injury would eliminate him from the series altogether, and Hooper, who remained in Australia to be with his ill infant son. In addition, Holder twisted his ankle on the opening day and had to use a runner in both his brief innings, limiting his footwork.

It meant West Indies didn't have the resources or the resolve to withstand the ruthless Australians, led for the first time in a Test by Steve Waugh. Bowlers appreciated a typically complex Queen's Park pitch and, in the fateful second innings, Waugh needed only the probing pace of McGrath and Gillespie. Once Campbell had been dismissed in the eighth over, the fast bowlers finished things off in the space of 11.4 overs The effect of their controlled pace and movement was reflected in the method of dismissals – one bowler, four leg befores and four slip catches. Only Dillon's run-out denied them a clean sweep.

'I expected to win but didn't expect it to be so easy,' captain Waugh admitted. 'You never expect to bowl a team out for 51 in a Test match.'

It was a sickening anticlimax for West Indies who held their own throughout the opening day. The inclusion of both leg-spinners influenced Waugh into batting on winning the toss and Australia were restricted to 174 for 6 off the 90 overs to close. The pitch, and the outfield, retained moisture from the previous day's persistent rain and, allied to disciplined bowling, made free-scoring difficult throughout.

Walsh's three wickets gained him membership of the elite 400 club, joining Kapil Dev and Hadlee, while the new left-armer was impressive on debut accounting for both openers. Elliott's 44 occupied four and a quarter hours before he was one of the 15 leg before victims in the match, padding out to the left-arm Collins who had an impressive debut. It typified the batsmen's difficulties.

Ambrose soon removed top-scorer Blewett and Warne on the second morning but West Indies' effort was frustrated by Gillespie and McGrath. The fast bowlers made the first of their many significant contributions to the match in a last-wicket stand of 66, both recording their highest Test scores.

In the conditions, Australia's 269 was a challenging total, and only while Joseph, with his uncomplicated style and forthright attitude, and Lara were together in the first innings did West Indies remotely look like matching it. Both met Warne and MacGill with positive assurance but once Joseph was leg before to the first ball of a new spell from McGrath, the batting folded.

FIRST TEST – WEST INDIES v. AUSTRALIA
5, 6, 7 and 8 March 1999 at Queen's Park Oval, Port-of-Spain

AUSTRALIA

	First Innings		Second Innings	
MJ Slater	c Dillon, b Collins	23	st Jacobs, b Adams	106
MTG Elliott	lbw, b Collins	44	c Joseph, b Walsh	0
JL Langer	c Jacobs, b Walsh	5	c Jacobs, b Dillon	24
ME Waugh	lbw, b Walsh	2	lbw, b Ambrose	33
SR Waugh (capt)	c Jacobs, b Dillon	14	c Jacobs, b Collins	0
GS Blewett	lbw, b Ambrose	58	st Jacobs, b Adams	28
*IA Healy	lbw, b Waugh	12	lbw, b Walsh	0
SK Warne	c Campbell, b Ambrose	21	b Walsh	25
JN Gillespie	not out	28	c Lara, b Ambrose	22
SCG MacGill	b Ambrose	0	b Walsh	0
GD McGrath	c Jacobs, b Dillon	39	not out	4
	lb 19, nb 4	23	b 4, lb 7, w 1, nb 7	19
		269		**261**

	First Innings				Second Innings			
	O	M	R	W	O	M	R	W
Walsh	31	9	60	3	25.2	2	67	4
Ambrose	27	15	35	3	18	8	25	2
Collins	23	8	45	2	21	2	72	1
Dillon	26.3	4	69	2	14	1	57	1
Adams	14	2	41	0	8	1	29	2

Fall of Wickets
1–42, 2–51, 3–53, 4–74, 5–118, 6–153, 7–186, 8–203, 9–203
1–7, 2–45, 3–126, 4–127, 5–193, 6–194, 7–227, 8–257, 9–257

WEST INDIES

	First Innings		Second Innings	
SL Campbell	lbw, b McGrath	9	c ME Waugh, b Gillespie	0
S Ragoonath	run out (McGrath)	9	lbw, b Gillespie	2
DR E Joseph	lbw, b McGrath	50	c Warne, b McGrath	5
BC Lara (capt)	run out (Langer)	62	c ME Waugh, b Gillespie	3
JC Adams	b MacGill	13	lbw, b McGrath	5
*RD Jacobs	lbw, b MacGill	6	lbw, b McGrath	19
PT Collins	lbw, b McGrath	1	(10) b Gillespie	0
RIC Holder	lbw, b MacGill	0	(7) c ME Waugh, b McGrath	4
CEL Ambrose	c Slater, b McGrath	0	(8) lbw, b McGrath	6
MV Dillon	b McGrath	0	(9) run out (Blewett)	0
CA Walsh	not out	0	not out	2
	b 4, lb 2, nb 11	17	b 4, lb 1	5
		167		**51**

	First Innings				Second Innings			
	O	M	R	W	O	M	R	W
McGrath	14	3	50	5	10	3	28	5
Gillespie	12	3	34	0	9.1	4	18	4
MacGill	16	5	41	3				
Warne	14	4	35	0				
Blewett	1	0	1	0				

Fall of Wickets
1–16, 2–28, 3–116, 4–149, 5–156, 6–163, 7–163, 8–163, 9–167
1–3, 2–8, 3–11, 4–16, 5–16, 6–31, 7–47, 8–47, 9–49

Umpires: EA Nicholls & P Willey
Toss: Australia

Australia won by 312 runs

Michael Slater celebrates his second-innings century in the first Test.

Gordon Brooks/Sportsline Photographic

Lara was 62 and his confidence growing with every stroke when he was run out by Langer's slick work from short leg after he was struck on the body by an on-drive off Warne. McGrath and MacGill then swiftly rounded off the innings, the last seven wickets tumbling for 18.

Australia's lead of 102 was enough virtually to guarantee victory but West Indies bowlers stuck stoically to their hopeless task. They collected wickets throughout the third afternoon but could do nothing to upset Slater who proceeded to his 12th hundred in his 46th Test, his fifth in his last nine. It was praised by his captain as 'one of the best Test match hundreds I have seen'.

His skillfully controlled 106, made out of 192 while he was at the wicket, was at the core of the Australian effort. He spent four and three-quarter chanceless hours making light of a slow pitch of uncertain bounce that was a challenge to his method and nature. He finally became that rare statistic on a West Indian scoreboard, a stumping, as he charged down to Adams' left-arm spin.

Australia, 227 for 7 at the start of the fourth day, stretched their lead to 362 before Walsh and Ambrose ended the innings with the second new ball half an hour into play. Even in that time, as the tail-enders again batted without bother, there was a hint that the fight had gone out of West Indies.

McGrath and Gillespie had to wait until halfway through the seventh over before they could initiate the rout. Once it was on, it was only temporarily interrupted by two brief rain breaks. The second brought an early lunch and, at 16 for 5, New Zealand's 26 against England that had stood for 44 years as Test cricket's lowest total was under threat.

It didn't come to that but the pain for West Indies cricket was none the less for that.

Ian Healy is out leg before wicket to give Courtney Walsh 400 Test wickets, in the first Test.

Gordon Brooks/Sportsline Photographic

SECOND TEST
13, 14, 15 and 16 March 1999 at Kingston

Bob Marley's 'Redemption Song' boomed out across Sabina Park from the celebrating Red Stripe Mound as West Indies completed one of their most remarkable and gratifying Test victories.

It was unimaginable a week earlier, when they had been toppled for 51 and beaten in their sixth successive Test by 312 runs. It was even more so after the opening day when, carrying the inexperience of six players with a mere nine Tests between them, they were tottering at 37 for 4 replying to Australia's 256.

Yet, galvanised on the second day by captain Brian Lara's magical 213, they recovered to beat the same powerful opponents who had so humbled them in the first Test, virtually by an innings less than an hour into the fourth day.

In the circumstances, Lara's performance was as significant as any ever staged in West Indies' cause. West Indies cricket had never experienced such lean times. No West Indies captain had ever endured as much pressure, most of it of his own making.

He had been pilloried right, left and centre for his team's preceding disgrace in South Africa, castigated by his Board for his weak leadership and placed on probation for two Tests. This was his last chance and, as he walked out to toss, he allegedly turned to Steve Waugh and said: 'I'm glad this is the last time I'll have to do this.'

Had he been overwhelmed by the responsibility and failed, there is no telling what his future, and the immediate future of West Indies cricket, would have been. Instead, he revealed a steely foundation to his cavalier persona.

It was not entirely a one-man show. As they did in the first Test, the bowlers did their duty, supported by flawless catching and sharp ground fielding. The tall Jamaican off-spinner, Perry, capitalising on a rare and substantial first-innings lead, gathered five second-innings wickets on his

SECOND TEST – WEST INDIES v. AUSTRALIA
13, 14, 15 and 16 March 1999 at Sabina Park, Kingston

AUSTRALIA

	First Innings		Second Innings	
MJ Slater	c Jacobs, b Walsh	22	(2) b Walsh	0
MTG Elliott	c Lara, b Walsh	0	(1) lbw, b Perry	16
JL Langer	c Jacobs, b Walsh	8	c Jacobs, b Perry	24
ME Waugh	b Perry	67	c Walsh, b Ambrose	21
SR Waugh (capt)	c Joseph, b Collins	100	c Jacobs, b Perry	9
GS Blewett	lbw, b Walsh	5	c Lara, b Perry	30
*IA Healy	run out (Joseph/Perry)	6	run out (Collins/Jacobs)	10
SK Warne	c Joseph, b Collins	24	c Joseph, b Walsh	23
JN Gillespie	b Ambrose	1	c Jacobs, b Walsh	7
SCG MacGill	c Joseph, b Collins	0	c Joseph, b Perry	7
GD McGrath	not out	2	not out	11
	b 1, lb 3, nb 17	21	lb 3, nb 16	19
		256		**177**

	First Innings				Second Innings			
	O	M	R	W	O	M	R	W
Ambrose	17	9	33	1	14	4	28	1
Walsh	20	6	55	4	18	3	52	3
Collins	16.3	2	79	3	8	0	24	0
Perry	17	1	79	1	26	8	70	5
Adams	1	0	6	0				

Fall of Wickets
1–8, 2–28, 3–46, 4–158, 5–171, 6–179, 7–227, 8–242, 9–248
1–4, 2–36, 3–51, 4–63, 5–86, 6–107, 7–137, 8–157, 9–159

WEST INDIES

	First Innings		Second Innings	
SL Campbell	b McGrath	12	not out	1
S Ragoonath	lbw, b Gillespie	0	not out	2
LA Roberts	c Warne, b McGrath	0		
BC Lara (capt)	c Healy, b McGrath	213		
DRE Joseph	c Blewett, b McGrath	14		
PT Collins	c ME Waugh, b MacGill	13		
JC Adams	c Elliott, b McGrath	94		
*RD Jacobs	c Gillespie, b Warne	25		
NO Perry	not out	15		
CEL Ambrose	b MacGill	3		
CA Walsh	lbw, b MacGill	0		
	b 12, lb 8, nb 22	42		
		431	(for 0 wicket)	**3**

	First Innings				Second Innings			
	O	M	R	W	O	M	R	W
McGrath	35	11	93	5	0.3	0	3	0
Gillespie	33	7	79	1				
Warne	30	8	94	1				
MacGill	22.3	3	84	3				
Blewett	10	1	48	0				
ME Waugh	2	0	13	0				

Fall of Wickets
1–4, 2–5, 3–17, 4–34, 5–378, 6–398, 7–420, 8–427, 9–431

Umpires: SA Bucknor & P Willey
Toss: Australia

West Indies won by ten wickets

Steve Waugh is congratulated by fans on completing a century in the second Test.
Gordon Brooks/Sportsline Photographic

debut. Walsh had four important victims in the first innings and seven in all and Collins ensured there was no tail-wagging as there was in Port-of-Spain.

Yet none of these were as substantial as the role of Jimmy Adams who remained steadfast by Lara's side in their day-long partnership of 322, a new West Indies record for the fifth wicket.

Steve Waugh's typically efficient, even hundred and his untroubled stand of 112 in two hours either side of lunch on the opening day were about all Australia could show for the advantage of winning the toss. 256 was at least 100 below par.

Walsh made the early breaks, removing Elliott, Langer and Slater in the first hour, and, after Mark was bowled by Perry's shooter, the last seven wickets could only muster 98. Captain Waugh had just recorded his 17th Test hundred when he was last out to the third of Joseph's first slip catches off Collins.

In the 14.3 overs available before the light deteriorated enough to end play, McGrath and Gillespie had run through the shaky West Indies' top order much as they had done a week earlier in Port-of-Spain – but they did not move Lara.

Throughout the following day, Lara emphatically changed the course of the match and the series with a withering assault on his startled rivals. As he

Nehemiah Perry is embraced by Brian Lara after bowling Mark Waugh for 67, to claim his first Test wicket, in the second Test at Sabina Park.
Gordon Brooks/Sportsline Photographic

arrived at his first hundred for 14 Tests, just making his ground on a sharp single before Langer's direct hit, he was engulfed in a mass of jubilant spectators. When he passed 200 for the third time in Tests, he had to seek sanctuary from another invasion in the dressing room. The despondency that had hung over him and West Indies cricket for so long had been dispelled in the space of a few hours.

For 40 minutes, the steady nightwatchman Collins kept Lara company, handing over to Adams after a blow to the box caused him to retire. Fully appreciating his role, Adams contributed 88 of the 321 the two left-handers added on the second day.

Content to watch Lara in full flight, he saw 29 fours in all directions, none better or more courageous than the 25th, a cover drive off McGrath the ball after his old adversary had temporarily floored him with a bouncer to the flap of the helmet. Lara was severest on MacGill and Warne who conceded 156 runs from 41 overs on the day, including Lara's two sixes off successive balls, one off MacGill and one off Warne.

At 377 for 4, West Indies were already 121 to the good at the start of the third day with Lara still unbeaten. Overnight thoughts turned to another triple-century but his masterpiece ended meekly within quarter of an hour, to a thin edge to Healy off McGrath off whom he had been dropped by Mark Waugh, wide to his left at second slip, when 44. There was further anticlimax as Adams missed his deserved hundred by two, also undone by McGrath who again had five wickets in the innings.

Although the innings quickly subsided on Lara's dismissal, the lead was substantial and the bowlers wasted no time exploiting it. Walsh bowled Slater off the inside edge with his fourth ball. Perry removed Elliott, Langer, Steve Waugh and, with the last ball of the day, Blewett. Ambrose lured Mark Waugh into hooking into long leg's lap and Healy ran himself out for the second time. Australia were still 18 short of an innings defeat with two tail-end wickets remaining when the fourth day began but the last pair, Gillespie and McGrath, just managed to avoid that indignity. Campbell and Ragoonath were left with the formality of scoring three runs to complete a great result for West Indies.

It was overdue compensation for the anguish to which they had been subjected throughout the series in South Africa and satisfying amends not only for the first Test loss, but also for the innings defeat on the same ground four years earlier that had surrendered the Frank Worrell Trophy to Australia for the first time in 17 years.

West Indies 'A' v. Australia
20, 21, 22 and 23 March 1999 at Antigua Recreation Ground, St John's
Australia 303 and 263 for 8 dec.
West Indies 'A' 102 and 310
Australia won by 154 runs

Another batting failure led to another heavy defeat for a team made up of West Indies Test hopefuls. The gap between them and the established players was emphasised by Hooper who, in his first match on return from Australia, had nine wickets and a second-innings hundred. Langer and Elliott secured their tenuous Test places with timely hundreds.

THIRD TEST
26, 27, 28, 29 and 30 March 1999 at Bridgetown

For Steve Waugh, it was 'the best Test I've ever played in' – and it was his 114th. For Clive Lloyd it was 'the stuff of which dreams are made'. The *Barbados Daily Nation* headlined it 'Test of the Century'. The *London Evening Standard* was not the only one wondering whether it was 'the greatest Test ever played'.

The contest, played out before near-full houses on each of the five days, was spell binding throughout. Its intensity and its quality never waned. Australia consistently held the advantage only to have it snatched away at the very end by a West Indies team that refused to yield. They repeatedly turned crisis into recovery and their extraordinary captain, Lara, composed one of the truly great match-winning innings on the last day, two weeks after his similar epic at Sabina.

The match was embellished by outstanding performances by the most distinguished players on each side. Steve Waugh's first-innings 199 was as typical of the gritty Australian captain as the decisive, unbeaten 153 was of the flamboyant Lara. The Herculean effort of McGrath, who bowled 77 incisive overs in the searing heat, was matched by those of Ambrose and Walsh on the other side. Yet there were also critical contributions from the lesser lights, principally Ponting and Gillespie for Australia, Campbell, Jacobs and Adams for West Indies.

As it approached its sensational conclusion, spectators hurried to Kensington from nearby Bridgetown city centre, rush-hour traffic came to a halt throughout the Caribbean and business slowed. Sky Sports in Britain, carrying live television coverage, reported record ratings.

When Lara finally lashed the winning boundary through the covers off Gillespie, the pent-up excitement in the stands exploded in a joyous invasion of the field. Several of his players were the first to get to Lara for an emotional embrace.

There was no hint of such a remarkable climax as Australia built the foundations of their imposing first-innings total on the first day. Captain Waugh was again their standard-bearer. His 19th Test century began, as so many have done, with Australia in disarray – at 36 for 3 with Ambrose and Walsh

Steve Waugh sweeping Perry in his innings of 199 in the third Test.

Gordon Brooks/Sportsline Photographic

enjoying a familiar pitch with early encouragement. By close, he was 141 and Australia, at 322 for 4, were already seemingly impregnable.

Waugh's example inspired positive responses from Langer, who helped steady things in a stand of 108 before Hooper bowled him with a straight one, and from Ponting, returning to the team only because of Blewett's hand injury. As the pitch rapidly developed into a beauty, Waugh and Ponting took charge, seldom in trouble as they stayed together for ten minutes under five hours in adding 281, a new Australian fifth-wicket record against West Indies.

Ponting's dismissal on the second day to a top-edged sweep off Perry quarter of an hour after he reached his third Test century set off a late-order collapse in which the last six wickets fell for 65. After nearly eight and a half chanceless hours, Waugh was one away from his second Test double-century when, back to Perry, he was leg before.

The Australians had a late-afternoon burst at their weary opponents and duly reduced them to 80 for 4 off the available 26 overs, among them Lara to Gillespie's wicked bouncer.

On resumption, McGrath soon accounted for Hooper and Adams to slip catches but Campbell and Jacobs then transformed Kensington from a Sunday morning morgue into a Caribbean carnival with a counter-attacking partnership of 153 in three and three-quarter hours that included 21 fours.

Campbell's third and most notable Test hundred, his second on home soil, was divided into two distinct parts. He managed only one scoring stroke in the first hour before taking the cue for attack from Jacobs who was typically belligerent from the start. They were separated when Jacobs edged a slip catch off Ponting, filling in for a few overs to rest McGrath prior to the new ball. Campbell's vital contribution was ended by the deserving Gillespie just after tea, but his stand with Jacobs was the catalyst for merry resistance from the tail. The last four wickets yielded 231, not only avoiding the follow-on but perceptively lifting West Indies' spirits.

In the brief time they had on the third evening, Walsh and Ambrose took a wicket apiece and the fightback, led by Walsh's five wickets, continued into the next day as Australia were dismissed by tea for 146. It was enough to open the door to the amazing events that were to follow.

West Indies were initially energised by Campbell's direct hit from 50 yards that ran out the dangerous Slater 35 minutes into the fourth day. They didn't let up until Warne came in at 81 for 7 to halt the collapse with a robust 32 off 48 balls.

THIRD TEST – WEST INDIES v. AUSTRALIA
26, 27, 28, 29 and 30 March 1999 at Kensington Oval, Bridgetown

AUSTRALIA

	First Innings		Second Innings	
MJ Slater	c Lara, b Ambrose	23	(2) run out (Campbell)	26
MTG Elliott	c Jacobs, b Walsh	9	(1) c Jacobs, b Walsh	0
JL Langer	b Hooper	51	(5) lbw, b Ambrose	1
ME Waugh	b Ambrose	0	(5) lbw, b Walsh	3
SR Waugh (capt)	lbw, b Perry	199	(6) b Collins	11
RT Ponting	c Hooper, b Perry	104	(7) c Griffith, b Walsh	22
*IA Healy	lbw, b Walsh	0	(8) c Jacobs, b Collins	3
SK Warne	c Lara, b Perry	13	(9) lbw, b Walsh	32
JN Gillespie	not out	23	(4) b Ambrose	14
SCG MacGill	run out (Ambrose)	17	c Campbell, b Walsh	1
GD McGrath	c Joseph, b Hooper	3	not out	8
	b 4, lb 10, nb 34	48	lb 5, w 1, nb 19	25
		490		**146**

	First Innings				Second Innings			
	O	M	R	W	O	M	R	W
Ambrose	31.3	7	93	2	20	2	60	2
Walsh	38	8	121	2	17.1	3	39	5
Perry	33	5	102	3	4	0	11	0
Collins	35.3	7	110	0	9	0	31	2
Hooper	15.4	4	50	2				

Fall of Wickets
1-31, 2-36, 3-36, 4-144, 5-425, 6-427, 7-429, 8-446, 9-483
1-0, 2-12, 3-35, 4-46, 5-48, 6-73, 7-81, 8-134, 9-137

WEST INDIES

	First Innings		Second Innings	
SL Campbell	c SR Waugh, b Gillespie	105	lbw, b McGrath	33
AFG Griffith	run out (Ponting)	0	lbw, b Gillespie	35
DRE Joseph	lbw, b McGrath	26	lbw, b MacGill	1
PT Collins	lbw, b McGrath	0	lbw, b McGrath	0
BC Lara (capt)	c Healy, b Gillespie	8	not out	153
CL Hooper	c Warne, b McGrath	25	c Healy, b Gillespie	6
JC Adams	c ME Waugh, b McGrath	0	b McGrath	38
*RD Jacobs	c ME Waugh, b Ponting	68	lbw, b McGrath	5
NO Perry	lbw, b Gillespie	24	lbw, b McGrath	0
CEL Ambrose	not out	28	c Elliott, b Gillespie	12
CA Walsh	c Slater, b Warne	12	not out	0
	b 10, lb 3, nb 20	33	b 8, lb 13, w 2, nb 5	28
		329	(for 9 wickets)	**311**

	First Innings				Second Innings			
	O	M	R	W	O	M	R	W
McGrath	33	5	128	4	44	13	92	5
Gillespie	28	14	48	3	26.1	8	62	3
Warne	15.5	2	70	1	24	4	69	0
MacGill	20	5	47	0	21	6	48	1
Ponting	4	1	12	1				
ME Waugh	3	0	11	0				
SR Waugh					5	0	19	0

Fall of Wickets
1-1, 2-50, 3-50, 4-64, 5-98, 6-98, 7-251, 8-265, 9-291
1-77, 2-77, 3-78, 4-91, 5-105, 6-238, 7-248, 8-248, 9-302

Umpires: EA Nicholls & DL Orchard
Toss: Australia

West Indies won by one wicket

The winning goal for the home team was 308, far from impossible but, everyone knew, heavily dependent on Lara. Campbell and the left-handed Griffith provided them with the best start of the series, adding 72, but three wickets in the last half-hour shifted the balance back to Australia. When the overnight 85 for 3 became 98 for 6 on the last morning, it seemed it had gone too far for it to swing again – except that Lara was still there and so too was Adams.

In the same way they had done in their record partnership in the second Test, they stopped the rot and then built a partnership of 133 that carried West Indies to within 70 of their target.

Lara inevitably took the lead. After battling through a compelling opening hour against McGrath and Gillespie during which he spent 47 balls over his first ten runs, he launched another calculated assault on Warne and MacGill who went wicketless on the day. With Gillespie in the pavilion following his opening spell for treatment to a back strain, Waugh was forced to recall McGrath for more work than planned.

The abrasive fast bowler never shirked from the challenge – and nor did Lara. A blow to the helmet as Lara ducked into a bouncer sparked a verbal joust between the two and brought Adams in as peacemaker. Two balls later, Lara's telling riposte was a fierce pull for four.

But McGrath was not finished. In space of ten runs, he changed the course of the game once more, bowling Adams with a beauty and claiming Jacobs and Perry leg before with successive balls. It left Lara to gather the 60 runs still required with only Ambrose and Walsh in support.

If it appeared an impossible mission, Ambrose did not think so. He defended diligently for an hour and 20 minutes with his captain while the score moved to within six of victory. As the tension rose, Gillespie returned and immediately had Lara dropped by Healy, wide to his left. Lara was 145 and seven more were needed, a decisive error by Test cricket's most successful wicketkeeper.

Gillespie did remove Ambrose to a slip catch at the same score but Lara would not be denied. Walsh, whose 32 ducks are a comfortable Test record, held out for five balls as the nervy Australians conceded two runs to a Gillespie no-ball and a wide from the tiring McGrath.

Lara tied the scores with a hooked single off McGrath and fittingly placed a final and expressive exclamation mark on a remarkable match with a trademark cover drive off Gillespie.

FOURTH TEST
3, 4, 5, 6 and 7 April 1999 at St. John's

The Frank Worrell Trophy – described afterwards by Steve Waugh as the equal of the Ashes – was slipping from Australia's grasp and their new captain was in danger of losing his first series in the considerable wake of Mark Taylor's retirement.

Warne, once their most feared weapon, was so out of sorts that he had managed only two wickets in the preceding three Tests. Gillespie, their young,

Brian Lara looks to the heavens after completing a century off 84 balls in the fourth Test.
Gordon Brooks/Sportsline Photographic

Justin Langer lifts Carl Hooper for four in his first innings in
the fourth Test. He scored 127 in the second innings.
Gordon Brooks/Sportsline Photographic

high-class fast bowler, was out of action with a
bothersome back.

The force was with their opponents. On an
emotional high following their sensational victory in
the third Test three days earlier, all they required
was a draw to reclaim the Trophy that had been
taken from them in the Caribbean in 1995 after 17
years in their keeping.

It is in such adversity that the character of true
champions is best judged. Australia proved theirs
with a commanding result so that Waugh, with a
rare and understandable smile, collected the Trophy
as Taylor had twice done before him.

Australia demonstrated their single-minded
purpose by dropping Warne, the vice-captain; a
difficult and once unthinkable decision. It so upset
the leg-spinner that, in the gloomy aftermath, he
openly hinted at retirement, but it better balanced
the attack.

Lara reeled off his mandatory
hundred but his mental and
physical energy had been
drained by his Bridgetown epic.
It was a dazzling 84-ball cameo
lasting less than two hours and it
could not deny the Australians
the time they needed to exploit
the general weakness of West
Indies batting.

Australia did take some time
to overcome their self-doubt. It
was reflected in their first-day
batting that left them 211 for 5
at close, their scoring limited by
their own caution, tight bowling
and a heavily-grassed outfield
that allowed only 13 fours.

Slater and Blewett, back to
replace Elliott, saw to it that
Australia had their best start of
the series but the innings was
faltering when they and Mark
Waugh were out before 100.
Waugh's captain brother
replaced him and set about
putting things back on track
with characteristic diligence.
He made a mockery of the
tired West Indies tactic of
bouncing him and passed another half-century
just before close. Along the way, he lost his two
partners in profit from the Bridgetown Test:
Langer ran himself out on the stroke that raised
his fifty, beaten by Perry's strong, accurate return
to bowler Hooper as he tried to convert a
comfortable two into a tight three; Ponting was
leg before as he padded out Ambrose's in-swinger
with the second new ball.

Ambrose soon had Australia shaky at 242 for 8
with three quick wickets next morning, all to slip
catches, but he met his match in the swashbuckling
Miller, in his first Test of the series. Encouraged by
his captain to have a go, he hooked Ambrose for
two long sixes and rushed to a run-a-ball 47 before
Adams' slow stuff snared him.

Once Ambrose rounded off the innings with his
fifth wicket, Miller was back out to make an impact
with his medium-pace swing – and then to spoil his
day by missing a simple and important catch. He
removed both openers to edged catches before
Lara's mistimed pull off McGrath found his lap and
then the grass at mid-on.

FOURTH TEST – WEST INDIES v. AUSTRALIA
3, 4, 5, 6 and 7 April 1999 at Recreation Ground, St John's

AUSTRALIA

	First Innings		Second Innings	
MJ Slater	c Joseph, b Perry	33	(2) b Walsh	44
GS Blewett	c Jacobs, b Collymore	32	(1) lbw, b Ambrose	7
JL Langer	run out (Perry/Hooper)	51	b Hooper	127
ME Waugh	c Hooper, b Walsh	11	c Jacobs, b Ambrose	65
SR Waugh (capt)	not out	72	c Jacobs, b Ambrose	4
RT Ponting	lbw, b Ambrose	21	not out	21
*IA Healy	c Hooper, b Ambrose	6	c Adams, b Hooper	16
AC Dale	c Hooper, b Ambrose	1	(9) c Hooper, b Walsh	0
SCG MacGill	c Joseph, b Ambrose	4	(10) c Perry, b Hooper	2
CR Miller	c Joseph, b Adams	43	(8) c Lara, b Walsh	1
GD McGrath	c Jacobs, b Ambrose	5	b Walsh	2
	lb 5, nb 19	24	b 2, lb 1, w 3, nb 11	17
		303		**306**

	First Innings				Second Innings			
	O	M	R	W	O	M	R	W
Ambrose	29.5	6	94	5	27	10	55	3
Walsh	26	1	67	1	32.4	6	78	4
Collymore	25	6	49	1	16	1	60	0
Perry	15	5	36	1	7	0	28	0
Adams	6	1	18	1	8.2	2	13	0
Hooper	10	1	34	0	30.4	7	69	3

Fall of Wickets
1–60, 2–76, 3–96, 4–155, 5–211, 6–226, 7–232, 8–242, 9–295
1–15, 2–76, 3–223, 4–241, 5–265, 6–287, 7–288, 8–288, 9–296

WEST INDIES

	First Innings		Second Innings	
SL Campbell	c ME Waugh, b Miller	8	c Healy, b McGrath	29
AFG Griffith	c Healy, b Miller	9	lbw, b MacGill	56
DRE Joseph	lbw, b Dale	28	c Miller, b Dale	17
BC Lara (capt)	c Healy, b McGrath	100	lbw, b McGrath	7
CL Hooper	run out (McGrath/Healy)	47	lbw, b Blewett	12
JC Adams	c Healy, b Dale	0	st Healy, b Miller	18
*RD Jacobs	lbw, b MacGill	4	lbw, b Blewett	16
NO Perry	b McGrath	6	c Slater, b MacGill	26
CEL Ambrose	c Ponting, b MacGill	0	b MacGill	4
CD Collymore	not out	11	c MacGill, b McGrath	6
CA Walsh	lbw, b McGrath	3	not out	0
	nb 6	6	b 5, lb 12, nb 3	20
		222		**211**

	First Innings				Second Innings			
	O	M	R	W	O	M	R	W
McGrath	27.2	9	64	3	35.5	15	50	3
Dale	18	7	67	2	12	5	28	1
Miller	17	5	39	2	21	10	27	1
MacGill	14	3	52	2	26	8	80	3
Blewett					8	3	9	2

Fall of Wickets
1–19, 2–20, 3–136, 4–176, 5–178, 6–192, 7–205, 8–206, 9–213
1–56, 2–58, 3–69, 4–87, 5–105, 6–145, 7–184, 8–190, 9–209

Umpires: SA Bucknor & DL Orchard
Toss: Australia

<u>Australia won by 176 runs</u>

It was the signal for stroke-play by Lara even more spectacular, if not as significant, as that in his two previous epics. He spent 13 balls over his first run but, once started, he devastated the bowling with drives, pulls, sweeps and cuts of bewildering power and perfection.

MacGill was plundered for 34 off three overs. Dale went for 22 in his first over as replacement. Lara arrived at his first fifty off 61 balls but required only 21 balls for his second. His hundred off 82 balls (with three sixes and 15 fours) was still 26 more than Viv Richards, watching from the commentary box, needed for Test cricket's fastest hundred against England in 1986 but it was no less exhilarating.

Two balls later, McGrath ended the entertainment – and virtually the West Indies resistance – as Lara's

Australian captain Steve Waugh holds aloft the Sir Frank Worrell Trophy which he retained after defeating the West Indies in the fourth Test to level the Series two–two.
Gordon Brooks / Sportsline Photographic

gloved leg-side deflection was gathered by Healy inches from the turf. Relieved at Lara's dismissal, Dale dismissed Joseph, whose part in a stand of 116 was 14, and Adams in quick succession and, in spite of Hooper's 47, West Indies were yielding a lead of 81.

After that, Australia made almost all the running even though West Indies did not concede easily. The left-handed Langer and Mark Waugh came together at 76 for 2 and carried their third-wicket partnership to 147 into the fourth day when Australia's advance was checked by an outstanding spell of ten consecutive overs by Ambrose.

He dismissed the Waugh brothers, repeatedly beat the bat and so stimulated West Indies that Australia had to labour 42.4 overs in adding 97, their last six wickets falling for 41. Langer soldiered on to his third Test century, remaining focused for just over six and a half hours before Hooper bowled him for 127.

In ordinary circumstances, a requirement of 388 to win or a minimum 138 overs to survive over the last four and a half sessions would have been considered out of the question but this had not been an ordinary series.

With Lara, nothing seemed beyond West Indies but it was too much to expect another miracle. The fate of the match and the Trophy was virtually settled 55 minutes into the final session of the fourth day when McGrath went through Lara's defence from round the wicket, straightening enough to gain a leg before verdict. It was the tenth time the combative fast bowler had dismissed his left-handed foe in Tests but his triumph was sullied by a spitting incident on the side of the pitch following the last ball of the day. It brought an angry dressing-room complaint from Lara and a penalty from match referee Raman Subba Row that cost him 30 per cent of his match fee.

Lara's wicket reduced West Indies to 69 for 3, which became 105 for 4 by stumps and 105 for 5 first thing next morning through Healy's slick leg-side stumping of Adams off Miller's off-spin.

Griffith, the tall left-hander who had been forced to retire hurt the previous day by a numbing blow to the forearm from McGrath, kept going for four hours, 40 minutes all told. He had just raised his first Test half-century when he was ninth out, padding away MacGill's leg-break. He and the lower order kept the Australians waiting until 40 minutes before tea before they could claim victory but the outcome was never in doubt once Lara had been removed.

TEST MATCH AVERAGES
West Indies v. Australia

WEST INDIES

Batting	M	Inns	NO	HS	Runs	Av	100	50
BC Lara	4	7	1	213	546	91.00	3	1
SL Campbell	4	8	1	105	197	28.14	1	-
AFG Griffith	2	4	-	56	100	25.00	-	1
JC Adams	4	7	-	94	168	24.00	-	1
CL Hooper	2	4	-	47	90	22.50	-	-
RD Jacobs	4	7	-	68	143	20.42	-	1
DRE Joseph	4	7	-	50	141	20.14	-	1
NO Perry	3	5	1	26	71	17.75	-	-
CEL Ambrose	4	7	1	28*	53	8.83	-	-
CA Walsh	4	7	4	12	17	5.66	-	-
S Ragoonath	2	4	1	9	13	4.33	-	-
PT Collins	3	5	-	13	14	2.80	-	-

Played in one Test: CD Collymore 11* & 6; M Dillon 0 & 0; RIC Holder 0 & 4; LA Roberts 0

Bowling	Overs	Mds	Runs	Wkcts	Av	Best	10/m	5/inns
CA Walsh	208.1	38	539	26	20.73	5-39	-	1
CEL Ambrose	184.2	61	423	19	22.26	5-94	-	1
CL Hooper	56.2	12	153	5	30.60	3-69	-	-
NO Perry	102	19	326	10	32.60	5-70	-	1
PT Collins	113	19	361	8	45.12	3-79	-	-

Also bowled: JC Adams 37.2-6-107-3; CD Collymore 41-7-109-1; M Dillon 40.3-5-126-3

Fielding Figures
19 – RD Jacobs (17 ct/2 st); 10 – DRE Joseph; 6 – BC Lara; 5 – CL Hooper;
2 – SL Campbell; 1 – JC Adams, M Dillon, AFG Griffith, NO Perry, CA Walsh

AUSTRALIA

Batting	M	Inns	NO	HS	Runs	Av	100	50
SR Waugh	4	8	1	199	409	58.42	2	1
RT Ponting	2	4	1	104	168	56.00	1	-
JL Langer	4	8	-	127	291	36.37	1	2
MJ Slater	4	8	-	106	277	34.62	1	-
GS Blewett	3	6	-	58	160	26.66	-	1
ME Waugh	4	8	-	67	202	25.25	-	2
JN Gillespie	3	6	2	28*	95	23.75	-	-
SK Warne	3	6	-	32	138	23.00	-	-
GD McGrath	4	8	4	39	74	18.50	-	-
MTG Elliott	3	6	-	44	69	11.50	-	-
IA Healy	4	8	-	16	53	6.62	-	-
SCG MacGill	4	8	-	17	31	3.87	-	-

Played in one Test: AC Dale 1 & 0; CR Miller 43 & 1

Bowling	Overs	Mds	Runs	Wkts	Av	Best	10/m	5/inns
GD McGrath	199.4	59	508	30	16.93	5-28	1	4
JN Gillespie	108.2	36	241	11	21.90	4-18	-	-
SCG MacGill	119.3	30	352	12	29.33	3-41	-	-

Also bowled: GS Blewett 19-4-58-2; AC Dale 30-12-95-3; CR Miller 38-15-66-3;
RT Ponting 4-1-12-1; SK Warne 83.5-18-268-2; ME Waugh 5-0-24-0; SR Waugh 5-0-19-0

Fielding Figures
8 – IA Healy (7 ct/1 st); 7 – ME Waugh; 3 – MJ Slater, SK Warne; 2 – MTG Elliott;
1 – GS Blewett, JN Gillespie, SCG MacGill, CR Miller, RT Ponting, SR Waugh

ONE-DAY INTERNATIONAL SERIES

A memorable series came to an ugly end as crowds, for differing reasons, disrupted two of the last three one-day internationals.

It left Australian captain Steve Waugh, who was in real physical danger both times, warning of the future certainty of death on the field and Barbados Prime Minister Owen Arthur apologising 'to the cricket world' for the second, and more serious, disturbance in the final match in Bridgetown.

In the fifth match in Georgetown, hundreds of frenzied spectators from the overcrowded stands on the eastern side of Bourda twice stampeded across the outfield prior to and at the end of a close, tense match. Players were jostled, stumps seized and mayhem reigned as Steve Waugh and Warne attempted to sprint an unlikely third run off the last ball that would have tied the match and kept the series level.

After several viewings of the television replays, match referee Subba Row ruled the match a tie.

At Kensington Oval four days later, an angry capacity crowd reacted by throwing bottles on to the field in protest against the run-out of local favourite, Campbell. Scampering a quick single, he fell to the ground after his path was impeded by Julian, the bowler, but was ruled out by standing umpire, Eddie Nicholls.

As the Australians made for the sanctuary of their dressing room, a bottle thrown from the Sir Garfield Sobers Pavilion, the most expensive seats in the house, was seen on the global television coverage whizzing inches past Steve Waugh's head. Play was held up 45 minutes until Sobers himself was led on to the field to announce that, with the agreement of the Australians, Campbell would be allowed to continue. It was a decision later derided by the West Indies Cricket Umpires' Association.

Nor was the strife over. Steve Waugh told the press that one of the reasons his players resumed play was because the police commissioner could give no guarantee of their safety. It prompted a libel suit from commissioner Grantley Watson who claimed he was not even at the match and was not involved in discussions about the players' safety.

Sherwin Campbell appeals for obstruction by Brendon Julian in seventh one-day international at Kensington Oval. The incident caused bottles to be thrown. Campbell was later voted Man of the Series.
Gordon Brooks/Sportsline Photographic

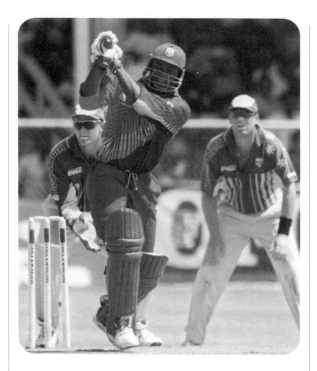

Ridley Jacobs hitting out in his knock of 54 in the seventh
one-day international at Kensington Oval.
Gordon Brooks/Sportsline Photographic

He sought costs and damages since Waugh's
comments had brought him into 'public ridicule'
and implied he was 'inept and not capable of
efficient performance of his duty'. The case
remained pending after several months.

Both teams hoped to use the seven matches as a
final dress rehearsal for the World Cup that
immediately followed but, well before the crowds
took over, such plans were rendered largely futile by
injuries to key players. McGrath did not play again
after spraining his ankle after one over of the opening
match and Dale not at all, returning to Australia to
recover from a bout of pneumonia. Lara took the last
three matches off to rest his injured right wrist and
Ambrose and Walsh were sparingly used.

Campbell was made Man of the Series for his
consistency (312 runs in the seven innings) but
Bevan's usual finishing power and Warne's return to
recognisable form challenged him hard.

There was only one century, Lehmann's unbeaten
110 at international cricket's newest venue, the
impressive new 20,000-capacity stadium in Grenada,
built on the site of the old first-class ground,
Queen's Park, that had staged a one-day
international against India in 1983.

Match One
11 April 1999 at Arnos Vale, Kingston, St Vincent
West Indies 209 (48.1 overs) SL Campbell 62
Australia 165 (41.5 overs) HR Bryan 4 for 24
West Indies won by 44 runs
Man of the Match: HR Bryan

Match Two
14 April 1999 at Queen's Park, St George's, Grenada
Australia 288 for 4 (50 overs) DS Lehmann 110*,
MB Bevan 72*
West Indies 242 (47.3 overs)
Australia won by 46 runs
Man of the Match: DS Lehmann

Match Three
17 April 1999 at Queen's Park Oval, Port-of-Spain
Australia 242 for 7 (50 overs) ME Waugh 74
West Indies 244 for 5 (49 overs) JC Adams 82,
SL Campbell 64, CL Hooper 56
West Indies won by five wickets
Man of the Match: JC Adams

Match Four
18 April 1999 at Queen's Park Oval, Port-of-Spain
Australia 189 for 9 (50 overs) MG Bevan 59*,
M Dillon 4 for 20
West Indies 169 (46.2 overs)
Australia won by 20 runs
Man of the Match: SK Warne

Match Five
21 April 1999 at Bourda, Georgetown
West Indies 173 for 5 (30 overs)
Australia 173 for 7 (30 overs) SR Waugh 72*
Match tied
Man of the Match: SR Waugh

Match Six
24 April 1999 at Kensington Oval, Bridgetown
West Indies 249 for 8 (50 overs) RD Jacobs 68
Australia 253 for 6 (48.3 overs) AC Gilchrist 64
Australia won by four wickets
Man of the Match: AC Gilchrist

Match Seven
25 April 1999 at Kensington Oval, Bridgetown
Australia 252 for 9 (50 overs) TM Moody 50*
West Indies 197 for 2 (37 overs) SL Campbell 62,
RD Jacobs 54
West Indies won by eight wickets (D/L Method)
Man of the Match: SL Campbell
Man of the Series: SL Campbell

BUSTA CUP
By Tony Cozier

'Something has to be done about our regional cricket before we start looking up again. Our problems are really deep-rooted.' Brian Lara's lament following West Indies' five-nil defeat in the Test series in South Africa was far from a lame excuse. It was a realistic assessment of a situation that was once more reflected in the 1999 first-class tournament, contested for the first time for the Busta Cup after the West Indies Cricket Board (WICB) gained new sponsorship from a Trinidad & Tobago soft-drink manufacturer.

A week later, Joey Carew, a selector and former Test opener, was echoing the sentiments of the man for whom he was an early tutor. 'We must raise the standard of our territorial cricket for us to be able to bridge the gap between first-class and Test cricket,' he said after watching a particularly limp batting performance by the Leeward Islands, the 1998 champions, against Barbados. 'If we are to judge by this performance, it is a sad day for West Indies batting.'

The statistics lent powerful support to such concerns. In the 17 matches of an extended season, including the semi-finals and final, there was only one total above 400 and four above 350. In contrast, there were 17 under 150. Only eight batsmen, half with Test experience, scored hundreds. Bowlers with five or more wickets in an innings numbered 16.

The problem had been identified by the former Test captain, Rohan Kanhai, and others some time ago as poor pitches that destroy the confidence and techniques of young batsmen. There was no improvement.

Winning four of their five preliminary matches, Barbados defeated Jamaica, the only team to hold out for an earlier draw, in the semi-final and beat Trinidad & Tobago by 160 runs in the final for their 16th championship since it was first initiated on an annual basis as the Shell Shield in 1966.

Trinidad & Tobago qualified in second place with 44 points and advanced to the final on first-innings lead in a rain-shortened semi-final. The Leeward Islands, the 1998 champions and a steady source of Test players in recent times, and the woeful Windward Islands occupied the nether reaches of the table.

Barbados were strongest in top-order batting and balanced bowling. Openers Sherwin Campbell and the left-handed Adrian Griffith were the highest scorers in the tournament and captain Roland Holder was among the eight batsmen in the tournament with over 300 runs. Campbell's 675 runs included two hundreds and were made at an average of 61.36. Griffith's 458 runs were at an average of 41.63. It was enough for all three to regain their Test places in the series against Australia although an ankle injury eliminated Holder after the first Test – and prevented him from playing in the Cup final as well.

Barbados' left-arm spinner Winston Reid, 36 and in his 14th season, was again a puzzle to opposing batsmen, collecting 47 wickets, only two fewer than the record of the Trinidad & Tobago leg-spinner Rajindra Dhanraj's record. It gained him the tournament's Most Valuable Player award. But, in spite of his effectiveness, season after season, Reid's age precluded him from the selectors' considerations.

He was an effective contrast to fast bowlers Corey Collymore, Hendy Bryan and Pedro Collins who claimed a collective 71 wickets. Their performances earned first Test caps for Collins, a slim left-armer who had done well on 'A' team tours to South Africa and India and Bangladesh, and for Collymore, 21 and in his first first-class season. Bryan, whose aggressive batting was a decisive factor in the Cup final, also made his international debut in the one-day internationals against Australia and was included in the World Cup squad.

Trinidad & Tobago were well led by the experienced Ian Bishop who got the best out of his younger players. Lincoln Roberts and Denis

Brian Lara.
David Munden/Sportsline Photographic

Rampersad, both attractive right-hand batsmen, accumulated more than 300 runs, the former attracting attention with a quality 151 against the Leewards Islands that brought him into the team for the second Test against Australia.

Trinidad & Tobago's chances in the final would have been appreciably boosted but for the wrist injury that prevented Brian Lara from joining them on his return from South Africa. Bishop himself, although past his best, Merv Dillon, back early from South Africa, and the strongly built Marlon Black formed a penetrative pace combination, consistently supported by the off-spin of Mookesh Prasad. Black, whose performances included a hat-trick against the Leeward Islands, and Prasad each had 24 wickets.

With Shivnarine Chanderpaul missing with the shoulder injury that also eliminated him from the Test series and Carl Hooper away with his ill infant son in Australia, the only Guyana batsman with more than 300 runs was the veteran left-hand opener, Clayton Lambert. Returning home after his omission from the one-day section of the ill-fated South African tour, he went past Desmond Haynes' record as the leading scorer in domestic cricket with 4,520 runs against Haynes' 4,431. He later announced his retirement. Their young batsmen were disappointing and Guyana had to rely more on an attack based on the pace of Colin Stuart (22 wickets) and Kevin Darlington (12) and the leg-spin of Mahendra Nagamatoo and off-spinner Garvin Nedd, who shared 40 wickets.

In Ricardo Powell, 20, Jamaica possessed the most exciting prospect of the year, a talented stroke-player who averaged 61 in his three matches, a tidy off-spinner and athletic fielder. When Hooper suddenly announced his retirement at the end of the season, Powell was drafted into the World Cup team in his place.

But Jamaica relied more on their established men. Jimmy Adams' tour to South Africa was ended before it began when he severed tendons on his right hand on the flight out but he recovered in time to skipper the team – and convince the Test selectors his left-handed versatility and experience were required for a team in need of rebuilding.

Nehemiah Perry, the tall 30-year-old off-spinner, enjoyed the best of his 12 first-class seasons with 30 wickets, another performance impressive enough for a place on the Test side for the first time.

The only consolation for the Leeward Islands for the loss of their championship was the batting of Dave Joseph that brought him into the Test side for

Barbados captain Philo Wallace.
David Munden/Sportsline Photographic

all four matches against the Australians. The heavy-set 29-year-old right-hander's 401 runs at 50.12 constituted his best season. But that had to be set against three losses in their five matches. One was against the Windward Islands when they were bowled out for 84 and 92.

The Windwards were no better. They were routed for 55 by Jamaica, 105 by Guyana, 119 and 131 by Barbados and 148 by Trinidad & Tobago. Nothing more emphatically accentuated Lara's concern over the standard of the tournament.

RED STRIPE BOWL

Off the field, the 1999 Red Stripe Bowl, the annual 50-overs championship, was spoiled by controversy and confusion in its showpiece climax, the Final Four Weekend. On it, bowling and fielding held sway.

Both the defending champions, the Leeward Islands, and Trinidad & Tobago turned up to contest the final against Guyana after the match referee's erroneous decision to award Trinidad & Tobago victory in the rain-shortened semi-final was overturned by a complaints committee on appeal.

The committee's verdict did stand but the Trinidadians were making a point. Their captain Brian Lara called the situation 'unprofessional'. The Leeward Islands' manager, Carlisle Powell, used the word 'farce'. One newspaper headlined it the 'Red Strife Bowl'.

The championship, at last, went to Guyana. They had reached the final in each of the previous three seasons without winning it. Now, they were the only unbeaten team, comfortably defeating the Leeward Islands by 52 runs, reversing the 1997 result to take the Bowl.

The Leewards could have no excuses. When they complained that two players had to share the same bed at a resort hotel on Jamaica's north coast designed for couples, not cricket teams, they were moved to suitable accommodation. One fast bowler noted he had never slept with a man before and didn't intend to start now. The other teams, presumably not as fussy, stayed where they were.

Guyana were assisted by the breaks that had previously eluded them. Their two most difficult matches, against Trinidad & Tobago in the qualifying round in Georgetown and against Barbados in the semi-final at the unpretentious Alpart Sports Club ground in Discovery Bay, Jamaica, were both abandoned to rain with the contests evenly balanced.

The format was reduced from the first year of the Bowl with only one round of group matches, instead of two, leading straight to the semi-finals, eliminating the redundant quarter-finals.

Guyana and Trinidad & Tobago were clear-cut qualifiers from the Guyana group although there was doubt whether the official decision that placed Guyana as group winners was correct. Both beat the disappointing Windward Islands and Bermuda who were missing several key players for disciplinary reasons and were soundly beaten in all three of their matches.

The Jamaica group was more competitive. The United States, solely comprising players of West Indian, Indian or Pakistani origin, were outclassed in their first entry under the pre-arrangement by which they alternate with Canada, leaving Barbados, the Leeward Islands and Jamaica to battle out the two semi-final places. In the end, Jamaica were eliminated, an ironic twist to the sponsors' demand that the Final Four Weekend – the semis and the final – be staged in Jamaica.

The 15 matches yielded only one total over 250 – the Leeward Islands' 330 for 4 against the USA – and only three individual hundreds. Two were against the USA by new Leeward Islands' opener Wilden Cornwall (126) and Barbados captain Philo Wallace (104 not out) and the other Shivnarine Chanderpaul's 112 for Guyana against Barbados in the first aborted semi-final.

Just a few days before their departure for the South African tour, the tournament was boosted by the participation of all the leading players. They generally dominated.

Guyana batsman Clayton Lambert.
David Munden/Sportsline Photographic

BRIAN LARA

West Indies cricket was in a state of depression it had never before experienced. The team had just been routed by Australia for 51, their lowest total in 71 years of Test cricket, losing their sixth successive Test, following the unprecedented five–nil drubbing in South Africa that was completed six weeks earlier. Three more Tests and seven one–day internationals lay ahead against the toughest opponents in the international game. The immediate future looked even bleaker than the recent past.

BY TONY COZIER

Brian Lara, opposite page, and below playing Australia in April.
Gordon Brooks/David Munden/Sportsline Photographic

Seldom far away from controversy throughout his turbulent career, Brian Lara had been stripped of his captaincy by the West Indies Cricket Board (WICB) less than six months earlier and then reinstated to end a players' strike that placed the much anticipated South African tour in jeopardy. Now he bore the brunt of the blame for the debacle that ensued.

The upshot was a stinging rebuke from the WICB which blamed 'weaknesses in leadership' for the defeat although it stopped short of bowing to widespread public demands that Lara be dismissed, this time for good.

Instead, it placed him on probation for two Tests and told him he needed 'to make significant improvement in his leadership skills'.

In the first Test, at the Queen's Park Oval where he had honed his extraordinary natural talent since he was a boy, Lara's world that had been in repeated danger of falling apart seemed to be finally crumbling around him.

Yet, for all the extraordinary pressure he was under, he for once saw clearly and simply what was required.

'I think it's important for myself and for West Indies cricket that I try my best to solve my batting problems

and see how best I can go out and get similar scores like I used to four years ago,' he told the assembled media on the day of the all-out 51.

The logic was self-evident, especially since two of his main batsmen, Shivnarine Chanderpaul and Carl Hooper, were missing. Chanderpaul's shoulder injury would eliminate him from the series altogether, Hooper would not return from his son's side in Australia until the third Test .

The challenge to Lara was to carry it out – and the evidence was unconvincing.

The scores of four years earlier to which he referred had carried him to heights no other batsman had reached before. His 375 in the final Test against England at the Antigua Recreation Ground and his unbeaten 501 for his English county, Warwickshire, against Durham were made in the space of six weeks, both new records.

The fame and fortune that immediately engulfed him proved bothersome distractions. His appetite for batting gradually, but certainly, deserted him. His average plummeted from over 60 to just under 50 and he had not managed a hundred for 15 Tests. There was justifiable concern about his future.

What happened next was nothing short of miraculous.

Less than a week after the Queen's Park collapse, Lara was making good his assertion to the press. In six hours of a sunlit Saturday afternoon at Kingston's Sabina Park, on the second day of the second Test, he set about the Australian bowlers with a devastating brilliance they had first experienced in the lithe left-hander's 277 at Sydney six years earlier, his maiden Test hundred. His boundary-filled 213 inspired an implausible but emphatic victory and instantly lifted the gloom hanging over him and West Indies.

There was yet more to come. In what was widely hailed as one of the greatest innings ever played in one of the greatest Tests ever played, Lara's unbeaten, last-day 153 virtually single-handedly carried West Indies to another stirring triumph, with a single wicket intact, in the next match at Kensington Oval.

They were mighty efforts, occupying 14 hours all told, that drained him physically and mentally. He still managed another breathtaking performance in the first innings of the final Test but his even hundred, from 84 balls, was a cameo, not an epic, and it could not save his still fragile team from the defeat that allowed Australia to retain the Frank Worrell Trophy.

It was as impossible to judge how much the whole episode had taken out of Lara as to identify the cause of his own regeneration and that of his team.

He could bring himself to play only three matches in the subsequent one-day internationals against Australia, citing a lingering wrist injury for his withdrawal. He made no impact on the World Cup that immediately followed.

Lara, no doubt conscious of the Board's admonition to improve his 'leadership skills', credited his team with the revival.

'It was a whole, all-round effort not only by me but by everyone,' he said. 'You've got to realise that no one individual could be responsible for something as disastrous as South Africa.'

'I've played a part and I must hold some sort of responsibility but I've improved as a person, even outside of cricket, living my life day-to-day, and that's important," he added. 'As you get older, you get wiser, I suppose.'

They were humble words from a superstar not previously associated with humility. West Indians wait impatiently to discover whether the change is permanent for they know that the fortunes of their Test team are inseparable from those of the mercurial captain.

They should have their answer by the time Lara leads the team to England in the first summer of the third millennium.

FIRST-CLASS AVERAGES

BATTING

	M	Inns	NO	HS	Runs	Av	100	50
BC Lara	4	7	1	213	546	91.00	3	1
RT Ponting	4	8	2	104	317	52.83	1	1
SL Campbell	11	21	3	169*	872	48.44	3	4
SR Waugh	6	11	1	199	483	48.30	2	2
AFG Griffith	10	19	3	93	596	37.25	-	5
RL Powell	5	8	1	114*	260	37.14	1	1
CB Lambert	5	9	0	102	334	37.11	1	1
DRE Joseph	10	18	1	123*	619	36.41	2	4
JL Langer	7	13	0	134	468	36.00	2	2
ME Waugh	5	9	0	106	308	34.22	1	2
CL Hooper	3	6	0	102	202	33.66	1	-
RIC Holder	7	12	1	72	370	33.63	-	4
JC Adams	10	18	2	100*	537	33.56	1	3
MJ Slater	7	13	0	106	428	32.92	1	-
LA Roberts	8	11	0	151	360	32.72	1	1
D Ganga	4	7	0	92	220	31.42	-	1
GS Blewett	6	11	1	58	343	31.18	-	3
DA Joseph	5	9	2	69*	218	31.14	-	1
SC Williams	5	9	0	145	275	30.55	1	1
PV Simmons	7	11	1	82*	299	29.90	-	3
D Rampersad	8	13	1	84	355	29.58	-	2
RAM Smith	7	11	2	98	243	27.00	-	1
TO Powell	6	10	1	95*	239	26.55	-	1
MV Nagamatoo	6	11	1	64	248	24.80	-	2
S Ragoonath	8	15	1	61	342	24.42	-	4
RR Sarwan	6	11	0	87	262	23.81	-	1
WW Hinds	8	15	1	126	328	23.42	1	1
DK Marshall	4	6	1	71	115	23.00	-	1
WE Reid	7	8	2	57	136	22.66	-	1
MTG Elliott	6	11	0	115	244	22.18	1	-
LC Romero	4	6	0	48	131	21.83	-	-
RJJ McLean	6	11	0	65	238	21.63	-	2
BS Murphy	5	7	1	39*	129	21.50	-	-
NO Perry	9	15	1	59	300	21.42	-	2
IR Bishop	7	9	1	52	165	20.62	-	1
JN Gillespie	4	7	2	28*	102	20.40	-	-
CO Browne	7	10	0	72	203	20.30	-	1
AR Percival	5	9	1	51	162	20.25	-	1
RO Hinds	8	13	2	58	213	19.36	-	1
SK Warne	6	10	0	32	190	19.00	-	-
RD Jacobs	5	8	0	68	149	18.62	-	1
DS Smith	5	9	0	79	166	18.44	-	1
CH Gayle	6	11	1	53	182	18.20	-	1
RS Morton	5	9	0	45	161	17.88	-	-
HR Waldron	3	5	0	31	86	17.20	-	-
LR Williams	6	10	1	40	148	16.44	-	-
NAM McLean	3	6	1	30	81	16.20	-	-
GD McGrath	5	9	4	39	78	15.60	-	-
WW Cornwall	3	5	0	38	78	15.60	-	-
PA Wallace	3	5	0	33	75	15.00	-	-
SC Joseph	3	6	0	31	89	14.83	-	-
FA Adams	3	6	0	46	87	14.50	-	-
J Parillon	5	9	0	41	122	13.55	-	-
LV Garrick	5	9	0	36	122	13.55	-	-
LJ Cush	6	11	0	59	148	13.45	-	-
MG Sinclair	5	7	1	44*	80	13.33	-	-
CM Tuckett	5	9	1	43	104	13.00	-	-
RA Marshall	5	9	0	47	117	13.00	-	-
J Williams	4	8	2	36*	78	13.00	-	-
D Williams	7	10	1	28	116	12.88	-	-
IA Healy	7	12	0	42	150	12.50	-	-
V Nagamatoo	5	9	0	36	112	12.44	-	-
KG Darlington	4	8	3	18	56	11.20	-	-
MD Ventura	3	6	1	21	56	11.20	-	-
WD Phillip	3	5	0	42	56	11.20	-	-
BM Watt	5	9	0	44	97	10.77	-	-
KCG Benjamin	4	7	1	28	63	10.50	-	-

Qualification: 5 completed innings, average 10.00

FIRST-CLASS AVERAGES

BOWLING

	Overs	Mds	Runs	Wkts	Av	Best	10m	5/inns
RA Marshall	160.3	42	302	21	14.38	6–32	1	2
SCG MacGill	187.4	54	493	32	15.40	7–29	1	2
HR Bryan	104.5	20	337	21	16.04	5–57	-	2
WE Reid	312.4	89	766	47	16.29	8–77	1	3
GD McGrath	221.4	64	567	33	17.18	5–28	1	4
CE Cuffy	121.1	26	264	15	17.60	4–49	-	-
MJ Morgan	93.2	18	252	14	18.00	4–42	-	-
CD Collymore	219.5	44	607	33	18.39	4–42	-	-
M Dillon	164.3	34	455	23	19.78	6–46	-	1
MV Nagamootoo	201.1	56	445	22	20.22	6–24	1	1
CEL Stuart	157	32	449	22	20.40	4–81	-	-
CA Walsh	208.1	38	539	26	20.73	5–39	-	1
MI Black	147.5	30	506	24	21.08	6–23	-	1
BS Murphy	166	39	405	19	21.31	4–85	-	-
M Persad	224.4	55	523	24	21.79	6–86	1	1
CEL Ambrose	184.2	61	423	19	22.26	5–94	-	1
NO Perry	372.5	98	896	40	22.40	7–49	1	3
LR Williams	145	36	354	15	23.60	4–36	-	-
D Mais	179.4	50	496	21	23.61	4–64	-	-
CM Tuckett	113.4	25	306	11	27.81	4–16	-	-
PT Collins	319	61	976	32	30.50	5–64	-	1
IR Bishop	161.2	22	456	14	32.57	3–47	-	-
PV Simmons	122.2	27	346	10	34.60	3–20	-	-
SK Warne	162.5	37	508	11	46.18	3–26	-	-

Qualification: 10 wickets in 8 innings

The following players took 10 wickets in fewer than 8 innings:-

AC Dale	102.4	41	232	18	12.88	7–24	-	2
WD Phillip	124.3	33	262	16	16.37	5–48	1	2
GH Nedd	136	32	315	18	17.50	6–23	-	1
NC McGarrell	115	31	228	13	17.53	5–21	-	1
CL Hooper	99.2	22	246	14	17.57	5–53	-	1
JC Maynard	67.1	5	238	11	21.63	5–24	-	1
RD King	77.2	15	221	10	22.10	5–75	-	1
CA Davis	78.3	20	222	10	22.20	5–60	-	1
KG Darlington	113	27	298	12	24.83	5–29	-	1
JN Gillespie	129.2	41	297	11	27.00	4–18	-	-
KCG Benjamin	136.4	24	384	14	27.42	4–34	-	-
NAM McLean	87.3	15	306	11	27.81	3–26	-	-
AJA Lake	148.5	26	472	10	47.20	4–50	-	-

FIELDING

32 – CO Browne (23 ct/9 st); 25 – RD Jacobs (22 ct/3 st); 21 – D Williams (19 ct/2 st);
20 – IA Healy (15 ct/5 st); 18 – MG Sinclair (17 ct/1 st); 13 – DRE Joseph, WD Phillip;
12 – TO Powell; 10 – LV Garrick, LC Romero; 9 – V Nagamatoo (7 ct/2 st), SL Campbell,
AFG Griffith, MV Nagamatoo, ME Waugh, J Williams; 8 – AR Percival, NO Perry, RAM Smith

INDIA

PAKISTAN IN INDIA
By Qamar Ahmed

After three previous attempts by Pakistan to tour India were called off because of the threats to disrupt the matches by Hindu extremists, Pakistan did well to take up the challenge and visit the neighbouring country at last for its first Test series in India in 12 years. The opposition to Pakistan touring India from Bal Thackeray and the followers of Shiv Sena was intense.

Their anger was directed at Pakistan because of their party's claim that Pakistan was responsible for the border skirmishes in the disputed region of Kashmir. Pakistan have always denied these allegations.

The pitch at the Feroze Shah Kotla Ground at Delhi was severely damaged by the activists prior to Pakistan's visit. Protesting demonstrators took to the streets of Mumbai and Delhi. So, too, did those in favour of the visit. The headquarters of the Board of Control for Cricket in India (BCCI) was ransacked and its officials manhandled as the anger escalated.

Venkatesh Prasad finished with figures 6 for 33 in the second innings of the first Test against Pakistan.

David Munden/Sportsline Photographic

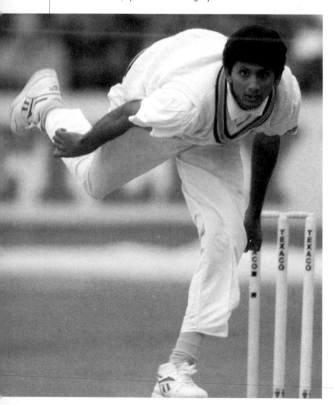

In danger of being declared an outcast from the coalition government of India, Bal Thackeray and his party relented and withdrew their threats only a day before Pakistan landed in India. They arrived amidst unprecedented security: even snake charmers were engaged in case the reptiles were unleashed during matches, as Shiv Sena had threatened.

The two-match Test series ended without any incident, which was a big victory for both cricket and diplomacy. The Tests at Chennai and Delhi were dominated by the spinners and ended on the fourth day. The matches were watched by packed houses: 50,000 turned up on each day at Chennai where Pakistan won a close match by only 12 runs, and nearly 35,000 turned up every day in Delhi where India squared the series. Thousands of security men guarded the grounds to prevent any unsavoury incidents.

The domination of the spinners was such that most of the wickets were shared by the off-spinner Saqlain Mushtaq and leg-spinner Anil Kumble. Taking five wickets in an innings four times, Saqlain finished with 20 wickets in two Tests at an average of 20.15 and Kumble bagged 21 at 14.66 apiece. In the second innings of the second Test, Kumble captured all ten wickets as Pakistan chased 420 to win. He devastated Pakistan with 10 for 74 to finish with 14 for 149 in the match, thus becoming only the second man in Test cricket's 122-year history to take all ten wickets. Surrey and England off-spinner Jim Laker had taken 10 for 53 against Australia at Old Trafford in 1956 to claim 19 for 90 in the match. Kumble's feat was watched by one Richard Stoke who had also happened to see Laker's great bowling performance as a ten-year-old.

The feature of the series was an innings of sterling quality by Sachin Tendulkar who made 136 in the first Test at Chennai to so nearly snatch victory from Pakistan. Shahid Afridi playing in only his second Test at Chennai scored a maiden Test century (141). Left-hander Sadagopan Ramesh, 24, who made his debut in the first Test, was unlucky to miss his maiden hundred in the second Test by four runs. He impressed everyone with his consistency and topped the averages with 204 runs in the series at an average of 51.00.

The drawn series was described by both captains, Wasim Akram and Mohammad Azharuddin, as a 'fair result'. In the end, hatred was defeated. So, too, were the detractors who had opposed the tour, and cricket succeeded once again in building bridges between the neighbouring countries.

FIRST TEST
28, 29, 30 and 31 January 1999 at Madras

In an exciting finish, Pakistan won the game by 12 runs. Saqlain Mushtaq with 10 for 187 was mainly responsible for providing Pakistan with a one-nil lead in the two-match series. India, after being set a target of 271 to win, were bowled out for 258 in their second innings. From a hopeless 85 for 5, India salvaged their innings through a 136-run sixth-wicket stand between Nayan Mongia and Sachin Tendulkar to get near to their target. But Mongia's dismissal by Wasim Akram when at 52 – and later

Mohammad Azharuddin captained India in both Test matches against Pakistan.

David Munden/Sportsline Photographic

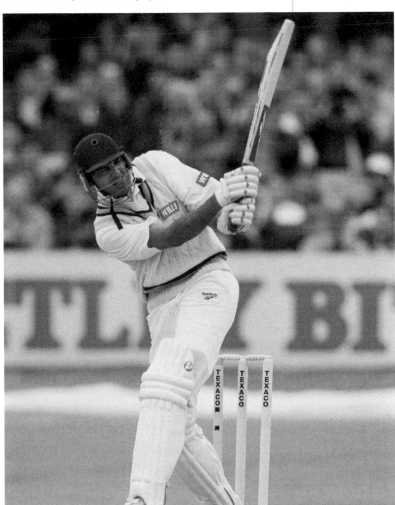

that of Tendulkar by Saqlain Mushtaq after he had made 136 – turned the game around. India had needed only 17 more runs to win the match when Tendulkar was out, but the tail failed to wag.

Struggling at 91 for 5 after having won the toss, Pakistan recovered remarkably to make 238 in their first innings. Moin Khan and Yousuf Youhana came to the rescue with 63 and 60 runs respectively. Moin added 63 runs for the sixth wicket with Youhana and 50 with Wasim Akram for the seventh wicket. Anil Kumble with 6 for 70, his 12th five-wicket haul in Tests did most of the damage. India, resuming at 48 for 0 from overnight, lost four wickets for 125 at lunch on the second day, but collapsed to be all out for 254 after tea. Tendulkar was out for 0 off Saqlain Mushtaq, his fourth duck in 98 Test innings. Saurav Ganguly scored 54 to add 53 for the fifth wicket with Rahul Dravid. Saqlain with 5 for 94 his sixth haul of five wickets, had put Pakistan back in the game.

At the start of play on the third morning, Pakistan led India by 18 runs with nine wickets in hand. Shahid Afridi, batting in an uncharacteristic fashion, added 97 with Inzamam-ul-Haq for the third wicket, and 106 for the fifth wicket with Salim Malik to reach his maiden Test century in only his second Test. He hit 21 fours and three sixes in his 141, which took him 305 minutes and 191 balls. After being 274 for 4, Pakistan slid to 286 all out as Venkatesh Prasad picked up five wickets in 18 balls without conceding a run. Prasad finished with 6 for 33, his best in Tests. India, at 40 for 2, were chasing 271 to win on the fourth day. The previous highest total that India had scored to win at home was 256 for 8 against Australia at the Brebourne Stadium at Mumbai in 1964. The odds were against them, but Tendulkar seemed intent on rewriting the record books. He made a brilliant 136 but, in the end, it was in vain.

FIRST TEST – INDIA v. PAKISTAN
28, 29, 30 and 31 January 1999 at MA Chidambaram Stadium, Madras

PAKISTAN

	First Innings			Second Innings	
Saeed Anwar	lbw, b Srinath	24		lbw, b Prasad	7
Shahid Afridi	c Ganguly, b Srinath	11		b Prasad	141
Ijaz Ahmed	lbw, b Kumble	13		c and b Kumble	11
Inzamam-ul-Haq	c and b Kumble	10		c Laxman, b Tendulkar	51
Yousuf Youhana	lbw, b Tendulkar	53		b Tendulkar	26
Salim Malik	b Srinath	8		c Dravid, b Joshi	32
*Moin Khan	c Ganguly, b Kumble	60		c Mongia, b Prasad	3
Wasim Akram (capt)	c Laxman, b Kumble	38		c Joshi, b Prasad	1
Saqlain Mushtaq	c Laxman, b Kumble	2		lbw, b Prasad	0
Nadeem Khan	c Dravid, b Kumble	8		not out	1
Waqar Younis	not out	0		c Ramesh, b Prasad	5
	lb 5, nb 6	11		b 1, lb 4, nb 3	8
		238			**286**

	First Innings				Second Innings			
	O	M	R	W	O	M	R	W
Srinath	15	3	63	3	16	1	68	-
Prasad	16	1	54	-	10.2	5	33	6
Kumble	24.5	7	70	6	22	4	93	1
Joshi	21	8	36	1	14	3	42	1
Tendulkar	3	0	10	1	7	1	35	2
Laxman					2	0	10	-

Fall of Wickets
1-32, 2-41, 3-61, 4-66, 5-91, 6-154, 7-214, 8-227, 9-237
1-11, 2-42, 3-139, 4-169, 5-275, 6-278, 7-279, 8-279, 9-280

INDIA

	First Innings			Second Innings	
S Ramesh	lbw, b Wasim Akram	43		c Inzamam-ul-Haq, b Waqar	5
VVS Laxman	lbw, b Wasim Akram	23		lbw, b Waqar Younis	0
RS Dravid	lbw, b Saqlain Mushtaq	53		b Wasim Khan	10
SR Tendulkar	c Salim Malik, b Saqlain	0		c Wasim Akram, b Saqlain	136
M Azharuddin (capt)	c Inzamam-ul-Haq, b Saqlain	11		lbw, b Saqlain Mushtaq	7
SC Ganguly	c Ijaz Ahmed, b Shahid Afridi	54		c Moin Khan, b Saqlain	2
*NR Mongia	st Moin Khan, b Saqlain	5		c Waqar Younis, b Wasim	52
A Kumble	c Yousuf Youhana, b Saqlain	4		(9) lbw, b Wasim Akram	1
SB Joshi	not out	25		(8) c and b Saqlain Mushtaq	8
J Srinath	c Ijaz Ahmed, b Shahid Afridi	10		b Saqlain Mushtaq	1
BKV Prasad	st Moin Khan, b Shahid Afridi	4		not out	0
	b 2, lb 2, nb 18	22		b 8, lb 10, nb 18	36
		254			**258**

	First Innings				Second Innings			
	O	M	R	W	O	M	R	W
Wasim Akram	20	4	60	2	22	4	80	3
Waqar Younis	12	2	48	-	12	6	26	2
Saqlain Mushtaq	35	8	94	5	32.2	8	93	5
Shahid Afridi	7.1	0	31	3	16	7	23	-
Nadeem Khan	7	0	17	-	13	5	18	-

Fall of Wickets
1-67, 2-71, 3-72, 4-103, 5-156, 6-166, 7-188, 8-229, 9-246
1-5, 2-6, 3-50, 4-73, 5-82, 6-218, 7-254, 8-256, 9-256

Umpires: VK Ramaswamy & RS Dunne
Toss: Pakistan

Pakistan won by 12 runs

SECOND TEST
4, 5, 6 and 7 February 1999 at Delhi

For the Indian leg-spinner Anil Kumble, this was a Test of which dreams are made. He took all ten wickets in the Pakistan second innings to return match figures of 14 for 149. His 10 for 74 in the Pakistan's run chase of 420 enabled him to become only the second man after England's Jim Laker to ten wickets in a single innings.

Pakistan, set a target of 420 to win, were all out for 207 on the fourth evening. At 101 for 0 at lunch, they seemed to have taken up the challenge. But in 20.3 overs, Kumble proceeded to dash their hopes. His ten wickets – all taken after lunch at a cost of 47 runs – turned the tide in India's favour as Pakistan batsmen succumbed on a pitch of uneven bounce and to a couple of debatable decisions by the home

Inzamam-ul-Haq is out, bowled by Kumble as Kumble takes all ten wickets in the second innings at the Delhi Test match.
Mueen-ud-din-Hameed/Sportsline Photographic

umpire AV Jayaprakash. Kumble had Shahid Afridi caught at the wicket for 41 and Ijaz Ahmed leg before next ball, but Inzamam-ul-Haq managed to avert the hat-trick. He later played on to his stumps, Yousuf Youhana was leg before and Moin Khan taken at slip as Pakistan slumped from 101 for 0 to 128 for 5. Saeed Anwar, having resisted for two and a half hours for his 69, was caught off bat and pad to give 6 for 27 in 44 balls. He was now well in sight of his record haul.

Resuming at 173 for 6 after tea, Salim Malik, having put on 56 for the seventh wicket with his captain Wasim Akram, was leg before as he pulled and missed. Kumble then had Mushtaq Ahmed taken at gully. Saqlain Mushtaq, hit on the toe, was leg before and, for the second time in the match, Kumble was on a hat-trick. At the other end, Javagal Srinath was instructed to bowl wide of the stumps to allow his partner to take his tenth wicket, Wasim Akram. The leg-spinner was mobbed by his colleagues, lifted on their shoulders and greeted with a standing ovation.

Mongia catches Afridi, another of Kumble's ten victims at the Delhi Test.
Mueen-ud-din-Hameed/Sportsline Photographic

PEPSI CUP TRI-NATION TOURNAMENT

Not long after their triumph in the Asian Test Championship, Pakistan added yet another trophy by winning the tri-nation one-day Pepsi Cup which had replaced the three-match one-day series in Pakistan's original tour itinerary of India. Maintaining their peak form, Pakistan won four of the matches including the final at Bangalore's KSCA stadium where they beat India by 123 runs. India had two victories – both against Sri Lanka who performed poorly to win only a solitary game against Pakistan at Vishakhapatnam.

The competition started with Pakistan beating Sri Lanka at Jamshedpur by nine runs. Pakistan made 246 for 9 with the help of two fine innings by Saeed Anwar and Shahid Afridi who put on 148 for the first wicket. Sri Lanka were bowled out for 237 in an exciting finish despite Aravinda de Silva's 81 and Mahela Jayawardene's 60. In the second match of the Cup at Nagpur, India beat Sri Lanka by 80 runs. For India, Saurav Ganguly carried his bat through for 130 and Rahul Dravid made 116 adding 236 for the second wicket with Ganguly who later took 4 for 21.

SECOND TEST – INDIA v. PAKISTAN
4, 5, 6 and 7 February 1999 at Feroze Shah Kotla, Delhi

INDIA

	First Innings		Second Innings	
S Ramesh	b Saqlain Mushtaq	60	c and b Mushtaq Ahmed	96
VVS Laxman	b Wasim Akram	35	b Wasim Akram	8
RS Dravid	lbw, b Saqlain Mushtaq	33	c Ijaz Ahmed, b Saqlain	29
SR Tendulkar	lbw, b Saqlain Mushtaq	6	c Wasim, b Mushtaq Ahmed	29
M Azharuddin (capt)	c Ijaz, b Mushtaq Ahmed	67	b Wasim Akram	14
SC Ganguly	lbw, b Mushtaq Ahmed	13	not out	62
*NR Mongia	run out (Shahid Afridi)	10	lbw, b Wasim Akram	0
A Kumble	c Yousuf Youhana, b Saqlain	0	c Ijaz Ahmed, b Saqlain	15
J Srinath	lbw, b Saqlain Mushtaq	0	lbw, b Saqlain Mushtaq	49
BKV Prasad	not out	1	b Saqlain Mushtaq	6
Harbhajan Singh	run out (Wasim Akram/ Moin Khan)	1	b Saqlain Mushtaq	0
	b 13, lb 7, nb 6	26	b 13, lb 9, nb 9	31
		252		**339**

	First Innings				Second Innings			
	O	M	R	W	O	M	R	W
Wasim Akram	13	3	23	1	21	3	43	3
Waqar Younis	13	5	37	-	12	2	42	-
Saqlain Mushtaq	35.5	9	94	5	46.4	12	122	5
Mushtaq Ahmed	26	5	64	2	26	4	86	2
Shahid Afridi	4	1	14	-	8	1	24	-

Fall of Wickets
1–88, 2–113, 3–122, 4–191, 5–231, 6–240, 7–243, 8–247, 9–248
1–15, 2–100, 3–168, 4–183, 5–199, 6–199, 7–231, 8–331, 9–339

PAKISTAN

	First Innings		Second Innings	
Saeed Anwar	c Mongia, b Prasad	1	c Laxman, b Kumble	69
Shahid Afridi	b Harbhajan Singh	32	c Mongia, b Kumble	41
Ijaz Ahmed	c Dravid, b Kumble	17	lbw, b Kumble	0
Inzamam-ul-Haq	b Kumble	26	b Kumble	6
Yousuf Youhana	c and b Kumble	3	lbw, b Kumble	0
Salim Malik	c Azharuddin, b Prasad	31	(7) b Kumble	15
*Moin Khan	lbw, b Srinath	14	(6) c Ganguly, b Kumble	3
Wasim Akram (capt)	lbw, b Harbhajan Singh	15	c Laxman, b Kumble	37
Mushtaq Ahmed	c Laxman, b Harbhajan Singh	12	c Dravid, b Kumble	1
Saqlain Mushtaq	lbw, b Kumble	2	lbw, b Kumble	0
Waqar Younis	not out	1	not out	6
	b 1, lb 8, nb 9	18	b 15, lb 2, w 2, nb 10	29
		172		**207**

	First Innings				Second Innings			
	O	M	R	W	O	M	R	W
Srinath	12	1	38	1	12	2	50	-
Prasad	11	2	20	2	4	1	15	-
Harbhajan Singh	17	5	30	3	18	5	51	-
Kumble	24.3	4	75	4	26.3	9	74	10

Fall of Wickets
1–1, 2–54, 3–54, 4–60, 5–114, 6–130, 7–139, 8–167, 9–168
1–101, 2–101, 3–115, 4–115, 5–127, 6–128, 7–186, 8–199, 9–199

Umpires: AV Jayaprakash & SA Bucknor
Toss: India

India won by 212 runs

TEST MATCH AVERAGES
India v. Pakistan

INDIA

Batting	M	Inns	NO	HS	Runs	Av	100	50
S Ramesh	2	4	-	96	204	51.00	-	2
SC Ganguly	2	4	1	62*	131	43.66	-	2
SR Tendulkar	2	4	-	136	171	42.75	1	-
RS Dravid	2	4	-	53	125	31.25	-	1
M Azharuddin	2	4	-	67	99	24.75	-	1
NR Mongia	2	4	-	52	67	16.75	-	1
VVS Laxman	2	4	-	35	66	16.50	-	-
J Srinath	2	4	-	49	60	15.00	-	-
BKV Prasad	2	4	2	6	11	5.50	-	-
A Kumble	2	4	-	15	20	5.00	-	-

Played in one Test: Harbhajan Singh 1 & 0; SB Joshi 25* & 8

Bowling	Overs	Mds	Runs	Wkts	Av	Best	10/m	5/inns
A Kumble	97.5	24	312	21	14.85	10–74	1	2
B K V Prasad	41.2	9	122	8	15.25	6–33	-	1

Also bowled: Harbhajan Singh 35–10–81–3; SB Joshi 35–11–78–1; VVS Laxman 2–0–10–0;
J Srinath 55–7–219–4; SR Tendulkar 10–1–45–3

Fielding Figures
6 – VVS Laxman; 4 – RS Dravid; 3 – SC Ganguly, A Kumble, NR Mongia;
1 – M Azharuddin, SB Joshi, S Ramesh

PAKISTAN

Batting	M	Inns	NO	HS	Runs	Av	100	50
Shahid Afridi	2	4	-	141	225	56.25	1	-
Saeed Anwar	2	4	-	69	101	25.25	-	1
Inzamam-ul-Haq	2	4	-	51	93	23.25	-	1
Wasim Akram	2	4	-	38	91	22.75	-	-
Salim Malik	2	4	-	32	86	21.50	-	-
Yousuf Youhana	2	4	-	53	82	20.50	-	1
Moin Khan	2	4	-	60	80	20.00	-	1
Waqar Younis	2	4	3	6*	12	12.00	-	-
Ijaz Ahmed	2	4	-	17	41	10.25	-	-
Saqlain Mushtaq	2	4	-	2	4	1.00	-	-

Played in one Test: Mushtaq Ahmed 12 & 1; Nadeem Khan 8 & l*

Bowling	Overs	Mds	Runs	Wkts	Av	Best	10/m	5/inns
Saqlain Mushtaq	149.5	37	403	20	20.15	5–93	2	4
Wasim Akram	76	14	206	9	22.88	3–43	-	-

Also bowled: Mushtaq Ahmed 52–9–150–4; Nadeem Khan 20–5–35–0;
Shahid Afridi 35.1–9–92–3; Waqar Younis 49–15–153–2

Fielding Figures
6 – Ijaz Ahmed; 3 – Moin Khan (1 ct/2 st); 2 – Inzamam-ul-Haq, Wasim Akram, Yousuf Youhana;
1 – Mushtaq Ahmed, Salim Malik, Saqlain Mushtaq, Waqar Younis

In the match at Jaipur, Pakistan had their second win of the Cup when they beat India by 143 runs. In reply to Pakistan's 278 for 9, India were bowled out for 135 in 36.1 overs. Off-spinner Arshad Khan claimed 3 for 22 while Saeed Anwar, in making 95, reached 6,000 runs in one-day games in his 164th international. At Vishakhapatnam, Sri Lanka had their only taste of victory. Their 253 for 8 was helped by 101 by Jayawardene. Pakistan were bowled out for 241 in the 47th over. However, Sri Lanka's joy was short-lived – in the next game they were beaten by India by 51 runs to go out of the contest. They allowed India to make 286 for 6, Ajay Jadeja hammering their bowling for 103 in 102 balls, and were then dismissed for 235 in the 46th over. Saurav Ganguly was the Man of the Series for his all-round performances. He made 298 runs at an average of 74.5, and took 6 wickets for 101 at 16.8.

Match One – Pakistan v. Sri Lanka
19 March 1999 at Keenan Stadium, Jamshedpur
Pakistan 246 for 9 (50 overs) Saeed Anwar 72, Shahid Afridi 71, GP Wickremasinghe 4 for 48
Sri Lanka 237 (49.3 overs) de Silva 81, Jayawardene 60
Pakistan won by 9 runs
Man of the Match: Wasim Akram

Match Two – India v. Sri Lanka
22 March 1999 at Vidarbha CA Ground, Nagpur
India 287 for 4 (50 overs) SC Ganguly 130*, RS Dravid 116
Sri Lanka 207 (38 overs) SC Ganguly 4 for 21
India won by 80 runs
Man of the Match: SC Ganguly

Match Three – India v. Pakistan
24 March 1999 at Mansarover Stadium, Jaipur
Pakistan 278 for 9 (50 overs) Saeed Anwar 95, A Kumble 4 for 53
India 135 (36.1 overs) AD Jadeja 61
Pakistan won by 143 runs
Man of the Match: Saeed Anwar

Match Four – Pakistan v. Sri Lanka
27 March 1999 at Indira Priyadarshani Stadium, Vishakhapatnam
Sri Lanka 253 for 8 (50 overs) DPMD Jayawardene 101, Azhar Mahmood 4 for 40

Pakistan 241 (46.3 overs) Wasim Akram 79
Sri Lanka won by 12 runs
Man of the Match: DPMD Jayawardene

Match Five – India v. Sri Lanka
30 March 1999 at Nehru Stadium, Pune
India 286 for 6 (50 overs) AD Jadeja 103*, SC Ganguly 65
Sri Lanka 235 (45.5 overs) PA de Silva 55
India won by 51 runs
Man of the Match: AD Jadeja

Match Six – India v. Pakistan
1 April 1999 at Punjab CS Stadium, Mohali
India 196 (49.5 overs) SC Ganguly 57
Pakistan 197 for 3 (42 overs) Ijaz Ahmed 89*,
Inzamam-ul-Haq 63*
Pakistan won by seven wickets
Man of the Match: Ijaz Ahmed

FINAL – INDIA v. PAKISTAN
4 April 1999 at Karnataka State CA Stadium, Bangalore

PAKISTAN

Batting

				Bowling	O	M	R	W
Saeed Anwar	lbw, b Prasad	13		Prasad	10	1	37	2
Shahid Afridi	c Jadeja, b Ganguly	65		Srinath	10	0	65	1
Ijaz Ahmed	b Srinath	3		Agarkar	10	1	63	1
Inzamam-ul-Haq	run out	91		Kumble	10	0	56	0
Yousuf Youhana	c Kumble, b Ganguly	16		Singh	3	0	30	0
*Moin Khan	c Mongia, b Prasad	35		Ganguly	7	0	35	2
Azhar Mahmood	c Srinath, b Agarkar	25						
Wasim Akram (capt)	not out	21						
Saqlain Mushtaq	run out	1		**Fall of Wickets**				
Arshad Khan	not out	6		1–23, 2–28, 3–122, 3–154, 5–217,				
Shoaib Akhtar				6–247, 7–273, 8–275				
	lb 5, w 5, nb 5	15						

50 overs (for 8 wickets) 291

INDIA

Batting

				Bowling	O	M	R	W
SC Ganguly	c Moin Khan, b Wasim	13		Wasim Akram	6	0	37	1
S Ramesh	c Moin, b Shoaib Akhtar	1		Shoaib Akhtar	8	3	22	2
RS Dravid	lbw, b Azhar Mahmood	25		Azhar Mahmood	10	1	38	5
AR Khurasiya	lbw, Shoaib Akhtar	3		Saqlain Mushtaq	9.1	2	29	1
AD Jadeja (capt)	c Moin, b Azhar Mahmood	41		Arshad Khan	6	0	23	0
RR Singh	c Moin, b Azhar Mahmood	5		Shahid Afridi	3	0	14	0
AB Agarkar	run out	13						
*NR Mongia	not out	27						
A Kumble	b Azhar Mahmood	1		**Fall of Wickets**				
J Srinath	lbw, b Azhar Mahmood	0		1–5, 2–41, 3–44, 4–56, 5–63, 6–104,				
BKV Prasad	b Saqlain Mushtaq	17		7–131, 8–135, 9–135				
	b 1, lb 4, w 9, nb 8	22						

42.1 overs   168

Umpires: K Parthasarathi & S Venkataraghavan
Man of the Match: Azhar Mahmood
Man of the Series: SC Ganguly

Pakistan won by 123 runs

INDIA DOMESTIC FIRST-CLASS SEASON
By Qamar Ahmed

A lack of quality cricket and falling attendances marked India's domestic season in 1998–99. The matches were unremarkable for various reasons, but particularly the absence of star players who were busy with international commitments. The board had talked of improving pitches to raise the standard of play but had not yet done so. On placid wickets some tall scores were attained and it was a pity that these performances against weak opposition were recognised and rewarded.

The Duleep Trophy was reverted to a knockout from a league format which was not a good move. There was plenty of action, though, because the players wanted to make the most of the packed international programme. This meant there were

Anil Kumble.
David Munden/Sportsline Photographic

Ajay Jadeja.
David Munden/Sportsline Photographic

frequent opportunities for the youngsters to grab a place in national teams. Compared to previous seasons, this was not one to transform the face of Indian cricket. The quality of play of the up-and-coming cricketers could not be gauged in the absence of such stalwarts as Anil Kumble, Javagal Srinath, Sachin Tendulkar or Rahul Dravid. This is underlined by the fact that Kumble and Srinath did not play a single match for the Ranji Trophy champions, Karnataka.

However, one highlight of the season was the consistency shown by the unsung cricketers from the Central Zone. In winning the Duleep Trophy and the Deodhar Trophy, the Zone spotlighted the flow of cricketers good enough to perform at this level. Madhya Pradesh, the prime team in the Central Zone, did wonderfully well to win the Wills Trophy and make the final of the Ranji Trophy. Although they did not win the title, the team could not complain because they had Karnataka gasping before a sensational spell of Vijay Raghvendra Bharadwaj, bowling off-spinners, took the match away from Madhya Pradesh.

There was a stunning development this season when Mumbai, the nursery of Indian cricket, failed to qualify. In the absence of Sachin Tendulkar for most of the season, the team was going to struggle since Vinod Kambli had shifted his loyalty from Mumbai.

In the final of the Ranji Trophy at Bangalore, Madhya Pradesh took the lead and were set to claim their first ever title when inexperience and poor tactics cost them dear. In the last session of the match, Vijay Raghvendra Bharadwaj, who had two half-centuries to his credit in the match, swung it in his team's favour by claiming six wickets. Madhya Pradesh were left frustrated and Karnataka deservedly won the Trophy. Vijay Raghvendra Bharadwaj, and J Arun Kumar were Karnataka's consistent performers and there was tremendous support from Dodda Ganesh who was clearly the best seamer in the country but failed to make an impression on the selectors.

The Duleep Trophy, the prime tournament for the selection in India, was again deprived of class participation because of the national players' engagements. The tournament, however, saw the confirmation of Madhya Pradesh as the best national team. In the final, Central Zone was hard pressed by a determined West Zone side with Manoj Mudgal, Mohammad Kaif, Gagan Khoda, AW Zaidi and Murali Kartik shining for the winning team. The final was held at a little-known cricket venue of Aurangabad and the players were critical of the playing conditions. A hastily prepared pitch began to crumble halfway through the five-day final and Central Zone, enjoying the advantage of the toss, bowled West Zone out for 144 when the target set had been a somewhat modest 266. It was an interesting competition in the sense that it brought the best out of a young, developing team and there was a touch of desperation in the ranks of the strong West Zone team as Central Zone came up with an excellent all-round performance.

Ever since the format was switched to a super national league and then a national knockout, the Ranji Trophy championship has gone up in the players' estimation. Though much of cricket is played on sub-standard pitches and with poor facilities, the major knockout matches are now held on Test grounds with the superior conditions the players have been asking for.

INDIA DOMESTIC ONE-DAY SEASON

Madhya Pradesh, the rising power in Indian cricket, won the Wills Trophy, which is by far the more attractive tournament for the players, who get good travel facilities and decent playing conditions thanks to a sponsorship deal with a tobacco company. Madhya Pradesh beat Bengal in the final by 32 runs with medium-pacer Jai Prakash Yadav hogging the limelight with a hat-trick and claiming five wickets. The most successful batsman for Madhya Pradesh was Amay Khurasiya, the left-hander, who forced his way into the side for the World Cup on the basis of his performances in national cricket in recent years.

Madhya Pradesh reaped the rewards for having attracted several top players from the mid-eighties onwards when it became possible for Ranji Trophy teams to field up to three professional cricketers from outside their own state. Players like Sundeep Patil and Chandrakant Pandit moved from Bombay and set up a system in which the younger players improved by their contact with the stars.

Poor planning hit the NKP Salve Trophy which in these days of limited-over cricket craze in India is supposed to be the highlight of the domestic one-day circuit. The tournament had been planned on a grand scale some seasons ago with live television coverage promised by those who wished to get a breakthrough in cricket in India. The tournament is just another on a lengthening domestic season, and was a farcical wash-out as cyclones ravaged Gujarat. Only one match of the several planned between the senior Indian teams, India 'A' and India 'B' could be played, and that on a restricted-overs basis. The match had to be called off because of the poor state of the pitch with both teams sharing honours.

There was a rare double for Central Zone, which contains several Madhya Pradesh players, when they won the Deodhar Trophy inter-zone tournament. Their record in the one-day tournament came in a clean slate of four straight victories while North Zone finished second, leaving East, West and South well behind.

Javagal Srinath.
David Munden/Sportsline Photographic

FIRST-CLASS AVERAGES

BATTING

	M	Inns	NO	HS	Runs	Av	100	50
JJ Martin	10	16	4	242	1152	96.00	5	3
RV Bhardwaj	13	21	3	200*	1463	81.27	4	8
BJ Bhatt	8	11	2	180	698	77.55	3	2
D Bundela	11	19	6	165	1008	77.53	2	7
D Gandhi	9	14	0	323	943	67.35	3	2
RR Panda	8	13	2	178	680	61.81	3	2
SH Kotak	11	17	1	129	961	60.06	3	5
V Rathore	13	20	0	207	1200	60.00	4	4
JM Gopal	7	9	0	199	534	59.33	2	2
AV Kale	10	16	2	151	828	59.14	3	4
V Shewag	11	17	0	163	979	57.58	3	7
BM Jadeja	8	11	1	203	567	56.70	3	–
JA Kumar	12	18	0	151	1004	55.77	5	2
Abbas Ali	9	13	3	112*	554	55.40	1	3
R Nayyar	7	14	2	118*	663	55.25	2	3
VVS Laxman	10	19	0	219	1014	53.36	3	4
P Mullick	8	13	1	113	638	53.16	2	5
Tariq-ur-Rehman	9	13	2	94	582	52.90	–	5
S Sriram	8	11	1	101	529	52.90	2	2
S Ramesh	13	21	1	145	1046	52.30	2	7
SS Bhave	8	12	1	164	569	51.72	2	2
N Haldipur	9	12	1	170	559	50.81	2	1
I Srinivas	5	8	0	105	391	48.87	2	2
PS Rawat	7	9	1	95	390	48.75	–	4
NS Sidhu	10	12	0	124	584	48.66	1	4
Saeed Anwar	5	10	1	188*	432	48.00	1	2
R Puri	7	12	2	103*	478	47.80	1	1
N Gaur	5	10	0	130	470	47.00	2	1
A Kaypee	9	15	1	148	647	46.21	2	2
MV Sridhu	10	15	0	128	691	46.06	1	5
Wasim Jaffer	6	10	1	180	411	45.66	1	2
S Kumar	8	13	2	124	498	45.27	1	3
CC Williams	8	12	0	96	539	44.91	–	6
HH Kinikar	6	9	1	129*	358	44.75	1	3
V Pratap	11	18	3	108*	664	44.26	1	4
A George	5	8	0	81	354	44.25	–	4
S Oasis	5	8	0	118	353	44.12	1	2
A Nandkishore	11	18	1	108	744	43.76	2	5
SS Tanna	7	11	1	151*	434	43.40	2	1
D Mongia	12	18	2	160	680	42.50	2	3
A Vijay	11	17	3	97	584	41.71	–	4
A Malhotra	9	15	3	111	499	41.58	2	3
R Kumar	8	13	1	164	497	41.41	1	2
KNA Padmanabhan	6	11	2	153	366	40.66	1	1
M Kaif	7	11	2	69	364	40.44	–	3
K Singh	5	10	0	133	403	40.30	2	1
AR Khurasiya	12	20	0	167	803	40.15	1	5
RS Sodhi	7	8	0	71	321	40.12	–	4
HK Bhadani	10	13	0	122	513	39.46	1	4
Jai Prakash Yadav	11	20	1	111*	743	39.10	1	5
R Kanwat	8	12	1	100*	429	39.00	1	2
HH Kanitkar	8	12	0	143	465	38.75	1	2
VST Naidu	8	11	1	125	387	38.70	2	1
S Dighe	6	9	0	153	348	38.66	1	1
DV Kumar	10	16	4	100*	462	38.50	1	2
V Dahiya	11	18	4	137	537	38.35	1	3
SS Das	9	15	0	178	575	38.33	2	2
AK Das	8	10	2	102*	299	37.37	1	2
S Bangar	9	13	0	131	485	37.30	1	2
RA Swaroop	8	11	2	77	334	37.11	–	4
C Sharma	5	10	1	96	330	36.66	–	3
S Somasunder	13	20	0	143	726	36.30	2	2
RVCH Prasad	5	8	0	94	289	36.12	–	2
S Arfi	8	11	0	72	396	36.00	–	3
S Godbole	7	9	1	87	286	35.75	–	2
Salim Malik	4	8	0	122	285	35.62	1	–
A Jain	6	10	0	100	353	35.30	1	2
R Ali	10	14	1	88	445	34.23	–	3
Jitender Singh	10	20	2	107*	614	34.11	2	3
P Sharma	9	15	1	154	473	33.78	1	2
RJ Gavaskar	10	14	1	190	435	33.46	1	2
S Sharath	12	16	1	100	500	33.33	1	7

FIRST-CLASS AVERAGES

BATTING

	M	Inns	NO	HS	Runs	Av	100	50
N Ranjan	8	13	0	114	429	33.00	1	4
HR Jadhav	8	13	2	88	362	32.90	–	2
Shahid Afridi	4	8	0	141	262	32.75	1	–
V Kolambkar	5	10	0	106	327	32.70	1	1
T Arothe	8	11	2	114	289	32.11	1	–
GK Khoda	10	18	1	107	544	32.00	1	3
HS Sodhi	10	15	4	100*	349	31.72	1	2
D Vasu	9	11	2	71	283	31.44	–	2
H Jagnu	11	15	1	90	440	31.42	–	4
A Shetty	10	17	1	87	496	31.00	–	4
Yousuf Youhana	5	10	0	124	308	30.80	1	2
N Chopra	8	11	2	82*	277	30.77	–	2
A Dani	11	19	0	140	584	30.73	1	3
S Shankar	5	9	1	54	244	30.50	–	2
PV Panajpe	6	9	0	89	267	29.66	–	1
A Sharma	7	10	1	78	266	29.55	–	2
P Dharmani	13	18	0	103	531	29.50	1	3
R Morris	7	10	1	90	265	29.44	–	2
KST Rai	5	8	0	124	233	29.12	1	–
S Shiraguppi	13	20	3	125	494	29.05	1	3
P Jayachandra	8	14	1	59	377	29.00	–	4
AFG Griffith	4	8	0	93	229	28.62	–	2
D Singh	7	11	1	55*	278	27.80	–	2
CS Pandit	10	15	0	111	416	27.73	1	2
MM Parmer	8	11	1	53	277	27.70	–	1
M Minhas	9	15	2	66	359	27.61	–	2
DS Manohar	9	16	1	132	413	27.53	1	–
A Kotecha	4	8	0	128	220	27.50	1	–
A Pathak	5	8	0	67	219	27.37	–	2
S Singh	5	10	0	69	268	26.80	–	2
S Verma	5	10	0	70	266	26.60	–	1
P Thakur	9	14	4	73*	263	26.30	–	1
HJ Parsana	7	10	1	115*	235	26.11	1	–
FR Khaleel	8	11	0	82	287	26.09	–	2
Moin Khan	5	10	0	70	260	26.00	–	3
RR Singh	7	10	1	56	230	25.55	–	1
I Siddiqui	9	11	2	116	229	25.44	1	–
N Modi	4	8	0	38	197	24.62	–	–
VN Kumar	5	9	0	49	221	24.55	–	1
DP Singh	7	10	0	74	243	24.30	–	2
S Sharma	5	10	1	91	216	24.00	–	1
AR Kapoor	8	11	0	108	263	23.90	1	2
Jyoti Prasad Yadav	7	10	0	84	234	23.40	–	2
M Parmer	4	8	0	58	186	23.25	–	1
CP Sahu	5	9	0	60	203	22.55	–	1
Wasim Akram	4	8	0	40	176	22.00	–	–
S Angurla	6	9	1	50*	175	21.87	–	1
Harbhajan Singh	9	13	4	67*	196	21.77	–	1
SS Raul	9	15	0	63	325	21.66	–	1
AR Yalvigi	11	14	1	95	280	21.53	–	2
S Kondhalkar	7	8	0	60	166	20.75	–	1
A Verma	5	10	1	81	186	20.66	–	1
A Gupta	4	8	0	54	160	20.00	–	1

Qualification: 8 completed innings, average 20.00

BOWLING

	Overs	Mds	Runs	Wkts	Av	Best	10m	5/inn
Robin Singh	203.1	55	510	28	18.21	5–26	1	3
BKV Prasad	151.3	39	377	20	18.85	6–33	–	2
A Sharma	125.1	23	329	17	19.35	6–34	–	2
N Singh	329.1	105	715	36	19.86	7–56	1	2
Wasim Akram	141.3	26	406	20	20.30	5–55	–	1
DS Mohanty	176.4	64	391	19	20.57	5–67	–	1
NP Singh	398	113	999	48	20.81	6–82	–	1
AW Zaidi	232.3	49	571	27	21.14	7–77	–	2
M Majithia	193.2	39	413	19	21.73	4–50	–	–
LR Shukla	190.3	48	610	28	21.78	5–100	–	1
MS Kulkarni	209	55	523	24	21.79	7–122	–	1
SS Godbole	94.4	29	219	10	21.90	4–20	–	–

FIRST-CLASS AVERAGES

BOWLING

	Overs	Mds	Runs	Wkts	Av	Best	10m	5/inn
RR Bose	155.1	38	395	18	21.94	7-24	-	2
Saqlain Mushtaq	203.5	47	555	25	22.20	5-93	2	4
T Kumeran	349.5	60	1028	46	22.34	6-56	-	1
M Kartik	465.1	156	944	42	22.47	5-55	-	3
S Mahesh	234	52	676	30	22.53	5-45	-	3
A Bhandari	305.3	54	936	41	22.82	6-70	-	2
H Ramkishen	347.4	85	977	42	23.26	6-141	1	4
SB Joshi	260.5	100	539	23	23.43	5-48	-	2
K Singh	497	130	1203	51	23.58	8-86	1	4
RV Bhardwaj	173.3	39	505	21	24.04	6-24	-	2
A Gupta	157.2	24	483	20	24.15	7-131	1	3
Harvinder Singh	219.5	63	611	25	24.44	7-53	-	1
Y Wakaskar	179.2	54	416	17	24.47	5-58	-	2
RR Singh	201.5	67	441	18	24.50	4-33	-	-
N Chopra	365.4	85	816	33	24.72	5-27	-	2
S Lahore	214.5	57	475	19	25.00	3-14	-	-
U Chatterjee	346.5	144	585	23	25.43	5-56	-	1
SS Singh	149.3	40	358	14	25.57	5-58	-	1
MA Khan	225	48	694	27	25.70	4-40	-	-
SS Raul	162	47	362	14	25.85	4-22	-	-
R Morris	146	35	365	14	26.07	4-65	-	-
Harbhajan Singh	381.3	88	1079	41	26.31	6-63	-	3
D Ganesh	618.2	104	1948	74	26.32	6-37	1	6
SLV Raju	578	257	1186	45	26.35	6-54	-	1
JP Pandey	138	28	427	16	26.68	5-87	-	1
V Shewag	212	47	590	22	26.81	4-32	-	-
A Nehra	315.1	78	871	32	27.21	6-63	-	1
DP Singh	215	56	495	18	27.50	6-67	-	1
KNA Padmanabhan	222.2	55	610	22	27.72	6-61	-	2
B Bushan	237.1	56	668	24	27.83	7-84	-	1
D Vasu	328.5	106	683	24	28.45	7-53	-	1
S Sharma	187.5	38	517	18	28.72	4-75	-	-
R Panta	109	21	376	13	28.92	3-33	-	-
HS Sodhi	261.2	50	733	25	29.32	5-78	-	1
P Thakur	411.1	81	1147	38	30.18	6-108	-	2
S Singh	192	54	454	15	30.26	4-58	-	-
N Gaur	127.2	33	340	11	30.90	3-49	-	-
SH Kotak	223.3	34	718	23	31.21	6-81	-	1
A Yalvigi	269.3	65	844	27	31.25	5-41	-	1
SK Kanwal	131.2	33	344	11	31.27	3-42	-	-
D Singh	146.1	42	377	12	31.41	3-74	-	-
S Satpathy	234.2	58	663	21	31.57	6-64	-	1
I Siddiqui	379.4	90	1079	34	31.67	7-81	-	2
SB Nair	180.4	29	608	19	32.00	5-48	-	1
PL Mhambrey	193	39	515	16	32.18	4-31	-	-
P Jain	297.4	79	812	25	32.48	4-24	-	-
YU Bambhaniya	138.1	28	329	10	32.90	3-40	-	-
Avinash Kumar	326.3	74	813	24	33.87	6-130	-	1
R Sanghvi	504	105	1567	46	34.06	7-68	-	2
W Majumder	156	37	446	13	34.30	4-66	-	-
KVP Rao	269.5	67	722	21	34.38	6-70	-	1
RA Swaroop	280.4	69	587	17	34.52	4-98	-	-
PV Gandhe	223.5	53	595	17	35.00	4-69	-	-
A Katti	300.1	89	774	22	35.18	4-111	-	-
NM Kulkami	317.2	112	649	18	36.05	6-48	-	-
A Kapoor	420.1	90	1047	29	36.10	6-111	-	-
V Jain	325.2	66	1132	31	36.51	4-117	-	-
DG Mulherkar	264.1	56	708	19	37.26	7-40	-	2

FIRST-CLASS AVERAGES

BOWLING

	Overs	Mds	Runs	Wkts	Av	Best	10m	5/inn
Z Hassan	192.4	52	488	13	37.53	3-43	-	-
Sahid Khan	265.3	71	652	17	38.35	3-37	-	-
J Rai	232.2	70	541	14	38.64	5-153	1	-
MO Kamal	162.5	49	400	10	40.00	4-49	-	-
RK Chauhan	384.2	87	908	22	41.27	4-92	-	-
T Arothe	199	36	540	13	41.53	4-79	-	-
P Subbiah	196.4	42	512	12	42.66	3-65	-	-
S Angurla	135.5	26	455	10	44.50	2-13	-	-
HJ Parsana	289.4	59	867	19	45.63	5-89	1	-
SV Bahutule	238.1	64	558	12	46.50	3-48	-	-
N Rana	137.2	29	493	10	49.30	4-66	-	-
S Panda	181	40	608	11	55.27	3-66	-	-
V Kumar	285.3	48	930	16	58.12	5-83	-	1

Qualification: 10 wickets in 8 innings

The following players took 10 wickets in fewer than 8 innings:

D Deverand	81.2	20	181	10	4-38	18.10	-	
P Sharma	101.4	18	344	18	4-42	19.11	-	-
IR Bishop	95.2	18	249	13	4-38	19.15	-	-
Shoaib Akhtar	73.3	8	241	12	4-47	20.08	-	-
A Kumble	144.1	36	451	22	10-74	20.50	1	2
J Srinath	101	17	351	17	8-46	20.64	1	2
A Shukla	95	27	245	11	5-92	22.27	-	1
M Kadri	87.1	22	236	10	5-33	23.60	-	1
S Sirsat	119.4	23	314	13	4-57	24.15	-	-
NC McGarrell	128	17	390	16	5-42	24.37	-	2
PT Collins	103.5	19	350	14	4-56	25.00	-	-
YS Raganath	133.4	37	352	14	4-59	25.14	-	-
T Chanda	77	3	320	12	3-47	26.66	-	-
B Patel	118	32	347	13	7-40	26.69	-	1
G Dutta	106	24	274	10	3-57	27.40	-	-
P Bali	114	25	339	12	5-81	28.25	-	1
KD Chavada	98.5	16	416	14	6-95	29.71	-	1
SK Nair	148	46	370	12	5-96	30.83	-	1
AR Tandon	127.1	36	340	11	5-86	30.90	-	1
D Parteki	157	46	376	12	5-85	31.33	-	1
SS Banerjee	156	38	422	13	6-72	32.46	-	1
A Barik	117.4	16	413	12	4-32	34.91	-	-
MV Rao	112.3	15	363	10	6-76	36.30	-	1
N Kalekan	140.1	29	404	11	4-34	36.72	-	-
N Odedra	158.4	40	401	10	3-147	40.10	-	-

FIELDING FIGURES

43 – V Dahiya (39 ct/4 st); 40 – S Shiraguppi (33 ct/7 st); 27 – MM Parmar (22 ct/5 st); 26 – S Kondhalkhar (25 ct/1 st); 25 – Yourav Singh (22 ct/3 st); 24 – P Dharmani (23 ct/1 st), MSK Prasad (22 ct/2 st); 23 – H Jagnu (22 ct/1 st); 22 – SS Karim (21 ct/1 st); 19 – CS Pandit (17 ct/2 st); 18 – CP Sahu; 17 – MS Mudgal; 15 – TR Arasu, D Ganesh, G Gopal, GK Khoda, D Mongia, R Paul, S Somasunder; 14 – CO Browne (11 ct/3 st), A Sharma (12 ct/2 st), Jitender Singh, VVS Laxman, A Nandkishore, V Shewag; 13 – S Dighe (12 ct/3 st), Moin Khan (10 ct/3 st), S Singh (10 ct/3 st), B Bundela, SS Das, A Kaypee; 12 – S Abbas Ali, S Arfi, HH Kanitkar, NR Mongia, A Vijay, Wasim Jaffer; 11 – S Kumar (9 ct/2 st), V R Samant (l0 ct/1 st), S Bangar, SH Kotak, DS Manohar, V Rathore; 10 – M Mewada (9 ct/1 st), Jai Prakash Yadav, AR Khurasiya, DV Kumar, M Minhas, Shafiq Khan

PAKISTAN

AUSTRALIA IN PAKISTAN
By Jim Maxwell

Intrigues off the field sustained stories in the press throughout a series that was dominated on the field by a committed and single-minded Australian team. And whereas Mark Taylor was decisively in control of his team's mission, his counterpart, Aamir Sohail, struggled. Beset by injuries, curious selections, wavering support, and the ongoing inquiry into allegations of bribery and match-fixing, Sohail's captaincy was doomed. In the power plays of Pakistan cricket his was an interregnum – Wasim Akram was the preferred natural leader – and his reputation had been sullied by his alleged association with match-fixing. The judicial inquiry and the palpable falling-out between Pakistan Board Chairman, Khalid Mahmood, and Chief Executive, Majid Khan, were distractions that revealed Pakistan's factionalised and chaotic condition. The decision to appoint Javed Miandad as coach also went awry. Well intentioned, he lacked the method and communication skills to be effective. Rumours that he was planning a comeback for the World Cup were probably unfounded, but the speculation damaged his perceived coaching commitment.

Mark Waugh too, appeared to be distracted by the official inquiry. And given subsequent revelations about his involvement with bookmakers, his edginess was understandable. After rejecting an initial request to appear before the inquiry, Waugh and Mark Taylor stealthily travelled to Lahore. At a specially convened court hearing they were surprised to see protagonist Salim Malik and his cross-examining lawyer. Waugh and Taylor reiterated the original evidence which accused Salim of offering bribes to Waugh and Shane Warne in 1994. In a remarkable public admission the presiding judge, Mohammad Malik Qayyum, said that if he believed Taylor's corroboration of Waugh's testimony, then Salim Malik was damned. Qayyum's admission raised questions about the legal process and its efficacy. After all it was supposed to be an official inquiry, and surely the judge's opinions were sub judice until the findings were made public? Hearings were held more formally in the Lahore High Court, where Pakistani players, officials and alleged bookmakers were arraigned, and often scolded by the judge for their amnesic performances. John Mortimer would have delighted in the real life 'misleading cases' and judicial showmanship.

Taylor stated bluntly that 'we're here to play cricket' at the start of the tour and having dealt with the inquiry straight after the first-Test victory in Rawalpindi, he produced a stunning endorsement of the tour motto in Peshawar. His record equalling 334 not out was a monumental innings. Monumental on two counts: that he was able to bat for two days in a Test match, and that his career had survived long enough even to attempt this accomplishment. Taylor's captaincy record vindicated the selectors' decision to stick with him during his batting decline, and just when it seemed another slump was imminent, he produced a huge innings. And damning the critics who suggested he should have kept batting, Taylor said, 'I want to win a series in the subcontinent, and this is the only way I can be bracketed with Bradman.' Altruistic? Certainly admirable. And in the words of his former opening partner and current coach, Geoff Marsh: 'he has put his team before his own record. That's why he is a great leader.'

Australia deservedly won the series, their first success in Pakistan for 39 years. And in the one-dayers the same hunger and organisation delivered a three-nil victory, including a record-equalling second-innings score in Lahore.

Australia v. Karachi City Cricket Association
26, 27, 28 and 29 September 1998 at National Stadium Karachi
Australia 540 for 9 dec. and 194 for 2 dec.
Karachi City Cricket Association 278 and 123
Australia won by 333 runs

Michael Slater's swashbuckling double century highlighted a one-sided match. Slater smacked 22 fours and six sixes in his highest first-class score, 221 from 260 balls. Taylor excepted, all the front-line Australian batsmen tuned up impressively for the first Test, with the number three elect, Justin Langer, compiling a solid second-innings century when Taylor took the option of batting practice in preference to enforcing the follow-on. McGrath, in his first match since January, showed form and fitness, in several lively spells. Conversely Waqar Younis looked badly underdone in his recovery from an elbow injury.

The match ended quickly on the last day when leg-spinner MacGill grabbed five wickets in 19 balls, as the locals were abjectly dispatched for 123. MacGill's 6 for 34 gave him nine match wickets, and Australia a confident momentum for the rest of the tour.

FIRST TEST
1, 2, 3, 4 and 5 October 1998 at Rawalpindi

Australia's first Test win in Pakistan for 39 years was inspired by four splendid individual performances in another outstanding team effort orchestrated by Mark Taylor. Steve Waugh and Michael Slater scored match-winning centuries. Glenn McGrath and Stuart MacGill bowled superbly, MacGill taking nine match wickets with his bouncy leg-spin. And Ian Healy snared the world wicketkeeping record, to boot. Pakistan's disarray certainly contributed to the outcome. In the lead-up, 18 players were picked in the initial squad, whittled down to 14 before the final unbalanced eleven was negotiated. For new captain Aamir Sohail it was a bad beginning, and his displeasure was plain when he preferred his own version of left-arm spin to that of the selected specialist Muhammad Hussain. Sohail should have been named Mahmood, because he was always in one. Not pretty! The more so in the field, where he deployed by numbers. It reminded me of Ted Dexter in 1962–63, who habitually positioned boundary riders after slow bowlers were hit for four. In Sohail's case he could not sustain the pressure once Steve Waugh and his disciplined accomplice Michael Slater cracked the infield, pushing men back and thus accommodating easily taken singles.

The match drew a refreshingly involved crowd. Recent home Tests had been poorly supported, so the sight of terrace-loads of shalwar qameez'd fans, banging drums and generally cavorting, lent atmosphere. Some were less supportive of their heroes when they failed. Wasim Akram, dismissed carelessly in Pakistan's first innings when he holed out off MacGill, was rebuked with taunts of: 'how much were you paid?' as he wandered off. So was Salim Malik when he edged Colin Miller's fifth ball to Taylor's swooping right hand at slip. Miller was the surprise debutant. Preferred over Gavin Robertson, the 34-year-old Miller completed a remarkable transition from journeyman Tasmanian-cum-Dutch league professional to Test cricket. Introduced after McGrath and Fleming had knocked the top off the Pakistan first innings, Miller bowled brisk out-swingers, alternating to off-spin when Saeed Anwar settled into his brilliantly productive innings. MacGill's three-for-none burst in seven balls read 147 for 8 on Pakistan's scoreboard, Anwar finding sane support from Mushtaq, their century stand ensuring respectability, with Anwar's 145 a gem of timing and wristy elegance.

Wasim hit back at the taunters by removing Taylor and Langer cheaply, and with Mark Waugh leg before padding up to Mushtaq, it was 28 for 3. A typically determined Steve Waugh came to the rescue, his 198-run partnership with the applied Slater repelling the threat of spin, especially Saqlain, who was periodically swatted over mid-wicket by Waugh. Pakistan's hopes of curtailing the lead were dashed by Lehmann, who batted boldly and belligerently, until an ambitious sweep gave up his wicket at 98. Healy kept the tail wagging and Australia were all out at stumps on the third day, 244 runs in front. Pakistan's second innings was a disaster. McGrath went after Sohail who, with two

Stuart MacGill took nine wickets in the first Test match at Rawalpindi.
David Munden/Sportsline Photographic

Darren Lehmann scored 98 for Australia in the first Test.
Mueen-ud-din-Hameed/Sportsline Photographic

men back on the hook, did not know whether to
evade, defend or attack. Tangled between all three he
deflected into his stumps, initiating another slide.
Proving that all umpires are neutral, Javed Akhtar
gave two leg befores in one Fleming over – and
then, going round the wicket, Miller got another
one from umpire Willey on Anwar. Miller's second
wicket was memorable. Bowling over the wicket to
Wasim, he pitched middle, the ball bounced, turned
and was deflected uncomfortably to Healy's left.
Healy's jubilant snare eclipsed Rod Marsh's record
of 355 Test dismissals, and when Healy eventually
got back to the dressing room at tea, a bottle of
celebratory champagne was awaiting him, courtesy
of Marsh.

In only his second Test, MacGill made a perfect
substitute for Warne, twirling out 9 for 109, with
McGrath finishing off Saqlain 13 minutes into the
final day, so Australia won by an innings. In the
neighbouring Islamic capital, the bar at the
Australian High Commission's Waltzing Matilda
watering hole was appropriately dry: the next
morning, that is!

Australia v. Rawalpindi District Cricket Association
8, 9, 10 and 11 October 1998 at Khan Research
Laboratories Ground, Rawalpindi
Australia 355 and 298
Rawalpindi District Cricket Association 261 and 263
for 3
Match drawn

Ringed by a high iron spiked fence the Rawalpindi
ground was on the edge of the compound where
Pakistan's nuclear bombs were allegedly engineered.
But the only explosions that took place over four
meandering days came from Darren Lehmann's bat.
Lehmann made a hundred in each innings, the
second struck from 95 balls. Sadly he strained a
groin muscle, an injury that ultimately forced him
out of the second Test. Taylor's return to form was
fortuitous. Dismissed cheaply in the first innings, he
went for a net. Attempting to climb the perimeter
fence, Taylor spiked his right hand. Held back to
number five in the second innings, he scored a
tenacious and, as it turned out, timely, 63 not out.
For the locals, left-arm spinner Shakeel Ahmed
troubled the right-handers, taking 7 for 71, and
Ijaz Ahmed did enough to earn a recall for the
Peshawar Test.

FIRST TEST – PAKISTAN v. AUSTRALIA
1, 2, 3, 4 and 5 October 1998 at Pindi Cricket Stadium, Rawalpindi

PAKISTAN

	First Innings		Second Innings	
Saeed Anwar	c Langer, b MacGill	145	lbw, b Miller	19
Aamir Sohail (capt)	c Healy, b McGrath	4	b McGrath	13
Mohammad Wasim	c Healy, b Fleming	1	lbw, b Fleming	0
Inzamam-ul-Haq	c Langer, b McGrath	14	lbw, b Fleming	0
Salim Malik	c Taylor, b Miller	10	not out	52
Azhar Mahmood	c McGrath, b MacGill	16	(7) c Langer, b MacGill	1
*Moin Khan	c Fleming, b MacGill	39	(6) c Taylor, b MacGill	18
Wasim Akram	c Fleming, b MacGill	0	c Healy, b Miller	15
Mohammad Hussain	b MacGill	1	c Miller, b MacGill	17
Mushtaq Ahmed	run out (Miller)	26	lbw, b MacGill	0
Saqlain Mushtaq	not out	2	lbw, b MacGill	7
	b 5, lb 2, nb 4	11	lb 3	3
		269		145

	First Innings				Second Innings			
	O	M	R	W	O	M	R	W
McGrath	26	3	83	2	15.5	6	24	2
Fleming	20	3	39	1	15	4	38	2
Miller	23	4	65	1	21	8	30	2
MacGill	22	5	66	5	21	7	47	4
Lehmann	4	1	3	-	3	2	3	-
SR Waugh	2	0	6	-				

Fall of Wickets
1–13, 2–18, 3–35, 4–50, 5–81, 6–140, 7–140, 8–147, 9–267
1–24, 2–32, 3–32, 4–32, 5–66, 6–68, 7–94, 8–126, 9–128

AUSTRALIA

	First Innings	
MJ Slater	c Mohammad Wasim, b Mohammad Hussain	108
MA Taylor (capt)	c Moin Khan, b Wasim Akram	3
JL Langer	lbw, b Wasim Akram	0
ME Waugh	lbw, b Mushtaq Ahmed	0
SR Waugh	c Mohammad Wasim, b Aamir Sohail	157
DS Lehmann	b Mohammad Hussain	98
*IA Healy	c Mohammad Wasim, b Saqlain Mushtaq	82
DW Fleming	b Wasim Akram	8
CR Miller	c and b Mushtaq Ahmed	3
SCG MacGill	b Saqlain Mushtaq	21
GD McGrath	not out	3
	lb 19, nb 11	30
		513

	First Innings			
	O	M	R	W
Wasim Akram	35	4	111	3
Azhar Mahmood	13	1	36	-
Mushtaq Ahmed	41	7	115	2
Saqlain Mushtaq	41.5	9	112	2
Mohammad Hussain	20	3	66	2
Aamir Sohail	23	3	54	1

Fall of Wickets
1–11, 2–11, 3–28, 4–226, 5–352, 6–443, 7–459, 8–464, 9–504

Umpires: Javed Akhtar & P Willey
Toss: Pakistan

Australia won by an innings and 99 runs

SECOND TEST
15, 16, 17, 18 and 19 October 1998 at Peshawar

It was the road Alexander the Great and Genghis Khan would have preferred to the rugged terrain of the nearby Khyber Pass. One Australian player quipped, 'have you paid ya' toll', as a media mob surveyed the Arbab Niaz Stadium pitch, or eponymously, the Peshawar freeway. The cliché, 'Taylor-made for batting', was an appropriate description. In a match where 1,468 runs were scored in three incomplete innings, Taylor made 334 not out and 92. He could have been out for a duck, and he should have been caught on 18 and 27 by the fumbling Anwar.

A crowd disturbance on Australia's 1994 tour ensured a strong security presence for the match,

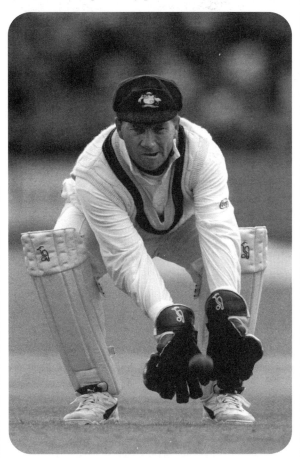

During the Pakistan tour, Australian wicketkeeper Ian Healy broke Rod Marsh's record of 355 Test dismissals.
David Munden/Sportsline Photographic

Mark Taylor reaches 300 during the first innings of the second Test match at Peshawar.

Mueen-ud-din-Hameed/Sportsline Photographic

the local police insisting 'no stones, no water bottles', during body searches at the gate. Bowlers felt similarly disarmed by the end of a high-scoring contest. Shoaib Akhtar shared the new ball with another potential missile-hurler, Mohammad Zahid, and was unlucky that at least

SECOND TEST – PAKISTAN v. AUSTRALIA
15, 16, 17, 18 and 19 October 1998 at Arbab Niaz Stadium, Peshawar

AUSTRALIA

	First Innings		Second Innings	
MA Taylor (capt)	not out	334	(2) b Aamir Nazir	92
MJ Slater	c Azhar Mahmood, b Shoaib Akhtar	2	(1) lbw, b Mushtaq Ahmed	21
JL Langer	c Moin Khan, b Azhar Mahmood	116	c Yousuf Youhana, b Mushtaq Ahmed	14
ME Waugh	c Salim Malik, b Aamir Sohail	42	b Shoaib Akhtar	43
SR Waugh	c Moin Khan, b Shoaib Akhtar	1	not out	49
RT Ponting	not out	76	lbw, b Ijaz Ahmed	43
*IA Healy			not out	14
DW Fleming				
CR Miller				
SCG MacGill				
GD McGrath				
	lb 9, w 3, nb 16	28	lb 4, nb 9	13
	(for 4 wickets dec.)	599	(for 5 wickets)	289

	First Innings				Second Innings			
	O	M	R	W	O	M	R	W
Shoaib Akhtar	31	6	107	2	16	2	68	1
Mohammad Zahid	16	0	74	–	10	2	42	–
Mushtaq Ahmed	46	3	153	–	20	1	59	2
Azhar Mahmood	23	2	82	1	3	0	18	–
Aamir Sohail	42	8	111	1	10	1	35	1
Salim Malik	16	0	63	–	15	1	30	–
Ijaz Ahmed					14	1	33	1

Fall of Wickets
1–16, 2–295, 3–418 , 4–431
1–39, 2–67, 3–170, 4–179, 5–269

PAKISTAN

	First Innings	
Saeed Anwar	c Healy, b Miller	126
Aamir Sohail (capt)	c Fleming, b McGrath	31
Ijaz Ahmed	c Healy, b MacGill	155
Inzamam-ul-Haq	c Healy, b SR Waugh	97
Salim Malik	c Taylor, b McGrath	49
Yousuf Youhana	c SR Waugh, b MacGill	28
*Moin Khan	c Healy, b Ponting	0
Azhar Mahmood	c Langer, b McGrath	26
Mushtaq Ahmed	not out	48
Mohammad Zahid	lbw, b Fleming	1
Shoaib Akhtar		
	b 5, lb 9, w 1, nb 4	19
	(for 9 wickets dec.)	580

	First Innings			
	O	M	R	W
McGrath	36	8	131	3
Fleming	35.1	6	103	1
MacGill	42	5	169	2
Miller	38	12	99	1
ME Waugh	8	0	32	–
SR Waugh	8	1	19	1
Ponting	5	1	13	1

Fall of Wickets
1–45, 2–256, 3–371, 4–454, 5–500, 6–501, 7–521, 8–571, 9–580

Umpires: Mohammad Nazir & SA Bucknor
Toss: Australia

Match drawn

one of his hollers for lbw to umpire Bucknor, did not remove either Taylor or Langer before they had scored. Wasim had cried off with the 'flu at the eleventh hour, and with Saqlain dropped and Mushtaq battling a knee injury, the bowling looked – and quickly became – underwhelming. The sinistral partners walloped the short ball, Taylor's innings a pulling and driving revelation. The true bounce must have reminded Langer of the WACA; he scored an attractive maiden Test century in a record stand of 279.

Taylor was remorseless, becoming the first Australian since Bob Cowper in 1965–66 to score a Test triple hundred. He seemed certain to top the Don's legendary 334 in the shadows of stumps on the second day, but a brilliant stop by Ijaz Ahmed at mid-wicket from the final delivery fatefully thwarted him.

Most pundits had already written the match off, reckoning the pitch was a road. Whether it was fatigue, captain's psychology or the bowlers' union at work, Taylor delayed the declaration until the next morning, putting the chance of victory above personal aggrandisement. His decision astounded local observers, who believed that the eclipse of Lara's record was a formality. Taylor said, 'I want to win a series in the subcontinent, and this is the only way I can be bracketed with Bradman. I have equalled Sir Donald Bradman's record, and that is enough for me'. He'd batted for two days; an innings of remarkable concentration and determination.

Within two days Taylor was back, chasing Gooch's record match aggregate of 456. By then the thought of an opportunity missed must have crossed his mind, watching Pakistan's batting plunder. Leg-spinner MacGill simply could not land them, feeding Ijaz on his favourite cuts and pulled baseball shots. Cheerleader Abdul's chanting posse and their orchestrated movements on the terraces became more entertaining than the 'roadworkers', as the match inevitably faded into a stalemate. Taylor stopped the sleepers snoring as he chased down the record. Having spent the best part of five days on the ground it was no surprise that weariness finally overcame him, playing on for 92, 31 runs shy of Gooch.

Taylor was the obvious Man of the Match, as much for his altruism as for an extraordinary innings.

THIRD TEST
22, 23, 24, 25 and 26 October 1998 at Karachi

With Allan Border's fearful analysis preying on the mind, Australia picked three spinners for the deciding match. Pakistan confirmed the visitors' suspicions by including two specialist finger spinners and the all-rounder, Shahid Afridi, who bowled wrist-spin. Border, who had been on three losing tours to Pakistan, was on hand as a television commentator, and in his alternate role as a selector. Taylor, too, was aware of the Karachi pitch's tendencies, having been on the end of a dramatic defeat by one wicket in 1994. Pakistan had never lost a Test at the National Stadium

Colin Miller took three wickets in 22 minutes on the last day of the third Test match in Karachi.
David Munden / Sportsline Photographic

in 31 matches since 1955, and had Taylor caught Ijaz Ahmed off McGrath's bowling before lunch on the final morning, it could well have been a loss instead of a draw. Pakistan would have been five down for less than 100 with two sessions to survive.

Test debutant Shahid Afridi captured 5 wickets for 52 in the first innings of the Karachi Test.
David Munden/Sportsline Photographic

The pitch held up, never threatening to become the turner some of the sages had forecast. Yes, it was slow and hard to score on: Australia squeezed a paltry 6 for 207 from it on the first day. But Michael Slater confirmed his class with another disciplined innings, and should have reached a hundred. He was distracted by a surprise burst of wrist-spin mayhem from Test debutant Afridi, who removed the Waughs and Lehmann in 13 balls; the score plummeting from a handy 169 for 2 to 179 for 5. Then Slater went aberrant, charged at Arshad and was stumped for 96.

Afridi had made his mark in one-day cricket as a slathering batsman, and his quick wrist-spin was known to most of the Australian batsmen from previous mortification of not picking the faster, quicker ball. That's how Steve Waugh went, plumb leg before. It was one of those rapid-fire dismissals that made one wonder why Steve had bothered to bring his bat from the dressing room, as the unused implement accompanied its cussed owner off.

Twin brother Mark was spectacularly caught by Pakistan's version of an airship, Inzamam, hurling himself at slip to grab a ricochet off Youhana in the gully. Inzamam was a legitimate passenger in the field, this brilliant catch aside, because he'd injured his ankle at practice. He did not bat long enough in Pakistan's first innings to demonstrate whether the injury could have affected his running. Probably not; just his immobility.

Healy and MacGill flirted and flashed, Arshad getting the benefit of the doubt on Healy for a catch at the wicket, and Afridi taking the last wicket to bag 5 for 52. Australia's 280 looked adequate, the more so by the close of play when Pakistan were alive only at one end, their captain preventing a rout on 83 not out at 170 for 6. McGrath defied the sluggish pitch in a tremendous spell of sustained pace and aggression, taking 3 for 6 in five overs. Afridi, crazily, flung his bat at the new ball, and Ijaz haphazardly hooked for Healy's benefit.

Aamir Sohail, in the curious absence of his henchman Saeed Anwar, who'd returned to Lahore with an illness or an injury (or both) played magnificently. Like so many left-handers with the felicitous gift of timing and a sharp eye, Sohail put the half-bad balls away after surviving the hesitancy of single figures. Moin and Wasim made up for the vanquished middle order of Inzamam, Salim and Youhana, although Miller dropped the aggressive all-rounder at long off on the third

THIRD TEST – PAKISTAN v. AUSTRALIA
22, 23, 24, 25 and 26 October 1998 at National Stadium, Karachi

AUSTRALIA

	First Innings		Second Innings	
MA Taylor (capt)	c Inzamam, b Arshad Khan	16	(2) b Arshad Khan	68
MJ Slater	st Moin Khan, b Arshad Khan	96	(1) c Yousuf, b Arshad Khan	11
JL Langer	lbw, b Shoaib Akhtar	30	run out (Ijaz Ahmed)	51
ME Waugh	c Inzamam-ul-Haq, b Shahid Afridi	26	st Moin Khan, b Shakeel Ahmed	117
SR Waugh	lbw, b Shahid Afridi	0	c Moin, b Shakeel Ahmed	28
DS Lehmann	b Shahid Afridi	3	c Ijaz Ahmed, b Wasim Akram	26
*IA Healy	c Moin Khan, b Arshad Khan	47	c Shahid, b Shoaib Akhtar	3
GR Robertson	c Yousuf Youhana, b Shahid Afridi	5	c Wasim Akram, b Shakeel Ahmed	45
CR Miller	b Wasim Akram	0	c Shahid Afridi, b Shakeel Ahmed	0
SCG MacGill	not out	24	run out (Salim Malik)	10
GD McGrath	c Shakeel Ahmed, b Shahid Afridi	6	not out	4
	b 1, lb 16, nb 10	27	b 4, lb 8, nb 15	27
		280		390

	First Innings				Second Innings			
	O	M	R	W	O	M	R	W
Wasim Akram	22	4	51	1	22	2	60	1
Shoaib Akhtar	14.2	3	39	1	17	3	37	1
Shakeel Ahmed	24.4	9	48	-	29.3	3	91	4
Arshad Khan	41	14	73	3	56	14	141	2
Shahid Afridi	23.3	6	52	5	18	3	49	-

Fall of Wickets
1-38, 2-105, 3-169, 4-169, 5-179, 6-189, 7-210, 8-211, 9-266
1-27, 2-136, 3-152, 4-208, 5-284, 6-294, 7-357, 8-357, 9-369

PAKISTAN

	First Innings		Second Innings	
Aamir Sohail (capt)	c Langer, b Miller	133	lbw, b Miller	25
Shahid Afridi	c Taylor, b McGrath	10	c Healy, b Miller	6
Ijaz Ahmed	c Healy, b McGrath	5	not out	120
Inzamam-ul-Haq	c Lehmann, b McGrath	9	(7) not out	21
Salim Malik	c McGrath, b MacGill	0	(4) lbw, b Miller	0
Yousuf Youhana	b Robertson	9	(5) c ME Waugh, b MacGill	11
*Moin Khan	c Slater, b McGrath	20	(6) c MacGill, b Lehmann	75
Wasim Akram	lbw, b MacGill	35		
Shakeel Ahmed	c Langer, b McGrath	1		
Arshad Khan	lbw, b MacGill	7		
Shoaib Akhtar	not out	6		
	b 6, lb 5, w 1, nb 5	17	b 2, nb 2	4
		252	(for 5 wickets)	262

	First Innings				Second Innings			
	O	M	R	W	O	M	R	W
McGrath	25	6	66	5	18	11	40	-
Miller	14	2	53	1	25	5	82	3
MacGill	25.4	5	64	3	17	2	66	1
Robertson	22	5	46	1	16	2	56	-
Lehmann	1	0	6	-	2	0	6	1
SR Waugh	2	0	6	-	8	5	10	-

Fall of Wickets
1-26, 2-40, 3-51, 4-54, 5-69, 6-116, 7-214, 8-239, 9-240
1-20, 2-33, 3-35, 4-75, 5-228

Umpires: Riazuddin & DL Orchard
Toss: Australia

Match drawn

morning at 6 for 183. MacGill, who lacked consistency, finally had Wasim leg before not offering, but by lunch Sohail had added 50 of 69 scored in the session to reach 133, and an invaluable fifth Test century. You can dine out on Big Macs in Lahore, but the locals found them indigestible in Karachi, McGrath claiming five and MacGill three wickets, with Pakistan trailing by 28 runs.

The Peshawar plunderers, Taylor and Langer, worked diligently via sweeps, nudges and keen running to urge the total to 1 for 130 with two days to go. Umpires Orchard and Riazuddin stood firm, denying the leg-before and bat-pad appellants, and reaffirming the importance of at least one arbiter being 'neutral'. Riazuddin was particularly impressive. Diminutive but never demeaned or intimidated, one wondered how much the staunchness of a solid partner like David Orchard made Riazuddin confident in his judgements.

Australia's batting was more applied than attractive, the run-out of Langer a wasted wicket, caused by Mark Waugh's casual push and run to the favoured left hand of Ijaz at square leg. Next time Langer might stand his ground and shout 'no', instead of falling into fatal indecision. Waugh made amends with a controlled dissection of the spinners.

Left-armer Shakeel was accurate, but predictable, darting through without ever hinting he might deceive Waugh in flight. By the time Mark's 15th Test century had been scored, his team was well placed, and with Robertson swinging judiciously for 45, a lead of 418 seemed more than enough to bowl at on the last day.

Colin Miller caused a stir grabbing three wickets in 22 balls in the first hour, two plumb leg befores and Afridi driving lusciously to Healy off a thin middle, but McGrath, feeling the pinch, could not repeat his first-innings brilliance. Certainly Taylor's missed catch off Ijaz was vital, but the combination of a slow pitch, some ineffective spin bowling, and the talented Moin in partnership with a defiantly counter-attacking Ijaz, made sure of the draw and a series win for Australia.

Taylor's team were better prepared, motivated and led. Pakistan's performance left one ruminating about the talented players who lacked purpose, and that sense of being a team that Wasim may have delivered. Put brutally, when it came to toughness, Australia won by knockout – or at least on points.

TEST MATCH AVERAGES
Pakistan v. Australia

PAKISTAN

Batting	M	Inns	NO	HS	Runs	Av	100	50
Ijaz Ahmed	2	3	1	155	280	140.00	2	-
Saeed Anwar	2	3	-	145	290	96.66	2	-
Aamir Sohail	3	5	-	133	206	41.20	1	-
Mushtaq Ahmed	2	3	1	48*	74	37.00	-	-
Inzamam-ul-Haq	3	5	1	97	141	35.25	-	1
Moin Khan	3	5	-	75	152	30.40	-	1
Salim Malik	3	5	1	52*	111	27.75	-	1
Wasim Akram	2	3	-	35	50	16.66	-	-
Yousuf Youhana	2	3	-	28	48	16.00	-	-
Azhar Mahmood	2	3	-	26	43	14.33	-	-

Played in one Test: Arshad Khan 7; Mohammad Wasim 1 & 0; Mohammad Zahid 1; Muhammad Hussain 1 & 17; Saqlain Mushtaq 2* & 7; Shahid Afridi 10 & 6; Shakil Ahmed 1
Played in two Tests: Shoaib Akhtar 6*

Bowling	Overs	Mds	Runs	Wkts	Av	Best	10/m	5/inns
Shahid Afridi	41.3	9	101	5	20.20	5-52	-	1
Arshad Khan	97	28	214	5	42.80	3-72	-	-
Wasim Akram	79	10	222	5	44.40	3-111	-	-
Shoaib Akhtar	78.2	14	251	5	50.20	2-107	-	-

Also bowled: Aamir Sohail 75-12-200-3; Azhar Mahmood 39-3-136-1; Ijaz Ahmed 14-1-33-1; Mohammad Zahid 26-2-116-0; Muhammad Hussain 20-3-66-2; Mushtaq Ahmed 107-11-327-4; Salim Malik 31-1-93-0; Saqlain Mushtaq 41.5-9-112-2; Shakil Ahmed 54.1-3-139-4

Fielding Figures
7 - Moin Khan (5 ct/2 st); 3 - Mohammad Wasim, Yousuf Youhana; 2 - Inzamam-ul-Haq, Shahid Afridi; 1 - Azhar Mahmood, Ijaz Ahmed, Mushtaq Ahmed, Salim Malik, Shakil Ahmed, Wasim Akram

AUSTRALIA

Batting	M	Inns	NO	HS	Runs	Av	100	50
MA Taylor	3	5	1	334*	513	128.25	1	2
SR Waugh	3	5	1	157	235	58.75	1	-
IA Healy	3	4	1	82	146	48.66	-	1
MJ Slater	3	5	-	108	238	47.60	1	1
ME Waugh	3	5	-	117	228	45.60	1	-
DS Lehmann	2	3	-	98	127	42.33	-	1
JL Langer	3	5	-	116	211	42.20	1	1
SCG MacGill	3	3	1	24*	55	27.5	-	-
GD McGrath	3	3	2	6	13	13.00	-	-
CR Miller	3	3	-	3	3	1.00	-	-

Played in two Tests: DW Fleming 8
Played in one Test: RT Ponting 76* & 43; GR Robertson 5 & 45

Bowling	Overs	Mds	Runs	Wkts	Av	Best	10/m	5/inns
SCG MacGill	127.4	24	412	15	27.46	5-66	-	1
GD McGrath	120.5	34	344	12	28.66	5-66	-	1
CR Miller	121	31	329	8	41.12	3-82	-	-

Also bowled: DW Fleming 70.1-13-180-4; DS Lehmann 10-3-18-1; RT Ponting 5-1-13-1; GR Robertson 38-6-102-1; ME Waugh 8-0-32-0; SR Waugh 20-6-41-1

Fielding Figures
9 - IA Healy; 6 - JL Langer; 4 - MA Taylor; 3 - DW Fleming; 2 - GD McGrath; 1 - DS Lehmann, SCG MacGill, CR Miller, MJ Slater, ME Waugh, SR Waugh

ONE-DAY INTERNATIONALS

Australia dominated Pakistan, in another series that underlined the exhibition nature of most one-day series. And an exhibition for which there was no reward by way of a trophy for the victors. It is easy cynically to pass these series off as mere revenue raisers, and they would have far more meaning if the results counted towards a broader competition or official ICC pecking order.

Australia's separation policy, introducing six fresh players, certainly energised their approach, whereas Pakistan floundered with their batting, missing the injured Saeed Anwar and Inzamam. Again the sustained quality of McGrath's bowling was a major factor, and other than Warne, Australia were at full strength.

Gilchrist set the tempo in the first match in Karachi, cueing an impressive sinistral performance from Lehmann and Bevan. Out in the 13th over for 45, Gilchrist was particularly savage on the wayward Kabir Khan. Lehmann scored his maiden international one-day century from 97 balls, adding a rollicking 157 with Bevan, who showed how aggressive running and clever placements can comfortably average six an over against spread fields. With 85 coming from the last ten overs, Australia reached their third-highest first-innings one-day total, 324 for 8. Pakistan's chase began disastrously when McGrath dismissed Elahi with his second ball, taking three wickets in an opening spell that sent Pakistan plummeting to 76 for 6 in the 16th over. Yousuf Youhana, one of only four Christians to play for Pakistan, kept the innings, but not the contest, alive, with 92 from 110 balls. Australia dropped seven catches but still won with 16 balls and 86 runs in hand. An eager crowd, estimated at 33,000, watched the action, some precariously perched on the corrugated iron roofs, until the police removed them. The roof parties certainly won more attention than the match as Pakistan meandered towards their inevitable defeat.

In Peshawar Pakistan's top order failed again. On the same pitch where Taylor had amassed his triple century, Australia's pace attack swung and bounced the ball in cool conditions, Azhar Mahmood saving the innings from a wipe-out at 5 for 59 with 65 sensible runs. Pakistan's 7 for 217 seemed inadequate as once again Gilchrist whirred into attack, clipping 42 from 48 balls. The skillful Saqlain, who had not played in Karachi, produced a fine spell of accurate, varied off-spin, teasing out

Moin Khan.
David Munden/Sportsline Photographic

hundreds from Ijaz and Yousuf. Challenged to achieve a record-chasing total, Australia's momentum was guaranteed by the effervescent Gilchrist and Ponting. Maintaining a rate above six runs per over in their 193-run stand meant only 59 were needed in the last ten overs, and Australia cruised in with seven balls to spare. It was the first time four players had made centuries in a one-day international. So Australia completed a clean sweep, three-nil, and with this rousing win maintained their undefeated tour record.

In the absence of an official trophy, the Australian media made an unofficial presentation of a local artefact to Steve Waugh's victorious team.

Match One
6 November 1998 at National Stadium, Karachi
Australia 324 for 8 (50 overs) DS Lehmann 103, MG Bevan 83
Pakistan 238 (47.2 overs) Yousuf Youhana 92
Australia won by 86 runs
Man of the Match: DS Lehmann

Match Two
8 November 1998 at Arbab Niaz Stadium, Peshawar
Pakistan 217 for 7 (50 overs) Azhar Mahmood 65*
Australia 220 for 5 (48.1 overs) MG Bevan 57*, RT Ponting 55
Australia won by five wickets
Man of the Match: BP Julian

Match Three
10 November 1998 at Gaddafi Stadium, Lahore
Pakistan 315 for 8 (50 overs) Ijaz Ahmed 111, Yousuf Youhana 100
Australia 316 for 4 (48.1 overs) RT Ponting 124*, AC Gilchrist 103
Australia won by six wickets
Man of the Match: RT Ponting

three victims in 14 balls, putting the clamp on Australia's advance. Ponting and Bevan assiduously consolidated from 90 for 4, and with the light fading, Lehmann struck four boundaries to clinch a five-wicket win.

On the flattest pitch of the series in Lahore Pakistan at last found batting form. A brilliant throw down run-out from Ricky Ponting removed Salim Malik at 3 for 73, whereupon Ijaz Ahmed and Yousuf Youhana scored effortlessly. Steve Waugh tried eight bowlers, but Ijaz kept hitting fours, eight in his fifty from as many balls. They thumped 87 from the final ten overs, Afridi swashbuckling a lively 40, behind run-a-ball

ZIMBABWE IN PAKISTAN
By Qamar Ahmed

Zimbabwe held on to a seven-wicket victory in the first Test at Peshawar to win their first overseas Test series. Interestingly, their first ever Test victory had also come against Pakistan when they beat them at Harare in 1994–95 by an innings and 64 runs.

For Pakistan it was a disappointing end to their international commitments at home. Ravaged by allegations of match-fixing, betting and bribery, and by internal unrest over the appointment of Aamir Sohail as captain, they were also deprived of the opportunity to level the series by inclement weather and unusual fog.

Pakistan had hoped to square the series at Lahore in the second Test, but 233 overs were lost because of bad light and fog, and the match ended in a draw. The final Test at Faisalabad had to be abandoned without a ball being bowled, again due to heavy fog.

Dissension in the Pakistan team reached such a crescendo that the captain Aamir Sohail had to pull out of the second Test match at Lahore complaining of 'stomach trouble'. The truth was, the selectors' choice of team for the second Test was not to his liking and the dressing room atmosphere had put even greater pressure on him. Moin Khan, his deputy, was handed the reins of the captaincy for the first time in a Test.

Zimbabwe's victory in a low-scoring match in the first Test at Peshawar was helped by left-hander Neil Johnson, who scored his maiden Test century. Medium-pacer Henry Olonga took 4 for 42 in the second innings to devastate Pakistan and bowl them out for 103. The target of 162 to win was achieved by the visitors for the loss of only three wickets. Pakistan's batting failure in the second innings wrecked the good work done by Wasim Akram and Waqar Younis, who had earned a decent 58-run first-innings lead through their attacking bowling.

Yousuf Youhana, who was named Man of the Series, scored 209 runs in two Tests including his maiden unbeaten 120 in the second Test to finish with an average of 104.50. Saeed Anwar and Ijaz Ahmed also batted well, but only in patches. Heath Streak bagged his 100th Test victim in his 25th Test, to become the first Zimbabwean bowler to reach that landmark. Salim Malik,

FIRST TEST – PAKISTAN v. ZIMBABWE
27, 28, 29 and 30 November 1998 at Arbab Niaz Stadium, Peshawar

PAKISTAN

	First Innings		Second Innings	
Saeed Anwar	b Johnson	36	(7) c A Flower, b Olonga	31
Aamir Sohail (capt)	c A Flower, b Mbangwa	15	(1) c and b Olonga	2
Ijaz Ahmed	C Whittall, b Mbangwa	87	c Johnson, b Streak	0
Inzamam-ul-Haq	lbw, b Mbangwa	19	b Olonga	2
Yousuf Youhana	c Campbell, b Streak	75	(5) b Mbangwa	14
*Moin Khan	c Mbangwa, b Olonga	15	(6) b Mbangwa	6
Azhar Mahmood	c A Flower, b Streak	11	(2) c A Flower, b Olonga	5
Wasim Akram	b Olonga	10	c Olonga, b Mbangwa	31
Mushtaq Ahmed	lbw, b Streak	0	run out (Johnson)	0
Waqar Younis	lbw, b Streak	6	not out	1
Aqib Javed	not out	1	c Wishart, b Streak	0
	b 4, lb 6, nb 11	21	b 4, lb 2, nb 5	11
		296		**103**

	First Innings				Second Innings			
	O	M	R	W	O	M	R	W
Streak	22.5	2	93	4	12.5	3	19	2
Olonga	17	3	47	2	11	1	42	4
Johnson	18	2	76	1	6	2	13	–
Mbangwa	23	9	40	3	7	2	23	3
Whittall	5	0	30	–				

Fall of Wickets
1–45, 2–56, 3–92, 4–210, 5–233, 6–268, 7–283, 8–283, 9–288
1–7, 2 12, 3–12, 4–15, 5–34, 6–41, 7–98, 8–102, 9–102

ZIMBABWE

	First Innings		Second Innings	
GJ Rennie	lbw, b Wasim Akram	2	c Ijaz Ahmed, b Wasim Akram	6
GW Flower	c Azhar Mahmood, b Waqar	15	c Moin Khan, b Wasim Akram	31
MW Goodwin	lbw, b Waqar Younis	29	not out	73
ADR Campbell (capt)	lbw, b Wasim Akram	16	c Ijaz Ahmed, b Wasim Akram	12
*A Flower	b Waqar Younis	0	not out	17
NC Johnson	c Azhar Mahmood, b Wasim	107		
CB Wishart	b Wasim Akram	3		
HH Streak	b Mushtaq Ahmed	24		
AR Whittall	c Azhar Mahmood, b Waqar	13		
HK Olonga	lbw, b Wasim Akram	3		
M Mbangwa	not out	1		
	lb 6, nb 19	25	b 4, lb 8, w 2, nb 9	23
		238	(for 3 wickets)	**162**

	First Innings				Second Innings			
	O	M	R	W	O	M	R	W
Wasim Akram	23	5	52	5	17	6	47	3
Waqar Younis	20.3	2	78	4	11	1	51	–
Aqib Javed	14	2	52	–	13.2	4	36	–
Azhar Mahmood	6	0	28	–	3	1	3	–
Mushtaq Ahmed	5	0	22	1	4	2	13	–

Fall of Wickets
1–3, 2–58, 3–63, 4–63, 5–106, 6–115, 7–218, 8–218, 9–236
1–13, 2–94, 3–130

Umpires: Athar Zaidi & G Sharp
Toss: Zimbabwe

Zimbabwe won by seven wickets

Left-hander Neil Johnson scored a maiden Test century for Zimbabwe against Pakistan at the Arbab Niaz Stadium, Peshawar. Zimbabwe eventually won the match by seven wickets.
Mueen-ud-din-Hameed/Sportsline Photographic

dropped from the first Test, returned for the second to appear in his 100th Test match but was unlucky to be run out for 2. Saqlain Mushtaq, with 5 for 32 and Waqar Younis with 4 for 54, bowled superbly in the second Test to earn Pakistan a lead of 142 runs. In the end poor weather spoiled their bid for win as the match petered out in a draw.

One other notable milestone reached in the series was by Wasim Akram who, in taking the wicket of Neil Johnson, reached the landmark of 350 Test wickets

Pakistan's had the consolation of a two-one win in the one-day series.

FIRST TEST
27, 28, 29 and 30 November 1998 at Peshawar

On a seaming pitch, Zimbabwe came from behind to bowl Pakistan out for 103 in their second innings to chase only 162 runs to win their first Test abroad. They did so at a canter losing only three wickets and thus taking a one-nil lead in the three-match series.

Pakistan owed their first innings total of 296 to Ijaz Ahmed who made 87 and Yousuf Youhana, who scored a fine 75. The two put on 118 for the fourth wicket after Pakistan were reduced to 92 for 3. Heath Streak, playing in his 25th Test, became the first Zimbabwean to take 100 wickets in Tests when he had Azhar Mahmood caught at the wicket. He picked up three more wickets on the second morning with the new ball to finish with 4 for 93 to bowl Pakistan out for 296. Mpumelelo Mbangwa claimed 3 for 40.

Zimbabwe, in turn, were reduced to 115 for 6 by some aggressive and attacking bowling by Waqar

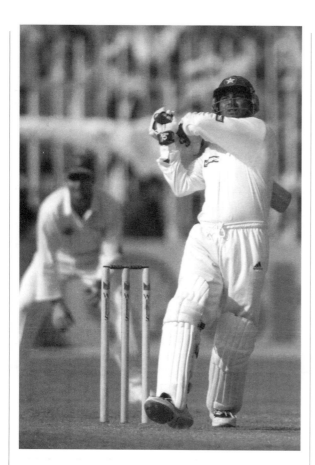

Aamir Sohail was appointed captain of Pakistan for the Test matches against Zimbabwe, but pulled out of the second Test complaining of 'stomach trouble'.

Mueen-ud-din-Hameed / Sportsline Photographic

Younis. The fast bowler was deprived of a hat-trick by Neil Johnson after he dismissed Murray Goodwin and Andy Flower with successive deliveries. Johnson revived Zimbabwean hopes with a seventh-wicket partnership of 103 with Heath Streak. Dropped at 9 by Azhar Mahmood off Wasim Akram, Johnson finally reached his maiden Test century with 15 fours, but was out to the second ball of the third morning to become Wasim Akram's 350th Test wicket. Wasim finished with 5 for 52, his 22nd haul of five wickets or more in a Test.

Henry Olonga's three wickets in ten balls left Pakistan reeling at 44 for 6 in the second innings. Wasim Akram and Saeed Anwar – who had batted late in the order because of a fever – then put on 57 for the seventh wicket. But Pakistan's last four wickets fell for five runs as they tumbled to 103 all out, their lowest against Zimbabwe. By the close of

the third day Zimbabwe, needing 162 to win, knocked up 70 for 1. Murray Goodwin, 34 overnight, and Andy Flower made brisk runs to wrap up the match on the fourth day within two hours of play.

'The victory is special for me as it comes against a top-class side. It took Australia 39 years to win a Test here, but we did it within only six years,' said the proud Zimbabwean captain, Alastair Campbell.

SECOND TEST
10, 11, 12, 13 and 14 December 1998 at Lahore

The Test match started on a controversial note as the captain of Pakistan, Aamir Sohail, did not turn up for the game and pulled out of the Test complaining of stomach trouble. His withdrawal at the last minute was, however, more to do with his differences with the selectors who had decided to play Salim Malik in his 100th Test. It was no secret that Sohail's team-mates were disenchanted with his style of leadership. Moin Khan, the vice-captain, took charge of the last two Tests. Unfortunately for Pakistan, the weather played a major part in the match, which ended in a draw. Only 13 overs were bowled on the third day, 45 on the fourth, and there was no play at all on the final day due to thick fog.

After putting Zimbabwe in to bat, Pakistan bowled the visitors out for 183 in their first innings. Waqar Younis picked up 4 for 78, taking all his wickets in his first spell and within the space of 25 balls. Off-spinner Saqlain Mushtaq had a haul of 5 for 32. An unbeaten 60 by Andy Flower had given Zimbabwe some respectability but bad light – a taste of what was to follow – brought a premature end to first day's play.

Pakistan's 325 for 9 was founded on a maiden Test century by Yousuf Youhana, who hit 15 fours and a six in his 120. Heavy fog allowed only 13 overs on the third day as Pakistan's innings dragged on into the fourth day. From 215 for 8, Pakistan managed to recover to take a first-innings lead of 142. Zimbabwe reached 48 without loss on the fourth afternoon, and were able to hang on for a draw as heavy fog engulfed the ground for the rest of the match.

THIRD TEST
Match abandoned

SECOND TEST – PAKISTAN v. ZIMBABWE
10, 11, 12, 13 and 14 December 1998 at Gaddafi Stadium, Lahore

ZIMBABWE

	First Innings		Second Innings	
GJ Rennie	c Ijaz Ahmed, b Waqar Younis	3	not out	16
GW Flower	lbw, b Waqar Younis	7	not out	17
MW Goodwin	c Moin Khan, b Waqar Younis	10		
ADR Campbell (capt)	c Yousuf Youhana, b Waqar	5		
*A Flower	not out	60		
NC Johnson	c and b Shoaib Akhtar	14		
CB Wishart	c Salim Malik, b Saqlain	28		
HH Streak	c Wasim Akram, b Saqlain	19		
HK Olonga	c Shoaib Akhtar, b Saqlain	3		
AG Huckle	c Saeed Anwar, b Saqlain	13		
M Mbangwa	c Ijaz Ahmed, b Saqlain	2		
	b 4, lb 3, nb 12	19	lb 5, nb 10	15
		183	(for 0 wicket)	**48**

	First Innings				Second Innings			
	O	M	R	W	O	M	R	W
Wasim Akram	20	6	42	–	6	0	23	–
Waqar Younis	18	3	54	4				
Shoaib Akhtar	15	1	48	1	5	1	15	–
Saqlain Mushtaq	13.5	3	32	5	1	0	5	–

Fall of Wickets
1–3, 2–16, 3–22, 4–28, 5–55, 6–104, 7–136, 8–140, 9–170

PAKISTAN

	First Innings	
Saeed Anwar	c A Flower, b Johnson	75
Naved Ashraf	b Streak	32
Ijaz Ahmed	c Huckle, b Johnson	16
Salim Malik	run out (Streak)	2
Yousuf Youhana	not out	120
Hasan Raza	c Rennie, b Huckle	3
*Moin Khan (capt)	lbw, b Olonga	25
Wasim Akram	c Johnson, b Olonga	2
Saqlain Mushtaq	b Olonga	0
Shoaib Akhtar	b Huckle	11
Waqar Younis	not out	24
	lb 10, nb 5	15
	(for 9 wickets, dec.)	**325**

	First Innings			
	O	M	R	W
Streak	33	8	75	1
Olonga	25	9	63	3
Mbangwa	24	4	66	–
Johnson	24	2	71	2
Huckle	7	0	40	2

Fall of Wickets
1–69, 2–121, 3–129, 4–132, 5–147, 6–213, 7–215, 8–215, 9–275

Umpires: Mian Mohammad Aslam & DB Hair
Toss: Pakistan

Match drawn

TEST MATCH AVERAGES
Pakistan v. Zimbabwe

PAKISTAN

Batting	M	Inns	NO	HS	Runs	Av	100	50
Yousuf Youhana	2	3	1	120*	209	104.50	1	1
Saeed Anwar	2	3	–	75	142	47.33	–	1
Ijaz Ahmed	2	3	–	87	103	34.33	–	1
Waqar Younis	2	3	2	24*	31	31.00	–	–
Moin Khan	2	3	–	25	46	15.33	–	–
Wasim Akram	2	3	–	31	43	14.33	–	–

Played in one Test: Aamir Sohail 15 & 2; Aqib Javed 1* & 0; Azhar Mahmood 11 & 5; Hasan Raza 3; Inzamam-ul-Haq 19 & 2; Mushtaq Ahmed 0 & 0; Naved Ashraf 32; Salim Malik 2; Saqlain Mushtaq 0; Shoaib Akhtar 11

Bowling	Overs	Mds	Runs	Wkts	Av	Best	10/m	5/inns
Saqlain Mushtaq	14.5	3	37	5	7.40	5–32	–	1
Wasim Akram	66	17	164	8	20.50	5–52	–	1
Waqar Younis	49.3	6	183	8	22.87	4–54	–	–

Also bowled: Aqib Javed 27.2–6–88–0; Azhar Mahmood 9–1–31–0; Mushtaq Ahmed 9–2–35–1; Shoaib Akhtar 20–2–63–1

Fielding Figures
4 – Ijaz Ahmed; 3 – Azhar Mahmood; 2 – Moin Khan, Shoaib Akhtar; 1 – Saeed Anwar, Salim Malik, Wasim Akram, Yousuf Youhana

ZIMBABWE

Batting	M	Inns	NO	HS	Runs	Av	100	50
A Flower	2	3	2	60*	77	77.00	–	1
MW Goodwill	2	3	1	73*	112	56.00	–	1
GW Flower	2	4	1	31	70	23.33	–	–
ADR Campbell	2	3	–	16	33	11.00	–	–
GJ Rennie	2	4	1	16*	27	9.00	–	–

Played in two Tests: NC Johnson 107 & 14; M Mbangwa 1* & 2; HK Olonga 3 & 3; HH Streak 24 & 19; CB Wishart 3 & 28
Played in one Test: AG Huckle 13; AR Whittall 13

Bowling	Overs	Mds	Runs	Wkts	Av	Best	10/m	5/inns
HK Olonga	53	13	152	9	16.88	4–42	–	–
M Mbangwa	54	15	129	6	21.50	3–23	–	–
HH Streak	68.4	13	187	7	26.71	4–93	–	–

Also bowled: AG Huckle 7–0–40–2; NC Johnson 48–6–160–3; AR Whittall 5–0–30–0

Fielding Figures
5 – A Flower; 2 – NC Johnson, HK Olonga; 1 – ADR Campbell, AG Huckle, M Mbangwa, GJ Rennie, AR Whittall, CB Wishart

ONE-DAY INTERNATIONALS

Following their defeats at the hands of Australia, Pakistan had the consolation of beating Zimbabwe two-one in the one-day series. The return of Aamir Sohail and Saeed Anwar as openers proved to be a bonus; they provided half-century starts in the victories at Gujranwala and Rawalpindi where Pakistan clinched the series.

In the first match, at Gujranwala, Pakistan bowled poorly to allow the visitors to make an impressive 237. Neil Johnson and Grant Flower put on 75 for the first wicket, Johnson scoring 74, Flower 24 and later the captain chipped in with a useful 42 in 57 balls as Saqlain Mushtaq and Shahid Afridi shared seven wickets between them. Pakistan reached the target in the 48th over with the help of a blistering 91 by Aamir Sohail, who hit nine fours and a six in his 105-ball innings. Moin Khan's catch to dismiss Grant

Flower made him the first Pakistan 'keeper to claim 100 victims in one-day internationals.

Zimbabwe were undaunted by the setback and won the second match at Sheikhupura by six wickets. Having put Pakistan in, Heath Streak, Andy Whittall and Neil Johnson reduced the home side to 98 for 5. But for young Hasan Raza's 46, Pakistan would have been humiliated. Later an opening stand of 101 between Neil Johnson (103) and Grant Flower (42) helped Zimbabwe reach the target of 212 in the 41st over. Johnson's maiden century in the one-day game was studded with 13 fours.

With one victory each under their belt the two teams arrived at Rawalpindi for the decider, which Pakistan won by 110 runs. After being put in Pakistan piled up 301 for 6 with the help of 132 by Ijaz Ahmed. His ninth one-day hundred had come in 103 balls. Saeed Anwar's 77 contained nine fours and a six. The opening stand of 77 with Aamir Sohail and the third-wicket stand of 97 in 117 balls between Ijaz Ahmed and Inzamam-ul-Haq had given Pakistan the launching pad for a sizeable score. Zimbabwe were bowled out for 191 in the 38th over. An innings of 61 by Andy Flower was the only notable feature of their rather patchy innings as Saqlain Mushtaq, with 3 for 27, was able to dent the middle order.

Match One
20 November 1998 at Jinnah Stadium, Gujranwala
Zimbabwe 237 (49.3 overs) NC Johnson 74, Saqlain Mushtaq 4 for 35
Pakistan 241 for 6 (47.4 overs) Aamir Sohail 91, Yousuf Youhana 55*
Pakistan won by four wickets
Man of the Match: Aamir Sohail

Match Two
22 November 1998 at Sheikhupura Cricket Stadium, Sheikhupura
Pakistan 211 (50 overs)
Zimbabwe 212 for 4 (40.4 overs) NC Johnson 103
Zimbabwe won by six wickets
Man of the Match: NC Johnson

Match Three
24 November 1998 at Pindi Cricket Stadium, Rawalpindi
Pakistan 301 for 6 (50 overs) Ijaz Ahmed 132, Saeed Anwar 73
Zimbabwe 191 (37.2 overs) A Flower 61
Pakistan won by 110 runs
Man of the Match: Ijaz Ahmed

Shoaib Akhtar.
David Munden/Sportsline Photographic

PAKISTAN DOMESTIC FIRST-CLASS SEASON
By Qamar Ahmed

The 1998–99 domestic season was one of the busiest in Pakistan's history. More than one hundred first-class games were played and there were visits by Australia, Zimbabwe and Sri Lanka. The season was particularly memorable for Peshawar who won the premier first-class tournament, the Quaid-e-Azam Trophy Grade 1, for the first time. The northerners beat Karachi Whites by an innings and 33 runs in the final at the National Stadium Karachi. Peshawar missed their star bowler Arshad Khan but, instead, they were successfully led by the medium-pacer Kabir Khan

Kabir Khan of Peshawar took 113 wickets in 18 matches, breaking the record for most first-class wickets by a bowler in Pakistan.

Mueen-ud-din-Hameed/Sportsline Photographic

who went on to create a new record for most first-class wickets by a bowler in Pakistan. His 113 wickets in 18 matches cost him 15.09, breaking Ijaz Faqih's record of 1985–86.

With Kabir Khan bowling so well for both Peshawar and Habib Bank, it was no wonder that the latter also featured prominently in the final honours list, winning the season's Patron's Trophy Grade 1. The champions made short work of the Agricultural Development Bank (ADBP) in the final at Karachi by an innings and 21 runs. Habib Bank had also taken this title in 1997–98 and are now the Patron's Trophy champions for the seventh time. Another young man from Peshawar broke a long-standing record: Wasim Yousufi, the wicketkeeper, dismissed 74 batsmen in 19 matches for the champions and for his new employers, Pakistan Customs. The previous record was held by Ashraf Ali, who claimed 70 dismissals in 1986–87 playing for the United Bank.

Two batsmen reached the landmark of scoring 1,000 runs in the season: Aamer Hanif of Karachi Whites and Allied Bank made 1,029 runs at an aggregate of 49.00 in 15 matches and Mohammad Ramzan of Faisalabad scored 1,017 runs in 17 matches at 35.06. The best bowling figures of the season were Athar Laeeq's 8 for 51 for Karachi Whites against Gujranwala and Kabir Khan's 8 for 52 for Peshawar against Hyderabad, while Manzoor Akhtar, a leg-spinner, had match figures of 12 for 152 in the Allied Bank's match against WAPDA.

Those are the statistics, but the season was clouded by confusion off the field. After Pakistan were defeated by Australia in the World Cup final, the cricket board was disbanded and an ad hoc committee was appointed by the President of Pakistan. This committee immediately announced a change in the first-class format for the 1999–2000 season, in which both the state teams and city teams would play alongside the commercial organisations' teams in one tournament called the Quaid-e-Azam Trophy. The Patron's Trophy, therefore, seems in danger of being scrapped. The officials of the ad hoc committee, led by a man who is totally unknown in cricket circles, Mr Mujeeb-ur-Rehman, also froze all the accounts of the state teams for scrutiny. His decision was later challenged in a court of law.

PAKISTAN DOMESTIC ONE-DAY SEASON

The Wills Cup, which had been sponsored by the Pakistan Tobacco Company for 19 years, was played under a new flag: Tissot. The tournament was won by Allied Bank who beat Pakistan Customs by four wickets in a day-and-night final at Lahore.

In the semi-finals, Allied Bank won by eight wickets against the Pakistan National Shipping Corporation (PNSC) with 15.3 overs to spare as they chased 237 to win. Humayun Farhat, the Man of the Match, made 112. In the other semi-final,

Customs, put in by Karachi Whites, clobbered their attack to the tune of 314 for 6. Hasan Raza made 109 and Azam Khan scored 75 as the two put on 163 in 184 balls for the third wicket. For Karachi Blues the target was unattainable and they were out for 253.

The final seemed to be heading for an easy win for the bankers following a fourth-wicket stand of 163 between Aamer Hanif and Ijaz Ahmed Junior, but a succession of wickets fell after the stand was broken to make the match an interesting one.

Customs, put in to bat, posted 259 for 9 in 50 overs after early hiccups. Following damage by Taimur Khan, who removed two batsmen within ten balls, Hasan Raza and Aamer Bashir added 60 for the fourth wicket. Hasan Raza made a lusty 50-ball fifty and later Aamer Bashir made 101 in 120 balls with eleven fours adding 89 more runs for the fifth wicket with Qayyumul Hasan. Chasing 260 to win, Allied Bank lost three wickets for 37, but Ijaz Ahmed Junior and Aamer Hanif steered the bank side with some fine batting. Hanif made an unbeaten 85 and Ijaz Junior slammed 84 in 86 balls with eight fours. The victory target was achieved through four leg-byes.

A total of 70 matches were played in three weeks which also featured Bangladesh. They could not progress beyond the preliminary stages. Other fancied teams like Habib Bank, Pakistan Airline and National Bank failed to reach the last four, largely because of the commitments of their players for Pakistan.

Salim Elahi of Habib Bank who scored three centuries, 152 against Bahawalpur, 144 against Multan and 172 against National Bank was the Player of the Tournament. The Bangladesh versus Quetta match ended in a tie: the first instance in 18 years of one-day cricket in Pakistan.

Aamir Sohail, who failed to be selected for Pakistan's World Cup squad.
David Munden/Sportsline Photographic

FIRST-CLASS AVERAGES

BATTING

	M	Inns	NO	HS	Runs	Av	100	50
Younas Khan	8	10	3	202	514	73.42	2	2
MJ Slater	5	8	0	221	507	63.37	2	1
Wajahatullah Wasti	6	11	1	135	614	61.40	3	2
Zaheer Abbasi	8	12	3	157	547	60.77	2	3
Saeed Anwar	5	8	0	145	477	59.62	2	1
Hasan Adnan	8	11	2	91	529	58.77	-	6
Hasan Raza	11	20	3	163*	925	54.41	3	2
Mahmood Hamid	14	21	3	138	939	52.16	2	6
Aamir Hanif	15	27	6	170*	1029	49.00	2	5
Zahid Fazal	12	16	1	201*	733	48.86	2	2
Bilal Khilji	11	17	3	106*	679	48.50	1	7
Ghulam Ali	8	14	0	141	676	48.28	1	4
J Langer	5	9	1	116	382	47.75	2	1
Abdul Basit Niazi	14	23	2	156*	978	46.57	3	5
Imran Farhat	6	11	0	172	472	42.90	1	3
Aamir Sohail	6	10	0	180	426	42.60	2	-
Intikhab Alam	10	16	2	95	594	42.42	-	4
Mohammad Nawaz	8	11	0	139	456	41.45	3	-
Zeeshan Parvez	9	16	3	127	517	39.76	2	2
ME Waugh	5	8	0	117	315	39.37	1	1
Akhtar Sarfraz	11	15	1	138*	541	38.64	1	3
Naeem Akhtar	14	21	3	157*	690	38.33	2	2
Atif Rauf	6	9	1	74	304	38.00	-	3
Asif Mujtaba	14	23	5	93*	680	37.77	-	6
Adil Nisar	11	17	0	129	642	37.76	1	4
Sohail Jaffar	8	14	1	100	483	37.15	1	2
Naveed Latif	14	22	1	161*	775	36.90	2	3
Ijaz Ahmed, Jr	16	28	3	110	921	36.84	1	9
Sher Ali	6	11	0	81	403	36.63	-	4
Taimur Khan	10	16	3	101*	474	36.46	1	2
Aamir Iqbal	9	15	2	74	474	36.46	-	3
Javed Hayat	7	12	1	89	398	36.18	-	3
Aaley Haider	6	11	0	123	393	35.72	2	1
Saeed Azad	17	30	3	110	964	35.70	3	3
Akram Raza	14	15	5	51*	354	35.40	-	1
Ehsan Shah	9	14	1	201*	456	35.07	1	-
Mohammad Ramzan	17	31	2	90	1017	35.06	-	6
Rehan Rafiq	9	12	3	128	314	34.88	1	1
Imran Naseer	13	19	1	96	625	34.72	-	6
Javed Sami Khan	16	27	1	121*	901	34.65	2	4
Tariq Aziz	7	10	0	75	343	34.30	-	3
Iqbal Imam	15	27	3	104	821	34.20	2	4
Azhar Shafiq	14	25	1	128*	816	34.00	2	3
Ali Naqvi	9	15	2	107	439	33.76	1	-
Zahid Umer	7	9	1	106	265	33.12	1	2
Azam Khan	10	18	1	84	555	32.64	-	5
Arif Mahmood	9	14	2	71	388	32.33	-	2
Naved Ashraf	11	19	1	115*	581	32.27	1	3
Taufeeq Umar	8	14	0	100	448	32.00	1	1
Faisal Athar	6	10	1	121	288	32.00	1	1
Zafar Jadoon	10	19	2	47	540	31.76	-	-
Salim Malik	7	12	1	149	342	31.09	1	2
Mansoor Rana	9	15	1	77*	425	30.35	-	3
Alamgir Khan	9	14	4	49	300	30.00	-	-
Amiruddin	11	20	0	130	591	29.55	1	2
Asif Mahmood	18	31	2	150	855	29.48	1	3
Iqbal Saleem	13	23	2	114	617	29.38	1	2
Iftikhar Hussain	9	16	1	139	435	29.00	1	2
Maqsood Ahmed	9	14	3	89*	314	28.54	-	2
Imran Abbas	14	26	3	91	656	28.52	-	6
Yasir Hameed	9	11	1	69	284	28.40	-	2
Aamir Wasim	13	19	1	79	505	28.05	-	3
Manzoor Akhtar	7	14	0	87	392	28.00	-	1
Mohammad Javed	11	19	1	75	502	27.88	-	4
Mohammad Nawaz	10	18	0	76	499	27.72	-	3
Farhan Adil	13	21	2	85	525	27.63	-	2
Imam-ul-Haq	9	17	1	57	438	27.37	-	2
Asadullah Butt	6	9	0	71	245	27.22	-	2
Ehsan Butt	10	18	1	106	461	27.11	1	1

FIRST-CLASS AVERAGES

BATTING

	M	Inns	NO	HS	Runs	Av	100	50
Shahid Afridi	8	15	1	73	378	27.00	-	2
Salim Elahi	8	12	2	82	270	27.00	-	2
Mehfooz Ali	6	10	0	106	268	26.80	1	1
Zahoor Elahi	9	17	0	157	453	26.64	1	1
Nadeem Abbasi	18	27	5	85	571	25.95	-	3
Moin Khan	6	10	0	75	257	25.70	-	2
Shadab Kabir	16	31	2	90	742	25.58	-	5
Tasanwar Hussain	6	10	1	61	230	25.55	-	1
Hafiz Majid	8	16	2	72*	357	25.50	-	1
Sajid Shah	17	21	10	51*	280	25.45	-	1
Aamir Butt	5	9	1	49	203	25.37	-	-
Naseer Ahmed	17	26	0	106	651	25.03	1	5
Usman Tariq	7	10	3	36	173	24.71	-	-
Aamir Bashir	17	27	4	76	567	24.65	-	5
Shahid Anwar	12	21	0	71	511	24.33	-	3
R Qayyum-ul-Hasan	14	24	1	96	555	24.13	-	3
Masroor Hussain	7	13	1	157*	289	24.08	1	-
Rizwan Ahmed Hassan	8	14	2	76	287	23.91	-	1
Aamir Akbar	5	9	1	95	188	23.50	-	1
Umar Rasheed	11	20	1	61*	444	23.36	-	3
Sajjad Akbar	15	22	3	114*	440	23.15	1	2
Kamran Hussain	8	12	2	89*	228	22.80	-	1
Shoaib Mohammad	7	13	0	70	296	22.76	-	3
Ahmer Saeed	5	10	0	101	224	22.40	1	-
Asfar Nawaz	6	11	0	66	245	22.27	-	1
Hanif-ur-Rehman	6	12	0	71	267	22.25	-	1
Babar Zaman	7	11	0	96	243	22.09	-	1
Hafiz Khalid	9	13	3	54	217	21.70	-	1
Majid Saeed	10	15	1	79*	303	21.64	-	2
Zafar Iqbal	8	13	2	57	237	21.54	-	1
Mohammad Hussain	8	11	0	64	236	21.45	-	1
Kamran Akmal	9	15	1	59	300	21.42	-	3
Naeem Ashraf	15	23	0	77	491	21.34	-	2
Jahangir Khan, Sr	11	16	0	89	341	21.31	-	3
Nadeem Afzaal	12	17	5	64	253	21.08	-	1
Shahid Javed	8	11	0	61	230	20.90	-	1
Naumanullah	6	10	0	90	208	20.80	-	1
Shahid Qambrani	8	14	0	105	286	20.42	1	1
Tahir Mahmood Mughal	15	22	2	64	404	20.20	-	2
Nadeem Hussain	12	20	4	63	313	19.56	-	2
Sajjad Ali	5	10	2	78	156	19.50	-	1
Murtaza Hussain	11	17	1	52	308	19.25	-	1
Inzamam-ul-Haq	6	10	1	97	171	19.00	-	1
Kabir Khan	18	20	2	55*	339	18.83	-	1
Naved Ahmad	8	13	0	63	244	18.76	-	2
Wasim Yousufi	19	25	2	58	428	18.60	-	2
Sajid Ali	9	17	0	60	315	18.52	-	1
Tahir Rasheed	9	14	2	56	222	18.50	-	1
Bilal Rana	6	11	1	59	182	18.20	-	1
Tariq Mahmood	5	9	0	56	159	17.66	-	1
Mohammad Asif	10	12	4	24*	139	17.37	-	-
Ijaz Mahmood	6	10	0	36	173	17.30	-	-
Mujahid Hameed	7	11	0	50	189	17.18	-	1
Qaiser Mahmood	7	11	2	37	150	16.66	-	-
Mubashir Nazir	11	15	7	27	133	16.62	-	-
Kashif Ahmed	9	17	0	48	280	16.47	-	1
Humayan Farhat	10	18	0	89	295	16.38	-	2
Shakeel Ahmed	14	19	7	44*	196	16.33	-	-
Sarfraz Ahmed	13	15	4	50	177	16.09	-	1
Shahid Mahboob	7	10	2	29	128	16.00	-	-
Tahir Shah	7	12	1	46*	174	15.81	-	-
Mujahid Jamshed	6	11	1	57	154	15.40	-	1
Mohammad Wasim	8	12	0	51	184	15.33	-	1
Shabbir Ahmed	9	12	1	37	167	15.18	-	-

Qualification: 8 completed innings, average 15.00

FIRST-CLASS AVERAGES

BOWLING

	Overs	Mds	Runs	Wkts	Av	Best	10m	5/inns
Babar Zaman	131.3	42	234	18	13.00	5–68	–	1
Naved Anjum	83	22	159	12	13.25	3–13	–	–
Bilal Rana	259.2	106	498	37	13.45	7–28	1	4
Ijaz Ahmed, Jr	146.2	47	297	20	14.85	6–74	–	1
Kabir Khan	559.4	105	1706	113	15.09	8–52	1	10
Asadullah Butt	107.1	21	277	18	15.38	5–39	–	1
Ali Raza	409.3	80	1009	62	16.27	8–55	3	7
Mohammad Hussain	168.3	56	377	23	16.39	7–53	–	2
Khalid Zafar	92	19	284	16	17.75	5–38	–	1
Fazl-e-Akbar	258.2	57	819	45	18.20	7–57	1	3
Sajid Shah	417.1	101	1222	67	18.23	6–30	2	4
Umar Rasheed	234.1	60	619	32	19.34	5–20	–	3
Naeem Akhtar	392.2	108	937	48	19.52	5–27	–	1
Arif Mahmood	199	70	394	20	19.70	5–61	–	1
Aamir Nazir	214	42	656	33	19.87	6–46	–	4
Nadeem Atzal	294.2	58	845	42	20.11	5–44	–	1
Manzoor Akhtar	123	22	385	19	20.26	8–89	1	1
Jaffar Nazir	518.1	106	1518	73	20.79	5–37	–	5
Naeem Ashraf	571.2	138	1500	72	20.83	6–36	–	6
Tahir Mahmood Mughal	453.3	75	1456	68	21.41	7–100	–	7
Naved Nazir	179.1	68	324	15	21.60	5–119	–	1
Nadeem Iqbal	392	68	1173	54	21.72	8–64	1	2
Shahid Mahboob	249.2	56	701	32	21.90	6–86	–	2
Lal Faraz	296.4	40	1023	46	22.23	7–96	1	4
Azhar Shafiq	381.5	85	1077	48	22.43	5–49	–	2
Athar Laiq	150.1	36	463	20	23.15	8–51	–	1
Mohammad Zahid, Jr	468	113	1146	49	23.38	5–34	1	3
Aamir Hanif	298.1	72	754	32	23.56	4–44	–	–
Tanvir Afzal	131.5	30	361	15	24.06	3–39	–	–
Murtaza Hussain	380.2	82	796	33	24.12	4–92	–	–
Mohammad Asif	367	81	842	34	24.76	5–86	–	1
Sarfraz Ahmed	510.5	136	1351	54	25.01	5–55	–	2
Wasim Akram	167.2	31	455	18	25.27	5–52	–	1
Sajjad Ali	123	19	433	17	25.47	5–74	–	1
Aamir Wasim	577.2	174	1353	53	25.52	5–60	–	3
Waqar Younis	121.3	19	437	17	25.70	5–54	–	1
Shakeel Ahmed	485.4	116	1238	48	25.79	7–71	1	3
Mohammad Javed	365.3	67	1034	39	26.51	6–103	–	2
Alamgir Khan	227.4	50	674	25	26.96	5–109	–	1
Ali Hussain Rizvi	271.1	46	852	31	27.48	6–98	–	2
Janwad Hameed	174	39	445	16	27.81	3–19	–	–
Kamran Hussain	184	36	588	21	28.00	7–44	–	2
Usman Tariq	96.2	13	311	11	28.27	2–0	–	–
Faisal Khan Afridi	243.4	33	851	30	28.36	5–43	–	2
Mohammad Akram	174.2	26	631	22	28.68	4–55	–	–
Akram Raza	373.1	88	959	33	29.06	7–65	–	2
Nadeem Khan	473.4	126	1090	37	29.45	5–69	–	2
Shahid Afridi	225.5	53	619	21	29.47	5–52	–	1
Shabbir Ahmed	340.1	62	1135	38	29.86	5–94	–	2
Sajjad Akbar	467.1	124	903	30	30.10	3–27	–	–

FIRST-CLASS AVERAGES

BOWLING

	Overs	Mds	Runs	Wkts	Av	Best	10m	5/inns
Naved Latif	123	25	370	12	30.83	3–41	–	–
Salman Fazal	240.1	84	497	16	31.06	4–56	–	–
Mohammad Zahid	161.2	28	571	18	31.72	4–40	–	–
Mubashir Nazir	289.4	45	960	30	32.00	5–71	–	1
Rizwan Ahmed Hassan	238	28	832	26	32.00	5–93	–	1
Zafar Iqbal	167.3	15	594	18	33.00	3–38	–	–
Ata-ur-Rehman	185.1	38	652	19	34.31	4–79	–	–
Hasnain Kazim	135.3	17	515	15	34.33	5–76	–	1
Arshad Khan	247	77	561	16	35.06	4–44	–	–
Nadeem Ghauri	199.4	48	463	13	35.61	5–80	–	1
Asfandyar Jafri	214.1	24	826	23	35.91	3–66	–	–
Danish Kaneria	106.5	19	366	10	36.60	4–55	–	–
Ali Gauhar	292.4	33	990	26	38.07	5–82	–	1
Javed Hayat	186	55	389	10	38.90	3–66	–	–
Zahid Saeed	153.3	27	546	14	39.00	4–55	–	–
Asif Mujtaba	227.3	52	557	14	39.78	3–101	–	–
Iqbal Imam	331.5	75	780	17	45.88	3–41	–	–
Raees Amjad	125.4	23	483	10	48.30	3–92	–	–

Qualification: 10 wickets in 8 innings

The following players took 10 wickets in fewer than 8 innings:

	Overs	Mds	Runs	Wkts	Av	Best	10m	5/inns
Farooq Iqbal	66.2	24	126	10	12.60	5–42	–	1
Anwar Ali	55.2	9	196	11	17.81	7–75	–	1
Ijaz Mahmood	105.4	28	265	14	18.92	6–40	–	1
SCG MacGill	169.1	32	537	24	22.37	6–34	–	2
Saqlain Mushtaq	128.2	48	429	19	22.57	5–32	–	2
Pervez Iqbal	98	24	258	11	23.45	4–91	–	–
GD McGrath	148.5	46	405	17	23.82	5–66	–	1
Waqas Ahmed	94	16	317	13	24.38	5–28	–	1
Abdur Razzaq	95.4	17	298	11	27.09	5–77	1	2
Haaris Khan	98	13	333	11	30.27	4–69	–	–
Manzoor Akhtar	109.3	22	336	11	30.54	5–69	–	1
Shoaib Malik	192.2	43	577	17	33.94	6–133	–	1
CR Miller	165	46	428	10	42.80	3–82	–	–

FIELDING

74 – Wasim Yousufi (72 ct/2 st); 53 – Nadeem Abbasi (51 ct/2 st); 34 – Kamran Akmal (33 ct/1 st) 32 – Humayan Farhat (30 ct/2 st); 31 – Ata-ur-Rehman (28 ct/3 st); 30 – Hafiz Khalid (29 ct/1 st), Iqbal Saleem (29 ct/1 st); 28– Nadeem Hussain (26 ct/2 st), Tahir Rasheed; 25 – Ehsan Shah (23 ct/2 st), Matahir Ali Shah; 24 – Mohammad Ramzan, Zahid Umar; 23 – Abdul Shakoor; 18 – Asif Mujtaba, Mahmood Hamid, Naseer Ahmed; 17 – Akram Raza, R Qayyum-al-Hasan; 16 – IA Healy (13 ct/3 st); 15 – Ahmed Zeeshan (13 ct/2 st), Zahid Fazal; 14 – Asfar Nawaz (12 ct/2 st), Aamir Bashir, Mohammad Nawaz; 13 – Alamgir Khan, Naved Ahmad; 12 – Wasim Arif (8 ct/4 st), Adil Nisar, Imran Abbas, Iqbal Imam, Qaiser Mahmood, Taufeeq Umar; 11 – Moin Khan (9 ct/2 st), Aamir Malik, Asif Mahmood, Bilal Khilji, Inlikhab Alam, Mohammad Javed, Naeem Ashraf, Zeeshan Parvez; 10 – Mohammad Wasim, Tariq Aziz, Zahoor Elahi

SRI LANKA

Sri Lanka Domestic First-Class Season
Sri Lanka Domestic One-Day Season

SRI LANKA DOMESTIC FIRST-CLASS SEASON
By Sa'adi Thawfeeq

Cricket in Sri Lanka had never been in such chaos as during the 1998–99 domestic season. At both administrative and domestic levels, conflicts and controversies raged. These remained unresolved because of a dispute regarding the functioning of the cricket board, and by the time the Australians visited Sri Lanka in September 1999, even the row over which team had won the Premier League tournament had not been settled. Far from it: the committee that had been set up to decide the argument between the two teams involved,

Roshan Mahanama: nearing the end of a distinguished career spanning 14 years.
David Munden/ Sportsline Photographic

Bloomfield Cricket Club and Colombo Cricket Club, was unable to come to a decision because of threats of court action from both teams.

The problems began immediately the following annual general meeting of the board on 30 March. Thilanga Sumathipala won the election to become the president of the board ahead of Clifford Ratawatte, an uncle of the President of the country, Chandrika Bandaranaike Kumaratunga. Ratawatte did not accept the result of the election and the problems began. A heated argument led, allegedly, to a near fist fight between the Presidential Security supporting Mr Ratawatte and the Chief Executive of the Board, Dhammika Ranatunga and his brother Prasana Ranatunga, who were rescued by their bodyguards.

Mr Ratawatte later challenged the election of Thalinga Sumathipala in the law courts and a stay order was given to stop the functioning of the board. Instead, an Interim Committee consisting of five people was appointed by the Sports Minister to run the board. The elected President challenged this action in another legal action, and the dispute continued even during the Test series against Australia.

The Premier League Tournament was disrupted as a result and a couple of matches had to be postponed until after the World Cup to decide the winner. Problems arose between Bloomfield and Colombo because several matches were postponed and eventually cancelled. Bloomfield, who consider themselves unofficial champions, had lodged a protest against the new tournament committee – which had directed Colombo to play their postponed game. However some clubs, including Bloomfield, had earlier been directed by the tournament committee not to play their postponed games in view of the enjoining order by the court.

Hence, at the time of going to press, this long, protracted argument is far from settled.

SRI LANKA DOMESTIC ONE-DAY SEASON
By Sa'adi Thawfeeq

Sri Lanka fast bowler Chaminda Vaas stole a march over his former captain Arjuna Ranatunga when he led his club Colombo Colts to victory over Singhalese SC in the final of the premier limited-overs tournament played at the R Premadasa Stadium on Boxing Day.

It was a fitting Christmas present for Colombo Colts in their 125th anniversary year. The margin of victory by 60 runs was comprehensive, and gave Colombo Colts their first-ever limited-overs title.

Colts lived up to the exceptional form they had shown throughout the tournament to rattle up an imposing total of 276 for 6 off 50 overs against an SSC side that included nine players who had represented the country in one-day internationals.

The pace was set by national wicketkeeper Romesh Kaluwitharana and Dulip Samaraweera in providing a launch pad for Colts's final total. The two batsmen put together an opening partnership of 123 off 20 overs with Kaluwitharana going on to make 70 and Samaraweera making 57 against an attack comprising Pramodya Wickremasinghe, Nuwan Zoysa and Ruchira Perera. Vaas and Erik

Upashantha took the game away from Singhalese SC when they indulged in a run-a-ball 63-run stand for the seventh wicket.

SSC's renowned batting line-up came a cropper to left-arm spinner Dinuka Hettiaratchi on the slow surface. Backed by sharp fielding, none of the top-order batsmen were allowed to make a substantial contribution.

Hettiaratchi had figures of 6 for 43, but the choice of Man of the Match went to Vaas, whose advice to his team members, 'let's play good cricket all the time', was followed to the letter that day.

SSC were dismissed for 216 in 44 overs with Upekha Fernando, Marvan Atapattu and Mahela Jayawardene all getting into the forties but none staying long enough to see it through.

Sixteen clubs participated in the tournament, which was conducted in two groups. Singhalese SC and Panadura SC qualified for the semi-finals from Group 'A', and Colombo Colts and Moors SC qualified from Group 'B'.

SSC suffered a shock five-wicket defeat in their final group match against Panadura SC. Panadura SC edged out Bloomfield, led by Sri Lanka captain Sanath Jayasuriya, by virtue of a higher run rate after both clubs tied with nine points each. Colts were in outstanding form throughout the tournament, running up the highest total – 328 for 4 in 50 overs – against Antonian SC and beating Panadura SC quite easily in the semi-finals.

Sri Lanka's explosive wicketkeeper/batsman, Romesh Kaluwitharana, lead the Colombo Colts to victory over Singhalese SC.
David Munden/Sportsline Photographic

FORM CHARTS

Derbyshire
Durham
Essex
Glamorgan
Gloucestershire
Hampshire
Kent
Lancashire
Leicestershire
Middlesex
Northamptonshire
Nottinghamshire
Somerset
Surrey
Sussex
Warwickshire
Worcestershire
Yorkshire

DERBYSHIRE CCC

FIRST-CLASS MATCHES

BATTING

	MJ Slater	AS Rollins	RMS Weston	SP Titchard	ME Cassar	DG Cork	PAJ DeFreitas	KM Krikken	P Aldred	TM Smith	KJ Dean	BJ Spendlove	SP Griffiths	AJ Harris	ID Blackwell	TA Tweats	SJ Lacey	M Newell	SD Stubbings	JP Pyemont	Extras	Total	Wickets	Result	Points	
v. Glamorgan	5	79*	3	14	5	45*	–	–	–	–	–										17	168	4	D	4	
(Derby) 20–23 April	–	–																								
v. Kent	65	71	2	4	0	82	2	24	17	0*	5										28	300	10	W	19	
(Canterbury) 28–30 April	20*	33*	–	–	–	–	–	–	–												9	62	0			
v. Warwickshire	39	51	16	23	5	9	13		10			63	16	7*							34	286	10	L	6	
(Edgbaston) 14–17 May	12	40	9	73	14	21	14		0			20	35	8*							18	264	10			
v. Northamptonshire	171	11	136	22	21	7				7*		20	13	4	28						26	466	10	W	20	
(Derby) 19–21 May	30	3		19*	8*																6	66	2			
v. Yorkshire	0	0	72	10	40	17	32					9*		6	4						15	206	10	D	9	A
(Derby) 2–5 June																										
v. Essex	27	129*	0	38	5							12			32	10					6	285	10	L	6	BCD
(Chelmsford) 9–11 June	22	22	41	1	8							9			4	0					15	131	10			BCD
v. Middlesex	53	6	124	45	0			17		10*		14		4	60		21				12	366	10	W	20	
(Lord's) 30 June–3 July	6	40*		16*																	4	66	1			
v. Somerset	20	5	156	5			56	0				51		7*	8		27				24	359	10	L	6	A
(Derby) 9–12 July	6	4	35	25			30*	26				8		0	30		0				20	194	10			A
v. Durham	9		0	3	14	53	88	15				7		3*	0			25			24	241	10	L	5	
(Chester-le-Street) 15–16 July	14		14	1	14	15	0	0				18		0*	33			7			14	130	10			
v. Sussex	18	29	7	17		4	25	3	29*			29		4	14						47	226	10	L	5	
(Derby) 21–23 July	23		0	8		37	3	15	0			8		6*	1						35	136	10			
v. Nottinghamshire		43	17	59	1	21	13	20	0*			28		5rh	13						43	263	9	W	18	
(Trent Bridge) 30 July–1 August		32	10	22	30*		4*					0			–						25	123	4			
v. Lancashire		43	6	20	27*	6	0	5	0			5					5				15	132	10	L	4	E
(Derby) 4–6 August		6	42	13*	21	5	10	2	0			22					0				14	135	9			E
v. Worcestershire		101	6	2	31		41	29	0	20*					48		28		24		52	382	10	W	20	
(Kidderminster) 18–21 August		13	1	36*	12										62*		–		40		19	183	4			
v. Surrey		22	11	0	1	18	38*	0	4						4				42		14	154	10	L	4	
(Derby) 24–27 August		53	3	37	4	53	10	6	1						4*				3	0	22	196	10			
v. Leicestershire		27	18	42	27	105			6						0		1*		0	3	19	308	10	W	19	
(Leicester) 1–3 September		113	0	29	4*			18*									2		45	13	11	235	6			
v. Gloucestershire		6	52	37		28	9	2	0	0*							4		36	7	22	203	10	W	17	
(Bristol) 8–10 September		95	43*	5		–			4								11			0*	3	161	4			
v. Hampshire		34	21	37	34	5	54	0	11	8*							31*		12		30	277	9	W	5	
(Derby) 15–18 September		5	37	26	0	51	61	27	2	1*							42		0		30	282	10			

	MJ Slater	AS Rollins	RMS Weston	SP Titchard	ME Cassar	DG Cork	PAJ DeFreitas	KM Krikken	P Aldred	TM Smith	KJ Dean	BJ Spendlove	SP Griffiths	AJ Harris	ID Blackwell	TA Tweats	SJ Lacey	M Newell	SD Stubbings	JP Pyemont
Matches	10	15	15	17	14	14	13	12	12	8	3	7	5	7	10	4	6	1	5	3
Innings	18	28	26	31	24	22	18	19	17	9	2	13	7	11	16	7	8	2	10	6
Not Out	1	3	2	4	3	2	1	3	2	6	1	0	1	7	2	0	2	0	0	1
Runs	540	965	838	752	393	535	441	389	122	52	15	279	108	48	347	21	154	32	213	23
Highest score	171	129*	156	136	42	82	105	88	29*	20*	10*	63	35	8*	62*	10	42	25	45	13
Average	31.76	38.6	34.91	27.85	18.71	26.75	25.94	24.31	8.13	17.33	15.00	21.46	18.00	12.00	24.78	3.00	25.66	16.00	21.30	4.6
100s	1	2	3	1	–	–	1	–	–	–	–	–	–	–	–	–	–	–	–	–
50s	2	5	2	2	–	4	2	3	–	–	–	2	–	–	2	–	–	–	–	–

A   MJ Deane 1; 0 & 10
B   AP Woolley 8 & 1
C   PA Thomas 1 & 0
D   SJ Base 17 & 8*
E   R Eagleson 0 & absent injured

DERBYSHIRE CCC

FIRST-CLASS MATCHES
BOWLING

	PAJ DeFreitas	KJ Dean	DG Cork	TM Smith	P Aldred	ME Cassar	AJ Harris	ID Blackwell	Overs	Totals	Byes/Leg-byes	Wickets	Run outs	
v. Kent	17-3-48-3	17-5-34-4	11-1-34-2	4-1-15-1					49	141	10	10	–	
(Canterbury) 28–30 April	19-4-58-1	16-3-60-3	9-3-23-2	14.4-4-38-4	12-6-30-0	2-1-6-0			72.4	220	5	10	–	
v. Warwickshire	33-5-92-6		17-3-37-0	17.2-2-64-3		7-0-45-1	17-4-75-0		91.2	315	2	10	–	
(Edgbaston) 14–17 May	25-4-78-2		34-8-88-5	15-4-57-0		3-0-25-0	16-5-42-2		93	319	29	10	1	A
v. Northamptonshire	21.1-5-48-5		21-4-75-2	21-5-85-2			17-1-47-1	1-0-1-0	81.1	270	14	10	–	
(Derby) 19–21 May	30-6-100-3		16-2-41-2	7-3-19-0			5.5-1-24-1	25-4-64-3	83.5	261	13	10	1	
v. Yorkshire	17.3-6-37-4		13-3-19-3			3-0-8-1	1-0-4-0		46.3	117	7	10	–	A
(Derby) 2–5 June	13.4-7-35-0		33.4-13-66-5			19-6-38-1		25-8-76-2	111	308	22	8	–	ABCD
v. Essex			24-9-52-3			27-4-51-5		15-2-40-0	96	281	6	10	–	EFG
(Chelmsford) 9–11 June			5-1-21-0			5-0-34-1		7.2-1-38-0	24.2	136	6	1	–	EG
v. Middlesex		16-2-44-1			22.5-4-54-4	6-1-29-0	25-5-63-5	3-2-7-0	76.5	210	4	10	–	H
(Lord's) 30 June–3 July		17.4-4-60-4			13-7-31-0		24-7-70-2	22-8-30-3	83.4	221	14	10	–	H
v. Somerset					33.4-8-74-5		36-9-101-5	40-14-69-0	138.4	361	24	10	–	AH
(Derby) 9–12 July					13-1-39-0		15-2-51-1	24-8-50-0	65	196	15	2	–	CH
v. Durham			30-5-106-5		15-3-66-1		23-1-108-2	21-4-60-2	89	346	6	10	–	
(Chester-le-Street) 15–16 July			5-1-14-2				4.5-1-15-1		9.5	29	–	3	–	
v. Sussex	14-0-61-1		24-2-113-6		12-4-40-1		12.5-1-51-2		62.5	271	6	10	–	
(Derby) 21–23 July	17.3-3-41-6		20-6-44-2		12-4-28-1		15-2-51-0		64.3	176	12	10	1	
v. Nottinghamshire	14-4-57-1		15-2-65-1		16.1-3-47-4		18-5-54-4		63.1	232	9	10	–	
(Trent Bridge) 30 July–1 August	22-7-39-3		14-1-46-4		14.3-2-50-3				53.3	153	6	10	–	
v. Lancashire	30-9-64-1		19-6-42-2		31-12-83-6				90.5	224	1	10	–	I
(Derby) 4–6 August	25-9-74-1		6-1-25-0		26.3-4-101-7	12-4-19-2		3-0-12-0	69.3	235	16	10	–	
v. Worcestershire	33-10-86-5			9-1-43-0	33-7-96-2	17.1-5-63-2			104.1	316	5	10	–	H
(Kidderminster) 18–21 August	26-10-51-2			3-1-10-0	25.4-5-81-6	13-5-23-1			103.4	245	17	10	–	
v. Surrey	25.1-3-76-3		20.3-4-69-2		15-5-40-1		24-3-97-3	10-3-21-1	101.3	350	8	9	–	
(Derby) 24–27 August	0.4-0-1-0		1-1-0-1					36-12-63-1	1.4	1	1	1	–	
v. Leicestershire	17.4-8-37-1		15.2-2-46-2	24.4-3-87-5		14-3-54-1		16.5-3-60-0	104.4	343	12	10	–	H
(Leicester) 1–3 September	16-8-21-2		20-3-59-2	18-2-63-5		1.5-0-12-1			61.5	187	23	10	–	H
v. Gloucestershire	13-3-57-2		15-3-42-1	3.1-1-12-1	17-4-34-6				48.1	150	5	10	–	
(Bristol) 8–10 September	21-7-35-4		16-2-42-1	21.5-1-69-5	15-1-46-0				73.5	212	20	10	–	
v. Hampshire	26-4-88-3		23-10-60-0	22-5-78-3	27-4-86-2	6-2-33-0			104	362	27	8	–	
(Derby) 15–18 September				3-1-6-2	8.2-1-37-1	4-0-35-0			34.4	199	11	5	–	

Overs	477.2	66.4	427.3	183.4	362.4	164	229.3	250.1
Maidens	125	14	96	34	85	34	44	69
Runs	1284	198	1229	646	1063	562	752	595
Wickets	59	12	55	31	50	19	26	12
Bowler's average	21.76	16.50	22.34	20.83	21.26	29.57	28.92	49.58

A   MJ Deane 12-4-42-2 & 12.4-2-40-0; 7-2-30-0
B   MJ Slater 4-0-23-0
C   SP Titchard 2-2-0-0; 6-1-19-0
D   RMS Weston 1-0-8-0; 5-1-15-1
E   PA Thomas 13-1-54-2 & 3-0-20-0
F   SJ Base 10-3-34-0
G   AP Woolley 7-1-44-0 & 4-0-17-0
H   SJ Lacey 4-0-9-0 & 7-0-16-1; 22-5-63-0 & 7-2-22-1; 2-1-2-0; 33-7-107-1 & 6-0-19-0
I   R Eagleson 10.5-2-34-1
J   SD Stubbings 5-0-41-0
K   KM Krikken 9.2-2-54-1

FIELDING

31 – KM Krikken (30 ct/1 st)	
18 – DG Cork	
17 – SP Griffiths (16 ct/1 st)	
9 – AS Rollins, MJ Slater, RMS Weston	
7 – PAJ DeFreitas	
6 – ID Blackwell, SJ Lacey (5 ct/1 st)	
5 – ME Cassar	
4 – P Aldred, AJ Harris	
3 – JP Pyemont, SD Stubbings	
2 – TM Smith, BJ Spendlove, SP Titchard, TA Tweats	
1 – KJ Dean, MJ Deane, RL Eagleson, M Newell	

DURHAM CCC

FIRST-CLASS MATCHES

BATTING

	JJB Lewis	MA Gough	JE Morris	JA Daley	DC Boon	PD Collingwood	MP Speight	MM Betts	J Wood	SJE Brown	SJ Harmison	N Killeen	GD Bridge	NJ Speak	NC Phillips	SA Chapman	Extras	Total	Wickets	Result	Points
v. Worcestershire	52	0	55	24	54	56	34*	19*	–	–	–						9	303	6	D	11
(Chester-le-Street) 13–16 April	–																–	–			
v. Hampshire	19	29	21	43*	5	1	0	11	0	6	8						24	167	10	L	4
(Chester-le-Street) 28–30 April	25	59	2	56	61*	1	0	13	0	4	3						40	264	10		
v. Kent	11	9	25	10	12	0	4	7	0	4	0*						11	93	10	L	3
(Stockton) 14–17 May	132	67	29	14	0	17	4	1	11	9	0*						41	325	10		
v. Yorkshire	20	4	8	22	0	9	25*	0	8	4	0						14	114	10	L	4
(Headingley) 27–29 May	74	23	8	0	10	0	46*	0	25	0	0						25	211	10		
v. Somerset	68	1	100	8	8	40	12		0	17	14*	18					26	312	10	D	11
(Chester-le-Street) 2–5 June	–																–				
v. Northamptonshire	29	29	29	40	57	0	31		49*	11	7	12					23	317	10	W	19
(Northampton) 9–12 June	34	9	4	3	5	72	7		0	15*	2	45					20	216	10		
v. Surrey	36	15	78	1	6	7	0			4*	2	29		6			33	217	10	L	5
(Oval) 30 June–3 July	46	0	22	6	25	0	8			0	0*	1		5			26	139	10		
v. Nottinghamshire	4	62	27		28	106	60	0		6*	1	2		41			55	392	10	W	20
(Chester-le-Street) 9–12 July	118			24	30	21*	0			12*	0	0					21	304	10		
v. Derbyshire	29	53	119		19	8	11	2		15*	0			57	6		27	346	10	W	19
(Chester-le-Street) 15–16 July	5	4	7		0*									13*	–		–	29	3		
v. Gloucestershire	59	11	74		139	14	56			2*	4	14		110	42		27	552	10		
(Cheltenham) 21–23 July	–																–			W	20
v. Glamorgan	50			5	48	29	97*			4	0	46		103	11	28	27	448	10	L	6
(Cardiff) 30 July–2 August	1			13	18	51	24			0	6*	12		21		32	6	185	10		
v. Sussex	18		42	6	8	11	8			4	0*	2		0	0		42	141	10	L	4
(Chester-le-Street) 4–8 August	5		12	80	42	50	3			9	1*	9		7	1		55	274	10		
v. Essex	29		105	75	4	70		6	0*		12*			8			41	350	8	D	12
(Colchester) 18–21 August	–																–				
v. Middlesex	98		15	25		47	11			0	0*	10		35	20	0	29	290	10	W	18
(Chester-le-Street) 24–27 August	14		25	14		23					25*	–	–	7*			5	113	4		
v. Lancashire	61		4	66	3	2	13		1		11*	2		34	20		29	226	10	L	4
(Old Trafford) 1–3 September	8		0	25	13	14	4		23		0	11*		66	4		29	197	10		
v. Warwickshire	76	6	8	54	20	0			0	29*	12	17		9			24	255	10	W	18
(Chester-le-Street) 8–11 September	25	7	5	72	42	15			6	5	4	19*		3			32	235	10		
v. Leicestershire		36	8	30	53	38	2	2*	10		4	1		38			56	278	10	D	10
(Leicester) 15–18 September																	–	–	–		
Matches	16	12	15	14	16	17	17	7	10	15	17	12	1	10	6	2					
Innings	28	20	25	24	27	28	27	11	15	23	24	19	2	17	9	4					
Not Out	0	0	0	1	2	0	5	2	1	8	9	3	0	2	0	1					
Runs	1146	424	792	609	839	692	566	55	139	160	79	251	11	561	105	67					
Highest score	132	67	119	105	139	106	97*	19*	49*	29*	14*	46	6	110	42	32					
Average	40.92	21.2	31.68	26.47	33.56	24.71	25.72	6.11	9.92	10.66	5.26	15.68	5.50	37.40	11.66	22.33					
100s	2	–	2	1	1	1	–	–	–	–	–	–	–	2	–	–					
50s	8	4	4	3	7	4	4	–	–	–	–	–	–	2	–	–					

DURHAM CCC

FIRST-CLASS MATCHES

BOWLING

	SJE Brown	MM Betts	J Wood	SJ Harmison	MA Gough	PD Collingwood	N Killeen	NC Phillips	Overs	Totals	Byes/Leg-byes	Wickets	Run outs
v. Worcestershire	15.1-6-25-6	12-2-46-2	12-2-39-0	8-2-20-2	3-1-7-0	2-0-12-0			52.1	152	3	10	–
(Chester-le-Street) 13–16 April	20-6-39-1	12-6-22-1	8-1-32-2	17-4-37-3	4.4-2-6-0				61.4	137	1	7	–
v. Hampshire	29.4-8-69-3	25-8-64-1	25-5-80-3	18-2-83-1	7-2-23-0	12-2-29-1			116.4	366	18	10	1
(Chester-le-Street) 28–30 April	6-0-17-1	4-0-23-1	2-0-11-0	3-1-14-0					15	66	1	2	–
v. Kent	24.1-7-66-3	23-7-64-3	23-5-78-2	20-2-67-0	4-1-15-0	1-1-0-0			95.1	301	11	8	–
(Stockton-on-Tees) 14–17 May	6-1-25-0	3-1-14-0	8.1-0-47-4	6-0-33-0					23.1	121	2	5	1
v. Yorkshire	26-10-72-3	19-3-81-0	23.2-8-58-7	16-2-70-0	4-0-17-0				90.2	310	9	10	– A
(Headingley) 27–29 May		3-0-6-1		3.2-1-10-0					6.2	16	–	1	–
v. Somerset	25.1-5-90-3		11-1-62-1	13-1-51-3	1-0-5-0	3-0-16-0	22-5-60-2		75.1	300	8	9	–
(Chester-le-Street) 2–5 June	20.3-7-49-3		24-6-67-3	17-5-43-2			10-4-29-2		71.3	199	11	10	0
v. Northamptonshire	15-1-55-0		16-4-50-0	18-3-58-4			14-8-20-6		63	190	7	10	–
(Northampton) 9–12 June	28-6-99-5		14-4-64-2	28-5-93-3		3-0-11-0	12-3-25-0		85	298	6	10	–
v. Surrey	20-1-97-2			24-4-76-5		9-7-9-1	24-7-85-1		106	335	8	10	– B
(The Oval) 30 June–3 July	14.1-4-42-2			14-4-62-2	11-0-41-0	2-0-15-0	8-1-35-1		64.1	247	2	6	1 B
v. Nottinghamshire	16-2-53-1	23-4-79-4		24-4-82-2	8-1-36-0	9-0-40-0	27-10-49-3		107	353	14	10	–
(Chester-le-Street) 9–12 July	10-2-39-0	15-2-47-1		15-2-33-3	14-2-49-4	5-2-19-1	14-1-59-1		73	248	2	10	–
v. Derbyshire	23.4-3-84-6	14-2-52-1		23-6-60-2				16-2-35-1	76.4	241	10	10	–
(Chester-le-Street) 15–16 July	8-1-27-3	6.1-1-34-4		14-4-65-3					28.1	130	4	10	–
v. Gloucestershire	20-5-78-5			19-6-40-2		4-1-8-1	10.1-4-23-1	13-2-51-0	66.1	202	2	10	I
(Cheltenham) 21–23 July	11-3-41-2			20.5-7-52-2	3-1-13-0		11.1-6-13-1	16-6-47-0	79.1	223	8	10	–
v. Glamorgan	17-4-55-0			18-1-68-0			19-5-55-1	52-9-171-6	119	387	20	10	– C
(Cardiff) 30 July–2 August	4-0-27-0			9.3-0-34-0		8-4-7-3	10-2-23-0	32-6-97-6	64.3	247	17	7	– C
v. Sussex	26.3-4-77-3			22-4-65-3			20-6-46-4	8-1-24-0	76.3	231	19	10	–
(Chester-le-Street) 4–7 August	25-5-64-6			21.5-4-80-3			16-6-28-1	5-2-4-0	67.5	192	16	10	–
v. Essex	16-4-55-1		14-3-37-2	18.5-4-57-3			20-5-61-4		69.5	215	2	10	– A
(Colchester) 18–21 August													
v. Middlesex	22-7-48-3			20.5-7-51-4			23-4-65-2	16-3-49-1	81.5	222	9	10	–
(Chester-le-Street) 25–27 August	18.5-8-38-1			30-12-49-4		3-0-6-0	29.2-11-50-5	8-0-28-0	89.1	180	9	10	–
v. Lancashire			10-4-11-0	39-11-96-2			34-8-90-3	46-10-171-4	142	437	18	10	– AD
(Old Trafford) 1–3 September													
v. Warwickshire (Chester-le-Street)	3.1-0-10-0		23.2-9-75-5	24-3-78-1	18-4-47-0	4-0-9-0	28-7-62-4		100.3	285	4	10	–
8–11 September	4-2-7-0		11-5-22-3	11.3-6-20-2				16-3-57-4	42.3	115	9	9	–
v. Leicestershire		13-4-48-0	11.5-1-48-1	25-5-100-2			11-1-34-0	30-7-85-7	90.5	322	7	10	–
(Leicester) 15–18 September		3-1-3-1	11-3-24-1	5-0-23-1		4-1-10-0	7-3-11-1		30	74	3	4	–

	SJE Brown	MM Betts	J Wood	SJ Harmison	MA Gough	PD Collingwood	N Killeen	NC Phillips
Overs	475	175.1	247.4	565.5	77.4	91.1	411.3	212
Maidens	112	41	61	120	14	25	114	41
Runs	1448	583	805	1775	259	238	1070	677
Wickets	63	20	36	64	4	8	58	18
Bowler's average	**22.98**	**29.15**	**22.36**	**27.73**	**64.75**	**29.75**	**18.44**	**37.61**

A   JA Daley 2-1-3-0; 1-0-3-0; 8-1-34-0
B   GD Bridge 29-10-60-1 & 15-2-50-0
C   S Chapman 5-1-11-0 & 9-0-49-1
D   DC Boon 5-1-17-1

FIELDING

50 – MP Speight (48 ct/2 st)
25 – PD Collingwood
17 – MA Gough
8 – DC Boon
7 – JA Daley, JJB Lewis, JE Morris
6 – NJ Speak
5 – NC Phillips
4 – MM Betts, SJ Harmison, J Wood
3 – SJE Brown, SA Chapman
1 – GD Bridge, N Killeen

ESSEX CCC

FIRST–CLASS MATCHES
BATTING

	PJ Prichard	DDJ Robinson	IN Flanagan	SG Law	RC Irani	AP Grayson	SD Peters	RJ Rollins	AP Cowan	MC Ilott	PM Such	JO Grove	JE Bishop	N Hussain	BJ Hyam	TC Walton	RSG Anderson	DR Law	DJ Thompson	TJ Phillips	Extras	Total	Wickets	Result	Points	Note
v. Leicestershire (Chelmsford) 13–16 April	91	13	0	49	10	0	0	3	17	16	18*										35	252	10	L	4	
	7	23	8	0	16	1	6	20	46	14	0*										9	150	10			
v. Cambridge University (Cambridge) 21–23 April	55	111		25rh	83	42*	9*		–	–	–	–									15	340	3	D	–	A
	–	–							–	–	–	–									–	–				A
v. Warwickshire (Chelmsford) 28–30 April	10	9		33	12	29			23*	30	1	7		7	26						4	191	10	W	16	
	59	5		33*	9*	–			–	–	–	–		59	–						3	168	3			
v. Surrey (The Oval) 14–17 May	103	1	29	36	14	22			23*	1	7	0			7						19	262	10	L	6	
	9	13	7	64	18	1			11	8	3	6*			51						13	204	10			
v. Yorkshire (Chelmsford) 19–22 May	7	28	2	159	48	22			10	7	4	0			31*						17	335	10	L	7	
	33	29	0	113*	11	0			8	23	2	4			1						13	237	10			
v. Gloucestershire (Gloucester) 26–29 May	61	0		4	0	62			7	43	10*			46	3	17					20	273	10	D	10	
	16	21		125	64	7			0	20*	–			4		71	9*				7	344	8			
v. Hampshire (Ilford) 2–5 June		4		56	9	159*			20	35				9	21	10	2				29	354	9	D	12	
		9		107*	6*	31			–	–				59							6	218	3			
v. Derbyshire (Chelmsford) 9–11 June		20		0	39	2			0	20	1*			141	43	0	5				10	281	10	W	18	
		0		–	–	74*			–	–	–			56*	–	–	–				6	136	1			
v. Oxford University (Chelmsford) 15–17 June		53	52	116			0	33			0				37	6	23*	abs inj			20	364	9	D	–	B
		–	–	–			–	–			–				–	–	–	–			–	–				
v. Lancashire (Old Trafford) 29 June–2 July		13		51	5	63	9		17	6	1*				1	8	1				32	207	10	L	5	
		11		2	9	76	32*		0	0	1				–	17	1				33	182	10			
v. Glamorgan (Cardiff) 9–11 July	73			140	4	27	81		2	44	0*			5	31	3					34	444	10	W	20	
	–			–	–	–	–		–	–	–			–	–	–					–	–				
v. Middlesex (Southend) 14–16 July	0			58	70	11	26		52*	abs inj	20			99	47	0					46	429	9	W	19	
	–			–	–	–	–		–	abs inj	–			–	–	–					–	–				
v. Sri Lanka 'A' (Chelmsford) 21–24 July		29		153	125	0					20	17		7				24		16	24	442	10	D	–	CD
		–		–	–	–					–	–		–				–		–	–	–				CD
v. Northamptonshire (Northampton) 30 July–1 August	74	27		117	35	22	42		5	0*				0			2	1			30	355	10	L	8	
	11	0		11	27	4	14		28	22*				0			0	22			4	143	10			
v. Kent (Canterbury) 4–7 August	14		36	29	127*	32	14		4						18		44	2	7		23	350	10	L	5	
	3		2	104*	52	8	1		7						20		18	3	0		25	243	10			
v. New Zealand (Chelmsford) 13–16 August	11	200		24	0		99							37	9		3	63*	8	4	35	493	10	W	–	
	–	–		–	–		–							–	–		–	–	–	–	–	–				
v. Durham (Colchester) 18–21 August	14	3		94	9	8			4	11	16*			0			20	26			10	215	10	D	8	
	–	–		–	–	–			–	–	–			–			–	–			–	–				
v. Somerset (Chelmsford) 24–27 August	4	112		263	35	50			14		3*			21	6		7	0			29	544	10	D	12	
	–	–		–	–	–			–		–			–	–		–	–			–	–				
v. Sussex (Chelmsford) 31 August–2 September	12	28		38	18	0			0		1			61	8		0*	0			13	179	10	L	4	
	0	15		18	17	42			18		4			0	8*		0	4			29	155	10			
v. Worcestershire (Chelmsford) 8–11 September	3	2		13	103	1			16		0			71	49*		5		15		25	303	10	D	11	
	46	10*		6	21*	105			–		–			65	–		–	–	–		12	265	4			
v. Nottinghamshire (Trent Bridge) 15–18 September	26	3		64	9	3			8		0*			28	10		4	0			33	188	10	W	16	
	110	23		46	5	12			4					143	42*		–	–			47	432	7			
Matches	16	17	6	17	20	20	11	3	17	12	19	4	2	9	18	6	15	4	8	3						
Innings	26	29	10	29	32	32	15	4	24	17	23	5	1	15	26	8	20	4	10	4						
Not Out	0	1	0	4	5	2	2	1	3	1	11	1	0	1	4	0	2	2	0	0						
Runs	852	786	165	1833	1111	1083	374	65	332	290	134	17	17	824	514	155	147	136	55	27						
Highest score	110	200	52	263	153	159*	99	33	52*	44	20	7	17	143	51	71	44	63*	22	16						
Average	32.76	28.07	16.50	73.32	41.14	36.10	28.76	21.66	15.80	18.12	11.16	4.25	17.00	58.85	23.36	19.37	8.16	68.00	5.50	6.75						
100s	2	3	–	8	4	3	–	–	–	–	–	–	–	2	–	–	–	–	–	–						
50s	6	1	1	6	3	6	2	–	1	–	–	–	–	7	1	1	–	1	–	–						

A   JC Powell (2 innings) did not bat
B   TP Hodgson 24
C   GR Napier 27
D   A McGarry 0*

ESSEX CCC

FIRST-CLASS MATCHES
BOWLING

	MC Ilott	AP Cowan	RC Irani	PM Such	AP Grayson	JO Grove	RSG Anderson	DJ Thompson	DR Law	TJ Phillips	Overs	Totals	Byes/Leg-byes	Wickets	Run outs	
v. Leicestershire	33–9–115–3	27–6–83–2	23.1–5–59–4	21.2–3–70–0	26–10–56–1						136.1	424	16	10	–	A
(Chelmsford) 13–16 April																
v. Cambridge University		14–7–17–2	6–3–13–0	18–9–21–1	13–4–33–3	17–3–63–1					75	191	11	7	–	B
(Cambridge) 21–23 April																
v. Warwickshire	21–8–43–3	18–4–60–2	17–2–40–2	17–2–37–0	7.5–3–15–2	13–3–59–1					93.5	271	17	10	–	
(Chelmsford) 28–30 April	14–4–38–6	7–1–25–2	6.3–2–17–2								27.3	86	6	10	–	
v. Surrey	20–8–44–4	13–1–38–1	18–2–48–2	6.4–2–8–2		14–2–52–1					71.4	195	5	10	–	
(The Oval) 14–17 May	20–10–50–2	13–1–54–1	9–1–31–0	34.4–12–65–2	18–5–42–1	5–1–22–0					99.4	272	8	6	–	
v. Yorkshire	20–8–54–2	19.2–2–52–3	14–4–45–0	23–9–48–3	26–14–47–1	12–1–53–1					114.2	311	12	10	–	
(Chelmsford) 19–22 May	9–0–51–0	12–0–48–2	13–0–71–1	20–1–78–1	25–4–117–0	13–4–55–1					92	435	15	5	–	
v. Gloucestershire	33–8–100–2	27–5–81–2	21–10–43–4	22–4–63–1	9–5–20–0		16–2–89–1				128	408	12	10	–	
(Gloucester) 26–29 May																
v. Hampshire	24–7–61–1	10.5–2–34–2	12–2–43–2	24–5–75–1	14–3–35–0		16–7–54–3				102.5	324	14	10	–	A
(Ilford) 2–5 June	5–2–4–2			6–2–14–0			3.4–0–13–0				14.4	36	5	2	–	
v. Derbyshire	14–1–49–2	20–2–70–3	17–6–41–2	32–14–69–3	7–1–14–0		12–3–36–0				102	285	6	10	–	
(Chelmsford) 9–11 June	10–0–27–0	8–1–28–1	7–1–14–1	10–4–10–2			12.1–2–37–5				47.1	131	15	10	1	
v. Oxford University			5–1–15–0	16–7–39–4			12–4–30–0	9–4–24–1	14–5–32–4		58.3	158	10	10	–	D
(Chelmsford) 15–17 June				33–9–80–4			18–3–54–1		17–5–49–0		87.5	268	6	7	–	CDEF
v. Lancashire	10–5–18–1	12–2–37–0	3–1–5–0	40.4–8–136–7	26–7–75–0		12–6–19–2				105.4	298	7	10	–	A
(Old Trafford) 29 June–2 July	6–2–13–0	4–0–12–0		32–8–77–6	25–2–80–1						71	209	14	7	–	A
v. Glamorgan	10–3–23–0	17–5–47–6	11–1–27–0	14–3–35–1			16–6–35–3				68	185	18	10	–	
(Cardiff) 9–11 July	9–3–14–3	6–1–20–0	13–5–29–4	19.1–7–29–2			5–0–20–0				53.1	122	7	10	–	A
v. Middlesex	5.4–0–22–2	12–2–33–1	8.2–4–13–2				13.1–3–36–5				39.1	113	9	10	–	
(Southend) 14–16 July		10–3–34–1	7–3–13–1	20.2–4–42–3	10–4–16–4		9–3–21–1				56.2	140	14	10	–	
v. Sri Lanka 'A'				18–5–40–0	10.3–6–29–2				18–3–94–1	17–7–42–4	103.3	364	9	10	–	BGH
(Chelmsford) 21–24 July				31–6–73–1					22–1–119–0	20–5–83–1	128.3	525	26	7	–	BHIJ
v. Northamptonshire		25–5–69–4	22–6–72–2	19–1–80–0	18–0–91–0		23–3–112–1	17–2–91–3			131	579	34	10	–	A
(Northampton) 30 July–1 August																
v. Kent		25–3–80–0	30–6–83–3		16.1–5–35–1		30–7–103–1	26–0–111–3		16–1–66–1	152.1	541	27	10	–	
(Canterbury) 4–7 August		5–0–17–2	3.2–1–12–0		3–0–15–1					1–0–5–0	12.2	53	4	3	–	
v. New Zealand			12–4–24–3		1–1–0–0		20–3–78–2	20–7–58–2	18–2–48–3		71	236	28	10	–	
(Chelmsford) 13–16 August			10–5–14–1		1–0–1–0		17–5–39–4	14–5–24–1	9–1–33–1	22–4–82–2	73	217	24	9	–	
v. Durham	16–1–53–0	23.4–3–79–2		31–9–69–2	5–1–19–0		22–7–70–4		7–0–43–0		104.4	350	17	8	–	
(Colchester) 18–21 August																
v. Somerset		13–3–51–2	11–1–43–0	17–6–27–1	4–0–16–1		11–2–44–2	16.3–2–46–4			72.3	246	19	10	–	
(Chelmsford) 24–27 August		5–0–21–0	10–2–19–2	35–15–69–1	19–15–10–1		22–8–66–4	17–3–49–1			112	256	9	9	–	A
v. Sussex (Chelmsford)		17–4–56–3	14–5–28–1	18–1–36–2	2–0–6–0		24.4–3–58–3	14–2–69–0			90.4	271	14	10	1	A
31 August–2 September		4–0–13–1	5–1–16–0				3.5–0–13–0	5–0–20–1			17.5	64	2	2	–	
v. Worcestershire		13.2–1–51–1	20–4–51–4	27–9–66–0	11–4–26–1		18–2–74–4	8–1–35–0			97.2	308	5	10	–	
(Chelmsford) 8–11 September		12–2–57–0	10–2–34–2	34–10–92–0	14.5–3–39–2		17–3–50–3	14–1–64–2			101.5	365	29	9	–	
v. Nottinghamshire	21–3–75–2		17–5–58–2	17–3–47–0	7–1–12–0		16–1–95–1	14.3–2–54–4			92.3	349	8	10	1	
(Trent Bridge) 15–18 September	10–3–46–3		9–3–25–3	4.1–3–1–1			9–2–27–0	0–1–10–2			41.1	151	12	10	1	

Overs	310.4	393.1	384.2	661	319.2	74	378.3	184	105	76
Maidens	85	66	98	181	98	14	85	30	17	17
Runs	900	1267	1046	1596	849	304	1273	685	418	273
Wickets	38	46	50	51	22	5	50	24	9	8
Bowler's average	**23.68**	**27.54**	**20.92**	**31.29**	**38.59**	**60.8**	**25.46**	**28.54**	**46.44**	**34.12**

A SG Law 5.4–0–25–0; 2–0–8–1; 2–1–1–0 & 4–1–13–0; 1–0–3–1; 7–1–30–0; 9–3–36–1; 4–0–13–0; 1–0–4–0
B JE Bishop 7–1–33–0; 17–3–58–1 & 19–3–89–2
C DDJ Robinson 2–1–6–0
D TC Walton 2.3–1–8–1 & 5–1–20–0
E SD Peters 3.5–0–19–1
F TP Hodgson 9–2–34–1
G GR Napier 3–0–20–0
H A McGarry 20–2–72–2 & 20–3–77–2
I IN Flanagan 14.3–4–50–1
J BJ Hyam 2–0–8–0

FIELDING

47 – BJ Hyam (46 ct/1 st)
29 – SG Law
13 – SD Peters, DDJ Robinson
10 – AP Cowan, N Hussain, RC Irani
8 – AP Grayson
7 – RJ Rollins (6 ct/1 st)
6 – PJ Prichard, TC Walton
5 – RSG Anderson, MC Ilott
4 – PM Such
3 – IN Flanagan
2 – DR Law, GR Napier, JC Powell
1 – TJ Phillips, DJ Thompson

GLAMORGAN CCC

FIRST–CLASS MATCHES

BATTING

Opponent / Venue	SP James	AW Evans	A Dale	MP Maynard	K Newell	RDB Croft	AD Shaw	DS Harrison	SD Thomas	SP Jones	SL Watkin	DA Cosker	I Dawood	MJ Powell	WL Law	O T Parkin	AP Davies	JH Kallis	MA Wallace	Extras	Total	Wickets	Result	Points
v. Derbyshire	–	–	–	–	–	–	–	–	–	–	–	–	–	–	–	–	–	–	–	–	–	–	D	5
(Derby) 20–23 April	–	–	–	–	–	–	–	–	–	–	–	–	–	–	–	–	–	–	–	–	–			
v. Sussex	14	14	12	abs inj	6	0	16		18	13	2*	49								5	149	9	W	16
(Cardiff) 28 April–1 May	153	5	49	abs inj	41	58*	15*													20	341	4		
v. Gloucestershire		4	108		38		12		5	6*	8	6	12	17	19					25	260	10	W	18
(Cardiff) 14–17 May		1	113		18		1		1*	–	–	–	102	41*	16					19	312	6		
v. Oxford University		46					140	13	32*			–		111	30	–				20	392	5	D	–
(Oxford) 19–21 May		33*						16		19*	15		58	6	7	5				10	171	7		
v. Worcestershire	3	1	8	2		2			0		7	23*	25	42		0				14	127	10	L	4
(Worcester) 26–28 May	5	29	8	9		45			2		2	16	5	26		0*				2	149	10		
v. Leicestershire	65	46	35	5	17	0	16		7		8		71*	2						19	291	10	D	10
(Leicester) 2–5 June	–	–	–	–	–	–	–		–		–		–	–						–	–	–		
v. Middlesex	36	8	6	1		1			2		7	4	14*	4		11				14	108	10	L	3
(Cardiff) 9–11 June	6	36	26	28		7			2		19	10	3	83*		0				21	241	10		
v. Kent	103	50	47	170		5	12		23	1	8*	15		43						67	544	10	D	11
(Canterbury) 15–18 June	–	–	–	–		–	–		–	–	–	–		–						–	–	–		
v. Hampshire	0	0	45	23		15			2	0	0*	1	19	21						36	162	10	L	4
(Swansea) 30 June–3 July	53	1	4	23		5			36	6	0*	32	7	0						10	177	10		
v. Essex	13	7	37	36		15			0	12*	3	2	5	33						22	185	10	L	3
(Cardiff) 9–11 July	2	29	4	0		18			10	1*	1	0	7	35						15	122	10		
v. Lancashire	33		112	9		9			54	2	2*	6	13	6	18					18	282	10	L	3
(Blackpool) 14–17 July	28		16	1		43			18	1	0*	1	1	96	53					31	289	10		
v. Durham	65	46	79	26	9		33		0		7	4*		42				45		31	387	10	W	18
(Cardiff) 30 July–2 August	28	88*	9	0	3*		19		11		–			12				60		17	247	7		
v. Surrey	3	2	24	12	0		0		23	6		4*		16		0				12	101	10	L	4
(The Oval) 4–5 August	5	13	9	7	8*		5		3	4		0		10		8				12	84	10		
v. Nottinghamshire	259*	11*	0	81										164				101		32	648	4	W	20
(Colwyn Bay) 18–21 August	–	–	–	–					–					–				–			–	–		
v. Warwickshire	1	1	22	72		57*	8		22	3*		5						94		15	300	8	D	11
(Cardiff) 24–27 August	–	–	–	–		–	–		–	–		–						–			–	–		
v. Somerset	11	31	1	1		3			17	0	0				0*			10	28	11	113	10	L	4
(Taunton) 2–4 September	0	10	10	28		15			24	8		40			0*			9	4	3	151	10		
v. Yorkshire	20			186	45	33			0		5	1		70		0		35	64*	39	498	10	W	20
(Headingley) 8–10 September	–			–	–	–			–		–			–		–		–	–		–	–		
v. Northamptonshire	0		20	6	46	1			7		16*	21		67	34				2	7	227	10	D	9
(Cardiff) 15–18 September	111	5	4*									5*			64					15	204	3		

	SP James	AW Evans	A Dale	MP Maynard	K Newell	RDB Croft	AD Shaw	DS Harrison	SD Thomas	SP Jones	SL Watkin	DA Cosker	I Dawood	MJ Powell	WL Law	O T Parkin	AP Davies	JH Kallis	MA Wallace					
Matches	16	15	16	13	8	15	12	2	18	10	15	13	7	16	5	7	1	6	3					
Innings	25	24	26	18	11	21	16	2	26	13	19	18	12	26	9	9	1	9	4					
Not Out	1	3	0	1	0	4	1	0	2	3	9	4	0	4	0	3	0	0	1					
Runs	1017	512	809	685	239	322	312	29	352	77	86	212	262	1060	240	11	5	362	98					
Highest score	259*	88*	113	186	46	58*	140	16	54	19*	16*	49	102	164	64	11	5	101	64*					
Average	42.37	24.38	31.11	40.29	21.72	18.94	20.8	14.50	14.66	7.70	8.60	15.14	21.83	48.18	26.66	3.50	5.00	40.22	32.66					
100s	4	–	3	2	–	–	1	–	–	–	–	–	1	2	–	–	–	2	–					
50s	3	2	1	2	–	2	–	–	1	–	–	1	1	5	2	–	–	2	1					

GLAMORGAN CCC

FIRST-CLASS MATCHES
BOWLING

	SL Watkin	SD Thomas	A Dale	SP Jones	RDB Croft	DA Cosker	OT Parkin	JH Kallis	Overs	Totals	Byes/Leg-byes	Wickets	Run outs	
v. Derbyshire (Derby) 20–23 April	15-6-16-1	15-4-36-1	11.5-5-23-1	9-2-18-1	9-2-35-0				69.5	168	7	4	–	A
v. Sussex (Cardiff) 28 April–1 May	18-5-43-0	18-4-54-3	10-3-40-1	13.3-3-31-5	19-7-35-1	10-1-13-0			88.3	222	6	10	–	
	15-6-25-0	15-2-58-3	7-5-11-0	9-1-21-0	37-12-82-5	22-6-52-1			105	265	16	10	1	
v. Gloucestershire (Cardiff) 14–17 May	12.5-2-31-5	12-1-42-2	7-2-10-2	6-1-15-1		1-1-0-0			38.5	109	11	10	–	
	25-9-49-3	23-3-81-4	9-3-42-1		13-1-62-0	22-11-40-2			92	291	17	10	–	
v. Oxford University (Oxford) 19–21 May		4-2-11-0		14-4-62-2		20-8-24-1	18.2-1-72-4		82.2	289	17	10	–	ABC
				3-0-12-0			8-4-15-1		32	106	5	2	–	ABC
v. Worcestershire (Worcester) 26–28 May	17-5-41-2	12.1-1-40-3	10-4-29-3			3-1-6-0	16-5-41-2		58.1	164	7	10	–	
	14-5-30-2	15-2-48-4	7-3-24-0				14-4-38-2		56	160	5	10	–	D
v. Leicestershire (Leicester) 2–5 June		18-3-66-4	10-3-32-2	12.3-2-70-4	10-2-32-0		10-1-44-0		62.3	259	8	10	–	D
v. Middlesex (Cardiff) 9–11 June	24-5-76-0	30-8-84-4	8-1-23-1		29-9-74-0	30.5-6-100-3	19-4-83-1		140.5	462	22	9	–	
v. Kent (Canterbury) 15–18 June	25.1-10-47-5	27-6-66-1	9-1-29-1	20-3-91-2	25-7-64-1	16-6-29-0			122.1	332	6	10	–	
	17-5-38-1	18-2-70-1	6-2-17-0	15-1-50-0	30-9-64-0	24-8-64-2			111	317	11	4	–	E
v. Hampshire (Swansea) 30 June–3 July	21.3-6-45-4	23-4-71-1	3-1-13-0	18-2-68-1	32-8-81-3	21-5-49-1			118.3	345	18	10	–	
v. Essex (Cardiff) 9–11 July	21-6-62-0	26-4-105-3	6-3-4-1	25-3-98-2	34-4-98-3	21-4-69-1			133	444	8	10	–	
v. Lancashire (Blackpool) 14–17 July	30-7-81-2	19-2-80-0		26-5-87-0	34-8-144-1	46-10-143-3			157	556	10	6	–	C
	4-3-1-0			3-0-10-0					8.1	19	4	–	–	FG
v. Durham 30 July–2 August	28-8-69-2	31-8-64-5	10-2-31-0		59-13-168-3	38-11-93-0			167	448	23	10	–	F
	11-2-28-1	5-0-18-0			30.4-12-70-7	12-1-41-1		5-0-22-1	63.4	185	6	10	–	
v. Surrey (The Oval) 4–5 August		16-0-67-1	3-1-10-1	21-3-81-1	28-6-46-2	15-0-48-2		12-2-41-2	95	309	16	9	–	
v. Nottinghamshire (Colwyn Bay) 18–21 August	18-6-75-6	15-2-59-2	4-3-12-0		9.2-2-35-1	2-0-2-0		11-3-38-1	59.2	228	7	10	–	
	14-4-53-0	17-3-50-2	5-1-11-0		32-9-60-5	18.1-2-71-2		15-2-53-1	101.1	302	4	10	–	
v. Warwickshire (Cardiff) 24–27 August	20-5-51-0	15.4-1-58-3	11-3-46-1		36-8-89-5		16-2-58-0		102.4	341	18	10	1	C
v. Somerset (Taunton) 2–4 September	14-3-53-1	12.3-4-40-4					14-4-38-4	16-3-54-0	56.3	203	18	10	1	
	9-1-55-0	13.4-2-77-3			20-7-59-3		13-5-26-1	13-1-52-3	68.4	280	11	10	–	
v. Yorkshire (Headingley) 8–10 September	12-2-35-4	8-1-31-2			5-2-17-0		7.2-2-22-2	7-0-23-2	39.2	140	12	10	–	
	14-4-36-1	12.2-0-52-2			20-5-86-2		20-7-54-4	16-1-62-1	82.2	306	16	10	–	
v. Northamptonshire (Cardiff) 15–18 September	22-6-47-3	26-9-52-3			22.4-3-73-3				75.4	204	16	10	1	D

	SL Watkin	SD Thomas	A Dale	SP Jones	RDB Croft	DA Cosker	OT Parkin	JH Kallis
Overs	421.3	447.2	136.5	208	521.4	322	155.4	95
Maidens	121	78	46	31	135	81	39	12
Runs	1087	1480	407	776	1412	844	491	345
Wickets	43	61	15	19	45	19	21	11
Bowler's average	**25.27**	**24.26**	**27.13**	**40.84**	**31.37**	**44.42**	**23.38**	**31.36**

A   DS Harrison 10-2-33-0; 7-1-16-0 & 5-0-15-1
B   AP Davies 11-3-48-1 & 10-1-30-0
C   MJ Powell 8-1-39-2 & 6-0-29-0; 2-0-11-0; 4-0-21-0
D   K Newell 6-0-15-2; 2-1-7-0; 5-0-16-0
E   AW Evans 1-0-3-0
F   MP Maynard 1-1-0-0; 1-1-0-0
G   WL Law 0.1-0-4-0

FIELDING

26 – AD Shaw (25 ct/1 st)
20 – I Dawood
14 – DA Cosker
12 – MA Wallace
10 – AW Evans
9 – SP James, MP Maynard, SD Thomas
7 – SL Watkin
5 – RDB Croft, MJ Powell
4 – A Dale
3 – JH Kallis, WL Law
2 – SP Jones, K Newell, OT Parkin

GLOUCESTERSHIRE CCC

FIRST–CLASS MATCHES

BATTING

	KJ Barnett	THC Hancock	DR Hewson	MW Alleyne	MGN Windows	JN Snape	RC Russell	MCJ Ball	J Lewis	IJ Harvey	AM Smith	RI Dawson	JMM Averis	BW Gannon	RJ Cunliffe	MJ Cawdron	MA Hardinges	TP Cotterell	Extras	Total	Wickets	Result	Points
v. Surrey	17	53	6	10	12	21	36*	0	6	30	0								22	213	10	D	9
(The Oval) 13–16 April	1	2	26	34	98*	18	20*	–	–	–	–								10	209	5		
v. Yorkshire	24	20	6	4	28	1	19	18	26*	0	6								17	169	10	L	4
(Headingley) 21–24 April	36	7	10	5	39	48	8*	4	0	6	0								17	180	10		
v. Middlesex	51	1	23	76	15	18	36		17		14	10	18*						18	297	10	L	6
(Bristol) 28 April–1 May	23	42	40	4	16	6	9		11		0*	36	4						24	215	10		
v. Glamorgan	1	13	4	16	5	1	13	8	14		12			3*					19	109	10	L	4
(Cardiff) 14–17 May	16	55	0	8	57	63*	29	2	0		4			18					39	291	10		
v. Sussex	4	66		12	0	15	64	43*	27	27	6			9					21	294	10	L	6
(Hove) 19–22 May	3	29		48	50	0	85	25*	12	26	7*			–					17	302	8		
v. Essex	17	25		43	118	98*	1	11	17	29	11			16					22	408	10	D	12
(Gloucester) 26–29 May	–	–	–	–	–	–	–	–	–	–	–			–									
v. Lancashire	–	–	–	–	–	–	–	–	–	–	–			–					–	–	–	D	8
(Bristol) 2–5 June	–	–	–	–	–	–	–	–	–	–	–			–									
v. Somerset	88	8		0	34	30	86	44	1	31	5		2*						17	346	10	W	19
(Bath) 9–12 June	8	29		40	0	17	0	17*	0*	19	–								14	144	7		
v. Nottinghamshire	56	5		35*	38	9	18	5	0	34				0	84				33	317	10	W	19
(Bristol) 30 June–3 July	2*	27		–	5*	46								–	45				29	154	3		
v. Worcestershire	53	58		0	9	23	37*	21	0	4	3				0				23	231	10	L	2
(Cheltenham) 14–17 July	106	64		34	21	0	12	70*	62	9	4				33				10	425	10		
v. Durham	3	26		39	27	4	35	8	13*	20	1				24				2	202	10	L	2
(Cheltenham) 21–23 July	12	4		64	53	1	16	22	19	0	10*				14				8	223	10		
v. Hampshire	30	22		75	6	5	94*	14		13				0	52	42			27	380	10	D	11
(Bristol) 5–8 August	0	32		2	1	27*	5		4		2*			–	14	4			5	96	8		
v. Northamptonshire	27	1		7	9	6	50							4	108	31*	1	0	16	260	10	D	10
(Northampton) 17–20 August	–	–		–	–	–	–							–	–	–	–	–					
v. Leicestershire		38		31	38	17*	9	0	1	0				4	5	0			23	166	10	L	4
(Leicester) 24–27 August		68		22	5	1	0	14	0	6				4*	20	0			30	170	10		
v. Warwickshire		20	4	5	0	57	2	0	0	33	4					5*			2	132	10	L	4
(Edgbaston) 2–4 September		1	25	36	37	6	7	32	9	37	0*					7			9	206	10		
v. Derbyshire	4	27		11	34	2	3	0					3	5*	18	36			7	150	10	L	4
(Bristol) 8–10 September	15	71		0	55	2	27*	3					9	5	4	1			20	212	10		
v. Kent	125	37		4	37	1*	13			123				6*	abs ill				4	350	6	D	12
(Canterbury) 15–18 September	5	7		7	113*	21*	10			0				–	abs ill				10	173	5		

	KJ Barnett	THC Hancock	DR Hewson	MW Alleyne	MGN Windows	JN Snape	RC Russell	MCJ Ball	J Lewis	IJ Harvey	AM Smith	RI Dawson	JMM Averis	BW Gannon	RJ Cunliffe	MJ Cawdron	MA Hardinges	TP Cotterell
Matches	15	17	5	17	17	17	17	12	14	12	14	1	3	11	7	6	1	1
Innings	26	30	10	29	30	29	30	19	23	19	21	2	5	12	13	9	1	1
Not Out	1	0	0	1	3	6	6	4	3	0	5	0	2	4	0	2	0	0
Runs	727	858	144	672	960	518	790	333	266	429	108	46	40	70	421	126	1	0
Highest score	125	71	40	76	118	98*	94*	70*	62	123	14	36	18*	18	108	42	1	0
Average	29.08	28.6	14.40	24.00	35.55	22.52	32.91	22.20	13.30	22.57	6.75	23.00	13.33	8.75	32.38	18.00	1.00	–
100s	2	–	–	–	2	–	–	–	–	1	–	–	–	–	1	–	–	–
50s	4	7	–	3	5	3	5	1	1	–	–	–	–	–	2	–	–	–

GLOUCESTERSHIRE CCC

FIRST-CLASS MATCHES

BOWLING

Match	AM Smith	J Lewis	IJ Harvey	MW Alleyne	MCJ Ball	JN Snape	JMM Averis	BW Gannon	MJ Cawdron	Overs	Totals	Byes/Leg-byes	Wickets	Run outs
v. Surrey	32-9-93-4	32-12-76-1	26-10-77-3	20.2-8-44-1	14-4-36-1	5-1-16-0				129.2	342	–	10	–
(The Oval) 13-16 April	17-3-42-5	12-2-56-1			13-1-47-0	4-0-24-0				58	229	10	7	–
v. Yorkshire	27-6-73-4	24-4-58-0	27-10-58-3	15.4-6-32-2	3-1-15-0					113.4	282	15	10	AB
(Headingley) 21-24 April	16-6-58-2	20-6-60-4	6-2-13-0	2-0-13-0						44	148	4	6	–
v. Middlesex	25-5-62-1	27.1-9-79-5		23-7-36-3		18-7-22-1	15-3-44-0			110.1	268	17	10	B
(Bristol) 28 April-1 May	25-5-70-1	27.4-8-74-3				14-1-54-2	9-1-30-0			78.4	245	5	8	2 AC
v. Gloucestershire	18-7-36-1	25.3-8-69-3		3-1-7-0	13-4-42-0	4-1-13-0		26-3-80-6		89.3	260	13	10	–
(Cardiff) 14-17 May	9-2-26-1	11-3-35-0		9-2-28-0	9-2-40-1	16-2-67-3		14-3-57-1		79	312	11	6	AB
v. Sussex	15-4-36-4	17.5-6-34-2	13-5-24-3	14-2-45-1	29-5-67-0	19-5-54-1	10-2-37-1			55.5	145	14	10	–
(Hove) 19-22 May	23.3-5-60-1	15-1-70-2	30-4-109-3				8-0-33-0			138.3	455	17	8	–
v. Essex	22-7-45-4	21-7-54-2	16-5-43-1	14-5-36-1	6-3-12-0		15.3-2-71-2			94.3	273	12	10	–
(Gloucester) 26-29 May	17-7-32-2	20-8-51-2	10-1-39-0		32-9-75-3	24.1-7-52-0	8-0-33-0			132.1	344	7	8	B
v. Lancashire	16-6-34-2	20.1-4-101-4	11-0-45-1	10-1-72-1		2-0-25-0	11-1-59-1			78.1	351	4	9	B
(Bristol) 2-5 June														
v. Somerset	11-5-10-1	14-6-24-1	15-6-41-4	9-2-19-0				13.3-1-38-4		62.3	138	6	10	–
(Bath) 9-12 June	6-1-15-1	29.4-11-67-3	22-4-84-0	16-5-30-0	24-8-50-1	9-4-9-0		29-8-88-3		138.4	351	3	10	1 A
v. Nottinghamshire		24.4-9-36-3	29-7-76-5	19-8-31-1	12-4-25-0	7-1-27-0		16-5-53-1		108.4	269	17	10	–
(Bristol) 30 June-3 July		27.5-7-56-7	6-0-16-0	7-1-25-0	9-1-30-0	17-7-35-1		6-2-36-1		72.5	201	3	10	1 A
v. Worcestershire	25-10-44-0	22-2-96-0	21-7-57-1	22-4-81-0	36-5-133-1	26-6-91-1				164.3	591	22	7	1 AB
(Cheltenham) 14-17 July	8-0-47-4	5-2-10-0			3.1-1-10-1	1-1-0-0				17.1	68	1	5	–
v. Durham	29-7-81-3	26-3-122-1	34-7-112-3	36-9-113-3	14-3-42-0	8-2-24-0				157	552	19	10	A
(Cheltenham) 21-23 July														
v. Hampshire	23-8-69-2	13-4-38-1		7-3-11-0		16-6-21-0		16-1-75-2	19.1-6-35-5	94.1	253	4	10	–
(Bristol) 5-8 August														
v. Northamptonshire				17-8-28-1		22-4-60-0		19-4-73-1	22.4-5-54-5	118.4	341	6	10	DE
(Northampton) 17-20 August						8.2-0-25-1		9-2-23-1	8-4-8-0	43.2	84	–	3	DEF
v. Leicestershire	17-7-43-2	16.2-6-48-2	17-5-56-1	9-3-25-0				6-1-38-1	16-7-54-5	64.2	214	6	10	–
(Leicester) 24-27 August	18-2-65-2	20-3-73-1		12-1-52-1		27.4-6-82-2			4-0-17-0	98.4	347	2	7	–
v. Warwickshire	15.4-4-41-5	9.3-2-25-0		15-5-33-1	20.3-10-38-3				8-2-23-1	68.4	167	7	10	–
(Edgbaston) 2-4 September	20-8-42-3	11-1-32-1	13-4-26-2		19.2-4-48-1					77.2	174	5	9	–
v. Derbyshire				18-7-43-2			17-4-46-3	18.3-5-42-5	18-5-55-0	76.3	203	5	10	A
(Bristol) 8-10 September				7-2-24-0	9-4-13-1		9.2-3-42-3	10-1-61-0	6-1-20-0	41.2	161	1	4	–
v. Kent	15-3-44-2		0.1-0-0-1	19-5-58-1		29-10-103-0	22-5-99-2	24-6-95-3		127.1	483	9	10	A
(Canterbury) 15-18 September														

	AM Smith	J Lewis	IJ Harvey	MW Alleyne	MCJ Ball	JN Snape	JMM Averis	BW Gannon	MJ Cawdron
Overs	450.1	492.2	296.1	367	266	277.1	72.2	259.3	101.5
Maidens	127	134	77	109	69	71	16	47	30
Runs	1168	1444	876	1000	723	804	261	992	266
Wickets	57	49	31	23	13	12	8	33	16
Bowler's average	20.49	29.46	28.25	43.47	55.61	67	32.62	30.06	16.62

A THC Hancock 8-4-15-1; 2-0-12-0; 3-0-13-0; 3-1-5-1; 1-0-4-0; 3-1-15-1; 10-1-39-0; 5-0-12-0; 18-5-75-1
B KJ Barnett 9-3-16-0; 2-0-8-0; 8-0-35-0; 4-1-12-0; 8-2-11-0; 9.3-0-52-2
C DR Hewson 1-1-0-0
D MA Hardinges 17-4-51-0 & 6-2-9-1
E TP Cotterell 21-4-69-3 & 11-4-12-0
F MGN Windows 1-0-7-0

FIELDING

60 – RC Russell (55 ct/5 st)
20 – MW Alleyne
15 – KJ Barnett
11 – MCJ Ball
8 – RJ Cunliffe, JN Snape
7 – THC Hancock
6 – IJ Harvey
5 – MGN Windows
4 – BW Gannon, AM Smith
3 – DR Hewson
2 – J Lewis
1 – MJ Cawdron, RI Dawson

HAMPSHIRE CCC

FIRST–CLASS MATCHES

BATTING

	JP Stephenson	GW White	WS Kendall	RA Smith	AN Aymes	S Lugsden	DA Kenway	AD Mascarenhas	SD Udal	AC Morris	SJ Renshaw	NAM McLean	M Keech	PJ Hartley	KD James	JS Laney	M Garaway	SRG Francis	TM Hansen	ZC Morris	Extras	Total	Wickets	Result	Points
v. Oxford University	136	5	24	45rh	69rh	16	56*	5	28*	–	–										13	397	5	D	–
(Oxford) 14–16 April	–	39*	–	–	–	–	–	–	58*	–												97	–		
v. Kent	17	6	93	18	18		45	15	11	0	1*	11									17	252	10	D	9
(Southampton) 21–23 April	–	–	–	–	–		–	–	–	–	–	–													
v. Durham	7	25	105	10	51		70*	44	1	2	4	5									42	366	10	W	20
(Chester-le-Street) 28–30 April		8	2	30*			19*														7	66	2		
v. Worcestershire	4	17	33	69	14		41	62		13	9*		26	35							29	352	10	W	20
(Southampton) 14–17 May	8	30	39*	11	1*						–		–	–							2	91	3		
v. Middlesex	15	17	85	23	2		75*	22	12	17		11	58								42	379	10	W	20
(Lord's) 19–22 May	8	64	78*	13			17*						19								20	219	4		
v. Nottinghamshire	0	27	12	68	4		7	13		22		6*	14	4							26	203	10	L	5
(Trent Bridge) 27–29 May	20	17	2	55	1		3	6	19*			4	21	18							27	193	10		
v. Essex	38	4	15	96	6		47	40			4	3	48	5*							18	324	10	D	11
(Ilford) 2–5 June	17*	0	2	12*	–		–	–			–	–	–	–							5	36	2		
v. Yorkshire	1	16	46	24	7		14	20		4*	9	37	4								24	206	10	L	5
(Basingstoke) 9–11 June	0	8	9	17	2		4	2		28	6	42*	6								–	124	10		
v. Leicestershire	17		52	78	60		1	49			7*		0	32	5	50					31	382	10	D	11
(Southampton) 15–18 June	29		29	0	16		0	15*					1*	12	0	99					21	222	8		
v. Glamorgan	2		37	63	89		12	22	12				0	43	4*	29					32	345	10	W	19
(Swansea) 30 June–3 July	–		–	–	–		–	–	–				–	–	–	–					–	–	–		
v. New Zealand	54	121	13			8	35	9					10*	0		18	2	1			26	297	10	D	–
(Southampton) 9–12 July	9*	25	28			1*	42	2					4	50		5	1	55			5	227	9		
v. Surrey	4		17	40	1		63	26	30				70	11	15	0					45	322	10	L	7
(Guildford) 14–17 July	26		9	46	5		20		0*				4	8	1	7					28	175	10		
v. Lancashire	4	29	23	29	17		12	0					3	0*		49		1			14	181	10	L	2
(Southampton) 21–24 July	6	47	0	77	4		92	11					4	4*		95		0			62	402	10		
v. Gloucestershire	0	25	55	14	14		11	13					0			97		0*			24	253	10	D	8
(Bristol) 4–8 August	–	–	–	–	–		–	–					–			–		–			–	–	–		
v. Warwickshire	3	92	51	15	45		102	8*	8*							14					15	353	7	D	12
(Southampton) 17–20 August	–	–	–	–	–		22*									23*					1	46	1		
v. Sussex		0	2	17	3		4	3	4				0	4*		20		8			11	76	10	D	8
(Southampton) 24–27 August		77	201	66	111*		24	28	16*							24					23	570	6		
v. Northamptonshire		55	98	94	7		39	0	0				44*	0		0			1	1	18	357	10	L	7
(Northampton) 1–4 September		32	8	5	4		52	10	2*				0			43			0	0	11	167	10		
v. Somerset		5	10	11	115*		61	35	21				28			63		11	24		29	413	10	D	7
(Southampton) 8–11 September		–	–	–	–		–	–	–				–			–		–	–		–	–	–		
v. Derbyshire		0	8	64	86		21	51	3				24*			67					38	362	8	W	20
(Derby) 15–18 September		27	0	–	39*		44	45	19*							8					17	199	5		

	JP Stephenson	GW White	WS Kendall	RA Smith	AN Aymes	S Lugsden	DA Kenway	AD Mascarenhas	SD Udal	AC Morris	SJ Renshaw	NAM McLean	M Keech	PJ Hartley	KD James	JS Laney	M Garaway	SRG Francis	TM Hansen	ZC Morris
Matches	15	16	19	18	18	2	19	14	15	6	12	14	8	12	2	11	1	3	3	1
Innings	24	28	32	29	27	3	31	20	21	7	13	19	13	15	4	19	2	4	4	2
Not Out	2	1	2	3	5	1	6	2	6	2	6	3	1	6	0	1	0	1	0	0
Runs	425	818	1186	1110	791	25	1055	465	261	131	101	206	353	183	28	691	56	12	33	1
Highest score	136	121	201	96	115*	25	1055	465	261	131	101	206	353	183	28	691	56	12	33	1
Average	19.31	30.29	39.53	42.69	35.95	12.50	42.20	25.83	17.40	26.20	14.42	12.87	29.41	20.33	7.00	38.38	28.00	4.00	8.25	0.50
100s	1	1	2	–	2	–	1	–	–	–	–	–	–	–	–	–	–	–	–	–
50s	1	4	7	10	5	–	7	2	–	1	–	1	1	1	–	6	1	–	–	–

HAMPSHIRE CCC

FIRST-CLASS MATCHES
BOWLING

	AC Morris	SJ Renshaw	AD Mascarenhas	SD Udal	JP Stephenson	NAM McLean	PJ Hartley	KD James	SRG Francis	TM Hansen	Overs	Totals	Byes/Leg-byes	Wickets	Run outs	
v. Oxford University	20–7–30–4	11–5–13–1	14–5–38–2	18–7–36–2	7–3–19–1						84	191	17	10	–	AB
(Oxford) 14–16 April		6–3–12–1	3–1–2–2	2–0–5–0	5–0–11–0						16	30	–	3	–	
v. Kent	13–8–19–2	10–3–25–2	9–4–24–0		7–1–27–2	12.4–3–35–1					51.4	135	5	7	–	
(Southampton) 21–24 April																
v. Durham	13–4–33–2	16–4–43–4	10–5–8–1	3–0–9–0	5.4–0–20–2	12–0–44–1					59.4	167	10	10	–	
(Chester-le-Street) 28–30 April	15–2–39–0	23–12–38–0	18–5–35–2	12–4–26–1	19–6–48–4	20.1–8–57–3					107.1	264	21	10	–	
v. Worcestershire	15–3–59–5	10.3–4–40–1	16–7–31–2		12–6–20–1	17–6–50–3					54.3	184	15	10	–	
(Southampton) 14–17 May	19–6–52–5	20–3–61–1			11–0–56–1	18–5–48–1					84	258	10	10	–	
v. Middlesex	16–7–52–2		16–7–43–2	7–3–16–0	9–3–23–2	20.5–6–65–2	16–6–41–1				84.5	256	16	10	1	
(Lord's) 19–22 May	30–8–79–5	9–3–18–0	26–7–55–1		17–3–48–1	24.1–4–65–3	17–3–52–0				123.1	339	22	10	–	
v. Nottinghamshire	19–3–78–2		18–3–70–2		11–3–37–1	18.3–5–55–2	19–6–34–3				86.3	324	43	10	1	C
(Trent Bridge) 27–29 May	12–3–56–1		9–2–49–0		16–2–66–1	15–4–54–1	19–3–70–3				78.4	333	15	10	1	B
v. Essex		21–4–76–3		27.5–7–92–2	8–0–54–0	26–5–65–2	18–6–57–1				101.5	354	7	9	–	B
(Ilford) 2–5 June		16–1–71–1		20–2–66–2		4–3–6–0					54	218	6	3	–	BC
v. Yorkshire		12–3–34–0		10–2–20–0	7–1–29–0	20–9–33–2	26.5–5–65–8				75.5	192	11	10	–	
(Basingstoke) 9–11 June		3–0–23–0		9.2–1–34–0		12–4–27–1	17–5–52–3				41.2	141	5	4	–	
v. Leicestershire		31–4–124–4	19–5–42–1		22–3–79–1	31–8–79–1		16.1–5–38–3			126	405	23	10	–	CD
(Southampton) 15–18 June		18–6–50–0	2–0–21–0		17–0–67–4	19–1–78–1		13–0–61–3			75	317	12	8	–	E
v. Glamorgan			5–0–16–0	15.2–3–32–3	5–1–21–0	14–4–33–3	14–5–54–4				53.2	162	6	10	–	
(Swansea) 30 June–3 July			7–2–14–0	16.5–2–47–6	5–2–17–1	17–2–89–1	7–3–14–2				52.5	177	2	10	–	
v. New Zealand		36–14–91–3		21.4–7–60–2	11–3–29–0			21–8–69–0			120.4	370	13	9	1	AB
(Southampton) 9–12 July		18–3–39–1		33.2–10–102–5	17–8–47–2			4–0–33–0			80.2	247	1	9	–	A
v. Surrey			9–2–26–0	1.3–0–2–2	2–0–8–0	12–1–63–4	17–6–66–4				41.3	171	6	10	–	
(Guildford) 14–17 July			19–7–50–0	16–2–46–1	27–0–132–2	30.4–0–118–2	31–8–88–3				135.4	482	16	10	1	E
v. Lancashire			25–7–84–1		28.5–4–102–3	29–4–98–1	29–5–102–3		28–6–94–2		139.5	492	12	10	–	
(Southampton) 21–24 July					5.3–1–43–1	5–2–5–0			5–0–32–1		19.3	93	1	2	–	
v. Gloucestershire		23–6–69–0		39.5–10–96–5	26–6–60–5		28–7–70–0		22–3–62–0		138.5	380	23	10	–	
(Bristol) 5–8 August		8–1–29–1		11–4–16–3	6–1–22–1		9–4–10–2		5–1–16–1		39	96	3	8	–	
v. Warwickshire			24–8–54–0	26–9–66–2	3–0–7–1	26–4–100–2	27.1–3–88–5			17–5–59–3	108.1	351	26	10	–	D
(Southampton) 17–20 August																
v. Sussex			8–2–48–0	39.3–9–102–4		22–4–85–2	17–2–59–1				105.3	375	11	10	–	B
(Southampton) 24–27 August																
v. Northamptonshire		16–4–41–3		34.5–11–95–2			22.3–5–59–4			13–2–47–0	116.3	342	13	10	–	EF
(Northampton) 1–4 September		9–2–20–1		21.3–3–80–4			12–2–2–1				54.3	183	11	6	–	EF
v. Somerset		39–6–107–3	29–6–103–1	40–8–115–0					29–6–81–0	27–9–66–2	165	493	20	6	–	G
(Southampton) 8–11 September		15–2–44–0	9–2–30–0	16–5–34–0					8–0–47–1	7–1–24–0	82	255	1	2	1	BDEHI
v. Derbyshire		11–2–32–0	17–10–34–0	11–2–49–1		19–5–50–3	19–4–78–3				79	277	18	9	1	B
(Derby) 15–18 September		9–1–43–0	13–5–28–1	18–6–35–2		26–8–87–4	23.3–5–77				89.3	282	12	10	–	

	AC Morris	SJ Renshaw	AD Mascarenhas	SD Udal	JP Stephenson	NAM McLean	PJ Hartley	KD James	SRG Francis	TM Hansen
Overs	172	381.3	308	497.3	310	471	393	54.1	97	64
Maidens	51	93	98	124	57	105	93	13	16	17
Runs	497	1125	868	1336	1086	1489	1176	201	332	196
Wickets	28	30	17	50	37	46	54	6	5	5
Bowler's average	17.75	37.5	51.05	26.72	29.35	32.36	21.77	33.50	66.90	39.20

A S Lugsden 13–5–31–0; 30–6–105–3 & 8–1–25–1
B GW White 1–0–7–0; 7.4–0–23–3; 1–0–3–1 & 11–0–54–1; 1–0–3–0; 2–0–11–0; 12–2–41–0; 2–0–16–1
C M Keech 1–0–7–0; 3–0–15–0; 5–1–15–0
D WS Kendall 1.5–0–5–0; 2–0–10–0; 1–0–2–0
E JS Laney 6–0–28–0; 12–2–32–1; 7–2–24–1 & 2–0–13–0; 12–1–29–0
F ZC Morris 23.1–5–63–0 & 10–2–31–0
G DA Kenway 1–0–1–0
H RA Smith 1–0–2–0
I AN Aymes 1–0–1–0

FIELDING

53 – AN Aymes (51 ct/2 st)	
25 – WS Kendall	
17 – JP Stephenson	
13 – DA Kenway	
11 – GW White	
9 – RA Smith	
8 – M Keech	
7 – JS Laney, SJ Renshaw	
6 – NAM McLean	
5 – M Garaway (4 ct/1 st)	
4 – AD Mascarenhas	
3 – PJ Hartley	
2 – KD James	
1 – SD Udal	

KENT CCC

FIRST-CLASS MATCHES

BATTING

Match	RWT Key	ET Smith	TR Ward	AP Wells	A Symonds	MJ Walker	SA Marsh	MV Fleming	DW Headley	MM Patel	JB Thompson	MJ McCague	DP Fulton	MA Ealham	WJ House	SC Willis	DA Scott	MJ Saggers	MJ Banes	JM Golding	Extras	Total	Wickets	Result	Points
v. Middlesex	86	3	1	9	69	1	43	18	12	18	0*										26	286	10	D	10
(Lord's) 13–16 April	–	–	–	–	–	–	–	–	–	–	–														
v. Hampshire	2		10	33	4	10*	6	16*	–	0		–	41								13	135	7	D	8
(Southampton) 21–24 April	–		–	–	–	–	–	–		–			–												
v. Derbyshire	11		11		8	53	7	4	10	6	11*	4	2								14	141	10	L	4
(Canterbury) 28–30 April	9		7		25	3	0	41	1	9		30	0	88*							7	220	10		
v. Durham	1	2	111	78	42	4	11	13*	8*	–			6								25	301	8	W	19
(Stockton-on-Tees) 14–17 May	21	42		–	6	12	0	26*	–	–			10*								4	121	5		
v. Cambridge University	–	44	101		103*								99								21	368	3	W	–
(Cambridge) 20–22 May	91	89			–										22*	10*	–	–			33	245	2		
v. Leicestershire	22		41	177	5	24	24	20*	2	1			64				0				40	420	10	D	11
(Canterbury) 26–29 May	29*		20	15*	16								1								11	92	3		
v. Surrey	0		0	2	16	1		10	13	1	1		5			12*					10	71	10	L	4
(Tunbridge Wells) 2–5 June	31		10	3	27	0		37*	14	3	3		22			9					13	172	10		
v. Sussex	11	36		54	51	15	1	15	21*	0			4	74							54	336	10	D	11
(Hove) 9–12 June	24*	16*		–	–								–	–							2	42	–		
v. Glamorgan	92	49		26	11	7	94	3	2*	1			0	9							38	332	10	D	9
(Canterbury) 15–18 June	0	61		0	93		–	–		–			126*	17*							20	317	4		
v. Warwickshire	17	30	0	11			15	0		4	3*	46	0	21							17	164	10	W	16
(Maidstone) 30 June – 2 July	7	52	2	0			44	9		19	3*	10	33	1							19	199	10		
v. Worcestershire	0	6	0	0			9	45	33	1	0*		8	5							12	119	10	W	16
(Worcester) 9–12 July	33	19	11	0			4	138	22	7	23*		41	28							24	350	10		
v. New Zealand	4	72		9			37					4	43	0		9	0		0	0*	23	201	10	D	–
(Canterbury) 15–18 July	27	111		102			21*					4	15	43		10	0*		53	3	28	417	9		
v. Nottinghamshire	50	10		32		2	26		1	0	6*	29	1						5		29	191	10	W	16
(Trent Bridge) 21–23 July	17	38		37		32*	25		10	4	6	3	20						2		28	222	10		
v. Essex	77	33		132	41	14	14	17		27	6*	48	13	80							53	541	10	W	20
(Canterbury) 4–7 August	0	17*		5*	21	–								4							6	53	3		
v. Somerset	33	83	2			43	73*	50		3	2	31	86	75							23	504	10	D	10
(Taunton) 18–21 August	125	37	49			5	–			–	43		0*								5	279	6		
v. Northamptonshire	1	19	11		0			3		12	22*	19	2	2	67						9	167	10	W	16
(Canterbury) 24–26 August	–	–	–		–			–		–	–	–	–	–	–										
v. Yorkshire	9	10	26	0		46		0	49	8*	53	19	59								23	302	10	L	6
(Scarborough) 1–4 September	2	55	23		25	31		0*	0	44	4	5	9								28	226	10		
v. Lancashire	1	11	86	99	4		12	55	72	14				21				12*			23	410	10	L	8
(Old Trafford) 8–11 September	2	13	17	8	13		18	23	30	6				7				4*			18	159	10		
v. Gloucestershire	1	17	100				60	99	5	67	12*		24	23							41	483	10	D	10 A
(Canterbury) 15–18 September	–	–	–				–			–	–		–	–											

	RWT Key	ET Smith	TR Ward	AP Wells	A Symonds	MJ Walker	SA Marsh	MV Fleming	DW Headley	MM Patel	JB Thompson	MJ McCague	DP Fulton	MA Ealham	WJ House	SC Willis	DA Scott	MJ Saggers	MJ Banes	JM Golding
Matches	19	14	8	10	14	14	15	17	12	18	14	10	17	13	1	4	3	2	2	1
Innings	33	25	13	15	25	23	22	25	16	24	19	13	29	22	1	6	4	1	4	2
Not Out	2	2	0	0	2	2	2	4	3	3	9	2	2	3	1	2	3	0	0	1
Runs	836	931	240	490	940	553	466	830	263	290	176	272	722	585	22	117	16	0	60	3
Highest score	125	111	101	111	177	103*	73*	138	72	67	44	53	126*	88*	22*	67	12*	0	53	3
Average	26.96	40.47	18.46	32.66	40.86	26.33	23.3	39.52	20.23	13.8	17.6	24.72	26.74	30.78	–	29.25	16	–	15	3
100s	1	1	1	2	3	1	–	1	–	–	–	–	1	–	–	–	–	–	–	–
50s	5	6	–	1	4	3	2	4	1	1	–	1	3	5	–	1	–	–	1	

A   JB Hockley 34

KENT CCC

FIRST–CLASS MATCHES
BOWLING

	DW Headley	JBD Thompson	MV Fleming	A Symonds	MM Patel	MJ McCague	MA Ealham	MJ Saggers	DA Scott	Overs	Totals	Byes/Leg-byes	Wickets	Run outs	
v. Middlesex	26-4-79-1	23.5-5-61-4	21-9-42-2	15-3-40-0	10-3-21-3					95.5	254	11	10	–	
(Lord's) 13-16 April	15-2-45-1	10-3-21-0	15-2-44-0	18-1-116-1	31-2-130-2					92.1	381	8	4	–	AB
v. Hampshire	20-8-42-2		18-3-63-2	14-7-39-1	13.1-4-32-1	21-3-65-4				86.1	252	11	10	–	
(Southampton) 21-24 April															
v. Derbyshire	27.1-3-103-4		12-4-29-0	7-0-26-1	11-4-27-0	10-2-34-0	23-4-75-4			90.1	300	6	10	1	
(Canterbury) 28-30 April	2-0-25-0		2.1-0-8-0	3-0-9-0		3-1-18-0				10.1	62	2	–	–	
v. Durham	7-2-29-0	10-5-14-2	7-3-11-2	6.1-1-12-1	17-7-18-5					47.1	93	9	10	–	
(Stockton-on-Tees) 14-17 May	34-9-86-2	33.4-10-89-7	16-4-49-1	17-5-40-0	39-25-38-0					139.4	325	23	10	–	
v. Cambridge University					10.5-9-4-2	21-5-36-4		16-4-35-3	5-2-6-1	58.5	102	9	10	–	C
(Cambridge) 20-22 May					26-7-58-4	3-1-9-0		10.1-3-26-4	21-4-58-2	60.1	160	9	10	–	
v. Leicestershire	31-11-78-2	26-16-67-2	11-3-34-1	21-3-59-2	27-6-57-1			12.4-1-55-2		128.4	369	19	10	–	
(Canterbury) 26-29 May	16-4-46-1	18-3-79-4		8-0-38-0	42.4-12-87-1			21-5-76-3		105.4	346	20	9	–	
v. Surrey	21-8-53-2	23-8-47-1	17-3-49-2	10-2-42-1	28.1-6-59-3					99.1	271	21	10	1	
(Tunbridge Wells) 2-5 June															
v. Sussex	28-2-74-4	25.3-7-82-2	14-3-43-1	13-3-49-0	9-2-16-0		23-4-58-3			112.3	336	14	10	–	
(Hove) 9-12 June	21-6-60-1	24.4-3-77-4	2-1-2-1	6-0-30-0	34-6-95-2		10-3-32-0			97.4	317	21	8	–	
v. Glamorgan	34-5-127-2	23-3-68-0	23-5-63-0	17-1-69-1	30.3-6-93-4		32-9-79-2			159.3	544	45	10	1	
(Canterbury) 15-18 June															
v. Warwickshire		13-0-48-4	3-3-0-1			8.4-1-40-2	8-1-22-3			32.4	116	6	10	–	
(Maidstone) 30 June-2 July		12-5-22-2	6.1-2-13-1		17-8-43-6	14-2-42-0	13-1-33-0			62.1	156	3	10	1	
v. Worcestershire	12-3-35-3	7-3-13-0			16-5-31-4		9-4-18-2			44	106	9	10	1	
(Worcester) 9-12 July	24-2-89-1	24-6-58-4		5-0-38-1	37-14-80-1		20-5-59-2			110	343	19	10	1	
v. New Zealand			23.4-4-72-2	25-6-66-0		38-8-120-1	31-6-89-2		42-10-151-4	181.4	591	19	10	–	D
(Canterbury) 15-18 July															
v. Nottinghamshire		11-1-18-2				17.1-4-33-3	11-1-30-5			39.1	88	7	10	–	
(Trent Bridge) 21-23 July		18.3-6-63-6	9-0-36-1	7-1-22-1	2-1-4-0	12-3-36-0	17-3-52-2			65.3	237	24	10	–	
v. Essex		22-2-87-3	21-5-48-0	7-4-18-0	45-18-60-3	17-5-62-0	18.5-5-51-4			134.5	350	21	10	1	A
(Canterbury) 4-7 August		17-6-49-2	3.3-2-1-2		37-14-74-1	19-4-66-3	20-8-44-1			96.3	243	9	10	1	
v. Somerset		24-8-64-2	10-1-27-0		37-13-90-1	18-1-86-1	17-1-51-1			111	361	20	6	1	A
(Taunton) 18-21 August															
v. Northamptonshire		11-4-27-6				3-0-21-0	9.1-4-18-3			23.1	69	3	10	1	
(Canterbury) 24-26 August		10-0-24-2	7-4-13-1			5-2-10-1	11.2-1-35-6			33.2	86	4	10	–	
v. Yorkshire	30-7-105-4	12-4-46-2			34-11-72-1	20.1-1-59-2	26-6-71-1			130.1	389	12	10	–	A
(Scarborough) 1-4 September	8.4-0-32-1	8-2-39-1			14-4-40-3	5-1-17-0	9-3-9-0			44.4	141	4	5	–	
v. Lancashire	16-0-52-1		10-3-20-0	8-0-48-2	41-12-115-8		11-1-38-0		20.2-2-83-1	88.2	312	24	10	–	
(Old Trafford) 8-11 September	8-2-21-0		15-0-59-3		30.2-3-120-4				7-0-34-0	63.2	258	15	6	–	
v. Gloucestershire	15-3-64-1	18-3-83-1			10.5-1-36-1		19-3-104-0			77.5	350	4	6	–	
(Canterbury) 15-18 September	4-1-8-0	9-3-19-1			24-6-68-2		1-0-13-0			50	173	8	5	1	E

	DW Headley	JBD Thompson	MV Fleming	A Symonds	MM Patel	MJ McCague	MA Ealham	MJ Saggers	DA Scott
Overs	399.5	434.1	266.3	207.1	674.3	235	339.2	59.5	95.2
Maidens	82	116	64	37	209	44	73	13	18
Runs	1253	1265	726	761	1568	754	981	192	332
Wickets	33	64	23	12	63	21	41	12	8
Bowler's average	37.96	19.76	31.56	63.41	24.88	35.9	23.92	16	41.5

A   MJ Walker 2.1-0-14-0; 4-1-3-0; 5-1-23-0; 8-1-24-0
B   ET Smith 1-0-3-0
C   WJ House 6-0-12-0
D   JM Golding 22-4-74-1
E   JB Hockley 12-1-57-1

FIELDING

35 – SA Marsh (28 ct/7 st)
18 – DA Fulton, RWT Key
15 – A Symonds
13 – MK Walker
11 – SC Willis (10 ct/1 st)
9 – DW Headley, TR Ward
7 – MJ McCague
6 – MM Patel
4 – MV Fleming
3 – MA Ealham
2 – ET Smith
1 – MJ Banes, DA Scott, JB DeC Thompson, AP Wells

LANCASHIRE CCC

FIRST–CLASS MATCHES
BATTING

	MJ Chilton	NT Wood	PC McKeown	GD Lloyd	M Watkinson	JJ Haynes	CP Schofield	G Chapple	RJ Green	MP Smethurst	JP Crawley	WK Hegg	PJ Martin	A Flintoff	G Keedy	M Muralitharan	NH Fairbrother	ID Austin	MA Atherton	G Yates	Extras	Total	Wickets	Result	Points
v. Cambridge University	106*	46	74*																		19	245	1	W	
(Cambridge) 8–10 April	31	–	75	52	10*	–	4*														5	216	4		A
v. Sussex	87	22	10	46	0	–	35	33*	–	–	0	14	30*								24	301	8	D	10
(Old Trafford) 14–16 April	–	–	–	–	––	–	––														–				
v. Leicestershire	3	24	9	18	15	2	14*	2			11	36		86							21	241	10	L	5
(Leicester) 28 April–1 May	15	82	1	37	39*	22	10	3			13	9		1							23	255	10		
v. Northamptonshire	102	15	2	12	116		21*				19	37*	–	–							26	350	6	L	6
(Old Trafford) 19–22 May	12	22	12	2	23		13	0			2	11	12	1*							11	121	10		
v. Nottinghamshire	20	8	8	0	24		2	4			0	28	26	0*							21	141	10	W	16
(Old Trafford) 19–22 May	2	0	27	120*	28		55				49	8	0*								43	332	7		
v. Gloucestershire	28	6		8	55		24	8*			13	6		158	9						28	351	9	D	8 B
(Bristol) 2–5 June	–																				–				
v. Warwickshire	18			0	8						55	6*	0	34	2	3	3				15	144	10	L	4 B
(Southport) 9–11 June	11			4	49						76	58	3	18	5	6	1				33	265	10		B
v. Surrey	15			11	23						36	25	23*	0	1	0	6		24		30	194	10	L	4
(The Oval) 15–18 June	37			18	2						0	94	18	8	3*	0	2		52		26	260	10		
v. Essex	71			25	0						51	43	3	52	0*	0	37	1			15	298	10	W	18
(Old Trafford) 29 June–2 July	0			11	8						64	23*	14*	0			40	31			18	209	7		
v. Sri Lanka 'A'	9			37	80	18				0				11	9*		55	6	1	0	45	271	10	L	–
(Old Trafford) 9–11 July	1			17	34*	17				0				0	3		12	4	5		8	101	10		
v. Glamorgan	71			3							34	53	12	59			34*		268*		22	556	6	W	20
(Blackpool) 14–17 July	2*																13*				4	19	–		
v. Hampshire	51			85	8						101	2	23	27	4		83	45*	39		24	492	10	W	20
(Southampton) 21–24 July											24*		49*			4	–	15			1	93	2		
v. Derbyshire	11			5	12	83	27				0	41	0	31	0*	9					5	224	10	W	17
(Derby) 4–6 August	3			104	0	0	19*				1	48	1	29	10	0					20	235	10		
v. Yorkshire	6			31	10	41	7*				2	0	12	160			12			21	12	314	10	W	19
(Old Trafford) 19–21 August	20*										14*										–	34	–		
v. Worcestershire	8			26	32		5				30	27	22*	30			12	6		4	15	217	10	D	9
(Worcester) 24–27 August	–																				–				
v. Durham	47			86	14		37				158	24	9	0	0*		21	15			26	437	10	W	20
(Old Trafford) 1–3 September	–																				–				
v. Kent	29			81	37*		6				9	21	14	18	0		63			0	34	312	10	W	19
(Old Trafford) 8–11 September	5			84	0*		9				57	21		3*			38			–	41	258	6		
v. Somerset	6			144	1		13	2*			64	28	4				41	7		0	12	322	10	D	9
(Taunton) 15–18 September																									

	MJ Chilton	NT Wood	PC McKeown	GD Lloyd	M Watkinson	JJ Haynes	CP Schofield	G Chapple	RJ Green	MP Smethurst	JP Crawley	WK Hegg	PJ Martin	A Flintoff	G Keedy	M Muralitharan	NH Fairbrother	ID Austin	MA Atherton	G Yates
Matches	18	6	5	17	17	8	10	13	10	5	15	16	14	13	7	7	12	5	7	5
Innings	30	9	8	26	26	13	14	18	10	4	25	24	19	21	9	9	19	8	11	6
Not Out	3	0	1	1	1	1	4	2	2	5	2	3	5	2	6	1	0	2	2	0
Runs	827	225	216	1066	1066	345	205	402	96	5	870	670	220	727	17	30	503	125	445	25
Highest score	106*	82	75	144	144	39*	83	27	3	158	94	30*	160	9*	10	83	45*	268*	125	25
Average	30.62	25.00	30.85	42.64	42.64	28.75	20.50	25.12	19.2	1.25	37.82	31.90	15.71	38.26	5.66	3.75	26.47	20.83	49.44	4.16
100s	2	–	–	3	3	1	–	–	–	–	2	–	–	2	–	–	–	–	1	–
50s	4	1	2	6	6	–	–	2	–	–	6	3	–	2	–	–	4	–	1	–

A ME Harvey 39
B PM Ridgway 8*; 0 & 1*

LANCASHIRE CCC

FIRST-CLASS MATCHES
BOWLING

	G Chapple	MP Smethurst	M Watkinson	RJ Green	CP Schofield	PJ Martin	A Flintoff	G Keedy	M Muralitharan	ID Austin	Overs	Totals	Byes/Leg-byes	Wickets	Run outs	
v. Cambridge University (Cambridge) 8–10 April	21–7–38–0	17–3–41–2	19–8–41–2	12–4–20–0	25–5–89–2						98	261	13	7	–	A
	8–4–8–0	22–11–44–4	16–2–54–2	18–9–39–2	12.3–4–36–2						80.3	197	3	10	–	A
v. Sussex (Old Trafford) 13–16 April	30–8–73–2	21–1–67–1	17–5–42–1		19.4–1–96–1	31–7–62–3					118.4	351	11	8	–	
v. Leicestershire (Leicester) 28 April–1 May	31–9–92–5	16–3–46–1	8–1–33–0	32–7–86–4	13–2–53–0		13–2–48–0				115	388	21	10	–	A
	19–8–45–2	19.1–7–47–4		19–4–51–1	4–0–16–0		17–4–46–3				78.1	215	10	10	–	
v. Northamptonshire (Old Trafford) 14–17 May	35.1–11–70–3		5–1–18–1	29–5–104–1		34–10–82–1		25–1–103–2			130.1	404	20	8	–	A
	2–0–7–0		9–2–31–0			3–2–4–0		8–1–22–0			44	256	5	0	–	BCD
v. Nottinghamshire (Old Trafford) 19–22 May	12–3–36–0		14–2–43–3	9–2–40–1		21.3–8–43–5		2–0–7–1			58.3	181	12	10	–	
	11.4–4–27–0		20–5–60–2	12.2–0–51–1		21–4–71–1		25.5–5–67–5			90.5	291	15	10	1	
v. Warwickshire (Southport) 9–11 June			6–1–17–0			18–9–24–3	4–0–19–0		34.5–16–44–7	19–4–65–0	85.5	217	11	10	–	E
			4–1–8–0			30.5–9–72–3			34–13–73–7	11–1–32–0	84.5	211	8	10	–	E
v. Surrey (The Oval) 15–18 June	10–3–31–0					10–2–53–0	11–3–29–1	25–3–87–3	41.5–15–87–6		97.5	298	11	10	–	
	3–0–15–0						3–1–10–0	31–10–67–2	31.5–10–61–4		68.5	161	2	6	–	
v. Essex (Old Trafford) 29 June–1 July			6–0–30–0			9–5–7–0	2–0–10–0	16–6–43–3	30–8–73–7	6–0–24–0	69	207	20	10	–	
			13–2–36–1			7–1–19–0		24–8–47–2	34.2–11–61–6		78.2	182	19	10	1	
v. Sri Lanka 'A' (Old Trafford) 9–11 July		11–0–52–1			28–5–96–1		4–1–5–0	20–5–46–1		18–8–43–6	87	277	15	10	1	G
		8–1–36–0			28–8–68–3		5–1–12–0	14–6–35–0		6–0–36–0	95	274	32	10	1	AG
v. Glamorgan (Blackpool) 14–17 July		6–2–22–0		8–2–34–0	25.2–7–55–4				48–9–104–6	19–5–51–0	106.2	282	16	10	–	
		6–1–22–0		5–1–20–0	31–13–71–4		4–1–7–0		40.3–14–72–4	18–3–74–2	107.3	289	23	10	1	A
v. Hampshire (Southampton) 21–24 July	14–2–38–0					18–5–52–3	10.1–3–24–5		12–4–21–1	13–4–40–1	67.1	181	6	10	–	
	25–7–78–2					26–10–54–0	19–2–58–0		48.2–11–114–7	19–4–78–0	137.2	402	20	10	1	
v. Derbyshire (Derby) 4–6 August	11–3–39–1			3–0–9–0		23.5–10–51–5			15–6–22–4		52.5	132	11	10	–	
	7–1–32–0			7–0–31–0		4–4–29–2			15.4–5 39–7		43.4	135	4	9	–	
v. Yorkshire (Old Trafford) 19–21 August	10–2–22–3			9–3–21–4	20–5–56–0	11.2–7–9–3	8–6–11–0				38.2	67	4	10	–	
	16–6–47–0			8–2–24–1		28.1–5–67–5	12–2 29 2				118.1	277	16	10	–	G
v. Worcestershire (Worcester) 24–27 August	16–5–61–1			16–2–62–1		24–8–52–5	8.3–1–27–3				72.3	227	13	10	–	AG
	2–1–1–0			7–1–30–2		2–0–12–0	5–0–28–0				26	88	2	2	–	AFG
v. Durham (Old Trafford) 1–3 September	16–3–52–1				26.3–7–66–5	20–8–27–2	9–2–17–1	16–7–47–1			87.3	226	17	10	–	
	8–1–32–2				24–5–72–3	18–5–44–2	6–1–20–0	6–3–10–1			62	197	19	10	1	
v. Kent (Old Trafford) 8–11 September	13–0–60–2				38–10–103–4	30–5–84–1	5–0–19–0	20.5–3–71–3			117.5	410	19	10	–	G
					1–0–9–0	14–4–19–2		32–15–59–2			64.1	159	8	10	–	G
v. Somerset (Taunton) 15–18 September	17–5–60–0			18–4–70–2	28–10–65–0	32–6–91–3					118	376	27	6	–	G

	G Chapple	MP Smethurst	M Watkinson	RJ Green	CP Schofield	PJ Martin	A Flintoff	G Keedy	M Muralitharan	ID Austin
Overs	337.5	126.1	137	212.2	324	446.4	145.4	265.4	386.2	129
Maidens	93	29	30	46	82	134	30	73	122	29
Runs	964	377	413	692	951	1028	419	711	777	443
Wickets	24	13	12	20	29	50	15	26	66	9
Bowler's average	40.16	29.00	34.41	34.6	32.79	20.56	27.93	27.34	11.77	49.22

A   MJ Chilton 4–1–19–1 & 4–0–13–0; 2–1–9–0; 2–0–7–0; 1–0–1–1; 3–3–0–0; 7–3–12–0 & 2–1–1–0
B   JP Crawley 6–0–51–0
C   GD Lloyd 10–0–100–0
D   NT Wood 6–0–36–0
E   PM Ridgway 4–0–37–0 & 5–1–18–0
F   NH Fairbrother 2–0–2–0
G   G Yates 6–2–20–0 & 33–15–54–5; 34–15–48–2; 1–1–0–0 & 6–2–12–0; 11–2–54–0 & 17.1–1–64–6; 23–4–63–1

FIELDING

49 – WK Hegg (45 ct/4 st)	
25 – A Flintoff	
21 – MJ Chilton	
17 – NH Fairbrother	
10 – JP Crawley	
9 – JJ Haynes (8 ct/1 st)	
8 – CP Schofield	
7 – GD Lloyd	
4 – PC McKeown, M Watkinson, G Yates	
3 – MA Atherton	
2 – ID Austin, G Chapple, PJ Martin, M Muralitharan	
1 – RJ Green, ME Harvey, G Keedy, MP Smethurst, NT Wood	

LEICESTERSHIRE CCC

FIRST–CLASS MATCHES
BATTING

Match	DL Maddy	IJ Sutcliffe	Aftab Habib	BF Smith	JJ Whitaker	PA Nixon	CC Lewis	JM Dakin	MS Kasprowicz	J Ormond	MT Brimson	VJ Wells	AD Mullally	DJ Millns	DI Stevens	CD Crowe	D Williamson	TJ Mason	AA Khan	SAJ Boswell	Extras	Total	Wickets	Result	Points
v. Essex (Chelmsford) 13–16 April	46	11	3	14	44	121	139	8	9	6	1*										22	424	10	W	20
	–	–	–	–	–	–	–	–	–	–	–										–	–	–		
v. Nottinghamshire (Leicester) 20–23 April	–	–	–	–	–	–	–	–	–	–	–										–	–	–	D	6
	–	–	–	–	–	–	–	–	–	–	–														
v. Lancashire (Leicester) 28 April–1 May	86	6	12	17	14	25	108	–	5	–	36*	44	0								35	388	10	W	20
	0	2	79	15	11	38*	37	–	3	–	11	4	3								12	215	10		
v. Somerset (Taunton) 19–21 May	21	40	0	4	27	0	46*	6	8	11	0										10	173	10	L	3
	23	40	147	0	1	12	10	62	1*	10	1										6	313	10		
v. Kent (Canterbury) 26–29 May	18	55	60	73	0	26	–	5	32*	18	2			47							33	369	10	D	11
	93	27	13	49	33	7	–	12	52*	7	9*			6							38	346	9		
v. Glamorgan (Leicester) 2–5 June	10	4	73	82		28	0	4	0	0		13		15*							30	259	10	D	10
	–	–	–	–		–	–	–	–	–		–		–											
v. Surrey (Leicester) 9–12 June	23	17	60	3		33	56		0		1	44	3*	0							32	272	10	D	9
	52	18	70*	0		47	20*	–	–	–	–	–									32	239	4		
v. Hampshire (Southampton) 15–18 June	38	12	16	154		6		73	4	1*		13	22	32							34	405	10	D	11
	108	18	28	36		2		13	8			1*	18*	61							24	317	8		
v. Yorkshire (Leicester) 1–3 July	158*			10		4	23	17	16	13	5	2		9	12						28	297	10	W	18
	5*	–	–	–	–	–	–	–	–	–	–	–		–	2						–	7	1		
v. Sussex (Arundel) 14–17 July	30		160*	34		8	51		52			51	11*		130	23					16	566	8	W	20
	–		–	–		–	–		–			–	–		–	–									
v. Worcestershire (Worcester) 22–25 July	38	110		4		37		5			1		19	2		16	31*	5			23	291	10	D	10
	35	5	138	7		19						14		0*		31	14	36	–		17	316	9		
v. New Zealand (Leicester) 30 July – 1 August	7	18	5	17		19		10		5	5*	4		0						15	20	125	10	L	–
	38	0	4	37		99		18		1	2*	101		9						0	24	333	10		
v. Warwickshire (Leicester) 6–9 August	59	0	12	43		29			2	50*	33	109*	–	0							16	353	8	D	12
	–		–	–		–			–	–	–	–		–											
v. Middlesex (Lord's) 18–21 August		58	14	2		28	0	56*	49	0	0	8		7							6	228	10	D	9
		21	21	6		15	0	57*	54*			41		0							16	225	7		
v. Gloucestershire (Leicester) 24–27 August	33	13	0			31	19	61	8	17			1*			11	0				20	214	10	W	17
	0	6	141			32	124	8								25	7*				4	347	7		
v. Derbyshire (Derby) 1–3 September	22	9	35			72	16	44	23			68			2	32					20	343	10	L	7 (A)
	5	0	6			51	9	5	16*			11			60	7					27	197	10		(A)
v. Northampton (Leicester) 8–10 September	40	40	51			5		10				4			39	44*	10	11		15	42	311	10	L	6
	31	3	2			0		10				12			19	22	19	1		9*	15	143	10		
v. Durham (Leicester) 15–18 September	13	45	2			37	30	7	0	3*	3	57			98						27	322	10	D	11
	9	12	15*			9*	–	–	–	–	–	0			22						7	74	4		

	DL Maddy	IJ Sutcliffe	Aftab Habib	BF Smith	JJ Whitaker	PA Nixon	CC Lewis	JM Dakin	MS Kasprowicz	J Ormond	MT Brimson	VJ Wells	AD Mullally	DJ Millns	DI Stevens	CD Crowe	D Williamson	TJ Mason	AA Khan	SAJ Boswell
Matches	17	16	16	14	5	18	10	11	16	13	14	13	6	6	11	4	2	2	1	2
Innings	28	27	26	21	7	29	13	18	23	17	16	20	7	9	20	7	4	4	1	4
Not Out	2	0	3	0	0	2	2	2	4	3	6	2	4	3	0	2	0	1	0	1
Runs	1041	590	1029	732	130	828	520	454	507	183	127	588	32	136	562	135	59	79	5	15
Highest score	158*	110	160*	154	44	121	139	124	73	50*	36*	109*	13	47	130	44	19	36	5	39
Average	40.03	21.85	44.73	34.85	18.57	30.66	47.27	28.37	26.68	13.07	12.7	32.66	10.66	22.66	28.10	27.00	14.75	26.33	5.00	13.00
100s	2	1	3	2	–	1	2	1	–	–	–	2	–	–	1	–	–	–	–	–
50s	4	2	6	2	–	3	2	3	5	1	–	3	–	–	3	–	–	–	–	–

A   A Sachdeva 0* & 0

LEICESTERSHIRE CCC

FIRST-CLASS MATCHES
BOWLING

	MS Kasprowicz	CC Lewis	J Ormond	JM Dakin	MT Brimson	VJ Wells	AD Mullally	DL Maddy	DJ Millns	CD Crowe	Overs	Totals	Byes/Leg-byes	Wickets	Run outs
v. Essex (Chelmsford) 13–16 April	28–10–78–3	27–6–85–2	18.1–4–39–2	11–3–31–1	2–1–9–1						86.1	252	10	10	1
	19–3–39–3	15–5–49–3	10–1–26–1	10.1–3–23–3	3–1–12–0						57.1	150	1	10	–
v. Nottinghamshire (Leicester) 20–23 April	11–3–31–2	11–3–23–2	6–1–32–0		5–1–9–0	7–3–14–1					40	117	8	5	–
v. Lancashire (Leicester) 28 April–1 May	25–5–71–1	15.1–8–18–3			5–0–24–1	19–3–58–2	17–6–52–2	2–0–9–0			83.1	241	9	10	1
	22–5–84–3	18–6–42–1			13.4–4–33–2	13–2–48–2	23–8–37–1	1–0–2–0			90.4	255	9	10	1
v. Somerset (Taunton) 19–21 May	32–10–116–1	17–2–75–0	28.2–6–85–5	31–12–58–2	23–6–77–1			6–0–23–1			137.2	453	19	10	–
	3–0–7–0		4.4–0–20–0	2–0–8–1							9.4	37	2	1	–
v. Kent (Canterbury) 26–29 May	31–8–81–2		32–6–102–3	19–4–59–0	24–6–76–0			3–0–18–0	15.5–1–62–5		124.5	420	22	10	–
	2–0–7–0		10–3–24–1	4–0–20–0	7–1–13–1				9–2–21–1		32	92	7	3	–
v. Glamorgan (??) 2–5 June	20–6–55–2	16–3–48–1	26–6–85–2	10–1–32–0		14–3–30–1			16.1–5–30–4		102.1	291	11	10	–
v. Surrey (Leicester) 9–12 June	24–1–106–3	15–0–77–0			27–6–94–0		32–6–106–5	7–1–19–0	26.2–3–80–2		131.2	501	19	10	–
v. Hampshire (Southampton) 15–18 June	23–6–71–1		30–3–119–3		29–7–66–1		22–7–58–1	3–1–6–0	19–6–47–4		126	382	15	10	–
	3–0–10–0		28.5–6–93–4		32–16–56–1		12–2–27–1	9–4–13–2	2–0–6–0		87.5	222	17	8	A
v. Yorkshire (Leicester) 1–3 July	13–3–30–1		11–4–16–4			3–1–2–2			1.3–1–1–3		28.3	52	3	10	–
	12–1–32–1	16–8–32–0	13.2–3–43–3		31.1–12–43–3	19–9–28–0		5–2–7–2	20.4–7–54–1		117.1	251	12	10	–
v. Sussex (Arundel) 14–17 July	6.5–3–19–1	19–7–43–0			28–8–69–4	13–3–41–0	31–10–76–3	6–2–12–0		17–5–38–2	120.5	319	21	10	–
					30–13–51–5	15–7–24–0	14–6–27–1	9–4–19–3		19–2–87–1	87	214	6	10	–
v. Worcestershire (Worcester) 22–25 July				18–5–27–4		6–1–13–0		2–1–10–0	14–5–27–2		69.2	133	5	10	BCF
				25–7–70–0		14–2–38–0		6–3–15–0	18–5–44–1		142	353	27	4	BCF
v. New Zealand (Leicester) 30 July–1 August			19.4–6–63–5	12–3–37–1	13–5–23–1	6–0–35–0		2–0–18–0			67.4	260	13	10	–
			12–2–35–0	9–0–43–0	13–4–41–1			4–0–19–0			49.1	202	10	1	D
v. Warwickshire (Leicester) 6–9 August	21.5–0–72–3		31–7–108–5		4–1–13–0	10–5–19–0	31–14–54–2	5–1–14–0			102.5	306	26	10	–
v. Middlesex (Lord's) 18–21 August	17.3–5–42–5	6–0–33–3	16–1–59–2	1–1–0–0							40.3	137	3	10	–
	20.3–5–65–1	5–0–35–0	28–9–62–1	9–1–28–2	19–4–51–2	3–1–8–0					84.3	273	24	6	–
v. Gloucestershire (Leicester) 24–27 August	18–2–59–2		10–3–41–3	15–9–31–1			12–3–19–1	2.4–1–5–3			57.4	166	11	10	–
	18–5–61–4		14.1–5–34–4	8–1–22–2	3–1–10–0		5–2–15–0	1–0–2–0			49.1	170	26	10	–
v. Derbyshire (Leicester) 1–3 September	23–6–70–4		21–4–82–1	9–2–29–2		8–1–30–0		3–1–3–0		12–1–63–3	82	308	9	10	E
	17–4–52–2		7–2–32–0	12–2–34–0		3–0–22–0		6–1–27–1		12.2–3–25–2	63.2	235	11	6	E
v. Northamptonshire (Northampton) 8–10 September	41–9–125–3					14–3–42–1		3–0–19–0		31.4–3–135–3	133.4	509	25	10	BF
v. Durham (Leicester) 15–18 September	34.1–6–75–5	11–3–25–1	29–7–83–3	14–5–23–0	5–1–14–0	9–3–21–1					102.1	278	37	10	–

	MS Kasprowicz	CC Lewis	J Ormond	JM Dakin	MT Brimson	VJ Wells	AD Mullally	DL Maddy	DJ Millns	CD Crowe
Overs	485.5	191	406.1	219.1	316.5	176	199	85.4	142.3	92
Maidens	106	51	89	59	98	47	64	22	35	14
Runs	1458	585	1283	575	784	473	471	260	372	348
Wickets	53	16	52	19	24	10	17	12	23	11
Bowler's average	**27.5**	**36.56**	**24.67**	**30.26**	**32.66**	**47.30**	**27.70**	**21.66**	**16.17**	**31.63**

A   IJ Sutcliffe 1–1–0–0
B   D Williamson 5–0–8–0 & 8–3–14–0; 3–0–11–0
C   AA Khan 6.2–3–11–1 & 18–6–52–0
D   DI Stevens 1.1–0–6–0
E   A Sachdeva 6–1–22–0 & 6–0–32–1
F   TJ Mason 18–4–32–3 & 53–20–93–3; 20–4–57–1

FIELDING

50 – PA Nixon (46 ct/4 st)	
17 – DL Maddy	
13 – VJ Wells	
12 – DI Stevens	
10 – BF Smith	
9 – IJ Sutcliffe	
7 – CC Lewis	
5 – DJ Millns	
3 – MS Kasprowicz	
2 – Aftab Habib, MT Brimson, CD Crowe, JM Dakin, J Ormond, D Williamson	
1 – JJ Whitaker	

MIDDLESEX CCC

FIRST–CLASS MATCHES

BATTING

	MA Roseberry	JL Langer	MR Ramprakash	RA Kettleborough	O A Shah	PN Weekes	DC Nash	JP Hewitt	RL Johnson	SJ Cook	PCR Tufnell	ARC Fraser	TF Bloomfield	KP Dutch	AJ Strauss	DJ Goodchild	JK Maunders	MJ Brown	IN Blanchett	BL Hutton	Extras	Total	Wickets	Result	Points
v. Kent	6	55	12	0	16	14	62*	25	28	0	5										31	254	10	D	10
(Lord's) 13–16 April	–	241*	8	8	46	33*	–	25	–	–	–										20	381	4		
v. Gloucestershire	8	43	101	10	0	6	30	19	9*	13	0										29	268	10	W	18
(Bristol) 28 April–1 May	11	23	43	36	60	40	10*	5	4	–	6*										7	245	8		
v. Yorkshire	2	12	84	7	34	15	31*	5	0	9	16										34	249	10	W	17
(Headingley) 14–17 May	0	127*	10	4	0	65*	–	–	5	–	–										15	226	5		
v. Hampshire	44	14	2	13	0	61	11	7		51	19	0*									34	256	10	L	6
(Lord's) 19–22 May	116	17	62	1	19	0	33	11		20	8*	12									40	339	10		
v. Sussex	26	12	81	21	4	23	20		0	5	0*	12									29	233	10	D	7
(Lord's) 26–29 May	43	21	59	75	62	7		49*	0	6	1	15									20	358	10		
v. Warwickshire	8	43	2	▸9	57	22		7		8*				23							37	216	10	D	5
(Edgbaston) 2–5 June	5*				8*																2	15	–		
v. Glamorgan	84	20	19		10	140*	3			38	48	56rh	0	14							30	462	9	W	20
(Cardiff) 9–11 June	–	–	–		–	–	–			–	–	–	–	–											
v. Cambridge University				–	103	47	18							16	12	0	4	19*	5*		13	237	7	L	–
(Cambridge) 16–18 June				0	0	17	32							0	5	26	9	24*	6		5	128	10		A
v. Derbyshire	4	25		38	6	5	43	4		3		17*	0		61						4	210	10	L	5
(Lord's) 30 June–3 July	47	22		0	5	71*	1	32		0		6	5		4						28	221	10		
v. Northamptonshire	1	4	0	7	21	3	8			1		23*	0	22							6	96	10	W	16
(Lord's) 9–11 July		117*	5	24	40*							21									11	218	3		
v. Essex		0		30	0	2	1	8	15	4	7*	4								25	17	113	10	L	2
(Southend) 14–16 July		10		10	8	20	6	5	4	2	0*	42								9	24	140	10		
v. Somerset	2	96	40	9	65	46*	0		37	12	12	27									9	355	10	D	12
(Taunton) 21–23 July	15	127*			110*																19	271	1		
v. Nottinghamshire	3	19		14	5	92	27		9	9*	14	4								59	36	291	10	L	6
(Southgate) 4–6 August	7	0		1	12	9	3		0*	6	20	15									23	120	10		
v. Leicestershire				0	2	22	0	2	39	14	9*	19			12		5				13	137	10	D	8
(Lord's) 18–21 August				93	108	13	7*		4	6*		19			2						36	273	6		
v. Durham	22	53	17	33	52	0	24	3	14	1	0*										3	222	10	L	5
(Chester-le-Street) 24–27 August	29	2	6	17	18	56	28	5	5	1	0*										13	180	10		
v. Surrey			41	9	12	30	25*	0	25	14	1				98						18	284	10	D	8
(Lord's) 9–12 September			209*	69	15	34	56*			19					50						47	499	5		
v. Worcestershire			9	10	0	27	37		0	2	9*				62						21	235	10	D	7
(Worcester) 15–18 September			87*												71*					47	30	235	1		B
Matches	12	12	12	8	17	16	17	13	6	10	12	12	11	6	9	1	1	2	1	7					
Innings	21	22	22	15	32	28	27	21	8	16	15	16	17	10	17	2	2	3	2	13					
Not Out	1	4	2	0	2	4	8	1	0	3	1	5	9	0	1	0	0	2	1	0					
Runs	483	1048	929	300	829	828	696	350	86	237	184	142	80	119	488	26	13	48	11	307					
Highest score	116	241*	209*	93	110*	140*	92	49*	39	51	48	56rh	17*	23	98	26	9	24*	6	59					
Average	24.15	58.22	46.45	20.00	27.63	34.5	36.63	17.50	10.75	18.23	13.14	12.90	10.00	11.90	30.50	13.00	6.50	48.00	11.00	23.61					
100s	1	4	2	–	3	1	–	–	–	–	–	–	–	–	–	–	–	–	–	–					
50s	1	2	6	2	3	6	4	–	–	1	–	1	–	–	4	–	–	–	–	2					

A   M Creese 4
B   EC Joyce 9

MIDDLESEX CCC

FIRST-CLASS MATCHES

BOWLING

Match	SJ Cook	RL Johnson	JP Hewitt	OA Shah	PCR Tufnell	PN Weekes	ARC Fraser	TF Bloomfield	KP Dutch	Overs	Totals	Byes/Leg-byes	Wickets	Run outs
v. Kent (Lord's) 13–16 April	26-6-83-2	18-5-52-0	25.1-10-50-5	3-0-12-0	26-8-45-2	11-2-32-1				109.1	286	12	10	–
v. Gloucestershire (Bristol) 28 April–1 May	13-2-51-1		22-4-67-1	7.5-2-14-2	42-9-82-2	10-4-16-0	35-15-53-4			129.5	297	14	10	
	11-4-29-1		6-0-28-0	16-5-33-3	30-4-61-5		22.1-7-42-1			85.1	215	22	10	
v. Yorkshire (Headingley) 14–17 May	15-6-46-2	19-5-56-4	15-5-27-3		12.4-4-22-1	1-1-0-0				62.4	160	9	10	
	37-15-83-4	5-1-10-0	20.5-4-63-3	8-2-25-0	49-16-81-3	10-1-27-0				129.5	313	24	10	
v. Hampshire (Lord's) 19–22 May	25.4-4-108-4		9-0-56-1	4-0-20-0	17-7-27-0	20-1-46-1		29-4-109-4		104.4	379	13	10	
	8-1-42-1		7-1-35-0		7-0-39-0	1-0-10-0		14.3-0-81-3		37.3	219	12	4	
v. Sussex (Lord's) 26–29 May	35-3-95-2		28-4-87-2	12-0-37-2	26-11-46-2	23-3-75-1		22-3-62-1	3-0-16-0	149	430	12	10	
	9-0-35-3				8-5-6-2	5-4-2-0		11-1-36-2		33	81	2	7	–
v. Warwickshire (Edgbaston) 2–5 June	5-1-21-0	5-1-21-0			9-2-10-2	2-1-1-0	7-1-13-0			28	70	4	2	–
v. Glamorgan (Cardiff) 9–11 June	12-3-41-1					4.4-1-11-2	7-1-12-2	9-1-36-5		32.4	108	8	10	
	9-1-42-0				21-8-35-1	17.3-4-45-3	20-3-65-3	14-3-39-2		81.3	241	15	10	1
v. Cambridge University (Cambridge) 16–18 June			23-12-43-4	13-3-25-1					30-5-84-2	89.3	247	5	9	1 ABC
			16-5-31-1	2-0-7-0					21-5-75-2	68	241	3	5	AC
v. Derbyshire (Lord's) 30 June–3 July	18-2-80-3		17.2-2-76-3	10-1-38-1		18-8-25-0	33-9-77-2	17-4-51-0	3-1-12-0	117.2	366	4	10	1 D
	3-0-20-1		4.2-1-13-0				6-1-20-0	2-1-11-0		15.2	66	2	1	–
v. Northamptonshire (Lord's) 9–11 July			6.3-3-19-1			16-3-58-2	14-3-35-0	20-6-46-3	16-6-53-4	72.3	223	12	10	
			10-4-6-4	2-0-9-0		15.2-2-32-2	15-5-16-3	7-1-16-1		49.2	88	9	10	
v. Essex (Southend) 14–16 July			14-3-68-3		50-16-99-1	36-6-94-1	34-14-64-2	16-2-72-2		152	429	25	9	– E
v. Somerset (Taunton) 21–23 July	12-1-58-0		18-5-66-2	1-0-3-0		15.4-4-36-3	24-6-69-1	13-4-40-3		86.4	297	7	10	– E
	16-3-52-0		25-1-110-0	4-0-32-0		32-5-140-1	26-3-106-0	12-2-70-1		119	523	13	3	1
v. Nottinghamshire (Southgate) 4–6 August			11-2-34-1	11-1-31-1		23-7-50-4	24-7-54-0	10-3-36-1	23-6-63-3	110	306	7	10	– DE
			2-0-12-0			8-1-39-2	4-0-14-0	3-0-17-0	7-0-22-0	24	108	4	2	–
v. Leicestershire (Lord's) 18–21 August	12-4-45-1	15-3-50-4	6-0-38-1			4-0-12-2	22-6-54-2			68	228	6	10	– E
	10-4-23-1	20-8-59-1	10-0-40-0			9-2-17-0	23-8-63-5			76	225	14	7	– E
v. Durham (Chester-le-Street) 24–27 August		26.3-4-102-4			27-10-53-1	11-3-22-0	29-6-67-3	18-6-34-2		112.3	290	10	10	– F
		11-2-36-2			2.1-0-13-0	11-2-35-2		6-0-28-0		30.1	113	1	4	–
v. Surrey (Lord's) 9–12 September		14-1-67-1		5.2-0-40-1	38-6-90-3	23-3-105-0	34-5-111-3	29-3-128-2		150.2	585	14	10	– EF
v. Worcestershire (Worcester) 15–18 September			15-3-53-0		49-8-107-5	17.2-4-50-2	39-8-112-2	14-1-88-0		141.2	465	8	9	– EF

	SJ Cook	RL Johnson	JP Hewitt	OA Shah	PCR Tufnell	PN Weekes	ARC Fraser	TF Bloomfield	KP Dutch
Overs	276.4	133.3	311.1	99.1	445.1	316.1	435.1	266.3	87
Maidens	60	30	69	14	119	68	113	45	17
Runs	954	453	1022	326	906	890	1093	1007	278
Wickets	27	16	35	11	34	23	38	33	7
Bowler's average	**35.33**	**28.31**	**29.2**	**29.63**	**26.64**	**38.69**	**28.76**	**30.51**	**39.71**

A   IN Blanchett 8-0-52-0 & 12-1-64-2
B   RA Kettleborough 7-6-1-0
C   M Creese 8.3-2-37-1 & 17-5-61-0
D   JL Langer 1-0-3-0; 1-1-0-0
E   BL Hutton 2-0-7-0; 3-0-18-1; 7-2-25-0; 9-2-23-0 & 4-1-9-0; 2-0-10-0; 4-0-34-0
F   MR Ramprakash 1-0-2-0; 5-0-20-0; 3-0-13-0

FIELDING

50 – DC Nash (46 ct/4 st)	
19 – PN Weekes	
12 – JL Langer	
9 – OA Shah	
8 – MR Ramprakash	
7 – MA Roseberry	
6 – JP Hewitt	
5 – BL Hutton	
4 – RA Kettleborough	
3 – SJ Cook, AJ Strauss, PCR Tufnell	
2 – MJ Brown, KP Dutch	
1 – IN Blanchett, TF Bloomfield, RL Johnson, E Joyce, JK Maunders	

NORTHAMPTONSHIRE CCC

FIRST-CLASS MATCHES

BATTING

Match / Venue	ML Hayden	RJ Bailey	MB Loye	RJ Warren	DJG Sales	AL Penberthy	GP Swann	D Ripley	JP Taylor	D Follett	DE Malcolm	AJ Swann	DJ Roberts	KJ Innes	TMB Bailey	MK Davies	RJ Logan	RV Sutcliffe	JP Brown	KM Curran	Extras	Total	Wickets	Result	Points
v. Warwickshire	29	14	6	41	49*	5	8	3*	–	–	–										12	167	6	D	8
(Edgbaston) 14–17 April	–	–																			–	–			
v. Sussex	119	26	9	88	5	26	13	50*	21	10*	–										24	391	8	D	12
(Hove) 21–24 April				–			–														–	–			
v. Surrey	11	75	1	0	16	3	0	13	71	19	0*										39	248	10	L	5
(Northampton) 28 April–1 May	0	45	47	12	69	88	1	13*	2	11	0										50	338	10		
v. Cambridge University		25	102			29*	–					116	6	22*	–	–	–	–			23	323	4	D	–
(Cambridge) 9–11 May	85*			–			12					34*	33	–							5	169	2		
v. Lancashire	5	40	100	16	96	33	36	29*	19												30	404	8	W	18
(Old Trafford) 14–17 May	130*	113*	–	–																	13	256	–		
v. Derbyshire	13	30	0	33	7	98	24	5	26	4	10*										20	270	10	L	6
(Derby) 19–21 May	111	5	6	40	18	20	4	35	0	0	5*										17	261	10		
v. Nottinghamshire	170	11		57*	81*	–	–					154		–							11	484	3	D	12
(Northampton) 2–5 June	–																				–	–			
v. Durham	68	14	16	8	10	1	0	24	6		0					32*					11	190	10	L	4
(Northampton) 9–12 June	25	15	13	55	84	0	62	1	16		1					7*					19	298	10		
v. Worcestershire	37	17	0	35	8	6	62	17	6		0*					0					9	197	10	L	4
(Northampton) 30 June–2 July	1	8	0	40	16	31	27*	18	19		4					0					13	177	10		
v. Middlesex				6	3	5	78	36*	21		7	2	9	14	6						36	223	10	L	5
(Lord's) 9–11 July				25		0	13	6	17*		0	4	4	4	1						11	88	10		
v. Sri Lanka 'A'			29	13	87		75*	28				29		0	0	6	0	0			47	314	10	W	–
(Northampton) 15–17 July			–	51	48		130*	2				41		5	–	7	1	9*			19	313	7		
v. Yorkshire	8			87	37	123*	37	107	–			0	1	–							53	517	7	D	12
(Scarborough) 20–23 July	18*			0*	3		38		–			–	–	–							2	61	2		
v. Essex			5	8	303*	0	4	94	12			5	0	40		10					98	579	10	W	20
(Northampton) 30 July–1 August			–																		–	–			
v. Somerset			2	10	17	16	0	4	12			0	2	27*		2					19	111	10	L	3
(Northampton) 4–6 August			32	11	7	53	32	0	8*			15	17	23		3					25	226	10		
v. Gloucestershire		25	25	44	39	92			0		0*	57			24	0			8		27	341	10	D	11
(Northampton) 17–20 August		22	38	12*	4*				–			4									4	84	3		
v. Kent		22		3	0	1	5		0		4	8			8	15*				0		369	10	1	4
(Canterbury) 24–26 August		0		1	11	20	23		14		1*	8			1	0				1	6	86	10		
v. Hampshire			92	2	110		67		0		0	44			12*						15	342	10	W	18
(Northampton) 1–4 September		46	0	39*	0	4	26*		–			57			0						11	183	6		
v. Leicestershire			8	18	205	22	0	105	32		0	29		47*		0					43	509	10	W	20
(Northampton) 8–10 September																					–	–			
v. Glamorgan		5		72	4	29	24	15	24*		0	4	2			9					16	204	10	D	9
(Cardiff) 15–18 September																					–	–			

	ML Hayden	RJ Bailey	MB Loye	RJ Warren	DJG Sales	AL Penberthy	GP Swann	D Ripley	JP Taylor	D Follett	DE Malcolm	AJ Swann	DJ Roberts	KJ Innes	TMB Bailey	MK Davies	RJ Logan	RV Sutcliffe	JP Brown	KM Curran
Matches	9	14	13	18	18	18	18	15	17	5	15	12	5	8	5	13	2	2	1	1
Innings	15	23	20	29	29	25	27	22	21	5	16	18	8	11	4	18	2	2	1	2
Not Out	2	2	0	4	4	2	4	6	2	1	6	0	1	3	0	4	0	1	0	0
Runs	745	743	433	935	1291	718	727	683	316	44	32	573	73	217	33	110	1	9	8	1
Highest score	170	113*	102	110	303*	123*	130*	107	71	19	10*	154	34*	47*	24	32*	1	9*	8	1
Average	57.30	35.38	21.65	37.40	51.64	31.21	31.60	42.68	16.63	11.00	3.20	31.83	10.42	27.12	8.25	7.85	0.50	9.00	8.00	0.50
100s	4	1	2	1	3	1	1	2	–	–	–	2	–	–	–	–	–	–	–	–
50s	1	3	–	6	5	4	4	3	1	–	–	2	–	–	–	–	–	–	–	–

NORTHAMPTONSHIRE CCC

FIRST-CLASS MATCHES

BOWLING

	DE Malcolm	JP Taylor	GP Swann	D Follett	AL Penberthy	DJG Sales	ML Hayden	RJ Logan	KJ Innes	MK Davies	Overs	Totals	Byes/Leg-byes	Wickets	Run outs
v. Warwickshire (Edgbaston) 14–17 April	29-3-116-6	33.1-11-70-3	18-7-43-1	18-2-55-0	14-7-32-0						112.1	323	7	10	–
v. Sussex (Hove) 21–24 April	17.2-4-39-6	11-4-16-1	13-3-30-2	8-3-16-1		1-1-0-0					50.2	104	3	10	–
	11-2-47-0	12-4-31-0	16-3-62-1	12-5-22-0	7-2-19-0	4-1-3-0	4-1-14-0				69	209	7	1	– A
v. Surrey (Northampton) 28 April–1 May	23.3-3-82-3	18-3-63-2	22-2-64-3		6-2-35-1						79.3	286	19	10	1
	17-2-71-1	11-3-38-0		26.1-4-87-1	15-2-69-0	1-0-6-0					82.1	301	5	2	– A
Cambridge University (Cambridge) 9–11 May			17-6-39-2		4-1-9-0			17-9-35-2	4-0-8-0	12-5-35-0	66	181	9	4	– E
			20-3-87-2			6-2-14-0		11-4-42-3	8-5-9-1	16-3-34-0	80	251	12	7	– AE
v. Lancashire (Old Trafford) 14–17 May	20-5-68-1	26-5-76-0	22-5-88-3	17-3-54-2	14-5-49-0	1-0-1-0					100	350	14	6	–
	14.2-3-37-4	12-4-22-2	12-4-22-3	10-2-29-1							48.2	121	11	10	–
v. Derbyshire (Derby) 19–21 May	24-2-139-3	19-3-84-1	19-0-98-2	15-4-61-1	15-3-39-1		6-0-19-1				101	466	22	10	–
	5-0-28-0	7.3-1-27-2		3-0-7-0							15.3	66	4	2	– A
v. Nottinghamshire (Trent Bridge) 2–5 June	19-3-52-4	16.3-2-62-1	18-1-57-2		6-1-15-0					15-6-20-3	74.3	220	14	10	
	17-6-59-0	20-8-45-1	18-5-51-1				8-2-21-0			17-7-23-0	80	209	10	3	1
v. Durham (Northampton) 9–12 June	26-6-78-2	18-2-58-1	24-2-88-2		16-4-43-3					15-6-33-2	99	317	17	10	
	12-0-52-0	22-4-51-3	26-8-62-1		9.2-5-13-3					13-1-22-3	82.2	216	16	10	–
v. Worcestershire (Northampton) 30 June–2 July	12-5-35-3	11-3-32-3			8-3-22-1		7-4-10-3				38	102	3	10	
	27.5-6-83-2	30-5-105-5	15-3-51-2		18-8-63-1		5-0-28-0			13-2-41-0	108.5	384	13	10	–
v. Middlesex (Lord's) 9–11 July	10.4-1-49-4	14-3-23-4	2-0-8-0		5-0-8-1					1-0-4-0	32.4	96	4	10	1
	15-1-61-1	17-1-41-1	8.3-1-33-0		5-1-12-0				5-2-9-0	17-3-53-1	67.3	218	9	3	–
v. Sri Lanka 'A' (Northampton) 15–17 July						6-2-25-4		8-2-24-2	6.4-2-23-3		28.4	86	1	10	– E
			4-0-20-0			4-1-15-1		22-3-77-1	25-4-85-4	18-3-63-1	102	385	18	10	– BE
v. Yorkshire (Scarborough) 20–23 July	25-3-106-4	24-11-54-1	19.5-2-61-3		13-6-16-1				13-6-35-1		94.5	289	17	10	
	21-3-80-2	31-7-90-3	45-9-110-3		11-5-34-0	3.5-0-7-2			11-2-46-0		127.5	407	14	10	– B
v. Essex (Northampton) 30 July–1 August		19-3-69-0	30-9-98-3		22-8-52-2	3-1-8-0			6-0-37-0	35.1-13-61-5	115.1	355	30	10	
		11-3-24-2	15.3-2-46-2		7-2-13-1				11-5-33-1	21-13-23-4	65.3	143	4	10	–
v. Somerset (Northampton) 4–6 August			12-5-40-0	38-13-94-3	26.3-6-76-3		5.4-1-29-0		23.2-7-73-2	55-18-88-1	164.3	422	12	9	– B
v. Gloucestershire (Northampton) 17–20 August	20-4-68-1	13-1-37-1			6-2-16-0					42-18-65-6	110.5	260	10	10	– C
v. Kent (Canterbury) 24–26 August	21-6-65-5	18.2-5-55-4			6-2-14-0						53.2	167	7	10	1 D
										3-1-5-0					
v. Hampshire (Northampton) 1–4 September	22-6-73-2	18-2-65-2	31-6-88-3		7-2-22-0	2-0-5-1				44-14-90-2	124	357	14	10	
	3-0-15-0	5-2-9-0	23-7-46-4		4-0-23-0					19.2-4-49-6	59.2	167	11	10	– B
v. Leicestershire (Leicester) 8–10 September	21-6-57-0	9.4-1-34-1	39-13-85-5		3-1-9-0					37-10-87-4	112.4	311	28	10	–
	5-2-26-0	9-4-19-1	18.1-5-41-6						3-1-10-0	15-4-32-2	50.1	143	15	10	1
v. Glamorgan (Cardiff) 15–18 September	24-6-68-3	20.1-4-52-3			13-3-42-1				14-1-45-3	5-1-13-0	76.1	227	7	10	–
	22.1-2-72-3	19-5-35-0	12-5-23-0		6-0-27-0				7-2-16-0	10-5-16-0	76.1	204	15	3	–

	DE Malcolm	JP Taylor	GP Swann	D Follett	AL Penberthy	DJG Sales	ML Hayden	RJ Logan	KJ Innes	MK Davies
Overs	484.5	507.2	560.1	120	266.5	31.3	'30	58	137	423.3
Maidens	90	119	131	23	85	7	7	18	37	137
Runs	1726	1427	1641	377	735	99	92	178	429	857
Wickets	60	48	57	8	19	8	4	0	15	40
Bowler's average	28.76	29.72	28.78	47.12	38.68	12.37	23.00	22.25	28.60	21.42

A   RJ Bailey 3-0-4-0; 3-0-7-0; 10-0-36-0; 3-1-4-1
B   AJ Swann 3-0-19-1; 5-1-26-0; 4-2-10-0; 5-0-14-0; 3-0-11-0
C   JP Brown 29.5-8-64-2
D   KM Curran 5-1-21-1
E   RV Sutcliffe 12-1-46-0 & 9-3-17-1; 8-3-13-1 & 26-7-88-2

FIELDING

43 – D Ripley (40 ct/3 st)
15 – DJG Sales
13 – GP Swann
12 – RJ Warren
11 – AJ Swann
9 – RJ Bailey
6 – TMB Bailey (5 ct/1 st), ML Hayden, AL Penberthy
5 – JP Taylor
4 – KJ Innes, MB Loye, DE Malcolm, DJ Roberts
3 – MK Davies
1 – RJ Logan

NOTTINGHAMSHIRE CCC

FIRST–CLASS MATCHES

BATTING

	GE Welton	U Afzaal	JER Gallian	P Johnson	NA Gie	MP Dowman	CMW Read	AG Wharf	KP Evans	DS Lucas	RD Stemp	RT Robinson	VC Drakes	PJ Franks	MN Bowen	GF Archer	RT Bates	CM Tolley	WM Noon	SJ Randall	Extras	Total	Wickets	Result	Points
v. Cambridge University	–	–	–	–	–	–	–														–	–	–	D	–
(Cambridge) 12–14 April	38	18	1		14	59*	52	12*													18	212	5		
v. Leicestershire		4	9	8	33*	28						12	1*								22	117	5	D	4
(Leicester) 20–23 April		–																			–	–			
v. Worcestershire		12	82	126	36		41	20		0*		0	26	3	5						66	417	10	W	20
(Trent Bridge) 28–30 April		14*										19*									2	35	2		
v. Oxford University	34	1	49*	13		67	31	4		3*						132					22	356	7	D	–
(Oxford) 5–7 May	21*	29*																				50	–		
v. Somerset		5	16	26	0		17	42			49	18	24	16*	4						34	251	10	W	18
(Trent Bridge) 14–17 May		9	76	18	3		0	7			31	55*	0	0	2						45	246	10		
v. Lancashire	0		0	14			28	54*		1	37	4	6	14	7						16	181	10	L	4
(Old Trafford) 19–22 May	12	120*		2			38	9		16	22	5	17	19	12						19	291	10		
v. Hampshire	16	12	45	37			14	9			7	1	61	1*	48						73	324	10	W	19
(Trent Bridge) 27–29 May	15	8	92	67*	37		0				6	33	12	0	42						21	333	10		
v. Northamptonshire			0	61	22		10	8		2*		61	2	13		27	0				14	220	10	D	6
(Northampton) 2–5 June			39	83*	30		4									43*	1				10	209	3		
v. Warwickshire		32	16	13	0		160	5				10	11	5*	3			51			21	327	10	L	7
(Trent Bridge) 15–17 June		5	11	9	0		1	14*				14	5	2							1	76	10		
v. Gloucestershire		9	20	85		7				10*		64	11	19	14	0		7			23	269	10	L	6
(Bristol) 30 June–3 July		59	11	59		26*				2		10	13	0	5	8		1			7	201	10		
v. Durham		60	41	83		3	12*			1	12	9	7			81		14			30	353	10	L	8
(Chester-le-Street) 9–12 July		4	69	70*		0	0			0		80	0	0		0		19			6	248	10		
v. Kent	30	2	1	13			0			2		8*	4	1		12	8				7	88	10	L	4
(Trent Bridge) 21–23 July	9	62	8	1			11			9		80	18	0			0				39	237	10		
v. Derbyshire	11	28	4	85		0	67	3				10	0	0*		9					15	232	10	L	5
(Derby) 30 July–1 August	20	39	26	2		32	15	1				0	0	1*		3					14	153	10		
v. Middlesex	2	28	74	55		44*	0					4	8			56		6		0	29	306	10	W	19
(Southgate) 4–6 August	12	52	26*	14*																	4	108	2		
v. Glamorgan		52	0	0		0	5	78		17		0	49*			0				20	7	228	10	L	1
(Colwyn Bay) 18–21 August		97	24	53		28	20	10				8	27			25				4*	6	302	10		
v. Yorkshire		23	50	10			1	4		0	0*	30	5			32					29	184	10	L	4
(Trent Bridge) 24–26 August		0	21	22			1	19		5	4*	6	4	9		28					25	144	10		
v. Surrey	4	47	6	0			14	11			2	0	11	6*							14	115	10	L	4
(The Oval) 1–2 September	16	104	0	41			17	1			1	0	15*	6		8					24	233	10		
v. Sussex		18	7				0	20			18	32	28	13	18*	23	4				18	199	10	L	4
(Hove) 9–11 September		0	31				15				3	0	26	16*		25	11				5	132	10		
v. Essex	76	15	118				1	12		3*		66	14			5	5				34	349	10	L	7
(Trent Bridge) 15–18 September	0	0	9				39	32		24*		0	13			0				6	28	151	10		
Matches	9	16	19	16	5	9	16	16	1	6	13	12	17	16	11	15	1	4	3	3					
Innings	17	30	34	29	6	15	27	26	–	7	17	22	30	27	21	28	1	8	5	5					
Not Out	1	2	3	3	2	3	1	3	–	3	5	1	3	3	8	1	0	0	0	1					
Runs	316	828	985	1104	144	412	615	370	–	58	74	525	427	348	130	635	0	106	22	30					
Highest score	76	104	120*	126	59*	67*	160	78	–	24*	18	80	80	61	19	132	0	51	8	20					
Average	19.75	29.57	31.77	42.46	36.00	34.33	23.65	16.08	–	14.50	6.16	25.00	15.81	14.50	10.00	23.51	–	13.25	4.40	7.50					
100s	–	1	2	1	–	–	1	–	–	–	–	–	–	–	–	1	–	–	–	–					
50s	1	6	5	10	1	3	1	2	–	–	–	4	2	1	–	2	–	1	–	–					

A   MJA Whiley (2 innings) did not bat

NOTTINGHAMSHIRE CCC

FIRST-CLASS MATCHES

BOWLING

	DS Lucas	AG Wharf	JER Gallian	RD Stemp	U Afzaal	VC Drakes	PJ Franks	MN Bowen	CM Tolley	Overs	Totals	Byes/Leg-byes	Wickets	Run outs	
v. Cambridge University	22-11-62-3	22-5-66-1	7-4-14-0	17-8-38-0	2-1-2-0					96	287	10	8	–	AB
(Cambridge) 12-14 April					2-1-2-0					7	38	0	0	–	CD
v. Worcestershire		13-2-44-2				18.4-6-49-5	14-3-42-1	12-5-23-1		57.4	172	14	9	–	
(Trent Bridge) 28-30 April		16-3-52-0	6-4-7-1	8-3-22-0		27-8-60-4	26-4-78-1	14-2-50-3		97	279	10	9	–	
v. Oxford University	14-3-63-3	16-4-50-0		20-10-31-1	4-0-22-0					67	219	8	5	–	CE
(Oxford) 5-7 May															
v. Somerset		10-1-37-1	2-1-6-0			19.3-4-66-2	15-4-52-2	20-3-66-5		66.3	234	7	10	–	
(Trent Bridge) 14-17 May		11-0-40-2	3-0-14-1			21-4-70-4	15-5-38-1	14-2-63-2		64	232	7	10	–	
v. Lancashire		6-5-7-0		17-9-33-2		18-3-55-4	12.2-4-24-4	3-1-11-0		56.2	141	11	10	–	
(Old Trafford) 19-22 May		5-0-30-0		31.5-7-114-4		23-5-94-1	13-3-33-2	11-2-46-0		83.5	332	15	7	–	
v. Hampshire		14-4-52-2	1-1-0-0			22.5-4-63-4	18-4-34-3	17-3-49-1		72.5	203	5	10	–	
(Trent Bridge) 27-29 May		13-4-41-2	5.4-0-27-1			12-0-41-0	13-4-25-4	11-2-31-3		58.4	193	15	10	–	B
v. Northamptonshire		13-0-78-1		30-4-158-0		16-3-63-1	16-2-80-1			94	484	7	3	–	BF
(Northampton) 2-5 June															
v. Warwickshire		17-3-73-0	9-1-28-2			25.3-4-71-6	22-4-64-1	17-5-49-1	8-1-20-0	98.3	316	11	10	–	
(Northampton) 15-17 June						22.4-9-39-6	21-6-52-4	8-1-30-0	3-0-9-0	54.4	142	12	10	–	
v. Gloucestershire				34-9-87-2	1-0-2-0	23-7-84-3	25-9-49-3	18-3-80-2		101	317	15	10	–	
(Bristol) 30 June-3 July				20-7-38-2	14.1-5-42-1	4-1-7-0		2-0-9-0		48.1	154	21	3	–	
v. Durham		17-3-87-1	3-0-16-0	14-0-45-1	4-0-19-0	30-5-88-4	33-7-80-4		20-8-36-0	121	392	21	10	–	
(Chester-le-Street) 9-12 July		8-1-32-0		24-7-63-2	4-0-17-1	22-1-70-4	23-5-81-1		10-1-30-0	91	304	11	8	–	
v. Kent		12-1-39-3				19-4-61-2	20-6-53-3	10.2-2-23-2		61.2	191	15	10	–	
(Trent Bridge) 21-23 July		18-3-75-4				15.5-3-63-1	14-4-53-2	9-4-21-2		56.5	222	10	10	1	
v. Derbyshire		13-3-63-1				22-7-58-2	24.5-9-77-4	13-1-41-2		76.5	263	13	9	–	B
(Trent Bridge) 30 July-1 August		7-1-22-1				8-0-50-1	9-2-31-0	3-1-10-2		27	123	10	4	–	
v. Middlesex				27-7-64-0		36.3-13-64-6	28-4-96-4			118.3	291	14	10	–	BG
(Southgate) 4-6 August				8-2-23-2		18.5-5-49-5	16-5-32-3			48.5	120	6	10	–	G
v. Glamorgan		30-7-98-1		38-9-120-0	12-0-52-1	32-7-95-0	37-5-134-2			187	648	14	4	–	BG
(Colwyn Bay) 18-21 August															
v. Yorkshire	8-1-37-0	10.1-2-34-2				23-7-55-2	25-5-52-5			66.1	185	7	10	1	
(Trent Bridge) 24-26 August		11-2-32-2				15-2-79-2	18-8-32-3			44	144	1	7	–	
v. Surrey		11-3-40-0		9-3-30-0		19-7-53-4	11.5-2-32-2	8-1-30-3		58.5	199	14	10	1	
(The Oval) 1 & 2 September		4-0-29-0		4-0-29-0	1-0-13-0	7.4-0-46-0	3-1-20-0	3-0-9-0		22.4	153	7	0	–	
v. Sussex	13-2-44-1			14-3-35-0		27-7-68-4		22.4-9-48-3	11-2-33-2	103.4	275	9	10	–	
(Hove) 9-11 September	15-2-53-2			10-1-44-0	1-0-9-0	17.2-3-54-3	16-2-70-3	17-2-60-2	4-0-18-0	80.2	315	7	10	–	
v. Essex	9-2-31-1	16.2-6-30-4	1-0-1-0				11-2-44-0	14-3-54-2	10-3-15-3	61.2	188	13	10	–	
(Trent Bridge) 15-18 September	22.5-2-104-5	22-3-65-1	21-7-83-0		4-1-18-0	9-0-35-0		17-1-69-1	19-5-38-0	114.5	432	20	7	–	

	DS Lucas	AG Wharf	JER Gallian	RD Stemp	U Afzaal	VC Drakes	PJ Franks	MN Bowen	CM Tolley
Overs	103.6	335.3	36.4	325.5	49.1	586.2	513	264	85
Maidens	23	65	11	89	9	131	124	53	20
Runs	394	1216	112	974	198	1794	1489	872	199
Wickets	15	31	5	16	3	80	63	37	5
Bowler's average	**26.26**	**39.22**	**22.40**	**60.87**	**66.00**	**22.42**	**23.63**	**23.56**	**39.80**

A   KP Evans 21-5-70-3
B   MP Dowman 5-0-25-1; 4-1-13-0; 6-1-15-0; 4-1-11-0; 9-4-17-0; 7-1-28-0
C   NA Gie 4-0-26-0; 1-0-1-0
D   P Johnson 1-0-10-0
E   MJA Whiley 12-3-44-1
F   RT Bates 13-0-83-0
G   SJ Randall 18-5-36-0 & 6-3-10-0; 31-3-107-0

FIELDING

50 – CMW Read (49 ct/1 st)
27 – GF Archer
19 – JER Gallian
11 – P Johnson
10 – RT Robinson
9 – WM Noon
8 – AG Wharf
6 – MP Dowman
5 – VC Drakes
4 – U Afzaal, GE Welton
3 – SJ Randall
2 – MN Bowen, PJ Franks
1 – RD Stemp

SOMERSET CCC

FIRST–CLASS MATCHES

BATTING

	J Cox	PD Bowler	JID Kerr	PCL Holloway	ME Trescothick	M Burns	RJ Turner	GD Rose	MPL Bulbeck	ARK Pierson	PW Jarvis	AR Caddick	KA Parsons	PS Jones	GJ Kennis	I Jones	Saqib Mahmood	Extras	Total	Wickets	Result	Points
v. Cambridge University	139	140*	30*	–	–	–	–	–	–	–								29	338	1	D	–
(Cambridge) 15–17 April	–	–	–	62 rh	26	24	79	48*	–	–								22	261	3		
v. Warwickshire												–						–	–	–	D	7
(Edgbaston) 19–22 April	–																					
v. Yorkshire	173	4	12	26	34	63	53	44*				22	15	–				22	468	9	W	20
(Taunton) 29 April–2 May	12	–	0	5*	0	6	1*											2	26	4		
v. Nottinghamshire	0	0	51	38	0	14	36		12		12	31		9*				31	234	10	L	5
(Trent Bridge) 14–17 May	83	–	11	8	7	13	27		26		1	18	9*	4				25	232	10		
v. Leicestershire	19	138	22	7	8	109	52*		3			9	20	0				66	453	10	W	20
(Taunton) 19–21 May	7	19*		9*														2	37	1		
v. Surrey	6	24	21	9	0	31	67		12*	3		1	15					10	199	10	L	1
(The Oval) 26–28 May	54	22*	35	1	76	27	68		3	0		21	77					21	405	10		
v. Durham	25		11	8		1	95		76*			0	18	0	24	18*		24	300	9	D	11
(Chester-le-Street) 2–5 June	25		0	9	50*		0	0				17	5	25	8	35		25	199	10		
v. Gloucestershire	14	23	10	9		9	36	9	0	5		1*						16	138	10	L	4
(Bath) 9–12 June	58	4	18	3		53	107	0	25*	37		14	18					14	351	10		
v. Worcestershire	30	26	9	3		23	63		4*	0	7	7			7			14	193	10	L	3
(Worcester) 15–18 June	7	44	11	18		105	58		8*	5	4				7			22	289	10		
v. New Zealand			16	4	43	0	59			66			16	105	175	23	7*	40	554	10	L	–
(Taunton) 25–28 June			48	5	0	39	32*			0			8	1	4	2	0	7	146	10		
v. Sussex	111	42	15	110	12	35	9	–			20		43*	40*				66	503	8	W	20
(Taunton) 30 June–3 July	28	0*	–	22*	30	–						–						14	94	2		
v. Derbyshire	15	149		11	4	72	45		17	1	1	6*	12					28	361	10	M	18
(Derby) 9–12 July	89*	43*		30	19	–												15	196	2		
v. Middlesex	19	0	0	1	8	74	73		43*		2		30	28				19	297	10	D	10
(Taunton) 21–24 July	114	36*	–	114*	190	–			–				–	46				23	523	3		
v. Northamptonshire	69	40	64	32	7	33	31	37	17*	–			80					12	422	9	W	19
(Northampton) 4–6 August	–	–	–	–									–					–	–	–		
v. Kent	0	36	–	65		29	138*	23		–			32	14*		–		24	361	6	D	10
(Taunton) 18–21 August	–		–										–					–	–	–		
v. Essex	49	0		60	20	18	24	36	0		1*	5	4					29	246	10	D	6
(Chelmsford) 24–27 August	54	23		52	0	29	27	2	7*		10*	21	0					31	256	9		
v. Glamorgan	31	1		37	32	4	5	50	1*		1	11	2					28	203	10	W	17
(Taunton) 2–4 September	9	2		18	167	11	1	0	4*		44	4	3					17	280	10		
v. Hampshire	216	103*		58	45	25	0	14	–			–	7*					25	493	6	D	11
(Southampton) 8–11 September	129*	1*		36	86	–												3	255	2		
v. Lancashire	32	0		0	78	4	32	123*	–			–	76*					31	376	6	D	12
(Taunton) 15–18 September	–	0	–															–	–	–		

	J Cox	PD Bowler	JID Kerr	PCL Holloway	ME Trescothick	M Burns	RJ Turner	GD Rose	MPL Bulbeck	ARK Pierson	PW Jarvis	AR Caddick	KA Parsons	PS Jones	GJ Kennis	I Jones	Saqib Mahmood
Matches	18	17	14	19	15	19	19	9	15	13	7	13	15	9	3	3	1
Innings	30	27	19	32	24	27	27	11	15	13	8	17	21	14	6	4	2
Not Out	2	8	1	5	0	1	4	2	8	3	0	5	3	3	0	1	1
Runs	1617	931	381	869	898	915	1217	342	265	129	73	205	499	281	225	78	7
Highest score	216	149	64	114*	190	109	138*	123*	76*	66	20	44	80	105	175	35	7*
Average	57.75	49.00	21.16	32.18	37.41	35.19	52.91	38.00	37.85	12.90	9.12	17.08	27.72	25.54	37.50	26.00	7.00
100s	6	4	–	2	2	2	2	1	–	–	–	–	–	–	1	1	–
50s	6	–	2	5	3	5	10	1	1	1	–	–	3	–	–	–	–

SOMERSET CCC

FIRST–CLASS MATCHES

BOWLING

Match	PW Jarvis	MPL Bulbeck	J Cox	GD Rose	ARK Pierson	JID Kerr	M Burns	AR Caddick	PS Jones	KA Parsons	Overs	Totals	Byes/Leg-byes	Wickets	Run outs	
v. Cambridge University (Cambridge) 15–17 April	9.3–4–20–1	15–1–63–0	7.3–1–36–0	13–6–21–0	20–8–35–1	11–3–45–1	5–1–19–1				81	247	8	4	1	
		8–2–17–1					7–4–11–1				15	29	1	2	–	
v. Warwickshire (Edgbaston) 19–22 April		23–6–83–2		24–5–90–1	2–0–11–0	15–5–44–2	8–2–29–0	32–10–90–2			104	356	9	7	–	
v. Yorkshire (Taunton) 29 April–2 May		16–3–49–0	1–0–1–0			4–1–7–0		20–12–24–4	14.2–4–40–3	8–3–17–3	63.2	148	10	10	–	
		21–4–79–4	3–0–9–0			18–7–49–3	7–1–28–0	28–12–60–2	22–6–60–0	11.5–1–45–1	110.5	345	15	10	–	
v. Nottinghamshire (Trent Bridge) 14–17 May	16–3–43–3	14.2–4–58–5				7–1–26–0		23–5–78–2	9–2–22–0		69.2	251	24	10	–	
	24–6–76–4	12–3–57–1				6–0–29–0	2–0–4–0	31.5–17–31–3	13–4–32–2		88.5	246	17	10	–	
v. Leicestershire (Taunton) 19–22 May	8–0–36–0	9–3–36–1				10.5–4–23–7		18–4–59–2		4–1–17–0	49.5	173	2	10	–	C
	8.4–1–41–1	18–3–67–1				16–2–73–1		31–8–79–5		19.2–9–25–0	105	313	2	10	–	
v. Surrey (The Oval) 26–29 May		21–3–88–1			37–7–95–0	32–4–114–1	4–0–17–1	45–10–132–3		29–5–86–1	172	558	8	9	1	C
						2–0–26–0					4.5	49	2	3	2	
v. Durham (Chester-le-Street) 2–5 June		8–1–29–0				7–1–21–2		22.5–4–77–2	15–0–62–0	16–2–57–5 1	81.5	312	18	10	–	D
v. Gloucestershire (Bath) 9–12 June		24–4–83–3		23–10–47–1	7–2–15–1	13–4–48–1		34.1–8–100–3		17–6–44–1	118.1	346	9	10	–	
		13–6–22–0		8–1–25–1		9.3–2–40–2		25–10–55–4			55.3	144	2	7	–	
v. Worcestershire (Worcester) 15–18 June	26–6–80–1	29–10–69–3			15–3–33–0	18–5–43–1	5–1–12–0	35.4–18–55–4			128.4	308	16	10	1	
	24–7–68–0	7–2–32–1			1.3–1–1–1	13–2–36–2		26–11–48–5			71.3	200	15	10	1	
v. New Zealand (Taunton) 25–28 June					17–2–79–1	15–4–65–3	9–3–42–1		16–2–76–2	10–2–39–0	88.2	420	4	10	–	AD
					8–0–47–0	13–3–51–0	3–0–28–0		11–2–34–0	12–2–61–4	59	282	12	4	–	AD
v. Sussex (Taunton) 30 June–3 July	12.5–0–55–3	7–3–29–1				8–0–31–0			10–2–31–3	4–0–15–2	41.5	165	4	10	1	
	18–4–58–1	30–7–101–4	6–0–32–1			24–3–101–0			23–4–55–1	21.4–7–69–3	125.4	431	8	10	–	B
v. Derbyshire (Derby) 9–12 July	25–3–86–1	25–5–83–3			17–4–31–0		3–0–9–0	36–14–72–4		15–5–53–2	124	359	14	10	–	C
	20.2–8–30–3	15–2–59–2			7–4–16–0			27–8–56–4		10–6–19–1	79.2	194	14	10	–	
v. Middlesex (Taunton) 21–24 July	9–1–26–1	25–5–82–3	11–2–46–3			18–5–56–0	5–0–17–0		23–7–53–2	13–3–33–0	109	355	24	10	–	C
		11–3–25–0	10–0–51–0			20–8–54–1	8–1–28–0		14–3–53–0	7–1–16–0	79	271	7	1	–	BC
v. Northamptonshire (Northampton) 4–6 August		14–4–45–5		11.2–3–20–3		9–3–18–2				8–1–30–2	40.2	111	13	10	–	
		18–4–63–5	1–0–2–0	12–2–36–0	10–6–21–1	11–1–51–2				8.1–0–30–2	60.1	226	23	10	–	
v. Kent (Taunton) 18–21 August				24–6–72–0	37.1–7–131–4	5–0–24–0	11–1–46–2		27–6–99–1	10–3–19–0	134.1	504	11	10	1	D
				8–3–9–0	13–3–32–0	23–5–51–1	11–2–37–0		17–2–46–2	13–5–27–1	106.5	279	3	6	–	BD
v. Essex (Chelmsford) 24–27 August					21–3–111–2	36.4–2–119–2	4–0–14–0	39–8–128–2	26–2–126–4	13–3–33–0	139.4	544	13	10	–	
v. Glamorgan (Taunton) 2–4 September				11–6–14–4				16–4–42–2	10–3–38–1	5.1–3–10–2	42.1	113	9	10	1	
				16–3–56–4				20.2–3–47–6	5–1–18–0	6–0–24–0	49.2	151	1	10	–	C
v. Hampshire (Southampton) 8–11 September		27.2–9–58–4	2–1–2–0	22–7–61–1	33–1–104–1	2–1–6–0	2–1–6–0	41–14–121–3		19–8–37–0	150.2	413	11	10	–	C
v. Lancashire (Taunton) 15–18 September		15–4–79–1		21–6–72–0		6–1–18–1	6–1–18–1	35–7–113–8		7–3–32–0	84	322	8	10	–	

	PW Jarvis	MPL Bulbeck	J Cox	GD Rose	ARK Pierson	JID Kerr	M Burns	AR Caddick	PS Jones	KA Parsons
Overs	201.2	425.4	49.3	219.2	271.2	305.2	100	589.4	255.2	285.1
Maidens	43	101	7	61	52	68	18	187	50	80
Runs	619	1456	188	657	789	1075	365	1488	845	823
Wickets	19	51	4	17	13	31	7	71	21	28
Bowler's average	32.57	28.54	47.00	38.64	60.69	34.67	52.14	20.95	40.23	29.39

A Saqib Mahmood 2–0–34–0 & 1–0–9–0
B PD Bowler 3–1–7–0; 1–0–1–0; 5.5–1–4–2
C ME Tresothick 12–3–26–2; 4–0–18–1; 3–1–11–0; 5–1–18–1 & 8–0–36–0; 2–0–5–0; 4–2–13–1
D I Jones 13–0–48–1; 19.2–7–81–3 & 11–13–40–0; 20–1–102–2 & 16–2–70–0

FIELDING

69 –	RJ Turner
27 –	ME Trescothick
12 –	KA Parsons
11 –	M Burns
9 –	PCL Holloway
8 –	PD Bowler
7 –	J Cox
5 –	JID Kerr, ARK Pierson
3 –	PS Jones
2 –	AR Caddick, PW Jarvis, GJ Kennis, GD Rose
1 –	MPL Bulbeck, Saqib Mahmood

SURREY CCC

FIRST–CLASS MATCHES
BATTING

Match	MA Butcher	IJ Ward	JD Ratcliffe	Nadeem Shahid	AD Brown	BC Hollioake	JN Batty	GP Butcher	AJ Tudor	IDK Salisbury	MP Bicknell	AJ Stewart	GP Thorpe	AJ Hollioake	DJ Bicknell	RM Amin	JE Benjamin	Saqlain Mushtaq	CG Greenidge, Jr	IE Bishop	Extras	Total	Wickets	Result	Points
v. Gloucestershire	68	78	0	12	11	49	37	9	6	17	49*										6	342	10	D	11
(The Oval) 13–16 April	101	0	6	23	4	10	39*	27	9*	–	–										10	229	7		
v. Worcestershire	30	31			26	55	5		0	20	7*	6	4	7							32	223	10	D	5
(Worcester) 20–23 April					–	–	–		–	–	–	–	–	–											
v. Northamptonshire	52	7	1*		27	25	5		2	8	0		32	96							31	286	10	W	18
(Northampton) 28 April–1 May	13	63	–		66*	–	–		–	–		138*	–								21	301	7		
v. Essex	39	1	6		26	0	8	33	14	27*				10	2						29	195	10	W	16
(The Oval) 14–17 May	25	32	32		110*	24	16*	–	1					6	–						26	272	6		
v. Somerset	12	76	86		42	36	0	4	100*	69				114	3*						16	558	9	W	19
(The Oval) 26–29 May	1	0*	27		8*	9	–	–	–												4	49	3		
v. Kent	32	6	22		11	30	0	4	38*	27				57			5				39	271	10	W	18
(Tunbridge Wells) 2–5 June	–	–	–		–	–	–		–	–															
Leicestershire	259	57			25	21	21	7*	14	9			23	1	1						63	501	10	D	12
(Leicester) 9–12 June	–	–			–	–	–		–	–			–												
v. Lancashire	40	30			14	11	0	9	2			95	38	37	1*						21	298	10	W	18
(The Oval) 15–18 June	40	43			1	14	23*	–	–			0	4	24*							12	161	6		
v. Durham		51	28		24	50	44	25	53	25*			2	3			4				26	335	10	W	19
(The Oval) 30 June–3 July		17	91		14*	71	–	6	1					40							7	247	10		
v. Hampshire	1	0			17	15		17	0	15	23	4	63*				0				16	171	10	W	16
(Guildford) 14–17 July	94	55			40	0		0	12	35	19	164	23				10*				30	482	10		
v. Warwickshire		82	37		108	34	38	70	11	20			43	16			0*				24	483	10	W	20
(Edgbaston) 21–23 July		–	–		–	–	–		–	–			–	–			–								
v. Sri Lanka 'A'		50	0			69	21	54		19			16	18				14		0	36	322	10	W	–	A
(The Oval) 30 July–2 August		14	22			1	64	4		15			32	8				4		0*	7	182	10			A
v. Glamorgan		41	9		124	14	0rh	4	0	57			10	19			3*				28	309	9	W	19
(The Oval) 4–5 August		–	–		–	–	–		–	–			–	–			–								
v. Sussex	5	0	14		0	8			11	67			61	11			4	25*			18	224	10	W	17
(Hove) 18–21 August	24	23	16		59	45*			–	0			24	115			–				9	315	7		
v. Derbyshire		103	5		43				12	25	18	89	4	25			0*			0*	26	350	9	W	20
(Derby) 24–27 August		1*	0*		–				–	–	–	–	–	0			–			–	–	1	1		
v. Nottinghamshire	22	12	4		34				2		49	7	24				4			0*	41	199	10	W	16	B
(The Oval) 1–2 September	81*	55*	–		–				–		–	–	–				–			–	17	153	0		
v. Middlesex	43	48	2		265	5			38	0	27	0	116							7*	34	585	10	D	12
(Lord's) 9–12 September	–	–	–		–		–		–	–	–	–	–							–					
v. Yorkshire	7	27	0		18	0			0	0	0	58*	5					2			11	128	10	D	8
(The Oval) 15–18 September	2	15	–		5	–			–	–	25*	0	6*					–			4	57	4		

	MA Butcher	IJ Ward	JD Ratcliffe	Nadeem Shahid	AD Brown	BC Hollioake	JN Batty	GP Butcher	AJ Tudor	IDK Salisbury	MP Bicknell	AJ Stewart	GP Thorpe	AJ Hollioake	DJ Bicknell	RM Amin	JE Benjamin	Saqlain Mushtaq	CG Greenidge, Jr	IE Bishop
Matches	13	18	13	2	17	13	15	5	9	17	15	8	9	13	11	3	2	7	2	4
Innings	22	30	20	3	26	20	20	8	11	17	17	12	13	18	17	3	2	8	3	5
Not Out	1	3	1	1	4	0	5	0	2	2	4	1	2	2	1	2	0	5	–	4
Runs	991	1018	402	36	1127	538	379	199	91	353	432	296	561	534	504	6	9	46	20	7
Highest score	259	103	91	23	265	71	64	70	33	100*	69	95	164	116	115	3*	5	25*	14	7*
Average	47.19	37.7	21.15	18.00	51.22	26.90	25.26	24.87	10.11	20.76	33.23	26.90	51.00	33.37	31.50	6.00	4.50	15.33	6.66	7.00
100s	2	1	–	–	4	–	–	–	–	1	–	–	2	1	2	–	–	–	–	–
50s	4	9	2	–	2	4	1	2	–	1	3	1	2	3	1	–	–	–	–	–

A   GJ Batty 25* & 11
B   MW Patterson 0

SURREY CCC

FIRST-CLASS MATCHES
BOWLING

	MP Bicknell	AJ Tudor	IDK Salisbury	BC Hollioake	MA Butcher	AJ Hollioake	RM Amin	JD Ratcliffe	Saqlain Mushtaq	CG Greenidge, Jr	Overs	Totals	Byes/Leg-byes	Wickets	Run outs	
v. Gloucestershire	22-7-56-3	17-2-46-0	17.2-6-44-5	7-1-42-1							72.2	213	6	10	–	A
(The Oval) 13-16 April	14-2-46-2	13-1-54-1	17-7-30-1	8.3-2-28-0	8-2-27-1						64.3	209	2	5	–	A
v. Worcestershire	3-1-7-0	2-0-7-1									5	15	1	1	–	
(Worcester) 20-23 April																
v. Northamptonshire	21-8-48-4	19-6-59-2	14.1-3-39-1	12-2-53-0	11-3-19-2	6-1-19-0					83.1	248	11	10	1	
(Northampton) 28 April–1 May	26.5-9-78-4	27-9-64-5	33-9-84-0	20-4-63-1	4-0-27-0						110.5	338	22	10	–	
v. Essex	23-3-70-2	24-11-50-1	17.5-4-49-3	19-5-40-0	15-8-18-3		10-4-22-1				108.5	262	13	10	–	
(The Oval) 14–17 May	17-3-63-2	14-3-42-4	12-3-29-1	8-2-39-2	7-1-22-1						58	204	9	10	–	
v. Somerset	18-3-72-4	15-3-47-1	19-6-35-3	7.3-0-26-2	5-2-10-0		3-2-3-0				67.3	199	6	10	–	
(The Oval) 26–29 May	27-8-51-1	19-3-66-0	49-15-95-3	19-5-58-2	4-1-15-0		54-30-87-4	2-0-16-0			174	405	17	10	–	
v. Kent	18-5-32-4	14.3-5-30-5		3-1-3-1							35.3	71	6	10	–	
(Tunbridge Wells) 2–5 June	18.5-9-23-3	17-4-39-2	10-1-25-1	15-1-29-1	3-1-2-0			12-4-28-3			84.5	172	5	10	–	B
v. Leicestershire	23-5-68-1	20.2-2-77-7	14-2-33-0	10-1-41-1	13-2-24-0	5-1-19-1					85.2	272	10	10	–	
(Leicester) 9–12 June	23-8-57-0	12-4-29-1	35-9-71-3	9-4-24-0	7-1-22-0	4-1-14-0					90	239	22	4	–	
v. Lancashire		20-6-60-4	11.2-3-28-3	17-5-46-0	13-7-21-1		12-1-35-2				73.2	194	4	10	–	
(The Oval) 15–18 June		24.4-4-81-4	36-9-81-0	8-5-11-0	14-4-30-4		22-8-43-2				104.4	260	14	10	–	
v. Durham	15-3-31-0		29-11-57-4	10-1-40-1					38.5-13-72-5		92.5	217	17	10	–	
(The Oval) 30 June–3 July	12-4-31-2		24.4-11-34-1	8-3-20-0					21-10-38-7		65.4	139	16	10	–	
v. Hampshire	24-5-75-4	17-2-69-1	15-3-45-2	5.5-0-31-2	2-0-4-0				28-10-77-1		91.5	322	21	10	–	
(Guildford) 14–17 July	17-3-50-3	6-1-16-0	7.1-2-19-1	4-0-17-0	5-3-7-0				17-3-44-6		56.1	175	22	10	–	
v. Warwickshire	12-4-23-1		22.1-5-49-5	9-0-48-0		4-0-30-1		4-1-11-0	24-6-58-2		75.1	227	8	10	1	
(Edgbaston) 21–23 July	9-2-29-1		16-6-46-4	-1-20-0		2-0-2-0			16.1-5-32-5		50.1	133	4	10	–	
v. Sri Lanka 'A'						7.5-0-27-1		17-4-48-6		14-4-42-0	69.5	232	12	10	–	ACJ
(The Oval) 30 July–2 August			15-2-47-3			5-1-16-0		7-2-11-1		16.4-2-65-3	76.4	251	7	10	1	CJ
v. Glamorgan	15-6-24-3			20-3-51-5					5.5-1-14-2		40.5	101	12	10	–	
(The Oval) 4–5 August	9-2-18-3		6-1-12-1	8-1-24-1					7-1-18-5		30	84	12	10	–	
v. Sussex	18-7-46-3				9-2-17-0				14-8-19-7		45	115	7	10	0	B
(Hove) 18–21 August	18-7-46-2		15-2-45-4						28.2-9-78-3		65.2	217	17	10	–	B
v. Derbyshire			12-3-33-1					5-1-9-2	18.2-3-36-3		57.2	154	12	10	–	J
(Derby) 24–27 August						5-2-14-0		2-0-8-0	25.5-7-59-5		77.5	196	14	10	–	J
v. Nottinghamshire			11-1-29-3					13.3-6-15-3	9-1-27-1		44.3	115	8	10	–	DJ
(The Oval) 1 & 2 September			26.1-5-66-4				8-3-21-2	33-8-100-4	6-1-12-0		78.1	233	20	10	–	DJ
v. Middlesex	26-9-47-2		34-7-74-3		1.2-0-7-1		18-7-48-1		6-1-29-0		107.2	284	10	10	–	EJ
(Lord's) 9–12 September	30-8-80-2		31-6-117-0		11-3-46-1		11-2-42-0				148	499	33	5	–	EFGHI
v. Yorkshire	18-7-38-4		1.2-0-1-1		2-0-12-0		3-0-4-0			20-7-60-5	44.2	115	0	10	–	
(The Oval) 15–18 September	24-9-39-3		22.1-5-45-2		5-1-14-1		10-3-23-0			26-7-64-3	92.1	213	9	9	–	

	MP Bicknell	AJ Tudor	IDK Salisbury	BC Hollioake	MA Butcher	AJ Hollioake	RM Amin	JD Ratcliffe	Saqlain Mushtaq	CG Greenidge, Jr
Overs	545.4	281.3	558.2	249.5	168	58.1	101	99	290.5	76.4
Maidens	167	66	145	49	50	10	45	27	90	20
Runs	1346	836	1315	801	500	220	190	269	660	231
Wickets	71	39	60	23	16	6	9	15	58	11
Bowler's average	18.95	21.43	21.91	34.82	25.00	36.66	21.11	17.93	11.37	21.00

A   GP Butcher 9-4-19-1 & 4-0-22-0; 8-0-36-1
B   JE Benjamin 9-2-21-0; 4-0-26-0 & 4-0-31-1
C   GJ Batty 5-1-13-0 & 16-1-45-2
D   MW Patterson 8-1-25-3 & 5-1-14-0
E   AD Brown 3-0-15-0 & 23-3-65-0
F   IJ Ward 4-2-8-0
G   GP Thorpe 13-0-42-0
H   AJ Stewart 2-0-6-0
I   JN Batty 2-1-9-0
J   IE Bishop 18-3-54-2 & 17-4-60-0; 11-0-45-2 & 12-4-22-0; 9-1-27-1 & 6-1-12-0; 6-1-29-0

FIELDING

56 – JN Batty (49 ct/7 st)
31 – AD Brown (30 ct/1 st)
13 – MA Butcher, AJ Stewart (11 ct/2 st), GP Thorpe
12 – BC Hollioake
8 – AJ Hollioake
7 – IJ Ward
6 – JD Ratcliffe
5 – MP Bicknell, IDK Salisbury
3 – DJ Bicknell, IE Bishop, CG Greenidge, Jr, AJ Tudor
2 – GP Butcher, Nadeem Shahid
1 – RM Amin, JE Benjamin, Saqlain Mushtaq

SUSSEX CCC

FIRST-CLASS MATCHES

BATTING

	RR Montgomerie	MTE Peirce	CJ Adams	MJ Di Venuto	PA Cottey	RK Rao	RJ Kirtley	RSC Martin-Jenkins	S Humphries	UBA Rashid	MA Robinson	AD Edwards	WG Khan	JD Lewry	MR Strong	NJ Wilton	GR Haywood	JJ Bates	WV Taylor	Extras	Total	Wickets	Result	Points
v. Lancashire	62	77	26	31	46	13	30*	1	0	22*	–									43	351	8	D	11
(Old Trafford) 13–16 April	–	–	–	–	–	–	–	–	–	–	–													
v. Northamptonshire	8	9	4	0	10	52*	0	15	1		0	0								5	104	10	D	7
(Hove) 21–24 April	113*	48	35*	–	–	–	–	–	–		–	–								13	209	1		
v. Glamorgan	28	13	41	12	6	8	4	0	57	43	0*									10	222	10	L	5
(Cardiff) 28 April–1 May	16	123	24	4	9	0	0	52	15	4	0*									18	265	10		
v. Gloucestershire	12	14	9	10	20	1	11*	22	7	13	10									16	145	10	W	16
(Hove) 19–22 May	6	26	15	162	126	13	5*	15	12	44*	–									31	455	8		
v. Middlesex	69	98	130	31	10		9*	0	9	18	8	22								26	430	10	D	12
(Lord's) 26–29 May	0	1	35	24	1	–	0	4*	12*	–	0									4	81	7		
v. Worcestershire	66	75	40	64	0		13	16*	0		0*		8	1						18	301	9	D	11
(Horsham) 2–5 June	–	–	–	–	–		–	–	–		–		–	–										
v. Kent	70	25	0	136	11		6	5	0	38	0*			13						32	336	10	D	11
(Hove) 9–12 June	34	1	7	71	26		32	12	18*	73	–			–						43	317	8		
v. Yorkshire	35	5	28	9	34		0	42	1	8	0*			10						20	192	10	W	16
(Headingley) 15–17 June	110	6	58	12*	38*		–	1	–	–	–			–						14	239	5		
v. Somerset		0	56	52	0		0	0	29	10	0*		4	4						10	165	10	L	1
(Taunton) 30 June–3 July		41	42	105	4		25	70	0	69	2		51	0*						22	431	10		
v. Leicestershire		1	28	29	42						0		88	1	35*	9	14	43		29	319	10	L	4
(Arundel) 14–17 July		14	22	2	44						0		16	23*	16	55	1	5		16	214	10		
v. Derbyshire	42	16	92	24	22						1*		0	3		39		4	14	20	271	10	W	18
(Derby) 21–23 July	40	55	16	13	11						0		0	10*		0		15	0	16	176	10		
v. Durham	10	16	14	23	53		24	5		19	2*			6		26				33	231	10	W	17
(Chester-le-Street) 4–7 August	4	15	49	2	2		0	14		55	10			6*		13				22	192	10		
v. Surrey	19	51	14	1	1		0	3*		4	3			0		0				19	115	10	L	4
(Hove) 18–21 August	14	4	72	41	25		3*	2		4	7			4		10				31	217	10		
v. Hampshire	16	1	53	93	54		15			18	7			30*		4		57		27	375	10	D	12
(Southampton) 24–27 August	–	–	–	–	–		–			–	–			–		–		–						
v. Essex (Chelmsford)	83	6	12	0	72		0	31			2*			4		0		19		42	271	10	W	18
31 August–2 September	1	23	6*	26*	–		–	–			–			–		–		–		8	64	10		
v. Nottinghamshire	59	25	7	0	14		9	46	0		8			27*				39		41	275	10	W	18
(Hove) 9–11 September	14	95	12	90	15		1	28	2		2			8*				4		44	315	10		
v. Warwickshire	28	2	9		11		2	23	11	1*	0		0					0		12	99	10	L	4
(Edgbaston) 15–16 September	3	39			73		5	10	10	0*	0		13					4		19	176	10		

	RR Montgomerie	MTE Peirce	CJ Adams	MJ Di Venuto	PA Cottey	RK Rao	RJ Kirtley	RSC Martin-Jenkins	S Humphries	UBA Rashid	MA Robinson	AD Edwards	WG Khan	JD Lewry	MR Strong	NJ Wilton	GR Haywood	JJ Bates	WV Taylor
Matches	15	17	17	16	17	4	15	14	11	10	17	2	5	12	1	6	1	6	1
Innings	27	31	31	28	29	6	23	24	18	18	24	3	9	19	2	10	2	10	2
Not Out	1	0	2	1	1	1	5	2	2	3	11	0	0	7	1	0	0	0	0
Runs	962	919	956	1067	780	87	194	413	176	454	63	22	167	163	51	156	15	190	14
Highest score	113*	123	130	162	126	52*	32	70	57	73	10	22	88	30*	35*	55	14	57	14
Average	37.00	29.64	32.96	41.03	27.85	17.40	10.77	18.77	11.00	30.26	4.84	7.33	18.55	13.58	51.00	15.60	7.50	19.00	7.00
100s	2	1	1	3	1	–	–	–	–	–	–	–	–	–	–	–	–	–	–
50s	6	6	5	5	4	1	–	2	1	3	–	–	2	–	–	1	–	1	–

SUSSEX CCC

FIRST-CLASS MATCHES
BOWLING

	RJ Kirtley	RSC Martin-Jenkins	MA Robinson	UBA Rashid	CJ Adams	JD Lewry	JJ Bates	Overs	Totals	Byes/Leg-byes	Wickets	Run outs	
v. Lancashire	20-5-70-1	15-0-63-0	15-0-62-4	8.3-4-90-3				69.3	301	12	8	–	A
(Old Trafford) 13–16 April													
v. Northamptonshire	27-4-92-0	28-5-94-2	25-8-67-0		6-2-14-0			116	391	14	8	2	ABC
(Hove) 21–24 April													
v. Glamorgan	23-6-49-5	10-2-24-1	20.1-7-27-3	10-1-31-0				66.1	149	3	9	–	AC
(Cardiff) 28 April–1 May	28-5-101-2	13-5-32-0	21-3-74-0	19-7-57-0		13-2-49-2		98.5	341	8	4	–	A
v. Gloucestershire	31-10-77-0	24-5-85-3	24.2-6-45-2	21-10-38-2		14-2-37-3		115.2	294	11	10	–	A
(Hove) 19–22 May	20-4-75-4	20-6-66-1	22-7-79-3	12-4-36-0		11-3-31-0		85	302	15	8	–	
v. Middlesex	24-10-67-3	20-8-36-3	26-5-85-4	4-1-10-0				83	233	11	10	–	B
(Lord's) 26–29 May	32-8-63-3	24.2-7-58-4	27-5-81-1	10-4-39-0		13-2-35-1		126.2	358	16	10	–	B
v. Worcestershire	13-3-26-3	8-3-12-1	10-4-18-0			17.4-4-63-6		48.4	124	5	10	–	
(Horsham) 2–5 June	23-6-50-1	15.2-3-61-2	18-7-38-2		3-1-5-1	19-2-96-3		78.2	255	5	9	–	
v. Kent	23-9-49-2	8-1-39-1	29.5-7-75-4	23-10-41-3	12-3-25-0	20-5-87-0		115.5	336	20	10	–	
(Hove) 9–12 June	4-0-25-0		3.2-2-4-0	5-3-6-0		6-3-7-0		18.2	42	0	0	–	
v. Yorkshire	21-7-45-3	16-7-28-1	17.3-3-72-1	20-8-41-4	4-2-6-1	19-4-65-0		97.3	271	14	10	–	
(Headingley) 15–17 June	21-9-31-3	12-6-22-2	7-3-27-0		6-2-8-1	20.3-2-59-4		66.3	157	10	10	–	
v. Somerset	29-6-104-2	27-6-61-2	34-16-72-1	20-2-83-0	15-5-45-0	30-7-102-2		156	503	36	8	1	D
(Taunton) 30 June–3 July	3-0-15-0		5-2-21-0	6.1-3-15-0		4-0-34-0		20.1	94	6	2	1	E
v. Leicestershire			23.4-4-56-1		10-2-39-1	33-6-110-1	60-22-154-5	172	566	14	8	–	DFG
(Arundel) 14–17 July													
v. Derbyshire			21.5-4-88-6			18-2-75-3		54.4	226	9	10	–	H
(Derby) 21–23 July			15-4-35-2			12.1-3-38-7		37.1	136	9	10	–	H
v. Durham	10.2-4-19-3	7-0-22-1	13-3-46-2			14-2-36-4		44.2	141	18	10	–	
(Chester-le-Street) 4–7 August	23-10-53-1	14-2-36-1	27-12-52-2	8-5-8-0	5-1-12-0	19.4-3-86-5		96.4	274	27	10	1	
v. Surrey	18-2-61-4	19.3-6-50-4	13-1-46-1		4-0-18-0	15-5-43-1		69.3	224	6	10	–	
(Hove) 18–21 August	18-0-96-3	10-2-52-0	13-2-46-2	17.5-1-76-2		11-3-40-0		69.5	315	5	7	–	
v. Hampshire	14.1-6-21-7				4-1-9-0	14-2-46-3	2-2-0-0	30.1	76	9	10	–	
(Southampton) 24–27 August	24-1-105-0		27-6-70-1	24-4-93-1		32-11-77-1	62-17-166-3	185	570	7	6	–	EI
v. Essex (Chelmsford)	10-1-30-2	17.2-2-58-4	15-5-29-0			10-6-31-1	10-3-24-3	62.2	179	7	10	–	
31 August–2 September	15.3-5-37-6	17-9-28-2	14-7-22-0			13-3-44-2	4-2-3-0	63.3	155	21	10	–	
v. Nottinghamshire	14-4-37-2	19.5-11-39-2	17-4-36-3			18-4-72-3	3-0-9-0	71.5	199	6	10	–	
(Hove) 9–11 September	7-4-25-1	13-2-50-2	11-2-33-3			9.3-4-23-4		40.3	132	1	10	–	
v. Warwickshire	12-3-56-2	12-2-58-3	5-1-32-0			19.1-3-59-5		48.1	207	2	10	–	
(Edgbaston) 15–16 September	6.3-1-25-2					7-0-37-1		13.3	71	9	3	–	

	RJ Kirtley	RSC Martin-Jenkins	MA Robinson	UBA Rashid	CJ Adams	JD Lewry	JJ Bates
Overs	514.3	370.2	520.4	218.3	120	381.4	141
Maidens	133	100	140	67	28	84	46
Runs	1504	1074	1438	664	333	1330	356
Wickets	65	42	48	15	10	56	11
Bowler's average	23.13	25.57	29.95	44.26	33.3	23.75	32.36

A   RK Rao 1-0-4-0; 6-0-27-1; 2-1-1-0 & 4.5-1-20-0; 1-0-1-0
B   AD Edwards 19-5-67-2; 9-4-24-0 & 20-3-66-1
C   MTE Peirce 5-1-16-1; 1-0-14-0
D   PA Cottey 1-1-0-0; 1-0-3-0
E   MJ Di Venuto 2-0-3-1; 11-2-37-0
F   MR Strong 31-5-124-0
G   GR Haywood 13.2-1-66-0
H   WV Taylor 15-3-54-1 & 10-1-54-1
I   RR Montgomerie 1-0-6-0

FIELDING

23 – CJ Adams
20 – MJ Di Venuto, S Humphries (18 ct/2 st)
19 – RR Montgomerie
15 – NJ Wilton (13 ct/2 st)
11 – PA Cottey
5 – MTE Peirce, UBA Rashid
2 – JJ Bates, RJ Kirtley, JD Lewry, RSC Martin-Jenkins
1 – AD Edwards, WG Khan, RK Rao, MA Robinson,
    MR Strong, WV Taylor

WARWICKSHIRE CCC

FIRST–CLASS MATCHES

BATTING

Opponent / (Venue, Date)	MA Wagh	MJ Powell	DL Hemp	TL Penney	KJ Piper	DR Brown	NMK Smith	AF Giles	G Welch	TA Munton	ESH Giddins	NV Knight	T Frost	A Singh	CE Dagnall	MD Edmond	A Richardson	M Sheikh	DP Ostler	AA Donald	Extras	Total	Wickets	Result	Points
v. Northamptonshire	0	20	64	6	34	142	8	8	23	1	10*										7	323	10	D	9
(Edgbaston) 14–17 April	–	–	–	–	–	–	–	–	–	–	–										–	–	–		
v. Somerset	44		47	73	66	55*	37	1	23*	–	–		1								9	356	7	D	8
(Edgbaston) 19–22 April	–		–	–	–	–	–	–	–												–	–	–		
v. Essex	3	30	19			8	69	30	48*	24	6	2	11								21	271	10	L	6
(Chelmsford) 28–30 April	18	20	4			0	18	2	5	0	0*	5	8												
v. Derbyshire	25	28	31			51	51	7	27*	1	5		25	58							6	86	10	W	19
(Edgbaston) 14–17 May	20	18	59			74	6	26	31	5*	6		35	6							6	315	10		
v. Worcestershire	60	30	144	8		4	22	0	33*	1	abs ill			6							3	319	10	W	19
(Edgbaston) 19–22 May	41	16	9	71*		22	4	–	5*	–				69							13	321	9		
v. Oxford University	216*		94	24*			–	–	–						–	–	–				16	253	6	W	–
(Oxford) 25–27 May	–	27	–	–			13	123*	5				17		0	31	0*				3	337	2		
v. Middlesex	32		2	3*		–	–	–	–	–	–	27*									6	222	6	D	7
(Edgbaston) 2–5 June	–		–	–								–									6	70	2		
v. Lancashire	32	18	0			5	15	24	2	3	0*	82	19								17	217	10	W	17
(Southport) 9–11 June	30	36	4			11	4	1	36	2	6*	64	3								14	211	10		
v. Nottinghamshire	41	100	45			4	41	27	8	3*	11	8	38*								33	316	10	W	19
(Trent Bridge) 15–17 June	1	6	2			23	39	3	0	9	1	8									12	142	10		
v. Kent	16	20	6			1			3	10	0*	12	28	2				12			6	116	10	L	4
(Maidstone) 30 June–3 July	10	0	30			3			21	14	18	40	10	0				7*			3	156	10		
v. Yorkshire	19	53	14	10		37		10	15	0*	0	59		4							32	253	10	L	6
(Edgbaston) 13–16 July	0	0	37	1		36		29	2	4	0*	51		9							13	182	10		
v. Surrey	0	26		5		42		4*	7		4	94		0					21	10	14	227	10	L	3
(Edgbaston) 21–23 July	24	15		14		27		7	19		4*	13		0					1	3	6	133	10		
v. Leicestershire	11	52	8	22		3	29	20*			7	29						0	87		38	306	10	D	10
(Leicester) 6–9 August	–	–	–	–		–	–	–			–	–							–		–	–	–		
v. Hampshire		33	69	49		32	33	26	5*			28	21					2	2		51	351	10	D	11
(Southampton) 17–20 August		–	–	–		–	–	–	–			–	–						–		–	–	–		
v. Glamorgan		136	73	0			22	0	8	1*		64	9					1	3		24	341	10	D	10
(Cardiff) 24–27 August		–	–	–			–	–	–			–	–						–		–	–	–		
v. Gloucestershire		4	16	6		21	21	0	2*			39	12					2	35		9	167	10	W	16
(Edgbaston) 2–4 September		40	9	0		1	1	11*	0			1	26					0*	76		9	174	9		
v. Durham		117	51	1		35	0		1			35	12					4	19	1*	9	285	10	L	6
(Chester-le-Street) 8–11 September		5	49	25		16	0		0			0	8					0*	1	0rh	11	115	9		
v. Sussex		3	8			13	71	15	0	5*		14	66						0		12	207	10	W	17	A
(Edgbaston) 15–16 September		11	1			–	–	1*	–	–		40*							5		13	71	3		

	MA Wagh	MJ Powell	DL Hemp	TL Penney	KJ Piper	DR Brown	NMK Smith	AF Giles	G Welch	TA Munton	ESH Giddins	NV Knight	T Frost	A Singh	CE Dagnall	MD Edmond	A Richardson	M Sheikh	DP Ostler	AA Donald
Matches	13	9	18	15	5	16	15	16	14	13	14	14	12	5	1	1	6	1	7	2
Innings	21	14	29	24	7	25	21	23	21	19	18	23	18	10	1	1	8	2	11	4
Not Out	1	0	0	3	0	1	0	5	6	3	10	2	1	0	0		3	1	0	2
Runs	643	494	1014	517	152	666	504	375	326	80	76	719	348	154	0	31	9	19	250	14
Highest score	216*	136	144	73	66	142	71	123*	48*	24	18	94	66	69	0	31	4	12	87	10
Average	32.15	35.28	34.96	24.61	21.71	27.75	24.00	20.83	21.73	5.00	9.50	34.23	20.47	15.40	–	31.00	1.80	19.00	22.72	7.00
100s	1	2	2	–	–	1	–	1	–	–	–	–	–	–	–	–	–	–	–	–
50s	1	1	6	3	1	3	3	–	–	–	–	6	1	2	–	–	–	–	2	–

A   IR Bell 0

WARWICKSHIRE CCC

FIRST-CLASS MATCHES

BOWLING

Match	ESH Giddins	TA Munton	G Welch	DR Brown	AF Giles	NMK Smith	A Richardson	CE Dagnall	MA Waugh	Overs	Totals	Byes/Leg-byes	Wickets	Run outs	
v. Northamptonshire (Edgbaston) 14–17 April	14-4-41-1	15.4-2-62-0	16-5-47-5	2-0-9-0						47.4	167	8	6	–	
v. Essex (Chelmsford) 28–30 April	23-6-42-4	21.1-8-44-3	21-8-47-1		32-15-45-0	8-4-11-2				105.1	191	2	10	–	
	10-2-42-1	14-5-37-0	8-1-28-0		9-0-30-1	11.3-2-30-1				52.3	168	1	3	–	
v. Derbyshire (Edgbaston) 14–17 May	18-5-71-2	13.5-1-53-1	8-2-29-1		28-9-63-4	14-2-58-1				81.5	286	12	10	1	
	17-5-46-1	11-1-36-1	3-0-16-0		45-17-62-4	36-13-90-4				112	264	14	10	–	
v. Worcestershire (Edgbaston) 19–22 May	9-0-73-0	24-6-55-1	15-1-57-4	10-3-11-0	31-12-48-3	15-7-24-2				95	203	8	10	–	
		21-6-46-3			47-20-64-4	34-5-82-2				121.5	320	23	10	–	
v. Oxford University (Oxford) 25–27 May			10-1-47-0			16-5-28-5	19-5-51-1	12.5-5-20-4	1-0-4-0	62.5	158	18	10	–	AB
					17-7-26-0	8-2-15-0	15-2-54-2	14-2-68-2	11.1-3-33-4	81.1	272	11	10	1	B
v. Middlesex (Edgbaston) 2–5 June	22-6-55-0	26.3-10-45-2	17-3-66-3		15-3-33-1	4-1-8-1				84.3	216	9	8	1	
	2.1-1-1-0									4.1	15	0	0	–	B
v. Lancashire (Southport) 9–11 June	18-5-50-5	14-4-57-1	5-2-11-1		12-4-25-3					49	144	1	10	–	
	28-11-65-3	25-6-60-2	11-2-39-1		9.1-2-36-3	13-2-24-0	3-0-22-0			89.1	265	19	10	1	
v. Nottinghamshire (Trent Bridge) 15–17 June	20-6-46-4	24-6-62-2	22-0-97-3	18-5-67-1	6-0-26-0	3-0-20-0				93	327	9	10	–	
	11-3-31-4	11-5-20-4	4.5-0-14-1	4-1-10-1						30.5	76	1	10	–	
v. Kent (Maidstone) 30 June–2 July	13-3-27-0	15-3-44-6	12-2-38-1		15.2-4-18-2					55.2	164	7	10	1	
	17-5-52-2	16-3-34-1	16.2-5-46-3		18-6-37-4					73.2	199	9	10	0	C
v. Yorkshire (Edgbaston) 13–16 July	18-3-59-4	12-1-41-2	15-1-70-1	12.3-3-25-2	6-1-12-1					63.3	213	6	10	–	
	22.5-5-71-3	21-3-61-2	8-1-23-0	11-0-39-0	8-2-22-0					70.5	224	7	7	2	
v. Surrey (Edgbaston) 21–23 July	33-13-90-6		9-0-42-0	31-8-121-2	29-4-108-1				9-1-29-1	136	483	18	10	–	D
v. Leicestershire (Leicester) 6–9 August	21-2-111-3			22-5-84-2	24-11-59-0	2-1-4-0	20-3-81-2			89	353	14	8	1	
v. Hampshire (Southampton) 17–20 August			36-3-120-4	26-6-77-1	16-4-48-1		32-8-78-1			120	353	15	7	–	E
							4-1-6-0			16	46	1	0	–	BEFG
v. Glamorgan (Cardiff) 24–27 August	5.3-1-16-0		21.3-8-58-1		39-13-87-2	11-4-42-0	36-9-75-4			118	300	7	8	1	E
v. Gloucestershire (Edgbaston) 2–4 September		13-3-29-1		6-1-30-0	7-1-22-1		15.5-4-51-8			41.5	132	0	10	–	
		17-6-28-3			23.3-10-43-3	19-5-74-2	17-3-56-2			76.3	206	5	10	–	
v. Durham (Chester-le-Street) 8–11 September		37-6-91-7		17-5-25-1		8-0-20-0	21.4-4-63-2			100.4	255	18	10	–	D
		20-3-57-1		22.5-8-66-7		4-0-13-0	14-5-30-1			76.5	235	30	10	1	DE
v. Sussex (Edgbaston) 15–16 September	17-4-41-3	20-10-36-7		3-0-20-0						40	99	2	10	–	
	16-5-33-2	17-9-30-2		5-1-12-0	24.1-5-63-5	6-0-21-1				68.1	176	17	10	–	

	ESH Giddins	TA Munton	G Welch	DR Brown	AF Giles	NMK Smith	A Richardson	CE Dagnall	MA Waugh
Overs	355.3	409.1	269.3	232.5	447.4	190.3	190.3	26.5	21.1
Maidens	95	107	47	57	145	47	43	7	4
Runs	1063	1028	927	717	938	540	539	88	66
Wickets	48	52	31	26	39	16	23	6	5
Bowler's average	22.14	19.76	29.90	27.57	24.05	33.75	23.43	14.66	13.20

A MD Edmond 8-3-24-0
B DL Hemp 6-2-13-0 & 6-2-18-1; 2-0-14-0; 7-1-26-0
C M Sheikh 6-0-21-0
D AA Donald 25-8-75-0; 17-5-38-0 & 8-2-23-0
E MJ Powell 10-2-15-0 & 2-0-10-0; 5-1-15-0; 8-3-16-0
F TL Penney 2-1-1-0
G DP Ostler 1-0-2-0

FIELDING

30 – NV Knight
24 – T Frost (23 ct/1 st)
13 – DR Brown
11 – DL Hemp
9 – KJ Piper (8 ct/1 st)
8 – TL Penney (6 ct/2 st), NMK Smith
6 – AF Giles
5 – TA Munton, DP Ostler, MJ Powell, G Welch
3 – MA Wagh
2 – IR Bell, ESH Giddins
1 – AA Donald, MD Edmond, A Richardson

WORCESTERSHIRE CCC

FIRST–CLASS MATCHES
BATTING

	WPC Weston	PR Pollard	VS Solanki	DA Leatherdale	GR Haynes	SJ Rhodes	SR Lampitt	RK Illingworth	A Sheriyar	CG Liptrot	JM de la Pena	EJ Wilson	GA Hick	KR Spring	Abdul Hafeez	NE Batson	PJ Newport	TM Moody	MJ Rawnsley	DN Catterall	Extras	Total	Wickets	Result	Points	
v. Oxford University	84	60	19	71	10	15	14*	0*	–	–	–										11	284	6	W	–	
(Oxford) 8–10 April	28	31	74*	0*	–	–	–														2	135	2			
v. Durham	2	14	4	85		15	1	13	11	0*	0	0									7	152	10	D	6	
(Chester-le-Street) 13–16 April	0	4	27	8		0	15	13	1*			58*									11	137	7			
v. Surrey	0	0*						8*					–								7	15	1	D	8	
(Worcester) 20–23 April	–																									
v. Nottinghamshire	45	20	8	6	7	11		6*	0	2			23								44	172	9	L	3	
(Trent Bridge) 28–30 April	2	14	91	0	29	0		12	2	1*			89								39	279	9			
v. Hampshire			1	33	4	1	91*	16	13	0				0	0	6					19	184	10	L	4	
(Southampton) 14–17 May			84	30	16	45*	7	6	12	0				12	0	19					27	258	10			
v. Warwickshire		43	20	1	0	46	26	18	11*						0	0	12				26	203	10	L	5	
(Edgbaston) 19–22 May		58	1	46	5	28	34*			61					8	42	12				25	320	10			
v. Glamorgan		52	35	0		2	22	6	0*	2				11		8	15				11	164	10	W	16	
(Worcester) 26–28 May		8	39	18		14	15	9	5	2*				18		16	9				7	160	10			
v. Sussex		22	4	11		9	26	5	1*	4			0	1		4					37	124	10	D	8	
(Horsham) 2–5 June		0	10	28		29*	0	0	0*	0			134	16		0					38	255	9			
v. Somerset		12	30	25		12	30	31	1	19			50	3			65*				30	308	10	W	18	
(Worcester) 15–18 June		0	7	11		25	15	23	0	4			17	4			33				25	200	10			
v. Northamptonshire		0	0	9		16	0	0	9				2	0			0	63*			3	102	10	W	16	
(Northampton) 30 June–2 July		0	126	35		45	11	13	10*				20	4			42	63			15	384	10			
v. Kent	23	10	11			20	5	4	1*				10	0			7	0			15	106	10	L	4	
(Worcester) 9–12 July	34	35	31			46*	19	11	0				99	3			0	8			57	343	10			
v. Gloucestershire	139	171	41			4*	46						122	32			4				32	591	7	W	20	
(Cheltenham) 14–17 July	0	13	11*			4*							4	0			29				7	60	5			
v. Leicestershire	1	13	12			24	1	12	8			7	4				29		15*		7	133	10	D	8	
(Worcester) 22–25 July	157	16	12*									36	59				34*		–		39	353	4			
v. Yorkshire	8	4	4			7	20*		13				0	10			26	0	5		2	90	10	L	4	
(Headingley) 4–6 August	0	70	19			32	66*		5				16				1	5	56		17	287	10			
v. Sri Lanka 'A'	5	22	50	52	9*					4*			0				72		–		18	237	7	D	–	A
(Worcester) 11–13 August	0	7	49	0	60*					6			22				16*		21		25	222	8			A
v. Derbyshire	10	3	75	14		19	47*		1				54	51			27		6		9	316	10	L	4	
(Kidderminster) 18–21 August	4	7*	9	40		4	48		0				12	60			6		20		35	245	10			
v. Lancashire	0	0	0		15	74	22	12	3		22	31					22*				17	227	10	D	9	
(Worcester) 24–27 August	12		40*									21*	5				–				10	88	2			
v. Essex			37	10	17	0	29	10*				22	101				5			12	23	308	10	D	11	B
(Chelmsford) 8–11 September			12	3	5	31	29					18	150				5*			60	40	365	9			B
v. Middlesex			155	7		13	17	8*	1*			20	116							60	34	465	9	D	12	BC
(Worcester) 15–18 September			–			–														–						

	WPC Weston	PR Pollard	VS Solanki	DA Leatherdale	GR Haynes	SJ Rhodes	SR Lampitt	RK Illingworth	A Sheriyar	CG Liptrot	JM de la Pena	EJ Wilson	GA Hick	KR Spring	Abdul Hafeez	NE Batson	PJ Newport	TM Moody	MJ Rawnsley	DN Catterall
Matches	11	11	19	19	8	18	14	16	19	11	3	8	12	5	4	5	11	5	4	2
Innings	21	21	35	34	12	30	19	26	26	16	3	15	21	10	8	10	19	10	6	3
Not Out	0	2	2	3	2	5	5	5	8	6	0	2	0	0	0	1	3	2	1	0
Runs	554	377	1339	693	177	591	413	457	129	142	0	404	1051	69	43	181	295	286	67	132
Highest score	157	60	171	85	60*	74	66*	91*	18	61	0	116	150	18	32	72	65*	63*	21	60
Average	26.38	19.84	40.57	22.35	17.70	23.64	29.50	21.76	7.16	14.20	–	31.07	50.04	6.90	5.37	20.11	18.43	35.75	13.40	44.00
100s	2	–	3	–	–	–	–	–	–	–	–	1	4	–	–	–	–	–	–	–
50s	1	3	6	3	1	1	2	1	–	1	–	2	6	–	–	1	1	3	–	2

A DJ Pipe 5 & 16
B RC Driver 42 & 12; 23
C Kabir Ali 11

WORCESTERSHIRE CCC

FIRST-CLASS MATCHES
BOWLING

Match	A Sheriyar	SR Lampitt	CG Liptrot	RK Illingworth	VS Solanki	DA Leatherdale	GR Haynes	PJ Newport	TM Moody	MJ Rawnsley	Overs	Totals	Byes/Leg-byes	Wickets	Run outs	
v. Oxford University (Oxford) 8–10 April	13-4-25-2	6-5-1-1	5.3-1-18-1	5-1-8-0	4-0-21-0	4-1-9-0					43.3	81	11	10	–	A
	12-4-35-2	11-3-36-3	11-2-32-1	5-3-7-0							61.5	182	8	10	–	A
v. Durham (Chester-le-Street) 13–16 April	18-2-69-2	13-6-30-1	5-0-32-0	16-3-49-1	3-1-10-0	1-0-2-0					78	303	5	6	–	A
v. Surrey (Worcester) 20–23 April	10-0-63-0	9-1-47-4	12.4-2-51-5			3-1-14-0	9-1-36-1				43.4	223	12	10	–	
v. Nottinghamshire (Trent Bridge) 28–30 April	28.5-7-94-4	21-4-56-2	25-7-71-2	21-3-60-1	2-0-19-0	14-1-48-1	11-3-28-0				122.5	417	39	10	–	
	4.2-0-26-0		4-2-9-0								8.2	35	0	0	–	
v. Hampshire (Southampton) 14–17 May	40-12-130-7		24-10-70-1	5-2-9-0		3.2-0-13-1	11-3-35-0				96.2	352	13	10	–	
	16-6-42-3		9-1-35-0				6.1-2-12-0				31.1	91	2	3	–	
v. Warwickshire (Edgbaston) 19–22 May	31-2-104-6		19-9-46-1	22-5-47-1	3-2-10-0	11-3-20-0	10-1-33-0	15-3-52-0			111	321	9	9	1	
	20-0-76-1			12-2-41-1	17-5-38-1	2-0-8-0	13-4-27-0	10-0-51-3			74	253	12	6	–	
v. Glamorgan (Worcester) 26–28 May	16-3-49-4	8-2-14-3	8-3-13-1	2-1-4-0			3-2-5-0	9-1-34-2			46	127	8	10	–	
	18.3-2-82-3	12-4-18-3	7-2-21-0			3-1-4-1		11-2-24-3			51.3	149	0	10	–	
v. Sussex (Horsham) 2–5 June	27-3-102-4	22.2-4-83-2	10-1-45-2	6-1-15-0			6-1-29-0	12-3-25-0			83.2	301	2	9	1	
v. Somerset (Worcester) 15–18 June	15.2-3-49-4	13-2-31-1	14-2-57-2	6-0-12-0			6-2-14-2	7-2-16-1			61.2	193	14	10		
	29.2-7-96-5	16-2-79-1	6-2-21-1	8-1-17-1			2-0-18-0	16-5-42-2			77.2	289	16	10	–	
v. Northamptonshire (Northampton) 30 June–3 July	15-4-70-2	9.5-1-28-4				1-0-1-0		16-6-41-3	10-2-50-0		51.5	197	7	10	1	
	18-5-56-3	12-4-29-2		17-4-58-3				12-4-29-2			59	177	5	10	–	
v. Kent (Worcester) 9–12 July	18-9-43-4	10-4-15-1		1-0-3-0				14-6-23-1	12.55-6-27-4		55.5	119	8	10	–	
	25.2-3-117-3	18-5-43-1		25.4-12-29-1	22.2-10-62-4			14-3-48-0	12-3-29-1		117.2	350	22	10	–	
v. Gloucestershire (Cheltenham) 11–14 July	23.1-1-101-6	22-6-47-3		8-2-15-0	9-6-10-0			12-6-23-1	10-3-32-0		84.1	231	3	10	–	
	29-8-136-3	13-3-56-0		29-17-38-0	15.3-4-40-1	4-0-7-1		18-6-57-4	17-2-62-0		137.3	425	4	10	–	B
v. Leicestershire (Worcester) 22–25 July	21-4-62-2	8-3-11-1		19-4-34-0	26.5-7-64-4	4-1-12-0			15-6-43-1	19-3-46-2	115.5	291	17	10	–	B
	5-2-12-0	10-0-36-0		25-4-85-3	18.5-5-64-3				5-1-9-0	18-7-43-2	95.5	316	17	9	–	B
v. Yorkshire (Headingley) 4–6 August	23.5-3-94-4	15-1-79-1			11-5-18-0			17-1-62-2	8-2-15-0	32-8-84-3	108.5	374	17	10	–	
						0.2-0-4-1					0.2	4	0	1	–	
v. Sri Lanka 'A' (Worcester) 11–13 August	20-4-51-2		14-2-55-2		13.5-4-41-4	4-1-19-0	11-4-27-0			15-5-34-0	77.5	243	16	9	1	
	8-1-34-0				3-0-15-0	4-0-31-0					15	84	4	0	–	
v. Derbyshire (Kidderminster) 18–21 August	29.5-3-142-4	20-5-57-1			3-0-22-0	6-2-20-1		27-9-65-2		19-4-58-1	104.5	382	18	10	1	
	10-0-57-2	9-1-38-2			3-0-29-0			8.4-2-28-0		7-1-26-0	37.4	183	5	4	–	
v. Lancashire (Worcester) 24–27 August	18-6-86-4	9-4-54-2		1-0-4-1		13-2-35-2		14-3-33-1								
v. Essex (Chelmsford) 8–11 September	14.1-4-70-4			29-14-47-1	13-2-32-1	9-1-28-0		23-9-47-3			102.1	303	9	10	–	C
	8.5-4-17-0			23-6-64-1	5.1-1-45-0	6-1-17-0		19-6-47-1			91	265	10	4	–	BC
v. Middlesex (Worcester) 15–18 September	12.5-2-42-2		3-1-16-0	28-3-80-1	2-0-12-0						66.5	235	9	10	1	BCD
	10-1-39-0		5-0-32-0	18-1-44-0							66	235	10	1	–	BCD

	A Sheriyar	SR Lampitt	CG Liptrot	RK Illingworth	VS Solanki	DA Leatherdale	GR Haynes	PJ Newport	TM Moody	MJ Rawnsley
Overs	809.2	287.1	194.1	336.4	150.3	83.4	88.1	271.4	89.5	110
Maidens	119	70	49	92	47	17	22	77	25	28
Runs	2273	888	665	767	514	283	278	747	267	291
Wickets	92	39	20	15	17	8	3	31	6	8
Bowler's average	24.70	22.76	33.25	51.13	30.23	35.37	92.66	24.09	44.5	36.37

A   JM de la Pena 14-6-18-6 & 14.5-5-34-4; 22-5-106-2; 13-3-82-1
B   GA Hick 12-5-25-1; 3-1-2-0 & 14-0-50-1; 18-6-49-1; 2-1-8-2 & 11-5-21-0
C   DN Catterall 14-2-70-1 & 11-3-16-2; 10-2-32-2 & 11-3-67-0
D   Kabir Ali 9-1-36-2 & 11-7-22-1

FIELDING

53 – SJ Rhodes (5 ct/2 st)	
21 – VS Solanki	
18 – GA Hick	
9 – DA Leatherdale	
7 – SR Lampitt	
5 – NE Batson, RK Illingworth, TM Moody, EJ Wilson	
3 – PJ Newport, A Sheriyar, KR Spiring, WPC Weston	
2 – Abdul Haafeez, PR Pollard	
1 – JM de la Pena, MJ Rawnsley	

YORKSHIRE CCC

FIRST-CLASS MATCHES

BATTING

	GS Blewett	MP Vaughan	D Byas	MJ Wood	RJ Harden	C White	RJ Blakey	GM Hamilton	D Gough	RJ Sidebottom	MJ Hoggard	A McGrath	CEW Silverwood	ID Fisher	PM Hutchison	GM Fellows	Extras	Total	Wickets	Result	Points
v. Gloucestershire	6	2	11	36	43	15	21	81*	33	1	8						25	282	10	W	18
(Headingley) 21–24 April	12	3	16	42	4rh	40	0	14*	7*	–	–						10	148	6		
v. Somerset	27	17	0	25		28	32	3		0	0*	0	4				12	148	10	L	3
(Taunton) 29 April–2 May	22	4	90	35		3	28	4		21*	21	75	7				35	345	10		
v. Middlesex	2	32	62	5		4	1			6	0*	10	6	2			30	160	10	L	4
(Headingley) 14–17 May	73	10	6	4		5	1			4	6	142*	0	26			36	313	10		
v. Essex	4	100	44	53		44	8			2	0	0	11	3*			42	311	10	W	19
(Chelmsford) 19–22 May	44*	151	90	10		47	6*			–	–	54	–	–			33	435	5		
v. Durham	34	8	68	8		9	28			3	8	62	39	22*			21	310	10	W	19
(Headingley) 27–29 May	6*	9	1*	–		–	–			–	–	–	–	–			–	16	1		
v. Derbyshire	4	15	0	1		34	6			6	5*	17	19	1			9	117	10	D	8
(Derby) 2–5 June	34	13	9	20		6	70*			0	–	76	25	25*			30	308	8		
v. Hampshire	0	1	37	2		0	59	35			1	34	4	0*			19	192	10	W	16
(Basingstoke) 9–11 June	4	4	95	24		0*	–	–			–	9*	–	–			5	141	4		
v. Sussex	6	71	29	11		36	6	13*	21	0	0	27					51	271	10	L	6
(Headingley) 15–17 June	11	11	38	27		12	1	30*	5	0	4	2					16	157	10		
v. Leicestershire	13	4	4	17	1	5	0	4		1*		0	0				3	52	10	L	4
(Leicester) 1–3 July	8	43	17	5	69	52	0	10		26*		0	3				18	251	10		
v. Warwickshire	16	24	21	0	8	4	21*	8	0			75	12				24	213	10	W	17
(Edgbaston) 13–16 July	4	52	12	20	25	0	17*	75*	–			5	–				14	224	7		
v. Northamptonshire	98	4	50	5	25	23	13	16		0*		30	2				23	289	10	D	8
(Scarborough) 20–23 July	190	18	14	0	50	8	2	84*		1		13	13				14	407	10		
v. Worcestershire	37	44	67	4	2	24	22	94*				51		0	0		29	374	10	W	20
(Headingley) 4–6 August	–	0*	0*	2		–	–					–	–	–	–		2	4	1		
v. Lancashire		14	0	9	10	0	19	0		0		0		1	0*		14	67	10	L	4
(Old Trafford) 19–21 August		25	66	35	26	34	5	20		5		28		17	4*		12	277	10		
v. Nottinghamshire		2	0	2	2	36	60	23				16	1	14	2*		27	185	10	W	16
(Trent Bridge) 24–26 August		2	4	4	11	0	20	43*				14	25*	–	–		21	144	7		
v. Kent		153	1	6	64	20	0			13		13	53*	38		0	28	389	10	W	20
(Scarborough) 1–4 September		50	5	21	10*		15			–		0	–	–		34*	6	141	5		
v. Glamorgan		1	10	2	39	7	20			9		7	12	14*		5	14	140	10	L	3
(Headingley) 8–10 September		1	6	2	10	11	123			48*		16	18	16		26	29	306	10		
v. Surrey		0	2	12	36*	1	9	0				17	5	31		0	2	115	10	D	8
(The Oval) 15–18 September		7	0	2	3	13*	71	10				38	–	51		9	9	213	9		

	GS Blewett	MP Vaughan	D Byas	MJ Wood	RJ Harden	C White	RJ Blakey	GM Hamilton	D Gough	RJ Sidebottom	MJ Hoggard	A McGrath	CEW Silverwood	ID Fisher	PM Hutchison	GM Fellows
Matches	12	17	17	17	10	17	17	11	3	12	8	16	13	11	3	3
Innings	23	34	34	33	19	31	31	20	5	20	11	30	20	16	4	6
Not Out	2	1	2	0	3	2	4	8	1	5	3	2	2	5	3	1
Runs	655	895	875	451	438	521	684	567	66	146	53	831	259	261	6	74
Highest score	190	153	95	53	69	52	123	94*	33	48*	21	142*	53*	51	4*	34*
Average	31.19	27.12	27.34	13.66	27.37	17.96	25.33	47.25	16.50	9.73	6.62	29.67	14.38	23.72	6.00	14.80
100s	1	3	–	–	–	–	1	–	–	–	–	1	–	–	–	–
50s	2	3	8	1	3	1	4	4	–	–	–	6	1	1	–	–

YORKSHIRE CCC

FIRST-CLASS MATCHES
BOWLING

	D Gough	MJ Hoggard	GM Hamilton	RJ Sidebottom	C White	CEW Silverwood	MP Vaughan	GS Blewett	ID Fisher	PM Hutchison	Overs	Totals	Byes/Leg-byes	Wickets	Run outs
v. Gloucestershire	16-3-51-2	6-0-32-0	8-2-26-4	8-2-33-1	4.2-2-14-3						42.2	169	13	10	–
(Headingley) 21–24 April	16-6-27-4	14-3-53-0	12-5-33-3	13-3-34-2	7-1-16-1						62	180	17	10	–
v. Somerset		22-3-56-2		27-5-88-0		25-7-96-2	6-0-24-0				137	468	9	9	–
(Taunton) 29 April–2 May		3.2-0-13-0				4-0-11-4					7.2	26	2	4	–
v. Middlesex		26-8-56-4		20-7-38-1	18-7-23-0	23.2-3-72-3		3-0-12-0	12-4-18-2		102.2	249	30	10	–
(Headingley) 14–17 May		17.2-6-49-2		13-2-44-0	8-1-36-0	20-6-50-2	4-1-7-0		5-1-29-1		67.2	226	11	5	–
v. Essex		21-5-63-3		12-0-39-2	13-2-50-3	18-2-64-1	8-0-32-0	3-0-19-1	15-3-59-0		90	335	9	10	–
(Chelmsford) 19–22 May		11.4-3-43-2		12-5-14-1	12-2-36-1	19-4-46-1	4-0-16-0		25-7-73-5		83.4	237	9	10	–
v. Durham		10-1-41-3		7-2-16-1	4-2-10-2	8-2-30-3		5-2-8-0			37	114	6	10	–
(Headingley) 27–29 May		8-1-27-0		10-4-30-1	18-3-63-4	18.4-5-45-3		9-2-16-2	6-2-11-0		69.4	211	19	10	–
v. Derbyshire		23-10-47-5		10-2-33-0	8-1-32-0	21.2-4-59-4		6-2-15-0	3-0-7-1		72.2	206	7	10	–
(Derby) 2–5 June															
v. Hampshire		17-8-35-1	16-5-45-2		11-3-27-1	17-6-43-5		5-1-17-0	11-2-26-1		77	206	13	10	–
(Basingstoke) 9–11 June		16.4-5-45-4	10-1-22-3		12.2-5-27-1	12.4-6-23-1			2-0-7-0		53.4	124	0	10	1
v. Sussex	13.3-2-59-3			7-0-17-1	9.3-1-32-2		5-2-6-0				58.1	192	6	10	–
(Headingley) 15–17 June	20-3-75-1	11-3-35-1		12-2-35-0			5.5-0-19-2	7-0-29-0			71.5	239	2	5	1
v. Leicestershire			23.4-4-55-3	19-4-54-3	17-2-58-1	24-3-61-3	8-1-29-0	6-2-16-0			97.4	297	24	10	–
(Leicester) 1–3 July			0.2-0-5-0			1-0-2-1					1.2	7	0	1	–
v. Warwickshire	20.2-3-62-4		18-7-29-3		16-3-50-0	22-8-60-3	6-1-17-0	5-0-23-0			87.2	253	12	10	–
(Edgbaston) 13–16 July	11-3-45-3		9.3-1-29-1		9-1-26-3	11-1-68-2	5-3-9-1				45.3	182	5	10	–
v. Northamptonshire			35-9-83-3	32-6-118-0	20-3-66-1	37-4-92-1	15-2-58-1				159.4	517	31	7	–
(Scarborough) 20–23 July			2-0-15-0	1.3-0-11-2		4-0-33-0			11.4-2-44-1		7.3	61	2	2	–
v. Worcestershire			10-3-35-3		4-0-18-1				6-2-13-1	12-5-35-6	26	90	2	10	–
(Headingley) 4–6 August			16-3-56-2		20-7-37-2	25-8-45-2			28-10-48-0	19-5-68-3	117	287	17	10	–
v. Lancashire			15-4-73-2	10-1-36-0	18.3-4-36-3		7-0-41-2	7-0-44-0	12-2-66-3		71.3	314	4	10	–
(Old Trafford) 19–21 August			4-0-15-0							3.5-1-19-0	7.5	34	0	0	–
v. Nottinghamshire			10.4-3-30-5		13-3-44-4	12-3-44-0				9-0-49-1	44.4	184	17	10	–
(Trent Bridge) 24–26 August			14-5-29-3		11.2-2-32-4	15-4-38-3				10-3-26-0	50.2	144	19	10	
v. Kent				23-7-65-2	25-2-90-0	26.2-9-67-5			7-1-40-1		96.2	302	9	10	1
(Scarborough) 1–4 September				18-11-16-3	14-3-24-0	20-3-57-4	19-6-50-0		19-11-28-2		109	226	18	10	–
v. Glamorgan			23-6-69-1		22-3-83-1	30-5-89-2	18.2-1-71-2		21-1-85-1		140.2	498	14	10	– A
(Headingley) 8–10 September															
v. Surrey			9-0-49-1		7-0-28-1	10-2-28-5					33	128	5	10	–
(The Oval) 15–18 September			6-1-16-2		4-2-7-0	6-0-26-1	1-1-0-0		1-0-1-0		22	57	0	4	–

	D Gough	MJ Hoggard	GM Hamilton	RJ Sidebottom	C White	CEW Silverwood	MP Vaughan	GS Blewett	ID Fisher	PM Hutchison
Overs	96.5	215.1	277.1	275.3	354	405.2	137.1	86	66.4	162
Maidens	20	58	64	70	70	87	26	26	13	42
Runs	319	619	825	789	1058	1204	424	204	212	476
Wickets	17	28	43	24	41	59	10	9	5	14
Bowler's average	18.76	22.10	19.18	32.87	25.80	20.40	42.40	22.66	42.40	34.00

A   GM Fellows 7-0-38-1

FIELDING

41 – RJ Blakey
24 – D Byas
15 – A McGrath
12 – C White
10 – MJ Wood
6 – RJ Sidebottom
5 – GS Blewett, MP Vaughan
3 – GM Hamilton, CEW Silverwood
2 – RJ Harden, MJ Hoggard
1 – GM Fellows